The Hip Hop and Religion Reader

Edited by two recognized scholars of African-American religion and culture, this reader, the first of its kind, provides the essential texts for an important and emerging field of study—religion and hip hop. Until now, the discipline of religious studies lacked a consistent and coherent text that highlights the developing work at the intersections of hip hop, religion, and theology. Moving beyond an institutional understanding of religion and offering a multidimensional assortment of essays, this new volume charts new ground by bringing together voices who, to this point, have been a disparate and scattered few. Comprehensively organized with the foundational and most influential works that continue to provide a base for current scholarship, *The Hip Hop and Religion Reader* frames the lively and expanding conversation on hip hop's influence on the academic study of religion.

Monica R. Miller is currently Assistant Professor of Religion and Africana Studies and Director of Women, Gender and Sexuality Studies at Lehigh University. Among other publications, she is the author of *Religion and Hip Hop* (Routledge, 2012) and currently serves as a Senior Research Fellow with the Institute for Humanist Studies (Washington, DC), Co-Chair/Founder of the "Critical Approaches to Hip Hop and Religion Group" (AAR), member of the Culture on the Edge international scholarly collaborative, and editorial board member of Culture on the Edge: Studies in Identity Formation book series (Equinox).

Anthony B. Pinn is currently the Agnes Cullen Arnold Professor of Humanities and Professor of Religious Studies at Rice University, founding director of Rice's Center for Engaged Research and Collaborative Learning and Director of Research for the Institute for Humanist Studies (Washington, DC). He is the author/editor of thirty books, including *Noise and Spirit: The Religious and Spiritual Sensibilities of Rap Music* (NYU Press, 2003).

The Hip Hop and Religion Reader

Edited by
Monica R. Miller and Anthony B. Pinn

Routledge
Taylor & Francis Group

NEW YORK AND LONDON

First published 2015 by Routledge
711 Third Avenue, New York, NY 10017

and by Routledge
2 Park Square, Milton Park, Abingdon, Oxon, OX14 4RN

Routledge is an imprint of the Taylor & Francis Group, an informa business

Library of Congress Cataloging in Publication Data
The hip hop and religion reader:/[edited by] Monica R. Miller & Anthony B. Pinn. — 1 [edition].
pages cm
Includes bibliographical references and index.
1. African Americans—Religion. 2. Hip-hop. I. Miller, Monica R., 1981- editor.
II. Pinn, Anthony B., editor.
BL2525.H56 2014
201′.7—dc23
2014016348

ISBN: 978-0-415-74100-2 (hbk)
ISBN: 978-0-415-74101-9 (pbk)

Typeset in Minion Pro and Trade Gothic
by Swales & Willis Ltd, Exeter, Devon, UK

Contents

List of Figures   viii

Acknowledgments   ix

General Introduction   1
Monica R. Miller and Anthony B. Pinn

Part I   **Setting the Context, Framing the Discussion**   **7**

1   Michael Eric Dyson: "Performance, Protest, and Prophecy in the Culture of Hip-Hop"   11

2   Anthony B. Pinn: "Making a World with a Beat: Musical Expression's Relationship to Religious Identity and Experience"   20

3   Greg Dimitriadis: "Hip Hop to Rap: Some Implications of an Historically Situated Approach to Performance"   38

4   H. Samy Alim: "A New Research Agenda: Exploring the Transglobal Hip Hop *Umma*"   53

Part II   **What's the "Religion" in Hip Hop?**   **63**

5   Monica R. Miller: "Don't Judge a Book By Its Cover"   65

6   Joseph Winters: "Unstrange Bedfellows: Hip Hop and Religion"   73

7   John L. Jackson Jr.: "Peter Piper Picked Peppers, but Humpty Dumpty Got Pushed: The Productively Paranoid Stylings of Hip-hop's Spirituality"   85

Part III   **The Religious Aesthetics of Hip Hop Culture**   **99**

8   Margarita L. Simon Guillory: "Intersecting Points:
The 'Erotic as Religious' in the Lyrics of Missy Elliott"   101

9   Elonda Clay: "Two Turntables and a Microphone:
Turntablism, Ritual and Implicit Religion"   115

10   Angela M. Nelson: "'God's Smiling on You and He's
Frowning Too': Rap and the Problem of Evil"   129

11   Martina Viljoen: "'Wrapped Up': Ideological Setting and
Figurative Meaning in African-American Gospel Rap"   140

12   Racquel Cepeda: "AfroBlue: Incanting Yoruba Gods
in Hip Hop's Isms"   159

Part IV   **Hip Hop and/in Religious Traditions**   **165**

Islam

13   Juan M. Floyd-Thomas: "A Jihad of Words: The Evolution
of African American Islam and Contemporary Hip-Hop"   167

14   H. Samy Alim: "Re-inventing Islam with Unique Modern
Tones: Muslim Hip Hop Artists as Verbal Mujahidin"   183

15   Felicia Miyakawa: "The Five Percenter 'Way of Life'"   197

16   Dervla Sara Shannahan and Qurra Hussain:
"Rap on L'avenue': Islam, Aesthetics, Authenticity and
Masculinities in the Tunisian Rap Scene"   213

Christianity

17   Josef Sorett: "Believe Me, This Pimp Game Is Very
Religious: Toward a Religious History of Hip Hop"   234

18   Cheryl Kirk-Duggan and Marlon F. Hall: "Put Down
the Pimp Stick to Pick Up the Pulpit"   245

19   John B. Hatch: "Rhetorical Synthesis through a
(Rap)Prochement of Identities: Hip-Hop and the Gospel
According to the Gospel Gangstaz"   263

20   Daniel White Hodge: "Where Are My Dawgs At?:
A Theology of Community"   288

Judaism

21   Judah Cohen: "Hip-Hop Judaica: The Politics of Representin' Heebster Heritage"   302

22   Malka Shabtay: "'RaGap': Music and Identity Among Young Ethiopians in Israel"   321

Eastern Religion

23   Steven J. Rosen: "Hip-Hop Hinduism: The Spiritual Journey of MC Yogi"   331

24   Ian Condry: "Battling Hip-Hop Samurai"   337

25   Anthony Y. H. Fung: "Western Style, Chinese Pop: Jay Chou's Rap and Hip-Hop in China"   364

Part V   **Hip Hop as Religion**   **375**

26   Siphiwe Ignatius Dube: "Hate Me Now: An Instance of NAS as Hip-Hop's Self-proclaimed Prophet and Messiah"   377

27   James Perkinson: "Tupac Shakur as Ogou Achade: Hip Hop Anger and Postcolonial Rancour Read from the Other Side"   392

28   Robin Sylvan: "Rap Music, Hip-Hop Culture and 'the Future Religion of the World'"   407

Conclusion: Hip Hop *and* or *in* Religion and Other Questions   421
Monica R. Miller and Anthony B. Pinn

Contributors   427

Permissions   434

Index   437

List of Figures

Chapter 11

Example 1 *Wrapped Up*, simplified voice-leading reduction, bars 1–6   149
Example 2 *Wrapped Up*, voice-leading reduction, Hook I (bars 14–21)   149
Example 3 *Wrapped Up*, bridge, oscillating harmonies, bars 38–47   150
Example 4 *Middle-ground voice-leading graph, bars 1–47*   151

Chapter 15

Figure 15.1   Nation of Islam and Five Percent Nation lessons   199
Figure 15.2   Science of Supreme Mathematics   200
Figure 15.3   Solar Facts   201
Figure 15.4   Universal Flag of the Five Percent Nation   202
Figure 15.5   The Supreme Alphabet   203

Chapter 20

Figure 20.1   The Spatial Identity Formation Model   292
Table 20.1   Post-soul Urban Language Differentiations   294

Acknowledgments

We are grateful to the numerous individuals and contributors who have, since the inception of this project, offered their sustained support for *The Hip Hop and Religion Reader*. We would especially like to thank the Series Editor to whom we first presented this project—Steve Wiggins, former editor for Religious Studies and Anthropology at Routledge whose enthusiasm and eagerness to see this work through helped to make this volume possible—we are grateful for the time, energy and support offered. We're especially grateful to and for Andrew Beck, Senior Philosophy Editor at Routledge for all of his attention to and sustained support of this work—we appreciate much your patience and conscientious diligence throughout the production process! We'd also like to thank the various presses that provided permission to reprint the materials and the contributors who enthusiastically supported our reprinting of their work. To everyone involved in the project on the publishing end, your support and energy have made this project enjoyable.

We are deeply appreciative to The Center for Engaged Research and Collaborative Learning at Rice University, including Assistant Director for Programming and Administration Maya Reine and the graduate students associated with the African American religious studies Ph.D. concentration at Rice. Over the years, CERCL has done much to solidify southern hip hop's contribution to the academic arena. Today, these efforts provide blueprints for engagement now used across the country. We would also like to specifically thank recent Rice Ph.D. graduate, Dr. Christopher Driscoll who offered assistance with many aspects of this project. We appreciate his efforts. We also thank both of our institutions, Rice University and Lehigh University, for providing space, resource, and collegial support as this project unfolded.

Finally—we would like to give a huge shout out to hip hop and the many constituents who've helped to make this growing area of study a palpable reality in the academy, classroom and beyond. We hope *The Hip Hop and Religion Reader* demonstrates our celebration of critical engagement, love for hip hop, and ongoing commitment to the sights, voices, times, and spaces that gave the world this thing we call hip hop culture.

Monica R. Miller
Anthony B. Pinn

General Introduction

Monica R. Miller and Anthony B. Pinn

This reader taps into a young but potent story that is, according to many, about 40 years old: the story of hip hop culture—a prevailing transnational force that has fundamentally changed and altered the ways in which we see and understand the world. It is a story with local roots, beginning in a nondescript area of the South Bronx, on 1520 Sedgwick Avenue, on August 11, 1973, due to a need for music for a party.

From this very specific block and time in American history to the rise of the global hip hop generation today, the universal presence of hip hop culture has exceeded the expectations of its consumers, critics, producers, and founders. Whether one self-identifies as hip hop or not, this cultural production and practice can't be ignored and is now cited along with other powerful cultural developments and movements such as the spirituals, blues, jazz, the Civil Rights Movement, Black Arts and Power Movement, and the power behind what some are calling the Post-Civil Rights and Post-Soul generations. Representing the best and worst of American society, hip hop culture is as American as apple pie, and yet, it troubles traditional associations of what, where, why, how, and who is the face of America. This reader contributes to discussions and discourses about the shifting scope of social and cultural identity in the late twentieth and early twenty-first century focused on that cultural artifact we have come to know as hip hop.

Hip Hop Studies

Hip hop studies begins as those who had come to appreciate and participate in hip hop culture made their way into the academy and were determined to bring their hip hop sensibilities with them. As the generation of academics before them were doing work that reflected their adherence to Civil Rights Movement postures and intellectual questions, many late baby boomers and members of "Generation X" vowed to shape the academy around the richness and depth of hip hop culture. Hip hop scholars and students owe a debt of gratitude to a long list of journalists and academics who worked hard to prove the public and academic merit and weight of hip hop. Dissertations, books, articles, academic lectures, and meetings ignored arguments that attention to popular culture—like rap music—was academic fluff, not the real stuff of scholarship. Classes on hip hop in various forms would follow this growing literature. And as books about hip hop culture gained more widespread attention, such as Tricia Rose's *Black Noise* (1994) winning the American Book Award in 1995, it became so much more difficult to resist: hip hop had bum rushed the academy.

Out of this early work has emerged a more fully formed canon rightly called hip hop stud-ies. The burgeoning development of hip hop studies, from its inception, is interdisciplinary, multi-vocal, and layered. The wide variety of topics and concerns taken up in hip hop studies scholarship has given hip hop culture an academic home in many fields today.

Hip hop studies, like other interdisciplinary modes of analyses, was meant to unpack the contributions of hip hop culture to the larger body of Western knowledge in a way that would allow hip hop to find a solid place within the US academy—as both resource material and cultural development demanding scholarly interrogation. That is to say, hip hop studies was meant to appreciate the earthy and urban origins of hip hop while also transporting this cul-tural development to institutions of higher learning. Courses on hip hop culture continue to emerge across the globe, with many rap artists doubling as distinguished lecturers and visit-ing scholars in departments across the academy today.

The journalistic and academic study of hip hop culture now spans well over twenty years and includes scholarship in a wide variety of disciplines and sub-interests. In 1978, the main trade magazine *Billboard* published an essay about the phenomenon that was becoming pop-ularized through the street parties and performances of many people following the pioneer-ing work of DJ Kool Herc.[1] In addition to journalists who were working hard to explore and report on the emergent cultural practices, personalities, ways of life, attitudes and behaviors that were shaping and shifting hip hop culture, film makers such as Charlie Ahearn were also taking note—consider the immense contribution that his film *Wild Style* (1982) made and continues to make in the teaching and learning of hip hop cultural elements.[2] And while media, filmmakers, and journalists like Robert Ford were taking note through public com-mentary, scholars such as Nelson George, among others, were working hard to give hip hop culture academic legs and feet. In 1984, David Toop published the text *Rap Attack: African Jove to New York Hip-Hop* which, according to Murray Forman, "presented a focused exami-nation of the cultural contexts within which hip-hop evolved and flourished."[3] The late 1990s and early 2000s gave rise to not only a new cadre of hip hop inspired academics—but also what we'd come to cite as the most foundational works for the development of hip hop stud-ies today. Scholars such as Robin D. G. Kelley, Russell A. Potter, Michael Eric Dyson, Mark Anthony Neal, Murray Forman, Joan Morgan, S. Craig Watkins, Nelson George, Tricia Rose, Imani Perry and Todd Boyd, among others, constitute black intellectuals within the univer-sity system who would come to produce articles and books that now stand as pioneering clas-sics within hip hop studies and bear witness to hip hop's academic legitimation.

Like African American studies, and women's and gender studies, it was only a matter of time before this attention to hip hop culture would gain a formal and systematic presence as a constituted field of study.

Religion and Hip Hop

Despite such growth and development, certain areas of thought such as religion were only slowly taken up. Many within hip hop studies, as had been the case in African American stud-ies or black studies, assumed that religion was a tricky topic—too often ministerial in nature and without rigor. Those perhaps interested in the embodied dimensions of hip hop culture and the production of meaning within and among this cultural geography would touch on such issues from positions of performance but rarely would attention to religion be offered in such work. Significant attention to perspectives on the study of religion outside religious studies departments and programs is beyond the scope of this introduction, but suffice it to say that this assumption, of course, is wrong; yet, it requires a corrective in the form of books, articles, classes, and so on that counter this flawed ideological position. That is, scholars of religion concerned with hip hop had to produce materials that were academically rich and intellectually thoughtful. They had to explore and excavate the religious language and theological conversations and foundations in hip hop that others overlooked or assumed to have limited significance and import for understanding more fully the importance of hip hop as a postmodern cultural development.

Religion is a significant cultural development in the United States, and the communities that gave birth to hip hop culture also formed and nurtured religious institutions, practices, and thought patterns. That is to say, religion and hip hop are organic to both black and brown communities and cannot be separated from them. For instance, hip hop pioneers like Afrika Bambaataa made use of a wide ranging spiritual and philosophical eclecticism for local cultural and social change in postindustrial America. And one might suggest that it is impossible to understand the social and existential weight of rap music and hip hop without understanding something about the formation and impact of Islam and Christianity (among many others) in urban communities of color. Both hip hop and religion spoke to and from the predicaments of life that shaped these communities. Yet, as religious institutions in African American communities, for instance, declined in significance and importance in the post-civil rights era, hip hop, as did the arts more generally, emerged as a new and viable way of seeing and speaking to the absurdities of life—the socio-political and economic arrangements of life and the weighty questions (the who, what, when, where, and why questions) that such circumstances encourage and necessitate. By the 1970s, the study of religion had been on solid footing for some time in U.S. colleges and universities, and the study of African American religion was gaining ground—with faculty appointments in that area of study at a variety of institutions across the country. By the late 1980s, some of those holding such appointments in the study of African American culture were also fans and participants of hip hop—and like their colleagues in English departments, history departments and so on—they were determined to bring the realities of hip hop to the exploration of religious studies. Hip hop had something to say to and about religion, and religion had something to say to and about hip hop. These scholars argued that there were creative and compelling intellectual links between these two cultural worlds—hip hop and religion—that demanded systematic and sustained intellectual attention.

Much of the credit for this turn to religion and/in hip hop is owed to a host of thinkers in the study of religion and related fields who mined the benefits of hip hop for understanding important topics in the study of religion such as human suffering and redemption, but who also saw within religious studies ways to unpack the importance of hip hop as a means to build community and make meaning. Much of this early conversation took place within the pages of the now defunct journal *Black Sacred Music: A Journal of Theomusicology* edited by John Michael Spencer who, in 1991, devoted a special issue of that journal to the topic of "The Emergence of Black and the Emergence of Rap." This special issue in particular and the journal in general gave scholars like Michael Dyson, Angela Nelson, and William Perkins the opportunity to engage religion, theology, spirituality and hip hop culture within an academic space.

During the 1990s and 2000s foundational work at the intersections of hip hop, religion, and theology grounded within a social criticism methodology was produced. Thinkers such as Dyson, Cornel West, and Anthony B. Pinn began to offer attention to the socio-religious dimensions and rhetoric grounding much of the production of rap music. In 1995, Dyson published *Between God and Gangsta Rap: Bearing Witness to Black Popular Culture*, a groundbreaking text that put hip hop on the religious studies map—this academic contribution became a signpost and formative contribution upon which religion and hip hop studies would build. This text focused on rap music and popular icons of color—making use of cultural criticism as its main approach. With an eye toward the problem of evil and suffering in black religion, Pinn broke ground with his text *Why Lord: Suffering and Evil in Black Theology* (1995) in which he developed a "nitty-gritty hermeneutic"[4]—a way to tap into and unearth life meaning in the seemingly secular and profane. In this work, Pinn offered robust attention to rap music and situated it as cultural source material alongside folktales, the spirituals, and the blues. With a working theory and method in hand, and a reconciling of the sacred and profane, what would became clear for religious studies more generally and African American religion and theology in particular was recognition that it was impossible to understand and chart the uses and function of religion in society without attention to culture itself—the very "stuff" that makes something like religion possible.

The push for the expansion of sources continues in Pinn's 2003 text *Noise & Spirit: The Religious and Spiritual Sensibilities of Rap Music*, which broadened the conversation to include attention to the varieties of religion in rap music. This text put rap music on the religious and theological studies terrain by placing rap music at the center of its analysis while highlighting the depth and breadth of religious sensibilities in rap—including attention to Christianity, Islam, Humanism, and more. Texts such as James Perkinson's *Shamanism, Racism, and Hip Hop Culture: Essays on White Supremacy and Black Subversion* (2005) pushed for greater attention and detail to both race and religion in hip hop culture. The growing attention to religion in rap music and hip hop culture assisted in the emergence of more theologically focused texts such as Ralph Watkins's *The Gospel Remix: Reaching the Hip Hop Generation* (2007), Daniel White Hodge's *The Soul of Hip Hop: Rims, Tims, and a Cultural Theology* (2010) and Cheryl Kirk-Duggan and Marlon F. Hall's most recent work *Wake Up!: Hip Hop Christianity and the Black Church* (2011).

The emergence of these scholars undertaking sustained, critical gazes at hip hop culture is surely influenced by personal and contextual concerns for many of these authors, but undergirding this growing body of scholarship—and helping to produce a market for it—have been longstanding efforts by some (and support from too many to name) within the American Academy of Religion (AAR).

Between the years of 2003 and 2010, over fifteen presentations touching on religion and hip hop culture were presented at the AAR as either single presentations or panels devoted to the theme. Attention to hip hop during such scholarly meetings indicates a clear trend toward increased participation and interest over the last decade. Born out of two panels at the AAR that focused exclusively on religion and theology in hip hop culture in 2007, a 2009 special issue of *Culture and Religion: An Interdisciplinary Journal* (Taylor & Francis) was dedicated to the theme of Hip Hop and Religion (Pinn and Miller, co-editors). This issue took up a variety of approaches from African American studies, cultural studies, and postcolonial analysis in order to examine the category of religion in hip hop culture in a more sustained way by broadening the data of hip hop beyond a sole focus on rap music. To be sure, the lyrics of hip hop account for a vast array of cultural data and interest, but only now are scholars—many appearing in this volume— taking a fuller account of the "look" of hip hop in all its varied dimensions.

A major marker of hip hop's solid footing in the academy was the formation of the AAR group on hip hop culture, *Critical Approaches to the Study of Hip Hop and Religion*, co-chaired and founded by Miller and Christopher Driscoll. This group set out to establish an intellectual "home" within the AAR for those interested in hip hop and religion scholarship, but on the premise—and promise—that such a focus necessitated a rigorous critical attention to the theories and methods used in the study of hip hop and religion. Groups, like this one, provide ongoing intellectual space within the AAR for addressing some of the more compelling contemporary topics and themes, checking in with scholars engaged in such efforts in terms of support, and for sustained reflexive dialogue between those who study religion and hip hop, and those who study religion more broadly.

Thanks to all of these efforts collectively, what was once a "bum rush" from a select group of courageous scholars has become a growing yet established subfield where those within it have the space to ask what "keeping it real" means as much for hip hop studies as religious studies. The continued work of a growing group of scholars, course offerings, scholar–artist collaborations, and emerging publications contribute toward and mark a substantial body of work addressing various dimensions of religion and hip hop. Because of the proliferation of these ongoing efforts, we believe it is time to begin the work of archiving and producing texts that can assist students and scholars alike with charting out and understanding more fully the theories, approaches, arguments and data that comprise what should be recognized as the area of research and teaching we call *religion and hip hop studies*.

The Hip Hop and Religion Reader

The Hip Hop and Religion Reader is the most substantial effort to date to contextualize and present this new and growing area of study—religion and hip hop studies—with attention to the significance of the collaborations and debates between hip hop and religion, as well as the ways in which hip hop has fostered, for some, an alternative form of religiosity.

Our concern is not to debate whether this constitutes a division of hip hop studies or of religious studies, but rather to simply indicate that the study of religion and hip hop has reached a point where reflection on its content, attentions, and scope is necessary. Mindful of this, this reader brings together foundational scholarship (both local, national and international) on religion and hip hop across a wide variety of data, approaches, themes, and concerns. In this way, this reader offers a comprehensive and interdisciplinary take on the relationship between two powerful cultural developments—religion and hip hop. Of course, constraints of space limit and prevent us from including all articles that have contributed to this important conversation. Yet, we have worked to make certain the pieces included are representative of the types of questions, concerns, approaches, theories, and methods that guide this area of study today. To wit, this canon is not closed; these mark, however, foundational pieces of continued significance.

The volume is organized thematically with attention to: (1) setting the context and framing the discussion, (2) what's the "religion" in hip hop? (3) the religious aesthetics of hip hop culture, (4) hip hop and/in religious traditions, and (5) hip hop as religion. Additionally, each section includes an original introductory essay with brief conclusions that raise questions for future study and research, summaries of the particular pieces, and study questions to assist further evaluation and exploration. Finally, we offer a brief, concluding essay that explores the future of the study of religion and hip hop.

It is our hope that *The Hip Hop and Religion Reader* will be of use to students and scholars alike, as a source book that provides a conceptual roadmap for where we've been and the places we're headed as religion and hip hop scholarship continues to grow. As such, we see this text as beginning and initiating a wider conversation, a small contribution to what we hope this field will become in the years to come.

Stories live on in powerful ways. What went down on August 11, 1973 at 1520 Sedgwick Avenue in the South Bronx, New York has become a sacred story, tale, fiction, legend, and narrative that continues on, in new and exciting ways, in the cultural pockets and imaginations of society today. The story of hip hop culture—its cathartic, existential, religious, secular, complex and material legacy—is a shape-shifting and evolving one. This reader seeks to capture a bit of that history, a dimension of that story. In the parlance of hip hop culture, we hope that many will be inspired to continue building, doing the math, and dropping knowledge about one of society's most powerful and enduring cultural wonders.

Notes

1. Forman, Murray, and Mark Anthony Neal. *That's the Joint!: The Hip-Hop Studies Reader*. New York: Routledge, 2012, 41–2.
2. Ahearn, Charlie. *Wild Style 30th Anniversary Collector's Edition*. Music Box Films, 2013.
3. Forman and Neal, *That's the Joint!*, 2.
4. Pinn, Anthony B. *Why Lord?: Suffering and Evil in Black Theology*. New York: Continuum International Publishing Group, 1999.

Part I
Setting the Context,
Framing the Discussion

"It's bigger than hip hop" is an oft rehearsed shout-out specific to hip hop culture meant to raise questions about hip hop's social, cultural and political role and imaging in changing historical moments and climates. How do we, whether insiders, outsiders, or both, go about the business of defining *what* hip hop is, *who* is hip hop and *what* hip hop ought to do in and for the world, if anything at all? Think for a moment about the many raging and partisan debates about hip hop culture and the ever-changing and wide variety of niches that define hip hop cultural practices—whether hip hop *ought* to be "conscious," "political" or about "pleasure" and "desire"; whether rap artists in particular ought to be fully responsible and accountable for marketing and perpetuating social ills such as misogyny, sexism, and homophobia. Such queries have been productive *and* constricting—generative in terms of asking relevant questions and initiating important conversations while also, at times, compressing hip hop culture into boxes it most likely hadn't anticipated fitting.

These issues become particularly heightened in conversations and scholarship that seek to examine the use, roles, and functions of religion in hip hop culture, rap music in particular. As some of the thinkers in this part rightfully note, religious sensibilities have never been separate from the emergence and birth of hip hop culture and one would be correct to suggest that religion, spirituality, esotericism and philosophy are and always have been major stock ingredients in the building up and expression of hip hop culture, so much so that some have alluded to hip hop *as* a "new religion" (i.e., Kanye West and Jay Z's song "No Church in the Wild," Lupe Fiasco's song "Hip-Hop Saved My Life," Killer Mike's "R.A.P. Music" and KRS ONE's text *The Gospel of Hip Hop*). However, such a gesture requires and necessitates further thought about the role of the sacred and the profane in the "stuff" we call culture—that is, one's view of placing hip hop culture within the "sacred" or as an avenue for discovery of the "sacred" is often contingent upon how such categories are constructed, examined, understood and theorized among artists, producers, consumers, critics and so on. Similarly, such queries also entail a larger and more complex conversation regarding historical context and antecedents, methodological approaches, disciplinary norms, and changing definitions within and among hip hop studies today.

This part introduces foundational and preeminent essays that have become cornerstones and guideposts in the growing body of religion and hip hop scholarship. Taken together, these essays introduce and highlight not only initial concerns (i.e., sacred vs. profane) in this growing area of study, but also raise pressing questions that continue to stand as major areas of debate, consensus and growth in the field today. This part begins by introducing major questions of orientation such as what does hip hop *do*, how does society perceive it, and what does it signify?

Many know that "represent!" is a key term in hip hop communities and cosmology and such demand for *representation* or *bearing witness* is explored throughout this part by using hip hop not only as cultural data but also as a lens of analysis in exploring the role of religion, meaning, signification, class, and race, among a host of other areas in marginal communities—especially communities of color. But just what *is represented* in/by hip hop or the scholars who study it?

Earlier analysis of religion and hip hop (rap music in particular) offered hip hop culture a seat at the table of diasporic historical continuity—thus, legitimating it as the next logical cultural step and progression in communities of struggle and the subsequent demand to understand it through scholarship. Among a number of the essays, we see a connection made between rap music and the spirituals and the blues, and that close attention to "What the Music Said" (to borrow the title of Mark Anthony Neal's 1998 text on black popular music and black public culture) also says something about life and life options. And like life—as pointed out by a number of the essays in this part—rap music and hip hop are ... complex, messy and vulnerable to structural and social inequities. Hip hop *represents* the grittiness of life, and the bars, beats, breaks and railway boxcars remixed by this thing we've come to call hip hop represent a life examined.

But, for those convinced of the perpetual argument that rap music and hip hop culture are deterministically harmful and detrimental to the flourishing of certain communities (i.e., black life), some of the following essays strongly suggest that rap artists are in fact modern day griots—truth tellers and seekers who emulate and borrow artists' rhetorical and cultural practices that have been vital and endemic to the maintenance of black life in the diaspora and serve an important utility in the continual reclamation of historical, social, political and cultural forces that seek to threaten marginal groups. Through the strategy of constructing historical continuity and cultural progression for survival and expression—legitimation of rap music and hip hop as a proper object of study is solidified. With a rightful link forged, we begin to see the exploration of rap music expressive of the rich tradition of "black orality" within the context of historical struggle (i.e., slavery)—a permanent feature much animated in the traditions of black culture for the procurement and production of hope, meaning, questioning, existence and agency among a host of other themes that become key components of religion and hip hop scholarship. As the essays here move along, more focused attention is offered to expanding the varieties of religion explored in rap music and hip hop culture, as earlier work tended to hyper-focus on Christianity and Christian themes and theologies. Later scholarship begins to boast wider attention to other religious and spiritual sensibilities endemic to hip hop culture—such as Humanism and Islam.

Much earlier work, with an important eye toward legitimating rap music as a rightful object of study in religion and theology, often assumed the meaning and form of religion as *a priori*. That is, it often succeeded in legitimating hip hop's "religious" dimensions as viable and valuable for study through a tacit (or explicit) assumption that religion was its own thing, removed somehow from the more mundane stuff of culture. As this part progresses, we begin to see more forceful attention to theory and method as it concerns the category of religion in culture and a reconciling of the sacred and the profane—even a push to offer a theory of how religion moves in and through culture and life. Other theoretical challenges further opened the intellectual terrain. Often, earlier work tended to over-focus on rap music in particular and thus approaches to such data were often limited to textual approaches which often ignored other hip hop elements such as graffiti and dance—that is, the performance aspects of hip hop as experience, event, and movement. Such queries and interests require new theories, approaches and interdisciplinarity in order to examine things such as the impact of historical shifts on hip hop culture itself. Thus, we begin to see a broadening of variables in the area of study which begin to chart hip hop not only as product (of meaning) but also context (of use) and a heightened awareness that, like anything else, "interpretation" carries along with it a wide variety of agendas, motivations and interests—the struggle over meaning takes place not only within culture itself but also through the hermeneutical lenses that we bring to such cartographies.

With legitimation and refining in place, we begin to move outside of religious studies proper to focus on cultivating alternative approaches to hip hop, such as embodiment and performance. All of that to say, what hip hop "means" (to one scholar or another or one field or another) becomes a matter of debate and interpretation, not only within hip hop, but among those who study it. And in a fashion befitting hip hop's aesthetic foundation in the art of sampling, scholarship on religion and hip hop has often sampled itself as data, to date, constantly remade and remixed into expanding arenas with a growing theoretical dexterity and might coming from a humility expressed in and through arrogant stylings. Rightfully, this part ends with a gesture toward broadening the agenda of refining and expanding the study of hip hop—beyond the local and toward under-engaged components and dimensions of hip hops' existential textures, borders and boundaries. Some thinkers, not only in this first part but also in subsequent ones throughout this reader, have suggested that Islam in hip hop is not only largely ignored in scholarship, but that Islamic sensibilities were quite unique and germane to the founders and founding of hip hop culture itself. What might it be to think of hip hop (and religion, we might add) as context, product, text, event, authority, performance, community, and nation?

Early scholarship in this area (and others) worked hard to give the study of hip hop a viable academic stage, and in doing so initial challenges and concerns were often expressed in and through proving hip hop's public merit and existential weight—that it deserved to be studied from areas like religion and theology with themes such as embodiment, prophecy, community, nation, protest, meaning and transformation in mind—social ills notwithstanding nor placated, but certainly no different than complexities and contradictions to life in general terms. Such an effort was, and continues to be, accomplished through carefully and strategically constructing historical continuity among hip hop and rap music and other black cultural productions that have made possible the sustaining, management, and expression of black life throughout history. That religion would intrinsically be a formative dimension of, and rhetorically articulated through, the cultural product of hip hop is, according to the historical record of people of color in the New World, of little to no surprise.

Finally, this part introduces and marks the early archiving of key ideas and terms that have become endemic to the conversation on and study of religion and hip hop—notions such as prophetic, meaning-making and life meaning, complex subjectivity, global community and nation, bearing witness, commodity and commodification, among a host of others. Such crucial ideas and terms did much heavy lifting in terms of carving and crafting the terms of engagement, debate, and nuance which were never—from the beginning—disconnected from the study of black culture and religion in particular. Where and how do we locate such terms, contests and themes today when studying religion in hip hop? What aspects of these ideas and arguments continue in utility and purpose? Which ones stand in need of revision, expansion and challenge in light of hip hop's global and transnational growth?

1

Performance, Protest, and Prophecy in the Culture of Hip-Hop

Michael Eric Dyson considers the evolution and development of hip hop culture and rap music with attention to its role, function and outside perception in American society. Dyson argues that the emergence and sustaining of this cultural phenomenon represents aesthetic sensibilities that reflect fragmentation, generational divides, socio-economic and political destruction of inner cities and class fissures among black communities. Mindful of this troubled context, rap music and hip hop culture in general reflect the frustrations of a growing black underclass. Moving through various forms of rap music, and earlier markers such as the blues of African American articulation of life as filled with joy and pain, Dyson argues that, despite growing commercialism, hip hop and rap music represent logical progressions of black cultural products that express the realities of black life through musical expression. He then explores rap groups who maintain such a commitment, but one that is colored and conflicted by the ebbs and flows of increased violence, sexism and misogyny in rap music. He finds promising the preoccupation with literacy (wordplay, flow, creativity, linguistic innovation, and so on) borrowed from and rooted in rhetorical practices honed and perfected in black music and African American religious experiences as modern day "griots" of truth-telling and bearing witness. Dyson concludes that, despite its pitfalls and dangers, rap music is the most powerful form of black music today. It offers young people a means by which to reclaim history, a tradition of activism, and examines pressing social issues that continue to threaten black life.

Performance, Protest, and Prophecy in the Culture of Hip-Hop

Michael Eric Dyson

From the very beginning of its history, hip-hop music—or "rap," as it has come to be known—has faced various obstacles. Initially, rap was deemed a passing fad, a playful, harmlessly non-sensical, and ephemeral form of cultural high jinks that steamed off the musical energies of urban black teens. As it became obvious that rap was here to stay, a permanent fixture in black ghetto youths' musical landscape, the reactions changed from dismissal to denigration, and rap music came under attack from both white *and* black quarters. Is rap really as dangerous as many would have us believe? Or are there redeeming characteristics to rap that warrant serious, critical attention, as opposed to dismissive condescension? I will attempt to answer these and other questions as I explore the culture of hip-hop.

Trying to pinpoint the exact origin of rap is a tricky process that depends on when one acknowledges a particular cultural expression or product as rap. Rap has been traced back to the revolutionary verse of Gil Scott-Heron and the Last Poets, to Pigmeat Markham's "Heah Comes de Judge," and even to Bessie Smith's rapping to a beat in some of her blues. Some have gone back even further, citing ancient African oral traditions as the antecedents to various contemporary African-American cultural practices. In any case, the modern history of rap probably begins in 1979 with the rap song "Rapper's Delight," by the Sugarhill Gang. Although there were other (mostly underground) examples of rap, this record is regarded as the signal barrier-breaker, birthing hip-hop and consolidating the infant art form's popularity. This first stage in rap record production was characterized by rappers placing their rhythmic repetitive speech and staccatoed syllabic dexterity over well-known black music hits (mostly R&B). "Rapper's Delight" was rapped over the music to a song made by the popular seventies R&B group Chic, entitled "Good Times." Though rap would later expand and perfect its technical virtuosity through instrumentation, drum machines, and "sampling" existing records—thus making it creatively symbiotic—the first stage was benignly parasitic.

As rap grew, its expanded expression was still limited to mostly inner-city neighborhoods and particularly to its place of origin, New York City. Rap artists like Funky 4 Plus 1, Kool Moe Dee, Busy Bee, Afrika Bambaataa, Cold Rush Brothers, Kurtis Blow, DJ Kool Herc, and Grandmaster Melle Mel were experimenting with this developing musical genre. As it evolved, rap began to reflect critically upon the terrain of its genesis, describing and scrutinizing the social, economic, and political constituents that led to its emergence and development: drug addiction, police brutality, teen pregnancy, and various forms of material deprivation. This new development was both expressed and precipitated by Kurtis Blow's

"The Breaks," and by the most influential and important rap song to emerge in this period of rap history, "The Message," by Grandmaster Flash and the Furious Five. The picture this song painted of inner-city life for black Americans—the hues of dark social misery and stains of profound urban catastrophe—screeched against the canvas of most suburban sensibilities.

> Now you'll grow up in the ghetto livin' second rate
> And your eyes will sing a song of deep hate
> The places you play and where you stay
> Looks like one great big alleyway
> You'll admire all the number booktakers
> Thugs, pimps and pushers, and the big money makers
> Drivin' big cars, spendin' twenties and tens
> And you want to grow up to be just like them?
> (It's like a jungle sometimes)
> It makes me wonder how I keep from goin' under.

"The Message," along with Flash's "New York, New York," pioneered the social awakening of rap, catalyzing its maturation into a form combining social protest, musical creation, and cultural expression.

As its fortunes slowly grew, rap was still viewed by the music industry as an epiphenomenal cultural production that would cease as black youths became bored and moved on, as they had done with break dancing and graffiti art. But the successes of the group Run-DMC moved rap into a different sphere of artistic expression that signaled its increasing control of its own destiny. Run-DMC is widely recognized as the progenitor of modern rap's integration of social commentary, creatively diverse musical elements, and uncompromised cultural identification—an integration that pushed the music into the mainstream and secured its future as an American musical genre with an identifiable tradition. Run-DMC's stunning commercial and critical success almost singlehandedly landed rap in the homes of many black and nonblack youths across America by producing the first rap album to be certified gold (five hundred thousand copies sold), the first rap song to be featured on the twenty-four-hour music video channel MTV, and the first rap album (1987's *Raising Hell*) to go triple platinum (3 million copies sold).

On *Raising Hell*, Run-DMC showcased the sophisticated technical virtuosity of its DJ Jam Master Jay—the raw shrieks, scratches, glitches, and language of the street, plus the innovative and ingenious appropriation of hard-rock guitar riffs. In doing this, Run-DMC symbolically and substantively wedded two traditions—the waning subversion of rock music and the rising, incendiary aesthetic of hip-hop music—to produce a poignant and provocative hybrid of fiery lyricism and potent critique. *Raising Hell* ended with the rap anthem "Proud to Be Black," intoning its unabashed racial pride:

> Ya know I'm proud to be black ya'll
> And that's a fact ya'll
> Now Harriet Tubman was born a slave
> She was a tiny black woman when she was raised
> She was livin' to be givin' there's a lot that she gave
> There's not a slave in this day and age
> I'm proud to be black.

At the same time, rap, propelled by Run-DMC's epochal success, found an arena in which to concentrate its subversive cultural didacticism aimed at addressing racism, classism, social neglect, and urban pain; and rap discovered a place that allowed it to engage in ritualistic refusals of censored speech: the rap concert. The rap concert creates space for cultural resistance and personal agency, loosing the strictures of tyrannizing surveillance and demoralizing condemnation and substituting autonomous, often enabling, forms of self-expression and cultural creativity.

However, Run-DMC's success, which greatly increased the visibility and viability of rap music through record sales and rap concerts, brought along another charge which has had a negative impact on rap's perception by the general public the claim that rap expresses and causes violence. Tipper Gore has repeatedly said that rap music appeals to "angry, disillusioned, unloved kids" and tells them it is "okay to beat people up." Violent incidents at rap concerts in Los Angeles, Pittsburgh, Cleveland, Atlanta, Cincinnati, and New York have only reinforced the popular perception that rap is intimately linked to violent social behavior by mostly black and Latino inner-city kids. Countless black parents, too, have had negative reactions to rap, and the black radio and media establishment, although not as vocal as Gore, have voted on her side—with their silent allocation of much less airplay and print coverage to rap than is warranted by its impressive record sales.

Such reactions indicate a shallow understanding of rap, and in many cases result in people's unwillingness to listen to rap lyrics, many of which counsel antiviolent and antidrug behavior among the youths who are their avid audience. Many rappers have spoken directly against violence, such as KRS-One in his "Stop the Violence." A top-selling rap record produced by KRS-One in 1989, *Self Destruction*, insists that violence predates rap and speaks against escalating black-on-black crime, which erodes the social and communal fabric of already debased black inner cities across America:

> Well today's topic is self-destruction
> It really ain't the rap audience that's buggin'
> It's one or two suckers, ignorant brothers
> Tryin' to rob and steal from one another …
> 'Cause the way we live is positive
> We don't kill our relatives …
> Back in the sixties our brothers and sisters were hanged
> How could you gang-bang?
> I never ever ran from the Ku Klux Klan
> And I shouldn't have to run from a black man
> 'Cause that's self-destruction
> Ya headed for self-destruction.

Despite such potent messages, many mainstream blacks and whites persist in categorically negative appraisals of rap, displaying an inability to distinguish between enabling, productive rap messages and the social violence that exists in many inner-city communities and that is often reflected in rap songs. Of course, it is difficult for a culture that is serious about the maintenance of social arrangements, economic conditions, and political choices that create and reproduce poverty, racism, sexism, classism, and violence to display a significant appreciation for musical expressions that contest and scandalize the existence of such problems in black and Latino communities. What is doubly disappointing is the continued complicity of black radio stations in this sordid equivalent to Alan Bloom's and E. D. Hirsch's elitist cultural and intellectual agenda, which amounts to opprobrious bases for judging the suitability and propriety of musical tastes. The conspiracy of silence is not limited to black radio: expressions of conservative black cultural sensibilities pervade the print media as well. Although rapper MC Shan believes that most antirap bias arises from outside the black community, he faults black radio for depriving rap of adequate airplay and laments the fact that "if a white rock 'n' roll magazine like *Rolling Stone* or *Spin* can put a rapper on the cover and *Ebony* and *Jet* won't, that means there's really something wrong."

In this regard, rap music is emblematic of the glacier shift in aesthetic sensibilities that divides blacks intergenerationally, and it also emphasizes the brazen economic barriers that increasingly blockade underclass blacks from middle– and upper–middle–class blacks. Rap, in short, is a testimony to the intraracial class division that has plagued African-American communities for the last thirty years. The increasing social isolation, economic desperation, political degradation, and cultural exploitation undergone by most underclass communities in the past few decades have given rise to a form of musical expression that captures the terms of underclass existence. This is not to suggest that rap has been limited to the "ghetto poor," but only that its main ingredients (major themes and styles) continue to be drawn from the complexities, conflicts, and contradictions of urban black life.

One of the newer trends in rap music is the development of "pop" rap by groups like JJ Fad, the Fat Boys, DJ Jazzy Jeff and the Fresh Prince, and Tone Lōc. DJ Jazzy Jeff and the Fresh Prince, for example, are two suburbanites from South West Philadelphia and Winfield. (For that matter, the most radical rap group, Public Enemy, are suburbanites from Long Island.) DJ Jazzy Jeff and the Fresh Prince's album, *He's the DJ, I'm the Rapper*, has sold over 3 million copies, primarily due to their enormously successful single "Parents Just Don't Understand." This record, which rapped humorously about various crises associated with being a teen, struck a chord with teenagers across racial and class spectra, signaling the exploration of rap's populist terrain.

Tone Lōc's success also expresses rap's division between hard-core (social consciousness and racial pride backed by driving rhythms) and pop (exploration of common territory between races and classes, usually devoid of a social message). This division, while expressing the expansion of rap, also means that companies and willing radio executives have increasingly chosen pop rap as more acceptable than its more realistic, politically conscious counterpart. Tone Lōc is a Los Angeles rapper whose first single, "Wild Thing," sold over 2 million copies, topping Billboard's Hot Singles Chart, the first rap song to achieve this height. Tone Lōc's success was sparked by his video's placement in heavy rotation on MTV, which devotes an hour on Saturdays to "Yo! MTV Raps," a show that has become so popular that a daily half-hour segment has been added.

The success of such artists as Tone Lōc or DJ Jazzy Jeff and the Fresh Prince inevitably raises the specter of mainstream dilution, the threat to every emergent form of cultural production in American culture, particularly the fecund musical tradition that comes from black America. For many, this means the sanitizing of rap's expression of urban realities, resulting in sterile hip-hop which, devoid of its original fire, will offend no one. This scenario, of course, is a familiar denouement to the story of most formerly subversive musical genres. Also, MTV's increasing acceptance of rap and the staging of rap concerts run by white promoters willing to take a chance on rap artists add further commentary to the sad state of cultural affairs in many black communities, whose continued refusal to acknowledge authentic (not to mention desirable) forms of rap artistry ensures rap's existence on the margins of many black communities. More tragically, black businesses, by turning their backs on rap and the promotion of rap concerts and charity benefits utilizing the talents and influence of rap artists, have closed the door on viable ways of strengthening the weak economic infrastructure of many inner, city black communities.

Perhaps the example of another neglected and devalued black musical tradition, the blues, can be helpful for understanding what is occurring between rap, segments of the black community, and the mainstream. The blues now has a mostly young white audience. Blacks do not support the blues through concert patronage or record buying, thus neglecting a musical genre that was once closely identified with devalued, degraded, and despised people: poor southern, agrarian blacks and the northern, urban black poor, the first stratum of the developing underclass. The blues functioned for another generation of blacks similarly to the way rap functions for young blacks today: as a source of racial identity, permitting forms of boasting and machismo for devalued black men suffering from social emasculation, allowing commentary on social and personal conditions in uncensored language, and fostering the ability to transform hurt and anguish into art and commerce. Even in its heyday, however, the blues existed as a secular musical genre over against the religious sensibilities that described the blues as "devil's music" and the conservative black cultural sensibilities that viewed the blues as rather barbaric. These feelings, along with the direction of southern agrarian musical energies into a somewhat more accessible and populist soul music, ensured the contraction of the economic and cultural basis for expressing life experience in the blues idiom.

Robert Cray's newfound success in mainstreaming the blues perhaps completes the cycle of survival for devalued forms of black music: it originates in a context of anguish and pain and joy and happiness, it expresses those emotions and ideas in a musical language and idiom peculiar to its view of life, it is altered due to cultural sensibilities and economic factors/ realities, and it is refracted to the world through the prism of mainstream distribution, packaging, and consumption for leisurely or cathartic pleasure through concert attendance or record buying. Also, in the process, artists are removed from the immediate context and original site of their artistic production. Moreover, besides the everyday ways in which the music is employed in a variety of entertainment functions, it may occasionally be employed in contexts that truncate and vitiate its subversive critique of the status quo and may be used to legitimize a setting that, in negative ways, has partially given rise to its expression. The most recent example of this is Lee Atwater's positioning of himself as a privileged patron of the blues and soul music traditions in the 1989 Bush inauguration festivities, which was preceded by his racist use of the Willie Horton case. Atwater's use of Willie Horton viciously played on the very prejudice against black men that has often led blues musicians to express the psychic, personal, and social pain occasioned by racism in American (political) culture. Rap's visibility may alter this pattern as it continues to grow, but its self-defined, continuing challenge is to maintain its aesthetic, cultural, and political proximity to its site of original expression: the "ghetto poor."

Interestingly, a new wave of rap artists may be accomplishing this goal, but with foreboding consequences. For example, NWA (Niggaz With Attitudes) reflects the brutal circumstances that define the boundaries within which most underclass black kids in Los Angeles must live. For the most part they—unlike their socially conscientious counterparts Public Enemy, Boogie Down Productions, and Stetsasonic—have no ethical remove from the violence, gang bangin', and drugs in L.A.'s inner city. In their song "F— tha Police," NWA gives a sample of their reality:

> Fuck the police, comin' straight from the underground
> A young nigger got it bad 'cause I'm brown
> And not the other color, so police think
> They have the authority to kill a minority …
> Searchin' my car looking for the product
> Thinkin' every nigger is sellin' narcotics
> But don't let it be a black and a white one, 'cause they'll slam ya down to the street top
> Black police showin' out for the white cop.

Such expressions of violence certainly reflect the actual life circumstances of many black and Latino youths caught in the desperate cycle of drugs and gangs that constitute L.A. ghetto living. NWA portrays a view of life that celebrates a lethal mix of civil terrorism and personal cynicism. Their attitude is both one answer to and the logical outcome of the violence, racism, and oppression in American culture. On the other hand, their vision must be criticized for the stakes are too high for the luxury of moral neutrality. Having lived the life they rap about, NWA understands the viciousness of police brutality. However, they must also be challenged to develop an ethical perspective on the drug gangs that duplicate police violence in black-on-black crime. While rappers like NWA perform an invaluable service by rapping in poignant and realistic terms about urban underclass existence, they must be challenged to expand their moral vocabulary and to be more sophisticated in their understanding that description alone is insufficient in addressing the crises of black urban life. They must become critically aware that blacks are victims of the violence of both state repression *and* gang violence, that one form of violence is often the response to the other, and that blacks continue to be held captive to disenabling lifestyles (gang bangin' and drug dealing) that cripple the life of black communities.

Also problematic is the sexist sentiment that pervades so much of rap music. It is a rampant sexism that continues to mediate relations within the younger black generation with lamentable intensity. As Harry Allen says in an *Essence* magazine article: "As I once told a sister, hip-hop lyrics are, among other things, what a lot of Black men say about Black women when Black women aren't around … Because women are the ones best able to define sexism, they will have to challenge the music—tell it how to change and make it change–if change is to come. Only then will record companies cease the release of cuts that call for bitch-smacking." While it is true that rap's sexism is indeed a barometer of the general tenor and mood that mediates black male/female relations in the inner city, it is not the role of women alone to challenge it. Reproach must flow from women *and* men who are sensitive to the ongoing sexist attitudes and behaviors that dominate black male/female relationships. Because women by and large do not run record companies, or even head independent labels that have their records distributed by larger corporations, it is naive to assume that protest by women alone will arrest the spread of sexism in rap. Female rappers are certainly a potential resource for challenging existing sexist attitudes, but given the sexist barriers that patrol rap's borders, men who rap must be challenged by non-sexist men, especially male rappers who contest the portrayal of women in most rap music. The constant references to women as "skeezers," "bitches," and "ho's" only reinforces the perverted expression of male dominance and patriarchy and reasserts the coerced inferiority and objectification of women as sexual "things" exclusively intended for male pleasure.

Fortunately, many of the problems related to rap—particularly with black radio, media, and community acceptance—have helped to foster a sense of camaraderie that transcends in crucial ways the fierce competitive streak in rap (which, at its best moments, urges rappers on to creative musical heights). While the "dis'" rap (which humorously musicalizes the dozens) is alive and well, the overall feeling among rap artists that rap must exist and flourish outside the sanctions of traditional institutional means of garnering high visibility or securing record sales has directed a communal energy into the production of their music. The current state of affairs has also precipitated cooperative entrepreneurial activity among young black persons. The rap industry has spawned a number of independent labels, providing young blacks (mostly men) with experience as heads of their own businesses and with exposure as managers of talent, positions that otherwise might be unavailable to them. It also means that rap has flourished, for the most part, independently of the tight constraints imposed by major music corporations and independently of the patronage relations that develop under the severely regimented distribution of capital to specific genres of music in these corporations.

Although many independent companies have struck distribution deals with major labels— such as Atlantic, MCA, Columbia, and Warner Brothers—it is usually the case that, given the inexperience of major labels with rap and their continued conservatism in musical taste and in anticipating trends in rap, the independent labels continue to control their destinies by teaching the major companies invaluable lessons about street sales, the necessity of having a fast rate of delivery from the production of a record to its date of distribution, and remaining close to the sensibilities of the street, as well as about willingness to experiment and be diverse in their marketing approach as rap itself continues to diversify its style.

Also gratifying is the expression in rap of the ongoing preoccupation with literacy that has impelled the African-American community forward since the inception of legally coerced illiteracy during slavery. Rap artists explore grammatical creativity, verbal wizardry, and linguistic innovation in the art of oral communication with a welcome vengeance. The rap artist, as Cornel West has indicated, is a bridge figure who combines the two potent traditions in black culture, preaching and music: the rapper appeals to the rhetorical practices eloquently honed in African-American religious experiences and the cultural potency of black singing/ musical traditions to produce an engaging hybrid. In a sense, rappers are truly urban griots dispensing social and cultural critiques, verbal shamans exorcising the demons of "hiphopcrisy" and a laissez-faire orality that refuses to participate in the media of cultural exploration and social provocation. The culture of hip-hop has generated a lexicon of life that expresses rap's b-boy/b-girl *Weltanschauung,* a perspective that takes delight in the postmodern practice of demystifying high-classical strictures on language and celebrates the culturally encoded twists of phrases that communicate in their own idiom.

It is also refreshing to watch hip-hop culture revive an explicit historicism that combats the amnesia threatening to further consign the measured achievements of the recent black past into disabling lapses of memory. Hip-hop has infused a revived sense of historical pride into young black minds that is salutary insofar as it provides a solid base for self-esteem. Rap music has also focused renewed attention on black nationalist discourse and black radical thought. This revival has been best represented by the rap group Public Enemy.

Public Enemy announced their black nationalism in embryonic form on their first album, *Yo! Bum Rush the Show,* but their vision sprang forward full-blown in their important *It Takes a Nation of Millions to Hold Us Back.* The album's explicit black nationalist language and cultural sensibilities were joined with a powerful mix of music, beats, screams, noise, and rhythms from the street. Its message is provocative, even jarring, a precis of the contained chaos and channeled rage that informs the most politically astute rappers. On the cut "Bring the Noise," they intone:

> We got to demonstrate
> Come on now, they're gonna have to wait till we get it right
> Radio stations I question their blackness
> They call themselves black but we'll see if they'll play this
> turn it up! Bring the noise!

Public Enemy also speaks of the criminality of prison conditions and how dope dealers fail the black community. Their historical revivalism is noteworthy, for instance, as they rap on "Party for Your Right to Fight:"

> Power equality, and we're out to get it
> I know some of you ain't wit' it
> This party started right in sixty-six
> With a pro-black radical mix.

Public Enemy troubled even more sociocultural waters with their Nation of Islam views in "Don't Believe the Hype," saying, "The followers of Farrakhan/Don't tell me that you understand until you hear the man."

Such rap displays the power and pitfalls associated with the revival of earlier forms of black radicalism, nationalism, and cultural expression. The salutary aspect of the historical revival is that it raises consciousness about important figures, movements, and ideas that prompted the racial, social, and political progress that permits rappers to express their visions of life in American culture. This renewed historicism permits young blacks to discern links between the past and their own present circumstances, using the past as a fertile source of social reflection, cultural creation, and political resistance. On the other hand, it has also led to some forms of historical recuperation that do not provide critical distance from that past but are rather unquestioningly mimetic, attempting to replicate the past without challenging or expanding it. Thus, their historical revival fails to illumine as powerfully as it might, and the present generation of black youths, including rappers, fails to benefit as fully from the lessons that it so powerfully recuperates and appeals to. This of course is one result of the lack of dialogue, understanding, and communication between various segments of the black community, particularly along generational and class lines, problems symbolized in the black community's response to rap. Historical revival cries out for contexts that will provide the bases for revision and expansion that render the past understandable and usable. This cannot occur if large segments of the black community continue to be segregated from the most exciting cultural transformation occurring in contemporary African-American life: in the artistic expression, cultural exploration, social activity, and historical revival of hip-hop artists.

Rap is a form of profound musical, cultural, and social creativity. It expresses the desire of young black people to reclaim their history, reactivate forms of black radicalism, and contest the powers of despair, hopelessness, and genocide that presently besiege the black community. Besides being the most powerful form of black music today, rap projects a style of self onto the world that disciplines ultimate social despair into forms of cultural resistance, and transforms the ugly terrain of ghetto existence into a searing portrait of life as it is lived by millions of voiceless people. For this reason alone, rap deserves attention and should be taken seriously; and for its productive healthy expressions, it should be promoted as a worthy form of artistic expression and cultural projection, and as an enabling source of communal solidarity.

Study Questions

1. How does Dyson characterize the beginning of rap music's development and origins in black culture and life? Why is it difficult to pinpoint exactly when rap music emerges?
2. How does rap music evolve and expand and what challenges and advancements does hip hop's message experience and face during its transitional moments? How do societal demands of the music industry limit and advance rap music and the proliferation of its many messages?
3. How does Dyson connect rap music and religion as expressed in African American culture? What do the spirituals and the blues have to do with the function of religion in rap music?

2

Making a World with a Beat
Musical Expression's Relationship to Religious Identity and Experience

Historically, the oral tradition in black culture has been the primary mode of expressing themes related to survival and the quest for greater life meaning and increased agency. Written with an eye on the historical context of struggle and slavery spanning the spirituals, gospels, blues to rap music, this introduction situates the tradition, role, function, themes, and initial concerns that emerge from the tradition of music in black life. As such, artists function as modern day griots of praise and protest. This essay introduces major themes (such as survival, life meaning (religion), style, balance, and confrontation), key stock ingredients (African American history and varieties of religious sensibilities in black life), historical trajectories (Middle Passage to New World), and models and approaches (sacred vs. profane, theology & belief, and religion as meaning-making) that guide the contemporary academic study of religion in rap music and hip hop today.

Making a World with a Beat: Musical Expression's Relationship to Religious Identity and Experience*

Anthony B. Pinn

Recently, Reverend Paul Scott of Durham, North Carolina, renewed the attack on rap music initiated by Reverend Calvin Butts and C. Delores Tucker.

Butts and Tucker argued that groups such as 2 Live Crew promote a culture of disrespect and immorality that is not in keeping with the best American values and principles of life. Reverend Butts thought some rap music so foul that only a steamroller could adequately deal with the "music." Presenting a mild version of the perspective held by Tucker and Butts, Reverend Scott urged "black people to put black power back into hip-hop ... to counter the negativity" through giving attention to the positive forms of rap music.[1]

While there is much of questionable social value in rap music as a genre, statements issued by figures such as Reverend Scott, Reverend Butts, and C. Delores Tucker tend to lack any understanding of the complexity of its message, assuming rap can be neatly divided into rigid categories of "good" and "bad" styles. Over the years I've taught my "Religion and Popular Culture" course, some of the students have raised similar questions concerning the content of rap music. For my students, as with Scott and Butts, rap music is most problematic when viewed from the vantage point of religiously charged sensibilities. The two—rap music and religion—are seen as polar opposites. Though there is no doubt that the music is raw, is it not possible that rap artists are modern griots, as Houston Baker and Michael Dyson argue, in keeping with the earlier traditions of the spirituals and the blues? Is it not possible that these artists are continuing a tradition of social critique using an "organic" vocabulary? Hence, at its best, perhaps rap music is a continuation of the creative manner in which meaning is made out of an absurd world by promoting a style of living through which a sense of self and community is forged in a hostile environment.

Noise and Spirit (1995), the book from which this essay is taken, recognizes the deep and messy connections between religious concerns and rap music often expressed in the form of a wrestling between the "sacred" and "secular" that cut across rap style typologies. The field of religious studies needs to get up to speed with respect to rap music and hip-hop culture in more general terms. Is there anything of religious significance in rap music?

Before addressing this question, however, a bit of musical context is necessary. The ultimate questions and concerns of human existence and meaning are played out in many "secular" modes of musical expression, and that paying attention to these strands and what they say about religion and religious experience is important. I begin this process of exploration with the beginning, with the musical expression initiated as slaves first encountered the "New World."

Existential Concerns and "New World" Music

The "middle passage," the path by which enslaved Africans were brought to the Americas, is littered with bodies devoured by the waves and resting on the ocean's floor. Those who survived this journey found themselves in new and strange locations, among a new people. Perhaps the sounds and sights of this experience, this journey, remained alive in the new rhythms of their new world musical expression, first presented through the spirituals.

Stepping off slave ships, weak and shackled, enslaved Africans began to forge a new understanding of life—its pain and possibility—through musical expression. Spirituals recorded in the nineteenth century echo this encounter with an absurd world:

> Sometimes I feel like a motherless child,
> Sometimes I feel like a motherless child,
> Sometimes I feel like a motherless child,
> A long ways from home;
> A long ways from home.[2]

Such songs existed for some time before they were recognized as "rich" in beauty and content, representing the beginning of an African American cultural tradition and experience.

It was through this cultural expression enslaved Africans' efforts to express a sense of self in a hostile world—that memories of a former home were maintained and were used to make sense of their new existential and ontological space. It was a way of humanizing a dehumanizing environment. The music (and folk tales, decorative arts, and visual arts that make up this new Black culture) represents a style of interpretation, a stylized wrestling with life. It is a way of "moving" through harsh circumstances with dignity and integrity. Through songs developed very early in their "New World" experience, enslaved Africans addressed the harsh and hypocritical practices of white Americans and envisioned the possibility of a better and richer existence. The songs called into question the nastiness of life and provided a vision of fulfillment, expressed with an eye toward the promises of the Christian faith.

> I'm a-rolling, I'm a-rolling
> I'm a-rolling thro' an unfriendly world,
> I'm a-rolling, I'm a-rolling thro' an unfriendly world.[3]

Those who did not find meaning in Christian community and its teachings, as represented in the spirituals, made their presence known through the swaying and sultry sounds of the blues. Just as we cannot accurately date the development of the spirituals as a musical form, we also are uncertain as to when the blues emerged. However, many scholars argue that the blues developed long before they were recorded on "race records" during the early twentieth century. It is likely that the blues emerged during the antebellum period alongside the spirituals, in the fields and during more private moments of slave life.

There are links between the blues and spirituals; for example, country or southern blues, like spirituals, make use of an eight- or sixteen-bar form. In addition, the existential realities encountered in the spirituals—abusive whites and hard work—are also the subject matter of many blues tones. Yet while there are notable similarities between the blues and spirituals in terms of form and thematic structure, there are also major differences. In addition to a shift from communal concerns as expressed in the spirituals, to a radical individualism in the blues, the latter also expresses a rejection of many of the transcendental and supernatural assumptions found in the spirituals. Differing epistemological sensibilities and social codes resulted in friction between these two musical forms—the spirituals and the blues. The shift from a God-based understanding of the world to a human-experience-centered and more pessimistic orientation (including a celebration of sexuality in ways that troubled born-again Christians) resulted in the labeling of the blues as "devil" music by those committed to the spirituals and the black church.[4]

Taken as part of a larger pattern of cultural presence, blues, like spirituals, speak to the creative potential of blacks and to the way in which they made meaning out of a rather meaningless world. What else could they do?

> I worked all the winter
> And I worked all fall
> I got to wait til' spring
> To get my ashes hauled
> And now I'm tired
> Tired as I can be
> And I'm going back home
> Where these blues don't worry me.[5]

After the period of slavery, in an attempt by blacks to respond to the existential condition of being free yet oppressed, nascent forms of the blues were spread through popular entertainment venues such as carnivals, medicine shows, gin joints, house parties, and vaudeville shows. With increased mobility, the blues traveled and further developed in northern cities such as Chicago and New York. However, this geographic movement, together with increased exposure, did not translate into a wider acceptance by black Christians, who continued to question its spiritual value. Even blues fans and artists who participated in church activities during the day and swayed to the blues rhythms at night were said to be "flirting with the devil." The blues met with the disapproval of black churches because the lyrical content and seductive nature of the music fell outside the norms, values, and morality advocated by the black church tradition.

Within blues songs, the promises of the spirituals were weighed and tested in light of life's controlling hardships, and utopian ideals were found wanting. Raw or "gutbucket" experiences were poetically presented, critiqued, and synthesized; yet, they were understood as full and unavoidable. No subject was taboo, although most were shrouded and creatively worded. For example, Muddy Waters demonstrates a sexual tone using metaphorical language to mask sexual contact. The symbolism suggested by Muddy Waters was often extended to culinary images such as "jelly-roll" to represent sexual intercourse.[6] Blues men and women such as Robert Johnson, Muddy Waters, Bessie Smith, Ma Rainey, and Koko Taylor preached a politics of pleasure that worked to rethink the beauty and value of black bodies, at least in a limited sense. Using coded language, Ma Rainey had this to say:

> If you don't like my ocean don't fish in my sea,
> Don't like my ocean, don't fish in my sea
> Stay out of my valley, and let my mountain be.[7]

Many may recall the use of gospel music in the Civil Rights movement as a way of creatively expressing outrage with the status quo as well as determination to change oppressive social structures, but of course the social impulse in music predates this iteration. The blues had a humanizing effect, pointing to the tenacity of the human spirit. They were not simply a matter of survival, allowing the musician and listeners to lose themselves in sexual conquest and forget the world around them. Blues also served as a social force by offering a way of creating balance through a recognition of wrongdoing, while suggesting better ways of being in the world.

> Good mornin', blues,
> Blues, how do you do?
> Yes, blues, how do you do?
> I'm doing all right,
> Good mornin', how are you?[8]

The blues played an important role in the formation of consciousness in African American communities. They contain worlds of meaning forged as an early mode of expression born in enslaved Africans as they contemplated the crossing of water in a slave ship named "Jesus."

The blues present an early African American response to the absurdity of the "New World" and an expression of dignity in spite of its dehumanizing tendencies. When things were falling apart, the blues kept body and soul together. The music rejected the dualism (mind versus body) that marked the modern age and served as a humanizing device. In creative ways, this mode of music rejected much of what the "New World" attempted to force upon those of African descent through the creative reworking of cultural expressiveness within the context of a new environment. The formation of healthy consciousness through the use of musical forms such as the blues was deep, so deep that white cultural voyeurs missed much of its meaning and content. While "Uncle Jim" sang his song to white consumers, black listeners received subversive bits of information, such as the miseries of black life based on the hypocrisy of white economic, social, and political dealings. When the blues were played, enjoyment by white folks often entailed a process of signification they failed to "get." Even some black folks could not appreciate the serious nature of play at work in the blues. In fact, just when we think we have dug to the core and really "dig" the music, we discover another layer of complex meaning and vision, another layer of speculation on the meaning of life.

The blues and other musical forms such as the spirituals speak to a style of living, the rhythmic "sway" by which many African Americans have walked through this world. Embedded in the words and the rhythm exists an impulse, a musically defined drive that speaks to the manner in which African Americans have felt the nature of life, measured it, and harnessed it with purpose. It is a meaning that runs counter to the dominant society's efforts to limit the human and cultural worth of black people. As a blues artist notes:

> I wrote these blues, gonna sing 'em as I please,
> I wrote these blues, gonna sing 'em as I please,
> I'm the only one like the way I'm singin' 'em,
> I'll swear to goodness ain't no one else to please.[9]

Through this music one can question, prod, flip, and examine existential circumstances until something useful surfaces. There is in the blues an unflinching confrontation with life, as Ralph Ellison described: "The blues is an impulse to keep the painful details and episodes of a brutal experience alive in one's aching consciousness, to finger its jagged grain, and to transcend it." But this is not a push toward the metaphysical or a type of transhistorical enlightenment. Rather, as Ellison continues, this is a movement of consciousness done by "squeezing from it a near-tragic, near-comic lyricism."[10] The blues, then, is recognition of the value of

African Americans through their ability to shape and control language and thus a world—a world full of sarcasm and tenacious black bodies. This has been a mature depiction of life that recognizes the often absurd nature of encounter in a way that avoids nihilism and calls into question the nature of social crisis. This music teaches that life can be harsh, but these crises are not always "unto death," and in some cases are quite laughable.

> I got the world in a jug,
> The stopper in my hand.[11]

It teaches that life is survivable and more. One need only face it with vision, imagination, and tenacity. Connected to this style of making meaning is a posturing of the body. With the blues, this posture often entailed the sensual movement of bodies across dance floors, while those devoted to spirituals did the "ring shout" across "sacred" space.

For the blues, humanity is fragile, but this is not the problem. The problem is the manner in which fragility is often shown in illusions of superiority and guarded through the aggressive and destructive patterns that whites practice against blacks (and more vulnerable whites), and blacks practice as well. It is an honest depiction in that the music does not paint African Americans in heroic tones. Rather, the blues recognize flaws and point out shortcomings. In this sense, the cruel white landlord is rivaled by the exploiter Stagger Lee (Stackolee or Stack O'Lee). Their crimes are far from the same, but both crimes are rooted in a lack of comfort with fragility and vulnerability. The landlord is exercising a systematically reinforced power. Stagger Lee's exercise of control over his environment does not come with the same systemic backing, but it is vicious:

> I told Stack O'Lee please don't take my life,
> I got two li'l babes and a darling, loving wife.
> [Stack O'Lee remarks] What l care about your two babies and your loving, darling wife?
> You done stole my Stetson hat and I'm bound to take your life.[12]

Continuation of Religious Orientation in Gospel, Rock, and Jazz

I am not as pessimistic about popular music as, say, Martha Bayles, who writes: "Just as assaultive as the lyrics and images of contemporary popular music are many of the sounds. From the shrieking clamor of thrash metal to the murky din of grunge, from the cheap, synthesized tinsel of pop ballads to the deadly pounding of computerized rhythm tracks, popular music seems terminally hostile to any sound traditionally associated with music."[13] I find a hermeneutic based on a "whatever happened to the *good* music?" sensibility suspect. True, there are lamentable elements in popular music—racism, homophobia, sexism, misogyny, and so on—and these elements must be critiqued. But this critical attention must also appreciate the manner in which some of this music speaks to deeply rooted concerns with hard and pressing questions of life, questions of ultimate value and ultimate meaning. No particular genre can be disregarded for the sake of some type of musical "purity."

Music is a "fluid" art, a mode of cultural production marked by perpetual movement. The general aesthetic and musical quality of the blues, along with the spirituals, flows in a variety of directions—gospel, rhythm and blues, rock 'n' roll, rock, and so on—because, as Ralph Ellison notes in response to Amiri Baraka's *Blues People,* "the master artisans of the South were slaves, and white Americans have been walking Negro walks, talking Negro-flavored talk (and prizing it when spoken by Southern belles), dancing Negro dances and singing

Negro melodies far too long to talk of a 'mainstream' of American culture to which they're alien."[14] That is to say, the "American" musical idiom of the United States is indebted to and drawn heavily from the creativity and ingenuity of African Americans, and from this community of sun-kissed skin it moved outward.

Gospel, rock, and so forth owe something to earlier musical forms such as the blues and maintain their commitment on some level to exploring the ultimate questions of life, speaking about religious, or what some might refer to as a spiritual, orientation. There is a confirmed wrestling between sacred and secular in musical production, and the resulting friction represents an attempt to address the deeper issues of life. (How else could the creator of the blues hit "It's Tight Like That" also be the creator of the gospel song "Take My Hand Precious Lord"?) This wrestling is presented in the friction between the spirituals and the blues, and it continues in the often uneasy tension between the "sacred" and the "secular" within contemporary forms of music such as gospel, rock, and jazz that marks the presence of religious sensibilities and commitments in popular music.

Many of those who sang the blues were also religious in a traditional, church-derived way. Twentieth-century "born-again" blues folks, most notably Thomas Andrew Dorsey, were responsible for the development of a blues-influenced form of religious music called "Gospel Blues" or "Gospel Music" that got underway in 1921 with Dorsey's first song, "Someday, Somewhere." Gospel music became a part of black church worship because Dorsey and gospel singer Sallie Martin traveled across the nation singing and helping congregations develop gospel choirs. The music would change, influenced by new technology and social circumstances such as the Civil Rights movement.[15] The gospel sound changed the aesthetics of black church worship as choirs imitated the music on Sundays and the choir's attire became more dramatic to compliment the more explosive sound.

Sensitive to the theological claims of traditional gospel music, contemporary gospel music during the 1970s attempted to reach the unchurched, to draw them in by avoiding a message of repentance and salvation that was too confrontational. Contemporary gospel, as written by figures such as Andre Crouch, contained a subtle message of Jesus Christ and the merits of salvation that addressed the ethos created by the Black Power movement, Black Arts movement, and other movements developed with respect to growing black consciousness.[16] Contemporary gospel has offered the "traditional" message in a new package, with a more subdued approach to evangelization. It was because of this more subtle message, combined with the funk and rock of contemporary music, that one could hear gospel singer Tramaine Hawkins's proclamation of the Holy Spirit's presence being pumped into nightclubs during the early eighties, and on gospel-format radio stations during the same period.

Soulful singers such as Al Green have moved between gospel and more "secular" modes of music, while Little Richard expressed a call to ministry.[17] Sam Cooke was the son of a minister and sang with the Soul Stirrers, and some suggest: that "to compare his gospel recordings with his better secular recordings is to be struck by the resemblance, and in some cases, the identity between the two."[18] Cooke's "A Change Is Gonna Come" influenced other musicians such as Curtis Mayfield to address the deeper questions of life in important yet subtle ways, not with explicit utilization of Christian theological categories but with a wrestling over issues of self-consciousness.[19] And who can forget the musical importance of Marvin Gaye? His "What's Going On" incorporates a grappling with existential and ontological concerns plaguing humanity, and concludes with a prayer that undoubtedly connected Gaye with his childhood religious encounters and framed them in terms of his musical successes.

Are these and other examples really odd when one considers that R & B is a child of gospel, swing, and the blues? So many musicians have roots in various religious communities, and the questions and concerns generated within these communities continue to maintain a hold on the epistemological rings of these artists. According to a recent article in *Vibe* magazine:

> Historically, most R&B singers have grown up singing in church; still today, artists from Snoop to Lil' Kim have sung in the choir as kids. And the two genres have met in the middle any number of times, from the Teddy Riley-produced Return by the Winans, in 1990, to L. L. Cool J's 1991 track "The Power of God." … The Edwin Hawkins Singers' "Oh, Happy Day" was a chart smash in 1972, and the Clark Sisters' "You Brought the Sunshine" lit up discos in 1982. And who could forget M. C. Hammer's 1990 "Pray"?[20]

From gospel to the Christianity-influenced lyrics of R & B, to its "kissing cousin" rock, religious sensibilities and visions bleed through the lyrics and lives of blues-indebted musicians.[21]

Emerging in the 1950s, with figures such as Chuck Berry and Elvis Presley, rock defines a hybrid musical form and cultural sensibility drawn from a variety of sources, including the blues and gospel music that was popular in churches. Over the years, rock artists have used technological advances such as multitrack recording and drum machines to give expression to questions of ultimate meaning and place in the world. This discussion often took place through the language of religiosity. Who can forget, for example, the religious sensitivities put on public display by Elvis Presley on numerous occasions? Or the magic Jimi Hendrix performed with his electric guitar, though he did not live long enough to develop the "Electric Sky Church" he talked about:

> We're trying to save the kids … to help them realize a little more what their goals should be. We want them to realize that our music is just as spiritual as going to church. The soul must rule, not money or drugs. You should rule yourself and give God a chance.[22]

In response to some of the excesses of rock culture, including the type of drug use that took Jimi Hendrix's life, new movements within rock emerged as alternatives to the dominant ethos. Rather than advocating a radical Individualism and hedonism as the language of this musical form, groups emerging in the 1980s such as U2 sought to present a more complex and socially conscious message often expressed in the language of religious commitment. While the religious orientation or commitments of some artists has been questioned by music critics and fans, U2's allegiance to the Christian faith has been for the most part simply a given, shaping its music and message. Even those within formal religious institutions speak to this; in fact, as one minister deeply familiar with the group notes:

"Whether on records, on stage, on video or in interviews—they have never denied their faith, even if at times they have questioned how that faith fits with the events of their generation. They have constantly kept spiritual issues at the heart of all they have done, whether looking at the light or the darkness around them."[23] There is an ethical accountability, a musical articulation of liberation theology, tied to the Christianity of this group that is not as developed in the religious wrestling of most. According to Bono, "Faith in Jesus Christ that is not aligned to social justice—that is not aligned with the poor—it's nothing."[24] CDs such as the 1987 *Joshua Tree* point to the importance of religious questions and concerns for U2, tied as they are to a perpetual search for more meaning, and so Bono sings, "but I still haven't found what I'm looking for."[25]

Questions of a religious nature continue to find expression in musical production. What Michael Dyson says concerning Michael Jackson is true for a larger range of artists, including

U2, insofar as much of their music has clear links "to the spiritual roots that have nourished its beginning and that continue to sustain its expanding identity."[26] The words and images associated with these songs are pregnant with religiously based wonderings.

Jazz also has been involved in this struggle with religiosity and with the ultimate meaning of life. First articulated in the 1830s and 1840s through plantation brass bands and minstrel troupes and through the later development of ragtime in the 1890s, jazz marks a blending of African American musical sensibilities from the blues, for example, and European harmonic structures. Finding a home in places such as New Orleans and Chicago, jazz greats like the New Orleans Rhythm Kings, Jelly Roll Morton, and Louis Armstrong refined this musical art form. With time, the improvisation that marked Jelly Roll Morton's work among others was further developed into the swing style exemplified by figures such as Duke Ellington. Religious themes and issues were not lost on jazz musicians. For example, in Duke Ellington's "Sacred Concerts" as well as Billie Holiday's "God Bless the Child" and Nina Simone's "Sinner Man" religious questions are at play.

The music continued to evolve from swing through incarnations such as bebop and cool jazz, each bringing a creative take on the relationship between music and existential realities. But perhaps one of the best known examples of jazz's religious sensibilities is John Coltrane's album *A Love Supreme*, recorded in 1964. As Coltrane writes to listeners, the religious preoccupation that guides this musical project is clear: "This album is a humble offering to Him. An attempt to say 'thank you God' through our work, even as we do in our hearts and with our tongues." This struggle with the presence of divinity was inspired, Coltrane notes, during his "spiritual awakening" in 1957. As a result of this conversion experience, Coltrane "asked to be given the means and privilege to make others happy through music. I feel this has been granted through His grace."[27] The importance of this particular jazz recording for those seeking religious (or, as some put it, "spiritual") fulfillment has taken numerous forms, but none is more attention grabbing than the Church of Saint John Coltrane African Orthodox Church in San Francisco.

In 1971, Bishop F. W. King organized a chapel called the One Mind Temple Evolutionary Transitional Body of Christ as a religious community dedicated to "live cleanly, do right … offering praise to God and service to man." This development was inspired by "the dedicated triumph of John Coltrane's life over many obstacles, his music, and his testimony."[28] This church, dedicated to the example of John Coltrane, became an affiliate of the African Orthodox Church in 1982, and the name was changed to Church of St. John Coltrane African Orthodox Church. Over the course of the past two decades, numerous programs and projects such as the Human Outreach Program have developed as a way of extending the call for righteousness and proper living outlined in *A Love Supreme*.[29]

Rap Music's Religious Sensibilities and Concerns

What happened to musical movement and intent during the late twentieth century, in urban areas? Where does one turn for a raw and "natural" presentation for an extension of the nitty-gritty expressivity found during earlier periods? The answer is easily located. It manifested itself anew in rap music, the mode of musical expression developed first in New York City during the late 1970s.[30]

Through the spirit of the spirituals and the blues came a variety of musical forms with creative alterations of existing styles and with sensitivity to the existential circumstances of their creators. There should be no wondering, then, about the birth of rap music as a vital—and often troubled and troubling—mode of musical expression. "Rapper's Delight," the 1979 hit by the Sugar Hill Gang, brought what had been the skills of the streets, parks, basements, and clubs to the attention of a much larger audience—including Canada and Europe, where the single reached the top five and top ten, respectively. Eventually it became the "black single of the year" in 1980, with earnings of more than $3 million on sales of over 2 million records.[31] "In retrospect," cultural critic George Nelson notes, "rap or something like it should have been predicted. Each decade since World War II has seen the emergence of some new approach to black dance music [and more, I suspect]. The 1940s brought forth rhythm & blues, the 1950s rock & roll, the 1960s soul, the 1970s funk and disco. Something was due in the 1980s."[32] This "something due" expressed in clear terms the hybridization of music through a bold and creative manipulation of established genres. It brought together without apology jazz, disco, rhythm & blues, and so on; and in the process, through high-tech conjuration, presented musical ancestors within a new context. These conjurers looked at what they had produced and could not help but say, "Damn, it's dope!"

While the music is important, Houston Baker is correct to note that the voice finalizes the process. Language and the spoken word have their own materiality that moves the music because "the voice, some commentators have suggested, echoes African griots, black preachers, Apollo DJs, Birdland MCs, Muhammed Ali, black street corner males' signifying, oratory of the Nation of Islam, and get-down ghetto vernacular. The voice becomes the thing in which, finally, rap technology catches the consciousness of the young."[33]

Indebted to U.S. and Jamaican aesthetics and oral traditions, rap artists, as "new-style troubadours,"[34] expressed the concerns and preoccupations of young people living in urban centers of late-capitalism's America using linguistic manipulations and alterations fed through a system of creative technological arrangements. As Mark Costello and David Foster Wallace have noted: "Rap, like the avant-garde, deploys digital multi-tracked sampling to blow open the musical and political boundaries of the soul and funk that are the rapper's Bach and Beethoven."[35] The lyrical wing of a larger movement, referred to as hip-hop culture (which includes dance, the visual arts, and an aesthetic displayed through creative clothing choices), rap would grow and multiply into a variety of styles, with a complex typology–progressive, gangsta, and so on. Many assumed it was a fad, a stylistic virus easily contained and ended; but instead, rap artists have grown in stature, created production companies and record labels, and have moved into other areas of popular culture. These artists have used technological advances to signify the American vision of life and labor, and in so doing captured the imagination and dollars of an eager public.

As pop artists such as Andy Warhol produced work that raised philosophical questions concerning the nature of the visual arts, rap music raised a host of questions concerning the form and content of musical expression. Some, like the abstract expressionists who despised the innovations of pop art, lamented the substitution of "noise" for "music," while more insightful listeners recognized the musical creativity and compelling (though often troubling) presentation of sociohistorical and psychological realities and fantasies of life in the post civil rights years. At its best, rap music provides listeners with critical insights "as energetically productive as those manned by our most celebrated black critics and award winning writers."[36] But we must also acknowledge that when not at its best, rap music provides a celebration of radical individualism and nihilism over against community and hope.

In the early years, "back in tha day," this stylized depiction of life's meaning was rapped in the grab and poetry of Grand Master Flash and the Furious Five, KRS-One, Public Enemy, and others who looked at the world and critiqued it in "black." Rap music has changed since those days. Like many others, I lament some of its current lyrical and visual twists, such as the more objectifying videos. But I see glimmers of the quest for meaning, a stylized defense of subjectivity, an aesthetic that serves to harness and interpret human interaction and the world in which it takes place.

Continuation and experimentation with black orality is the hallmark of rap, taking the themes and sensibilities housed in musical expression for centuries and giving them a postindustrial twist. Rap music explores "grammatical creativity, verbal wizardry, and linguistic innovation in refining the art of oral communication."[37] Yet, what is most significant about rap for the purposes of this book is expressed not simply in terms of the process of fusion—grammatical, verbal, and linguistic manipulations—but through the morphing of content. The importance of rap music rests on this morphing process because "the rap artist appeals to the rhetorical practices eloquently honed in *African-American religious experiences* and the cultural potency of *black singing/musical traditions* to produce an engaging hybrid."[38] Michael Dyson points to an interesting interaction, a stylization of self and community, addressing ultimate meaning within the context of a musically significant "process of repetition and recontextualization,"[39] deserving greater attention.

The implicit claim here must be made explicit: one of the major and documented functions of musical production such as rap has been the articulation of responses to the "ultimate" questions of life. In this sense, it has engaged religious traditions and religious issues in both overt and covert ways. There are explicit examples in efforts to foreground Nation of Islam and Nation of Earths and Gods theologies within the music of Queen Mother Rage, Eric B. & Rakim, Isis, Paris, Public Enemy, and Poor Righteous Teachers, among others. While one may question the consistency, sophistication, and "thickness" of the presentation, references to Islam abound within rap music. The educational process such rap music seeks has had benefit. According to Sister Souljah, "hip-hop is a blessing because the [Poor] Righteous Teachers, Brand Nubian and KRS-One have actually been the educational system for Black kids, in place of the so-called educational system that is entirely financed *by* the American government. And in the absence of the voice of young people in hip-hop, we would have even more chaos than we have today."[40]

From the nebulous celebrations of Malcolm X to the more explicit and focused attention to the teachings of the Honorable Elijah Muhammad and Minister Louis Farrakhan, rappers highlight the commonly recognizable elements of the Nation of Islam's faith, such as the importance of self-knowledge as the key to all other developments. Others, moving from the early days of Africa Bambaataa to more recent figures, point to the teachings of the Nation of Earths and Gods (also known as the Five Percent Nation), highlighting the cosmic value and importance of blacks. Yet, "orthodox" Islam represents one of the fastest-growing religious groups in the United States among African Americans, and it too is represented in rap music. As rap artist Mos Def, a Sunni Muslim, notes in projects such as *Black on Both Sides* (1999), individual fulfillment and communal development are dependent upon spiritual awareness, a recognition of God, a devotion to prayer. In his words:

> I really believe that none of our efforts are gonna work until we turn our attention to the Creator … and really start to have a spiritual program, as opposed to a political program. To even have a spiritual program, first, you have to be attentive to what's in us, before we can say, "Okay this is how we can affect public policy." We gotta be going inside first, and then come out. … There's a Creator of all this and for me, and this is true for everyone, that when you focus your attention on trying to be as close, or as cognizant or as mindful of that presence, then all those other things fall into place.[41]

Not every artist presents religious sensitivities and theological vocabulary in such a straight-forward manner. Rap artist Nuwine, for example, argues that his music is not necessarily religious (in the strict sense). Rather, it is his attempt to discuss the events of his life that eventually lead him to the church. During various interviews, Nuwine, who records on boxer Evander Holyfield's label, talks about his early childhood. As a preteen he dropped out of school and became involved in gang activity. In 1990 this activity resulted in gunfire: "I was shaking hands with a guy when a rival gang saw us, and started shooting. They got me with the first shot." This experience did not stop the activities that eventually took him before a judge. At that point, while awaiting his court appearance, "I noticed a white guy across the room staring at me. After a while, he boldly interrupted me. 'You don't know me,' he said, 'but God loves you, man. God forgives you and has a purpose for you.' Suddenly my whole macho attitude caved in. I fell on my knees and cried."[42]

After this conversion experience, Nuwine began using his rap abilities to spread the story of his transformed life. Beginning with CDs sold from his trunk, to a record deal, Nuwine is concerned with music that moves beyond the mere nihilism present in some rap to a modest optimism based on the Christian faith. Nuwine argues that his music may be a little "hard," but this is appropriate because it speaks to people who are in need. In his words: "That's what ministry is about. Reachin' out to those who don't know God. Reachin' out to the sick, the rebellious, the angry, the hurting. That's what it's for. Jesus did it. He spent very little time in the synagogue. Why do the well people need a physician? It's the sick people that need a physician."[43] In another interview he elaborates on this point by clarifying the meaning behind the title of his 2001 CD, *Ghetto Mission*. He says: "The meaning speaks for itself. Look at the world the world is a ghetto. You have problems in suburbs and the cities, and that problem is people are hurting, man. People want answers, they want to know why they're here, why they're broke, why people are killing each other. So *[Ghetto] Mission* is like a mission statement. I'm reaching out to the ghettos, you know, and saying that God loves you."[44]

A few, such as Reverend Run (Joey Simmons of Run-DMC) have taken this concern with spreading a Christian message even further by entering a formal Christian ministry. Reflecting on his life prior to his conversion, Reverend Run critiques the materialism and radical attitude of consumption that marks so much rap music, the effort to uncover meaning through goods: "I thought I had all the riches, but I was really poor. It was then the Lord came into my life and raised me up, and I started to feel better and all those worldly things didn't mean anything to me anymore."[45]

Educator and part-time rapper from the 1990s, Sister Souljah, made a similar message clear by presenting a centered life marked by respect or self and community and a relationship with God as the hallmark of existence. The title track from her album, *360 Degrees of Power,* and other tracks such as "My God Is a Powerful God" speak to this reevaluation of life purpose and meaning.[46] Regarding the connections between her conviction and lyrics, Sister Souljah says:

> Having grown up on hip hop, I always considered the drum and beats and bass to be strong and moving. It captured the feeling of the energy of our experience in white America and reestablished Black masculinity, rebellion, self-instruction and information distribution. I believe that Chuck D and Hank Schocklee asked me to be a member of Public Enemy because my life represented what they were rhyming about. Not only had I lived it, I challenged it, rebelled against it, organized and created solutions, and stayed rooted and humble in my blackness.[47]

For some, there is a paradox at work, a form of existential slippage between stated commitments to a particular religious vision and the system of ethics expressed in the music. Take, for example, Snoop Dogg, whose lyrics often portray an image not necessarily in keeping with religious sensibilities claimed for his personal life: "I've got a responsibility to God. He put me here. He'll take me down in a heartbeat the minute I start tripping on myself and how great I must be because of all the people telling me all the time. … I tried to keep it real, never to sell the truth, but always to tell the truth. And if there's one reason why you know the name Snoop Dogg and I don't know yours, it's because telling the truth has given me the props I need to carry out God's purpose and plan."[48] One might wonder about the nature and meaning of central terms here: Truth? Providence? What is the doctrine of God represented here? And, what are the ramifications with respect to ethics, even if we dismiss, as we should, warped puritanical ethics? Yet, regardless of one's take on such matters, as vital as they are, there remains here an important tension, a battle between existential realities and religious sensibilities. We may not find the resolution offered by certain artists appealing, when such sensibilities do not raise a critique concerning oppressive attitudes and behaviors. Nonetheless, this should not mean a lack of attention paid to the nature of confrontation with the "religious" that is expressed in their work. Snoop Dogg and others provide rudimentary elements of a theological system, a theology of rap, complete with an epistemology of encounter:

> Thinking back on it now, I understand that God was reaching out to me, even then, It wasn't like I saw His face in a cloud or heard His voice thundering in my ear, like fucking Charlton Heston in a Bible movie or something. In my experience, God doesn't work that way. He lets His will and His plan be known to His children by the people and situations He brings across their paths. At the right time, and the right place, there was always someone there to guide me, to point me in the right direction. And even when I chose to go my own way, I still had the clear choice laid out in front of me. It takes time to learn to do the right thing, but God is patient and He'll bring you along, if you let Him.[49]

The line between religious belief and life practice is often blurred. The lyrical content with its expressed religious vision often creates a paradox. But this is not a problem that wipes out the value or vitality of the religious imagination within rap music. Rather, it might point to the linguistic "playfulness" within the music, drawn from vernacular practices within black oral and aesthetic traditions. In other words, it is quite likely that much of what is expressed in rap music is not meant to be taken literally, in the same manner in which numerous biblical stories are quite troubling if taken literally.[50] The sexism expressed by Saint Paul and other biblical figures and the homophobia that marks both testaments have not resulted in a huge theological backlash requiring the destruction of the Bible as a viable and sacred text. The same hermeneutic of multiple meanings may extend to rap lyrics and their creators. This is not to say these artists should not be held accountable, or should not be critiqued with regard to behavior and opinions. It simply means that we should recognize the often problematic relationship between theological pronouncements and arguments, and practice that plagues the history of religion in *and outside* hip-hop culture. Recognizing the great difficulty with which humans exercise and explain the religious, explicit theological or religious pronouncements in rap music are worth one's time and attention not because of perfection of practice but because of what they say about the musically expressed encounter with questions of meaning, those with great existential and ontological weight. Such consideration fosters, for the benefit of those in religious studies, cultural studies, and so forth an opportunity to follow the *flow* of the religious within cultural production, and in this way to better recognize and analyze both religiosity (themes, practices, etc.) and an important cultural ethos marking our new century.

In addition to explicit moments that reflect a type of hip-hop evangelicalism, there are also more "shadowed" engagements with religious themes and religious traditions in rap music, often lyrically fused in metaphor, signs, and symbols. Perhaps this approach is what rapper Big Boi of OutKast has in mind when discussing the need to address pressing issues and themes within the music: "We feel that—just like KRS-One said—when you get on this microphone, you have to educate as well as entertain. We feel that responsibility, but not in a preachy way. We're gonna party with y'all and slip something in there every now and then— maybe a word or a phrase or a question. And you might be like, Damn, I wonder why they said that?"[51] The rapper known as Common addresses a similar sensibility, one that moves from self-consciousness outward. When speaking about the motivation and intent behind his CD *Resurrection*, Common says:

> At that point I was just tryin' to become a better artist. At the same time l started becoming a better person. Just the things I exposed myself to. Or the things I got exposed to. … I started getting more in tune with myself spiritually and not just following the Christian upbringing that I had. Not just sayin' Jesus is God for this reason. I'll put it this way: Resurrection was more of an understanding. I started understanding things more and actually started to apply 'em more too. But it was an understanding. And the focus on that album was just to be creative and put a mark on this Hip Hop Game. And make people notice what myself and No ID was doin'.[52]

Rap music often fails in its effort to transform thought and action because artists forget their work must begin with self-consciousness. Otherwise, what is the lesson being taught to others? For the student of rap music and hip-hop culture, wondering "why" often points to religious sensibilities and themes within rap music that are not limited to Christianity and Islam. One must also be mindful of the meaning of Buddhism and humanism, for example, within the lives of particular artists. This is certainly the case with the Beastie Boys' Adam Yauch's conversion from Judaism to Tibetan Buddhism, and underground artist Sage Francis's apparent embrace of free thought (or humanism). It is worth noting that the influence of religiosity on rap music and hip-hop culture in more general terms is not limited to those at the microphone. Pioneers such as Russell Simmons recognize the importance of spiritual practice. (He uses the term "spiritual" as opposed to "religion" to connote the noninstitutional basis of his practice.) In his autobiography, *Life and Def: Sex, Drugs, and Money, + God*, he speaks to the importance of yoga for a sense of centeredness. In his words:

> The practice of yoga changed my life. Over the past six years I've been practicing yoga, and in that time found a spiritual center to my life. My spiritual sense IS stronger than ever, so the teachings of all the great religions sound good to me. The yoga practice of quieting the mind through asana practice, as well as meditation, is about clearing the mind of fluctuation so that you can one day know your true self. … My experiences with yoga have taught me the practice of finding God everywhere—especially within myself.[53]

The impact of this quest for greater meaning holds consequences for Simmons's perspective on hip-hop culture:

> Over the last few years I have begun to walk toward God or service to God, whether it is through promoting political initiatives that I believe could help the masses—from reforming the prison industrial complex to increased involvement in electoral politics—or by focusing more on the numerous charities I am involved with. I am in a unique position to organize some hip-hop for the better of the masses.[54]

Locating the Discussion

What is the significance of religious or spiritual considerations in the world of rap music? How should such considerations affect the manner in which we understand, explore, and discuss rap music and religion?

A good deal of academic work has been done on rap music, particularly using the methodological tools of literary theory, musicology, history, sociology, and so on. Work by scholars such as Tricia Rose, William Perkins, and Brian Cross and more "popular" treatments by Nelson George, James Spady, and David Toop discuss rap along these lines. Within these studies, which represent only a small sampling of the available literature, primary attention is given to the historical development of this musical genre as a creative, cultural response to certain social, political, and economic forces. The emphasis is most often on rap music as a secular response to pressing issues. However, as Jon Michael Spencer and others argue, there is no clear distinction between the sacred and the secular; they flow together, merging in unexpected places. Hence, "Locations within the secular world must also be examined for disclosures of the religious if we are ever to be able to understand what people are really thinking religiously and how those thoughts influence their behavior in the real world."[55]

Some, such as Ernest Allen, have explored rap music with respect to issues of black nationalism, noting connections with the Nation of Islam and the Five Percent Nation. Although this work has been extremely important and insightful, there is something religious/theological in much of this music that is not fully captured with this approach. Like the spirituals, the blues, and gospel, rap music has profound connections to the various religious traditions found within African American communities. It grapples with the questions of meaning that are intimately connected to religious organizations and their thoughts and practices. Those in religious studies are in a unique position to isolate and explore connections between rap music and religious faith. In addition, those with primary expertise in other areas enhance their discussion of rap music by employing the questions, concerns, and frameworks associated with religious studies.

There are a few treatments that address the need for a religious-studies (e.g., theological) analysis of rap music. Two prominent examples are several issues of Jon Michael Spencer's now defunct journal *Black Sacred Music* and Michael Eric Dyson's *Between Gad and Gangsta Rap*. Work by Dyson and Spencer is invaluable because it creates dialogue between popular culture and religious studies. However, these treatments of religion and rap are limited to a discussion of religious themes related to the Christian tradition and, in some cases, the Nation of Islam. If this exploration is to grow, we must also consider rap's relationship to a variety of other religious traditions and sensibilities—both institutional and noninstitutional.

Study Questions

1. How can the study of religion and music in African American culture and life help to contextualize the study of religion in hip hop today?
2. What types of themes (e.g., evil, pain, suffering, life meaning) have been present in the black musical tradition from the spirituals to the emergence of rap music in the late twentieth century in urban centers?
3. Anthony B. Pinn suggests that the black musical tradition often provides a "social critique" using organic vocabulary by which meaning is made. As such, how have religious themes in music helped to transform thought and action in black culture and life?

Notes

* Portions of this chapter from the text *Noise & Spirit* (Pinn, 2003) have been omitted and/or altered for style, consistency and flow.

1. *African Americans for Humanism Examiner* 12, no. 1 (Spring 2002): 8.
2. James Weldon Johnson and I. Rosamond Johnson, eds., *The Books of American Negro Spirituals* (New York: Da Capo Press, 1969), ii, 30–31.
3. R. Nathaniel Dett, ed., *Religious Folk-Songs of the Negro as Sung at Hampton Institute* (Hampton, VA: Hampton Institute Press, 1927), 186.
4. For additional information on the spirituals and blues, see Paul Oliver, *The Meaning of the Blues* (New York: Collier Books, 1960, 1963); Charles Keil, *Urban Blues* (Chicago: University of Chicago Press, 1966); Eileen Southern, *The Music of Black Americans: A History* (New York: W. W. Norton, 1971; 2nd edn, 1983); William Barlow, "Looking Up at Down": *The Emergence of Blues Culture* (Philadelphia: Temple University Press, 1989); Christa K. Dixon, *Negro Spirituals: From Bible to Folk Song* (Philadelphia: Fortress Press, 1976); Dena J. Epstein, *Sinful Tunes and Spirituals: Black Folk Music to the Civil War* (Urbana: University of Illinois Press, 1977); John Lovell, Jr., *Black Song: The Forge and the Flame; The Story of How the Afro-American Spiritual Was Hammered Out* (New York: Macmillan, 1972); Robert Palmer, *Deep Blues* (New York: Viking Press, 1981); Jon Michael Spencer, *Blues in Evil* (Knoxville: University of Tennessee Press, 1993); Howard Thurman, *The Negro Spirituals Speak of Life and Death* (Richmond, VA: Friends United Press, 1975).
5. Eric Sackheim, compiler, *The Blues Line: A Collection of Blues Lyrics* (Hopewell, NJ: Ecco Press, 1993), 45.
6. Paul Oliver, *The Blues Fell This Morning: The Meaning of the Blues* (New York: Cambridge University Press, 1979, 1990), 109–114.
7. Ma Rainey's "Don't Fish in My Sea," in Eric Sackheim, ed., *The Blues Line: A Collection of Blues Lyrics from Leadbelly to Muddy Waters* (New York: Ecco Press, 1993), 47.
8. James H. Cones, *The Spirituals and the Blues* (Maryknoll, NY: Orbis Books, 1972, 1991), 110.
9. Ibid., 97–98.
10. Ralph Ellison, "Richard Wright's Blues," in Robert G. O'Meally, ed., *Living with Music: Ralph Ellison's Jazz Writings* (New York: Modern Library Edition/ Random House, 2001), 103.
11. Ibid., 114.
12. Mississippi John Hurt, "Stack O'Lee Blues," in *The Blues, vol. 2* (Washington, DC: Smithsonian Collection of Recordings, 1993).
13. Martha Bayles, *Hole in the Soul: The Loss of Beauty and Meaning in American Popular Music* (Chicago: University of Chicago Press, 1996), 4.
14. Ralph Ellison, "Blues People," in Robert G. O'Meally, ed., *Living with Music: Ralph Ellison's Jazz Writings* (New York: Modern Library Edition/Random House, 2001), 130.

15. Melva Wilson Costen, *African American Christian Worship* (Nashville: Abingdon Press, 1995), 103–104.
16. Issues related to the mass appeal of contemporary gospel fostered questions related to White appreciation of this art form. The interplay between black musical production and Whites has always been an issue. Beginning with the debate over the origin of black spirituals and the origin of gospel music, African Americans have fought off claims to their musical production. Add to this the movement of White musicians into various areas of jazz and hip-hop. In recent years, a new challenge has arisen. It is the presence of White artists in gospel music and it has resulted in a question probed in numerous publications and in more private conversations: Are whites co-opting gospel music? Evidence of this "crossover" has been apparent. For example, Angelo Petrucci and Veronica Torres won the Dove Award for the best contemporary black gospel recorded song in 1995! Resentment over this development is heightened by what some artists understand as the industry's racism. White executives over black gospel divisions of labels have caused tension that is matched by the episodes of racism at major gospel festivals. Black artists eventually formed a new organization to address their interests, named the United Gospel Industry Council. Although white artists have made inroads into gospel music, it remains clear that African Americans dominate the market and in their recordings and concerts offer a somewhat "personalized" connection to a particular history of suffering based on race and celebration of triumph over racialized suffering.
17. "R. Kelly: From Raunch to Religion," *Ebony* magazine, June 1997, 106.
18. Bayles, *Hole in the Soul*, 156.
19. Ibid., 228–229.
20. Alan Light, "Say Amen, Somebody!" *Vibe* magazine, October 1997, 92.
21. One cannot forget the religious imagery and symbolism present in countless music videos such as R.E.M.'s "Losing My Religion," Tupac Shakur's "I Ain't Mad at Cha," Madonna's "Like a Prayer," or Joan Osborne's "One of Us." One could certainly add Moby to the list of artists for whom religious themes and ideals are fair musical "game." His recent recordings play off the religious aesthetics of the spirituals (and blues) as a way of exploring his sense of "spiritual" awareness. His present stance may be a matter of evolution—a movement from youthful years in the Presbyterian Church, to time spent as a rather conservative Christian, to a philosophical preoccupation with Marxism, to a more recent incarnation as one who is spiritually aware and appreciative of the teachings of Christ. Much of this comes across, for example, in a recent project titled Play that is heavily indebted to the African American spirituals tradition. Many of Moby's fans claim his music promotes a type of "spiritual" reaction. Yet for some there is an ambiguity or opaque quality to Moby's spiritual self-description that makes categorizing him rather difficult and the intended epistemological focus of his work hard to capture with any certainty.
22. Quoted in Bayles, *Hole in the Soul*, 236.
23. Steve Stockman, *Walk On: The Spiritual Journey of U2* (Lake Mary, FL: Relevant Books, 2001), 5.
24. Quoted in Ibid., 53.
25. U2, "I Still Haven't Found What I'm Looking For," on *The Joshua Tree*, Polygram Records; ASIN: B000001FS3.
26. Michael Eric Dyson, *Reflecting Black: African American Cultural Criticism* (Minneapolis: University of Minnesota Press, 1993), 40.
27. John Coltrane, liner notes to *A Love Supreme*, AS-77, MCA Records, 1964/MCA Records 1995/GRO Records, Inc., 1995.
28. Church of St. John Coltrane African Orthodox Church, "Saint John Will-I-Am Coltrane." Found at: <http://www.saintjohncoltrane.org>.
29. Finally, one might turn to Sun Ra and the "cosmic" as well as "New Age" sensibilities informing what makes up "Cosmic Tones for Mental Therapy/Art Form for Dimensions Tomorrow." Sun Ra's spirituality, a stretch for most people, I would imagine, involved claims to birth on Saturn and elements of the Egyptian mystery systems and cosmological structures.
30. A presentation of rap music's social and intellectual history is beyond the scope of this essay. For an excellent presentation of rap music's origins and development, see Tricia Rose, *Black Noise: Rap Music and Black Culture in Contemporary America* (Hanover, NH: University Press of New England,

1994). Also see Mark Costello and David Foster Wallace, *Signifying Rappers: Rap and Race in the Urban Present* (New York: Ecco Press, 1990); Brian Cross, *It's Not about a Salary … Rap, Race und Resistance in Los Angeles* (New York: Verso, 1993); Adam Krims, *Rap Music and the Poetics of Identity* (New York: Cambridge University Press, 2000); Jon Michael Spencer, ed., The Emergency of Black and the Emergence of Rap, a special issue of *Black Sacred Music: A Journal of Theomusicology* 5/1 (Spring 1991); William Eric Perkins, ed., *Droppin' Science: Critical Essays on Rap Music and Hip Hop Culture* (Philadelphia: Temple University Press, 1996).

31. Nelson George, *The Death of Rhythm & Blues* (New York: Pantheon Books, 1988), 169, 191.

32. Ibid., 188.

33. Houston A. Baker, Jr., *Rap, Black Studies, and the Academy* (Chicago: University of Chicago Press, 1993), 91.

34. Sherley Anne Williams, "Two Words on Music: Black Community," in Gina Dent, ed., *Black Popular Culture* (Seattle: Bay Press, 1992), 167.

35. Costello and Wallace, *Signifying Rappers*, 58.

36. Baker, *Rap, Black Studies, and the Academy*, 59–60.

37. Dyson, *Reflecting Black*, 12.

38. Ibid.

39. Rose, *Black Noise*, 73.

40. Quoted in Ernest Allen, Jr., "Making the Strong Survive: The Contours and Contradictions of Message Rap," in William Eric Perkins, ed., *Droppin' Science: Critical Essays on Rap Music and Hip Hop Culture* (Philadelphia: Temple University Press, 1996), 182.

41. Interview of Mos Def. Found on http://www.poundmag.com/magazine/features/articles/mighty/mosdef.html.

42. http://search.netscape.com/google.tmpl?search=nuwine.

43. Manhunt.com. Manhunt features: Interview by S2.

44. Nuwine Chat, February 1, 2000. Twec.com.

45. Quoted in Russell Simmons, with Nelson George, *Life and Def: Sex, Drugs, Money, God* (New York: Crown, 2001), 217.

46. Sister Souljah, *360 Degrees of Power* (New York: Epic ET48713).

47. Quoted in William Eric Perkins, "The Rap Attack: An Introduction," in Perkins, ed., *Droppin' Science: Critical Essays on Rap Music und Hip Hop Culture* (Philadelphia: Temple University Press, 1996), 35.

48. Snoop Dogg, with Davin Seay, *The Doggfather: The Times, Trials, and Hardcore Truths of Snoop Dogg* (New York: William Morrow, 1999), 2–3.

49. Ibid., 106.

50. Robin D. G. Kelley, *Yo' Mama's Disfunktional!: Fighting the Culture Wars in Urban America* (Boston: Beacon Press, 1997), 38–39.

51. Sacha Jenkins, "The End of the Ice Age?" SPIN magazine, March 2001, 85.

52. Meshack Blaq, interview with Common. Posted on *Kroniek Magazine* Online: <http://www.kronick.com/2.o/issue3o/common.shtm1>.

53. Simmons, *Life and Def*, 217–218.

54. Ibid., 219.

55. Jon Michael Spencer, "Overview of American Popular Music in Theological Perspective," in *Theomusicology* a special issue of *Black Sacred Music: A journal of Theomusicology* 8, no. 1 (Spring 1994): 216. The intertwining of the "sacred" and "secular" that I suggest throughout this introduction is embraced to varying degrees by the contributors to this volume.

3
Hip Hop to Rap
Some Implications of an Historically Situated Approach to Performance

Interested in the performance aspect of hip hop, Greg Dimitriadis argues that contemporary approaches to music criticism have often focused on the product rather than the contextual processes by which such musical products emerge. Beginning with performance theory and music criticism, Dimitriadis examines hip hop as event, the commodity form of hip hop, the transitional history of the 1980s and its impact on hip hop culture. This essay theoretically and methodologically brings together performance studies and postmodern thought to analyze localized black musical practices and presentations with the goal of carving out a new approach that can hold in tension the historical realties of commodification *and* the localized organic roots of black musical practices through a more complex analysis of music-making practices in the ever-unfolding historical recitations of contexts of use.

Hip Hop to Rap: Some Implications of an Historically Situated Approach to Performance

Greg Dimitriadis

Singin' on 'n on 'n on
The beat don't stop until the break of dawn
    —"Rapper's Delight" (1979) by the Sugarhill Gang

When we're on the tape, we're fresh out the box
You can hear our sounds, for blocks and blocks
    —"King of Rock" (1985) by Run-D.M.C.

From its inception, hip hop has been marked by a complex constellation of performance practices including D.J.-ing, M.C.-ing, breakdancing, and graffiti writing. However, the release of Run-D.M.C.'s first singles and albums (including "King of Rock"), helped change all this. Run-D.M.C.'s songs were typically three to five minutes long and had choruses and themes. They were self-contained texts meant to be consumed in privatized contexts. Hence, the above lyric from "King of Rock" was not at all anomalous when it was first released in 1985. Most people did receive hip hop culture by way of tapes played on personal stereo systems (including then-ubiquitous "boom boxes"). The lyric would, however, have sounded quite strange to those immersed in hip hop's earliest years, to those who hung out in clubs partying "until the break of dawn." Hip hop moved, in short, from an event-driven activity to a product-driven one with the release and overwhelming commercial success of Run-D.M.C.'s first recordings in the early 1980s. Situated and place-bound activity, which demanded active and engaged agents to sustain it, was eclipsed by the proliferation of self-contained musical texts by artists including Whodini, the Fat Boys, L.L. Cool J, the Beastie Boys and others—all of whom thrived in the discursive and material space opened up by the group. These recordings became the focus of hip hop, moving it to privatized contexts and encouraging more passive productive and consumptive practices.

Such historical shifts, as I will argue here, have been largely ignored in extant criticism on rap (specifically) and popular music (generally). This body of work tends to operate at, and fluctuate between, two poles—the micro-level analysis of song lyrics and music textures (e.g. Kellner) and/or the broad-brushed interrogation of macro-level historical and political contexts and currents (e.g., Breen; Grossberg; Straw). Attempts to bridge these paradigms often result in the stark juxtaposition of the two approaches—content analysis up close and context from afar—with little effort to integrate them in productive ways (e.g., Rose). What is needed, it seems, is a treatment of musical and performative processes that pays careful attention to the historical evolution of concrete contexts of production and consumption, acknowledging that the division between the two is no longer easy or self-evident. Drawing on (among others) de Certeau's notion of practices as "enunciations" imbricated in "contexts of use," this article attempts to develop such an approach by interrogating one defining moment of hip hop history—the moment when the popular imperatives of commodity-culture largely eclipsed the art's roots in localized performance (de Certeau 33).

Performance Theory and Music Criticism

Textual criticism, until very recently, has been stressed in both popular and classical strands of music criticism. Informed by various strains of formalism, textual criticism assumes that music texts are self-contained and referential entities. They exist ultimately outside of the variances of live production and performance and can be read as such. They are assumed fully decipherable, an assumption which has been read through "high art" as well as popular art traditions. This textual approach has its roots in structuralist models of communication, models which tend to assume all necessary contexts can be located in the texts themselves. Simon Frith echoes these concerns in his treatment of classical American composer Leonard Bernstein:

> [Leonard Bernstein's] question is *how* does music communicate (which is, for him, a prior question to what it does), and his starting assumption is that it must "mean" the same thing to composer, performer, and listener, otherwise communication would be impossible. In investigating this problem Bernstein draws on linguistics, on Chomskyan linguistics, in particular, on a theory of what makes communication *possible*: an underlying human capacity to grasp the "deep structure" of the communication process.
>
> (104)

Like many "classical" composers, Bernstein draws on a deep structure communicative model, one which assumes that *langue*, the language system abstracted from individual users, is most important (certainly more important than emergent performance or *parole*). This deep structure transcends particular and various performances.

In large measure, Western music criticism (of whatever variant) has imported the dominant *langue* model and thus has remained locked into textual kinds of criticism. The score or recording has remained a primary unit of analysis here, particular performances in historical context relegated to the sidelines of concern. The examples from cultural studies and cultural studies-inspired work—especially vis-à-vis rap—are plentiful (Allen, Jr.; Decker; Irving; Kellner). This work tends not to be interested in situated, consumptive practices, valorizing de-contextualized content analysis first and foremost. The most striking example in this regard is Douglas Kellner's recent *Media Cultures*.

In this text, Kellner explores the lyrics of a number of rap artists in an effort to provide a "diagnostic critique of the situation of African Americans in the United States today" (Kellner 157). Deploying close readings of a handful of texts, he stresses that the personalities and moral universes of many rap artists are more complex than the often monolithically negative ones stressed by the media. He argues, when discussing the prototypical "gangsta rapper" Ice-T, that "[a] close listening to Ice-T's *Original Gangster* evidences moralistic condemnation of those who devote themselves to a life of crime and drugs." He goes on to look at the song "Midnight," which narrates the story of a drive-by shooting and retaliation: "Ice-T's 'Midnight' tells of the all-night adventures with violence and police of a gangsta crew and although the rapper character gets home safely, he went off to sleep and at six in morning the police broke through his door—riffing off the message that the gangsta life don't pay" (Kellner 182–83). Kellner stresses that the song's last few lines bring a kind of moral closure to the violent narrative, one that condemns the life style seemingly glorified by the "gangsta." Kellner's warrants are, again, textual. He relies on his own "close listening" to reach his conclusions not providing sufficient historical context to understand how these texts might function vis-à-vis complex evolving idioms in particular consumptive sites.

These kinds of readings proliferate in music criticism, both popular and academic, and have been used to justify or condemn a broad range of political and personal agendas (e.g., Allen, Jr.; Decker; Irving). The problem, however, is that such readings assume *a priori* the kind of work lyrics perform and do not consider these lyrics as complex enunciations of situated practices, picked up and consumed in particular historical moments and contexts. In response to these and related issues, many critics have downplayed the importance of texts, looking at context more broadly. Influenced by the work of Stuart Hall, "articulation" approaches to popular culture, the most notable being that of Lawrence Grossberg, have become particularly important here (Morley and Chen). According to these critics, different cultural texts play into different political agendas at select historical moments, in ways difficult to prefigure based on lyric content alone. Popular culture is a site of intense affective investments that are articulated to and with each other in complex ways. As Grossberg writes, "the politics of the rock and roll apparatus cannot be located solely in its ideology [e.g., as located through textual content] but depends as well on the empowering effects of an affective economy" (Grossberg 88). In his own research, Grossberg looks at how the Right has picked up and redeployed the energies of popular culture in particular—and particularly repressive—ways. Grossberg eschews textual readings, looking instead at political currents and trends, stressing an exploration of "context" above all else.

As Marcus Breen posits, these articulation theories have enabled a whole host of global approaches that interrogate changing music industry structures, and what they will and will not allow: "Articulation theory now provides a means of giving broader expression to the ways in which culture and the market economy, values and commodity, are in rapid transition" (Breen 487). The music industry is a primary site for interrogation here, as are global patterns of production and consumption. The collection, *Rock and Popular Music: Politics, Policies, and Institutions*, edited by Tony Bennett, Simon Frith, Lawrence Grossberg, John Shepherd, and Graeme Turner, all notable cultural studies scholars, is broadly indicative of how these concerns have come to the forefront of popular music criticism. These approaches have been useful in helping critics to avoid the traps of de-contextualized textual analysis. However, like micro-level analysis, such approaches tend to treat music idioms in fairly monolithic and often ahistorical ways. Instead of ignoring context, however, these readings ignore the particular work of texts in situated contexts.

I want to suggest here that a focus on the changing histories of production and consumption might provide a good complement to these approaches, bridging the dichotomy between "text" and "context," opting for historically grounded treatments of music as realized in situated contexts, in performance. The work of de Certeau proves helpful here. Drawing on analogies between language-use and a host of other practices, he argues that we must interrogate "acts" or practices as situated enunciations of deeper syntactical structures, while elaborating on their contexts of production and consumption (or "use") as clearly as possible. The construct is helpful: "By situating the act in relation to its circumstances, 'contexts of use' draw attention to the traits that specify the act of speaking (or practice of language) and are its effects" (de Certeau 33). A number of important theorists and researchers have brought related concerns to ethnomusicology. In key exemplars, Charles Keil, John Chernoff, and Christopher Small have all similarly challenged the syntax-based logic still dominant in music criticism, pushing the field towards more situated understandings of performance and music process. However, as I will note, this work tends not to extend the study of these musical practices along historical lines.

Much of this work was inspired by the important writings of Charles Keil. Keil argued in the mid-1960s that the tools on which music critics typically draw are ground in a particularly European "high art" understanding of what music is all about. As such, these tools do not work well with other kinds of music, most specifically (for his argument) performance driven non-elite Western musics. In his classic discussion of Leonard Meyer's *Emotion and Feeling in Music* Keil writes:

> [Meyer's] procedure assumes that for analytic purposes music can be fixed or frozen as an object, a score, or a recording, and it implies not only a one-to-one relationship between syntactic form and expression but a weighting in favor of the former to the detriment of the latter.

> (54)

The syntax of the piece, the score as it is represented as a "fixed or frozen … object," is the primary unit of analysis. Here, music is removed from its situated context and treated as a self-contained object, one which can be explored and evaluated on its own. As Keil argues, such an approach equates form and expression. In other words, the score is considered internally consistent and entirely self-referential. It is all on the page so to speak. All the important relationships can be traced or explored between the notes themselves. Meaning or musical affect can be located within the score or recording itself, eliding the importance of local contexts of use.

These largely formalist criteria and assumptions have been used to illuminate an entire tradition of "classical" European score-driven music. However, these approaches, as Keil argues, have been particularly unhelpful in illuminating non-elite Western musics, musics which rely on performance for their ultimate realization.

These musics—like most popular musics rooted in dance—have been wholly ignored in the Western academy up until recently (McClary), Keil goes on:

> In some music, and I am thinking specifically of African and African-derived genres, illumination of syntactic relationships or of form will not go far in accounting for expression. The one-to-one relationship postulated by Meyer will not hold; syntactic analysis is a necessary condition for understanding such music, but it is not in itself sufficient.

> (54)

Musical/performative relationships are not fully contained or realized in the syntax alone. They cannot be captured in ideal form, out of context.

To understand these musics—as well as any other music performance, really—we must take the performance itself as the primary unit of analysis, expanding it to encompass all the situated activities which help constitute the event itself. This means appreciating all the ways various participants conspire to sustain the event, from musicians to listeners to dancers. Indeed, musical practices like all collective activities are sustained by particular communities in particular times and places, and must be understood as such. Howard Becker's *Art Worlds* is quite helpful here. Becker, in this seminal text, critiques the idea that art is created by isolated artists in historical vacuums. He writes, "All artistic work, like all human activity, involves the joint activity of a number, often a large number, of people" (Becker 1). Becker stresses that participants sustain artistic events in complex ways, mutually constituting the situated activity (so defined) in one way and not others. The autonomous artist creating his or her work in isolation, secluded from the vibrancy and variance of the social, is largely a fallacy of Western aesthetic criticism, and a particularly regressive one at that. More people than the musicians alone count here. Understanding the roles of the audience as active agents becomes increasingly important for understanding the music-making activity, as realized beyond the scope of the text alone. We are thus pushed towards an interrogation of contexts of use.

Christopher Small takes a similar activity-centered approach in *Music of the Common Tongue: Survival and Celebration in Afro-American Music*. He notes here that "music is not primarily a thing or a collection of things, but an activity in which we engage," continuing "I define [musicking] to include not only performing and composing ... but also listening and even dancing to music; all those involved in any way in a musical performance can be thought of as musicking" (Small 50). Indeed, Keil and others have stressed that many non-elite Western musics cannot be understood outside of their relationship with, and connections to, dance, something that can be said for most popular musics as well (see McClary). As John Chernoff writes, African music is, quite literally, only realized through the participation of dancers:

> In African music, it is largely the listener or dancer who has to supply the beat: the listener must be *actively engaged* in making sense of the music; the music itself does not become the concentrated focus of an event, as at a concert. It is for this fundamental reason that African music should not be studied out of its context or as "music": the African orchestra is not complete without a participant on the other side.
>
> (Chernoff 50)

Dancers do not simply accompany drummers as they perform. Rather, dancers become integral parts of the event, supplying an additional rhythm, through the pounding of their feet, to the poly-rhythmic event. Rhythms play off of each other, dancers interacting with drummers and drummers interacting with dancers in entirely recursive ways. All are responsible for sustaining the event.

These concerns have begun to resonate in popular music study, most especially in the study of contemporary dance cultures. Good examples here include Sarah Thornton's *Club Cultures* and Steve Redhead's collection *Rave Off* (Redhead; Thornton). A less obvious but equally important example is Robert Walser's *Running with the Devil: Power, Gender, and Madness in Heavy Metal Music*. Walser, who draws explicitly on Small's notion of "musicking," notes that his "interest is less in explicating texts or defining the history of a style than in analyzing the musical activities that produce texts and styles and make them socially significant." These activities are broad ranging. Walser writes that he "attended concerts, studied recordings, interviewed fans and musicians, took heavy metal guitar lessons, and read fan magazines, industry reports, and denunciations" to fashion a study that brought together cultural analysis, ethnography, and textual interpretation (Walser xiii). Walser, like Small, sees music not as a series of texts to be decoded, nor as empty slates to be articulated with particular political/contextual concerns. Musical processes, rather, are performative processes, sustained by multiple audiences in myriad and complex ways, in situated contexts of use.

The move to study situated performance has thus resonated throughout popular music as well as ethnomusicological studies. Yet, with the exception of some work in ethnomusicology (e.g., Manuel; Waterman), there has been little effort to trace historical, shifting contexts of consumption and production (or "use") on a local level. Contemporary currents in performance theory—particularly the work of Della Pollock and the authors in her recent *Exceptional Spaces*—prove helpful in beginning to fill this void. Pollock argues, in this important collection, that "conventional distinctions between performance and texts" in performance studies have fallen aside "in favor of a dynamic reception of texts as inseparable from the processes by which they are made, understood, and deployed." This notion, as I noted above, has also become central for certain currents in ethnomusicology, including the works of Keil, Small, and Chernoff. Yet, drawing on Foucault's notion of "genealogy," Pollock extends these concerns, arguing, as well, that performance theorists must begin to look at how texts "evoke their place within a history of tools, uses, and action" (Pollock 21). All the authors in *Exceptional Spaces* interrogate this mutual articulation of history and performance in different ways and to different ends, filling a central chasm in performance studies and opening up a potentially fruitful avenue of inquiry in music studies. Operating in this space, this essay will focus, specifically, on changing contexts of production and consumption in hip hop performance.

I will look at one defining moment in hip hop history, interrogating historically select contexts of use, noting how they resonate in and across multiple musical texts. I will begin with the period marked roughly from 1979–1982, when hip hop existed as a performance-based idiom, thriving in clubs in and around New York City. I will then trace the shift that took place circa 1983 with the rise of Run-D.M.C., as hip hop became more of a mass-disseminated popular art, one which circulated by way of privatized media forms. While deploying textual analysis, I will link these "readings" to concrete, situated contexts, arguing that one must understand their mutual imbrication to speak in any kind of informed way about these most powerful practices.

From Hip Hop to Rap

Hip Hop as Event

Hip hop began as a situated cultural practice, one dependent upon a whole series of artistic activities or competencies (Dimitriadis). Dance, music, and graffiti were all equally important in helping to sustain the event. Like many African musics and popular dance musics, early hip hop cannot be understood as aural text alone but must be approached and appreciated as multi-tiered event, in particular contexts of consumption and production. Tricia Rose gets at some of this interplay in *Black Noise*:

> Stylistic continuities were sustained by internal cross-fertilization between rapping, breakdancing, and graffiti writing. Some graffiti writers, such as black American Phase 2, Haitian Jean-Michel Basquiat, Futura, and black American Fab Five Freddy produced rap records. Other writers drew murals that celebrated favorite rap songs (e.g., Futura's mural "The Breaks" was a whole car mural that paid homage to Kurtis Blow's rap of the same name). Breakdancers, DJs, and rappers wore graffiti-painted jackets and tee-shirts. DJ Kool Herc was a graffiti writer and dancer first before he began playing records. Hip hop events featured breakdancers, rappers, and DJs as triple-bill entertainment. Graffiti writers drew murals for DJ's stage platforms and designed posters and flyers to advertise hip hop events.
>
> (Rose 35)

The artistic activities which helped constitute hip hop, thus, were multiple and varied, though entirely integrated by and through these "stylistic continuities" (Rose uses, later, flow, layer, and rupture metaphors to describe these continuities [38]). In a recent issue of

Rappages, Harry Allen notes that these were "mutually supporting art forms" and "each gave the other resonance and depth" (Allen 41). This sense of stylistic continuity was implicitly acknowledged by writers such as Steven Hager, whose 1984 book *Hip Hop* was subtitled "The Illustrated History of Break Dancing, Rap Music, and Graffiti."

The role of artist was relatively dispersed at this point in time. There were many ways to participate in the culture, though they all demanded engaging in situated activity (Lave and Wenger). Events took place in parks, tenement basements, high school gyms, and, most especially, clubs like Harlem World, Club 371, Disco Fever, and the Funhouse. Accessing the scene meant accessing such places. Unlike the current rap scene, this participation went beyond the production and circulation of musical texts alone to include practices such as dance and other face-to-face community building activities.

Rap's indissoluble connection with live performance is evinced, quite clearly, on early rap singles (1979–1982) as well as bootleg tapes from early shows. The performative spaces mentioned above thus resonated in and across these early texts. Singles such as the afore-mentioned "Rapper's Delight" (1979), for example, were full of the kinds of "floating" or "stock" phrases which circulated in and throughout NYC hip hop parties during the mid-1970s. Examples include the now-famous "you don't stop," a then-ubiquitous party chant. Such phrases were public domain at this point in time, called upon and deployed by numer-ous artists in varied contexts. Producing an original text was less important than the rapper's or DJ.'s ability to "move a crowd." Producing coherent and autonomous texts was simply not valued. Bootleg tapes, when available, were a by-product of this activity, as were early singles. The performance itself was most important.

Like the live events themselves, the earliest rap singles were long and sprawling, with little sense of internal lyrical (or musical) progression. "Rapper's Delight" is, in fact, over 15 min-utes long. These early recordings were entirely unlike the self-contained 3–5 minute narrative tracks which would become popular in the late eighties. Such singles seemed to run on and on and at some point simply end—as if someone abruptly ended the party. The closure implied in the three-part narrative form was missing. Each, rather, intertwined loose boasts and brags, with longer narratives and with (canned) artist-audience chants—tools ubiquitous in live hip hop events. Such tools were loosely combined and delivered in live contexts as rap was a more fluid and open-ended music or art at that point, a practice imbricated in live events. These singles indexed such events as unfolding activities, situations where a clearly delivered and thematic narrative might not be entirely appropriate to help "move" an ever-shifting and milling crowd.

The earliest hip hop singles evidence this indissoluble focus on the occasion or event in a number of ways. First and foremost, the prevailing theme throughout these singles is party-ing, getting crowds involved in the unfolding event. Lines like "Come alive y'all and give me what you got" abound throughout, flowing in and out of the more structured narrative sequences, as in a live show. Concurrently, the pronoun "you"—i.e., the live hip hop crowd—betrays a familiar and friendly relationship between artist and audience. This holds true for "Rapper's Delight" as well as nearly all early singles, including "Spoonin' Rap" (1980) by Spoonie Gee, "Money (Dollar Bill Y'all)" (1981) by Jimmy Spicer and "Supperrappin" (1980) by Grandmaster Flash and the Furious Five. In all these examples, the "you" indexes the par-ticipants necessary to sustain the event, active agents who engage and sustain the culture in complex and multiple ways in particular sites.

In a helpful counter-example, the pronoun "you" would come to reference a very different audience in years hence, as the form and function of the music changed. Most specifically, the "you" would often interpellate dominant society as a whole—for example, as in KRS-One's line "You built up a race on the concept of violence/Now in 90 you want silence?" or Ice-T's "You don't like my lifestyle? Fuck you. I'm rolling with the New Jack Crew." Quite clearly, these were not the active agents who sustained the event by engaging in collective and situated activity. They were nameless representatives of dominant society to whom these products were increasingly available for consumption outside of clubs. Indeed, the early "Rapper's Delight" speaks to a music still aware of itself as a dance or party music, as a music realized in situated performance. It speaks to a music which indexes embodied participation in complex social activities, not wide dissemination in disembodied texts. Any other use of "you" would have been entirely anomalous.

This sense of the event, of the recursive nature of interaction and communication, is evidenced, as well, in the use of "call and response" routines. These routines were ubiquitous in live hip hop shows and are also featured on nearly all the earliest rap singles. Examples include:

> Go Hotel, Motel, What ch'a gonna do today? *Say what? (in-studio* audience)
> Say I'm gonna get a fly girl, gonna get some spank, and drive off in a def O.J.
> —"Rapper's Delight" (1979) by the Sugarhill Gang

> When I say "rock," you say "roll" When I say "ice," then you say "cold"
> Then when I say "disco," you say "the beat"
> I say it's "like honey," then you say "it's sweet"
> —"Adventures of Super Rhymes" (1979) by Jimmy Spicer

> Before you hear the party people yell "Sugarhill" So what's the deal? *Sugarhill!*
> So what's the deal? *Sugarhill!*
> —"That's the Joint" (1979) by Funky Four + One More

These call and response routines give clear testimony to the intimacy of the club or party situation that these performers were coming out of. Rap grew out of a dialogic and interactive tradition, one that linked artists and audiences in some concrete fashion (Dimitriadis). These important but largely ignored aspects of early hip hop become evident when we begin mutually interrogating early texts and contexts of use.

Run-D.M.C. and Rap as Commodity Form

These call and response routines disappeared from hip hop during the early-to-mid-eighties, a period marked by the rise of Run-D.M.C. and related artists. Run-D.M.C. was the first mega-successful rap group, earning rap's first gold, platinum, and multi-platinum album awards (for *Run-D.M.C.* [1984], *King of Rock* [1985], and *Raising Hell* [1986] respectively). They were the first rappers to appear on MTV, the first to grace the cover of *Rolling Stone*, and the first to have a major endorsement deal with an athletic wear company. Rap became a popular American music with the ascent of Run-D.M.C., one which circulated widely in self-contained commodity form. Rap came to rely more and more on the in-studio producer (specifically) and the music industry (generally) at this critical juncture. Producing self-contained texts became more important than sustaining the live and often multi-tiered event. The voice of the crowd, the voice of response and participation, was silenced as rap entered this much wider and more commercial sphere, most especially by way of privatized contexts of use.

Run-D.M.C. was the first in a line of rap artists for whom the recording—not the party—became the all-important focus. The history of Run-D.M.C. is, in fact, inseparable from the history of Def Jam Recordings and its various behind the scenes producers and business-people. Def Jam Recordings was founded in the early 1980s by Rick Rubin and Russell Simmons. Like other famous producers including Berry Gordy (from Motown) and Phil Specter, Rubin and Simmons helped craft and develop their artists and their images in unique ways. In many respects, the cast of characters necessary to sustain hip hop/rap as an event shifted at this point. As Howard Becker writes, "Every art … rests on an extensive division of labor" (13) and this division is contingent over time. Thus, while breakdancers and graffiti artists, as I noted else-where, became less crucial for constituting the art during this period, producers like Rick Rubin became more so, crafting the art from behind the scenes in important ways (Dimitriadis).

In a particularly telling interview, Rick Rubin comments that his "biggest contribution to rap was the structured-song element." He notes further, "Prior to that, a lot of rap songs were seven minutes long; the guy would keep rapping until he ran out of words." By separating songs into "verses and choruses," Rubin, along with Russell Simmons, helped to turn rap into much more traditional pop music, one with a focused lyric content (quoted in Light, 110). Rubin and Simmons brought an explicitly producer-based aesthetic to hip hop, streamlining this otherwise more open-ended music into a more commodity-driven one. Many of their efforts reached platinum-plus sales status, due, in large part, to this popular approach. The move to self-contained commodity form and away from the particulars of the event is evinced from the very beginning of Run-D.M.C.'s career, on their very first single, "It's Like That."

This single, like many that would follow, marked a sea change in the art. Many of the earli-est hip hop tracks, tracks like "Rapper's Delight," did not feature focused thematic content nor organizing choruses. Such songs were a loose mix of boasts, brags, artist-audience routines, and short narratives. In contrast however, "It's Like That" (1983) is a tight, a thematic track, one which explores the trials and tribulations of poverty. Lines like "Bills fly higher everyday/We receive much lower pay" abound throughout and are divided up by the collectively delivered chorus "IT'S LIKE THAT." This chorus is used in traditional "pop" fashion, to organize the track thematically. Such choruses would become a staple of Run-D.M.C. (e.g., "My Adidas"), fellow Def Jam artists like L.L. *Cool J* (e.g., "I'm Bad"), as well as many other rap artists.

It is crucial to mention that Run-D.M.C. also re-worked this practice of "collective delivery" in key ways. Many early collectives like the Cold Crush Brothers and the Fantastic Five used collective delivery freely in face-to-face performance. Chants like "THE COLD CRUSHIN' MOTHER FUCKIN' TOUGH ASS FOUR M.C.'S" were used to frame loosely delivered boasts and brags, traded between members in live interactive contexts. These collective chants were not used to organize individual raps thematically but to sustain collective performance, a practice carried over onto wax by groups like the Treacherous Three (e.g., "BECAUSE WE ROCK NONSTOP" from "The Body Rock"). Run-D.M.C., however, uses collective delivery here to push the message of this song forward, to make it louder, to proclaim it more clearly. "IT'S LIKE THAT" is a clear, meaningful refrain or chorus used to divide up, organize, and accentuate this more focused, more organized pop cut.

This move towards rap-as-self-contained-commodity is evinced perhaps most clearly in Run-D.M.C.'s acknowledgment of mass-media forms in many of their songs. Indeed, as with early hip hop, the activity and practices surrounding this moment in hip hop registered in these singles in ways that blur the line between text and context. Hence, the line "When we're on the tape, we're fresh out the box/You can hear our sounds, for blocks and blocks." Rap was now mass-disseminated, capable of being configured and mediated in new ways in a number of different settings and places. The event as a place-specific and dependent activity was now radically re-worked as disembodied texts, capable of being consumed and disseminated in a wide number of contexts, became most important. Hip hop moved, in short, from a place-dependent art to a more mobile one.

This move to rap music and away from hip hop enabled the art's locus of production to expand. Hip hop had been a localized music. Specific clubs such as Harlem World, T-Connection, Disco Fever, Rooftop, and Funworld, all in the South Bronx or Harlem, were at the center of early hip hop activity. However, during the early-to-mid-eighties, the outlying areas of New York City, such as Hollis, Queens (the home of Run-D.M.C.) became increasingly important, as did areas around the country like Los Angeles (the home of Uncle Jam's Army and the World Class Wreckin' Crew). The so-called suburbanization of hip hop began during this period, as a much wider group of performers and audiences began to have access to the art. Rap was now a separable discourse that did not demand strict integration in live multi-media production. Artists were no longer performers first and recording artists second. In the face of this massive commercial success, the event was largely overshadowed by the promotion and propagation of select and iconic figures through commodity form, in ways that had implications for the idiom as a whole.

These recordings were often consumed by way of boom boxes. These large and bass-heavy radios allowed young people to take music with them, to play· it anywhere they chose. Yet, unlike privatized walkman radios, these radios projected music to people who might not want to hear it. Hence, crucial questions about public space and the ownership of space through sound became increasingly important in the eighties—questions we can trace as emerging in and through select texts. Indeed, L.L. Cool J (also on Def Jam Recordings) places the radio at the center of his musical universe on cuts like "I Can't Live Without my Radio," articulating his vision of race and masculinity through technology with lines like "Walking down the street to the hardcore beat while my J.V.C. vibrates the concrete." L.L. appropriates and celebrates this sense of rebellion when he raps of claiming space in his neighborhood by putting his "volume way past 10." A politics of public space and the ownership of public space became increasingly important and evident at this point in time. As Robin Kelley writes:

> The movement of young blacks, their music and expressive styles have literally become weapons in a battle over the right to occupy public space. Frequently employing high-decibel car stereos and boom boxes, they "pump up the volume" not only for their own listening pleasure but also as part of an indirect, ad hoc war of position to take back public space.
>
> (Kelley 134)

Again, with the rise of artists like L.L. Cool J and Run-D.M.C., hip hop moved away from a more place-bound activity to a more mobile one, allowing for a qualitatively new activity, with new political possibilities and constraints. Most clearly, however, we begin to see particular constructions of masculinity emerge, constructions which would play a defining role in the history of the idiom.

L.L.'s lyrics would have been anomalous early on, when rap was a more place-bound and in-group art form. Yet, these changing activities registered on myriad levels here, including in rap's vocal content. In key instance, rap lyrics focused on partying during the late seventies. The "you," as argued above, was typically directed towards other party-goers, as in "you don't stop!" Yet on this track, L.L. raps "I'm sorry if you can't understand, but I need a radio inside my hand." Clearly, the "you" represents an outside audience, one which would not share L.L.'s love for rap music. The move from face-to-face activity (as embodied in dance) to the production and dissemination of self-contained narrative texts changed the nature of the activity here in fundamental ways. The texts themselves became increasingly self-contained and structured, participants less easily identifiable. The dominant paradigm, where artists transfer messages to audiences, became more important than indexing the quality of the musical event or occasion itself. Indeed, even when artists addressed seemingly "live" audiences in their songs (e.g., on tracks like Eric B. and Rakim's early "I Know You Got Soul"), it was always from in and within self-contained and densely verbal texts, with clear choruses and verses, targeted to largely hypothetical audiences. The linear model, in large measure, eclipsed a more circular and recursive one at this point, though it opened up the possibility for addressing wider audiences with select concerns.

The more mobile use of self-contained texts is evinced, as well, in the increasing importance accrued to media-specific producer styles in the late eighties, as media forms other than boom boxes became important. When asked where "the most important place for hiphop is," Cypress Hill producer DJ Muggs comments: "it's the muthafuckers just poppin' the cassette in the box. You gotta be in your car, in your walkman, in your house, fuck a club, fuck a radio" (qtd. in Cross 247). Indeed, walkmans, cars, and homes became key sites for hip hop beginning in the mid-to-late 1980s, as rap moved towards commodity-driven forms. Different production styles began to reflect different regions of the country and their means of listening to music. For example, West Coast rap has become more bass and beat heavy, as it is targeted for consumption in ubiquitous cars and jeeps. East Coast rap, in contrast, has become more mid-range as it is often consumed by way of private stereos with small speakers. Producer DJ Pooh, who has worked most notably with West Coast act Ice Cube, comments:

> L.A. is on a car trip, and if the shit don't sound good in my car, fuck it, I don't want to hear it, so I make my music for your car. The East Coast is way different. They're looking for something they can play at home.
>
> (qtd. in D-Dub 11)

The sound is aimed at the listener's technology, technology which was most often consumed in dispersed and mobile settings. These sonic shifts began to occur during the mid-to-late 1980s with the rise of a rap-as-commodity from. The form and function of the music shifted, as self-contained and internally consistent texts became ever-ubiquitous and live performance became increasingly obsolete.

Rap's oft-noted move to masculinist ideals and values came as a parallel phenomenon to the proliferation of producer-based technologies as explored above. With the means of producing rap increasingly consolidated, questions of access (or lack thereof) became crucial. Tricia Rose writes:

> [Y]oung women [are] not especially welcome in male social spaces where technological knowledge is shared. Today's studios are extremely male-dominated spaces where technological discourse merges with a culture of male bonding that inordinately problematizes female apprenticeship. Both of these factors had a serious impact on the contributions of women in contemporary rap music production.
>
> (Rose 58)

By many accounts, including Rose's, women were an active part of early rap (see Guevara). Early rap artists included Sha-Rock (who recorded a few very early singles with the Funky Four + One), Pebbily Poo, Sequence (featuring Blondie, Cheryl "The Pearl" Cook, and Angie

B), Lisa Lee, Debbie Dee, and Wanda Dee (all associated with Afrika Bambaataa's Zulu Nation). Early breakers include Baby Love and early graffiti artists include Lady Pink. Yet, none of these artists had much financial success and their careers petered out during the early eighties, right at the point Run-D.M.C. entered the picture. Rap began to be constructed as a more masculinist art form during this period, one which allowed few opportunities for female access and thus agency, one which opened a space for the proliferation of already existing and deeply misogynist cultural discourses.

L.L. Cool J, especially, began to wed aggression against dominant society—as noted above—with an often racialized masculinity. The following is from his 1987 cut "I'm Bad,"

> M.C.'s retreat
> Cause they know I can beat 'em
> And eat 'em in a battle and the ref won't cheat 'em
> I'm the baddest
> Taking out all rookies
> So forget Oreos, eat *Cool J* cookies
> I'm bad

By noting that his competitors are "oreos," L.L. equates a lack of aggressive vocal prowess and presence with "whiteness." The implication, hence, is that being (metaphorically) aggressive, violent, and "bad" would make one "authentically" black. L.L. Cool J's image is thus tied into a kind of racialized macho posturing. Indeed, he embraced these ideals in full force, often posing shirtless in order to show off his muscular figure, and often boasting of his boxing prowess. His second album, *Bigger and Deffer,* sports a photo of him working out on a heavy bag, complete with thick gold chains and Kango hat. This image—the violent and aggressive young black male—would lodge itself in the collective psyche of America and its perception of rap music, drawing, as it did, on decades of affectively-invested, dominant cultural discourses and ideologies.

As noted, there were many different ways to participate in hip hop early on, many different ways to engage the culture. However, L.L. Cool J's (and others') popular racialized macho posturing, coupled with the lack of female access to increasingly important and consolidated producer technology, helped elide these. In fact, Simmons and Rubin alone effectively defined the face of rap from the early-to-mid-eighties. Dance and other event-oriented practices were eclipsed by commercial and (popular American) cultural imperatives. Rap became less an embodied practice and more about the production and dissemination of self-contained products. These came to be consumed, not in communal, dance-oriented sites (such as clubs), but in privatized spaces where particular kinds of activities were enabled and constrained. As Gilroy so succinctly put it, "it is not possible to dance in a car, however large and loud a system it may contain" (Gilroy 22). Concurrently, particular constructions of masculinity and race began to emerge in rap texts in ways that would help "define" the idiom. We see these, again, when we start looking closely at complex cultural forms in situated, historical contexts of use. When we do so, these constructs no longer seem immutable but the products of actors and institutions operating in particular moments in complex, over-determined ways.

Implications

As I have argued throughout, music criticism—both popular and academic—tends either to focus on texts too narrowly or context too broadly. Little attention is paid to music-making practices in historically unfolding contexts of use. In the case of rap, the result has been a focus on either specific and de-contextualized rap lyrics or broad social critique, questions of performance and activity nearly elided. Indeed, rap's early years have been all-but excluded from "serious" treatments of rap. It was, so the story goes, "just" about partying then. The implication, quite clearly, is that rap has since "progressed." As a result, the constructs that emerged in the art during the early part of the 1980s are taken as givens, in often debilitating and paralyzing ways. The story, however, is more complex. Sustaining the multi-tiered activity, as noted above, gave way to the production of self-contained texts, meant to be explored in more individualized contexts. The importance of agents in sustaining situated music-making activity was eclipsed by the consumption of commodities imbricated in, and within dominant cultural imperatives. These crucial (though largely ignored) shifts are brought into sharp relief if we begin treating musical events in situated, historical context. We begin to see the idiom as complex and evolving, registering and responding to history in the concrete. Hence, we begin to see how particular constructions of race, class, and gender begin to emerge in texts and practices as they unfold in performative contexts, thus opening up spaces for resistance and negotiation. When we take such an approach, we can no longer treat rap as a static, ahistorical signifier in the service of particular political or methodological agendas.

Study Questions

1. What are the advantages and disadvantages of both micro and macro approaches to the study of music criticism?
2. How does bringing in the work of social theorist of practice, Michel de Certeau, help to contextualize the settings of consumption and uses in hip hop culture?
3. What impact did the early 1980's have on hip hop and how does Dimitriadis make use of this historical trajectory in carving out an approach to the study of hip hop and black music?

Works Cited

Allen, Harry. "The Destruction of Hip-Hop Culture: 1970–2020." *Rappages* (June 1994): 35–43. Allen, Jr., Ernest. "Making the Strong Survive: The Contours and Contradictions of Message Rap." *Droppin' Science: Critical Essays on Rap Music and Hip Hop Culture*. Ed. William Eric Perkins. Philadelphia: Temple UP, 1996. 159–91.

Becker, Howard. *Art Worlds*. Berkeley: U of California P, 1982.

Bennett, Tony, et al. Eds. *Rock and Popular Music: Politics, Policies, and Institutions*. London: Routledge, 1993.

Breen, Marcus. "The End of the World as We Know It: Popular Music's Cultural Mobility." *Cultural Studies* 9.3 (1995): 486–504.

de Certeau, Michel. The *Practice of Everyday Life*. Berkeley: U of California P, 1984.

Chernoff, John. *African Rhythm and African Sensibility: Aesthetics and Social Action in African Musical Idioms*. Chicago: U of Chicago P, 1979.

Cross, Brian. *It's Not About a Salary ...: Rap, Race and Resistance in Los Angeles*. London: Verso, 1993.

D-Dub. "So YaStill Wannabe a Record Producer?" *Rappages* June 1992: 10–11.

Decker, Jeffrey Louis. "The State of Rap: Time and Place in Hip Hop Nationalism." *Microphone Fiends: Youth Music & Youth Culture*. Eds. Andrew Ross and Tricia Rose. New Yark: Routledge, 1994. 99–121.

Dimitriadis, Greg. "Hip Hop: From Live Performance to Mediated Narrative." *Popular Music* 15.2 (1996): 179–94.

Frith, Simon. *Performance Rites*. Cambridge: Harvard University P, 1996.

Gilroy, Paul. "Exer(or)cising Power: Black Bodies in the Black Public Sphere." *Dance in the City*. Ed. Helen Thomas. New York: St. Martin's P, 1997. 21–34.

Grossberg, Lawrence. *Dancing in Spite of Myself: Essays on Popular Culture*. Durham: Duke UP, 1997.

Guevara, Nancy. "Women Writin' Rappin' Breakin.'" *Droppin' Science: Critical Essays on Rap Music and Hip Hop Culture*. Ed. William Eric Perkins. Philadelphia: Temple UP, 1996. 49–62.

Hager, Steven. *Hip Hop: The Illustrated History of Break Dancing, Rap Music, and Graffiti*. New York: St. Martin's P, 1984.

Irving, Katrina. "'I Want Your Hands on Me': Building Equivalencies Through Rap Music." *Popular Music* 12.2 (1993): 105–21.

Keil, Charles. "Motion and Feeling Through Music." *Music Grooves*. Eds. Charles Keil and Steven Feld. Chicago: U of Chicago P, 1994. 53–76.

Kelley, Robin. "Kickin' Reality, Kickin' Ballistics: Gangsta Rap and Postindustrial Los Angeles." *Droppin' Science: Critical Essays on Rap Music and Hip Hop Culture*. Ed. William Eric Perkins. Philadelphia: Temple P, 1996. 117–58.

Kellner, Douglas. *Media Cultures: Cultural Studies, Identity and Politics Between the Modern and the Postmodern*. London: Routledge, 1995.

Lave, Jean and Etienne Wenger. *Situated Learning: Legitimate Peripheral Participation*. Cambridge: Cambridge UP, 1991.

Light, Alan. "Kings of Rap." *Rolling Stone* (15 November 1990): 110+.

McClary, Susan. "Same As It Ever Was." *Microphone Fiends: Youth Music & Youth Culture*. Eds. Andrew Ross and Tricia Rose. New York: Routledge, 1994. 29–40.

Manuel, Peter. *Cassette Culture: Popular Music and Technology in North India*. Chicago: U of Chicago P, 1993.

Morley, David and Chen, Kuan-Hsing. Eds. *Stuart Hall: Critical Dialogues in Cultural Studies*. London: Routledge, 1996.

Pollock, Della. "Introduction: Making History Go." *Exceptional Spaces: Essays in Performance & History*. Ed. Della Pollock. Durham: U of North Carolina P, 1988. 1–45.

Redhead, Steve. Ed. *Rave Off: Politics and Deviance in Contemporary Youth Culture*. Aldershot: Avebury, 1993.

Rose, Tricia. *Black Noise: Rap Music and Black Culture in Contemporary America*. Hanover, EG: Wesleyan UP, 1994.

Small, Christopher. *Music of the Common Tongue: Survival and Celebration in Afro-American Music*. London: John Calder, 1987.

Straw, Wili. "Systems of Articulation, Logics of Change: Communities and Scenes in Popular Music." *Cultural Studies* 5.3 (1992): 368–88.

Thornton, Sarah. *Club Cultures*. Hanover: Wesleyan UP, 1996.

Walser, Robert. *Running with the Devil: Power, Gender, and Madness in Heavy Metal Music*. Hanover: Wesleyan UP, 1994.

Waterman, Christopher Alan. *JuJu: A Social History and Ethnography of an African Popular Music*. Chicago: U of Chicago P, 1990.

4

A New Research Agenda
Exploring the Transglobal Hip Hop *Umma*

Often referred to as hip hop's "official religion"—Islam continues to play a major role in the development of hip hop culture and rap music. Given the presence, centrality, and under-engagement of Islam in hip hop studies, Alim paves the way for a communal "transglobal hip hop *umma*"—an Islamic nation of sorts that defies boundaries, borders and singularity. Here, Alim relies upon the Prophet Muhammad's imagined Islamic community or "*umma*" to reconceptualize hip hop as a global network. Focusing on both uses of Islam in hip hop and the self-identification of Islam among hip hop artists, Alim contextualizes and broadens Islam as expressed in hip hop (through focus on groups such as, Nation of Islam, The Nation of Gods and Earths, and the Sunni Muslim community in particular). He concludes that charting the movement of Islam in the hip hop *umma* uncovers the "highly misunderstood" aspects of its cultural uses and encourages not only the revision of Islamic pedagogy and scholarship, but also, the transformative global impact this holds for both a local and worldwide hip hop community.

A New Research Agenda: Exploring the Transglobal Hip Hop *Umma**

H. Samy Alim

Alim: When did you come into your Islamic knowledge?

Mos Def: I took my *shahada* four years ago.

A: I noticed in "Fear Not of Man" you opened up with *"Bismillah Al-Rahman Al-Rahim?"* Was that important for the album?

M: Well, I had been advised that when you do works that go out to the public—written works or spoken works—that you should bless them *like* that, you know. It makes *sense* to *me*. The spiritual *level* just puts the seal on it. Like I'm making a effort to reach Allah with this. And, *Insha'Allah,* my efforts will *be* accepted.

                        —MOS DEF, interview by the author, quoted in part in Alim 2001b

"I believe that there is no God but Allah, and I believe that Muhammad is his Messenger." These are the words that rappers Mos Def, Beanie Sigel, Freeway, Common, Chuck D, Napoleon of the Outlawz, and the Rza, along with over one billion other Muslims around the world, proclaimed, upon accepting the Islamic faith. Implicit in these words is a commitment to a way of life that is governed, regulated, and mediated by the precepts of Islam, by which Muslims are taught to "fear not of man," but to fear Allah alone (as Brooklyn rapper Mos Def makes clear above). Despite the fact that Islam has been a normative practice in African America since slavery, the full story of African American Muslim movements remains untold. In particular, despite journalist Harry Allen's description of Islam as hip hop's "official religion," Islam's dynamic presence and central role in the hip hop nation have been largely unexplored.

In this exploratory essay, I will be raising a number of issues and questions for further exploration in our ongoing attempt to gain an understanding of what I am calling the "transglobal hip hop *umma*" within a borderless Islamic nation. That is, the Prophet Muhammad did not speak of an "Islamic Iraq" or of a "Muslim Senegal"; he imagined a transglobal Muslim community, an *umma* where citizenship was based on faith rather than on contemporary nation-state distinctions, or rather, on how colonizing cartographers cut up the global landscape. The original goal of the *umma* was to be a network that was fixed in faith but mobile in all its parts.

We can begin with general questions: How much do we know about the relationship between "hip hop" and "Islam"? Do we even see these two communities as compatible? We can further problematize the notion of "Islamic hip hop" by reconsidering what it means to be an "Islamic artist" more generally. And we can delve deeper into the history of the hip hop cultural movement and ask questions like the following: Given the fact that Islamic civilization has been at once "transnational" and "connective" (as Cooke and Lawrence write in their introduction), how has this transnational connectivity been manifested within the hip hop cultural movement?[1] Further, given the transglobal nature of the hip hop cultural movement, which developed at least two decades ago in the movement's early period (Spady and Eure 1991; Mitchell 2001)—what Perkins (1996) referred to as "youth's global village" and Osumare (2002) as the "Hip Hop Global 'Hood"—how has this cultural nation without traditional borders served the purposes of spreading Islamic knowledge, values, teachings, ideas and ideals?

Before we can consider the transglobal hip hop *umma*, we need to explore the hidden histories of African American Muslim movements in the hip hop nation. As, Spady (2002) argues, "It is helpful to examine the current spread of Hip Hop Culture throughout Algeria and other African countries within the historical context of the Pan African, Pan Islamic and PanBanegritude movements of the 20th century."[2] Through the use of primary sources, namely oral histories and life history narratives, we can begin to develop a deeper understanding of the social, political, and cultural consciousness that is central to the philosophy of the hip hop cultural movement. At the same time, my research draws upon ethnographic techniques and demands direct engagement with hip hop artists wherever hip hop is practiced, that is, from the stadiums to the streets.

"Islam" needs to be broadly conceived, encompassing a spectrum of ideologies and schools of thought. I will focus on the three most dominant forms of Islam in the hip hop nation in the United States—the Nation of Islam, the Nation of Gods and Earths (or the Five Percent Nation of Islam), and the Sunni Muslim community. While there are theological and terminological differences between these communities, all view Islam as a transformative force in the lives of its practitioners, and the data reveal similarities among the views of their adherents. For example, the belief in Allah and the revelation of the Qur'an through the Prophet Muhammad is a tenet of all Muslim communities. These similarities are revealed through discussions with hip hop artists about the various creative processes involved in their craft.

Hip Hop Texts and the Qur'anic Text: Structural and Symbolic Similarities

Just as Mecca remains the metaphoric center of the global Muslim network, so do the concepts of the Qur'an and its revelation to the Prophet Muhammad remain at the core of Muslim beliefs. Members of the hip hop nation who represent the three African American Muslim movements I mentioned above have independently observed that the very means by which the Qur'an was revealed to the Prophet—that is, orally and, in large part, through rhymed prose-exhibits parallels to the linguistic and literary mode of delivery found in hip hop lyrical production. The African American oral tradition has rarely been interpreted in this way, yet Muslim artists have creatively conceptualized links between their mode of production and their Islamic faith. Through dozens of ethnographic interviews with hip hop artists in the United States, it became clear to me that Muslim hip hop artists were making new connections between hip hop lyrical production and the method and means by which Allah revealed the Qur'an to the Prophet. They were forging a new transnational network even while acknowledging and privileging its historical antecedents.

Engaged in a conversation about how black youth, often as early as preschool, are familiar with "rap language," rapper Wise Intelligent (a member of the Nation of Gods and Earths and of the rap group Poor Righteous Teachers) claimed: "You have to understand that the potency of the melanin in the black man makes him naturally rhythmic. So when he hears anything that has that rhythm he's going to become a part of that instantly. Anything that rhymes. Many of our ancestors were poets. Imhotep, who built the first step pyramid. The pharaoh Akhenaton, he was a poet. The Prophet Muhammad even wrote poetry. This is our blood" (Spady and Eure 1991, 74). Rapper Mos Def, who is a member of the Sunni Muslim community, discussed the reasons why he believes hip hop lyrics can be an effective medium in educational practice. In the midst of his animated description, he drew a bridge between hip hop poetics and the Qur'anic text as forms of poetry, each possessing a rhyme scheme and an ability to transmit "vital information" in a relatively short amount of time. His knowledge of the Qur'an and the Arabic language through which it was revealed were evident in his comments:

Alim: What do you feel the larger relationship between hip hop and education could be?
Mos Def: I mean, hip hop could be *phenomenal*. Hip hop's relationship to education could be phenomenal. It could be extremely phenomenal in the sense that hip hop is a medium where you can get a lot of information into a very small space. And make it hold fast to people's memory. It's *just* a very radical form of information transferal.
A: So, you see it as being a vehicle for transferring information?
M: Oh, hell, yeah! I mean, do you know how much information—vital information—you could get across in three minutes?! You know, and make it so that … I mean, the Qur'an is like that. The reason that people are able to be *hafiz* [one who memorizes the entire Qur'an through constant repetition and study] is because the entire *Qur'an* rhymes. [Mos Def begins reciting Islamic verses from the *Qur'an*.] *"Bismillah Al-Rahman Al-Rahim. Al-hamdulillahi Rabb Al-Alameen."* Like everything … Like, you see what I'm saying? I mean, it's any *surah* that I could name. *"Qul huwa Allahu ahad, Allahu samud. Lam yalid wa lam yulad wa lam yakun lahu kufwan ahad."* It all like that. Like, you don't even notice it. *"Idha ja'a nasru Allahi wal fath. Wa ra'aita al-nas yadkhuluna fi dini Allahi afwajan. Fa sabbih bi hamdi rabbika wa istaghfirhu innahu kana tawwab."* Like, there's a rhyme scheme in all of it. You see what I'm saying? And it holds fast to your memory. And then you start to have a deeper relationship with it on recitation. Like, you know, you learn *Surat Al-Ikhlas*, right. You learn *Al-Fatiha*. And you learn it and you recite it. And you learn it and you recite it. Then one day you're reciting it, and you start to understand! You really have a deeper relationship with what you're reciting. *"A'udhu billahi min al-shaitan al-rajim …"* You be like, "Wow!" You understand what I'm saying? Hip Hop has the ability to do that—on a poetic level. (Interview by the author, quoted in part in Alim 2001b)

Bay Area rapper JT the Bigga Figga, a registered member of the Nation of Islam, also refers to the literary similarities between what young African Americans are doing with language (see Alim 2002, 2003, 2004) and the purposeful use of creative language by Allah as a pedagogical tool to reach the hearts and minds of humankind. In a discussion of the relationship between the "language of the streets" and the "language of hip hop," JT drew on his knowledge of the *Qur'an* and linked it to his Bay Area comrade rapper E-40's inventive and metaphorical use of language:

Lim: How does he [E-40] come up with all this different stuff, man?
JT: Just hangin out and just different people talkin. And, you know, "fo sheezy, off da heezy!" Me and you, what we doin right now, to him, it's called marinatin.

A: Yeah, I hear him say that.

J: Marinatin. We marinatin right now. We goin over … Like, it's almost like with Allah how he'll describe his prophets as moonlight. He'll describe his word that he speaks in a metaphoric phrasing. Where he'll say the clouds and when they swell up heavy and the water goes back to the earth, distilling back to the earth. The water's heavier than gravity so it distills back to the earth on dry land, producing vegetation and herbs comin up out the ground, you feel me? And results is happening, you feel me? And the Disbelievers, how they dry land and the sun's scorching it. …

A: *So* he's describing the Believers when things start growing, right.

J: Yeah, yeah. He describe the different conditions, you know what I'm saying? And it can be related to nature, you feel me? *Nature.* And what we see, how we conduct ourself, can be related to some aspect of nature. … And that's kinda like what E-40 do when he take something and take a word and apply it, you feel me? (Interview by the author)

Whether engaged in conversations about young black children's familiarity with "rap language," the pedagogical potential of hip hop music, or the inventive and innovative use of language by specific artists within the hip hop nation, these hip hop artists invoke Islamic knowledge to accomplish diverse tasks. For Wise Intelligent, it makes sense that young black children would be so attentive to "rap language," because their, ancestry (as he describes it), including the Prophet Muhammad, has always been attentive to poetry, and to rhyme in particular. For Mos Def, hip hop's ability to function as what he calls a "radical form of information transferal" is similar to the poetic and pedagogical means by which Allah revealed the *Qur'an* to humankind through the Prophet Muhammad. Finally, JT the Bigga Figga refers to Allah's use of metaphoric phrasing in order to clarify his description of E-40's lexical innovation and semantic expansion. Muslim hip hop artists' descriptions of their craft often recalls the function of the *Qur'an*. In many of my interviews, I heard Islamic knowledge being invoked spontaneously in the flow of conversation (as often occurs in Muslim–Muslim conversations), pointing to the fact that members of the hip hop nation are studying and applying Islam in their everyday lives.

The Agents of the Transglobal Hip Hop Umma: Some Thoughts for Future Research

Hip hop music has been an active vehicle for social protest in the United States. Its targets have been racism, discrimination, police brutality, miseducation, and other social ills (Rose 1994). Many of the artists involved in the global manifestations of the hip-hop cultural movement—in places like France, Canada, Japan, Italy, South America, and Palestine—resist the multifarious forms of oppression in global societies. When hip hop pioneer Afrika Bambaataa launched the Muslim-influenced Zulu Nation in the United States in the 1970s and expanded the movement globally in places like France in the early 1980s (Prevos 2001), he was networking to help spread socially and politically conscious ideas and ideals, to build a community of people who would actively resist social, political, and economic subordination. Exploring what he refers to as the "transglobal Islamic underground" and commenting in particular on England's Fun-Da-Mental and France's IAM, Ted Swedenburg writes: "In both countries Muslims are attempting to construct cultural, social and political spaces for themselves as ethnic groups (of sorts), and are massively involved in anti-racist mobilizations against white supremacy. Hip-hop activism has been an important arena for anti-Islamophobic mobilization for both French and British Muslims" (2002, 16).

These brief but remarkable examples of anti-imperial; antiracist activities offer a range of sites for us to explore a fundamental question: How do the Muslim members of the hip hop cultural movement make the move from discursive to practical consciousness? In other words, how do these agents go from, as some hip hoppers would say, "*talkin* about it, to *bein* about it?" What is it that makes Public Enemy's Chuck D "try to do some of the things that he talks about" (Spady and Eure 1991, 191)? When San Francisco's JT The Bigga Figga states, "I could sit here and talk to you and tell you what I think I'm seeing, but to really know that in your heart mean you gon *act* on it now, even in a bigger way:" what is mediating the move to an active, practical nation-consciousness? Clearly, from these narratives, we can see that such moves are predicated upon faith. JT continues, "And have faith in yourself and in the God who brought you into existence to know that, 'I'm behind you. Do the inspiring thing" (interview by the author).

My research reveals that not only are these artists studying Islam (as demonstrated by their ability to quote and vividly describe Qur'anic passages) and applying it to their everyday lives, they are also operationalizing Islam, that is, acting upon what they have learned in order to help build a nation. Mos Def not only raps about issues like consciousness and justice, he lives them. His Islamic consciousness moved him and partner Talib Kweli to rescue Nkiru Bookstore, a black-owned bookstore in his home community of Brooklyn, from having to shut down. It guided him to actively participate in the creation of a hip hop album (*Hip Hop for Respect*) dedicated to obtaining justice for police brutality victims and the immoral murder of Amadou Diallo, a Muslim immigrant from Guinea who was killed by officers of the New York Police Department in 1999. Mos paraphrased the Qur'an and expressed his faith in Allah at a public rally against the acquittal of the officers who fired forty-one shots at the brother: "To people who seek justice, to the Amadou Diallo family, and to everyone who speaks against oppression, I say, *fear not*, Allah is the best of judges."

Similarly, Public Enemy front man Chuck D's Islamic consciousness moved him from giving live performances in concert halls to giving talks about nation building in the streets, prisons, and schools of black communities. It is what moved him to become perhaps the most well-known advocate for "cutting out the middle man" in the hip hop record industry by circumventing major record labels and distributors, building independent labels, and engaging in e-commerce. JT the Bigga Figga not only realized that he "had a bigger work to do through this music," but he has also helped to revitalize his local communities of Fillmore and Bay's View-Hunter's Point through filling speaking engagements and providing business classes to youth. He not only actively supported and attended the Million Man March and the Million Family March, as well as the many Nation of Islam-sponsored Hip-Hop Summits that have been organized since 1997, he has also assembled a group of young blacks, Latinos, and Pacific Islanders into a national cooperative business venture named Black Wall Street (in commemoration of the United States government's bombing of Oklahoma's Black Wall Street in 1934), thereby providing networking and economic growth opportunities to those traditionally excluded from such enterprises.

I am currently conducting research to uncover more of these Islamic nation-building activities within the hip hop nation. More attention needs to be directed, however, at exploring the role of Muslim female artists who are covering in the name of Allah. What do we know about Philadelphia rapper Eve's struggle and search for inner peace in a male-dominated recording industry? As she reminds us, "Heaven Only Knows." But we can start by engaging Eve and other Muslim female artists in informal conversation. Eve, who opened up the liner notes on her album *Eve of Destruction* with "All Praise Is Due To Allah," speaks about her relationship with Islam: "It's not strong like it should be. I'm striving. When I get to the point where I'm stable I definitely want to cover and go to the *masjid*. But now it's hard. It is really hard. But it definitely has a grip on me. I pray to Allah every night, every morning, all during the day, know what I'm saying? If it wasn't for him I wouldn't be blessed" (interview by the author, quoted in part in Spady, Lee, and Alim 1999). What do we know about New York City's Egyptian female rapper Mutamassik (meaning "tenacious" in Arabic)? What are her personal struggles, and how has she contributed to nation-building activities through and beyond her music (see Swedenburg 2001)?

International Context

What is the relationship between African American Muslim movements in the hip hop cultural movement and the global Islamic world? What kinds of nation-building activities are occurring when Wu-Tang Clan's Rza visits with his Muslim brethren in Egypt, or when the Sunz of Man meet up with IAM in France? What happens when Palestinian rhymer and graffiti artist Masari writes a graff on a San Francisco city wall reading "Liberate Palestine," then spits out these lines on the concrete streets of the United States to note that "back in Ramallah, my brothers are straight strugglin" (Interview by the author, 2001):

> Those gone souls are in my soul
> So now my mission's to be plottin
> Let the evil rot in …
> And our people live forever, cuz souls are not to be forgotten.

What are we to make of the many sons and daughters of Muslim immigrants to the United States who have been hiphopitized by this African American cultural movement? Will academic centers like Duke University's Center for the Study of Muslim Networks begin examining the role that hip hop has played in networking Muslims around the globe, from South Asia to South Philly, from South Africa to South Carolina? These are issues and questions for future research.

Researchers are needed to study the trilingual (Arabic, Hebrew, and English) rappers in Palestine as they rail against what they perceive to be the tyranny of the Israeli state, to explore the struggles of Muslim rappers in Algeria as they wage war on what they believe are corrupt regimes (rappers with African American-inspired names like Ole Dirty Shame, MC Ghosto, and Killa Dox), and to examine how Muslim artists in South Africa are critiquing what they perceive as the hypocrisy of their nation's new democracy. How are these groups networked? How are they communicating with each other and the world? How has the Internet helped network Muslim artists and practitioners in the hip hop cultural movement? How are newsgroups such as Yahoo's "Muslims in Hip Hop" contributing to nation-building activities within the transglobal hip hop *umma*?

Conclusion

In conclusion, the hip hop cultural movement needs to be examined with a seriousness of purpose and a methodology that considers the networked nature of Islam in order to reveal the hidden aspects of this highly misunderstood transglobal phenomenon, a cultural movement whose practitioners represent, arguably, some of the most cutting-edge conveyors of contemporary Islam. What will the new knowledge that is revealed mean for Islamic scholars who teach courses on *fiqh* (jurisprudence), Qur'anic exegesis, Islamic civilization, or Islam and modernity? Will it transform our view of the impact of popular culture, particularly hip hop culture, in constructing an Islam appropriate to the needs of contemporary society? Further, will imams revise their pedagogies in efforts to engage Muslim youth who are living in this postmodern hip hop world?

There will undoubtedly be many changes in the way that hip hop culture is studied in the academy within the next five to ten years. Hip hop culture's global impact has helped to transform public opinion (including opinion within the academy) of the art form. Only a decade ago, hip hop culture occupied a shunned pariah status in the academy; today, universities like Stanford, Harvard, Berkeley, Duke, and the University of Pennsylvania are offering hip hop courses in departments as diverse as linguistics, religious studies, philosophy, and African American studies. Hip hop culture is being widely recognized as the most recent instantiation of an African American oral tradition that has "gone global," become syncretized with other world cultures and musics as new manifestations of hip hop form worldwide (see Egyptian singer Hakim's latest offering, *Tamenny Alaik,* which combines French and Spanish-language rap with contemporary Egyptian *sha'abi* music), and galvanized an entire generation of youth to become more involved in social and political causes.

Many questions remain for what Jamillah Karim calls the "American *umma.*" Will hip hop culture's profound impact on Muslim immigrants to the United States, and their sons and daughters, help to reduce the current divide between the African American Muslim communities and immigrant Muslim communities? Will hip hop culture be the vehicle that helps unite the "American *umma*"? Or will the transformative, resistive power of hip hop culture be undercut by its widely gained acceptance and co-optation by some of the very institutions it was created to resist? For now we will continue to document the nation-building activities that are occurring around a world that is more and more tightly networked by these two seemingly contradictory communities—Islam and the hip hop nation—or, as we have conceived it here, the transglobal hip hop *umma.*

Study Questions

1. How have scholars, traditionally, approached Islam in hip hop studies and what are the ways in which Alim attempts to broaden and advance this area of study?
2. What does a transformative global Islamic hip hop community look like according to Alim's claims?
3. Why has Islam, as expressed in hip hop and black culture been grossly misunderstood?
4. What types of Islamic sensibilities does Alim uncover and how does he chart their movement in and through the hip hop *umma*?

Notes

*Portions of this chapter from the text *Muslim Networks from Hajj to Hip Hop* (Miriam Cooke and Bruce B. Lawrence, 2005) have been omitted and/or altered for style, consistency and flow.

1. Hip hop culture is sometimes defined as having four major elements: MCing (rapping), DJing (spinning records), break dancing (also known as "street dancing," an array of acrobatic dances associated with the hip hop cultural domain), and graffiti art (also known as "writing" or "tagging" by its practitioners). To these, pioneering hip hop artist KRS-One adds knowledge and Afrika Bambaataa, founder of the hip hop cultural movement, adds "overstanding," a word used frequently by Rastafarians to mean more than a cursory understanding, an ability to read between the lines to arrive at a deeper, say hidden, meaning. Even with six elements, this definition of hip hop culture is quite limited in scope. It is useful to distinguish between the terms "hip hop" and "rap." Rapping, one aspect of hip hop culture, consists of the aesthetic placement of verbal rhymes over musical beats. "Hip hop culture" refers not only to the various elements listed above but also to the entire range of

cultural activity and modes of being that encompass the hip hop culture-world. This is why Bloods say, "Hip hop ain't just music, it's a whole way of life!"

2. "PanBanegritude" is an anticolonial movement that had its origins among francophone Africans and Asians in France and Belgium during the 1920s. Kojo Touvalou Houenou, a Dahomean lawyer trained at the University of Bordeaux in France and a leader of the Universal Negro Improvement Association organized by Marcus Garvey, was a forerunner of the Pan African movement who claimed his negritude a decade before the literary negritude movement organized by Leopold Senghor, Leon Damas, and Aime Cesaire. Houenou's Ligue Universelle de la Defense de la Race Noire (Universal League for the Defense of the Black Race) and Ho Chi Minh's organization, Union Internationale, contributed to PanBanegritude unity. The Asian African caucus, founded at the inaugural conference of the League against Imperialism held in Brussels, Belgium, in 1927, predated the better-known Bandung Conference of Asians and Africans held in Indonesia by nearly three decades.

Bibliography

Alim, H. Samy, ed. 2001a. "Hip Hop Culture: Language, Literature, Literacy and the Lives of Black Youth." Special Issue, *Black Arts Quarterly* 6(2).

—— 2001b. "Three-X-Black: Mos Def, Mr. Nigga (Nigga, Nigga) and Big Black Afrika X-amine Hip Hop's Cultural Consciousness." In "Hip Hop Culture: Language, Literature, Literacy, and the Lives of Black Youth," edited by H. Samy Alim. Special issue, *Black Arts Quarterly* 6(2): 6–9.

—— 2002. "Street Conscious Copula Variation in the Hip Hop Nation." *American Speech* 77(3): 228–301.

—— 2003." On Some Serious Next Millennium Rap Ishhh: Pharoahe Monch, Hip Hop Poetics, and the Internal Rhymes of Internal Affairs." *Journal of English Linguistics* 31(1).

—— 2004. "Rap and Hip Hop." In *Language in the USA: Themes for the Twenty-First Century*, edited by Edward Finnegan and John R. Rickford. New York: Cambridge University Press.

Mitchell, Tony, ed. 2001 *Global Noise: Rap and Hip-Hop Outside the USA*, Middletown, Conn.: Wesleyan University Press.

Osumare, Halifu. 2002. "Troping Blackness in the Hip Hop Global" 'Hood. In "Black Culture's Global Impact," edited by H. Samy Alim. Special Issue, *Black Arts Quarterly* 7(1): 24–26.

Perkins, William Eric, ed. 1996. *Droppin' Science: Critical Essays on Rap Music and Hip Hop Culture*. Philadelphia: Temple University Press.

Prevos, Andre J. M. 2001. "Postcolonial Popular Music in France: Rap Music and Popular Culture in the 1980s and 1990s." In *Global Noise: Rap and Hip-Hop Outside the USA*, edited by Tony Mitchell. Middletown, Conn.: Wesleyan University Press.

Rose, Tricia. 1994. *Black Noise: Rap Music and Black Culture in Contemporary America*. Middletown, Conn.: Wesleyan University Press.

Spady, James G., and Joseph Eure. 1991. *Nation Conscious Rap: The Hip Hop Vision*. Philadelphia: Black History Museum.

Swedenburg, Ted. 2011. "Islamic Hip-Hop Versus Islamophobia." In *Global Noise: Rap and Hip-Hop Outside the USA*, edited by Tony Mitchell. Middletown, Conn.: Wesleyan University Press.

—— 2002. "Hip Hop Music in the Transglobal Islamic Underground." In "Black Culture's Global Impact," edited by H. Samy Alim. Special issue, *Black Arts Quarterly* 7(1): 16–18.

Part II
What's the "Religion" in Hip Hop?

No longer having to legitimate the study of religion in hip hop as two seeming *competing* and *colliding* forces and ideas, scholars working in and around this area began to think more closely about the category of religion—that is, how it is approached theoretically, methodologically and what sources within hip hop become utilized for such a study. In comparison to earlier and foundational scholarship which worked hard to prove, in many ways, that rap wasn't and need not be relegated to the "secular" void of the "sacred," emerging scholarship to follow stood firmly within and upon this provocative mandate and began to expand the terms and shape of the discourse in terms of theory, data and method.

This part introduces essays that extend beyond the query of what might be of religious value in (the study of) hip hop to press further the question of what we purport to mean and seek to accomplish in and through the use of the category of religion as a lens of analysis. That is— how might we, or do we, as scholars, commentators and analysts recognize the religious, on what terms, and further, what do we claim uses and appearances of religion in hip hop culture realize, point to, mark, and mean? How do we know? Is such meaning intentional among the producers themselves, the artists, the fans—and if so, how do we know? As some of the essays in Part I begin to discuss, this part too is marked by thinkers who call for new approaches, more theory, and an expansion of hip hop analysis beyond lyrical attention and focus.

From its inception, hip hop, in its many elements and constitution, has been characterized and marked by extensive and sometimes logic-defying flow, linguistic innovation, embodied movement and rhetorical wordplay for a wide variety of interests and motivations—constructing meaning, battle, one upping, humor and entertainment, performance, and social techniques like sleights of hand, trickster spooks, and making something out of nothing—or as hip hop calls it, a dolla out of fifteen cents. Some call this magic, others call it ability—some call it survival and some might even call it religious or spiritual. No matter how we slice and dice it, making "sense" of the brevity and (in)coherence of hip hop data can be quite the task.

In hip hop, things are rarely, as some of the essays below suggest, what they appear to be (or what we think they are) in time and space. With such coherent incoherence in the data under study, how then might the scholar go about the academic business of analyzing domains of religion—or religion understood more broadly as the search or quest for meaning in hip hop? Do uses of religion in hip hop always point toward something affirmative, unequivocally meaningful, and intentional? How do we know? Could the dizzying collection and uses of religion and esoteric philosophies in hip hop culture be representative of something more *or less* than meaning itself (i.e., marketing purposes, power and authority, and so on)? When is religion and meaning in hip hop *not* religion and meaning? What does analyzing the complexity and multifarious witty techniques in and of hip hop practices require and call for in terms of tools and approaches of study? These and other issues are taken up in the following part.

We begin with a challenge that scholars of religion have, in many cases, over-determined and oversold: religion in hip hop. Often, they raise the question of what attention to religion in hip hop says and reveals about the category we call religion. Such a question calls for new modes and models of approaching religion in culture more broadly in order to rethink not so much what religion *is* (and looks like) but more so what it *does* through *effect* and presentation. With theory and method at the helm, we then move into a more focused study and mapping of the challenges and possibilities of religion and hip hop's intellectual archive by using a trope that suggests hip hop and religion are not irreconcilable and that, it is time to develop thick and robust systems of analysis that speak to such fluidity—ones that are careful not to privilege one religion over another or arrest religion to and within institutional confines. After all, hip hop emerges outside of the four walls, so to speak—a life force powered in and through community and bodies on street corners and stoops—a cultural topography that is anything but flat, neat, coherent, and always intelligible if seeking neat arrangements and easy solutions. On the contrary, hip hop—like any other form of art or culture, as these essays here gesture—is, and always has been, multifaceted, conflicting, and ambiguous. So too are the beat, rhyme, and hook of its wide ranging play and thinking with religion—thus we might guard against, as suggested below, constricting hip hop's religious sensibilities to those solely represented within mainstream institutions, formal faith traditions, popularized and over-privileged sects such as Christianity or an assumption that belief is religion's logical counterpart. In like manner, we might also cordon off any tendency to suggest that hip hop is sui generis, either, although the line between fan and scholar—on this particular point—often causes difficulty in not situating hip hop as distinct and transhistorical.

Here, we are reminded of hip hop's coming to age in the 1970s and 1980s when codified and undercover talk of god, religion, esotericism, and spirituality in hip hop was just as voluminous as the beat itself. However, rather than understanding such references and narratives as indicative of belief in a strict sense, we are encouraged to think of these "incomprehensible" occurrences as artistic stylings that seek to manage racialized and classed suspicion and paranoia, particular in communities most vulnerable to, and historically harmed by, such social ill. In other words—what might it mean for us scholars and students to re-think how we imagine and study the sound, look, and posture of religion, applying such insights to the data of hip hop? And vice versa? That perhaps the "battles"—the noted and cited oppositionality and complexities in hip hop that some desire to flatten and make neat—are productively necessary, useful and given texture and form through the permanence of tension and fissures. The significance of "religion and hip hop" is that by placing them in productive antagonism, the seemingly competing data sets help expose new cultural threads and braids amongst each seemingly insular domain. Beyond a traditional focus on belief, in this part, we are encouraged to explore religion and belief in more complicated ways—as a means by which to think further about the social world in which we all find ourselves. In what ways do the alternative approaches suggested in this part build upon yet expand and challenge earlier ways of examining the category of religion in hip hop culture? How has the complexity involving talk of religion in hip hop continued and morphed? What might be at stake in rethinking the category of religion in such ways?

5

Don't Judge a Book By Its Cover

Concerned with the expansion of theory, method and data in the study of religion in hip hop, Miller's essay is framed by attention to the suspicious religious stylings of late rapper Tupac Shakur, the postmodern concerns over proper objects of study as exemplified by Judith Butler, and a methodological concern over how scholars ought to study religion according to the work of Russell T. McCutcheon. She suggests that religious analysis of hip hop culture often assumes and becomes arrested by a metaphysics of presence which privileges intentionality, meaning, and the affective nature of the inward look of subjective faculties. Moving to a prime example, she considers rapper 50 Cent's text *The 50th Law* (which was aesthetically fashioned after a bible) co-written with self-help guru Robert Greene, and one of three 2009 knowledge productions (artist produced hip hop books) which make use of religion. She argues that rather than analyzing religious uses in 50's text as evidence of or claims to belief, we ought to think about its use of religion as more strategic—a way of harnessing power and authority and securing particular ideological positionalities rooted in hip hop culture. Making use of the theoretical work of scholars of religion Anthony B. Pinn, Russell T. McCutcheon and social theorist Pierre Bourdieu among others, Miller shows varying dimensions of why and how using religion in *The 50th Law* (such as selling fearlessness and authorizing the thug's experience) requires an alternative theory and method to what has commonly been used in this area of study. How has religion in hip hop traditionally been examined and how and why does Miller critique such approaches for the study of hip hop today?

Don't Judge a Book By Its Cover

Monica R. Miller

I'm the religion that to me is the realist religion there is. I try to pray to God every night unless I pass out. I learned this in jail, I talked to every God [member of the Five Percent Nation] there was in jail. I think that if you take one of the "O's" out of "Good" it's "God," if you add a "D" to "Evil," it's the "Devil." I think some cool motherf**ker sat down a long time ago and said let's figure out a way to control motherf**kers.

(Tupac Shakur)

The institution of the "proper object" takes place, as usual, through a mundane sort of violence.
(Butler 1994, 1)

Believing religion somehow to provide privileged access to some posited transcendent realm of meaning, they search for their hermeneutic philosopher's stones and fail to understand feelings such as fear or awe as "taught" and therefore products of social life.

(McCutcheon 2001, 9)

The three quotes above bring together, in disparate and perhaps dizzying ways, the core themes engaged in this essay. Late rap artist Tupac Shakur expresses a rather esoteric and suspicious styling of religious musings, while queer theorist Judith Butler reminds us that the project of isolating "proper objects" of any field of study does not go without consequence, and lastly, religious studies scholar Russell T. McCutcheon cautions against fashioning the idea of religion *as* unique, interior, and therefore what he calls a "private affair" (2001, 9). While this essay explores the manner in which the religious is presented in hip hop culture—in moments such as these, we rarely question—or interrogate—the very object we claim to study. This essay, through empirical examples, offers an alternative rendering of investigating the religious among hip hop cultural modalities—thereby advocating for a redescription of the religious study of hip hop from assumptions of religious *presence* to religion as social formation and process. Instead of asking, what "is" religious about hip hop culture—I ask, what do *uses* of religion accomplish for competing social and cultural interests?

Borrowing from the work of scholars such as McCutcheon, I start from the assumption that there is nothing in and of itself "unique" (*sui generis*) about religion outside of its "disciplinary manufacturing." This work understands religion to be similar to other social constructions, such as race and gender; that is, they are real insomuch that society has come to categorize certain practices as "natural" and "innate" by the dominant culture. As most scholars agree, there's nothing *essentially* "real" about race or gender beyond an inculcated performativity of cultural, social, and political norms and values. Thought in this way (religion as non-unique social construction/formation), religion's dependency upon and intersections with class, social structure, and ideas of difference express themselves through a range of cultural practices. We must stay cognizant that, as McCutcheon argues, "efforts to privilege and protect any object of study, let alone the community of scholars that studies it, come with generally undetected social and political baggage" (10). While religion is often assumed and studied as a "self-evident" object of study, McCutcheon rings the bell of alarm when he reminds us that "sui generis religion is a constructed, analytical tool with an occluded manufacturing history" (5)—he reminds us that approaching religion as a social construction has potential to free this category outside of claims to (interiorized) uniqueness and authenticity—a quandary, he argues, that relies upon metaphysical abstractions such as "truth" and "personal experience." This perspective is also represented by social theorist James A. Beckford when he argues that to take up religion in this way is to abandon "the tendency to regard religion as a relatively well-defined object … examining critically the social processes whereby certain things are counted as religious." Moreover, this disposition emphasizes human activity and construction—remaining cognizant that sensibilities such as "public order, disorder, panics, and confidences are constructed as emergent products of myriad human interactions" (Beckford 2003, 2–3). With a focus on human activity, Beckford reminds us that "we *are* human beings who live in the medium of meanings, contested as well as shared, we are on firmer ground if we limit our investigations to what we can know about the social construction of religion as process and product" (4). The more common approach to exploring hip hop culture employs a religious and theological examination grounded in an erroneous occupation with preserving truth claims of what counts *as* religious among hip hop source material. This approach is problematic in its tendency to analytically separate what "is" and "isn't" religious—representative of a strategy maintaining religious uniqueness by asking what is decipherable about the religious.

By contending that there is something of value in studying the source material of popular culture, I am also suggesting that exploring the uses of religion in popular culture should add to the theoretical formation and critical interrogation of how scholars understand such categories. Jonathan Z. Smith reminds us,

> While there is a staggering amount of data, phenomena, of human experiences and expressions that might be characterized in one culture or another, by one criterion or another, as religion—there is no data for religion. Religion is solely the creation of the scholar's study. It is created for the scholar's analytic purposes by his imaginative acts of comparison and generalization. Religion has no existence apart from the academy.
>
> (1982, xi)

The Hard Questions of Life *As* Religious?

In an existentialist-like turn, the expression of particular rhetorical markers such as evil, pain, suffering, and the self in hip hop culture—what some have called the "hard questions of life" have often been thought of *as* religious. In a word, the religious analysis of hip hop cultural products has been arrested to and confined within a *metaphysics of presence*—the "unintended consequence" and *traces* of particular thought structures—that privilege intentionality and consciousness (of the subject), apprehension of meaning, and internal desire that give rise to religious activity grounded in affective faculties of subjectivity (inward feeling).

The religious analysis of hip hop culture at times seemingly retains an *unintended* taken-for-grantedness in the ways in which it figures the "quest for meaning" in hip hop as religious. By *unintended*, I simply mean that this effect is often unnoticed on behalf of the authors themselves; rather, the problematic of such thought is often the effect of inheriting particular intellectual heritages that seemingly work against the author's proposed trajectory. The logocentrism of such approach ubiquitously grounds the *experience of* or quest for meaning *as* a religious quest—remaining unaware that the presence of meaning itself cannot be fixed—rather, it always remains deferred within temporality. This perspective (the perpetual quest for meaning as a religious pursuit) can likewise be seen as searching for coherence and stability of presence to what is otherwise, in reality, unstable, unstructured, and characterized not by a center locus of intelligibility, but rather, in a Derridian sense, by "play," *aporia*, and an "undecidability"— sensibilities undecipherable through phenomenological and metaphysical quests for meaning (the science of presence). In other words, the phenomenological approach to religion acts upon its object of inquiry in a way that analyses (and assumes) essence of phenomena itself—the appearance and arrangement of what things *are* in time and space. The question is not what *is* religious about certain activity; rather, what are the effects of various uses of the religious? The redirection of this question has potential to yield interesting analyses beyond the simple citing of religion in cultural forms without privileging certain activity as "uniquely" religious over others.

In 2009, the literary market was flooded by a flurry of artist-produced hip hop knowledge productions which, in varied ways, use religious signifiers or existential themes as an entry into authorizing particular ideological positionalities of hip hop culture—albeit in very different ways. This essay considers one of three most recent 2009 productions: *The 50th Law* by 50 Cent and established author Robert Greene (author of self-help books that engage themes such as power, seduction, and strategy). Beyond celebrating the power of the "thugs" experience, this book markets an exterior aesthetic and style bringing attention to its mark on the world. Signifying power and authority, this book is fashioned after a black King James Version of the Bible; however, beyond the fascinating *styling* of this production, what do the *uses* of religious aesthetics and philosophical weight accomplish in this text?

Selling *Fearlessness*: Authorizing the Thug's Experience

Rapper Curtis "50 Cent" Jackson is no stranger to violence—dubbed as the rapper with "nine lives" after surviving a barrage of bullets and prior stabbings, 50 Cent has taken his street credibility to the publishing world of self-help. Having been influenced by his work in the past, 50 Cent teamed up with prolific self-help writer and guru Robert Greene, who has published works such as *The 48 Laws of Power, The Art of Seduction*, and *The 33 Strategies of War*, to unearth how complicated risky gangster ethics from his life have helped him succeed in the rap game. Each ethic is then applied to fifty sections of *The 50th Law* with the technical help and skills of Greene. Since it is fashioned after a bible, one may expect this book has something more "spiritual" or "religious" in mind; on the contrary, the main theme is *Fear Nothing* and maintain trust in not a higher power, but the self.

Greene plays many roles in this intellectual production: writer (of 50's life), ethnographer (of 50's life), translator (of 50's experiences as both a street "gangster" and successful entrepreneur), and artist (taking 50's experiences and packaging them alongside "established" truths from folks such as Malcolm X to philosopher Machiavelli). Rapper 50 Cent and self-help author Greene together have taken the best of two very different worlds (rapper and business/ marketing author) to accomplish a particular task—but what exactly does this work seek to accomplish? Here, I argue that 50 and Greene's work accomplishes three very different things: (1) Re-signifies *difference* and ideas of "properness" by authorizing 50's experience of "ghetto" life as the platform where his successful character of fearlessness contributes towards his ability to acquire social mobility, (2) Uses *aesthetic* and *philosophical* weight to establish an intellectual origin of the ideological marketing of "fearlessness," and lastly (3) Sets to accomplish a "thugged-out" New Age human-centered approach to life in more general terms. The thug's experience is central in this book, and marketing these experiences as "useful business tools" continues in its constitution through *aesthetic* and *philosophical* validation. Bruce Lincoln's work reminds us that authority in and of itself—like religion per se—is not an abstract concept, but rather, it occurs in the details and constitution of concretizing authority, more generally. In other words, authority is dynamic and constructed; it is not in and of itself, a natural or self-evident thing (1994, 11). More plainly stated, what gives 50's experiences, in this book, an intellectual authority that it would not otherwise have? I argue that beyond re-signifying *difference* and "deviance" there is yet another construction of authority at work here, one that provides the illusion and reliability of "hustler" legitimation and validation.

Stylistically fashioning *The 50th Law* after a bible visually provides authority and symbolic weight to what may otherwise be seen as less than a "proper" object of study. Textually speaking, the life experiences of 50 are given historical legitimation through the textual use of established philosophical and intellectual giants who are said to exemplify similar successful abilities as 50 Cent himself. Thus, using these authorities not only constructs authorization by means of textual assemblage, but likewise, offer a glimpse of "respectability" to a persona that dominant groups would not think twice of calling a "criminal." For example, 50 is compared to a modern-day Napoleon Bonaparte among others. Throughout *The 50th Law*, quotes from figures such as Malcolm X, Sun Tzu, Ralph Waldo Emerson, James Baldwin, Montesquieu, Dostoyevsky, Pascal, Nietzsche, and especially Machiavelli adorn each textual section. These established philosophy and intellectual sources validate 50's experience through the *effect* of historical authenticity. Greene writes, "I then expanded on these discussions with my own research, combining the example of Fifty with stories of other people throughout history who have displayed the same fearless quality" (Greene and 50 Cent 2009, x).

There is a market standard that must be met in order to effectively and persuasively sell the life world of 50—it has to be couched and delivered in a particular kind of way—not only do the poached intellectual quotes give "conventional" breadth and depth to 50's experiences, they also provide symbolic capital and weight by way of established epistemologies. The quotes and life worlds of already established philosophical persons like Nietzsche, for example, function almost ritualistically throughout the book. It is not strange that 50 and said intellectuals may embody or espouse similar philosophies of life, but the *poaching* of these quotes functions as an intellectual ritual of authority that provides symbolic capital and power to sell 50's life world. In a real sense, the troping of famous and "complex" quotes allows the reader to be more "acceptable" of the authorizing of 50's world—it allows the literary marketing of the "thug's" life, to "pass"—without being pathologized. In *Language and Symbolic Power*, Pierre Bourdieu reminds us of "the *social* function of ritual and the social significance of the boundaries or limits which the ritual allows one to pass over or transgress in a lawful way" (1991, 117)—in other words, as Michel Foucault points out in *The Archeology of Knowledge* (1972), what often gives shape, will, and power to the modes of existence of discourse itself is in and through the very construction of ideas themselves. The patchwork of 50's life, the authority of Greene, and the established intellectuals used to support 50's life world work together to shape the experience of authority and unity in this work. This works together to operationalize and provide persuasive power to the selling of the *50th Law*—here,

50's experiences of life are not "self-evident" in and of themselves; rather, they are mediated through, used in tension with, and grounded in intellectual authority, among other things. These "technologies of power, "if you will, help give shape to the authenticity of 50's authorship and help quell the deviance of his social world and practices. Foucault says it best when he writes, "Who is speaking? Who, among the totality of speaking individuals, is accorded the right to use this sort of language (*language*)? Who is qualified to do so? … What is the status of the individual who—alone—has the right, sanctioned by law or tradition, juridicially defined or spontaneously accepted, to proffer such a discourse?" (Foucault 1972, 50). Ultimately, *The 50th Law* (as a proven philosophy based on experience exemplified through the personification of 50) provides a philosophy that articulates *fearlessness*. The authors write, "Your fears are a kind of prison that confines you within a limited range of action. The less you fear, the more power you will have and the more fully you will live. It is our hope that *The 50th Law* will inspire you to discover this power for yourself" (Greene and 50 Cent 2009, x).

They suggest that *fear* hinders success to social mobility—likeable to an ir/rational emotion. Green and 50 suggest, "Out of fear, we also developed religion and various belief systems to comfort us. Fear is the oldest and strongest emotion known to man, something deeply inscribed in our nervous system and subconscious" (3). *The 50th Law* sells 50 Cent as the embodiment of this ideology, "The new fearless types, as represented by Fifty, move in the opposite direction"—it is these types that are not afraid, as they point out, to "hustle" and, "… let go of the past and create their own business model" (18). The construct of power is thus correlated with the "fearless" type—one must harness fearlessness in order to become, as this book suggests, a "free spirit."

Beyond the trope of *power*, *The 50th Law* esoterically buys into a New Age existential psychology where a premium is placed on total freedom and the power of the mind—notwithstanding structural issues. No matter what the circumstances one may face—whether a "thug" from Queens or a successful Hollywood socialite—what matters most is the power of the *mind*. While we may not, as they argue, be able to control our physical environments and the situations in which we are born into—what we can control is *how* the mind deals with events in the world and in our lives. In one sense, we have no control over the world—yet, we have full control of how the mind responds and reacts in various circumstances. Represented here is a melting of subjective differences into behavioral sameness, they write, "And the people that practice *The 50th Law* in their lives all share certain qualities—*supreme boldness, unconventional fluidity*, and *a sense of urgency*—that give them this unique ability to shape their circumstance" (19).

And, similar to the threat of transgressing any constructed belief, there is a consequence to those that fail to adhere to 50's law. They write, "It is all rather simple: when you transgress this fundamental law by bringing your usual fears into any encounter, you narrow your options and your capacity to shape events" (21). In an interesting turn away from the self to an invisible hand philosophy, they argue, "Observing *The 50th Law* creates the opposite dynamic—it opens possibilities, brings freedom of action, and helps create a forward momentum in life" (21).

Here, the troping of religious signifiers such as *observation* (adherence) and *transgression* construct the cost/benefit of not putting into practice such belief. In a Foucauldian sense, they construct what Foucault calls "truth obligations"—practices, such as confession, that work in accordance with belief. In a marketing sense, the play of language here constructs a formula for the metaphysics of seeing such belief into action. In a mythological sense the words "observing" and "transgress" become more than just words through their ideological manufacturing; rather, they are turned into action through the category of experience—50's life and success exemplifies a mythological meritocracy of capitalist progress. In addition to the construction of symbolic power, Bourdieu pushes us to consider how language becomes authorized. He writes, "The naïve question of the power of words is logically implicated in the initial suppression of the question of the uses of language, and therefore of the social conditions in which words are employed" (1996, 107). Words in and of themselves hold no power—more importantly, to make words powerful the speaker has to be authorized to do so. In this sense, the symbolic weight of words also have much to do with the subject. Bourdieu suggests that, "the symbolic efficacy of words is exercised only in so far as the person subjected to it recognizes the person who exercises it as authorized to do so" (116). Ultimately, in order to experience the fruits of *The 50th Law*, one must do what is thus required—*choose*, "Fifty *had* to confront his fears; you must *choose* to" (Greene and 50 Cent 2009, 22).

A philosophy and epistemology of realism is advanced here—and an enemy is named: the mind. The place where one can choose to confront or retreat. Fifty's realism matured when, "He decided to transform the hustler's words into a kind of code that he would live by." It is not situations that provide difficulty; rather, it's what Slavoj Žižek would call the "parallax view." The power to change and alter "shit into sugar," as they say in hip hop, remains in the power of the mind—mental alchemy sans fear. As Greene and 50 write, "With so many physical limitations, hustlers have learned to develop mental freedom … Their thoughts have to keep moving—creating new ventures, new hustles, new directions in music and clothes" (102). And, in a postmodern-like twist, they argue that one must not become frozen and fixed in stasis; rather, we must be more shape shifty than that—altering our strategies to each moment, we must keep the momentum—or what they call *flow* (mental, emotional, social, cultural) going. Here, belief is located in the materiality of the self.

At the point when 50 was no longer afraid of death, he reached his full potentiality and metamorphosis, "In not confronting our mortality, we tend to entertain certain illusions about death" (287). They further suggest that, "From the moment we are born we carry our death within ourselves as a continual possibility … if we are afraid of death, then we are afraid of life" (288). Fifty Cent embodies *The 50th Law*, but not on his own accord, for the processes of marketing the philosophy of *fearlessness* both constructs and buys into the authorization of myth-making based on universalizing the category of "experience."

Doing the Math …

> That book looks like a Bible!
> (Ramo, a blogger)

Perhaps, we were hustled—that book 'ain't no bible! The postmodern stylings of hip hop practices are indeed, as anthropologist John Jackson reminds us, paranoid by form (Jackson 2008). Hip hop is tricky, witty, and more often than not words and appearances are not what they always seem. This multi-positionality forces a new perspective to our intended "object" of inquiry—hip hop's paranoia, to use Jackson's language, forces a re-describing and new lens of analysis. A shift in disposition and approach is required to do justice to the stylings of popular culture.

In the spirit of *redescription*, McCutcheon reminds us, "In a word, we manufacture zones of significance and value in the so-called real world by means of our label *religion*; moreover, depending on the definition and theory of religion we employ, we often manufacture goods of questionable value" (2001, 12–13)—adding that if we leave the academic study of religion as "self-evident human impulse," then redescription is no longer necessary.

Within hip hop culture, religion is figured as many things, but rarely is a singular confessional approach taken. The paranoid stylings of hip hop material culture have challenged the object of the "theoriticians'" gaze (religion)—speaking back through cultural practices, hip hop reminds the scholar of religion on the quest for meaning that we must "recognize" and "do the math"—'cause looks ain't always what they seem, books cannot be judged by their covers, and we mustn't "believe the hype." Sometimes, what appears to be "religious" (*sui generis*) just *ain't* that religious after all.

Study Questions

1. What is the significance of the three disparate quotes used to open Miller's essay? How do they contribute to the construction and development of her argument?
2. How does rapper 50 Cent, according to Miller, make use of religion and philosophy in his text The 50th Law? What is significant about his use of religion for Miller's call for a redescription of the academic category of religion?
3. What does a methodological turn to analyzing religious rhetoric as **uses** and **effects** in this essay reveal (or not) about the study of religion in hip hop culture?

References

Beckford, James. 2003. *Social Theory and Religion*. Cambridge: Press Syndicate of the University of Cambridge.

Bourdieu, Pierre. 1991. *Language and Symbolic Power*. Oxford: Polity Press.

Butler, Judith. 1994. "Against Proper Objects." *Differences: A Journal of Feminist Cultural Studies* 6 (2+3): 1–27.

Foucault, Michel. 1972. *The Archaeology of Knowledge*. London: Tavistock.

Greene, Robert and 50 Cent. 2009. *The 50th Law*. New York: Harper.

Jackson, John. 2008. *Racial Paranoia: The Unintended Consequences of Political Correctness*. New York: Basic Civitas Books.

Lincoln, Bruce. 1994. *Authority: Construction and Corrosion*. Chicago: University of Chicago Press.

McCutcheon, Russell. 2001. *Critics Not Caretakers: Redescribing the Public Study of Religion*. Albany: State University of New York Press.

Ramo. 2009. "The 50th Law." *T.Magic World*, July 30. Accessed November 6, 2009. http://tmagicworld.com/2009/07/30/the-50th-law/

Shakur, Tupac. n.d. "Interview with 2pac." Accessed January 2, 2009. www.tupacnet.org/life/interview.htm

Smith, Jonathan. 1982. *Imagining Religion: From Babylon to Jonestown*. Chicago: University of Chicago Press.

Žižek, Slavoj. 2006. *The Parallax View*. Cambridge, Mass.: MIT Press.

6

Unstrange Bedfellows
Hip Hop and Religion

Winters thinks through the complexities and contours of religion and hip hop by using the trope "unstrange bedfellows" to trace the connections and trends in the intellectual archive of religion and hip hop scholarship. With an eye toward the development of Islam and Christianity and the impact of power on the cultural development of hip hop, Winters offers a robust engagement with Anthony B. Pinn's theory of religion, *Complex Subjectivity*, and hip hop culture. He concludes that the complexity, contradiction, and ambiguity that characterize the terrain of hip hop culture should likewise be applied beyond institutional religious forms in the study of religion and hip hop.

Unstrange Bedfellows: Hip Hop and Religion

Joseph Winters

Introduction

According to one strand of conventional wisdom, religion and hip hop are, at best, strange bedfellows. Hip hop culture, supposedly defined by avarice, the glorification of violence, demeaning representations of women, and a general irreverence toward traditional forms of authority, embodies a rejection of religious principles and values. The pervasive nihilism in hip hop, some suggest, is incompatible with virtues and qualities associated with religious practices and institutions, such as benevolence, discipline, self-respect, and hope. When Calvin Butts, the prominent minister of Abyssinian Baptist Church, initiated a campaign against gangsta rap in 1993, he assumed something like this stark dichotomy. According to Butts, gangsta rap "erodes the moral fabric" of Black communities (Lefevere 1993) and is out of joint with the best that American culture has to offer.[1] To be fair, Butts was referring to specific groups like NWA and 2 Live Crew,[2] groups widely known and lambasted for their violent and misogynist lyrics. He suggested that his concerns and criticisms did not apply to all rap groups, that a distinction can be made between good/ positive and bad/ negative rap music. Therefore, during this earlier phase of hip hop, he might have welcomed MC Hammer's "Pray" or a track like "Heavenly Father" by the eccentric rap group, the Fu-Schnickens. Yet, as Pinn (2003) admonishes, this neat distinction assumed by Butts and others falters. It ignores the complexities and ambiguities within rap music and hip hop culture. This neat divide neglects how hip hop music often compels us to redefine our categories and redraw boundaries (between good and evil, religious and secular, sacred and profane). In addition, Butts' endeavor to debunk gangsta rap obscures the ways in which the church is deeply invested in many of the disturbing practices, notions, and habits attributed to the former.[3]

Pinn represents a configuration of scholars who have endeavored to clear space within the academy for serious and creative discussions about hip hop culture. In the past two decades, scholars across the disciplinary spectrum (African American Studies, women's studies, music, literature, philosophy, theology) have deployed theoretical resources to trace the development, expansion, and perpetual transformation of hip hop. In addition to examining the social/historical forces through which hip hop emerged, contributors to the study of hip hop have drawn attention to the esthetic qualities of rhyming, storytelling, turn-table maneuvering, dance, graffiti, and other hip hop practices. Avoiding the tendency to blame rap artists for our social problems, thinkers like Robin Kelley, Tricia Rose, Imani Perry, and Michael

Eric Dyson have explored the ways in which rap music both reinforces and resists conditions, ideas and habits that are damaging to our lifeworlds. To study hip hop, they suggest, is to enter a cultural terrain replete with contradictions and tension-filled relationships.

One of these relationships, which continues to gain increasing interest but remains under-developed, is the relationship between hip hop and religion. In this article, I attempt to show the connections between this recent interest and broader concerns within hip hop scholar-ship. This article will not only trace the impact of institutional religions on hip hop, but will also interrogate what Pinn calls a general "quest for complex subjectivity" (Pinn 2003, p. 86) within this cultural form. For Pinn, rap music[4] is pervaded by a "religious sensibility" insofar as artists within this genre struggle to discover and create meaning and value against absurd, dehumanizing conditions that threaten the existence of ghetto dwellers. I suggest that the strength in this approach is that it brings into view a plurality of artists, lyrics, practices, and ideas that are not typically identified as "religious," thereby expanding and reconstructing our notion of this elusive category. Yet I contend that the complexity of this quest for meaning and identity is constrained by social arrangements that Pinn downplays.

Hip Hop Scholarship

In order to better understand the current endeavor to deepen and enrich our understanding of the relationship between hip hop and religion, we must briefly range over topics, themes, and motifs that have steered the general trajectory of hip hop scholarship. For the sake of brevity, I isolate three topics of interest: (1) The social / historical conditions underlying the formation of hip hop; (2) The relationship between hip hop and antecedent forms of Black cultural expression such as the blues and jazz; (3) The political implications of hip hop, the ways in which rap music exemplifies pernicious patterns of power and oppression but also carves out space where participants can voice resistance to the present state of things and imagine alternative worlds and possibilities. It is important to keep in mind that these con-cerns and interventions constitute variegated responses to ongoing rejections of hip hop as inartistic, unintellectual, apolitical, and regressive.[5]

According to George (1998, p. xiv), "Hip Hop is the spawn of many things. But most pro-foundly, it is a product of schizophrenic, post-civil rights movement America." Following George's formulation, this cultural phenomenon irrupted into the urban landscapes of New York City during a decade that, according to the telos of American progress, should have witnessed the actualization of the achievements of the civil rights movement. Although the civil rights struggles gave Black people unprecedented political and social power (protec-tion of electoral rights, opportunity to assume elected positions, wider educational, and job opportunities), the decade following the turbulent 1960s was marked by increasing levels of economic disparity for Blacks and Latinos situated in urban areas. Rose (1994, pp. 27–34) delineates several interlocking social factors that kept these subjects at the mar-gins of American life: deindustrialization and the loss of decent paying manufacturing jobs, the retrenchment of government funds for social services, urban renewal programs which disrupted relatively stable communities,[6] and the usurpation of affordable housing by profit-driven corporations. In the South Bronx, typically identified as the birthplace of hip hop, landlords would refuse to provide heat and water to tenants and destroy buildings, through arson, in order to collect insurance money (Chang 2005, pp. 13–5). Due to the accumulation of abandoned and burned down buildings and in light of the poverty, crime, and violence that this post-industrial condition produced, South Bronx was considered to be a wasteland by many outsiders.

Yet if waste connotes ruins, trash, and that which has been discarded, it also signifies excess, leftovers, remainders, and so forth. In other words, the duplicity inscribed in the meaning of term "waste" suggests that broken spaces of ruin and decay can become sites of transformation when these ruins or shards are reappropriated and rearticulated artistically.[7] Rose suggests this in her description of how the different elements of hip hop incorporate and reexpress the tensions and contradictions of post-industrial urban life. She writes:

> Hip hop replicates and reimagines the experiences of urban life and symbolically appropriates urban space through sampling, attitude, dance, style, and sound effects. Talk of subways, crews and posses, urban noise, economic stagnation leap out of hip hop lyrics, sounds, and themes. Graffiti artists spraypainted murals and name "tags" on trains, trucks, and playgrounds, claiming territories and inscribing otherwise contained identities on public property. Early breakdancers' elaborate street corner dances involving head spins on concrete sidewalks made the streets theatrically friendly and served as makeshift youth centers. DJs who initiated spontaneous street parties by attaching customized, makeshift turntables and speakers to street light electrical sources made "open-air" community centers where there were none. Hip hop gives voice to the tensions and contradictions in the public urban landscape and attempts to seize the shifting urban terrain, to make it work on behalf of the dispossessed.
>
> (1994, p. 22)

According to Rose, hip hop renders visible and audible social conflicts and inequalities in urban spaces; for the dispossessed youth who inhabit these spaces, it enables resistance to and readjustment of unjust arrangements. Think for instance of the classic hip hop track, "The Message," in which Melle Mel begins with a graphic description of his neighborhood: "Broken glass everywhere, people pissin on the stairs, you know they just don't care, I can't take the smell, can't take the noise, Got no money to move out, I guess I got no choice."[8] Throughout the song, the group makes brief, but poignant, references to drug addiction, poverty, homelessness, prostitution, labor strikes, police harassment, prison life, suicide, and low quality education. As the members articulate the tragic dimensions of their urban wasteland (through rhyme, story-telling, and chant), they temporarily establish a critical or reflective distance from the immediacy of these stark conditions. At the same time, Grandmaster Flash and the Furious Five create something beautiful, reminding us of the importance of pleasure in the experience of making and consuming music (Kelley 1997, p. 37).

If hip hop is born in the crucible of post-industrial urban America, it is also animated by and "in dialogue with" antecedent forms of Afro-diasporic cultural expression.[9] As Kelley (1997, p. 39) points out,

> From the outset, rap music embraced a variety of styles and cultural forms, from reggae and salsa to heavy metal and jazz. Hip Hop's hybridity reflected, in part, the increasingly international character of America's cities resulting from immigration as well as the inventive employment of technology in creating rap music.

Here we might advert to groups such as The Roots, Digable Planets, GangStarr, and A Tribe Called Quest who have routinely incorporated jazz into their music (in fact, Tribe collaborated with legendary bass player, Ron Carter, for a song entitled "Verses from the Abstract"[10]). In addition, the practice of free-styling, which often consists of an emcee combining spontaneous lyrics with written or memorized verses, is indebted to the improvisational aspects of the jazz tradition (Perry 2004, p. 33). One might think of how the conversational quality of rap is anticipated by the verbal performances and patterns of James Brown and Gill Scott Heron. One can also imagine affinities between the sultry sassiness of Lil Kim and the sensual audacity of early 20th century female blues singers like Ma Rainey and Bessie Smith (see Carby 1998, pp. 469–82). More generally, much of the musical production within hip hop has consisted of sampling from old jazz, blues, rock, funk, and soul records, leading some commentators to refer to hip hop as a form of post-modern pastiche (Potter 1995).

According to Perry (2004, p. 61), rap music's lyrical expressions participate in a broader black literary and musical tradition of *signifying*. Borrowing from Henry Louis Gates's magisterial work, *The Signifying Monkey*, Perry employs the term to illumine the ways in which irony, ambiguity, duplicity, reinterpretation, and play operate within rap music and contemporary black vernacular. The practice of signifying suggests that one can "say one thing and mean another" or reinterpret/ resignify familiar, everyday words, ideas, or utterances. On this reading, the signifying rapper is akin to the trickster figure embodied in West African oral traditions and the Brer Rabbit stories that circulated among African American slaves. By highlighting the signifying qualities of rap music, Perry resists the tendency to take all the claims of rap artists literally. To be sure, rap artists usually invite listeners to read them literally. The mantra, "Keep it real," has often tethered authenticity to lyrics that correspond to reality (and this "reality" is typically associated with the more sordid dimensions of our social worlds). Yet rappers exaggerate. They also fantasize (one obvious and deliberate example of this tendency would be Nas's "If I Ruled The World"). They use metaphors to captivate audiences, to amplify certain qualities about themselves, others, and their environment, and to outwit imagined competitors (Kelley 1997, p. 38). Buckshot Shorty's underground classic "Murder MC's," for instance, refers to the figurative obliteration of imaginary and potential rivals.[11] Signifying reminds us that words, terms, and concepts can be manipulated, reinterpreted, and turned against their ordinary meaning.

This playful quality of rap music should not overshadow the serious implications and effects of hip hop music with respect to the broader political/ social order. Some commentators, as intimated above, see hip hop as a form of youth rebellion (Rose 1994, Potter 1995) that has the potential for something like an organized political movement (Pough 2004b, Kitwana 2005). This hope is inspired by the critical awareness of certain artists who renounce police brutality, stark economic disparities, the race-informed injustices of the prison system, American empire, and so forth. According to Kitwana, hip hop, because it has become formative for youth located in different racial and ethnic groups, gestures toward the possibility of building coalitions across racial lines. One constant foil to this hope for a progressive political movement is the pervasive misogyny within hip hop. Hip hop is a male-dominated terrain that too often positions women, in songs and videos, as the objects and vehicles of male power and aggression (Perry 2004, p. 118; Rose 2008, p. 119). Whether women are relegated to being the objects of male fantasy and possession in rap lyrics or whether their bodies form the decorative backdrop of music videos, women are rarely depicted as subjects with agency and complexity. By making a stark distinction between "bitches and queens', male rappers frequently "divide women into groups that are worthy of protection and respect and those that are not" (Rose 2008, p. 119). Yet any arrangement of power, such as patriarchy, generates the possibility of its own undoing. As Pough (2004a) points out, women have seized spaces within hip hop to resist their erasure. Queen Latifah's 1993 track "U.N.I.T.Y," for instance, censures sexual assault and abusive relationships.[12] Salt n Pepa's music underscored the importance of "expressing" the female body in ways that violate the norms of female respectability as well as the expectations of men who reduce women to sexual prey (Rose 1994, pp. 166–8).

Despite ongoing interventions by women, hip hop remains a salient example of the broader patriarchal order.

Hip Hop and Religion

If complexity, contradiction, and ambiguity are qualities that define the topography of hip hop, it makes sense that these terms have become mantras in the emergent literature on religion and hip hop. The void in hip hop scholarship on this relationship has recently provoked commentators to explore, among other things, hip hop's indebtedness to gospel music, the structure and thematic content of Christian/Gospel rap, the prevalence of Islam within hip hop, and the religious sensibilities of artists who do not identify with a recognizable institution but address themes of "ultimate concern." Although I find the latter topic of interest the most promising, it is important to address the in/compatibility between hip hop and institutionalized forms of religion such as Islam and Christianity.

Any examination of the intersection of hip hop and religion must highlight Islam's influence on the religio-political imagination of rap artists (Perry 2004, pp. 148–50), even if Islam is adopted and practiced by these artists in non-traditional ways. Groups such as the Poor Righteous Teachers and Brand Nubian, for instance, have readily embraced the teachings of the Five Percent Nation, an organization that broke from the Nation of Islam under the leadership of Clarence X but retained some of the NOI's core doctrines. Crucial to the Five Percent Nation's theology is the notion that Black men are divine, that Black women are earths (signifying their fertility and their prescribed role as mothers), and that self-knowledge is a hallmark of this divine status. Five Percenters attribute the suffering of Black people to blindness and ignorance, conditions that are reproduced by the chicanery and manipulations of white people and other "bloodsuckers of the poor." Insofar as Christianity is perceived by Five Percenters as the religion of the oppressor and an ideology that compels adherents to worship a Mystery God, it is no surprise that Christianity has often been the object of critique in rap music. In Brand Nubian's "Wake Up," Grand Puba rhymes:

> Preacher got my aunt to put money in the pan, For the rest of the week now I'm eating out of soup cans; He has a home, drives a Caddy through town, Has my old earth believing that he's coming from the ground (Jesus).[13]

Here Grand Puba puts forth a quasi-Marxist critique of the material conditions and inequalities that the church reinforces. While his aunt invests her faith, hope, and money in the church by paying tithes and waiting patiently for the Resurrection, the disparity between the haves (those who own homes and drive fancy cars) and the have-nots remains intact. For Puba, the answer to this unjust situation lies in the recognition that divinity is the sole property of Black people ("The Asiatic black man is a dog spelled backwards"[14]) and in the realization of Black unity. Agency withers when Black people solicit help from an otherworldly source.

As Islam in America has expanded and changed, hip hop's relationship to Islam has also gone through shifts and transformations. According to Floyd-Thomas (2003, p. 67), "the development of a more 'orthodox' turn in rap's Islamic sensibilities mirrors the general shift in the Islamic orientation within the larger Black community." This turn is marked by a rejection of the racial separation that characterizes the NOI and the Five Percenters in addition to an acceptance of a more traditional notion of the divine. Artists like Mos Def and Lupe Fiasco represent this general drift within hip hop and the broader Black community toward Sunni Islam. In fact, Mos Def begins his first album, Black on Both Sides, uttering an Arabic prayer (the Basmala), inviting the listener into a musical world that has presumably been constructed in accordance with divine will (Floyd-Thomas 2003, p. 64). Lupe Fiasco, in his brilliant track "American Terrorist,"[15] disrupts the dichotomy between American democracy and Islamic fundamentalism by juxtaposing images of planes striking the Pentagon with allusions to the Middle Passage, the conquest of Native Americans, and the usurpation of land to further the interests of capital. These Sunni-influenced artists share with their Five Percenter counterparts a salient concern for the inequalities and injustices that beset Black people and denizens of the post-industrial urban landscape. As Floyd-Thomas notes, these artists also provide a counterpoint to the obsession with wealth and material gain within mainstream rap music.

This intra-religious shift has been accompanied by an inter-religious shift from Islamic sensibilities to Christian attachments. As Sorett (2009) suggests, Kanye West's hit song, "Jesus Walks," Mase's decision to become a pastor, Joseph Simmons' (of Run-DMC) name change to Reverend Run, and the recent release of KRS-One's The Gospel of Hip Hop, indicate an increasing tendency within hip hop to embrace Christian-informed ideas, symbols, and imagery. One artist, whose career trajectory exemplifies this transition, is Nas. As a guest artist on Main Source's 1991 classic, "Live at the Barbecue," Nas asserts: "Verbal assassin, my architect pleases, when I was 12, I went to hell for snuffin Jesus. Nasty Nas is a rebel to America."[16] In this lyrical fragment, Nas's position as a rebel or outsider vis-à-vis the broader American republic is accentuated by the image of him confronting and punching a sacred figure. This fantasized instance of blasphemy transgresses the boundary that protects this sacred body from being profaned. Perhaps Nas assumes that the image of Jesus (with its accompanying connotations and meanings) is consistent with the structures of American power that he rebels against. Yet as Nas's career develops, his relationship to Christianity and these structures of power changes. His 2002 album, for instance, is entitled God's Son which indicates some level of identification with the sacred figure that he imaginatively "snuffs" in his previous rhyme. On "The Cross," a track from this 2002 album, Nas depicts himself as bearing the cross, a self-portrait that signifies the pain and suffering he has endured and that locates his artistic creation as a source for the transformation/ redemption of hip hop (Miller 2009, pp. 51–2). To some extent, the two different renderings of Jesus within Nas's corpus (as an emblem of American power and as an icon of suffering and endurance, especially for the dispossessed) reflect the complex relationship that Christian practices and ideas have had with respect to empire, the nation-state, and so forth. Although it is not completely clear why this general drift within hip hop toward Christianity has occurred, Sorett (2009) offers a plausible explanation: as hip hop expands and becomes more mainstream, it appropriates available cultural capital to secure its success and relevance.[17]

If hip hop artists have become more willing to embrace Christian symbols, some churches have recently adopted elements from hip hop as a way to "spread the good news." Contra the tendency within the church to denigrate hip hop as a corrupter of youth, Jackson and Smith (2005) argue that hip hop and Christianity can co-exist. (To some extent, they suggest that they must coexist if the church wants to remain relevant to Black youth. Hip hop has become too pervasive and influential to simply dismiss.) According to Smith and Jackson, the more auspicious dimensions of hip hop (spirituality, blues-like tendency to express the raw stuff of life, emphasis on self-discovery) can be "hijacked" by the church and become a vehicle to advance Christian ideas and practices. Anticipating objections by those who desire to maintain a rigid divide between hip hop culture and the church, or secular and religious music, these pastors/authors remind us that Jesus identified with the pariahs and outcasts of his social world.

Reducing religion to its institutional modes, according to Anthony Pinn, prevents us from examining more subtle (and potentially more interesting) expressions of religiosity within hip hop and everyday culture. Borrowing from thinkers like Charles Long, Pinn (2003) suggests that

> religion's basic structure, embedded in history, is a general quest for complex subjectivity in the face of terror and dread associated with life within a historical context marked by dehumanization, objectification, abuse, intolerance, and captured most forcefully in the sign/symbol of the ghetto.

Notwithstanding the problems that accompany any attempt to define the structure of religion, there are several important facets to this quest for complex subjectivity. For one, Pinn foregrounds the tragic dimensions of human experience. Human finitude demands that we all must confront death and its various intimations. At the same time, certain constituencies bear the brunt of this confrontation while other groups are cushioned from socially produced forms of death (Perkinson 2003). Secondly, this description of religion as a quest for complex subjectivity dovetails nicely with Pinn's notion of religious humanism, a religious orientation that stresses human accountability and the potential for individual and social transformation without an appeal to a supernatural source (Pinn 2003, p. 87). Finally, Pinn emphasizes the modifier, "complex," in his formulation. This quest, which constantly runs up against tensions, ambiguities, and contradictions as subjects navigate their precarious lifeworlds, refuses closure or a final destination. A complex subjectivity acknowledges and welcomes the open-ended quality of human existence, the multiple layers and edges of our social worlds, life's dissonant notes and prospects for ongoing transformation. If this complex identity betokens the thick, layered quality of African American religiosity, then Pinn argues for a multidimensional approach to studying the religious dimensions of hip hop, an approach that does not privilege institutional religions and that reimagines categories like religion, culture, the sacred, and so forth (Miller and Pinn 2009).

Tupac Shakur's music is, according to Pinn, exemplary of this quest for complex subjectivity. Whereas Calvin Butts' diatribe against gangsta rappers would consign Tupac's celebration of "Thug Life" to one of the forces destroying Black communities, Pinn sees and hears something more complicated and interesting going on. Referring to tracks like "Black Jesus" and "Hail Mary," Pinn argues that Tupac unwittingly participates in a humanist tradition that casts suspicion on metaphysical categories that are disconnected from the messiness of human existence. Tupac's "black Jesus"[18] identifies with the everyday struggles of those who are hopeless; he identifies with and operates through communities that have been discarded as waste (thugs, drug dealers, crack addicts, impoverished single mothers), subjects who embody the underside of our social and political arrangements (Pinn 2003, p. 96). In "Hail Mary," Tupac resignifies this common Catholic prayer by integrating it into a configuration of sordid activities that are typically imagined as unholy.[19] This move exemplifies Tupac's unwillingness to countenance an intractable divide between good and evil (Perkinson 2009). Although he confesses, "Bow down, pray to God that he's listening," he also writes "On a one way trip to prison, Sellin drugs we all wrapped up in this livin" and "Hail til I reach hell, I don't care." According to TD Jakes, these contradictions in Tupac's music are indicative of a generation that is misguided and lost, a generation of black youth that has abandoned God's principles (Dyson 2002, p. 208). Yet, as Michael Eric Dyson (p. 229) rejoins, these contradictions are the product of a divided soul who refused to stop interrogating evil and suffering (including his own participation in these conditions). Tupac's inconsistency might be read as result of his fidelity to the broken, fractured nature of our world, a quality that cannot be easily resolved by the consolations and theodicies provided by institutional religions. Although Pinn and Dyson concede that Tupac's lyrics are at times reprehensible, they contend that Tupac's blues-inflected tendency to wrestle with existential dilemmas and matters of ultimate concern gives his music a religious sensibility.

Pinn's notion of a "quest for complex subjectivity" is productive insofar as it creates a bridge between the broader strands of hip hop scholarship and those particularly invested in the relationship between religion and hip hop. If Tricia Rose, for instance, reads hip hop as an artistic response by marginalized youth to the contradictions, absurdities, and modes of social neglect that characterize post-industrial urban America, Pinn's intervention suggests an affinity between the religious and the esthetic. Art, as Rose's analysis suggests, has a way of incorporating and reexpressing tensions, conflicts, and fissures that punctuate our social worlds. Art does not necessarily resolve these tensions and conflicts but through the reexpression of violent conditions (the dancer "breaking," the DJ "cutting," the graffiti artist "bombing" a train), those who participate in the art form are potentially able to relate to these conditions differently. This different way of relating to the social world is connected to art's ability to give participants pleasure, enjoyment, a sense of wonder, and even hope that the world might become less brutal. Pinn defines religion as a confrontation with the absurd, as the search for meaning amidst a world that denies meaning, recognition, and value to certain kinds of subjects. Like art, the religious sensibility in hip hop is a particular way of confronting, expressing, and working through the contradictions embodied by black subjects. Following Perry, we might read the practice of signifying (which entails reinterpretation, imagination, play, creativity, and an openness to ambiguity) as a vital strand of Pinn's notion of complex subjectivity, an always unfinished identity defined by tension, movement, and instability. Signifying, in other words, registers the ludic dimensions of living through ambiguity and contradiction.

Yet what are the conditions of possibility for this search or quest for complex identity? Does Pinn place too much emphasis on the Black subject's existential struggle with dehumanizing forces while downplaying the broader forces, mechanisms, and arrangements that shape, order, constrain, and enable the actions, quests, and aspirations of these subjects?[20] Borrowing from thinkers like Adorno and Marcuse, I argue that while social arrangements produce contradictions, they also produce the desire for consistency, stability, and clarity, a desire that often results in the repression and deflection of the very contradictions that would threaten a stable identity. Here we might think about the pervasive misogyny and homophobia within hip hop, the ways in which "complex" notions of gender and sexuality are foreclosed within a heteronormative, patriarchal order. In addition, within this epoch of late capitalism, the production of rap music seems increasingly regulated by the demands of the market, a trend that certainly has gripping (and flattening) effects on the desires, aspirations, and imaginations of rap artists and hip hop participants. If the notion of a quest invokes related concepts like desire, yearning, pursuit, and longing, my concern is that Pinn does not underscore the ways in which bodily desires, investments, and orientations are shaped, molded, and disciplined by mechanisms that facilitate the "smooth" flow of things. Here I am not endorsing or putting forth a declension narrative of hip hop. In other words, I am not suggesting that hip hop used to be creative, insurgent, and authentic and now it has simply been absorbed into the mainstream (becoming inauthentic and less pure). Although I occasionally feel nostalgic when I hear rap music from earlier periods, I also find allusions to a golden era of hip hop very problematic. Hip hop, like any cultural form, has always been constrained and limited by the dominant norms, expectations and standards of the broader social order, including those norms and standards that hip hop participants have attempted to challenge and undermine. Homophobia and misogyny have always been pervasive in hip hop culture; the desire to acquire and display wealth has also been a salient feature; "crossing over" to appeal to a wider audience or mimicking the popular styles of the day in order to remain relevant are not new phenomena within hip hop. My concluding response to Pinn is not meant to suggest that the present state of hip hop indicates a fall from a pristine era. I simply am concerned about his use of the term "complex subjectivity" and how the complexity of this subject (as she attempts to forge meaning in the face of dehumanizing conditions) is enabled and constrained by forces and trends that tend to produce reliable subjects (with similar preferences, desires, longings, and imaginative spectrums). This is not to suggest that centripetal forces like capital, the culture industry, or nationalism completely absorb or erase complexity, ambiguity, and creativity. Yet they do seem to impose stringent constraints on our ability to perform and embrace complexity in public spaces. More attention to these centripetal forces is crucial to understanding why so many artists feel a need to (in Lupe Fiasco's terms) "dumb down" their lyrical content and music in order to survive in the rap game.

Study Questions

1. What are the ways in which the "good/positive" and "bad/negative" classifications of rap music by the broader culture constrain the relationship and false distinction between rap music, hip hop, and religion?
2. What impact has the history of and attention to institutional religion had on understanding the role of religion in hip hop? Likewise, how has the work of Anthony B. Pinn, according to Winters, contributed to a more expansive approach to this area of study?
3. In thinking about theory and method in this growing area of thought, what does Winters suggest about Pinn's theory of *Complex Subjectivity*, its relationship to identity and attention to social arrangements as a way of exploring religion in rap music and hip hop culture?

Notes

1. For a critical response to this understanding of hip hop as an erosion of moral and religious values, see Pinn 2003, pp. 1–2. For a more in depth critique of the idea that hip hop is antithetical to American values, see Rose 2008.
2. NWA or "Niggas With Attitudes" was a group from Compton, California that included Ice Cube, Eazy-E, MC Ren, Dr. Dre, and DJ Yella. With songs like "F ck the Police" and "Gangsta, Gangsta," this group is typically hailed as being one of the pioneers of gangsta rap. 2 Live Crew was a Miami based rap group that sparked controversy in the early 1990s because of the sexually explicit content of their lyrics. Record stores were prohibited from selling the groups' records and members of the group were arrested after performing "obscene" lyrics at a concert. On the Black intellectual response to 2 Live Crew (including Henry Louis Gates' willingness to testify on the group's behalf), see Baker 1993, pp. 61–84.
3. Michael Eric Dyson makes this point, referring specifically to the deeply entrenched sexism within the Black church. See Dyson 1996, p. 185. One might also point to the affinities between the proponents of the prosperity gospel and contemporary rap artists obsessed with accumulating and displaying their riches. On this issue, see Sorett 2009.
4. Thus far, I have used the terms "hip hop" and "rap" somewhat interchangeably. This is certainly an anathema to many hip hop aficionados who make a clear distinction between the culture of hip

hop and rap music (which is one element of the broader culture). See for instance Pough 2004a, pp. 3–13. At the same time, this distinction can always be made to ease the minds of hip hop purists who want to safeguard authentic hip hop from the commercial interests of the rap music industry. On this issue, see Boyd 2002, pp. 44–8. For this article, I assume that rap music is one element of hip hop (alongside graffiti, breakdancing, and so forth). At the same time, I assume that rap music has proven to be one of the more durable elements. Most of my analysis in this article will privilege and refer to rap music, specifically its lyrical content.

5. By the term regressive, I am referring to cultural critics like Stanley Crouch who consider hip hop music to be contemporary form of minstrelsy.

6. The most famous example of this urban renewal program is the creation of the Cross-Bronx Expressway. Initiated by the powerful urban planner Robert Moses, the Cross-Bronx Expressway was designed to connect the boroughs of New York City with its surrounding suburbs. In the process of clearing space and razing houses for this project, over 50,000 Bronx residents were forced to relocate. On the effects of the Cross-Bronx Expressway, see Rose 1994, pp. 30–4. Also see Chang 2005, pp. 10–13.

7. Here I am indebted to the theories of members of the Frankfurt School, especially Theodor Adorno and Walter Benjamin. See for instance, Adorno 1978, p. 151.

8. Grandmaster Flash and the Furious Five, "The Message" The Message (Sugar Hill Records, 1982).

9. I am borrowing the term "Afro-diasporic" from Tricia Rose to acknowledge connections and affinities between Black American, Latino, and West Indian cultures, especially as these affinities are made visible within hip hop culture.

10. A Tribe Called Quest, "Verses From the Abstract," Low End Theory (Jive, 1991).

11. Black Moon, "Murder Mcs," Diggin in dah Vaults (Nervous, 1996).

12. Queen Latifah, "U.N.I.T.Y.," Black Reign (Motown/ PolyGram, 1993).

13. Brand Nubian, "Wake Up," One For All (Electra, 1990).

14. Brand Nubian, "Wake Up," One For All (Electra, 1990).

15. Lupe Fiasco, "American Terrorist," Food and Liquor (Atlantic, 2006).

16. Main Source, "Live at the Barbecue," Breakin Atoms (Wild Pitch, 1991). To snuff someone is to punch and knock them out.

17. Although space does not permit me to go into detail, it is important to mention the emergence of artists who deliberately identity their music as Christian rap. Artists such as Lil' Raskull, L.G. Wise, and Tru to Society deploy the language of sin, evil, salvation, and conversion as they lyrically navigate the problems and contradictions that plague their communities. See for instance Baker-Fletcher 2003.

18. Tupac, "Black Jesus," Still I Rise (Death Row Records, 1999).

19. Tupac, "Hail Mary," The Don Killuminati: The Seven Day Theory (Death Row Records, 1997).

20. Elonda Clay poses a similar set of questions and concerns. See Clay 2009.

Works Cited

Adorno, T. (1978). *Minima Moralia*. Translated by EFN Jephcott. New York: Verso.

Baker, H. (1993). *Black Studies, Rap, and the Academy*. Chicago: University of Chicago Press.

Baker-Fletcher, G. (2003). African American Christian Rap: Facing Truth and Resisting It. In: Anthony Pinn (ed.), *Noise and Spirit*, pp. 29–48. New York: NYU Press.

Boyd, T. (2002). *The New HNIC: The Death of Civil Rights and the Reign of Hip Hop*. New York: New York University Press.

Carby, H. (1998). It Jus Be's Dat Way Sometime: The Sexual Politics of Women's Blues. In: Robert O'Meally (ed.), *The Jazz Cadence of American Culture*, pp. 469–82. New York: Columbia University Press.

Chang, J. (2005). *Can't Stop, Won't Stop: A History of the Hip Hop Generation*. New York: St. Martin's Press.

Clay, E. (2009). Two Turntables and a Microphone: Turntablism, Ritual, and Implicit Religion, *Culture and Religion*, 10(1), pp. 23–38.

Dyson, M. (1996). *Between God and Gangsta Rap: Bearing Witness to Black Culture*. New York: Oxford University Press.

—— (2002). *Holler if You Hear Me: Searching for Tupac Shakur*. New York: Basic Civitas.

Floyd-Thomas, J. (2003). A Jihad of Words: The Evolution of African American Islam and Contemporary Hip Hop. In: Anthony Pinn (ed.), *Noise and Spirit*, pp. 49–70. New York: NYU Press.

Gates, H. (1989). *Signifying Monkey: A Theory of African American Literary Criticism*. Oxford: Oxford University Press.

George, N. (1998). *Hip Hop America*. New York: Viking Penguin.

Jackson, P. & Smith, E. (2005). *The Hip Hop Church: Connecting with the Movement Shaping our Culture*. Downers Grove, IL: IVP.

Kelley, R. (1997). *Yo Mama's Dysfunctional!: Fighting the Culture Wars in Urban America*. Boston: Beacon Press.

Kitwana, B. (2005). *Why White Kids Love Hip Hop: Wiggers, Wangstas, and the New Reality of Race in America*. New York: Basic Civitas Books.

Lefevere, P. (1993). NY Minister Combats Negative Rap Lyrics—Rev Calvin Butts III. *National Catholic Reporter*, 21 March.

Miller, M. (2009). The Promiscuous Gospel: The Religious Complexity and Theological Multiplicity of Rap Music. *Culture and Religion*, 10(1), pp. 39–61.

—— & Pinn, A. (2009). Introduction: Intersections of Culture and Religion in African-American Communities, *Culture and Religion*, 10(1) pp. 1–9.

Perkinson, J. (2003). Rap as Wrap and Rapture: North American Popular Culture and the Denial of Death. In: Anthony Pinn (ed.), *Noise and Spirit*, pp. 131–53. New York: NYU Press.

——. (2009). Tupac Shakur as Ogou Achade: Hip hop Anger and Postcolonial Rancour Read from the Other Side, Culture and Religion, 10(1) pp. 63–79.

Perry, I. (2004). *Prophets of the Hood: Politics and Poetics in Hip Hop*. Durham: Duke University Press.

Pinn, A. (ed.) (2003). *Noise and Spirit: The Religious and Spiritual Sensibilities of Rap Music*. New York: NYU Press.

Potter, Russell. (1995). *Spectacular Vernaculars: Hip Hop and the Politics of Postmodernism*. Albany: SUNY Press.

Pough, G. (2004a). *Check It, While I Wreck It: Black Womanhood, Hip Hop Culture, and the Public Sphere*. Boston: Northeastern University Press.

—— (2004b). Seeds and Legacies. In: M. Forman and M. Anthony Neal (eds.), *That's The Joint*, pp. 283–9. New York: Routledge.

Rose, T. (1994). *Black Noise: Rap Music and Black Culture in Contemporary America*. Middletown: Wesleyan University Press.

—— (2008). *Hip Hop Wars*. New York: Basic Books.

Sorett, J. (2009). Believe Me, This Pimp Game is Very Religious: Toward a Religious History of Hip Hop, *Culture and Religion*, 10(1) pp. 11–22.

Further Reading

Forman, M. & Neal, M. (eds.) (2004). *That's the Joint: The Hip Hop Studies Reader*. New York: Routledge.

Gilroy, P. (1993). *The Black Atlantic, Modernity, and Double Consciousness*. Cambridge: Harvard University Press.

hooks, bell. (1994). *Outlaw Culture: Resisting Representations*. New York: Routledge.

Jones, L. (1963). *Blues People*. New York: Morrow Quill Paperbacks.

Pinn, A. (2009). Rap Music, Culture and Religion: Concluding Thoughts, *Culture and Religion*, 10(1) pp. 97–108.

Ugwu, C. (ed.) (1995). *Let's Get It On: The Politics of Black Performance*. London: Institute for Contemporary Arts.

West, C. (2004). *Democracy Matters: Winning the Fight against Imperialism*. New York: Penguin.

7

Peter Piper Picked Peppers, but Humpty Dumpty Got Pushed
The Productively Paranoid Stylings of Hip-hop's Spirituality

Beginning with the memory of Brooklyn, New York in the 1970s and 80s, Jackson argues that talk of esoteric spirituality and references to god in hip hop song during this time were notable and capacious, an abundance that most certainly continues today. With a focus on the presence of The Five Percent Nation in hip hop culture, Jackson considers the role and weight of esoteric and codified narratives and lessons from within this group as a way to think further about the history and management of racial paranoia among communities of color today. Jackson considers the relationship between hip hop's esoteric and oppositional vernacular, its "useful incomprehensibility" and the transformation of belief into an organic heuristic of hip hop's paranoid spirituality and social relevance for the study of race in American society.

Peter Piper Picked Peppers, but Humpty Dumpty Got Pushed: The Productively Paranoid Stylings of Hip-hop's Spirituality

John L. Jackson, Jr.

When I was growing up in Brooklyn, New York, in the 1970s and 1980s, most of the young people who lived in the Bayview Houses (the housing project complex I called home for the bulk of my childhood) spent their weekends watching Saturday-afternoon kung fu movies on television, flicking clay—or wax-filled bottle caps across concrete sidewalks in "skelly" games, and listening to Mr. Magic or DJ Red Alert late at night on the radio. We were hip-hop's first youth generation, enthusiastic local guinea pigs for its unanticipated global influences.[1]

Before music came to television and hip-hop went mainstream, Mr. Magic and Red Alert were two of the most important official ambassadors for hip-hop music, spinning records by MC Lyte and Heavy D, Big Daddy Kane and Audio Two, UTFO and The Treacherous Three, records that you couldn't hear many other places on the radio dial. As passionate listeners, we memorized the artists' lyrics and recited their rhymes for one another—that is, when we weren't writing and performing our own original couplets in school cafeterias or during afternoon treks home. Everybody wanted to be an MC or a DJ, and that was long before most people fully realized just how financially lucrative hip-hop would turn out to be.

The hip-hop songs we memorized in the 1980s and 1990s were full of talk about "Gods and Earths" (i.e., black men and black women), references to the esoteric philosophies that MCs called "mathematics," tales of "grafted devils" (the theory that whites were genetically engineered by a black scientist long ago), and much more along those same lines.[2] This terminology and rhetoric grew out of another movement sprouting from the same fertile concrete that nurtured hip-hop.

Quite a few of the young black guys in Bayview Houses, these same hip-hop fans, were also Five Percenters. Members of the Five Percent Nation believe that the black man in America is god, a saintly energy and entity, and all their other philosophies spring from that premise. Five Percenters change their names (to things like "Wisdom Knowledge" "Righteous Born" and "Sincere Divine"), explicitly call one another gods, and memorize their daily "mathematics" right alongside their hip-hop lyrics. "Mathematics" represent the spiritual teachings that Five Percenters have to learn and recite on cue, the philosophical truths that provide them with "knowledge of self" about the black man's godly status.

Even though I was never a member of the Five Percent Nation, I did have enough Bayview friends in the group chat I was able to get some of my questions answered about their worldview. For instance, I learned about their conviction that certain powerful and elite social circles (which included high-level government officials and rich corporate tycoons) actually knew the truth about black people's celestial pedigree but purposefully hid the facts from wider public view. Most people don't realize this and won't accept it, Five Percenters will tell you, because there's an ongoing conspiracy organized by an evil 10 percent of the world's population to keep the masses (85 percent) in complete darkness. The job of the 5 percent left over is to dutifully pull the wool from over people's eyes and show them the black man's true divinity.

From the very beginning, hip-hop music was tailormade for disseminating Five Percenters' beliefs. For one thing, hip-hop and the Five Percent Nation were born at about the same time. Clarence 13X split from the Nation of Islam's Mosque Number 7 in Harlem (once Malcolm X's mosque) in 1968, at about the same time that blacks a few miles away (in the South Bronx) were first starting to combine urban Americana with Anglophone Caribbean and black British influences to form the earliest renditions of hip-hop style.[3] Some hip-hop artists explicitly considered themselves Five Percenters and attempted to use the new art form to help the masses find "truth."

Hip-hop with any apparent connection to Five Percenters' faith usually gets designated "conscious rap," a subgenre made up of songs specifically designed to endorse pro-black ideas (in the distinctive traditions of Afrocentrism, Pan-Africanism, and Black Nationalism).[4] The first conscious rap offerings of hip-hop acts such as Stetsasonic and Afrika Bambaataa existed on an ideological continuum with hip-hop groups made up of actual members from the Nation of Islam and the Five Percenters (including Brand Nubian and Poor Righteous Teachers). But conscious rappers didn't necessarily have to believe in the Five Percenters' theories of global religious conspiracies to sympathize with their educational bent or to invoke the organization's idiomatic expressions as a sign of authenticity and street credibility. A fan could have been listening to any number of hip-hop acts in the mid-1990s (not just "Nation" groups), and if they were listening closely enough, they would have learned more than a few of the basic beliefs central to Five Percenter and Nation of Islam theologies.

Even if all hip-hop artists didn't identify themselves as part of that enlightened 5 percent of "poor righteous teachers" tapped to save the world, many did position themselves explicitly as street professors espousing truths that went against the grain of conventional America's educational curricula, such as Jawanza Kunjufu, Frances Cress-Welsing, and Haki Madhubuti, to justify their own theoretical interventions on behalf of black America. For conscious rap groups such as X-Clan, the Jungle Brothers, and A Tribe Called Quest (as well as more mainstream acts, such as the Furious Five and Kool Moe Dee, who schooled listeners about life on the street), hip-hop was committed to reeducation in the wake of past miseducations of black people at the hands of public schools and elite colleges.

A critic might bookend this move to equate hip-hop MCs with teachers by citing KRS-One's late-1980s demand that his fans heed his ideas ("you must learn!") about ancient Egypt and black history, on the one hand, and a group like Dead Prez's early twenty-first-century dismissal of "They Schools" as little more than "brainwash camps," on the other. Neither of these last two acts has been affiliated with Islam as a foundational aspect of its reputation, but both represent the broader pedagogical metaphors that frame hip-hop artists' justifications for their work. Hip-hop is supposed to bring class into session, a new kind of class. The better the MC, the more irreproachable his or her teacherly credentials, with the listeners' homework being to study the lyrics and learn the lessons of these street philosophers. And one of the major themes in many of these lesson plans has always been a critical distrust of larger American society and its commitments to the urban communities that gave birth to hip-hop culture.

In contrast to a strictly romantic and utopian version of race relations in a post-civil rights context, one of the major themes of hip-hop music emphasizes the utility of a certain cynical paranoia vis-a-vis American society. Most of the earliest hip-hop songs played on the radio emphasized fun and good times, using easy-to-follow lyrics and a relatively slow verbal delivery to narrate tales about the horrors of dating and boasts about individual prowess. But as the genre got more technically sophisticated, its rhetoric and its very style became conducive to more suspicious readings of contemporary American life. As the rest of America sought to hide racism beneath a veneer of politically correct speech, hip-hop became increasingly paranoid about race, and not a small part of that diametrical difference is linked to the intrinsic racial skepticisms of groups such as the Five Percenters and the Nation of Islam, two of the earliest influences on hip-hop discourse.

If paranoia is usually dismissed by committed scholar activists, critics like political scientist Adolph Reed, as merely a distraction from real politics, something that dissipates the galvanizing energies required for true social transformation, hip-hop artists call on racial paranoia as a kind of lightning rod for politicizing otherwise disaffected black youth, asking them to wake up, recognize the global conspiracies afoot, and get their urban lives in order. The founding assumptions behind hip-hop's take on black America are often strikingly similar to Five Percenter philosophies and to race-based conspiracy theories more generally. For example, there is little mere coincidence in hip-hop rhetoric, especially when that rhetoric focuses on the plight of poor blacks. Nothing happens to African Americans simply by chance or due to the disinterested contingencies of history. Everything is chalked up to purposeful trickery and conniving, social insensitivity and self-serving disinterest.[5] For instance, when Grand Master Flash and the Furious Five released their megahit "The Message" in 1982, the song's talk of poverty and hopelessness emphasized uncaring teachers who provide little more than a "bum education" and highlighted all the conspicuous features of ghetto life that conspire to precipitate the early death of many young black children. Their message seemed to be that staying alive from day to day in America's ghettoes was a bona fide miracle.

"The Message" helped open hip-hop's political flood-gates, and many more rappers would provide snapshots of urban poverty in black America after Grand Master Flash's early salvo. Of course, most of these later accusations were "dropped" over heavy drumbeats and with recourse to intricate (sometimes very subtle) wordplay. Hip-hop lyricism is specifically about toying with the fact that words can have many different meanings, with the slightest change in tone and inflection redefining common terms, sometimes radically. Hip-hop revels in its own peculiar brand of linguistic sophistication, in the fact that words can imply any number of things, even the opposite of what uninitiated listeners might think.

Run-DMC offered a well-known vocabulary lesson in one of their early songs, explaining to outsiders that when they said the word "bad" it was "not 'bad' meaning 'bad' but 'bad' meaning 'good.'" From the nineteenth and early twentieth centuries, linguists such as Ferdinand de Saussure and Charles Sanders Peirce provided detailed explanations for the many reasons why "bad" can be made to mean "good," and those reasons all pivot on the basic arbitrariness of language. The sounds we make with our mouths only stand for the ideas they represent because of convention, because we all say they do. Societies (speech communities) agree on specific relationships between certain combinations of sounds and the concepts they symbolize, but such links aren't natural or "motivated" by logical connections fastening particular sounds to the ideas they sound out.[6]

Hip-hop uses that semantic slippage to popularize new sets of agreements (for those in the know) about the relationship between given words and what they "represent." "Bad meaning good" is particularly powerful, of course, because it turns a negative into a positive, like the hip-hop community's obsessive reclamation of "nigger/nigga" as a term of endearment, applying it in opposition to its venomous historical uses. Hip-hop embraces the "power to define" itself, and Run-DMC's one line alone speaks volumes about the group's desire to cross over, about their sense of themselves as teachers (responsible for teaching new fans how to listen accurately), and about hip-hop's emphasis on potential linguistic impenetrability as part of its cultural power.[7]

For fans to really make heads or tails of what hip-hop artists are saying, especially when the artists aren't explicitly defining their terms the way Run-DMC did above (and particularly after hip-hop MCs started to ratchet up the speed and lyrical complexity of their rhyming styles in the 1990s), they had to take their time deciphering what was mostly unintelligible to casual listeners or even to many serious fans. And that is a key part of hip-hop's story: its general "incomprehensibility."[8] Hip-hop as such potential conduit for conspiracy talk and racial paranoia in part because of its in-your-face secrecies, its ability to hide political views in plain sight. And this isn't just about euphemizing. The "Parental Advisory" stickers on their CDs prove that hip-hop artists can be clear and explicit when they want to be. However, fast rhyming, playing with the phonetics of language, and continually redefining words all conspire to make hip-hop almost as indecipherable as a foreign language for anyone not raised on its idiomatic expressions or committed to learning them. Fully comprehending hip-hop demands decoding its intricate use of language to the point where one is able to recognize relatively obscure and cloaked references to veiled philosophies found in African American versions of Islam or explicit invocations of alternative discourses on racism popularized by books such as *The Isis Papers*.

Hip-hop's useful incomprehensibility is also tied to the fact that it is hardly "easy listening." There is an obvious premium placed on lyrical flow and speed. But on top of that the layering of hip-hop music with scratching, cutting sampling, and other sound effects makes it that much more difficult to excavate all the hidden lyrical meanings beneath its complexly textured acoustic landscape.[9] Hip-hop plays with the very substance and texture of sound, reworking Jazz's "scat" tradition into "hip hop, a hippit, a hippit to the hip hip hop and you don't stop" nonsensicality, or transforming an MC's voice into a drum machine (in the form of a "human beat box"). Everything about hip-hop's aesthetic asks us to listen to the very materialities of meanings, which means hearing things in newfangled ways.

This all helps make hip-hop's form, its very structure and sensibility, conducive to a kind of conspiring in broad daylight. Incomprehensibility and the layering of beats, scratches, cuts, and the like, collude to make hip-hop a masterful secret keeper. At the same time, there is also a specific hip-hop mindset predicated on the dominant belief that you can't really trust what you see. If the genre has one mantra, it is that the eyes deceive—or prove downright ineffective: "You can't see me." "You're blind, baby." "Can't trust it." Hip-hoppers from Public Enemy to Jay-Z are adamant about the inadequacy of vision, which is part of the reason why matters of authenticity and credibility are endlessly debated.[10] You don't just spy a self-professed hip-hop "gangsta," say, and naively accept that he isn't, in fact, a "perpetrator," a "studio gangsta," someone who plays the role of criminal to raise record sales. In hip-hop, what you see is never what you get. Listeners have learned to be skeptical of spectacles, even as the spectacle is also a form of presentation that most hip-hop artists embrace. This is what makes things so complex. Hip-hop is invested in "appearances" even as it simultaneously denounces them for being misleading: distrust of the mere "image" is combined with fondness for making a fetish out of precisely those things (the artist's look, bling-bling fashions, etc.) that aren't supposed to be trusted. This is one of hip-hop's most productive and fascinating paradoxes.

So, if hip-hop doesn't trust eyewitnesses to supply it with evidence on authenticity and credibility, what does it use? In hip-hop, truth isn't seen; it is felt. It is a fact of the soul and spirit more than anything else. You are supposed to feel the "real" of that popular mandate to "keep it real." And if you don't feel it, there's nothing else you can do.

This hip-hop philosophy is succinctly captured in the question that hip-hop artists ask one another (and their listeners) almost neurotically: "You feel me?" Do you feel me? Can you feel me? That isn't just an idle inquiry. There is an important principle behind it. Hip-hop is offering up its own epistemology, its way of knowing the world. To "feel" means to test the world, but differently from what social scientists might label naive empiricism. "You feel me?" ensures that hip-hop doesn't rely too simplistically on what people can prove with mathematical formulas or scientific experiments. Something about the truth, about real life, is more powerfully felt than statistically proven, more intuited than seen, which is the precise sensibility that grounds racial paranoia. The racial slights are real (for Cynthia McKinney, for Dave Chappelle, for Gloria Naylor) at least partially because they feel real, and no visible displays to the contrary can completely refute that.

"Feeling" short-circuits more traditional corroboration techniques—and not just seeing. It is unreceptive to most forms of external verification. Hip-hop artist Jay-Z, for one, rhymes about this pointedly, crystallizing hip-hop's attitude to perfection: "I put my hand on my heart. That means I feel you. Real recognize real and you('re) looking familiar." To "feel" someone is to connect to them beyond words or otherwise superficial similarities. Familiarity is something you sense, not what your gullible eyes might try to validate. That isn't the same thing as saying that hip-hop advocates blindness. It imagines a way of knowing a person that can see inside them, can look past the surface and connect on some more fundamental ground.

This idea of seeing something that isn't observable to the naked eye is a classic motif for conspiracies and paranoia, which is why you can't just disabuse people of their seemingly misplaced paranoia by splashing them with the cool, crisp waters of reason. Racial paranoia exceeds rational debate. "You feel me" because you can feel me. That's it. You get a vibe, something as ephemeral and invisible as a hunch. It isn't about cognitive and intellectual vetting. You just sense, intuit, with something similar to the blinklike efficiency and immediacy Malcolm Gladwell described.[11] Hip-hop places a premium on such implicit feeling, treats it as obvious and self-evident, automatic and hardwired.

It is this feeling, this way of knowing by sensing, that also makes racial identity so real for people. Like anything else worthy of the designation "culture," racial identities work most efficiently when we can't even see them, when they become second nature and we can't even imagine ourselves otherwise. People don't believe in social identities just because they are logical or reasonable. "Believing" means using a very different heuristic entirely. And this privileging of belief is caught up in hip-hop's entrenched faith-based leanings more generally, in hip-hop's spiritual fundamentalisms.

Critics are far more interested in criticizing the music's obvious vulgarity than in talking about hip-hop's emphatic spirituality. They call hip-hop artists out for their shameless misogyny and homophobia. Detractors decry the violence and nihilism glamorized by hip-hop gangstas. Or they dismiss much of the music and culture for its embrace of commercialism and apolitical ostentation. Those are all important critiques, but they only begin to scratch the surface of more serious discussions about hip-hop's social relevance and spiritual ethic.[12]

When people do comment on the connection between hip-hop and religion, it is usually to puzzle over the dissonance of "Christian hip-hop" (as popularized by, say, Kirk Franklin and Compton Virtue), which proselytizes through Bible-inspired lyrics. Or they lampoon secular hip-hop artists who spend most of their albums cursing and depicting brutal forms of barbarity, only to turn around and solemnly thank God on nationally televised programs for helping them win prestigious music awards. Those award-show gestures are dismissed as insincere or hypocritical. But the thing to realize about hip-hop is that it is an unabashedly spiritual art form, even if it espouses a kind of spirituality very different from what a casual (or disinterested) listener might expect.

Hip-hop's spirituality is related to its emphasis on feeling over seeing, faith over sight, and that isn't just for converts to Islam and the Five Percent Nation. It is also about a profound kind of brutal Christianity, the kind that allows MCs to gun down "bitches" on one track and sincerely praise God on another, without this necessarily being a contradiction. Instead, hip-hop offers another kind of religiosity, hip-hop's "you feel me" spirituality. This emphasis on "feeling" provides the foundation for hip-hop's incessant spirituality, its ubiquitous invocations of God in songs penned by the likes of DMX, 50 Cent, and R. Kelly (to name just three of the people most criticized for religious hypocrisy). These artists would tell you that you can't judge them because you can't "see" them, can't "feel" them—not really, not what's inside. God knows my heart, they declare, which is why Tupac Shakur could believe that nobody else was in a position to judge him. God can see into hearts, definitively spying *de cardio* racisms (or any other secrets) with no problem at all. And so, it's what you feel (in your heart of hearts) in the place where you commune with God alone, not what someone else thinks he can see (or even prove), that serves as the basis for hip-hop's claims of social invulnerability and purposeful inaccessibility. Sometimes what's in that heart might be drastically different from what you see on the outside. What you see can be the exact opposite of what you get.

Hip-hop's serious commitment to spirituality reveals the ways in which this powerful cultural form helps to transmit contemporary racial paranoia across the globe. Through both the narratives that artists emphasize in their songs and the media's irrational responses to hip-hop's potential violence, we uncover an important story about how different forms of paranoia coalesce at the center of this vibrant cultural space. From a discussion of "grafted devils" to claims about corrupt police officers and the government-sanctioned introduction of drugs and diseases into black communities, hip-hop music has helped to popularize and disseminate some of the most dominant stories of racial paranoia making the rounds today.

Hip-hop is stocked with paranoid stylings, and it is also an art form about which many people, fans and nonfans alike, have become increasingly paranoid. Perhaps no person exemplifies the perceived dangers of hip-hop's corrosive influence more than John Walker Lindh, the twenty-one-year-old white suburbanite from Northern California captured in Afghanistan in 2001 while fighting for the Taliban. America was slowly beginning to recover from the wreckage of 9/11, and Lindh's soot-blackened and scraggly-bearded face represented the country's worst nightmare: one of its own lined up staunchly on the wrong side of the country's newly declared "war on terror." Not too long after Lindh was apprehended, once journalists started to piece together his story, it became a little clearer how he had ended up waging war against U.S. soldiers, how he had gotten seduced into high treason. Hip-hop made him do it.

Before he converted to Islam, before he took off for Yemen and Pakistan to study Arabic, Lindh was a serious hip-hop fan. He knew all the big MCs, studied and memorized their lyrics, and even entertained thoughts of becoming a hip-hop artist himself.[13] He was one of those teenage "wiggers" and "wannabes" that Bakari Kitwana analyzes in his examination of hip-hop culture's appeal to white youth, including and especially young activists.[14] But Lindh didn't just enjoy hip-hop; he was obsessed with it. Lindh appears to have been so enamored with black culture that he seemingly wanted to be black himself, to claim hip-hop as his racial birthright. At the very least, Lindh pretended to be black whenever he could get away with it, "passing" while posting his thoughts about hip-hop all over the Internet in the mid-1990s.[15] Under a string of pseudonyms, Lindh left revealing traces of his complicated beliefs about the music and its superstars.

From what he wrote as a young white teenager (again, claiming to be African American), Lindh was a bit of a rap purist, if not an outright hip-hop snob. He attacked artists for "spreading stereotypes" and selling out to corporate America, sacrificing black interests for a lucrative recording contract.[16] Lindh dismissed NWA for celebrating the self-destructiveness of mari-juana and malt liquor. He labeled Bay Area pimp-hop artist Too $hort a "house nigga" (a self-conscious reference to Malcolm X's already-mentioned critique). Too $hort, Lindh claimed, was "wacker than Marin County Caucasians," worse than the white folk Lindh knew and grew up with. In fact, Lindh was, himself, one of those very same Marin County Caucasians. Such low self-regard and disdain for his own local community undoubtedly played a crucial role in fomenting much of his angst, but hip-hop clearly provided the soundtrack.

Lindh had a problem with the politics of West Coast MCs, but he didn't just stick close to home. Old-schooler Marley Marl (one of hip-hop's New York pioneers) got blasted for "being fake like plastic" and crafting simplistic lyrics "to make money for the grafted." Lindh's reference to "the grafted" is important because it begins to hint at hip-hop's role in introduc-ing him to his earliest understanding of Islam, long before he ever took off for Afghanistan. One of Lindh's first bits of sustained exposure to the religion came from hip-hop's connec-tion to the Nation of Islam's version, where a diabolical black scientist named Yakub creates ("grafts") a demonic white race in his laboratory.[17]

While still in his mid-teens, Lindh seemed to so identify with hip-hop and some of the Nation of Islam-inflected beliefs of its early stars that he even attempted to embrace its myth-ological depiction of whites as laboratory-concocted devils, using that rhetoric to ground his criticisms of hip-hop artists as sellouts. Lindh was committed to blackness so thoroughly, so completely, that he felt immune to the sting of such antiwhite rhetoric, something similar to what neo-Nazi Leo Felton was able to pull off in New England at close to the same time.[18]

Felton, born to a black father and white mother in the 1960s, so identified with whiteness, with white identity, that he spent much of the late 1990s as an "Italian" neo-Nazi skinhead, starting fights with blacks (just because they were black) and plotting to blow up Jewish mon-uments in Boston. Felton actively and adamantly distanced himself from black Americans and clung to a relentless brand of white racism.

Questioned about this arguable contradiction, ostensibly being black while championing antiblack beliefs, Felton sounded like a seriously high-minded social theorist when he offered his response. Ask a group of academics in the sciences, humanities, and social sciences about race, ask them to define it for you and explain its significance, and chances are you'll get a potted answer about race being nothing more than "a social construction."[19] It isn't a real genetic and scientific fact, just a set of cultural beliefs hidden behind the facade of science. And Felton couldn't agree more. He doesn't think that race is biology, not at all.[20] In fact, he'd tell you, that is precisely the wrong way to understand it; you can't reduce racial identity to myths about genes and blood. Instead, Felton explains race as something you "feel" deep inside. It isn't material; it's spiritual, emotional. It is in your gut, your soul, your heart. And inside Felton's soul, deep down, he felt white, not black, regardless of his absentee black father or America's dogma about one drop of "black blood" disqualifying you from the purities of whiteness. Like Felton, Lindh seemed to invest in a version of race (at least as a teenager) that also cut against the grain of most people's assumptions about racial identification and even allowed him to spout (seemingly sincerely) racist principles about whites being "grafted" dev-ils. He espoused this while managing to envision himself, a young white kid from northern California, as somehow exempt from its condemnation—except, of course, for the fact that he had to pass for black to do it.

Lindh eventually distanced himself more and more from the Nation of Islam's transla-tion of that religion and from hip-hop culture altogether. But it had still been hip-hop that served as his point of entry into more orthodox forms of Islam. Hip-hop's expressions of religious belief started him out on his idiosyncratic journey to the frontlines of Afghanistan through the careful study of groups such as Public Enemy and dismissive criticisms of just about everyone else. Hip-hop brought him to the altar and taught him a certain sense of spiritual discipline and reverence. Hip-hop gave Lindh his first substantial taste of Islam, and an undeniably American brand at that. John Walker Lindh represents one of white America's biggest paranoias about hip-hop music: it will turn their children into crazed and violent troublemakers. With Lindh as an "enemy combatant" alternative, controversial hip-hop superstar Eminem might not seem all that bad to any suburban soccer moms terrified by their kids' obsessive interest in hip-hop music and culture. But soccer moms shouldn't be singled out. Hip-hop artists have always recognized what Public Enemy once described as white America's more general "fear of a black planet" (i.e., wide-ranging panic that hip-hop culture will contaminate all of white America, transforming the nation in fundamental ways), and many hip-hop artists challenge such (imagined or real) white xenophobia quite directly in their lyrics, helping to illustrate the music's tricky relationship to African American versions of racial paranoia. Public Enemy's lead MC, Chuck D, once called hip-hop black America's CNN. He was absolutely right—and not just because it disseminates news straight from "the streets." It also packages that news for us, providing a sensationalist and skeptical framework for its social interpretation.

There have been some very high-profile cases of songs explicitly dealing with racial issues that many people would consider newsworthy. For example, hip-hop has crafted many tunes emphasizing the fact that police in urban neighborhoods can't be trusted, black or white. The most famous version of this is NWA's 1991 anthem "Fuck tha police." NWA rails against the entire Los Angeles Police Department for racial profiling, excessive force, corruption and the attempted murder of innocent black men. And the police only seem to do this, the group argues, because they'd rather see black men struggling and in jail than thriving and successful.

While there are innumerable references to such institutionalized racist practices throughout hip-hop, "Fuck tha Police" transcends the topic, providing an example of the move from racism to racial paranoia. For Ice Cube and the rest of NWA, the fact that there are any crooked officers indicts the entire police department, which is why Cube can talk about the "bloodbath of cops" that he fantasizes about killing in Los Angeles—and without compunction. Any person with a badge is implicated in the racism of the few, and such a massive conspiracy is thought to necessitate an equally extensive response.

NWA was hardly a group of Five Percenter or conscious rappers, but many of their violent "gangsta" lyrics spoke directly to paranoia vis-a-vis the police department and other government agencies. There are no exceptions, and everybody from the district attorney to the judge and warden are in on it. Hip-hop's emphasis on race, to the point of racial paranoia, highlights what a conservative critic like John McWhorter would disparage as racial fetishization. But race was a fetish long before hip-hop got to the scene, and it'll probably stay that way well after the next new great musical genre has exceeded hip-hop's current popularity.

Like the Five Percenters and the Nation of Islam, many hip-hop artists believe that a good portion of what's most important about the workings of race in America are hidden, secret, even if they are actually quite "public secrets" that most people are simply afraid to invoke. Some hip-hop artists might actively distance themselves from (or downplay) the more mythical versions of these claims (about genetically "grafted devils" or a conspiring 10 percent literally working to help the devil gain world domination), but they still realize that racism is most powerful when it can't be seen, when it's lodged beneath the surface of things.

Hip-hoppers also highlight the *de cardio* subtleties of "perceived racism," of something qualitatively different from racisms of old. In his song "Mr. Nigger," for example, hip-hop

MC Mos Def takes on racial profiling and overt racism, but the title of the song stems from his realization that there are probably very few times when he'll ever come up against the most brutal and shameless versions of racism, the versions that would have found whites calling blacks "niggers" to their faces only a few generations ago. So, Mos Def raps about how a racist cop will never explicitly say that he stopped a young black man because of race, but they'll both still "know" the unsaid truth. Mos Def realizes that whites are no longer willing to call blacks "niggers" in mixed company, but he is sure that they must still be doing it when they are alone—the same fear that Eddie Murphy parodied when he put on whiteface and went undercover in that *Saturday Night Live* skit.

Contemporary hip-hop artist Mos Def also declares (and this is where "racial paranoia" shows its sharpest teeth) that even if whites never say the word "nigger," their everyday "actions reveal how their hearts really feel." Mos Def cites flight attendants putting less water in black passengers' water glasses and double-checking to make sure that they really belong in first class when he talks about the global dynamics of racism. His examples are mostly based on reading between the lines of social politeness, deciphering euphemisms and practiced civility. But Mos Def still characterizes these *de cardio* racialisms as though he were describing the explicitly de jure kind. Mos Def equates the aforementioned slights with white people explicitly calling him a "nigger." He pretends that such a connection is absolutely certain and self-evident, leaving no room for doubt—which, of course, it does (even if his assessments are right). For Mos Def, even when he claims to see the telltale racist heart revealed, the behavior he actually chronicles is much subtler than that which his parents and grandparents would have generally had to interpret, more contestable than his definitive conclusions admit. They aren't less significant than earlier versions of racism, only stubbornly resistant to older models of disclosure and proof.

Chicago-based rapper Kanye West provides a representative example of how hip-hop links de jure, de facto, and *de cardio* forms of racism while carefully concealing its racial accusations altogether. Although he famously proclaimed that President George W. Bush "doesn't care about black people," he isn't always so unambiguous about racial matters in his lyrics. In his song "Heard 'Em Say," he rhymes, "And I know that the government administer aids. So I guess we just pray like the ministers say." West uses the double meanings of "administer" and "aids" to talk the talk of racial paranoia long before Hurricane Katrina. On one level, West is expressing the obvious fact that a government is supposed to aid its people, to provide assistance to citizens. But he's simultaneously voicing a profound skepticism by inferring that all folks can do then is pray, ostensibly because the government is not doing its job. But the implications don't stop there.

West also implies something even more sinister: the government purposefully administered (spread) AIDS to people. Not "aids," as in assistance, but AIDS, as in the disease that attacks the immune system, disproportionately infecting black women and men. This belief in AIDS as a man-made (government-deployed) drug has a long history. In fact, the Nation of Islam spent most of the 1990s arguing not only that AIDS had a suspicious etiology but that the drug provided to help those suffering from the disease, AZT, might do more harm than good to black people, advocating interferon as a safer alternative. Kanye West isn't a Five Percenter or a member of the Nation of Islam, but he does offer a version of racial paranoia (and racial-conspiracy theorizing) that is strikingly similar to theirs, using hip-hop's aesthetic and acoustic characteristics to disguise his accusations with polyvalent terminology that demands a dose listen for complete comprehension.[21]

Are hip-hoppers right or just paranoid? If it is paranoia, is it "paranoia within reason" (as some anthropologists have labeled contemporary forms), another argument for not dismissing it out of hand?[22] With respect to African Americans, is this a "healthy paranoia" birthed from a cautious remembrance of America's sordid history of racial discrimination?[23] West's brand of paranoia is endemic to hip-hop, from the fears of crooked cops to DJs covering labels on the albums they "sample" so that other DJs can't steal their tunes. It isn't just the stuff of "grafted devils" that has hip-hop hardwired to deep-seated skepticism. Media outlets have exposed this skepticism and mistrust, some of which seems quite warranted. For example, those dramatic murders of Biggie Smalls and Tupac Shakur are shrouded in conspiracies and complicities. The 1990s have resulted less in fanciful Shakur sightings than in continued discussions about the possible depth of police complicity in his and Smalls's murders. Based on the work of investigative journalists following the Biggie Smalls case, there are certainly some strange ties linking major suspects to the Los Angeles Police Department.[24] This same adversarial relationship with law enforcement made it incredibly difficult to book hip-hop shows in many of the major venues throughout the 1980s and 1990s. There was a kind of "hip-hop tax" that raised the prices of those tickets relative to pop and heavy metal gatherings, even without hard evidence that hip-hop concerts produced markedly more actual violence. Sensationalized portrayals of hip-hop violence in the media seem to make concert promoters and city governments all the more paranoid about what might happen at a hip-hop performance in their town. Hip-hop has come to stand in for all kinds of potential violence, which means that hip-hop concerts are often treated differently, policed more stringently—and not just concerts.

I remember going to see the 50 Cent movie *Get Rich or Die Tryin'* in a suburb outside of Chicago in 2004 and being shocked to find police officers stationed inside the actual movie theater—not just in the lobby, not just on the sidewalk out front, but inside the movie theater itself. Six police officers stood at the front of the auditorium and watched us watch the film.[25] In some ways, it makes sense that hip-hop brings out the paranoia in people. After all, it is a musical genre that highlights the role of racial paranoia in its very style and storytelling. The aesthetics of hip-hop promote open secrecies, the kinds that conspiracy theories thrive on. The acoustic layerings, the purposeful redefining of terms, and the verbal dexterities of its rhetoricians all promote a rigorous insiderism that shields casual listeners from some of hip-hop's more paranoid claims and fools them into missing the spiritual emphasis of the music, an emphasis that starts with a fundamental faith in "feeling" over seeing.[26] The more you can feel, the less you need to see. Literally.

In the 1998 film *Belly*, hip-hop MC Nas plays a well-meaning gangster and thief named Sincere, a hoodlum with a heart of gold. Even though he robs clubs for extra cash, we can still tell that he's a good person, that he really means well. God knows his heart, but so do we, the movie-goers. Sincere's partner, Tommy, played by hip-hop star DMX, actually morphs, by the end of the film, from a cold-blooded assassin into a sincere believer in the Nation of Islam-like religious organization that he was supposed to infiltrate and bring down for the government.

Made by hip-hop music-video director Hype Williams, *Belly* is about the dark impossibility of knowing what's inside other people—in their minds, in their hearts, in their souls, even in their bellies.[27] That philosophy, just like the hip-hop aesthetic described above, is carried over into the way the film is shot. Williams purposefully shoots the scenes dark, some almost pitch black, to the point that they seem underexposed. This darkness even makes it hard to see the action during certain sequences. You squint uselessly, trying to figure out what is going on. This emphasis on darkness, this humbling of vision and the access to knowledge it provides, is at the heart of the impenetrabilities that hip-hop culture demands. And *Belly* is a great example of how those sensibilities—dark, spiritual and suspicious—follow hip-hop wherever it goes, even to the big screen.

Study Questions

1. What is the name of the "esoteric philosophies" often referred to by MCs in hip hop songs during the 1980s? What about this terminology does Jackson see as important and vital in understanding race and religion in hip hop culture?
2. What vision of society does the lessons of The Five Percent Nation as expressed through hip hop MCs advocate for and on behalf of? What type of semantic slippage, linguistic manipulations and altered ethics and meaning are involved in this lyrical process?
3. How are traditional notions of belief, spirituality and race altered in the trend of "conscious" hip hop culture and rap music?

Notes

1. Skelly is a street game we played on the sidewalk with bottle caps where you have to successfully negotiate a board (usually drawn out on the concrete itself) while hitting other competitors' bottle caps with your own and avoiding their attempts to do the same thing to you.
2. Although not a general Islamic principle, this idea of the black scientist Yakub's concocting whites in a laboratory is central to the Nation of Islam's traditional racial cosmology. For a look at African American versions of Islam that place that phenomenon into a larger global context, see Melani McAlister, *Epic Encounters: Culture, Media, and U.S. Interests in the Middle East, 1945–2000* (Berkeley: University of California Press, 2001), especially chapter 2, "The Middle East in African American Cultural Politics, 1955–1972," 84–124.
3. For a discussion of the Five Percenters and their relationship to New York City politics, see Barry Gottehrer, *The Mayor's Man* (Garden City, NY: Doubleday, 1975). Hip-hop's origin story is more complex and controversial than some believe, and "hip-hop experts" (in the academy and outside of it) have been debating its finer points for years.
4. There are many hip-hop artists who emphasize the belief that corporations are conspiring against "conscious rap," using their multinational power to promote the worst forms of self-degrading and depolitical rap. For some context to these accusations, see S. Craig Watkins, *Hip Hop Matters: Politics, Pop Culture, and the Struggle for the Soul of a Movement* (Boston: Beacon Press, 2005).
5. Everything is chalked up to what some hip-hop artists call "tricknology," a popular term birthed out of the tendency of groups like the Five Percenters, the Black Hebrews (in Israel), and the Rastafarians (in Jamaica) to coin new words as a way of challenging assumptions embedded in old ones (for instance, instead of "understanding" the world you are implored to "overstand" it). "Tricknology" marks technology's susceptibility to manipulation at the hands of secret groups hell-bent on engineering global (and racist) conspiracies.
6. We create meanings with words more than merely reflect them. Some advocates of political correctness argue that this is precisely why language matters—in the Sapir-Whorfian sense that they determine our world, rather that just passively reflecting it.
7. The African Hebrews of Jerusalem talk a lot about "the power to define," renaming many common terms that they believe are misnamed: a "diet" becomes a "live-it," the "Dead Sea" is the "Sea of Life," and you "rise" (not "fall") into love. My next book project is an extended ethnographic study of this fascinating and thriving transnational African American community based in southern Israel.
8. For a discussion of hip-hop's "impenetrability" in the context of a larger analysis of its politics and aesthetics, see Imani Perry, Prophets of the Hood: Politics and Poetics in Hip-Hop (Durham, NC: Duke University Press, 2004), especially 50–51.
9. Hip-hop's seemingly hurly-burly aesthetic actively promotes indecipherability and exclusion, making it much easier for artists to offer up their racial conspiracies in songs that can be played over the radio without many listeners being the wiser.

10. For more on vision, its imagined seductions and shortcomings, see Martin Jay, *Downcast Eyes: The Denigration of Vision in Twentieth-Century French Thought* (Berkeley: University of California Press, 1993), and David Michael Levin, ed., *Modernity and the Hegemony of Vision* (Berkeley: University of California Press, 1993).

11. Malcolm Gladwell, *Blink: The Power of Thinking without Thinking* (New York: Little, Brown, 2005).

12. There are many powerful books on hip-hop. For one recent anthology of hip-hop, see Murray Forman and Mark Anthony Neal, *That's the Joint! The Hip-Hop Studies Reader* (New York: Routledge, 2004). One of the canonical takes on hip-hop is Tricia Rose *Black Noise: Rap Music and Black Culture in Contemporary America* (Middletown, CT: Wesleyan University Press, 1994).

13. For an overview of John Walker Lindh's life (and an argument that links questions of sexuality to a theory about how he ended up in Afghanistan), read Sara Jess and Gabriel Beck, *John Walker Lindh: American Taliban* (California: University Press, 2002). For a look at Islam's emphasis on hip-hop, see Felicia Miyakawa, *Five Percenter Rap: God Hops Music, Message, and Black Muslim Mission* (Bloomington: Indiana University, 2005). For a general overview of hip-hop history, see Jeff Chang, *Can't Stop, Won't Stop: A History of the Hip-Hop Generation* (New York: St. Martin's Press, 2005).

14. Bakari Kitwana, *Why White Kids Love Hip-Hop: Wanksters, Wiggers, Wannabes, and the New Reality of Race in America* (New York: Basic Civitas, 2005).

15. James Best, "Black Like Me: John Walker Lindh's Hip-Hop Daze," *East Bay Express,* September 3, 2003. Also see Jess and Beck, *John Walker Lindh: American Taliban.*

16. Of course, even Dr. Dre sneaks conspiratorial references into his lyrics, and not just the kinds I discuss later in this chapter with respect to NWA, his former group. In "Been There, Done That," Dre rhymes, "If money is the root, I want the whole damn tree / Ain't trying to stick around for the Illuminati." Even his emphasis on making money doesn't stop him referencing one of global conspiracy theories' biggest culprits.

17. For a contextualized discussion of this religious group, see Edward E. Curtis IV, *Black Muslim Religion in the Nation of Islam, 1960–1975* (Chapel Hill: University of North Carolina Press, 2006). There are many significant books on African American Muslims not affiliated with the Nation of Islam; one of my favorites is Carolyn Rouse, *Engaged Surrender: African American Women and Islam* (Berkeley: University of California Press, 2004). This Nation of Islam invocation of genes and race (Yakub's grafting of whiteness) dovetails quite easily with Cress-Welsing and the other genetic arguments for interracial antagonism (even if Cress-Welsing doesn't necessarily posit the black origins of "recessive" whiteness in a laboratory.

18. Paul Touch, "The Black White Supremacist," In *The New York Times,* May 25, 2003.

19. The idea goes back as far as Emile Durkheim's notion of "social facts" (even to Georg Hegel and before), but one of the more recently canonized versions of the argument is found in Peter L. Berger and Thomas Luckmann, *The Social Construction of Reality: A Treatise in the Sociology of Knowledge* (New York: Anchor Books, 1967).

20. Tough, "The Black White Supremacist."

21. In yet another song, when Kanye West raps about racism being alive and hidden in contemporary America, the evidence he uses to make his case is the fact that he is even forced to show his ID when he goes to shop at a place like Sam's Club. Of course, Sam's Club makes everyone show their Sam's Club ID, don't they? But who has to show another form of ID on top of that, just to make sure that the faded-out Sam's Club ID is theirs?

22. See George Marcus, *Paranoia within Reason: A Casebook on Conspiracy as Explanation* (Chicago: University of Chicago Press, 1999).

23. See William H. Grier and Price M. Cobbs, *Black Rage* (New York: Basic Books, 1968); Eugene B. Redmond, "Introduction: The Ancient and Recent Voices within Henry Dumas," *Black American Literature Forum* 22, no. 2 (summer 1988): 143–54.

24. Randall Sullivan, *Labyrinth: A Detective Investigates the Murders of Tupac Shakur and Notorious B.I. G., the Implication of Death Row Records' Suge Knight, and the Origins of the Los Angeles Police Scandal* (New York: Grove Press, 2002).

25. We can also ask Detroit's so-called hip-hop mayor, Kwame Kirkpatrick, about the negative associations that glom onto hip-hop and its ambassadors, associations that have helped fuel attacks on

his administration since the first day he took office. For more discussion about him, see Natalie Hopkinson and Natalie Y. Moore, *Deconstructing Tyrone: A New Look at Black Masculinity in the Hip-Hop Generation* (San Francisco: Cleis Press, 2006).

26. I should just shout out to one twenty-eight-year-old hip hop fan who told me that he's sure the FBI isn't fooled by hip hop (or by its incomprehensibility): "They know," he said. "'They hire folks to know."

27. Even the movie poster is all black, all blackness, with just the two main actors' heads and hands indicating that they are even there.

Part III
The Religious Aesthetics of Hip Hop Culture

From an area of study that, at first, had to work hard to legitimate its merit for academic reflection, to prove its "secular" dimensions were worthy of "sacred" analysis and attention, this part bypasses altogether the field's initial concerns that dominated the early years of scholarship to explore more risky features of hip hop's religious aesthetics through untapped sources and underutilized methods of analysis. The challenges of what was once seemingly off-limits in academia writ large and slow to be taken up in areas such as religious studies is here obliterated with more provocative claims and productively risky hooks. Here we begin not by considering themes such as "protest" and "prophecy" as indicative of the formative years, but rather, with new approaches to (the often) forgotten elements of hip hop culture such as DJing or a consideration of not only pain and marginality but also sustained reflection of themes once considered too profane—such as pleasure and desire. Here—much like the preceding part—the search for meaning in hip hop, per se, is extended—in some cases further troubled—as attention to things such as the body, ritual activity and practice, human ingenuity, the problem of evil, musical composition and arrangement, dance, and visual production is offered sustained attention. That reconciling the sacred and the profane dominated much foundational work in religion and hip hop studies is of no surprise—for to keep them separate is to ultimately maintain lines of rigidity and division that sort and manage insider from outsider—i.e., what is legitimate for the study of religion and what is out of bounds. This part highlights such strides and advancements in the field while making room for a more specific conversation about formative yet under-engaged features—aesthetic in nature—often left untapped on the sidelines of religion and hip hop scholarship.

This part begins in and with a thought experiment of thinking the category of religion in and through the erotic—pleasure and sensuality. The perpetual rehearsal of calling attention to hip hop's social ills, such as the glorification of violence or the over-sexualization of bodies for instance (so much so that it is most difficult for some to conceive of the "sacred" in the "profane" of hip hop) has, quite often, shortchanged and stifled discussions and conversations on pleasure and desire in hip hop. Similarly, although earlier works tended to focus on Christianity, later moves to expand attention to religious sensibilities in hip hop often came at an expense of marginalization. Whether the erotic as a form of religion, DJing as unspoken religion, a consideration of the technical aesthetic patterns and relationships within music videos and musical composition or a reminder that the "spirit" that some argue holds together the African diaspora has always been connected to and with hip hop culture.

Here, we begin with the bold assertion that the erotic is religious—that the erotic as expressed in cultural modalities such as music, among others, deserves serious attention by scholars of religion—on its own terms. Rethinking the dimensions of the erotic—in embodied ways that mark movement, knowledge production and acquisition, and the attainment of power highlights that something like the erotic—as redefined through attention to rap music and located within human mobility in *this* world—can be seen as and understood through the religious. Throughout this part—we are reminded that a disproportionate attention to analyzing rap lyrics has often come at the expense of ignoring practices that were once considered foundational elements of hip hop culture—such as DJing and battling. Here, we revisit these historic elements as played out in contemporary ways on an international scale. Just like the erotic, DJ battles can, and often do, represent ritualization and practice through movement and sonic flow—another opportunity to rethink the religious by privileging hip hop practices. In this part, we not only revisit historical elements of hip hop culture, but also, influential claims and debates that emerged at the intersection of religion and music more generally and African American religion and culture in particular.

Talk of suffering has never been separate from religion and culture—in fact, suffering and its structural realities and effects has persisted as a key ingredient in the discourse and scholarship on hip hop culture and talk of suffering in hip hop, has, quite often, been weighed as somewhat religious in nature. But here, we consider the significance of human importance and centrality in rap music in lyrical engagement with and about god, evil or suffering as *secular* articulations of theodicy. In other words, here, the idea of theodicy which has long been hijacked *as* inherently religious and about god repositions humanity back at the center and attention on and to human concern over choice, ethics and the world. Questions of "why" are questions of and/or about meaning—a concept continually on trial in religion and hip hop scholarship by often focusing on the self-evident meaning in lyrics alone.

This third part begins the work of broadening and thickening aesthetic attention and analysis in hip hop culture which brings us to a consideration of gospel rap and how "irreconcilable" meaning, among other things, is shaped through the mechanics of musical composition. Again, the call for more robust frameworks and approaches emerges as the data under study become more varied, complex and robust. Finally, it is suggested that at its inception, hip hop—and the cypher that is hip hop—are held together through community, gods, enslavement and freedom of bodies and spirit that are further linked to African diasporic religions and cosmologies. Tracing the historic and aesthetic connections between the ties that bind between diasporic African religions and the birth of hip hop, we are reminded that some of hip hop's most important founders sampled, in their life and work, remixed and altered Africana religions. What does attention to the aesthetics of hip hop practices, broadly conceived, enable for thinking further about religion? Does attention to aesthetics from a posture of praise rather than protest limit or expand our ability to be critics of hip hop? How can thinking about the category of religion through untapped and far too often forgotten or ignored sources help to advance future study?

8

Intersecting Points
The "Erotic as Religious" in the Lyrics of Missy Elliott

Simon-Guillory explores the relationship between the erotic and religious by first considering previous work that makes use of literature and music to unpack the erotic as a viable source of the religious. She argues that previous scholarship explores the erotic polyvocally as politics and/or aesthetics but not clearly as one distinct thing or another, thus offering little attention to the erotic as sensuality and the ways in which the erotic acquires and actualizes certain types of religious knowledge. Simon-Guillory suggests rap music as a viable source for exploring the complexity of the erotic's nature, which she takes up by excavating the music of rapper Missy "Misdemeanor" Elliot to argue for the erotic as religious. Simon-Guillory uses the work of Missy Elliot as a case study through which she concludes the erotic is about movement toward the world, apprehension of knowledge, and a powerful force. Simon-Guillory ends by calling for an expansion of source material, such as rap music, for the study of the erotic and religious structure and multifaceted nature as expressed in culture.

Intersecting Points: The "Erotic as Religious" in the Lyrics of Missy Elliott

Margarita L. Simon Guillory

Published in 2004, *Loving the body: Black religious studies and the erotic* represented an early effort in African-American religious studies to explore the erotic across disciplines including ethics, biblical studies, pastoral studies, theology, musical studies, hermeneutics/ cultural criticism and sociology of religion. I am particularly interested in the ways in which musical production figured into the discussion of the nature and meaning of the erotic. Utilising literary narratives, biblical figures, and music as sources to explore the erotic, Baker-Fletcher and Kirk-Duggan advanced what Tricia Rose calls a "polyvocal approach." This approach creates a space of discussion in which the erotic is interpreted in multiple and distinctive ways. For instance, the erotic was not identified solely with sensuality, but instead these scholars presented the erotic as a source of power utilised in politics and aesthetics. While methodologically this polyvocal approach has allowed scholars to explore the erotic with more creativity and epistemological flexibility, certain complexities associated with the erotic's nature and function still remain under-explored, such as the erotic's role in the initiation, actualisation and apprehension of certain types of religious knowledge. What other material can be used to penetrate the deep recesses of the erotic's complexities? The lyrics of rap music offer scholars specialising in African-American religious experience in particular and larger audiences in general, yet another opportunity to explore the complexity of the erotic's nature as well as its function. My intention, then, is to excavate the lyrical content of rap music, specifically the work of Missy "Misdemeanor" Elliott, to demonstrate rap music's ability to operate as viable source material in exploring the "erotic as religious."

To accomplish this work, I find it important to delineate the complex way in which religion and the erotic intersect by looking at the work of historian of religion Charles Long, particularly his theory of religion as orientation. Secondly, I offer a synopsis of how womanist scholars approach the complexity of the erotic because this examination reveals progress made with respect to the erotic as well as an opportunity to problematise certain complexities related to the erotic's nature and function that remain under-explored. In addition, a comprehensive notion of the erotic—premised upon an understanding of the term by Lorde and Tillich—will be established in the third section. And, the last section utilises an "admixture-notion" of the erotic—developed in the previous section—as interpretative lens to magnify and explore the nature and operation of the erotic in the lyrical content of Missy "Misdemeanor" Elliott.

Intersecting Points: The Erotic and Religion

The erotic is a connective force, meaning that its very nature involves the pushing together of entities resulting in the formation of connections. The erotic seeks to move individual(s) towards the world—either through the formation of subject–subject or subject–object associations. It is important to note that both the position of object and subject, entities that the erotic moves one towards, can be one of materiality or metaphysically oriented. In order for this movement to occur the subject must undergo a movement or a positional change. In other words, the subject, in order to move towards a type of erotically driven unification with other entities of the world, is oriented. This orientation occurs as a result of the charging of one's centeredness through the process of actualisation by the erotic. Thus, orientation, in regards to the erotic, fosters movement, and this movement yields an apprehension of knowledge concerning the entities involved in the unitative process. It is this type of orientation that historian of religion Long equates to his understanding of religion. According to Long (1995, 7), religion represents a direct correlation between orientation and the way in which individuals or communities come to understand their specific position or "ultimate significance" in the world. Since the erotic is representative of one of the many driving forces which seeks to move entities towards this same world or ultimate significance, it can be concluded that this force is an integral dimension in gaining understanding of one's placement.

Not only does Long equate religion with a type of orientation, but he also refuses to restrict the sources which can be utilised in the investigation of religion in general and African-American religion in particular. After acknowledging the importance of, but not restriction to, Christianity in the formulation of certain aspect of African-American religion, he goes a step further by locating religious sensibilities in art, music, narratives, and other cultural productions operating within the African-American community (Long 1995, 2). Not only can these forms be utilised in exploring religion, that is, "orientation" in the world, but these forms also possess possibilities of gaining a more comprehensive understanding of the nature and operation of the erotic within lived experiences.

Womanist Engagement of the Erotic: Two Models

In defining eros, Baker-Fletcher—sifting through an extended conversation occurring between Phaedrus, Agathon and Socrates as explored in Plato's *Symposium*—presents eros as a force of unification. It is a force that connects both bodies as well as souls. Although Baker-Fletcher initiates her exploration of eros in dialogue with Plato's conception, she also utilises an interpretation of eros purported in Audre Lorde's essay, entitled Uses of the Erotic: The Erotic as Power, to further extend her understanding. Specifically, she incorporates Lorde's understanding of eros as a type of power. A force that Lorde maintains is harnessed within the interior cavity of women, which initiates creativity, knowledge, and the ability to recognize and fight systems of oppression that tends to suppress this power.

Baker-Fletcher identifies the "Hush Harbor" as a place where African American women freely express their views with respect to their sexuality. Baker-Fletcher begins by acknowledging a type of over-consuming silence in the lives of African American women concerning matters of sex in general—a silence reinforced by the advice of maternal figures who stressed the importance of keeping all matters pertaining to sex to themselves. Baker-Fletcher understands this silence as one that seems to "closet" and restrict the vocality of African American women regarding their sexual lives. However, the "Hush Harbor," as a space represented in both geographical and metaphorical forms, symbolises a safe haven in which "black women

[can] clearly hear their own voices and God's response" (Baker-Fletcher 2004, 206). Baker-Fletcher creatively illustrates how the literary work of African American women like Zora Neale Hurston and Alice Walker has served as "sacred" spaces, or "Hush Harbors" in which the discussion of the sexuality of African American women in particular and human sexuality in general is discussed without restriction or limitation. And with this utilisation of African American literary narrative Baker-Fletcher purports an understanding of sexuality that includes but is not limited to sex, an understanding in which sexuality serves a platform in which one becomes familiar with oneself, others, and life in general.

Like Baker-Fletcher, Kirk-Duggan initiates discourse on the erotic with Plato's understanding of the erotic as an impulse that embodies sensuality. She also pays tribute to Lorde's presentation of the erotic as an embodied female force—a force of creativity that embraces the totality of an individual—including the psychical, physical, and the cerebral dimensions. However, instead of employing literary works, Kirk-Duggan uses both biblical texts and music to explore the erotic. For example, the dance of Salome and David, according to Kirk-Duggan, illustrates the erotic in metaphorical form. The dances of both of these biblical figures symbolise the convoluted structure of the erotic one that includes the operation of the "political, spiritual physical, powerful aesthetic of embodied, sensual, intimate desire" (Kirk-Duggan 2004, 222).

Kirk-Duggan further uncoils the structure of the erotic by using Salome and David's dance as a hermeneutical lens by which to magnify the operation of the erotic in the music of Alberta Hunter, Marvin Gaye, Tupac Shakur and Shirley Caesar. For example, Kirk-Duggan presents Salome's dance as a metaphorical representation of the erotic in the form of sensuality and intimacy. Utilising these erotic representations as primers, she moves down the helical strands of music. What does she uncover? The music of Hunter and Caesar, although representing two different genres, serves as palette where the erotic expresses itself both as relational and transformative. With respect to Gaye, the erotic represents itself as one that encapsulates sensuality, connectivity, political/social protest and love. According to Kirk-Duggan, the music of Tupac, like the dance of Salome and David, is metaphorical. It is metaphorical in the sense that it contains in code form the daily-lived experiences that "connect with the senses, the body, life in community, and power in search of love and peace" (Kirk-Duggan 2004, 227).

Limiting the Complexity of the Erotic

In Baker-Fletcher's analysis of the erotic as found in literary writings of African American women, there is a specific type of relationship developed between eros and sexuality. Although she illustrates the unifying capabilities of the erotic with Walker's character Queen Anne (Baker-Fletcher 2004, 211)—a character that acknowledges the viability of body via union with creation—it seems that the exposition of the other tracts of literary works leads to an explicit discussion of the sexuality of African American women. In this respect are the terms erotic and sexuality synonymous? Are they interchangeable?

While the employment of literary sources written by African American women suggests a space, where sexuality can be discussed, is it possible to explore the multiple dimensions of the erotic based on the sole use of these sources without reducing the erotic itself as an identity based on just one of its properties, like sensuality or sexuality? The selected source material possesses a metaphorical structure. For instance, Baker-Fletcher's use of literary sources whose characters employ metaphorical language to express notions of sexuality further perpetuates an ethos of "quiet grace, unshouted courage, and invisible dignity" (Cannon 1988, 159). Within this type of ethos are African American women afforded a type of radical freedom that is needed when expressing some matters of sexuality like sexual orientation? How can one view the complexities of the erotic if there is a continuation of limiting analysis of sources that speak of the erotic in metaphorical language? In short, the erotic continues to wear a veil—a semi-transparent covering which exposes some parts of the face while hiding others. A veil that may allow one to see the shadowy outlines of the erotic's face while at the same time concealing an entire view of the naked face of the erotic.

Kirk-Duggan, in her exposition of the erotic in music, illustrates some of the complexities that surround the nature of the erotic. Although she gives a biographical sketch of each performer along with a description of styles utilised by each, the absence of more in-depth lyrical content seems to place the reader in a position in which he/she must trust that the descriptive accounts parallel with the repository of lyrics that each performer has built up over the years. In short, analysing a wider range of lyrics could have presented different images of the erotic, where by one can assess more fully the multidimensionality of the erotic. Without examining the lyrical content over each performer's career how can one paint a comprehensive picture of the erotic? For example, how does the erotic operate or show itself in Tupac's early works over against later materials?

In not treating each performer as a case study with respect to lyrical content, the structural composition of the erotic may be unintentionally narrowed. For instance, although Kirk-Duggan identifies a relationship between Tupac's music and lived experiences; commends him for his adoration of the body via personal tattoos; and celebrates his explicit protest against social and political forces of oppression, she portrays the erotic in Tupac's music as being one that "sensationalizes sex"—a quality that "skew[s] a healthy notion of the erotic" (Kirk-Duggan 2004, 227). Based on this conclusion, does an overarching understanding of the erotic as a force that contains both healthy and unhealthy elements parallel the author's overarching description of the erotic manifesting itself within Tupac as one who embraces aesthetics, embodies sexuality, and serves as an "energizing source for human integrating of mind, body, and spirit" (Kirk-Duggan 2004, 229)? In addition to Lorde's conception of the erotic, could not a Tillichian approach to the erotic—one that acknowledges both the constructive and destructive nature of eros—create a space in which the "healthiness" and "unhealthiness" within the lyrics of Tupac, or for that matter any other musician, be discussed? Or, does the multi-dimensionality of the erotic become stifled or labelled due to either the way in which the source material is utilised, or due to the amount of data, in this case musical content, actually utilised in the exploration of, for this article's purpose, the erotic?

Expanding the Erotic's Boundaries: Audre Lorde and Paul Tillich

The Greek notion of eros, especially as proposed by Plato, served as an instrumental factor in a particular understanding of the erotic offered by both Lorde and Tillich. In each of these thinkers' handling of the definition and function of the erotic there are some fundamental differences as well as distinct areas of overlap that are worth noting. According to Lorde, the erotic as an embodied force—a force located and operating in the deep recesses of the female—provides those who tap into it the necessary power to propagate change, specifically change regarding the eradication of oppressive structures in social, economical and political spheres. For Tillich the erotic does not represent a strictly gender-specific embodied force, but it is a divine–human driving force seeking to overcome estrangement—symbolising the creation of space between humanity and its original or true state, a pre-existing existence devoid of separation. While there may be some noticeable differences between Lorde's and Tillich's perception of the erotic, the similarities existing between the way in which these two thinkers approach the erotic, whether embodied or not, create a comprehensive view of the erotic, a view displaying the multi-dimensionality of the erotic itself.

As a way of addressing lingering questions connected to the approaches noted above, I propose a combination, an "admixture-notion," that is a methodological mixing of both Lorde and Tillich's understanding of the erotic—which combined displaying the erotic as a convoluted force that exhibits a specific nature, function, and place of manifestation. So conceived, the erotic is connective in nature, constantly pursuing union whether between person/self, person/person, person/object, person/world and/or person/divine with the hopes of achieving both an internal and external fulfilment. It is important to note that this type of union for Lorde involves the establishment of the inner self with the embodied erotic and it is this movement of self towards the erotic that creates a space for the development of other unions. For Tillich, the erotic's unitive nature involves overcoming a type of alienation he calls estrangement—a term symbolising the creation of space between humanity and its original state. And in its attempt to unify a type of knowledge—a knowledge that Lorde calls "erotic knowledge" (Lorde 2001, 237) and one that Tillich (1951, 95) acknowledges as "cognitive eros"—a term borrowed from Plato—is ascertained. Thus, a direct relationship exists between the erotic's nature and operation, for in its drive to continuously connect entities the erotic becomes the "driving force in all cultural creativity"; (1954, 117) and teaches one to strive towards excellence; initiates, strengthens, sustains, and promotes knowledge.

According to both thinkers, this type of knowledge is obtained via the movement of the erotic within life experiences. The erotic acts as a participatory force, manifesting itself in the "whole complex of persons, things, creatures, and ideas which constitute the "world" of human experience" (Irwin 1991, 85). It is a type of energy permeating one's life in that it, as Lorde attests, "heightens and sensitizes all my experiences" (Lorde 288). In short, the erotic connects, creates, and moves within the lived experiences of individuals as well as communities.

Erotic Expression and Function in the Lyrics of Missy "Misdemeanor" Elliott

Because the erotic manifests itself within the lived experiences of people, it is important to utilise sources that have the potential to encapsulate and highlight everyday experiences as lived. The lyrical arsenal of Missy "Misdemeanor" Elliott (Missy) presents an opportunity to investigate the erotic. Not only does Missy's work offer a multiplicity of data points, but her lyrics are also indicative of her life experiences. The latter is not an assumption because in an interview with Demitri Ehrlich of Interview she states "Music is what I live"[1] and in another interview shares with the interviewer that "If you listen to my songs, they tell stories."[2] It is because of this parallelism that Missy establishes between life and lyrics—in which such experiences occur—and moreover, provide the researcher with a more reliable source to explore the erotic as expressed in lived experiences. It is at this lyrical site where the erotic excavation begins.

The erotic, in order to drive humans towards the world, must initiate a process called actualisation. This process is indicative of a coming into self and accepting the distinct quality possessed by that same self (Jung 1959, 143). More specifically, Tillich defines this actualisation process as a movement from one's centre (Tillich 1963, 30). This centre symbolises a place of containment for actualisation in its passive state. Passivity of the centre equates to the state of the individual that contains the centre. The erotic serves as the necessary catalyst that initiates actualisation. This activation leads the individual to recognise his or her own centredness. It is this erotically charged actualisation—recognition of one's centredness—that creates a comfort within self, and it is this comfort that creates a sense of self-cohesion. Although examples of this process of activating one's centre is exemplified throughout Missy's lyrical arsenal, her last album entitled Cookbook explicitly presents the erotic's role in actualisation. In "Lose Control" she states, "I've got a cute face, chubby waist; Thick legs in shape, make you a double take; Plan rocka show stopa, flo froppa, head knocka; Beat stalla, tail droppa … Long weave sewed in; Say it again, sewed in …"[3] In "Joy" she proclaims, "They try to stop a chubby chick from comin through; My belly out and selling out these venues; My skills will fulfil those who drink booze; My attitude is super cool like I'm subdued."[4] According to these lyrics actualisation is manifested in the form of Missy's acceptance of her own physical body. It is this possession of a sense of self, propagated by the charging of her centre by the erotic, which supplies Missy with the tenacity to embrace her physical dimensions—expressed in the acknowledgement of a chubby waist, belly, thick legs, huge butt, and synthetic hair.

In response to this catalytic action submitted by the erotic, the human, or in this case Missy, apprehends self-awareness and it is in this identity of self that releases the individual from the bondage of self-centeredness. This freedom empowers the individual to "reach outward beyond the boundaries of [herself] toward communion [and] encounter with the world" (Irwin 1991, 85). The world is representative of organic forms like other humans and animals; inorganic forms as in material objects; and lastly other subjects whose forms may lie within the spiritual and/or psychical. In short, the erotic moves a person or subject world towards this point of connection, the world. Under the guidance of the erotic, the person possessing a charged centre, due to her/his desire to be in union with the world, moves toward the entity, whether temporal or non-temporal. In short, the subject or person moves toward the world.

Missy, in a rhyme called "Can You Hear Me?" expresses this type of movement—a movement occurring as a result of erotic-driven actualisation in which she has accepted and lyrically expressed—and desire for union outside of herself. This particular piece illustrates the erotic acting as a connective force in the unification of a subject, Missy, with another subject(s):

> I been checking on your moms and dad
> … since the day you left …
> But you mom its been so damn hard …
> Aaliyah she asked me why …
> Can you give me better words to say.
>
> Aaliyah can you hear me
> I hope that you're proud of me …
> I ain't never met a friend more incredible.[5]

As exhibited in this rap, the death of her best friend Aaliyah is an external reality for Missy, and in facing this reality she has had to become aware of the fragility associated with fragmented familial relationships, the toll of emotional hardships, and even questions concerning theodicy, presented by Aaliyah's mother. As shown in "Lose Control" and "Joy," Missy possesses the self-actualisation and self-acceptance needed in order to move outside of herself with respect to the death of her friend. An erotically charged desire for union causes Missy to attend to the needs of her friend's parents and siblings. She moves beyond herself. The erotic causes her to travel beyond the boundaries of her once passive centre. Even more than that, her movement outside of self causes her to desire union with her friend who is no longer living within the temporal realm. Yet, how does one characterize Aaliyah's "form"? Is she spiritual? Psychical?

According to Tillich, the erotic is not so much concerned with the form of the entity that Missy moves towards, whether it is between temporal subject and temporal subject(s) as in the case with Missy and Aaliyah's family or between temporal subject and non-temporal subject. Regardless of the form, both are subjects who possess the ability to undergo the connective force of the erotic. Thus, although Aaliyah may not be present with respect to materiality, the erotic still fuels the desire to move. Therefore, Missy, in her talking to Aaliyah in rap form, not only illustrates desire for union, but she also, through sharing career opportunities, re-playing of her friend's physical features and seeking a reply from Aaliyah, maintains that union has been achieved with her friend who has "passed on and went away with God."

While the nature of the erotic continuously drives one towards union with the world, the apprehension of a certain type of knowledge occurs via subject–object and subject–subject relationships. Hence, ascertaining this knowledge involves conjugation—a condition of being joined together—of subject–object and/or subject–subject. An eradication of space precedes the unification of two acting members via "cognitive eros," a driving force specifically occurring in the method of knowing (Tillich 1951, 94–5). In this, the erotic serves as an agent of connectivity between the subject–object and subject–subject. Under the driving force of the erotic, the mind is empowered breaking free from cognitive stagnation and complacency while moving towards cognitive enlightenment.

The erotic's drive to gradually eliminate the existing space between subject–object and subject–subject in the process of knowing utilises reciprocity. Reciprocity involves a state of mutuality. It represents a mutual exchange between the entities which are to be adjoined. The process of reciprocation symbolises an open communication occurring between, for example, a subject and an object. This process evolves as the erotic moves towards "intuition," the ability of the subject to visibly penetrate beyond the surface physicality of the object [or subject] (Tillich 1955, 129).

Missy and Genuwine, a male R&B singer, explicate this matter of ascertaining knowledge via reciprocity occurring between subject–subject in the following lyrical account in which she initiates by stating:

> You're so incredible
> Ever since the day we became … so personal …
> Take away your gold and platinum chains
> And I'm gonna love you baby …
> Not goin nowhere. …[6]

The move of the erotic causes Missy, i.e. "the subject," to see beyond Genuwine's surface which is representative in the form of material possessions. Thus Missy, because of the erotic, possesses the ability to see the engaging ontological elements of Genuwine—the sacrificing of his time to spend with her and his ability to show love via their various encounters. It is a combination of this insight into ontological and the driving force of the erotic that causes Missy to move towards the subject. And in this move she sees, she learns. Genuwine in the same lyrical poem responds,

> … let's make it national …
> I'm in love …[7]

With erotically-driven insight, Genuwine who symbolises the other subject possesses the ability to see past, see beyond, and see through the surface layers of Missy; he sees her beautiful ontological qualities. With this intuition he does not attempt to simply master her but instead acknowledges and respects these qualities. This he makes known in his announcement to both the world and other women who may attempt to wedge themselves between the two of them. Hence, it is this reciprocated exchange between the subject and subject that fosters the development of an "erotic knowledge," a wellspring of information that can unlock dimensions of the sensual, anatomical, emotional and psychical (Lorde 2001, 288). A reciprocated exchange serving as a catalyst in the creation of an ethos built upon a premise of sharing. A sharing of passion, joy, and an erotically charged unity is attested to in the terminating lyrics of this same song in which they both exclaim,

> I just want to be the perfect match
> You don't even have to ask ...[8]

Although the erotic places the subject in a specific posture with respect to the receptivity of knowledge, the subject's agency is vital in the determination of both union and the type of knowledge produced during this move towards union. Therefore, the subject has freedom of choice; this freedom illustrates a conditional element in the apprehension of knowledge during movement towards union. If the subject utilises the existential qualities of the object/subject gained through intuition while at the same time allowing these qualities to speak back, then reciprocity and union occurs producing erotic knowledge. However, in the formation of "controlling knowledge" (Tillich 1951, 89–90), the subject seeks control through the devaluation of ontological properties of the object/subject. In other words, the subject seeks conjugation based solely on principles of domination. This ethos of control can sometimes take place in spite of eros' drive towards intuition. The development of knowledge through the utilisation of control mechanisms foster a paradoxical relationship in which union is achieved, hence producing knowledge, but simultaneously a form of detachment also synthesizes, hence polluting the process of knowledge due to the subject's lack of involvement with the object/subject located on the other side of the union.

In "We Did It," a song released on Da Real World album, the presence of controlling knowledge can be detected in the melodic testimonial of Missy. She shares with her listeners:

> We made love, now you gone
> Now you don't wanna claim me no more
> Told your boys you never knew
> You never kissed or held me in your arms
> How dare you even leave, looking like I'm lying on you When you said it's all about me ...
> If you did it, then you did it
> Boy, you don't have to lie
> Once you hit it, then you hit it
> I'm no chick on the side
> Just forget it, gon' omit it
> Don't you, don't you dare try
> You done hit it, you done hit it
> More than, more than two times ...[9]

The lyrics suggest the establishment of a type of connectivity between two subjects, Missy and her unidentified partner. Based on the lyrical content, Missy's emotional despair due to the other subject's denial of their union suggest that she once saw in him certain properties which led tomultiple sexual encounters in which they made love, or in her words "he hit it." These interactions also included kissing, hugging, and conversation. Feelings of hurt and anger lace the lyricist words due to the lack of reciprocation from the other subject. According to the lyrics, Missy believed it was all about her and that the unidentified person saw some type of ontological properties within her beyond those associated with sensation. Thus, in this case, the lack of reciprocity reduces the erotic functionality to one of sensation. According to Lorde, this is not representative of the erotic, for this force cannot be reduced to a type of "plasticized sensation" (2001, 286) and it cannot be "relegated" to the bedroom alone (2001, 288). The unnamed subject's utilisation of Missy's ontological qualities is a matter of control, and this type of control yields detachment or in this case denial. Although the lyrics maintain the occurrence of union, Tillich would attest conjugation based solely on the basis of manipulation and control within the process of knowing produces a symbiotic relationship in which one party benefits, the unnamed person, while the other, Missy, is "transformed into a completely conditioned and calculable thing" (Tillich 1951, 97). Coupled with detachment, Missy is situated in both a posture of vulnerability and hurt. Her lyrical style testimony attests to how her ontological properties have been reduced and how her openness to the reception of erotic knowledge has not been reciprocated.

The nature of the erotic to serve as a connective force not only results in the apprehension of a certain type of knowledge and the formation of union between individual entities, but this force is also instrumental in driving an individual towards community. Hence, the erotic, due to its ability to charge individual centres through actualisation, is a vital substance found within the development of a community. A community represents a mutual meeting of centred selves. Each centre symbolizes a pole of necessity, which shares interdependence with another pole; therefore, the community is a place of participatory polarity (Tillich 1951, 41). These relationships between centres are not opportunistic, not seeking to overpower the other, because the formation of communal ties is built on the premise of mutualism. This mutualism of centres correlates to the interaction between subject/object and/or subject/subject in the apprehension of erotic knowledge initiated by the erotic. Similar to the exchange found in knowledge of conciliation, each centre participating in community building recognises the ontological reality and subjective qualities of the adjacent centre. This recognition propagates interaction, exchange and re-integration of the change in the formation of a group. Drawing from Durkheim (1995, 150), one might suggest that the erotic produces "a bond of mythical sympathy join[ing] each individual to other beings that are associated with him." Therefore, the erotic symbolises a binder; it is the cohesive force that establishes the group.

Deep within the recesses of Missy's lyrical cannon, the catalysts of this notion of actualisation-movement-participation by the erotic manifest itself in a rap called "Higher Ground." She begins the opening verse with a personal proclamation:

> Obstacles and situations, people places and things
> I must overcome ...
> I'm determined to reach my goal I need peace for my soul ...[10]

In this first verse, Missy allows her audience to peek further into her lived experiences—life moments that include "obstacles and situations, people, places, and things [that] she must overcome." It is in the recognition of these "obstacles" that allows the erotic to charge Missy's centre. This charging creates an ethos of actualisation in which she establishes a type of self-connectedness, one which grants her power and "becomes a lens through which [she] scrutinize all aspects of [her] existence, forcing [herself] to evaluate those aspects honestly in terms of their relative meaning within [her] life" (Lorde 2001, 288). Exposure to this erotically charged ethos of evaluation allows Missy to experience a stirring of her own individual psyche; she sets mind on higher things. Although these higher things are not labelled, based on the ending portion of verse one, Missy, due to the erotic's role in her actualisation process, moves.

Not only is she moving towards her inner self via self-actualisation, but she also candidly describes to her listeners in the second verse a movement towards "higher ground," stating, "I'm pressin on the upward way; … No higher place that I really have found; Lord plant my feet, plant my feet on higher ground …"[11] In this discourse there appears to be a desire to connect to what she calls "higher ground." What is this "higher ground?" Does it represent a mental apprehension of ease? Is it an emotional state? Or, yet is it representative of the Christian notion of heaven? Although this "ground" she seeks to move towards is draped in metaphorical garb, she identifies one source—Missy does not identify this source as one operating exclusively—that can empower her with the necessary strength required to move towards "higher ground." Despite her petitioning of the "Lord" to help her "plant her feet," does this petitioning nullify the erotic's role in the apprehension of union between Missy and the higher ground that she seeks? No. For example, Tillich would equate Missy's longing for higher ground with her desire to connect with the divine. Hence, the strategic positioning of the erotic towards a northern pole—"upward way"—orients Missy into a position in which conjugation or union with the divine is possible. With respect to Lorde, the erotic presence in Missy's desire results in the lyricist's seeking a movement away from a position of powerlessness into to one characterized by a sense of assurance, tenacity and courage. It is movement into a new position of self-assurance that creates a space in which participation in the communal takes place. Missy's participation with the communal realm is exhibited in the terminating verse of the same song. She shares with her listeners:

> The race is not given to the swift
> Nor the battle to the strong …
> Hold on and be strong …[12]

These lyrics exemplify a specific type of connection that the erotic has nurtured between Missy and her listeners. The utilisation of inclusive language, "we," illustrates that Missy's acceptance of the erotic within her own experiences allows her to "share the feelings of those others who participate in the experience with [her]" (Lorde 2001, 289). Hence, she encourages. She testifies concerning the erotic's ability to provide power in the midst of all that is "going on." She confirms that movement towards union with a goal is larger than the struggle. And, within this ethos of community, she tells them to "hold on and be strong."

Exploring this last segment of lyrics from one of Missy's songs entitled "Wake Up" is very instrumental because not only does it allow for a continued exploration of how the erotic's nature of connectivity yields movement of individual centres towards community, but these lyrics also illustrate a type of consciousness that is created when an individual is in touch with the moving force of the erotic. Missy exclaims:

> Motherfuckers betta wake up, stop sellin crack to the black
> Hope you bought a spare for your flat
> Can't accept me talking real facts
> Down the hill like Janet Jack …
> I'm creative to the fullest …

'Cause your talkin' never kill it
I hear but don't feel it thou ain't realest …
Yeah I'm a down diva done niva
Ya'll not xena heat'll squeeze into to a wife beater …
What ya teacher need to preach ya
It's time to get serious
Black people all areas who gon' carry us, it ain't time to bury us …[13]

Missy displays a type of comfort in her own self-connectedness, and this comfort with self allows her to take up concerns with the African-American community in particular. Unlike her approach in "Higher Ground," Missy moves past the metaphorical garb and presents her naked objections, refusing to "settle for the convenient, the shoddy, the conventionally expected, nor the merely safe." She boldly operates in the actualising power of the erotic calling out the "motherfuckers" who are poisoning the community with crack cocaine. Since she has acted against her own inner oppression—a theme exhibited in each of the songs presented in this essay either in an implicit or explicit form—the erotic creates within Missy the ability to reject denigrating factors operating against the community. She accepts the erotic operating in her life as a wellspring of power for she calls those who participate in the denigration, "weak," while synonymously presenting herself as a creative and strong leader, one who is infected with the "Martin Luther King fever." This type of positioning represents a type of consciousness. A consciousness of duality promoted and nurtured by the erotic's nature which allow Missy to possess both the ability to "self-connect" and the ability to move towards community with the hopes of "sharing the erotic's electrical charge" with others via reciprocity. Reciprocity, in this sense, creates opportunities for change within African-American communities specifically related to combating real social issues like intra/inter-communal violence, educational, economic, and healthcare disparities, as well as gentrification. Although these societal factors seek to bury various African-American communities across the United States, Missy erotically proclaims, "it ain't time to bury us."

Concluding Thoughts

Internal movement yielding self-actualisation, movement towards an external world, and the apprehension of knowledge via acceptance of ontological properties of one outside of self, are all acts operative as a result of the erotic. The erotic provides momentum. Its unitive force orientates individuals in such a way that they experience internal as well as external conjugations—unitive efforts yielding positive self-identity, friendships and/or communal activity in the form of political activism. In short, this connective force is dynamic in both its nature and function, and, as a result, demands attention that surpasses its surface. Thus, based on my analysis of the erotic represented in the lyrics of Missy Elliott, I argue that it therefore becomes imperative that scholars not only utilise a variety of sources, allowing for a creative approach to the erotic, but they should also move beyond surface examinations of these same sources by utilising methodological tools in a variety of ways. Selecting specific source material, the lyrics of Missy in the form of a case study and employing a combined methodological approach, one that is an admixture of Tillich and Lorde's understanding of the erotic, offers such an example of an in-depth examination of the erotic's multidimensionality. Specifically, applying this "admixture-notion" to Missy's lyrical displays of lived experiences vividly illustrates the erotic's nature, its desire to establish connectivity through movement, and how this movement propose certain complexities surrounding the activation of awareness, participation and knowledge. Thus, the thorough employment of a variety of sources, especially those provided in the domestic as well as the global hip hop community, whether expressed in dance, clothing, videos, or the lyrics of rap itself, provides ample source material in the investigation of the erotic's structure of multi-dimensionality.

Study Questions

1. How does the work of Charles Long offer a foundation whereby Simon can forge a connection between the erotic and the religious? How are both terms defined in this study?
2. What models of womanist engagement are explored and unpacked and how have these models both advanced and limited the discussion between both terms? What does she offer as a corrective and how does she expand the erotic's boundaries?
3. What of the erotic and religious does Simon find in the music and life of Missy Elliot? How does this impact Simon's conclusions?

Notes

1. Find Articles, "Missy Elliott—Interview," Find Articles, http://findarticles.com. (Accessed November 8, 2007).
2. Find Articles, "Master Missy—Writer, Singer, Producer and Label Head," Find Articles, http://findarticles.com.
3. Missy Elliott, "Lose Control," Cookbook, Atlantic Records, 2005.
4. Missy Elliott, "Joy," Cookbook, Atlantic Records, 2005.
5. Missy Elliott, "Can You Hear Me," Under Construction, Elektra/Wea, 2002.
6. Missy Elliott, "Take Away," Miss E … So Additive, Elektra/Wea, 2001.
7. Ibid.
8. Missy Elliott, "Take Away," Miss E … So Additive, Elektra/Wea, 2001.
9. Missy Elliott, "We Did It," Da Real World, East/West Records, 1999.
10. Missy Elliott, "Higher Ground," Miss E … So Addictive, Elektra/Wea, 2001.
11. Elliott, "Higher Ground."
12. Ibid.
13. Missy Elliott, "Wake Up," This Is Not A Test, Elektra/Wea, 2003.

References

Baker-Fletcher, K. 2004. The erotic in contemporary black women's writings. In *Loving the body: Black religious studies and the erotic*, ed. Anthony B. Pinn and Dwight N. Hopkins. New York: Palgrave Macmillan.

Cannon, K. G. 1988. *Black womanist ethics*. Atlanta, GA: Scholars Press.

Durkheim, E. 1995. *The elementary forms of religious life*. New York: The Free Press.

Ehrlich, D. 2001. Missy Elliott—interview. http://findarticles.com/p/articles/mi_m1285/is_5_31/ai_74583329?tag=content;col1.

Irwin, A.C. 1991. *Eros toward the world: Paul Tillich and the theology of the erotic*. Minneapolis, MN: Fortress Press.

Jung, C.G. 1959. *The basic writings of C.G. Jung*. New York: Modern Library.

Kirk-Duggan, C. 2004. Salome's veiled dance and David's full monty: A womanist reading on the black erotic in blues, rap, R&B, and Gospel music. In *Loving the body: Black religious studies and the erotic*, ed. Anthony B. Pinn and Dwight N. Hopkins. New York: Palgrave Macmillan.

Long, C. 1995. *Significations: Signs, symbols, and images in the interpretation of religion*. Aurora: The Davies Group.

Lorde, A. 2001. Uses of the erotic: The erotic as power. In *Black feminist cultural criticism*, ed. Jacqueline Bobo. Oxford: Blackwell Publishing.

MetroLyrics. Missy Elliott lyrics. http://www.metrolyrics.com.

Musto, M. 1999. Master Missy—writer, singer, producer and label head. http://findarticles.com/p/articles/mi_m1285/is_6_29/ai_54793382.

Tillich, P. 1951. *Systematic theology*. Vol. 1. Chicago, IL: University of Chicago Press.

—— 1954. *Love, power, and justice: Ontological analyses and ethical applications*. New York and London: Oxford University Press.

—— 1955. *The new being*. New York: Charles Scribner's Sons.

——1963. *Systematic theology. Vol. III*. Chicago: University of Chicago Press.

9

Two Turntables and a Microphone
Turntablism, Ritual and Implicit Religion

According to Clay, religion and hip hop scholarship has tended to methodologically over-focus on rap music and lyrics to the detriment of other historical hip hop elements such as graffiti and turntablism. Clay offers a corrective by considering the religious dimensions of DJ battles and turntablist practices. First considering connections between implicit religion and the practice of turntablism, Clay argues that the work of Charles H. Long on religion as *orientation* and Anthony B. Pinn's theory of religion as *complex subjectivity* expand the look of implicit religion in under-explored practices. Mindful of this, she argues battling is a ritual, and offers the Heineken Green Synergy competition and the DMC World DJ Championships in Europe as examples pointing to her assertion concerning implicit religion (e.g., rituals of meaning) found in the non-verbal dimensions of hip hop. In light of her data sets and findings, she argues that turntablism constitutes religious form and practice and that battle is an opportunity to extend the shape and form of hip hop religiosity.

Two Turntables and a Microphone: Turntablism, Ritual and Implicit Religion

Elonda Clay

Introduction

During the late 1970s, turntables were reinterpreted as musical instruments in the hands of the disc jockey (DJ). This artistic reinterpretation, what is now known as turntablism, is the rearrangement of pre-recorded music and sound samples to produce new musical soundscapes and complex performance routines by manipulating at least two turntables with an audio mixer and a crossfader. Disc jockeying techniques such as cutting, scratching, mixing and backspinning are foundational to hip hop music as a cultural production.

A pertinent starting point for this article begins with its title, where the material culture of disc jockeying practices is connected to the concept of implicit religion. One might immediately question what the two have to do with each other. After all, what are the religious dimensions of turntablism? How are we to understand the cultural manifestations of hip hop as a religious phenomena? What methods would be fruitful for our investigation, especially since music, dance, sound and embodied uses of technology do not produce the same explicitly religious expressions as those put forward in the spoken or textual content of rap lyrics?

At the heart of what religious scholar Bailey (2002, 2, 4) defines as implicit religion are commitment, integrating foci and "intensive concerns with extensive effects." This definition emphasises that the quest for meaning is not narrowly limited to that which is legitimated as officially religious; instead, everyday life and subjectivity become vital to the expression of individual and collective contemporary religiosity. Historian of religion Charles Long in his discussion of religion as orientation, and religious scholar Anthony Pinn in his discussion of complex subjectivity, provide insights that are congruent with implicit religion as a quest for meaning through their affirmation of informal and formal religious forms embedded in cultural practices.

This enquiry unfolds in four discursive movements in this essay. The first section presents a foundation for understanding battling as a form of ritual practice. Next, the characteristics of battling as expressed in turntablism and DJ battles are outlined. The third section is interpretive as it conveys empirical data from the mediated presentations of two distinct international DJ battle competitions. In the final section, I will apply implicit religion as a lens of analysis to DJ battles and turntablism, drawing comparisons from Bailey's work and Pinn's work to examine the religious dimensions of turntablism.

Battling as Ritual Process and Practice

My aim in this section is to show how the activity of battling in hip hop culture can be understood as both a process and a practice. Battling is a mode of social engagement that involves irony, competition, humour, double meanings, performance and humiliation. Although battling has a ludic quality, it is almost always serious fun because battling can also be a display of power or push for social positioning. Persons participate in battles to strengthen their battling skills, play around and provoke laughter, challenge a rival, humiliate a social "other" or address a personal or social breach.

Drawing from the work of ritual scholar Grimes (1990, 10), I first posit that battling should be understood as a ritualising process. Grimes proposes that the process of ritualising is "that which happens between institutions and in the margins and as such is alternately stigmatized and eulogized." He argues that ritual processes encompass forms of ritual change, which include the historical development or revision of a rite, changing relations between rites and their social context, and the process whereby rites give birth to other rites. Accordingly, a person engaged in ritualising is also a person who "invests surfaces (exteriors) with a sense of significance" (Grimes 1982, 56–64).

As a process, battling is loosely structured by time and performance. The timing and movement of battling is usually that of a back and forth, fast moving quid pro quo; the crack (a cutting insult and challenging action) must be responded to rapidly if the person being challenged does not want to lose face. Battles are informal contests that demonstrate the vitality and creativity of two or more competitors.

Two preceding cultural practices, which have been incorporated into battling, are playing the dozens, and cutting contests. The "dozens" is a form of competitive play where "put-downs"or insults, cleverness, boasting and humour are employed as the tools of competition. Cutting contests, contests in which musicians competed against one another in highly stylised ways, were popular during the height of jazz music. In battling, the older rites of playing the dozens and cutting are revised within hip hop, while battle events provide places for the public display of adeptly mastered musical or linguistic skills.

On the other hand, how might one address the dynamics of power and hierarchy also present in battling? Ritual theorist Bell (1992, 197), in her discussion on ritual practices, argues that ritualisation is a "strategy for the construction of certain types of power relationships effective within particular social organizations." Ritualisation as a process of performing rituals is characterised by "the differentiation and privileging of particular activities" (204–5). This approach to battling helps us to reveal the political or social implications of battling in hip hop. Practices such as signifying, rhetorical delivery style, improvisation, outrageousness, humour and crowd response are key elements incorporated into battles. The discursive aspects of battle performances are part of an individual's jockeying for increased social capital. Other battles may be of a more philosophical nature, dealing with the way hip hop should be practiced.

Signifying has implications for the political uses of music within hip hop battles. Signifying in this context is a symbolic game; a coded means of communicating in which power is deployed and negotiated in terms of who is signified upon and who is the signifier. It is not limited to language, as the body can also signify through gesturing, movement, modification and stylised dress. Signifying is expressed not only verbally in rap, but also non-verbally through dance, battle messages, music and visual images. What music is played and how bodies are signified in battling matters because the political uses of music can reinforce and challenge the values and perspectives embedded in mainstream society (Denisoff 1972, 2–3).

Battling is a predominately, but not exclusively, male activity. Hip hop battles are usually segregated based on gender. While there are no hard and fast rules explicitly in place to prevent such matches, men and women rarely battle each other in hip hop. Women are usually regulated to differentiated ways of participating; usually women are spatially situated in the margins and encouraged to take on supportive roles that benefit "real" men. For the women who do battle, some level of masculine posturing is usually required in order to be successful. Thus, the privileging and differentiation that is embedded in battling practices may speak more of socialisation, competition between the sexes or social taboo than the already recognised economic barriers to female participation in rap or turntablism.

Battle metaphors are pervasive in hip hop, making implicit the parallels between war and the competitiveness within hip hop. In hip hop battles, challenges are called "attacks"; battlers often described themselves as warriors, soldiers or samurai while describing their opponents as weak, stupid or limp (sexually impotent); and to beat a challenger is described as "catching wreck," cracking skulls or destroying the competition.

Battling in Turntablism

What sets battling in turntablism apart from other types of battling in hip hop culture is its particular pathway of ritualising and its subset of practices; battle messages, the order of battle routines, DJ techniques (mixing, scratching, beat juggling and cutting) and music selection for the battle routine. Battle messages are a means of communicating through cuts (short phrases) pulled from one song and placed into another song that is already playing. Battle routines usually begin with a signifying battle message, progress into a display of mastery of DJ techniques and conclude with another battle message. DJ battling is a creative process that encompasses prowess, technique, dissing and mental agility as a means to engage play and/or competition. Music selection is a type of evocative presentation of music, as DJs pull from rare or obscure pre-recorded sounds and various popular media including music, movies, speeches, street sounds and phrases to construct battle messages (Snapper 2004). Routines sometimes represent travelling through time with music, taking listeners on a sonic journey. Routines can also reconstruct cultural memory through the playing of songs identified as part of hip hop's heritage or serve as an act of tribute to a respected musician.

Signifying as it is re-appropriated by turntablists in battle competitions represents a fusion of competitive play, intense musical compositions, original messages and sounds, and stylised bodily movements referred to as "body tricks." Body tricks included in a routine serve several purposes, such as adding another layer of originality to the performance, the display of posturing and gestures that challenge one's opponent, increasing the visual appeal of a routine to incite loud crowd responses, and boosting the turntablist's reputation for outrageous or physically demanding moves. Symbolic violence is codified into turntablists' routines, often through tactics such as subliminal diss[1] or the use of feminising and insulting battle messages.

DJ battles are ceremonial celebrations because they combine ludic and competitive dimensions. Two or more DJs compete in front of a crowd and event judges. Important aspects of DJ battles are the exchange of energy, what Fikentscher (2000, 57–8) calls the DJ–dancer interaction and "digging in the crates," which is the pre-battle practice of amassing large music collections of both popular and obscure songs (Schloss 2004, 79–100). These activities require hours of dedicated time and practice, sometimes taking up much of a DJ's free time in preparation for the culminating event; the DJ battle competition.

Examples of the Ritual

For this section, I will consider two international DJ battle competitions as case studies; the first is the Heineken Green Synergy DJ Competition and the second is the DMC Technics World DJ Championships. DJ battles are collective ceremonies organised for the purpose of celebration, to spotlight the complex disc jockeying routines of turntablists, and to appoint a champion that has symbolically and strategically survived the "blows" of being in combat. The main reason for my inclusion of both events is the distinctive differences in the ethnic demographics and stylistic emphases of each event. There are many other large DJ battle events; however, there is a need to forego their inclusion in order to make this discussion manageable.

DJ Battling in the Caribbean: the Heineken Green Synergy Competition

The Heineken Green Synergy DJ Competition, which began in 2002, has grown in both popularity and attendance. The event considered was held on 8 October 2005 on the island of St Lucia. There were 18 competitors representing 18 countries from the Caribbean, such as Jamaica, Antigua, the British Virgin Islands, St Vincent, St Martin and Trinidad among others. During 2005, the grand prize was US$5000, however, in two short years the prize for the annual event has doubled to US$10,000 in 2007. DJ/producer DJ Rasta Roots, producer Frank Ramsey, Tony Nichols, local editor of Yo! Magazine, Gee Money and Phife Dawg, formerly of A Tribe Called Quest, co-hosted the event.

Prior to the competition, many of the DJs offered short interviews, during which they were given the opportunity to share their thoughts on the upcoming battle or the character of their competitors. Dancehall,[2] especially sound system clashes, has a dynamic influence on turntablists' performance style and musical aesthetics within the Caribbean. DJ Mr Mystic, a turntablist from the island of Dominica, focuses his discourse not on the usual braggadocio of annihilation of the competition, but instead on the unique contribution he brings to the battle:

> If we are to war tonight the way that the dancehall sound clash would war, there's nobody tonight to see me. But I'm bringing a different vibe, the other guys they are scratching and techniques and also, that works for them. My strength is my own stage personality the way I involve with the crowd, it's like energy. And that's what I'm going to bring, I'm gonna bring me, Mr Mystic, energy. That's what I'm going to bring, the hypeness. …
>
> (DJ Mr Mystic 2005)

Competitors received points from judges based on mixing precision, crowd reaction, crossover ability and cutting and scratching. The predominant ethnicity among the audience and the competitors was diasporic African, with a few European persons present throughout the audience or backstage handling technical details. Heineken beer flowed freely both throughout the crowd and backstage, with the crowd's responses after turntablists' performances becoming near deafening by the end of the competition.

The overall style of dress was casual and trendy, yet comfortable and colourful. The crowd was very high in energy; many participants danced and jumped, waving brightly coloured cloths in the air as the event progressed. The crowd did not stop making noise to observe the performance, in fact, the turntablists worked to increase the energy and noise among the crowd. Based on the crowd's reaction, body tricks and dancing were popular standard actions of performers. Many participants proudly exclaimed that they came to the battle to support their hometown favourite, DJ Webbie D.

Each DJ was given 10 minutes for their performance. The defending champion, DJ Ice Kid, in a dramatic enactment taken from the rap favourite "It Takes Two To Make A Thing Go Right" by Rob Base took off his shirt while mixing between two turntables the sampled phrase, "take off your shirt, just so it don't hit the dirt." The most physically deft competitor was Webbie D, who successfully executed several very difficult body tricks during his performance including standing on the DJ table while mixing two turntables between his legs, lifting one leg to mix a turntable with his right foot while mixing another turntable with his left hand, and sitting on a stack of crates while spinning vinyl with his feet. The competitors used various audio technologies ranging from vinyl to CDs to digital, yet vinyl was the predominant favourite.

Mix Master Pauly, the winner of the 2005 competition, was a very technical performer that benefited from fewer body tricks, incredible hand speed and excellent mixing skills. Hometown favourite Webbie D, in response to being awarded second place, exclaimed,

> Yo, trust me it's all good. Second, in the Caribbean, yo that's a dream come true! Although I wanted number one, but you know, I still placed second in the Caribbean. And I want to thank Heineken for doin' it so big yo, changing my whole life around. And yo trust me, I'm coming, I'm coming! Yo, we're doin' it big!

(2005)

DJ Battling in the United Kingdom and Europe: the DMC World DJ Championships

The Disco Music Club (DMC) World DJ Championships have a much longer history, having started in the United Kingdom in 1985. Over the years, the DMC Championship battles have accumulated a large group of sponsors; Technics/ Panasonic as a most visible sponsor, with LG Cellular, Ortofon DJ, Calvin Klein and MTV Base also sponsoring the event. The winners of the competition received US$10,000 and a framed golden vinyl record among other prizes. Competitors also received prizes, equipment and money from event sponsors.

The particular DJ battle event under consideration, which showcased both the team and individual competitor DJs, was held on 10 September 2006 at the Hammersmith Palais in London. The competitors, representing 18 countries in total, travelled from Europe (UK, France, Spain, Germany, etc.), USA and Canada, the Netherlands, Greece, China, Japan and Singapore among others.

The crowd was largely composed of Europeans, with other ethnicities, such as black or Asian also represented sparsely throughout the crowd. The crowd cheered for their favourite turntablists at the beginning of matches, however, their gestures and noise level during the DJ performances were very much like that of a jazz crowd; mostly quiet and rising in intensity only at appropriately signified intervals.

The competing performers executed their routines in a very precise and technical manner, making sure to include techniques with a level of difficulty. Body tricks were seldom included. During the first elimination matches, performers were given sixty seconds for their routines. Those who advanced to the second round were given 90 seconds, and in the final battle of two competitors the routines were also given 90 seconds. In each round, the competitors' tables were spaced at 90° angles from one another, an angle that provided competitors the opportunity to also direct gestures at one another during their face-off.

DJ Co-ma, a Japanese turntablist and winner of the individual Battle for World Supremacy competition, structured his first 60-second routine around the James Brown song, "I Feel Good." Exhibiting a markedly playful yet focused demeanour, he successfully demonstrated superior mixing skills while performing techniques such as backspinning, fading and crabbing. Co-ma saved body tricks for his final match performance against DJ Troubl' from France, who was awarded second place. The results were heavily weighted from the judges' opinions rather than crowd response. Although a few performers used CD turntables, the majority of turntablists expressed a clear preference for using vinyl. The debate over vinyl vs. digital appeared to be equally politicised and commodified in this setting, with one competitor, DJ Ego from Sweden, wearing an Ortofon DJ brand T-shirt that read, "F**k CD and MP3, Real DJs Play Vinyl."

The Two Events Analysed: DJ Battles and Implicit Religion (Commitment, Integrating Foci and Intensive Concerns with Extensive Effects)

I understand the religious dimensions of turntablism to be configured as implicit religion as defined by Bailey. In this section, I apply the three definitions of implicit religion, "commitments," "integrating foci" and "intensive concerns with extensive effects" to turntablism and DJ battles. Bailey argues that commitment, as a definitional component of implicit religion, suggests a concern with human intentionality, although he carefully acknowledges that commitments can also be deliberate, unconscious, plural, inherited and freely chosen (Bailey 2001, 3). Integrating processes, described by Bailey as integrating foci, are the mutually informing relationships and practices that aid in the construction of the self, community, society, nation and the world. The final definitional component of implicit religion, intensive concerns with extensive effects, is thoroughly grounded in everyday life and its concerns, seeing them as potentially religious in some way.

Commitment

In his discussion of personal depths or commitment as implicit religion, Bailey understands commitment as encompassing a range of experiences, including spontaneous experiences as well as individual and social experiences, whether they are transcendent or not (Bailey 1983, 72). What then are commitments to turntablism? Battle DJs make significant financial investments and extend tremendous amount of effort and time to become proficient at their craft. Commitment to turntables as a music technology is prevalent, but not totalising, as technological innovation is one way that DJs push themselves beyond their current limits. The preference for vinyl records should be seen not only as a commitment to an obsolete form of technology, but also as a commitment to communing with older musical styles and past musicians, an insistence to be in dialogue with important historical and contemporary figures, a sensory preference for handling records with your hands, and a desire to connect with participating listeners through music, image and sound.

Prior to competition, some DJs practice, collect music and focus on the composition of new musical routines all year long in preparation for an annual DJ world championship battle. During the week of the competition, DJs may spend one or more days competing in the preliminary elimination rounds. Finally, in an exchange metaphorically reminiscent of gladiator clashes, battle DJs fight to the finish until one DJ or DJ team is triumphant; all to the jolting sound of loud, cheering crowds.

Another outcome of the commitment to turntablism has been the creation of social networks; local, international and virtual, to facilitate activities related to disc jockeying (Valyi 2003). There has been an explosion of online resources for turntablism, such as blogs, battle-oriented sites (www.dmcdjchamps.com and www.heinekengreensynergy.com), indie multimedia music communities, e-zines (www.remixmag.com) and hybrid e-resource forms. In addition, there are countless websites created by individuals, organisations and retailers as well as member pages on other social networking websites, such as youtube.com and myspace.com that provide videos of DJ battles and DJ performances.

Integrating Foci

1. The imaginary,
2. Gift economy,
3. Social hierarchy, and
4. Ludic agency.

The Imaginary

The "Idea" of a Hip Hop Nation—Turntablism and the Hip Hop Imaginary

While there are many integrating foci that I might discuss from the data on DJ battles, I will limit my discussion to the hip hop imaginary, music and gift economy, social hierarchy and ludic agency.

Imagined community, as introduced by Anderson (1983), is helpful in explaining the tropes, performances, ethos and other actions that contribute to the self-understanding of turntable and hip hop practitioners. By perceiving hip hop in terms of interpersonal relationships rather than geographical boundaries, hip hop as a mode of cultural expression imagines and reproduces a community or nation united by its youthfulness, creativity, retail consumption and cultural diversity. Aspects of hip hop's imaginary often involve debates centred on authenticity, including the ways in which "real" hip hop is represented and enacted; the pillars of hip hop—a flexible list of practices and principles that are considered to be the original foundation of hip hop; the performance of "cool," ethnicity, sexuality, class and gender; stylised clothing, lifestyles of excess or poverty and adoption of hip hop as a way of life.

The broad frame of the hip hop imaginary consists of discourses of resistance and social transformation, although the smaller scale lived experiences of hip hop culture end up reflecting a dialectic of freedom and survival (Kalyan 2006). For example, hip hop is articulated as important to the forming of communities of struggle, where there is an emphasis on hip hop as a vehicle for education and political empowerment, a forum for marginal voices, and as a space for radical creativity or subversive social possibilities. Concurrently, violence, poverty and misogyny are often fetishised and celebrated, while criminal lifestyles become glamorised spectacles of consumption. Such displays, because of their transgressive nature and performance of uninhibited sexual abandon, can serve as initiatory fantasy and rites of reference or reclaiming by invoking focused attention on the body and bodily movement. The commodification of ghetto and gangster lifestyles provides social constructions of "dangerous" power, sexual competition and hypermasculinity that suggest a connection to existing American mythologies of race, gender, and class.

The interpersonal framing of hip hop community, which occurs on the sub-commercial or local levels, can be understood as an affirmation of life, a safer place for self-expression, a space of ritual renaming, a context of conflict and competition, and as sacred community. The scratch/DJ community or tablist community maintains its own sense of what it means to be a community and part of the global hip hop base. What is most prominent in turntablist discourses is the continuing development of turntablism as a serious and radical art form. Tablists view music as a barrier-breaking medium; an international language that brings diverse groups of people together in creative communion or sonic journey. The ethos of turntablism emphasises progressive creativity and musicianship, musical innovation, technical skill, technological consumption and strategic resistance from the hegemonic positioning of music conglomerates. Conversely, turntablists loathe biting[3], mediocre disc jockeying skills or unoriginal disc jockeying.

Gift Economy

The idea of gift economy (Mauss 1925), the mutual exchange of gifts as a structuring social activity, describes processes of reciprocal exchange that help to actualise music as an integrating focus for turntablism. I suggest that the experience of music is an ongoing gift to hip hop communities and that music is the gifting of DJs to listening crowds. Music is not only important in the creation of hip hop communal spaces; it is also a vehicle for community commentary and cultural memory. For some persons, music and dancing are significant factors in their decision to participate in DJ battles. The experience of the sonic as embodiment thus provide turntablists as well as hip hop heads with yet another mutual exchange; energy.

Energy plays a large role in the gift economy of hip hop culture. For live shows to be perceived as efficacious there is an expectation between performers and participating crowds to engage in the reciprocal exchange of energy and to work towards the increase of momentum in the ritual space, thus making room for the potential emergence of social intensity. The first phase of energy is establishing connection with the crowd. Establishing connection for a DJ might include an initial greeting and informal conversation with the crowd or a series of call and response exchanges that may be verbal or non-verbal. The second phase of energy is more difficult to achieve because it requires the DJ to "feel" what the crowd's tastes and disposition are in the present, then, respond to the crowd through the selection of certain songs. In "feeling" the crowd, DJs may develop a heightened responsiveness to symbolic interactions, allowing them to maintain a mood through the enactment of DJ techniques.

For example, the aforementioned DJ Mr. Mystic when establishing a connection with the crowd began his routine in a conversational tone by saying, "Blessings to ya! Mic [microphone] so nice, every'ting good, thanks to the creator. St Lucia, how are you then? Every'ting nice, every'ting merry?" (2005). He further explains how the second phase of energy, reciprocity, unfolds during his battle routine:

> It's like you give energy, you get back energy, and visa versa; that's how it's done. So it's like I feed off the crowd, at the same time, I have to feed the crowd … that's, where I get my energy from, the crowd. From the time to get go and I play my first tune, and I say, "Somebody say pull up!," trust me, from my first pull up, I gone.
>
> (2005)

Social Hierarchy

The process by which new champions are chosen is ordered: it begins with the gathering of the crowd and the announcing of contenders and it ends with the announcing of the competition's winner. The supervision of assessment sets up a traditionalising framework for the battle event, usually handled by judges who were former battle competitors. Battle competitors must seek the approval of the judges in order to be awarded the title of reigning contender. In addition to the material gains of winning the competition, such as prizes, equipment, and trips, the winning DJs are awarded bragging rights and their status within the social network of professional turntablists is elevated. With the attainment of such an award comes additional social capital including more opportunities to perform, more access and privilege, and greater recognition from others. The goal of the defending champion is to retire undefeated and possibly "graduate" to judge status. The authority of competition judges demonstrates a sense of formality. Christie Z-Pabon, a former event coordinator, explains the hierarchical status of judges by noting:

> Having hip hop DJ legends present as judges and honored guests is very important to the sense of community within hip hop DJ culture. The newer DJs basically try to gain the approval from the tribal elders as judges and the elders in turn, who have long since retired from battling, give their blessings to those who they feel best represent the art form.
>
> (Katz 2004, 122)

Ludic Agency and the Spectacle of DJ Battles

The commodification of hip hop and the construction of entertainment events as spectacular environments have implications for DJ battles and the battling space. As our two case studies show, larger and well-established DJ battle competitions are attracting major corporate sponsorship, and advertising from sponsors take up much of the visual space of the event. While turntablists have developed their own collective ethos, marketers participate in DJ battles hoping to cultivate a consumptive ethos for their products from battle attendees and DJs (Dowdy 2007, 77). The dispersing of prize money and other awards links the experiences of DJ battles to consumer products and consumption.

As a result, the dominant and indeed overwhelming presence of marketing at DJ battles and live hip hop shows have become a part of their ritual dynamics through the creation of "spectacular consumption environments" (Kozinets et al. 2004, 658). As the prevalence of corporate sponsorship of hip hop grows, questions concerning the intersection of consumer and ritual agency in light of sponsor's social construction of reality through spectacle rise to the surface.

Turntables and other music/visual technologies, clothing, advertising and websites for disc jockeying function as the material culture of turntablism as implicit religiosity. While there has been some discussion of the religious marketplace (Schofield-Clark), commercialised communitas (St John) and the spiritualised marketplace (Emerich); the convergence of implicit religiosity and economic life in late capitalism has received little attention. A unique approach to the commodification of everyday lived experience takes us in an unexpected direction; that of looking at DJ battles as spaces of ludic agency.

DJ Webbie D's statement that Heineken "changed my whole life around" speaks to his negotiation of the spectacular environment of international DJ battles and experience of battling as life-changing; Heineken's sponsorship was integral to actualising his goals of building a reputation as a battle DJ and his yearning for "doing it big." In their analysis of ludic agency and retail spectacle Kozinets et al. (2004, 659) have argued that even in spectacular environments, consumption is negotiated dialectically through moves and countermoves, making the relationship between marketers and consumers a complex and interactive one. Furthermore, Kent Grayson's theorisation of play and consumption suggests that "the rule-bound nature of play offers consumers paradoxical opportunities to be seduced or be subversive through rule following or rule breaking, playing along versus playing around" (659). Thus, "playing around" instead of "playing along," the struggle to have ludic agency, can be a transgressive response to the commodification of everyday life.

Intensive Concern with Extensive Effects

For implicit religion to have extensive effects, Bailey recognises the necessity of a phenomenon to have a particularly deep impact on the individual or group it affects (Bailey 1998, 23). According to Bailey, intensive personal experiences, such as conversion experiences, strong momentary emotional experiences or long standing interests are related in a reciprocal dialectic with wider constructions of individual and community identity. This suggests that the intensity of battling and competition, the emotional "high" from experiencing music or winning the DJ competition or the life-long interests in music technology could be what initially attracts DJs to turntablism. Those memorable experiences later become potential motives for individuals to join scratch/tablist communities.

UCLA anthropologist and hip hop scholar Alim offers more insight to the importance of intense experiences to hip hop events through his analysis of the process "multilayered totalizing expression" or MTE process. Alim describes MTE as "multiple levels of call and multiple levels of response, occurring simultaneously and synergistically, to create something even beyond total expression." He also posits that the creation of a continuum beyond the crowd and the performer has meaning, a meaning that is evidenced in the "spirited and spiritual response created during the climax of the performance." This spirited and spiritual response is reiterated in Alim's statement, "We witness a call and response on the oral/aural, physical (body), and spiritual/metaphysical level" (2006, 81).

The Religious Dimensions of the Battle

Our application of implicit religion as an analytical frame for DJ battles suggests that turntablism and DJ battles can have religious dimensions. To summarise, I contend that religious dimensions of the battle are: (1) the individual and collective commitments to hip hop culture and the art of turntablism, (2) the integrating foci of music, dance, energy exchange, consuming and play, and (3) memorable experiences of battling and other hip hop happenings connected to wider social spheres, such as scratch/tablist community or DJ battles.

DJ battles, hip hop concerts, block parties and smaller social gatherings where turntablists perform are experiences that structure social interactions and contribute to the idea of a hip hop as imagined community. These experiential opportunities, often occurring through a hub of ritual practices, become integral to the process of making life meaning for individuals and groups that identify with hip hop culture. In addition, hip hop events facilitate embodied ways of knowing and invite participation, because they are opportunities to experience movement of the body, feel sonic power and give/receive energy. World-renowned DJ and turntablist Grandmaster Flash, speaking upon his experience of disc jockeying, notes how music can become a vehicle for the spiritual:

> It's very spiritual [the experience of DJing]. When I am with a crowd, it takes me about 10 to 15 minutes to lock with the crowd. When we finally lock, I become you and you

become me. Sometimes it takes longer to connect and there are some nights where the connection just doesn't happen. Once I hit the groove, once I hit the flow, I'm good for about two hours. I don't think about what I'm doing. And you'll tell me, you'll tell me what you want to hear …

Yeah, there's definitely a spiritual flow; the music is just a vehicle for the spiritual. It's not even so much about playing records, it's about the spirituality of people coming together and sharing a common bond. Now, there are some people who perform and they just perform at you; I want to perform with you. It's also about the memories; I want to make you loose your cool, I want to make you remember what it felt like to be a kid again.[4]

The implicit religiosity of hip hop takes intensive concerns and connects them with the types of sociality reflected in the lived practices and experiences of hip hop artists and audiences. This reminds us that people contribute to the making of religion and are made by it, thus affording agency to hip hop heads and their religioning practices (Nye 2000). As contemporary forms of religiosity, the cultural practices of hip hop answers the desire for intensity and embodiment, provides a sense of belonging, creates a context for existential wrestling and truth-seeking, creates spaces to consume and play, promote values that groups or communities hold in common, and produce relevant representations of religious visual and material culture.

Critical Analysis of Complex Subjectivity in Light of the Case Study

Can the religious dimensions of battle competitions and turntablism also be understood as part of the larger quest for complex subjectivity, even though they are not explicitly religious? Religious theorist Pinn recognises the relationship between subjectivity and agency when he refers to complex subjectivity as "the creative struggle in history for increased agency, for fullness of life" (2003, 173). In this sense, the quest for complex subjectivity is understood as the continual yearning and pushing to move from: (1) being an object of exploitation and oppression controlled by essentialising social forces, to: (2) becoming a complex and creative human being and a conveyer of cultural meaning (158–9). As an activity of creative struggle, complex subjectivity is therefore both a paradox of being and a process of becoming.

A relevant question, then: what would complex subjectivity have to say about the lived paradoxes of hip hop? One of the paradoxes of hip hop that we have already mentioned is the commodification of hip hop and the construction of entertainment events as spectacular consumption environments. Another paradox related to hip hop as spectacle is the critique and celebration of late capitalism that is expressed in hip hop publics and counter-publics. Where Pinn examines the paradoxes of racialisation and racial identity, he says very little about the contradictions of questing for meaning in the current historical contexts of post-civil rights, postmodernity and late capitalism. How are heteronormativity and gender (as forms of fixed identities) rethought and reshaped in broader cultural contexts by complex subjects that practice hip hop as their way of life?

Also, complex subjectivity remains insufficient in explaining the tensions of contradictory or plural commitments. Pinn's definition of the quest for complex subjectivity as inner impulse or elemental feeling misses the dilemma of exercising agency in the face of inherited or multiple and conflicting commitments. Commitments are both conscious and unconscious, suggesting that individual or collective religiosity can be expressed both intentionally and unintentionally. Here is where the analytical framework of implicit religion might be a helpful tool to reframe the potentially religious experiences of complex subjects.

Lastly, as I have argued, play as employed in hip hop practices becomes a covert way to cloak the transgressive. In the case of DJ battles, battling as play showed how the signification from clothing, music routines and audiences, worked in serious ways to increase the social and economic status of the DJ, to reify gender, and to strategically position corporate marketing. The serious role of play and ludic agency in resolving or living with life's unresolved ambiguities is hinted at in Pinn's discussion of covert practices, expressive culture and visual arts; however, playing along or playing around with religiosity as part of a creative struggle for a fuller life is not mentioned as a viable response or recognition of complex subjectivity. Turner (1982, 29) suggests that play can be a response to the ambiguity of lived paradox when play is used to cover up social critique or engaged as a mode of sociability. As a consequence, play becomes paradoxical because its serious function is revealed. Turner states that "play in the guise of folly and in the ephemerality of its presence is licensed to comment on a great range of issues ... Play's flexibility contains within it the possibility of exploring new ways of doing things" (29). Here, I would emphasise that more attention should be given to the ludic recombination of religious experience.

Drawing on religious scholars such as Edward Bailey and Anthony Pinn, I have tried to show that turntablism, as part of the wider corpus of hip hop practices, can constitute a religious form and practice. Rituals, such as battling and DJ battles, are key experiential opportunities that assist in the development and continuity of hip hop religiosity. The idea of hip hop as a nation or a community provides multiple narratives, value systems, paradoxes and mythos within which to situate experiences of hip hop. As such, hip hop is a cultural practice that engenders complex subjectivity, helping its participants to find their place in the world.

Study Questions

1. How does Clay explore the work of Edward Bailey's theory of implicit religion and Anthony B. Pinn's theory of complex subjectivity within turntablism?
2. What does Clay mean when she suggests that we ought to view turntablism as a ritual process and practice? What elements and dimensions of turntablism does she use to make her claims?
3. What does her exploration of the two DJ battles (in the Caribbean and UK) suggest about implicit religion? How does she use these conclusions to offer a critical analysis of complex subjectivity in light of her case study?

Notes

1. Subliminal dissing is a tactic where the DJ buries an insulting phrase or sound within the layers of the music. It is meant to induce fear or publicly humiliate an opponent during a DJ's battle routine.
2. Sonjah Stanley-Niaah describes dancehall as a descendant of Jamaica's reggae music, an urban lifestyle and a cultural practice. Sound clashes (battles between sound systems) and toasting are competitive and celebratory rituals that travelled from Jamaica to New York, informing the shape of disc jockeying in hip hop through the innovations of Kool DJ Herc among others. See Stanley-Niaah 2004, 7, 102–18.
3. Biting is taking credit for something that you did not create or recreate. It's reusing the same sample or routine that belongs to someone else in an attempt to become popular.
4. Grandmaster Flash, pers. comm., July 26, 2008.

References

2005. Heineken Green Synergy DJ Competition. Directed by David Levine and Kurt Williamson. *TEMPO* television, a division of MTV Networks, a unit of Viacom International Inc. Available at http://www.youtube.com/watch?v=XtOuAsN-oYw.2005.

2006. DMC World DJ Championship: Battle for world supremacy. Directed by Doug Pray. London: DMC World, 2006.

Alim, S. 2006. *Roc the mic right: The language of hip hop culture*. New York: Routledge.

Anderson, B. 1983. *Imagined communities*. London: Verso.

Bailey, E.I. 1983. The implicit religion of contemporary society: An orientation and a plea for its study. *Religion*, no. 13: 69–83.

—— 1998. *Implicit religion: An introduction*. London: Middlesex.

—— 2002. Introduction—the notion of implicit religion: What it means, and does not mean. In *The secular quest for meaning in life: Denton papers in implicit religion*, ed. Edward Bailey. New York: Edwin Mellon Press.

Bell, C. 1992. *Ritual theory, ritual practice*. New York: Routledge.

Denisoff, R.S. 1972. *Sing a song of social significance*. Bowling Green, OH: Bowling Green University Popular Press.

Dowdy, M. 2007. Live hip hop, collective agency, and "acting in concert." *Popular Music and Society* 30, no. 1: 77–91.

Fikentscher, K. 2000. *You better work!: Underground dance music in New York city*. Hanover: Wesleyan University Press.

Grayson, K. 1999. The dangers and opportunities of playful consumption. In *Consumer value: A framework for analysis and research*, ed. Morris B. Holbrook. London: Routledge.

Grimes, R.L. 1982. *Beginnings in ritual studies*. Lanham, MD: University Press of America.

—— 1990. *Ritual criticism: Case studies in its practice, essays on its theory*. Columbia, SC: University of South Carolina Press.

Kalyan, R. 2006. Hip hop imaginaries: A genealogy of the present. *Journal For Cultural Research* 10, no. 3: 237–257.

Katz, M. 2004. *Capturing sound: How technology has changed music*. Berkeley: University of California Press.

Kozinets, R., John F. Sherry Jr., Diana Storm, Adam Duhachek, Krittinee Nuttavuthisit, and Be'net Deberry-Spence. 2004. Ludic agency and retail spectacle. *Journal of Consumer Research* 31: 658–72.

Long, C. 1986. *Significations: Signs, symbols, and images in the interpretation of religion*. Philadelphia: Fortress Press.

Nye, M. 2000. Religion, post-religionism, and religioning: Religious studies and contemporary cultural debates. *Method & Theory in the Study of Religion* 12, no. 4, 447–476.

Pinn, A. 2003. *Terror and triumph: The nature of black religion*. Minneapolis, MN: Fortress Press.

Schloss, J. 2004. *Making beats: The art of sample-based hip hop*. Middleton, CT: Wesley University Press.

Snapper, J. 2004. Scratching the surface: Spinning time and identity in hip hop turntablism. *European Journal of Cultural Studies* 7, no. 1: 9–25.

Stanley-Niaah, S. 2004. Kingston's dancehall: A story of space and celebration. *Space & Culture* 7, no. 1: 102–18.

Turner, V. 1982. *Celebration: Studies in festivity and ritual*. Washington, DC: Smithsonian Institution Press.

Valyi, G. 2003. Grass-roots cultural globalization: The case of the nu jazz DJ scene in east-central Europe. Paper presented at Net Culture Science/Netz Kultur Wissenschaft, December 10–13, in Budapest, Hungary.

10

"God's Smiling on You and He's Frowning Too"

Rap and the Problem of Evil

The theological conundrum of theodicy ("What can be said about God in light of moral evil in the world?") has been an enduring feature in the African American musical tradition. Interested in the secular articulation of theodicy, Nelson argues that rap music with its focus on the centrality and ultimacy of humans over God can appropriately be examined from a theodical framework. By considering how rappers talk about/make use of God, Satan, and black suffering, Nelson concludes that rappers' articulations of an evil world over and against a good God produce two secularized theodicies in rap music which serve to reconcile the tension in African American communities between belief in a good and just God and everyday suffering and evil. This is achieved by focusing on the fallibility of humanity and the ethical choice to do good or to produce harm.

"God's Smiling on You and He's Frowning Too": Rap and the Problem of Evil

Angela M. Nelson

Some African-American song lyrics illustrate a unique African-American conceptualization of a theological problem in Judea-Christian belief: theodicy. From the Greek words *theos* (God) and *dike* (justice), "theodicy" is the term for the propositional answers to the question or problem of evil. Theodicy is the defense or justification of God's justice and righteousness in the face of evil's existence in the world. Human beings posit different theodicies in an attempt to explain how a good God permits evil in the world.[1] African-American gospel music heralds the "harder the cross/brighter the crown" theodicy, which means one's suffering on earth pays off incrementally in heaven. Blues emphasizes the "reap what you sow" theodicy[2] which means suffering is brought on by one's own misdeeds. In the context of this study, I am interested in secular theodicies. I will draw on thought of black theological thinkers William R. Jones, in his book *Is God a White Racist?* and Jon Michael Spencer, in his essay on the theodicy of the blues.

Spencer especially influenced my resolve that theodicies do in fact exist in rap. In an essay titled "God in Secular Music Culture: The Theodicy of the Blues as the Paradigm of Proof," Spencer demonstrates that early blues singers reflected on both the cause of evil and the nature of suffering. They developed various theodicies addressing these "ultimate concerns."[3] Spencer identifies two blues theodicies to demonstrate that the ethos of the blues is in fact religious: the "reap what you sow" and "work of the devil" theodicies. The "reap what you sow" theodicy, the most typical of the blues theodicies, explains the suffering of "blues people" as derived from their living a life of reckless abandon—gambling, drinking, drug use, sexual promiscuity, and so forth.[4] The "work of the devil" theodicy made the devil a convenient means of explaining the existence of certain kinds of suffering in the lives of blues people.[5] In other words, blues people often blamed the devil for wreaking havoc in their lives.

As Spencer argues and demonstrates through analyzing blues texts, blues people, to the surprise of some scholars, unquestionably reflect on the cause of evil and the nature of human suffering. Indeed, for many African-Americans, an understanding of the cause and nature of suffering in their present and historical lives has framed most of their verbal discourse. For this reason, a black theodicy—one that not only exonerates and justifies God's purpose and works in the face of evil, but also determines the cause of black suffering or oppression[6]—has been central to the black experience in and beyond America. African-American music has been a major medium for the documentation of black theodicean reflection upon suffering, and today rap is one such medium.

As already mentioned, theodicy is a concept that operates in Western monotheism. Except for Judaism, it is almost entirely a Christian concern that dates back at least to the writings of the fifth-century theologian Augustine.[7] Traditional Christian belief in God describes the "ultimate reality" as the unique infinite, the uncreated, the eternal personal Spirit absolute in goodness and power.[8] The problem of theodicy is in acknowledging the goodness and power of God in a world with moral and natural evil.[9] The problem, as theodicist John Hick details it, is this: (1) If God is perfectly good, he must want to abolish all evil. (2) If God is unlimitedly powerful, he must be able to abolish all evil. (3) But evil exists. Therefore, either God is not perfectly good or his power is limited.[10] A theodicy, then, comprises the vindication of God in an evil-stricken world. The theodicy problem is a major concern of theologians across the world, but: it is not my intention to give any further detailed exposition of the endless discourse it has aroused. My task here is to demonstrate the inter-relatedness of the theodicy problem to the black experience in America and the existence of secular theodicy in African-American popular and folk music, particularly rap from the late 1980s and early 1990s.

The traditional definition of theodicy may seem to fall outside the periphery of black secular music (or any secular music for that matter) since it involves expressly the vindication of God. Rap appears to be centered on the ultimacy of human beings rather than God. If this is true, it seems to question the assumption that rap can be examined in a theodicean framework. However, rap can be examined in *this* framework *if* one embraces the notion of secular humanism or humanocentric theism. "Humanocentric theism" is a concept developed by theologian William R. Jones in response to the implied purpose and definition of black theology as a theology of liberation. Liberation assumes that human beings are oppressed in some manner and are suffering to some degree. African-Americans still wear the "stripes" of almost 250 years of enslavement in America. The lingering effects exist in the areas of education, housing, employment, health care, and law. Jones insists that we need to give special attention to black oppression and suffering. He also suggests that black theologians should embrace new models for treating black suffering and openly illustrate that God is not, in fact, a white racist, who willingly allows black people to suffer under white oppression.[11]

Jones contends that theodicy must be the controlling element in a black theology of liberation. Yet he demonstrates that it was already an implied and explicitly stated concern of leading black theologians James Cone, Joseph Washington, Albert Cleage, Major Jones, and J. Deotis Roberts because of their collective dialogues about black oppression and suffering.[12] Jones's theodicy, or humanocentric theism, and secular humanism both advocate the functional ultimacy of human beings. Human beings must act as if they were the ultimate valuators or ultimate agents in human history, or both. Humanocentric theism puts the responsibility for human actions and evil upon human beings. It removes God's overruling sovereignty from human history. In this way, Jones points out, God's responsibility for the crimes and errors of human history—Auschwitz, Native American genocide, the European slave trade—is reduced if not effectively eliminated.[13]

Humanocentric theism is based on thought from the writings of existentialist philosophers Martin Buber, Jean-Paul Sartre, and Albert Camus, and theologians Harvey Cox and Erich Fromm.[14] Although these scholars are not of African descent and have little personal knowledge of the black experience in America, they are significant to Jones's thesis because of their affirmation of the freedom of human beings to make choices that are best for them and in keeping with God's will. Human beings portray God's will and purpose for them by exercising human freedom, their freedom to choose. Human beings then become cocreators of human existence. In this respect, racism—probably the most oppressive circumstance for people of African descent—is traced to human rather than divine forces; God is not a white racist.[15] Therefore, the theodicies of such black secular music forms as rap can and should be interpreted under the rubric of humanocentric theism. No doubt, most (if not all) rappers would agree. I propose that rap has at least two secular or humanocentric theodicies that resolve the problem of black suffering without permitting the position that God is a white racist. I term these the "white supremacy" and "slave mentality" theodicies.

White Supremacy and Slave Mentality Theodicies

The white supremacy theodicy posited by rappers is derived from the blatant forms of European (white) dominance over nonwhite populations. "White supremacy" refers to the attitudes, ideologies, and policies associated with "white domination."[16] Although white supremacy was a primary factor in the enslavement system in America and in white–black relations in the Republic of South Africa, white supremacy as an institutionalization of written and unwritten policies in America did not fully come into being until the period of Reconstruction. Recognizing the economic, political, and educational gains of newly freed blacks following the Civil War, southern whites aggressively began campaigns to make African-Americans chattel, even though slavery was abolished. White supremacist acts included legislation that disenfranchised blacks, allowed rampant violence against blacks (fueled by the reorganization of the Ku Klux Klan in 1915), and enacted a series of Jim Crow laws and Black Codes similar to the old slave codes. These actions advanced the sharecropping system, which kept most black sharecroppers in debt, bound to the land, and bound to white landowners.[17]

The most developed form of white supremacy recently existed in the Republic of South Africa, with its color bars, apartheid, and citizenship rights restricted to privileged group members characterized by light skin pigmentarion.[18] The latter feature has been experienced in America to a lesser degree; however, color bars and racial segregation have been blatantly practiced and are only now showing concrete signs of being eliminated. Historian George M. Fredrickson states that white supremacy also suggests systematic and self-conscious efforts to make a person's race (or color) a qualification for membership in the dominant community.[19] Although white America shows evidence of a systematic exclusion of African-Americans, the sum of its efforts has not necessarily been self-conscious or government sanctioned. In fact, compared to South Africa's once well-devised policies, it almost seems coincidental that America has such a racist and discriminatory history. Nevertheless, the main concern here is that many whites, or people of European descent, have attitudes and ideologies that do not permit African-Americans to realize freedom. These attitudes and ideologies comprise what is called "white supremacy."

In rap music, African-American females and males express a theodicy that says the choices, values, and resulting actions of white Americans are the direct cause of the oppression and suffering of African-Americans. Consequently, black enslavement in North America was not an evil sent by the good Lord or a God who was a white racist. Instead, it was a circumstance created and augmented through decisions made by white people who also happened to have opposing worldviews on the meaning of humanity.

White American views on black humanity have affected and continue to affect African-Americans emotionally, mentally, physically, and socially. What results is a theodicy closely related to the white supremacy theodicy, one that places the perpetuation of black suffering squarely on the shoulders of African-Americans themselves: the slave mentality theodicy. "Slave mentality" refers to the residuals of slavery in the psyche of African-Americans. Amiri Baraka describes "slave mentality" as the mental adjustments slaves made during over two hundred years of slavery, the "marks" left by bending to the will of the white oppressor.[20] He further adds that a slave mentality encompasses some blacks accepting the superiority of the white oppressor and an accompanying contempt for other black people who do not possess the "refined" characteristics of the oppressor.[21]

In a more detailed description of this concept, William Jones comments on slave mentality while discussing theodicy, oppression, and quietism. His conclusion is that theodicies that say African-Americans are God's chosen vessels and that their suffering is God's means of disciplining them for his divine task are in fact "enslaving beliefs":

> At the base of oppression lies a complex of beliefs that define the role and status of the oppressor and the oppressed, and this complex of beliefs legitimates both. The oppressed, in part, are oppressed precisely because they buy, or are indoctrinated to accept, a set of beliefs that negate those attitudes and actions necessary for liberation. Accordingly, the purpose and first step of liberation is to effect a radical conversion of the mind of the oppressed, to free his mind from those destructive and enslaving beliefs that stifle the movement toward liberation.[22]

In other words, Jones contends that slave mentality also entails the oppressed accepting the goals and outcomes of the oppressor as equally profitable and advantageous for themselves. The slave mentality theodicy, which is humanocentric, puts the responsibility for continued black oppression and suffering upon African-Americans who are unable or refuse to realize that they carry the "scars" of the slavery experience in both their social and mental lives.[23]

Adding tremendously to the scholarship on slave mentalities is clinical psychologist Na'im Akbar. In his book *Chains and Images of Psychological Slavery,* Akbar says that slavery was a "severe psychological and social shock to the minds of African-Americans."[24] He then outlines nine areas in which the "slave mentality" is present in African-American social and mental life: (1) attitudes toward work; (2) mixed attitudes toward material objects and property; (3) disrespect of African-American leadership; (4) overwhelming tendency to become "clowns" or entertainers; (5) sense of inferiority; (6) disunited communities; (7) women choosing to become "breeders" and men seeking to prove their manhood through physical exploits sexual exploits or deviation; (8) excessive consciousness of skin color; and (9) psychological confusion from racial, religious, and symbolic imagery.[25]

African-American rappers comment on several of the manifest forms of slave mentality that Akbar describes. Many rappers believe, in general, that African-Americans are failing to make the best possible decisions for the lives and livelihood of themselves, their families, their communities, and their race. For example, in her rap entitled "Cappucino," female rapper MC Lyte tells the story of a girl named Berry, who would not listen to a social worker's warning about a notorious crack dealer. Lyte said Berry would not listen just as so many others do not listen to warnings about potential dangers to their lives.[26] In "Not Wit a Dealer," MC Lyte warns her friend Cecelia to stay away from a crack dealer named Born Supreme. Cecelia tells MC Lyte: "Girl, I love him, he treats me so good, he gets much respect in my neighborhood." Again MC Lyte tells us that Cecelia would not listen because she, like so many other black females, loves her man even more than herself.[27] Rappers such as MC Lyte believe that African-Americans are not living out God's divine decrees by discerning between good and evil, and by identifying societal elements that systematically hinder their racial progress. A slave mentality prevents African-Americans from attaining this liberation.

To summarize, the white supremacy theodicy, in view of humanocentric theism, says that ungodly decisions made by people of European origin in the past and present continue to result in black oppression and suffering. The slave mentality theodicy says that the residuals of white supremacy—especially from slavery—have left scars on the mental psyches of African-Americans, causing perpetual self-inflicted black oppression and suffering. Both theodicies are nonbiblical and noneschatological; rappers neither draw life narratives from Sacred Scripture nor find it feasible or comforting to expect a possible future reward at the end of time.

What makes the slave mentality theodicy a great burden to African-Americans, to emphasize the crucial point, is that it causes passivity or quietism (the refusal to undertake corrective action),[28] so much so that the slave mentality theodicy resembles otherworldiness. This otherworldliness is what Benjamin E. Mays terms "compensatory beliefs,"[29] which enable African-Americans to endure hardship, suffer pain, and withstand maladjustment. But such beliefs do not necessarily motivate them to eliminate the source of these ailments.[30] The slave mentality, indeed, prevents African-Americans from desiring to liberate themselves; however, this part is not precisely a compensatory belief. The important difference is that, since African-Americans have "enslaving beliefs" passed down through the generations over centuries, in some cases they do not recognize hardship, pain, and maladjustment. In other words, the psychic and social maladjustments of slavery are complete to the extent that some African-Americans today do not even recognize that they do not have the essential tools—such as education in African and African-American history—to eliminate the source of the ailments they suffer. The source of the ills they suffer, as rappers repeatedly point out, has been a racist ideology. Until African-Americans reach the state of awareness that rappers are questing for the masses, the slave mentality theodicy will continue to be a self-inflicted evil that is perhaps even more enduring than actual enslavement.

Accompanying the notions of the white supremacy and slave mentality theodicies are African-American conceptions of God and Satan and the nature of black suffering. Although there may be tremendous textual differences between the conceptions of these, in black sacred and secular music there still remains the past of slavery, which connects sacred and secular forms of music. Molefi Asante contends that in order to understand the role of vocal expressiveness within African-American communities, one must recognize slavery and *nommo* (the generative and dynamic quality of vocal expression).[31] Because of the shared historical experience of enslavement, African-Americans both in the sacred (church) and secular (non-church) context usually have the same concrete ideas about God and Satan and the circumstances of suffering. This fine line of what is sacred (and of God) and is not (and of Satan) is present even in rap music.

Conceptions of God and Satan

Jon Michael Spencer states that blues was ideologically "oppugnant."[32] One of the attitudes and ideologies that blues oppugned, or opposed, was Jim Crow ethics: the systematic discrimination, segregation, and oppression of people of color based on race. This particular oppugnancy is overwhelmingly evident in rap. Rappers view Jim Crow ethics as playing an influential part in the continual bombardment of black self-worth, self-esteem, and self-affirmation. Segregation, endorsed by Jim Crow ethics, was a successful breeding ground for white fears about blacks and their supposed inferiority. White disdain for blackness—both its color and its disposition—culminated in the highest code of separation, which was to prevent the "mongrelization" of the white race through so-called miscegenation. An excerpt from Mississippi Senator Theodore Bilbo's book *Take Your Choice: Separation or Mongrelization* (1947) is typical of white sentiment, not only in the past but also in the present, as the horrific killing of a black man in Jasper, Texas suggests. Bilbo says: "I'd rather see civilization blotted out with the atomic bomb than to see it slowly but surely destroyed in the maelstrom of miscegenation, interbreeding, intermarriage, and mongrelization."[33] Bilbo's preference for an atomic bomb is absurd and irrational, but it serves to illustrate the intensity with which many white Americans despised black people. It demonstrates that racism and white superiority complexes are entirely subjective and emotional decisions, based on a misreading of history.

Rappers Public Enemy comments on the problems of racism, white supremacist ideology, and the fear of so-called miscegenation in their rap "Pollywanacraka."[34] The title "Pollywanacraka" is a pun on a familiar phrase often spoken by parakeets in television and film ("Polly wants a cracker") and also a pejorative reference made by African-Americans about whites, especially economically poor ones—"crakas," or "crackers." The term derives its meaning from the skin color of people of European descent and (saltine) crackers. Chuck D, leader of Public Enemy, tells black people that they should not hate any "brother or sister" who is united with someone of another race. He argues, "No man is God," and "God … put us all here" in the first place. Chuck D says the system of white supremacy and the white fear of "mongrelization" have "no wisdom," and that "the devil" split the races by convincing black and white people that "White is good, Black is bad, and Black and White is still too bad."

While commenting on white supremacist ideology and slave mentality, Chuck D also shares his conceptions of God and the "devil." In saying, "No man is God," and that it was "God who put us all here," he implies that he has a fundamental belief in the omnipotence of God and belief in God as the infinite and sole creator of the universe. The concept of so-called miscegenation cannot be God's creation, since God is and possesses wisdom. Whites perceive so-called miscegenation to be the mixing of two distinct human species or races, as the Latin derivation of this word suggests. "Misce" comes from *miscere,* which means "to mix"; "genation" comes from *genus,* which means "species" or "genes": hence, "to mix species." Nevertheless, while there are many animal and plant species, there is only one living human species, Homo sapiens sapiens.[35] There are no distinct or different human species; all persons are human—period! "Miscegenation" therefore is a misnomer, only supporting the fact that, as Chuck D maintains, white supremacist ideologies are illogical and irrational.

Since "miscegenation" is not a concept related to God, it consequently falls within the domain of Satan's ideation. Public Enemy says "the devil" split the races in pairs with this lie of mixing races. Satan, or "the devil," taught all people that the union of two whites is good, that blacks are bad, and that the "mixture" of white and black persons is even worse. Rap group Public Enemy portrays Satan as an adversary who has no good in him. His evil ways have caused black people and white people to despise black–white relationships and caused people of white cultures especially to have contempt for white–black sexual unions. Basically, Chuck D's (Public Enemy's) conceptions of God and Satan are traditional and consistent with such older African-American portrayals found in spirituals, folktales, and legends.

Grandmaster Flash and the Furious Five offer a traditional conception of God as all-knowing (omniscient), all-powerful (omnipotent), and all-present (omnipresent) in their rap entitled "The Message." Lead MC, Melle Mel, speaks of the omniscience and omnipresence of God when referring to a black inner-city youth: "God's smiling on you and He's frowning too,/'Cause only God knows what you go through."[36] The power and presence of God is assumed by the mere fact that Melle Mel says God is "smiling and frowning" on this African-American teenager. God must be all-powerful and all-knowing if he is "everywhere and nowhere present" to see and know what this person *is* "going through."

Similarly, Kool Moe Dee comments on the omniscient, or all-knowing, character of God in his rap "Knowledge Is King."[37] Kool Moe Dee says the "knowledge of God" (Christ or

Allah) will teach African-Americans that money and fame are only temporary gains. He says the "knowledge of *God*" will give subliminal messages that free all human beings from the "criminal acts of the devil." Kool Moe Dee perceives the "acts of the devil" to be self-ambition, greed, ignorance, sexual promiscuity, and "slave mentality." Clearly, he sees knowledge as power and God as knowledge. The knowledge of God will prevent human beings from falling into the traps of Satan, particularly African-Americans making inappropriate decisions or choices at the expense of their own liberation. The acts of Satan, contends Kool Moe Dee, will continue to keep African-Americans oppressed if they do not obtain knowledge of God.

In a vein of thought similar to Kool Moe Dee, rappers 7A3 conceive of Satan as representing ignorance, physical violence, and the prevention of human liberation. They say people who are living with "Lucifer" need to quit this relationship. 7A3 says the issue of "ultimate concern" today is peace between the races, sexes, and classes of people who constitute America. They say cohabiting with Satan will not assist Americans in obtaining these goals.[38]

Conceptions of the Nature of Black Suffering

As shown above, the texts of African-American rappers illustrate their essentially traditional conceptions of God and Satan. While they reflect on the cause of black suffering with the white supremacy and slave mentality theodicies, they also reflect upon the essential character or nature of black suffering. An example is the frequently misquoted and misunderstood verses of Public Enemy's "Welcome to the Terrordome": "Apology made to whoever pleases/ Still they got me likeJesus."[39] A conception of the nature of black suffering is implied in the clause "They got me like Jesus." Based on descriptions in the Bible, the crucifixion of Jesus was excruciating but a necessary fulfillment of Old Testament prophecy. The nature of Jesus' suffering was that he had to endure cursings and violent physical reactions to his claim of being the Messiah. The significance here is that Jesus suffered horribly before he died. African-Americans have also endured a chronic suffering that seems just as unsubstantiated as that of Jesus. Rappers Public Enemy are saying that white American culture has still "got African-Americans like Jesus" in that African-Americans are enduring oppression and discrimination simply because of their culture and darker skin pigmentation.

James Cone documenting "ultimate concerns" of black spirituals almost twenty years before Public Enemy's release, finds similarly that enslaved African-Americans identified personally with Jesus. They believed he could save them from the oppression of slavery because he himself had suffered, died, and yet overcame death. Cone says:

> They were impressed by the Passion because they too had been rejected, beaten, shot without a chance to say a word in defense of their humanity. In Jesus' death black slaves saw themselves, and they unleashed their imagination, describing what they felt and saw.

His death was a symbol of their suffering, trials, and tribulations in an unfriendly world. They knew the agony of rejection and the pain of hanging from a tree ... Because black slaves knew the significance of the pain and shame of Jesus' death on the cross, they found themselves by his side. ... if Jesus was not alone in his suffering, they were not alone in their slavery. Jesus was with them![40]

Thus, eighteenth- and nineteenth-century African-Americans were using essentially the same rhetorical language as late twentieth-century African-Americans regarding the nature of their suffering in American society. The reason for the continuity of conception and language is the single experience of slavery and its residual effects. We can conclude, then, that the social, economic, and political contexts of African-American life have remained relatively the same, thus allowing a theological discourse surrounding the nature of suffering to stay alive. Cultural, social, economic, and political contexts are important in ascertaining an understanding of African-American music.

Another perspective on the nature of black suffering is illustrated in Naughty by Nature's brief case study of a young black male in a ghetto in their rap entitled "Ghetto Bastard (Everything's Gonna Be Alright)."[41] The protagonist, who has the point of view of Naughty by Nature's principal MC, Treach, recounts his life while growing up in the projects. Each stanza tells stories of suffering because of personal, familial, and especially, societal constraints. In his introductory stanza, Treach tells us he never knew his father, and that this explains why he is always angry. His mother was not able to keep him at home because she had too many mouths to feed; therefore, he had to "wander the streets." To express this despair and apparent sense of hopelessness, Treach revises a common "floating verse" in blues lyrics: "If not for bad luck, I would have none." In all of this, Treach cannot understand why he has had to suffer or what it means to his life in the present. As he continues, he speaks about contemplating suicide: "Sometimes I wish I could afford a pistol then though, /And stop the hell I would and ended things a while ago." Midway into his narration, Treach says that even while his neighborhood dictates a life of drug pushing and alcoholic intoxication and has caused him to consider suicide, he feels there must be a better way of life. He proclaims: "Hell no, I say there's gotta be a better way." He also decides that one way he can combat this reality is to "never gamble in any game" that he cannot play. In other words, he will not get involved in any activity that, within himself, he knows he cannot win. Even with his apparent resolve, the memories of suffering resurface and Treach asks, "How will I do or how will I make it?" And he answers, "I won't, that's how! Why me, huh?" Responding to all of Treach's questions of "Why me?" is a chorus of black women who reply, "Everything's gonna be alright."

In the last stanza of Treach's autobiographical account, he tells of his suffering but also illustrates how he responds to people who perpetually attack his self-worth. Treach's suffering is symptomatic of America's social ills. The only real hope that can be ascertained from his monologue is the reply by the chorus of black women: "Everything's gonna be alright." This refrain and specifically the use of black women portray the mandatory role and traditional response of African-American women in African-American culture especially in the black church. This role and response has been to build up their broken families and their broken men by affirming their fundamental humanity. Although Treach emphatically warns naive curiosity seekers to stay out of the ghetto, his story ends with a dialogue between himself ("Why me, huh?") and the chorus of black women ("Alright, alright").

The nature of Treach's suffering has been unsubstantiated, one with no logical answers as to the purpose of its occurrence since his suffering is the result of America's long history of systematic discrimination against black people on the basis of race. Treach's story is a microcosm of black suffering as a whole and illustrates clearly that African-Americans whether they are Saturday revelers or Sunday worshippers or both,[42] are reflecting on the nature of their suffering and devising resolutions to their oppression through song.

My analysis of theodicy in rap has drawn on thought by black theological thinkers: William R. Jones in his book *Is God a White Racist?* and Jon Michael Spencer in his essay on the theodicy of the blues. African-American rappers express concerns about evil in a world created by a good God, in the form of theodicean discourse, or theodicy. Theodicy, as specifically used in this study, examines the provisional means by which rappers exonerate and justify God's seeming inactivity in the face of evil, as well as determining the cause and nature of black oppression and suffering. Using William Jones's concept of "humanocentric theism," I found two secular theodicies in rap: the white supremacy theodicy and the slave mentality theodicy. These theodicies reconcile the tension between African-Americans' belief in an all-powerful good God and their actual suffering in the world. In other words, it is not God's fault that certain people, out of their free will, choose to oppress others, and that as a result certain other people have developed an enslaving mentality. Both sets of people work to perpetuate evil in the lives of African-Americans. I have also shown that the expression of the white supremacy and the slave mentality theodicies are evident in the rapper's traditional conceptions of God and Satan and in how they relate stories of the nature of black suffering.

Study Questions

1. Who are the formative black theological thinkers Nelson uses to build the case of theodicy and humanisms in her study of rap music and how does her conclusions of these sensibilities in rap music advance or challenge this stream of thought?
2. What two secular theodicies did Nelson find in her exploration of the problem of evil in rap music and what does she suggest they say about belief (i.e., God and Satan) and social suffering in the African American community?
3. How does (black) secular music challenge and advance traditional definitions and notions of theodicy in the study of black religion? How are theodical sensibilities in rap music identified?

Notes

1. John Hick, *Evil and the God of Love* (San Francisco: Harper & Row, 1978), 6.
2. Jon Michael Spencer, "God in Secular Music Culture: The Theodicy of the Blues as the Paradigm of Proof," *Black Sacred Music* 3, no. 2 (Fall 1989): 25, 34.
3. Ibid., 17–18.
4. Ibid., 27.
5. Ibid., 25.
6. William Jones, *Is God a White Racist?* (Garden City, NY: Anchor, 1973), xviii.
7. Hick, *Evil*, 3.
8. Ibid., 5.
9. Ibid., 12: "Moral evil is evil that we human beings originate: cruel, unjust, vicious, and perverse thoughts and deeds. Natural evil is the evil that originates independently of human actions: in disease bacilli, earthquakes, storms, droughts, tornadoes, etc."
10. Ibid., 5.
11. W. Jones, *White Racist?* xiii–xxii.
12. Ibid., 72–78.
13. Ibid., xxii.
14. See Martin Buber, *Tales of the Hasidim* (trans. Olga Marx; 2 vols.; New York: Schocken 1947–48); idem *The Eclipse of God: Studies in the Relation between Religion and Philosophy* (New York: Harper, 1952); Albert Camus, *The Plague* (trans. Stuart Gilbert; New York: Knopf, 1948); idem, *The Rebel* (trans. Anthony Bower; New York: Knopf, 1954); Harvey G. Cox, *The Secular City: Secularization and Urbanization in Theological Perspective* (rev. ed.; New York: Macmillan, 1966); Erich Fromm, *You Shall Be as Gods: A Radical Interpretation of the Old Testament and Its Tradition* (New York: Holt, Rinehart & Winston, 1966); and Jean-Paul Sartre, *Anti-Semite and Jew* (trans. George J. Becker; New York: Schocken Books, 1948).
15. W. Jones, *White Racist?* 185–95.

16. George M. Fredrickson, *White Supremacy: A Comparative Study in American and South African History* (New York: Oxford University Press, 1981), xi.

17. James A. Banks, *Teaching Strategies for Ethnic Studies* (Boston: Allyn & Bacon, 1991), 204–5.

18. Fredrickson, *White Supremacy,* xi.

19. Ibid.

20. LeRoi Jones (Amiri Baraka), *Blues People: The Negro Experience in White America and the Music That Developed from It* (New York: Morrow Quill, 1963), 57.

21. Ibid., 59.

22. W. Jones, *White Racist?* 41.

23. Na'im Akbar, *Chains and Images of Psychological Slavery* (Jersey City, NJ: New Mind Productions, 1984), 7.

24. Ibid.

25. Ibid., 9, 12, 15, 19, 20, 23, 30, 31, 38–42.

26. MC Lyte, "Cappucino," *Eyes on This* (New York: First Priority Records, distributed by Atlantic Recording, 1989).

27. Ibid., "Not Wit a Dealer."

28. W. Jones, *White Racist?* 44.

29. Cited in ibid., 40.

30. Ibid., 40–41.

31. Molefi Kete Asante, *The Afrocentric Idea* (Philadelphia: Temple University Press, 1987), 93.

32. Jon Michael Spencer, *Protest and Praise: Sacred Music of Black Religion* (Minneapolis: Fortress, 1990), 115.

33. Theodore Gilmore Bilbo, *Take Your Choice: Separation or Mongrelization* (Poplarville, MS: Dream House Publishing, 1947), 105.

34. Public Enemy, "Pollywanacraka," *Fear of a Black Planet* (New York: Def Jam Recordings, 1990).

35. See Acts 17:26.

36. Grandmaster Flash and the Furious Five, "The Message," *The Message* (Englewood, NJ: Sugarhill Records, 1982).

37. Kool Moe Dec, Knowledge Is King," *Knowledge Is King* (New York: Jive/Zomba Records, 1989).

38. 7A3, "Lucifer," *Coolin' in Cali* (London: Geffen Records, 1988).

39. Public Enemy, "Welcome to the Terrordome," *Fear of a Black Planet*.

40. James Cone, *The Spirituals and the Blues: An Interpretation* (San Francisco: Harper & Row, 1972), 52–54.

41. Naughty by Nature, "Ghetto Bastard (Everything's Gonna Be Alright)," *Naughty by Nature* (New York.: Tommy Boy Music, 1991).

42. Albert Murray, *Stomping the Blues* (New York: Da Capo, 1982), 27, 42.

11

"Wrapped Up"
Ideological Setting and Figurative Meaning in African-American Gospel Rap

Viljoen uses the gospel video *Wrapped Up* by Dawkins & Dawkins to explore incongruous meaning, negotiated ideologies, ritual activity, and symbolic reproduction. Viljoen works to more specifically chart patterns and relationships of domination, hidden imaginings, and narrative depictions within gospel rap. Despite the effort of some to discuss cultural forms, like rap music, through homogenizing tendencies, Viljoen suggests a move towards heterogeneous critical modes of inquiry and approaches that are more capacious and varied by bringing together a number of different frameworks and theories. By examining the lyrics, visuals, and musical composition of *Wrapped Up* through this multifaceted approach, Viljoen concludes that this embodied production (danced religion) is far more significant and layered than the common assumption of a commercialized and straightforward terrain.

"Wrapped Up": Ideological Setting and Figurative Meaning in African-American Gospel Rap

Martina Viljoen

Introduction

At first glance, the gospel video WRAPPED UP[1] by the African-American duo Dawkins & Dawkins is an uncomplicated and entertaining contemporary-religious mass culture text. However, subjected to a detailed scholarly analysis, this instance of gospel rap provides a visible site of conflict, offering an arena par excellence for the forging and negotiation of ideologies. Scholars such as Richard Shusterman (1992, p. 201ff) and Houston Baker (1994, p. 186) consider rap music and its analytical and pedagogical entailments a perfect case study for cultural criticism. As a trans-cultural and trans-national phenomenon, rap music is a particularly viable universal medium for such a theoretical/methodological endeavour. The special case of gospel rap presents a powerful embodiment of symbolic reproduction in its deployment of ritual activity, each symbol encompassing multiple, often contradictory meanings. As I would like to demonstrate in this article, it is exactly within these textual "contradictions" and "tensions" that strategies of symbolic construction and ideological modes of operation unfold.

For this reason my analysis of WRAPPED UP evolves around a speculative design for theorising the relationship between symbolic content and discursive socio-cultural contexts. This theoretical framework draws on the combined interpretative strengths of ideology critique and the analysis of figurative meaning, a methodology based on the philosopher Johann Visagie's (1994, 1996) approach to ideological culture.[2] Allowing for a detailed analysis of the semiotic layering surrounding and infiltrating all the various performative events that constitute symbolic expression, Visagie's interpretative framework furthermore facilitates the integration of relevant aspects of other theoretical models and approaches. This allows for the application of a relatively wide-ranging, even eclectic selection of analytical tools and methods, an aspect that is of considerable import for detailed musical and/or multimedia analysis.

While this strategy may appear to be no different from the generalised procedure of allowing disparate elements from different signifying practices to co-exist within cultural analysis, the most potent aspect of Visagie's framework is the fact that it focuses not only on the figurative content of texts, but more specifically on relations of domination between explicit or implicit images, metaphorical meanings, archetypal symbols, narrative representations, and so on. This kind of analysis is particularly productive in terms of a detailed and multi-layered reading of a complex text such as WRAPPED UP, illustrating that methods of formal or discursive analysis need to engage both creatively and critically in the construction of meaning for an interpretative explication of what is represented or "said" by symbolic forms. The primary aim of this article is thus to provide a scholarly reading of a commercialised mass-culture text—a reading that depends methodologically on a specialised theoretical approach.

Following the Cambridge ideology theorist John Thompson (1984, 1990), Visagie's notion of the concept of ideology is broadened to include the analysis and critique of important sites of domination and power other than those institutionalised in the modern state. Thus, the phenomenon of ideology is construed to be of more than merely political significance. Consequently, it facilitates specialised forms of discursive analysis in that it specifically enables the intensive exploration of links between all forms of conceptualisation (and thus all forms of "language") and ideology. In this broadened context, the complex "asymmetries" of social power relations may be interpreted in terms of a wide range of social forms and actions. These may include symbolic forms of various kinds, from everyday utterances to complex images and texts, as well as the contexts within which they are employed and deployed. Thus, the analysis of ideology is brought into a domain of conceptual and methodological issues of a considerably more general scope than was the case in the orthodox Marxian view (for instance).

Returning to the phenomenon of rap, it may be noted that a number of recent studies on rap music, including those of Rose (1994), Warner (1998), Griffin (1998) and Brown (1998) convincingly argue that consistent patterns of rhetorical appeal in rap music may be traced back to the traditions of African tribal music. As a powerful *aide-memoire* of black experience, rap music ignites an African cultural memory by drawing compellingly on such (figurative) strategies as story-telling, boasting, toasting, loud-talking, testifying and signifyin(g). While fully acknowledging features of African-American and diaspora discourse in rap and gospel music (and the more or less "culture-specific" approach of analysis they imply), my reading of WRAPPED UP simultaneously takes cognisance of the fact that rap texts are thoroughly postmodernist in their characteristic stylistic features. These include the flamboyant practices of sampling and recycling, the eclectic mixing of styles, and the enthusiastic embracing of technology and of mass culture (cf. Shustermann 1992, p. 201ff). Thus, I am convinced that syncretic popular forms (such as rap and the more commercialized forms of black gospel music) can no longer be studied only in terms of "traditional" cultural traits, but rather through heterogeneous, ideology-critical modes of inquiry. For this reason, I integrate in Visagie's framework an eclectic mix of critical interpretative grids, the most important of these being Adam Krims's (2000) system of rap genres, as well as Nicholas Cook's (1998) theory of multimedia analysis. Incorporated into Visagie's overarching framework, these theories serve to both specify and intensify a multi-layered ideology-critical analysis of "dominating discourses" in Dawkins & Dawkins's WRAPPED UP.

"Wrapped Up"

The song "Wrapped Up" by the brothers Anson and Eric Dawkins was first released on their album Focus during 1998. Distributed by Christian Art Music, the album was issued by Harmony Records, a division of Relativity Entertainment Inc. The song was written by Rodney Jerkins and the Dawkins brothers, and produced by Raina Bundy. A remix was included on the WoW Gospel 2000 album, rating thirteenth among the year's thirty top gospel songs. The soundtrack of the promotional video is a combination of the initial release on Focus and the remix version on WoW Gospel.[3] Liner notes on the WoW Gospel album describe Dawkins & Dawkins's style as "urban/contemporary."

The musical structure of WRAPPED UP conforms to standardised popular song structure. However, a Bridge and the already mentioned portion of rap text inserted between the third and fourth appearances of the Hook (chorus/refrain) disrupt this structure in terms of both meaning and musical style. Since these sections of the song are particularly significant in terms of figurative content, I shall return to them in more detail below.

For all the slickness of its deceptively smooth surface, the musical style of WRAPPED UP is a complex mix of styles drawing on both contemporary and earlier African-American and Latin American models. Already evident from the instrumental introduction, contemporary rhythm & blues is intermingled with a dominant Latin-American influence featuring a provocative rumba/tango mix. The sensuous mood of the music is intensified by a tight, prominent beat, directly traceable to an African rhythmic influence inherent in both the dance-styles featured and the intensive rhythms of rhythm & blues. The ensemble styles of the vocal and instrumental units are typical of this idiom, which, together with rap, is immensely popular in current gospel production. However, this subtle fusion of styles is dramatically disrupted by an aggressive "gangsta" rap idiom, representing the climax of the song as a whole. While such rap interventions are almost standardised features in rhythm & blues styles, in this specific context, the rap section fulfils an important function in terms of the figurative construction of meaning since it powerfully evokes the grim certainties of black urban ghetto life as embodied in the outlaw figure of the "gangsta."

My analysis below allows the figurative aspects of independent intra-textual levels of meaning (lyrics, visuals, and music) to interact performatively with one another. In this regard, I follow Nicholas Cook (1998, p. 24ff) in examining the various media components first as independent variables and consequently as interactive elements of the video text. Working systematically towards the final, most intuitive phase of my analysis, formalist aspects of my reading are creatively extended towards a speculative theorisation of figurative content. The first "level" of analysis concerns a discussion of the lyrics, the visuals, and the music of WRAPPED UP as multimedia constituents of this video.

The Lyrics

A discursive analysis of the lyrics of WRAPPED UP necessarily refers to both socio-historical contexts and to metaphor and narrative, woven so tightly into the fabric of the text that it becomes impossible to dissect it in terms of separate topics. These contextual frameworks, however, all work together in constructing meaning in this text, particularly with regard to its ambiguous representations of black religious identity. For this reason, I focus explicitly on historical hymnological models reverberating in this particular instance of gospel rap—a context often overlooked in studies of commercialised forms of contemporary hymnody. It should be noted, however, that despite its powerful projection of religious content, the lyrics of WRAPPED UP simultaneously construct implicit and explicit "bids" for ideological power through a constant contextual "refiguration" of metaphor and narrative.

Representing a testimony of confession and faith, the opening lines of WRAPPED UP's lyrics are typical of the beginnings of life-story narratives, thematically symbolising a transformation from darkness to light. This concurs with the tendency of gospel hymnody, drawing mainly on the hymnological model of Revivalism, to focus on individual spiritual experience, applied personally and re-lived inwardly and subjectively by the convert.

In representing the believer as "hopeless," "helpless," "even senseless" (complementing the metaphor of "Lord you've got me wrapped around Your finger"), the content of Verse I links this section of the lyrics with Wattsian hymnody rather than with the somewhat later model of Revivalist hymns, which are the historical precursor of gospel hymnody.[4] The rap lyrics reinforce this doctrinal orientation in presenting a range of Hebrew God-descriptions in rapid succession, all emphasising the greatness, the glory and the sovereignty of God ("Alpha, Omega"; "El Shaddai"; "Elohim"; "the great Addonai"). Note also that "Lion of Judah" refers to Christ the Messiah, again a focal point of Wattsian hymnody.

Influenced by Calvinistic theology, the content of Wattsian hymns was scriptural in nature, focusing on Christ as the very centre of objective worship. In the lyrics of WRAPPED UP, a Calvinist influence is also present in the connotations of power adduced by the metaphorical model of the "King" implicit in the Hebrew descriptions of God (also sustained by the reference to "Lion of Judah"). In itself, this kind of model or metaphor of God reduces the status of a complementary "intimate love" model: God as "Father"; "Friend"; "Husband"; "Shepherd."

Metaphorical content also points to a certain dualism between a "problem-filled" and a "Grace-saved" life. However, the phrases "how you always seem to come around ... in the nick of time ... to save the day" indicate a rather realistic approach acknowledging that life is (and even after the turn to faith remains) a "struggle." This moment reminds us of the assortment of metaphors serving to picture the essential content of life in relation to some or other origin or destination. One of these "master" metaphors does indeed depict life (in relation to God or another Ideal) as struggle, conflict or war.

In stark contrast with the model of the "King" the content of the Hook represents a subjective, emotional love-song to Jesus which, in the context of the video as a whole, is loaded with erotic suggestion ("You've got me wrapped up, tied up, tangled up"; and "You've got me wrapped around your Finger").[5] It is interesting to note that the content of the Bridge ("Lost here I am inside Your Love") also points to an underlying transformational duality (being lost in the Spirit, yet "found" in complete surrender—"Wrapped, tied up, tangled up"). Simultaneously, the "inside" metaphor may also serve to emphasise both the intimate closeness and the power of the Loving God: an example of two God-metaphors "deconstructing" each other, as it were. In representing a very existentialist kind of spirituality, the rap lyrics present yet another doctrinal model, the highly personal nature of which is evident from the "real-life testimony" by rapper T-bone, who refers openly to himself ("the Boney bone"; "I'm gone T-Bone") and to his conversion. Here, various metaphors are used to represent the Fallen Sinner, all relating to the metaphor of the streetwise gangster ("harder than concrete"; "playas, hustlas and addicts"; "put down the weed and the automatic"). However, in a manner appropriate to the medium of rap, the miracle of conversion is represented metaphorically by speed ("Fed Ex packages") and by heat ("type of heat movin' thugs on the street"). T-Bone's testimony also references the merits of Rhythm & Blues and rap as media for preaching the gospel:

> type of heat movin' thugs on the street that's harder than concrete
> with these R&B beats, baby

Note that the content of the rap also refers to the theme of religious transformation: "playas hustlas and addicts actin' charismatic."

The line "When I stop and meditate" (Verse I) suggests a contemplative posture, while "got me wrapped around your finger" (Verse I) is indicative of "falling and being held." The figural posture of suffering is suggested by the lines "Looking for solutions I can't find; any answers to my questions why" (Verse II). The content of " ... I gotta let you know just how I feel about you noon and day," on the other hand, is suggestive of praise, as is the line "... so throw your hand in the sky when we rockin" (Rap).

In terms of figurative content that may be linked with earlier hymnological models and with the blues, I interpret the "gangsta" images and the specific thematic figurative patterns in

the Rap lyrics as indicative of suffering in the specific context of black experience. These stereotypes point to an identity politics suggesting the hardships of particular social, economic,
and cultural experiences:

> Take it from this rap sanga, ex-gang banga
> I'll be wrapped around Your finger
> Like the Police, styles obese got playas hustlas and addicts actin' charismatic
> Put down the weed and the automatic
> my grammatic, fanatic steelo guaranteed to get you high like the addict

The Visuals

Drawing on ideology critique as well as on analysis of metaphor and narrative, I shall focus in
the following sections not only on the "contest" between the different media (cf. Cook 1998,
p. 106ff), but also on the conflict between different levels of signification.[6] Nicholas Cook's
notion of media contest is an important interpretative tool for the analysis and critique of
ideology, rendering possible an analysis of the way in which contest deconstructs media identities and familiar media hierarchies (and thus "meaning"). This approach dispenses with an
ethics of autonomy, implying that no particular media entity is automatically privileged, or
involuntarily assumed to "speak the truth" (Cook 1998, p. 128). My discussion of figurative
meaning in WRAPPED UP includes both general and specific features, illustrating that levels
of signification and their dialogic interaction with music, image and word performatively
"negotiate," "highlight," or "hide" meaning in this text.[7]

In WRAPPED UP, two powerful narratives operate simultaneously on the visual level,
influentially altering (refiguring) the musical metaphor that is operative throughout this text.
On the one hand, there is the star text, the meta-narrative framing the "story" of the gospel
duo Dawkins & Dawkins.[8] At the same time, a transformation story relating to the Biblical
master narrative of Creation, Fall and Redemption unfolds in the Bridge and Rap sections
of the video. These divergent narratives are intertwined in a very complex way, influentially
complicating (yet balancing) metaphorical and narrative allusion in the video.

The art historian Mieke Bal (1985, p. 142ff) describes narrative texts in which at a second
or third level a complete story is told as "embedded" texts. In such cases, the secondary story/
stories may explain the primary narrative, or resemble it. Often, the "mirror text" (or texts)
may determine the function of the primary text for the reader/listener/viewer. This function,
Bal (1985, p. 146) describes as "significance enhancing," implying that the second (or third)
narrative contains a suggestion as to how the text as a whole is to be understood.

Traceable from the very first shots of the video clip, the so-called star narrative strongly
dominates the visual materials of WRAPPED UP. Arriving by helicopter, Dawkins &
Dawkins, clothed in white, emerge on a beach set in an exotic location. While quite a few
MC's have featured helicopter landings in their videos, the white outfits of the stars seem to
suggest an intertextual referencing of the famous rap star P. Diddy's arrival by helicopter in
BEEN AROUND THE WORLD.

Interpreted in terms of Andrew Goodwin's (1992, p. 50ff) notion of the star meta-narrative,
a number of factors are of import here. First, by referencing well-known symbols associated
with a powerful "gangsta" rapper image, it is subliminally suggested that gospel duo Dawkins
& Dawkins too are "men of the world" and part of the star system of performers arriving in
jets, limousines and helicopters. The arrival scene is set (as is often the case in the star narrative) in an exotic location, suggesting the relaxed atmosphere and the luxuries associated

with the vacationing styles of the rich and famous.[9] Mieke Bal (1985, p. 43ff) observes that spatial elements indeed play a crucial role in narrative structures, pointing out the predominance of space and location in the human imagination. In this video text, as will become clear below, locational oppositions are also indicative of ideological conflict. Indeed, it may even be argued that, in WRAPPED UP, space is ideologically thematised. From these perspectives, it is clear that the visual parameters of the video, within its first few seconds, powerfully construct a particular identity (and the location of that identity) by suggesting difference and social boundaries by means of the phantasmagoric otherness of stardom.

Read in terms of the links between rap conventions and earlier Afro-centric rhetorical strategies, the opening shots of the video also signally represent an identification with and a challenge to "baadman" secular rappers. Potter (1995, p. 83ff) explains that, unlike Western signification, signifyin(g) assumes "a mistaking of meaning" (cf. Gates 1988), resulting in semantic slippages which function as a primary mechanism for meaning-making in rap. It may be argued that the ambiguous construction of figurative identity in this mass culture text represents an outstanding example of this rhetorical device through a deliberate "misconstruction" of meaning, and thus of the "product" being sold. This points to a profoundly "trans-actional" exchange where narrative and ideology interact, powerfully framing "interpellations" between text and implied listeners/viewers. In terms of Bal's (1985, p. 35ff) narrative theory, such "mistaking" of meaning may indeed be seen as an important element of narrative suspense.[10]

The projection of star identity is maintained throughout the entire video clip, the "journey" ending with the stars departing and the helicopter captured in a long shot against a magnificent sky. As Goodwin (1992, p. 107) observes, in music video, performance imagery is far from an innocent realist representation of the music itself. This implies that the various performance clips featuring the gospel duo Dawkins & Dawkins are actively part of the narrative strategies of the star text, intervening in a significant way in the construction of meaning in this text. The visual elements constructing the stage scene (subtle backlighting, the glamorous backing vocal team, professional dancers and an exuberant audience), all work together to create a generalised discourse of stardom-as-otherness. As will become clear in the ensuing argument, these (visual) narrative exchanges are not ideologically neutral, but reciprocally "transactional." Thus, in contrasting the different ideological "angles" of the star text, visual content powerfully establishes "relations of domination" in this video.[11]

It is also primarily in the visual content of this video text that certain (ideologically slanted) roles of fans are constructed or implied. As Berger's (1991, p. 4) study of media techniques emphasises, interpreters have to supply (both synchronically and diachronically) part of the meaning of texts.[12] Meaning thus construed, however, is complicit in establishing systemic asymmetries implied by the text. Even in the kind of camera shots employed, or in the angle that is used, ideology is present. An example of this kind of visual "manipulation" in WRAPPED UP is the series of performance scenes (stage scenes; see below), which are, in most cases, shot from an angle where the camera "looks up" at the stars. While this is typical of the "beatdown" scene (a common visual strategy of rap videos) from an ideology-critical point of view it may also be interpreted as an indication of the power and authority of the performers, established via a cliched media technique that seduces fans into the implied role of enthralled "admirers." Simultaneously, the audience is "viewed" by way of close-up shots. These suggest closeness and intimacy, implying that the camera acts as "representative" of individual "onlookers"/"participants" in the video "act."

Considering the structuring strategies of this video text, it is interesting to note that the first appearance of the gospel stars in the stage scene (medium long shot: stage scene with band and four professional dancers; dissolve and zoom-in: star duo centre stage) is used as a kind of visual hook. Featuring directly after the instrumental Introduction, it replaces the musical hook which is only featured after Verse I. Note that the visual hook of the stage scene is part of the materials building the star narrative framing this text, already suggested by visual materials displayed during the Introduction. This narrative is powerfully sustained throughout the video clip, and takes on special significance during the Bridge and the Rap.

The star narrative projected by the visual track of WRAPPED UP is complicated by the message of the lyrics and by the second embedded narrative, which tells not of glamour and stardom, but of the grace, love and sacrifice of God. Presented via the naive realist "gangsta" narrative of the Bridge section, it tells the story of a gangster (later morphed into real-life rapper T-Bone) being "literally" struck by the grace of God, and subsequently converted (monochrome close-up shot of gangster leaving car and donning a mask; panning monochrome long shot of robbery scene with masked gangster returning to car; dissolve to stars, colour returning and star duo appearing miraculously in flare). Following the Bridge section, the Rap text relates the story of T-Bone's conversion, and of how the media of R&B and rap are used to convert "thugs on the street that's harder than concrete." This reference to "R&B beats," together with the visuals of the Bridge, strongly suggest that the story of rapper T-Bone's conversion has been brought about by the gospel ministry of Dawkins & Dawkins.[13]

From the perspective of narrative theory and ideology critique, what is of importance here is that different kinds of oppositions are set up by these two "clashing" narrative structures, including opposing locations (slum scene/liturgical space/stage scenes), and the opposition between what Bal (1985, p. 37) calls "haves" and "have-nots." Describing characters as complex semantic units, Bal (1985, p. 79) suggests the ideological impact of predictability within the narrative structure. In this regard, the figure of the gangster functions as a powerful referential element, rhetorically not only presenting the myths and rituals of present-day gangsterism, but also referencing its lineage in earlier black cultural forms such as "baadman" narratives and the "blaxploitation" movie genre (cf. Kelley 1995, p. 127).

It is precisely at the point of rapper T-Bone's conversion that the ulterior motives of the star narrative interlock with the "gangsta" narrative in a highly complex manner. Used as a metaphor for the Fallen Life, the "gangsta" sequence takes a drastic turn as the grace of God, metaphorically represented by light, "strikes." Transformed from the ghetto scene to liturgical space, the visuals of the Bridge and the Rap metaphorically represent a spiritual version of the rags-to-riches narrative. However, in the very moment of conversion, it is not an image of God (or some God symbol) that is featured, but rather the star duo Dawkins & Dawkins; this is a striking case of the star text dominating the gospel ("gangsta") narrative. From the standpoint of ideology analysis, this moment indeed represents an ideology analogy as it literally "enacts" relations of domination within narratology.[14]

The Music

In the interpretation of structural and figurative meaning in the soundtrack of WRAPPED UP, I shall attempt to demonstrate that the musical parameters, at the above-described narrative point of "crisis," mirror the ideological complexities forged by this intersection of star text and "gospel" narrative. Moving between surface elements and deeper structure in the last subsection of this article, I shall discuss the meaning of this video as an emergent property of the musical text. Note that I follow Lawrence Kramer (1992, p. 140) in understanding musical representation in a very broad sense, acknowledging its rich interpretative ties to both musical and cultural processes. Kramer's (1992, p. 161) conviction that music becomes representational not in direct relation to social or physical reality but in relation to tropes is, to my mind, an analytical observation particularly pertinent to a figurative analysis of WRAPPED UP'S soundtrack and to my analytical strategy as a whole:

> A musical likeness is the equivalent of a metaphor, and more particularly of a metaphor with a substantial intertextual history. Once incorporated into a composition, such a metaphor is capable of influencing musical processes, which are in turn capable of extending, complicating or revising the metaphor.

In WRAPPED UP, interrelated layers of cultural signification contribute by shaping not only surface textural elements, but also structural events and, eventually, meaning in this text. Intertextuality is at play on various levels, specifically involving the musical soundtrack and the visuals.[15] Conforming to the practices of musical appropriation in jazz, the chordal and melodic structure of WRAPPED UP's Hook and Verses, already featured in the instrumental Introduction, is based on the materials from a rumba by the group Shaft, "Mucho mambo." In turn, this song borrows from the earlier dance-hit tune "Sway." It should also be noted that the song "Wrapped Up" explicitly tropes the Police song "Wrapped Around Your Finger." This trope might be interpreted to strengthen visual intertextuality referencing P. Diddy in that the rapper's first hit sampled a Police song as well. In terms of the construction of figurative meaning, it should be noted that the Police song to which "Wrapped Up" alludes refers to a reversal of a dependence relationship.

The multi-level layering of WRAPPED UP'S musical soundtrack, while building on simplistic formulas prescribed by cliched, standardised song structure, reveals a surprisingly complex formal texture, even an inclination towards formal experiment. Moreover, these compositional layers, apart from performing structural functions, refer on different levels to metaphor and narrative, and thus, ultimately, to the construction of meaning in this text.

As has been pointed out above, the soundtrack of WRAPPED UP conforms to standardised popular song structure, with the exception of the Bridge and the Rap text inserted between Hooks 3 and 4:

Instrumental Intro (bars 1–5)
Verse I (bars 6–13)
Hook I (x2) (bars 14–21)
Verse II (bars 22–29)
Hook I (x2) (bars 30–37)
Bridge (bars 38–47)
Hook II (incomplete) (bars 48–51)
Rap (bars 51–67)
Hook II (x6) (bars 68–91)

The soundtrack of WRAPPED UP powerfully emphasises relationships of V and I. Indeed, throughout the song, V may be seen as figuratively representing "expectation" while I is "resolution." Introduced by the rhythm section, the first bar of the instrumental Introduction is based on I of C minor, except for an A-flat augmented VI neighbour-note chord on the upbeat of bar 2 (strummed on acoustic guitar), immediately resolving to V7. The rest of the five-bar Introduction consists of two-bar appearances of V and I respectively. The elided resolution of the A-flat augmented VI chord in bar 2 (to V7 of C Minor) heightens the sensuous timbral and rhythmic effect of the first guitar chord, prolonged in a syncopated strumming effect almost reminiscent of the flamenco style, and intensified also by the overall rhythmic impulse of the music. This A-flat-G neighbour-note figure, the beginning of the melodic progression G-A-flat-G-F-D-E-flat-C,[16] a slightly varied melodic progression of the clichéd "tango" progression G-A-flat-G-F-E-flat-D-C, is also a structural figure in the musical text of

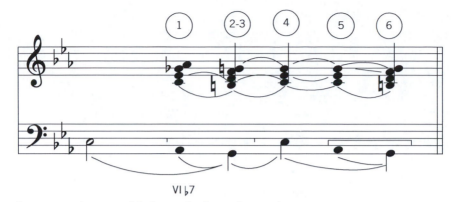

VI♭7

Example 1 Wrapped Up, simplified voice-leading reduction, bars 1–6

WRAPPED UP, acting not only as a recurring feature of the bass line of the Hook, but also as a middle-ground prolongation in the Bridge (Example 1).

The main melodic materials of Verses I and II may be reduced to sequential two-note figures descending from G to E-flat, built on the melodically embellished suspension figures G–F; F–E-flat, pointing both to melodic materials from "Sway" and "Mucho mambo" and to the neighbour-note motif A-flat-G of bar 2.[17] The melodic content of the Verses is a slight improvisational elaboration of Hook I. On the word "defenceless" in Verse I, the melodic movement G-F, F-E-flat deviates to B-flat, lending the music a somewhat ecstatic affect.[18]

This effect is intensified on the word "finger," where the melodic line rises to C, followed by G, as well as on the word "so" at the end of the Bridge. In Hook I, these ecstatic effects are echoed in rhythmic interjections by the backing vocals (among others) on the words "You got me tied up," rapidly moving between B-flat and G. Note that these (and other) interjections are part of the typically African heritage of call-and-response patterns, as well as the shouting practice ("getting happy"; "getting religion"; "having church"; "like fire shut up in my bones") typical of Holy Ghost Pentecostal singing in early African-American worship (Spencer 1990, p. 194; note that these are representative of the "transformational" theme). This "singing-testifying" formed part of the spiritual, mental and physical transmutation into the ritual celebration called "danced religion," inextricably bound with the shouting practice, a ritual Cusic (1990, p. 87) describes as "a physical and emotional activity at fever pitch."[19]

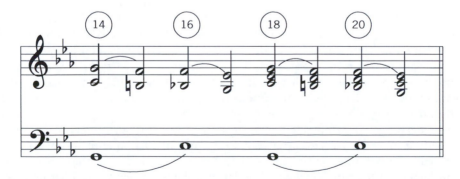

Example 2 Wrapped Up, voice-leading reduction, Hook I (bars 14–21)

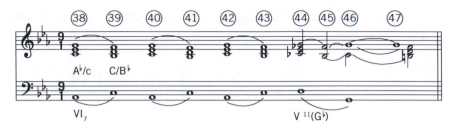

Example 3 *Wrapped Up*, Bridge, oscillating harmonies, bars 38–47

I have already alluded to the structural significance of the neighbour-note figure A-flat-G, first occurring in bars 1–2 of the Introduction. This figure functions as a "precursor" to its recurrence on the bass-line upbeat of respective versions of Hook I (Example 2). Its effect is intensified by an increase in percussive effects (the maraca is added), and by interjections by the backing vocals accompanied by an arpeggiated version of the underlying chordal structure, performed on an electronic keyboard. Again, these devices create effects of ecstasy and celebration, enhanced by the rhythmic effect of the backing vocals moving in parallel chord motion. However, from a structural viewpoint it should be noted that, in Hook I, the resulting neighbouring chord is now a major seventh, resulting from a C minor triad superimposed above the A-flat bass. On the melodic "chunks" G-F, F-E-flat, two parallel triads are featured, representing a kind of "sectional" harmony typical of jazz idioms.

The G suspension features a C minor triad, while on the F suspension, a B-flat triad is present, forming a polychord. As will be illustrated below, these polychordal elements take on special significance in the Bridge.

The Bridge is musically the most intricate part of this text, simultaneously highlighting and protracting elements from Hook I, while at the same time featuring materials which anticipate elements from the Rap section. Starting on B-flat, the melodic line moves to G via A-flat, referring again to melodic materials used earlier (compare "defenceless" in Verse I), appearing here, however, in a different tonal context. The melodic materials F-D-E-flat-F following this progression form an inversion of the same motif.

Harmonically deviating from the now familiar V-I chord structure, the Bridge starts on VI, involving both the bass A-flat and the C minor triad already mentioned (Example 3). While referencing the neighbour-note figure of bars 1–2, this A-flat does not immediately resolve to G, but instead moves to C with a B-flat major triad above it, thereby facilitating a recurrence of the C minor and B-flat major triads featured earlier on the G-F suspension in Hook I. Indeed, the Bridge continuously oscillates between the pitches A-flat and C. This tonal context seems to highlight the C minor triad above the A-flat bass, not only as part of the A-flat major seventh chord, but also as part of an oscillation of the C minor and B-flat major triads, respectively positioned above A-flat and C in the bass. Thus, the A-flat major seventh chord may also be interpreted (albeit rather precariously) as an A-flat/C polychord which is complemented by the C/B-flat polychord, performing an "inward" motion. With the motion of C back to A-flat, however, it moves "outward" again.

Characterised by tonal ambiguity, even a sense of tonal "loss," there is a further surprise in the Bridge.[20] After the third occurrence of the A-flat/C oscillation, the C/B-flat polychord unexpectedly moves up half a tone to D-flat/C-flat, apparently functioning as a secondary VII harmony on D-flat which instead of resolving to the presumed G-flat I harmony, suddenly reverts back to V of C minor, with the bass plunging down a tritone (D-flat-G-natural).

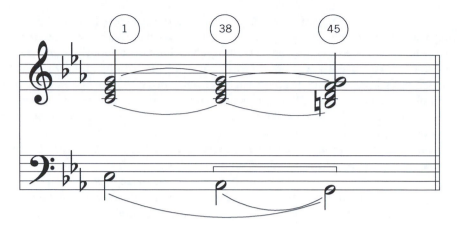

Example 4 Middle-ground voice-leading graph, bars 1–47

However, this dramatic plunge must be regarded as a "surface" harmonic motion. At a deeper level, a case may be made out for a resolution of the A-flat major 7th harmony to G, representing a large "middle-ground" parallelism of the A-flat-G harmonies in bars 1–2, 5–6, and the A-flat 7-G motions in Hook I.

This implies that the underlying prolonged harmony throughout the Bridge is A-flat, VI of C minor, a finding which may be substantiated in two ways. First, the A-flat/C bass motions must be regarded as motions to and from an inner voice of A-flat major, while the B-flat major triads in the triadic oscillations serve as lower neighbour chords to the C minor constituent of the A-flat/C polychord. The subsequent motion to D-flat is a further outgrowth of the C/B-flat polychord, which is, in turn, embedded within the A-flat prolongation.

Thus, the harmonic progression which might have moved from A-flat to D-flat to G is in fact a massive prolongation of A-flat to G, but with chord interpolations. It is interesting to note that the vocal style of the Bridge is unison, the chords being more sustained and presented without rhythmic patterns. This lends the music a certain starkness. Below, I will return to the figurative meaning of this musical gesture.

On the level of the foreground, at the point of conversion projected in the visual narrative in the Bridge, a 4–3 suspension is featured on V, representing a kind of shock element emphasising both V and the cadential plunge to D. This may be interpreted as a musical narration of the dramatic impact of the conversion. The conversion is very crudely symbolised by a crude scratch sound familiar to rap music,[21] with the musical style now featuring a hard-core, secular rap-rock style. While the spiritual transformation is effectively portrayed by this radical break in musical style, from the viewpoint of ideology critique, this simultaneous referencing of spiritual transformation and secular star text powerfully highlights the ambiguities of this text. The musical portrayal of a radical conversion and a break with the past furthermore symbolises a particular kind of triumphalist theology underlying the text of WRAPPED UP as a whole.

The musical style of the Bridge references the theme song of the film *Men in Black*.[22] This metaphor (the "black" men; the "thugs on the street") is juxtaposed with the metaphor of light in the visual materials, metaphorically representing the conversion. Note that the juxtaposition of the monochrome colours of the Bridge to the rich visual contrast of the liturgical space is also part of this metaphorical allusion to the spiritual transformation from darkness to light, simultaneously referencing a "being lost" and "being found."[23]

By way of a very crude tonal gesture, the Rap section abruptly moves to D minor, tonally representing a radical break with all previous materials. This musical transformation also manifests itself in a somewhat increased tempo and an electric guitar chord continuously emphasising I of D minor. The Rap consists of a descending baseline, moving between I and V (D-C-B-flat-A), and functioning as an ostinato figure accentuated by syncopated rhythmic figures.

The Hook of the Rap section (Hook II) also features an ostinato figure in the accompaniment. Here, a riff featured on the keyboard accompanies the words "Keep on wrappin' me, keep on wrappin' me with your love, Lord." The riff consists of a two-part figure in D minor with F in the upper voice, while the lower voice moves from A-B-C and from C-B-A. This is a transformation of the ecstasy motif featured on the word "defenceless" (G-B-flat-G) in Verse I, also referencing the melodic material from the Bridge.[24] The riff repeatedly ends on a B and F, referring to the triton implicit in the V7 chord of C minor and the dramatic tritone motion from D-flat to G at the end of the Bridge. At the same time, it functions as a colouring device typical of jazz idioms.

The ground bass movement in both the Rap section and the repeats of Hook II featuring the above-mentioned progression of I to V reverses the tonal axis of the music, creating the impression that the music stays in I. This effect is intensified by a riff in the vocals featuring a melodic progression D-F-A-G-A-G-F, the last three notes of which refer to the underlying melodic motion of the Verses. This continuously circling movement of the music, also represented by the repetition of Hook II (repeated six times before it is faded out) is intensified by the repetition of the ground bass figure and an "endless" repetition of the two riffs, creating the impression that the music is moving in a cycle based on I. Within the particular symbolic context, this musical gesture is traceable to African religious aesthetic and elements symbolic of traditional African music practices, and in particular to the African religious ring ritual. Note that Hook II does not "end," but is eventually faded out. This is of course also a cliched strategy of popular music, presenting us once more with an ambiguous mix of cultural layering and symbolic capital.

Finally, perhaps the most startling tonal symbolisation of WRAPPED UP can be seen in the relationship between the descending ostinato bass of the Rap section and Hook II and the overall middle-ground progression of the first part of the song (bars 1–47). Not only are the underlying harmonies the same (I-V), but the essential notes in the ostinato bass (D-B-flat-A) match the C-A-flat-G bass tones of the middle-ground progression. In fact, it is as if the ostinato bass reiterates the essential tonal motion of the first part of the song on the musical surface, enhanced by its "endless" repetition, while at the same time, it is retrospectively "wrapped up" tonally by the large middle-ground progression.

In terms of Krims's (2000) categories of rap flows, it is interesting to note that, in the rap section, speech-effusive and percussion-effusive styles are mixed, and that a sung rhythmic style is used only on the ecstatic words "wrapped around Your Finger." The latter expression suggests a certain sustainability in the text, linking it also with the lyrics of the R&B song. On the other hand, a consideration of word-tone relation-ship reveals that a percussive delivery is most often present when the lyrics project a sense of urgency (for instance "Fed Ex packages"; "I know You trippin I come up with lyrical styles/you never heard in English or Espagnol, mommy/that's how we spread the Word").

Music, Words and Images

In the above discussion of the musical parameters of WRAPPED UP, I have mentioned that the chordal and melodic structure of the soundtrack of this video draws on the earlier dance

hits "Mucho Mumbo" and "Sway." By way of a number of musical gestures, the most important of which is a rhythmic, timbral and melodic reference to the tango style, a "subliminal"
tango is suggested.[25] In terms of marketing ideology, I believe this representation to be an
example of a certain (implicit) propositional syntax, both "highlighting" and "hiding" erotic
associations explicit in the musical text of this video clip.[26]

The quotation of tango elements and of well-known dance-hit chord progressions, points
to the presence of an all-pervasive structural metaphor in this work. In terms of metaphor
and narrative analysis, it is important to note that narrative "development" in the music is
powerfully sustained through a "composing" with style and genre, evoking figurative content
overabundant in cultural meaning and associations.

Though expressed by way of mass-cultural structural cliches, a metaphorical interpretation of the subliminal tango in WRAPPED UP unveils the spiritual dimensions of this text,
in which it functions as a metaphor for "being touched by the grace of God." The many references to African religious ritual celebration and African-American cultural memory point
to the ring ritual and the phenomenon of holy dancing, also known as the "walk in Egypt"
(Spencer 1990, p. 194). Thus dance, in secular idioms often a sexual metaphor, becomes here a
powerful metaphor for spiritual liberation, pointing to the phenomenon of "danced religion."
Referenced in both the superficial and the deeper structural elements of the musical text of
WRAPPED UP, this metaphor is predominantly and almost constantly represented by a mixture of African and Latin American dance elements. Towards the end of the Hook, however,
the rhythm becomes less Latin American and more African; more basic, as it were. Here, the
two riffs (based on transformations of the ecstasy figure) mentioned in my musical analysis
above, "endlessly" move in a circular motion, the former tonal emphasis on V (expectation)
now replaced by a continuous resolution into I (transformation).[27] Note that the concept of
transformation is also present in the quotation of black religious suffering culminating in the
musico-dramatic construction of an ecstatic "danced" liturgy.[28]

Returning to Bal's (1985, p. 142) notion of the "embedded" text, one may argue that
WRAPPED UP'S musical parameters, in performative alignment with the visuals of the star
text, figuratively construct a third narrative level through the extended narrative emplotment metaphor of "danced religion." Similarly, the "gangsta" narrative may be viewed as an
extended metaphor, representing in its compact structure a narrative "crisis" that constructs a
certain (ideological) perspective on reality (cf. Bal's 1985, p. 100ff concept of "focalisation"—
the monochrome visuals; the slum environment; the implied socio-historical "construction"
of ghetto life—drug-related crime, "numbers running," prostitution, fencing and robbery).
Thus, both the "gangsta" narrative and the narrative emplotment metaphor of danced religion powerfully determine meaning in this text.[29]

On a figurative level, WRAPPED UP's primary message is that of spiritual transformation,
illustrated via metaphors of darkness and light, but also via a structural metaphor pointing to
the phenomenon of danced religion and its elements of physical and spiritual transmutation.
Thematically, transformation is present also in various motivic, topical and structural events
of this text. These "transformations," however, reflect a certain ambiguity, primarily by means
of the conflict imposed by a constant foregrounding of the frame narrative, the commercialised star meta-narrative.

I have argued that a figurative analysis of WRAPPED UP highlights ideological tensions
and ambiguities inherent in this text. In closing, I interpret this video clip as an exceptionally
complex example of metaphorical emplotment, moving from the surface to deeper levels, and
connecting spheres of figurative and prefigured meaning operative at various levels of the
text. In this regard, I view the typical framing devices of gospel video (symbols, signs, icons,

models, images, metaphors, etc.) as surface metaphors, connecting meaningfully in this text with archetypal figures which function as "root metaphors." Again, my focus is on ambiguity, and on a constant contextual refiguration of metaphor and narrative.

First, it should be noted that the lyrics of the rap section powerfully portray the (Calvinist) model of God as "King." This God model is in tension with the commercialised Lord (compare the Hook) who appears as "Lover" ("Wrapped up, tied up, tangled up"; "You've got me wrapped around your Finger").[30] More importantly, however, it clashes violently with the musical poetics of the rap soundtrack that represents the so-called hip hop sublime of "hardness" (cf. Krims 2000, p. 15). In the ambiguous erotic context of the video, however, the concept of God as "King" may be linked with the notion of sublime "hardness," opposing the concept of the Lord as "beautiful Lover."

The star text of the duo Dawkins & Dawkins projects the archetypal figure of the "Player." While in terms of religious archetypes this figure may be linked to the archetype of the carefree "Child" (finding acceptance and love in his Father's home), its symbolic entanglement with secular "gansta" rap styles strongly emphasises the role of the "Player" not only as an "Entertainer," but also as a "Power Player," possibly involved in real-life gangster activity.

A figurative and ideological analysis of WRAPPED UP highlights not only its ambiguous juxtapositions of "God as King" and "Lord as Lover" as well as those of "King" and "Player" (= "Star"/"Entertainer"), but, in particular, relations of domination in terms of these identity-related "roles" in the text, of which the most dramatic and critical instance is the domination of the star text over the Biblical narrative in the Bridge—indeed, a striking and most ambiguous instance of Johann Visagie's (1996, p. 94) notion of power as an effect of autonomisation, that is, power as an effect of value domination.

In terms of clashing identities, the ambiguous presence of both the dominating star narrative and the all-pervasive danced religion metaphor evokes a complex set of dominating ideological discourses within this text. While structural relationships visually foreground associations related to the star text and the commercialised pleasures of musical performance and dance, a more sophisticated (embedded) metaphorical cluster invokes the darker dimensions of black religious life and African-American cultural history, acting powerfully through the application of the "gangsta" figure.

Read in terms of the link between specific Afro-American rhetorical strategies and authenticity in gospel rap, the "gangsta" narrative, by "being real," powerfully suggests a variety of ideological discourses by means of an implied social criticism. Note that, again, the "gangsta" narrative is musically supported via a persistent application of style and genre in positioning oppositional figurative constructs as ideologically conflicting discourses.

The above interpretation of WRAPPED UP problematises its reading as an uncomplicated, commercialised excursion into the pleasures of an embodied, danced religion. In both "highlighting" and "hiding" the layers of cultural meaning built into the metaphor of danced religion, it celebrates black religious identity without distancing it from underlying ideological formations associated with collective suffering and social injustice. I believe that this "balance" between human hardship and the "lightness" of redemption is represented in this video, as a thoroughly commercialised mass-culture "intertext," in a highly complex fashion. The ambiguous figure of the "gangsta" with his darker socio-historical dimensions is powerfully counterpoised by the metaphor of ecstatic, eroticised danced religion. As an African-religious figurative construct framed by a commercialised mass-produced star text, the concept of danced religion is constantly suggested by densely layered intertextual mass-cultural clichés and Afro-diasporic significations, as well as by a spectrum of figural postures related to Christian praise and worship.

Original Copyright Acknowledgements: "I am indebted to Anson and Eric Dawkins for permission to quote lyrics and musical transcripts from the WRAPPED UP music video. Written and Produced by Rodney Jerkins and the Dawkins brothers, Executive Produced by Raina Bundy."

Study Questions

1. How are music, words, images, and religious meaning as expressed in "Wrapped Up" by Dawkins & Dawkins examined in this article?
2. What types of theories and methods does Viljoen use to accomplish her task of diversifying and complicating the traditional understanding of cultural products, like rap music, as uncomplicated and over-commercialized?
3. What are the advantages and disadvantages of analyzing syncretic popular cultural forms, like rap music, beyond the context of and sole focus on "cultural traits" to include ideological critical modes of inquiry (as exemplified in the application of Visagie's framework in this essay)?

Notes

* For the video "Wrapped Up", see: http://www.artistdirect.com/video/dawkins-dawkins-wrapped-up/35800

1. Following Andrew Goodwin (1992), I identify music videos by small uppercase letters in order to distinguish them from song titles, which appear in quotation marks. Following the conventions of scholarship and cultural criticism, album titles are italicised.

2. See Viljoen 2004c for a detailed explication of this interpretative framework. In Viljoen 2004a and 2004b, the model is applied in the context of multimedia analyses of gospel rap and kwaito music.

3. The video was produced for promotional purposes, and was not marketed commercially. The rendition used in this analysis was broadcast during 2000 as part of the BET Gospel programme "Lift Every Voice." BET Gospel is a twenty-four-hour cable channel offering spiritual and uplifting programming which showcases gospel videos, religious programming, motivational speakers and high-profile musical artists, interspersed with intensive advertising of all these various religious "products."

4. Though Revivalist hymns represent practically every mood of the Christian soul in an expressive, even passionate way, their style is simple and direct, suggesting an intimacy in addressing God as "Friend" (cf. Eskew and McElrath 1980, pp. 124–5). The Wattsian hymn, on the other hand, emphasises the glory and sovereignty of God, the depravity of human nature, and the all-sufficient atonement of Christ on the Cross for the sins of humanity.

5. The phrase "You've got me wrapped around Your finger" has, arguably, misogynistic connotations. The unconcealed corporeality of gospel music is directly traceable to the African-religious model; see, for instance, Floyd's (1995, p. 27ff) discussion. Sylvan (1998, p. 67ff) links West African possession religion with all manifestations of beat-driven contemporary popular music.

6. As part of his extended theory of meaning in multimedia, Nicholas Cook (1998, p. 100ff) proposes a metaphor model in which asymmetries between multimedia components may be ascertained via the principles of *conformance, complementation* or *contest*. Cook observes that conformance tends towards essentialism and stasis, and, as mentioned above, he finds that contest, an intrinsically dynamic and contextual model of meaning, is the paradigmatic model of multimedia. Among these hypothetical positions, complementation is the uncontested "mid-point."

7. Within these two "visible" narrative levels, yet another (embedded) level figuratively unfolds; see the discussion below.

8. I classify the Rap section as belonging to both star and "gangsta" narratives.

9. Typical rags-to-riches narratives, on the other hand, often feature slum scenes. As I will explain below, in the rap-section of WRAPPED UP, such a ghetto scene takes on special significance in terms of metaphor, narrative and ideology.

10. Bal suggests that secret, lie and suspense are important structural strategies of the fabula, that is the series of logically and chronologically related events that are caused or experienced by actors in a narrative.

11. The star text constructed by the performance imagery is already intertwined with a second "embedded" narrative unfolding through the metaphor of "danced religion"; see the discussion below.

12. This is a view propounded commonly in early video theory; cf. Kinder (1984) and Jones (1988). Cook (1998, p. 104ff) emphasises the "gapped" nature of multimedia texts which he describes as "zones of indeterminacy that allow readers to fill in the missing aspects and so interpret the text in the light of their own experience and inclination"; cf. also Iser (1978) and Jauss (1982).

13. In fact, the title of the song "Wrapped Up" may be a play on words meaning also "rapped up," the latter pointing to the black American preaching style which is a poignant influence on the virtuoso verbal style of rap. In the context of this song, the rap text indeed takes on dimensions of both testifying and preaching.

14. Fowles (1996, p. 6) critically observes that, in advertising, the symbol representing the product may never take on too large a significance in its own right, for fear of overwhelming what is being sold.

15. Here, I refer to intertextuality in its more conventional sense, alluding to a text's quotation of prior texts. However, the notion of intertextuality may be understood also in Culler's (1981, p. 103) broader definition, that is, as a designation of the text's participation in the discursive space, and its relationship with the various signifying practices of a culture which articulate possibilities of meaning for a culture; see also under 1. For an exploration of this (broadened) kind of intertextuality in relation to mass-culture texts, see Viljoen (2004a, p. 80ff).

16. In the longer Introduction of the CD version, this progression is anticipated by a "mirror" melodic progression in the guitar, C-D-E-flat-F-G-A-flat-G.

17. These figures are a stylisation (not a transcription) of melodic materials from "Sway" and "Mucho Mambo." I am indebted to Nicol Viljoen for this observation, as well as for his generous contribution towards the musical analysis of WRAPPED UP.

18. The B-flat is a typical case of the so-called blue note; a flattened note, usually the third or seventh degree of the scale, recurring frequently in jazz or blues.

19. Multi-layered backing vocals and shouts are part of the black gospel tradition, the latter referring to the practice of the so-called ring-shout in African religion.

20. Note that tonal ambiguity is a normal condition of some popular music styles. In this tonal context, harmonic progressions are not only structurally ambiguous, but also tonally conflicting.

21. Davis (1995, p. 92) points out the cultural links between the practice of scratching in rap music and the buzzing textures produced by home-made or non-musical instruments in African ceremonial music.

22. Note again the pertinence of Bal's (1985, p. 79) notion of "character predictability" as a narrative agent.

23. I am indebted to Nicholas Cook for pointing out that monochrome colours may signify not only loss and sadness, but also "long ago," which, in this religious context, points as much to gain as it does to loss.

24. Transformation, on many different levels, is a salient feature of this text.

25. *Tangere*; to touch.

26. In advertising, visual displays are often used to convey meanings that would be unacceptable if they were spelled out verbally. With regard to musical multimedia, Nicholas Cook (1998, pp. 16, 22) observes that verbal messages may be subordinated by a series of far more comprehensive attitudinal messages that are communicated by means of music. This implies that music is a profoundly powerful medium, generating meaning beyond anything that, as Cook puts it, "can be said in words."

27. As pointed out above, this is also a thoroughly commercialized cliche.

28. This interpretation links the metaphor with ideological formations of a moral and political nature.
29. However, such speculatively constructed meaning does not necessarily determine the functions of the text for implied listeners/viewers; see my discussion below.
30. The image of Jesus as a "Lover" is found in heavily commercialised gospel music; compare, for instance, Andrae Crouch's "Can't Nobody Do Me Like Jesus" (1999).

References

Baker, H. 1994. "Beyond artefacts: cultural studies and the new hybridity of rap," in *Cultural Artefacts and the Production of Meaning: The Page, the Image and the Body*, ed. M.J.M. Ezell and K. O'Brien O'Keefe (Ann Arbor, University of Michigan Press), pp. 183–98

Bal, M. 1985. *Narratology: Introduction to the Theory of Narrative*, trans. C. van Boheemen (Toronto, University of Toronto Press)

Berger, A.A. 1991. *Media Analysis Techniques* (London, Sage Publications)

Brown, S.M. 1998. *Alternative Explanations: A Textual Analysis of Rap Music Lyrics*, M.A., California State University (Ann Arbor, Michigan, UMI Dissertation Services)

Cook, N. 1998. *Analysing Musical Multimedia* (Oxford, Clarendon Press) 2001. "Theorising musical meaning," *Music Theory Spectrum*, 23/2, pp. 170–95

Culler, J. 1981. *The Pursuit of Signs: Semiotics, Literature, Deconstruction* (London, Routledge & Kegan Paul)

Cusic, D. 1990. *The Sound of Light: A History of Gospel Music* (Bowling Green, Ohio, Bowling Green State University Popular Press)

Davis, F. 1995. *The History of the Blues. The Roots, the Music, the People from Charley Patton to Robert Cray* (London, Secker & Warburg)

Eskew, H., and McElrath, H.T. 1980. *Sing with Understanding: An Introduction to Christian Hymnody* (Nashville, Broadman Press)

Floyd, S.A. 1995. *The Power of Black Music: Interpreting its History from Africa to the United States* (New York: Oxford University Press)

Fowles, J. 1996. *Advertising and Popular Culture* (Thousand Oaks: Sage Publications)

Gates, H.L. 1988. *The Signifying Monkey: A Theory of African-American Literary Criticism* (New York, Oxford University Press)

Goodwin, A. 1992. *Dancing in the Distraction Factory: Music Television and Popular Culture* (Minneapolis, University of Minnesota Press)

Griffin, M.D. 1998. *The Rap on Rap Music: The Social Construction of African-American Identity* M.A., University of Virginia (Ann Arbor, Michigan, UMI Dissertation Services)

Iser, W. 1978. *The Act of Reading: A Theory of Aesthetic Response* (London, Routledge & Kegan Paul)

Jauss, H.R. 1982. *Toward an Aesthetic of Reception*, trans. T. Bahti (Brighton, Sussex, Harvester Press)

Jones, S. 1988. "Cohesive but not coherent: music videos, narrative and culture," *Popular Music & Society*, 12/4, pp. 15–29

Kelley, R.D.G. 1995. "Kickin" reality, kickin" ballistics: "gangsta" rap and postindustrial Los Angeles," in *Droppin" Science: Critical Essays on Rap Music and Hip Hop Culture*, ed. E. Perkins (Philadelphia, Temple University Press), pp. 117–58

Kinder, M. 1984. "Music video and the spectator: television, ideology and dream," *Film Quarterly*, 38/1, pp. 2–15

Kramer, L. 1990. *Music as Cultural Practice 1800–1900* (Berkeley, University of California Press)

——.1992. "Music and representation: the instance of Haydn's Creation," in *Music and Text: Critical Inquiries*, ed. S.P. Scher (Cambridge, Cambridge University Press), pp. 139–62

Krims, A. 2000. *Rap Music and the Poetics of Identity* (Cambridge, Cambridge University Press)

Lakoff, G., and Johnson, M. 1980. *Metaphors We Live By* (Chicago, University of Chicago Press)

Potter, R.A. 1995. *Spectacular Vernaculars: Hip-hop and the Politics of Postmodernism* (Albany, State University of New York Press)

Reid, I. 1992. *Narrative Exchanges* (London, Routledge)

Rose, T. 1994. *Black Noise: Rap Music and Black Culture in Contemporary America* (Hanover, NH, University Press of New England)

Shusterman, R. 1992. *Pragmatist Aesthetics: Living Beauty, Rethinking Art* (Oxford, Blackwell Publishers)

Spencer, J.M. 1990. *Protest and Praise: Sacred Music of Black Religion* (Minneapolis, Fortress Press)

Sylvan, R.D. 1998. *Traces of the Spirit: the Religious Dimensions of Popular Music*. Ph.D., University of California (Ann Arbor, Michigan, UMI Dissertation Services)

Thompson, J. 1984. *Studies in the Theory of Ideology* (Berkeley, University of California Press)

——. 1990. *Ideology and Modern Culture: Critical Social Theory in the Era of Mass Communication* (Cambridge, Polity Press)

Viljoen, M. 2004a. Ideology and textuality: speculating on the boundaries of music, *Scrutiny2*, 9/1, pp. 68–87

——. 2004b. Two reflections on urban discourse: holy hip as social symbolism, *Muziki: Journal of Music Research in Africa*, 36/1, pp. 42–59

——. 2004c. Questions of musical meaning: an ideology-critical approach, *The International Review of the Aesthetics and Sociology of Music*, 35/1, pp. 3–27

Visagie, P.J. 1994. *The Name of the Game in Ideology Theory*, unpublished MS, University of the Free State

——. 1996. Power, meaning and culture: John Thompson's depth hermeneutics and the ideological topography of modernity, *South African Journal of Philosophy*, 15/2, pp. 73–83

Warner, E. 1998. *Searching for a Pragmatic Aesthetic: The Rhetorical Strategies of "gangsta" Rappers. Myths, Rituals, and Drama of an Outlaw Music*, Ph.D., Wayne State University (Ann Arbor, Michigan, UMI Dissertation Services)

Discography

Andrae Crouch, *Andrae Crouch*. Gospel Music Hall of Fame, CGI Platinum 5338 2. 1999

Dawkins & Dawkins, *Focus*. Harmony 1696–2. 1998

Gospel Gangstaz, *I Can See Clearly Now*. B-rite Music 606949025328. 1999

WoW Gospel 2000, Sarepta Music 01241–43149–2. Shaft, *Mucho Mambo*—Ltd. Mambo 721555. 1999

The Police, "Wrapped Around Your Finger." *Synchronicity*. A&M Records SP17264. 1983

Videography

Stefly, D.A. (Dir.) Wrapped Up. Music video. Released and aired for promotional purposes only. 1998

12

AfroBlue
Incanting Yoruba Gods in Hip-Hop's Isms

Cepeda argues rap music in particular and hip hop culture in general is marked by "spirit" through its undeniable connection to West African religions and philosophies. This essay charts the aesthetic, historical, geographic, and cultural connections between hip hop culture and African diasporic religions. Tracing the birth of gods and spirit along the treacherous route of the transatlantic slave trade, Cepeda makes unique connections in the study of hip hop and diasporic aesthetics by arguing that *Yoruba* philosophy undergirds hip hop elements such as graffiti, dance, fashion, and breaking. This, Cepeda suggests, can be observed in the work of Afrika Bambaataa (e.g., *Shango Funk Theology*), one of the founding figures in hip hop. This essay exposes readers to the secrets and remixes of Africana religions at the heart of hip hop cultural production.

AfroBlue: Incanting Yoruba Gods in Hip-Hop's Isms

Racquel Cepeda

Art historian Robert Farris Thompson once concluded that "popular music of the world is informed by a flash of the spirit." There is a collective memory in rock, jazz, salsa, highlife, juju, mambo, and other kinds of music with roots in improvisation and ingenuity that extends well beyond their soundscapes. The principles of song and dance inherently present in these aesthetics were founded by a source initially acquainted to this relatively New World by way of slavery. If we were to adhere to Farris Thompson's definition of the principles of flash—the dominance of a percussive performance style, a penchant for multiple meter, overlapping call and response in singing, inner pulse control, suspended accentuation patterning, songs and dances of social illusion—we might make the argument for hip-hop's initiation into the coolness of this spirit. Rap, and hip-hop culture as a whole, is linked to this spirit, not only through its innovation in artistic expression but also due to the manner in which its syncretic relationship with West African religion and philosophy planted an ancestral frequency into this chilled-out generation of heads.

Black Africa's most populous areas in the western regions of Nigeria and the eastern Benin Republic somehow survived to beget a tradition that has borne many spirits under one God in the New World via the transatlantic slave trade. Known in its Latino form as *La Regla Lùkùmí*, *Santeria*, and *La Regla de Ocha*; in Brazil as *Candomblé*; inTrinidad as *Shàngó* (Baptist); and through the more popular African American nationalist term *Yoruba*, the tradition has many names. And although they differ slightly from place to place, these indigenous religions, including the Haitian *Voudon*, or Voodoo, are all branches from the same proverbial tree in that they are vicissitudes of slavery.

Throughout hip-hop's still embryonic life, Yoruba religious philosophy and aesthetics have consistently informed graffiti art, fashion, rap music, and breakdancing. Hip-hop now again witnesses the "changing same" to sample Amiri Baraka, a curiosity with the intoxicating aesthetic that has inspired popular music for generations: Yoruba iconography and music. "I think that [it works] because it's so clear, so down to earth," says Farris Thompson, "and powerful because the symbols are so flexible that they will expand into any high-tech thing you want."

In the very first generation of commercial hip-hop music, Our Father Afrika Bambaataa experimented with allusions of Yoruba philosophy when teaming up with a group called Shango for the LP *Shango Funk Theology*. On the cover, an Ice Man, an abstracted orisha Obàtálá, hovers over earth and emits, from his hands, a deep freeze, chilling out the planet.

Afrika himself postures above in the shape of a double-headed ax, an *oshe*, emanating fire, synchronizing himself with the thunder god, Chango. "His fingers are arranged in the funk sign with two fingers up and the rest all curled down," points out Farris Thompson. "The fingers are witty because they are also the two meteorites that [in folklore] were hurled for moral vengeance by Lord Shàngó." The use of a futuristic robot looking down on the left side of these divinities, and a mortal on the right, symbolizes the special relationship that coexists between man and the supernatural.

Popular examples of African retention in our collective memory lie in the Brazilian martial art called *Capoeira*, in the Afro-Cuban street dancing by the *rumberos callejeros*, and the acrobatic mambo dancers in New York City circa 1950s, all forms that could arguably have sired what we know today as break dancing. The West African griot and the Cuban *sonero* are progenitors of the MC who share a (pre)disposition of improvising witty rhymes echoing generations past each time she summons the ancestral spirit known in its boundless nom de plume as "freestyling." Hip-hop fashion statements and hairstyles like cornrows are as bold as the African royalty and the gods and spirits in whom they are descended, our huge gold medallions and opulent taste in jewelry markers of our allegiance to this holy trinity. This flash even exists in our vernacular. The idea of being "chill," "cool," and "fresh" embraces the fundamental Yoruba philosophy of cultivating *ìwà pèlé*, or good character, by keeping our heads *cool* under circumstances that challenge our character.

Cuban immigrants and Afro-Cuban musicians first introduced this religion, however subliminally, to America in the 1940s. By the late 1950s, Mongo Santamaria's "Afro-Blue" had become just one of the many Latin jazz mainstays. According to historians John Mason and Henry John Drewal in *Beads, Body and Soul: Art and Light in the Yoruba Universe*, the first known African Americans to be initiated in Cuba dated back to August 1959—three months after the recorded release of "Afro-Blue." Although the exact number of Yoruba patrons living in the States is unknown, the late professor Dr. Mary Curry estimated the head count as being anywhere from 250,000 to one million in her book, *Making the Gods in New York: The Yoruba Religion in the African-American Community*. Today across the United States, there are whites, Blacks, Mexicans, Dominicans, Puerto Ricans, Panamanians, West and East Indians, Jews, African Americans, *all* kinds of people who have been "called" into this spiritual connector to God.

Santamaria's "Afro-Blue" conceptualized its melodies from an *oriki*, or praise song, dedicated to the orisha of creativity and coolness, Obàtálá. It was adopted by American artists like John Coltrane and Dizzy Gillespie, Abbey Lincoln, Cal Tjader, and many others. The *bata* drums, or "talking drums," sacred to patrons of the tradition, have belted out enchanted messages from Cuba's shores before Fidel Castro reigned and the ensuing U.S.-imposed embargo dubbed the "Special Period" halted the cultural exchange program between musicians who previous were awakened to the flash of spirit memory.

Cadres of hip-hop's finest continue to innovate the traditions and superior musical and visual aesthetics rooted in Yoruba and Congo religious philosophy. Just listen to the revolutionary sounds of the Cuban hip-hop group Los Orishas, who fused Afro-Cuban music with the universality of rap beats and rhymes, or the praise lyrics for the river rain goddess of beauty known as Ochùn by Queen Pen and Hurricane G.—the latter being an initiated priestess of this divinity—in their rhymes, reawakening the atmospheric connection to their transmissible rite. The sampling and experimentation of Yoruba praise songs are seamless with rap because at the most basic level the principal ideal of the dominance of a percussive performance style, polyrhythms, and the call-and-response model fits into the musical paradigms of *orikis* and rap.

In 1999, Common traveled to Cuba to perform at the yearly hip-hop festival in the neighborhood of Alamar in Havana. There he performed in front of an enormous acrylic painting called *El Mensajero,* dedicated to the divinity Elegba's abstracted, looming figure. It was a striking contrast: Elegbas abstracted, looming figure offset by Common in a Cuban-style *guayabera* outfit hat, holding a *cohiba,* and his Cuban counterparts wearing boots, baggy jeans, and oversize T-shirts by PNB. By the end of the trip, Common had been deeply moved by the culture and music, particularly the *orikis,* sung in a Creolization of the Yoruba language that came to be known as *Lùkùmí.*

Common's experience, and his desire to *test* himself musically with more of a melodic base, coupled with singer Vinia Mojica's *ashe,* or spiritual command, resulted in the befitting introduction to his millennial release, *Like Water for Chocolate.* Mojica—an initiated priestess of the orisha Yemayá, the archetypal mother to the world and source of all life who can also be heard singing the intro on Common's *Electric Circus*-combined two incantations dedicated to Elegba, translated here from the featured *Lùkùmí:*

> Talk a little time
> Talk a little
> He wanders around separating
> Make way He's separating
> The Owner of Vital Force
> He shoots, kicks, He pierces
> He ties the knot
> He darts out
> But He does not speak
> He wanders around separating
> Make way, He's wandering, separating
> The Owner of Vital Force

Elegba, one of the most important divinities to survive slavery, is the messenger of our prayers to Olódùmarè, the Supreme Being and Creator. The owner of the crossroads, the trickster who can dear and cause chaos in a whim, is the inaugural divinity to be invoked in a Yoruba religious context.

"Common was having a lot of blockage during the creation of [*Electric Circus*];" remembers Mojica, "so I immediately thought about Ogùn." The blacksmith divinity who cuts down obstacles with his iron implements, while mimicking warlike dances similar to those incorporated into breakdancing, becomes a perfect inspiration for hip-hop. The intro to *Electric Circus,* titled "Ferris Wheel" features Mojica belting out praise names for Ogùn, as he gets ready for battle and the spiritual cleansing of his host ridding him of indecision and negative energy. Author Ivor Miller was astonished to find that The Last Poets libated their album *Chastisement* with a chant for Ogùn. In his book *Aerosol Kingdom,* he wrote: "The significance of Ogùn to New York City, the trains, and the continuity of African-derived culture can hard be over stated ... The Last Poets were leading the way not only for future rappers, but for a reconnection to West African spirituality via the Caribbean."

Over the years, Yoruba philosophy and aesthetics have roused the aerosol art of DOZE GREEN, EZO, TOXIC TDS, and other artists who, like their ancestors of African American and Caribbean descent, Ivor Miller wrote, "related to trains as symbols and metaphors ... [and] worshipped gods of iron." The Ogùn connection exists between graffiti artists and the iron implements empowering their lives, these faceless youngsters with names becoming as legendary as the force that dominated their spirits. "As in all art, including graffiti, the connection between Yoruba art and philosophy is that they are both in the business of explaining man's place in the universe and his connection to a creator," affirms EZO, who began bombing in the late 1970s. "Spirituality is an important part of Latino culture, and the Latino influence on graffiti is incalculable, so references to faith topics were inevitable."

In one of DOZE Green's paper pieces, "Untitled (1999)," a b-boy blurs the lines between mortality and divinity, sporting a halo while receiving a libation from a Supreme Being. On the lower-right-hand side, there is a figure representing Elegba that features both Yoruba and Catholic symbols associated with this divinity, including an enormous penis (embodying fertility and infinite potential), the number three, and a devil-like horn representing the dark forces associated with this trickster by zealous missionaries. In the center of the acrylic canvas painting *Ghetto Resilient* (1998), DOZE features a more traditional image of Elegba—the form of a small cement head with cowrie shell eyes and mouth, protector of all that is Caribbean. The word *Chango* is also featured on the painting. Hip-hop-influenced visual artists find that Yoruba art and philosophy, and the children of Ogùn, with nerves of steel, are propagated from the same source.

Yoruba philosophy and art are rooted in individuality and style, which can be a seductive quality for artists. Imbued with the mystery of adventure, of the unknown, the paths toward expression become infinite. It is common to find a hip-hop head rocking a huge gold pendant of the Catholic saint Lazarus—depicted as a sore-riddled man on crutches accompanied by two dogs—synchronized with the divinity of sickness, Bàbàlù Ayé. Even fashion runways and lifestyle magazines have used models sporting colorful bead necklaces that are oftentimes specially "prepared" *collares* or *ilékes*, representing the protection of the Yoruba divinities, as well as linking the wearer to his or her godparent. The origins and history of this beaded set of spiritual armor are reflected in the colors and patterns used to make them.

At the outset of 2001, neosoul singer D'Angelo, a rapper literally possessed with a resonant voice, released the follow-up to his 1995 debut, *Brown Sugar*, ironically christened *Voodoo*. Fundamentally, the title did not reflect the concept of its namesake. Its Yoruba aesthetic was featured on the pages of the album's accompanying CD booklet. D'Angelo skates over the fine line between inspiration and religious insensitivity by sporting an *ídé*, an intricately beaded sacred bracelet worn by initiated priests in the orisha community that identifies their divinities, in this case Shàngó. Rather than depicting a voodoo ceremony, a staged *tambor*—or a religious fete—was given by a group of priests in Havana on the one-day photo shoot.

In all fairness, D'Angelo's goal was not malicious. He did not intend to further inflate the stereotypes associated with African religion. He wanted to create an atmosphere that showed a continuum between blues music—commonly referred to as the "devil's music"—and what has, to him, an extension of the soul he aimed to capture on this excellent collection. A few weeks before the album was released, D'Angelo, whose father and grandfather are preacher men, commented on Baraka's "changing same," noting that "the thing that came to mind was basically church [because] when we in church we catch the holy ghost and start speaking in tongue. And that's real similar to me."

Roots drummer Ahmir "Questlove" Thompson, who coproduced both Common's aforementioned albums and D'Angelo's *Voodoo*, says, "I feel that a more spiritual base coming around to combat the materialism that is slowly plaguing hip hop. I wouldn't say 'religion' per se. But I definitely feel a spiritual based feeling coming around." This explains the rise of hip-hop's pop-culture shamans.

But D'Angelo's case proves this newfound visibility to be a double-edged sword in the case of Yoruba, Congo, and Voodoo religions, which remain insular by nature. Many of the reports about the religions have been riddled with misinformation and taken out of context, in both mainstream and urban media outlets. Hollywood movies—too numerous to name—that exaggerate stereotypes of all that is African, recasting indigenous religions as negative or Satanic, keep many of the religions' patrons "underground," so to speak.

Cypress Hill rapper B-Real is a *babalawo,* or "father of secrets," in the Ifà system of the Yoruba religion. He says, "Like *Los Orishas* did in the Spanish-speaking countries on their records, eventually somebody will put it out for the English-speaking people to understand." But after eight albums, Cypress Hill has not purposely infused any religious elements into their music or visuals. Ironically, though, their use of skulls and cemeteries, B-Real says, "is linked to where I've fallen into with Ifà."

He believes that the complexity of the religion's secrets are better left to those who "are supposed to be exposed [to them] and those who need it." He adds, "I think people [have to] be careful with the lines they cross" when using Yoruba iconography unless "you're using it to bless your project and give light to the culture."

There are no right answers for what road to travel because of the spiritual conduit that is working, informing each individual that it chooses to possess with the flash of the spirit, or with ancestral intuition. The connection is atmospheric. The culture concentric with time, and "while how we code it may change," said a Congo priest to Farris Thompson, "what is coded *never* changes."

Study Questions

1. What role does slavery have on the ways in which Cepeda examines and understands the influence of African diasporic religions in hip hop culture?
2. What West African religions and philosophies does she note as being evidenced in hip hop cultural elements? Are traditional meanings of these religions held in place or do they emerge in a more eclectic and complex manner among diasporic cultural products of the New World?
3. How does Cepeda chart the movement of the "flash of the spirit" in hip hop from its emergence with Afrika Bambaataa to contemporary figures such as rapper Common?

Part IV
Hip Hop and/in Religious Traditions

As earlier essays in this Reader have suggested, Islam has been a key feature of hip hop culture. In fact, some contributors in this volume have suggested that Islam is hip hop's "original" religion—that is to say, that it's been present from its inception. This suggestion comes as no surprise, as some scholars of African American religion, for example, have suggested that Islam, although not always acknowledged, was a key feature of slave religion. And like much of black culture in the larger diaspora—traditions and customs were borrowed, sampled, remixed, and repurposed.

The religious traditions and sensibilities represented in hip hop culture are thick and varied—local and global; national and international. That is not to say we're suggesting that hip hop is self-consciously and overwhelmingly religious or spiritual at its core. On the contrary, uses of religion in hip hop culture reflect and refract a wide variety of interests, purposes, means, and ends—sorting and charting this terrain is part and parcel of the work in and around this area of study. More often than not, attention to religious sensibilities, samples, and traditions have often been limited to Christian analysis or confessional approaches with an eye toward institutionalized religious forms. Continued work in and around this area has complicated the posture and placement of religion in hip hop culture with attention to underexplored religious sensibilities like eastern religions to new age thought and practice. This part samples the wide variety of religious rhetoric, ideas, and themes in hip hop culture today—all of which raises a productive question about hip hop and the role of religion *in* and *as* tradition.

We begin with the exploration of Islam as rhetorically represented specifically in African American culture with the idea of battle vis-à-vis the Islamic notion of "Jihad," and consider the manner in which the affective output of anger, rage, and righteous indignation is often expressed in and through the use of religious language—Islam in particular. One will note that such a suggestion doesn't assume that all artists appropriating Islamic sensibilities do so out of firm belief in and practice of the tradition itself. Certainly there are those within hip hop that explicitly claim Islam as theirs; others, however, might simply repurpose the religious ideas and traditions of Islamic concepts and themes to develop their own syncretic iteration. Notable here among a number of these essays is attention beyond a focus on a single formulation of "Islam" or otherwise. That is, increased attention has been given throughout and over the years to carefully parsing the wide ranging iterations of religious sensibilities expressed in and highlighted throughout various hip hop customs and practices. One begins to note here the religio-cultural foundation and lineage of commonly troped hip hop references such as "do for self," "knowledge of self," and "peace, god"—among others. What have become commonly used, cited, rehearsed, and emulated greetings, shout-outs, customs, and fine points of style quite often have roots religious in nature.

Subsequent essays in this part build upon contested Islamic notions, such as "verbal muja-hidin" as a way to describe and think further about the bold enunciations of social and political critique of things such as suffering and the nation-state. Here, you'll note a reclamation of notoriously contentious phrases (i.e., "weapons of mass destruction") through re-appropriation and repurposing—techniques germane and apropos to how the audacious attitude of hip hop is expressed and understood. Here and throughout this reader we see not only the expansion of frameworks and methods in religion and hip hop study, but also, a fuller engagement with art-ists themselves through methods and opportunities such as interviews and primary data. From an examination of Islamic varieties and iterations in hip hop we arrive at a full consideration of one of the most influential variants of Islam in hip hop culture, the Nation of Gods and Earths, commonly referred to as "Five Percenters." In and through focus on Islamic variations whether five percent concepts or sensibilities orthodox in nature, the paranoid and suspicious stylings of life as expressed in and through esoteric and sometimes religious rhetoric among marginal groups in particular is persuasively evidenced. From the streets of urban centers in the US we then arrive on the international rap scene in Tunis where the significance of orthodox Islamic sensibilities is very much a part of hip hop participants' lives, output and identity construction.

Part IV then explores various dimensions of Christian-framed scholarship and hip hop, first with a historiographic assessment of religion in hip hop. With such a context in focus, the next essays situate Christian concerns in and through hip hop, underscoring the necessity of inter/intra-cultural exchange between Christian communities and hip hop heads, on the one hand, and the pervasive impact of hip hop on what many understand to be "Christian" beliefs, ritu-als, theologies, and the like. Clear from these more contemporary pieces is that early academic focus on or influence by Christianity does not imply scholars look elsewhere, but these essays all do well to help explain early trends in the field and how to move forward in light of expand-ing arenas of engagement.

The part is further broken down into Judaism and Eastern religious "traditions," not as a mandate that these are either cohesive "traditions" or that they warrant study above another, but because the theoretical merit of these pieces and international focus help to engage these very tough and necessary questions about tradition, place, geography, time, and representa-tion. Spanning the globe and stopping in Israel to explore Ethiopian youth appropriation and adoption of hip hop, followed by a brief stint in San Francisco to catch up with a Hindu yogi turned MC, the part concludes by traveling to Japan and China, respectively, looking at J-hop and Chinese hip hop expressions to better understand the circuitous trajectory of hip hop, reli-gion, and culture more generally. How does examining religion in hip hop culture globally shift and broaden perspective and approach to these areas of study? What similarities between the local and the global might be registered as significant and how might the role of new forms of technology and travel (i.e., virtual) shift access to and mobility of how religious knowledge and interpretation travels and broadens in understanding among a wide array of demographics and populations? How does geopolitical context impact the practice of hip hop and the expressions of religion within it? What are the ways in which East meets up with West and vice versa in and through the growing rise and power of hip hop cultural influence and import?

13

A Jihad of Words

The Evolution of African American Islam and Contemporary Hip-Hop

Floyd-Thomas highlights a "jihad of words" framework embodied by Malcolm X to explore the manner in which rappers both express and address rage through religious rhetoric. Throughout, he examines Islamic influences on the work of rap groups and artists such as Public Enemy and KRS-ONE. Expanding the content of Black Islam beyond a sole focus on The Nation of Islam (NOI), Floyd-Thomas broadly considers seldom engaged Islamic iterations such as The Five Percent Nation and the ways in which themes such as "knowledge of self" and "supreme mathematics"—a form of African American gnosticism—have provided enduring philosophies of humanity, origins, cosmos, and the nature of evil. Paying close attention to varied African American Islamic codes, consciousness, and diversity, Floyd-Thomas argues that the analytical rubric of "jihad of words" assists us in getting beyond a "unilateral imposition of Islamic influences upon this African American art form" which speaks to the powerful ways in which religion and popular culture provide a strong basis for communities and people working toward social justice.

A Jihad of Words: The Evolution of African American Islam and Contemporary Hip-Hop

Juan M. Floyd-Thomas

A Jihad of Words

Malcolm X gained international prominence through his role as the controversial spokesperson for the Nation of Islam (NOI). Malcolm's notoriety was largely driven by his relentless attack on the causes and consequences of racism as the nation's civil rights struggle gradually reached its apex. Coupled with his fiery invectives against the cruel injustices of Jim Crow in America, Malcolm's ascendancy in public life was also fueled by his representation of a growing Islamic presence in the United States. In a postwar America struggling to come to terms with its racial and religious transformations, Malcolm emerged as an enigmatic celebrity for the American public. In order to satisfy the public's growing interest in his life and career, in addition to chronicling his own personal quest for social justice and spiritual wholeness, Malcolm X agreed to compile his personal recollections into a book-length project.

In the wake of Malcolm X's untimely death, *The Autobiography of Malcolm X* stood as a testament to the formation of Black racial identity. Malcolm X's collaboration with author Alex Haley during the last years of Malcolm's life has served as the definitive articulation of the rage, struggle, and hope of African Americans in the late twentieth century as illustrated through personal tales of pain, loss, and rebirth.[1] Furthermore, for countless readers, Malcolm's memoirs provided unprecedented insights into African American Islam "as a religion as well as a weapon of protest and a means of self-definition."[2] Within the narrative of Malcolm's life, readers found a wellspring of frank, honest, and scathing indictments of American society from a person who had seen the worst side of life.

Malcolm's social critique and political vision, couched within a religious commitment, attacked the destructive tendencies of American culture. In fact, it has been suggested that Malcolm was engaged in a verbal jihad marked by a "talking back at white America—which translated as offering blacks a psychological alternative, a perhaps nonpacifist plan for fighting back."[3] Theologian Richard Brent Turner asserts that Malcolm X's "jihad of words" was advanced by his "extensive and thoughtful reading, debating, and serious contemplation" of the racial inequality and social injustice which eventually "raised his religious and political consciousness about the situation of black people in America and the world."[4]

Even as Malcolm used his mastery of logical exposition, reasoned disputation, and moral persuasion to attack white supremacy, capitalist exploitation, neocolonialism, and a multitude of comparable societal ills in an outward manner, such an enterprise had an indelible inward effect. This is also in keeping within the greater Islamic tradition of a dual essence to jihad: the *first— jihad bil nafs—addresses* "striving within the self"; the *second—jihad fi sabil Allah*—emphasizes "striving in the path of Allah."[5] Turner indicates that Malcolm's realization of and response to such negative aspects of the human condition eventually instilled him with the virtues, discipline, and wisdom needed to submit himself more fully to the will of Allah. Therefore, even as he sought to end oppression both here and abroad, Malcolm's jihad of words gradually made him a better, more devout Muslim. In many regards, the events and circumstances that defined the last few years of Malcolm's life demonstrated how political and moral concerns were contingent on one another. In his history of the Black Power movement and its relationship to American culture, William Van Deburg notes: "Following his death, Malcolm's influence expanded in dramatic, almost logarithmic fashion. He came to be far more than a martyr for the militant, separatist faith. He became a Black Power paradigm—the archetype, reference point, and spiritual adviser in absentia for a generation of Afro-American activists."[6]

What is of primary importance for this chapter is the manner in which Malcolm X's jihad of words provides the framework by which many rappers address both their religious sensibilities and social outrage. It must also be noted that this jihad of words, although initiated through the rhetoric of Malcolm X, is continued in the religious rhetoric and social critique offered by his most noteworthy successors such as the Honorable Minister Louis Farrakhan of the Nation of Islam, Father Allah of the Five Percent Nation, and Imam Warith Deen Muhammad of the American Muslim Mission. This essay argues that there has been a synergy of African American Islam and hip-hop over the past few decades which has forged a profound and complicated relationship between these two phenomenological forces that must be studied more closely by students of religion and popular culture in the contemporary world. I make an effort to develop this argument through attention to *both* the historical development of various modalities of Islam in black communities and the articulation of these developments in the lyrical content of rap music.

Application of the Jihad of Words, I: Nation of Islam

Although many scholars have written about the rap group Public Enemy (PE), little attention has been given to PE's overt references to NOI doctrine, icons, and rhetoric. The lyrics, for example, from "Party for Your Right to Fight," on PE's 1988 album *It Takes a Nation of Millions to Hold Us Back* reflect an open adoption of Malcolm X's "jihad of words." Many of the lyrical insights in this song are patent examples of NOI ideology within a hip-hop idiom: "It was your so called government/That made this occur/Like the grafted devils they were … Word from the honorable Elijah Muhammad."[7] A few years later, Public Enemy's song "White Man's Heaven Is a Black Man's Hell," from their 1994 album, *Muse-Sick-N-Hour-Message*, served as a tribute both in title and spirit to a classic calypso tune of the same name recorded by Louis Farrakhan.

The rapper KRS-One offers another manifestation of Malcolm's jihad of words. When KRS-One and DJ/producer Scott La Rock, as the seminal group Boogie Down Productions (BDP), released their debut album, *Criminal Minded*, in 1987, they were among the vanguard of East Coast rappers who anticipated the advent of gangsta rap through rhymes filled with murderous violence, sexual braggadocio, and youthful frustration. On the brink of commercial success and critical acclaim within gangsta rap, the group underwent a profound transformation largely marked by the murder of Scott La Rock, in 1987, as he attempted to break up an altercation in the Bronx. With the release of *By All Means Necessary*, BDP's sophomore album, in 1989, it was evident that the group had drastically altered its sense of purpose.

Both the cover art and title of the album reflected KRS-One's desire to appropriate much of Malcolm's symbolic and rhetorical arsenal. The album's title mimics one of Malcolm's most recognizable slogans, "By any means necessary." Moreover, the album's cover art consists of KRS-One standing with an automatic weapon next to a window in a state of constant readiness, serving as a direct visual allusion to a classic photo of an armed Malcolm X that was popularized during the 1960s. With these two gestures, KRS-One initiates a process wherein he infuses his aspirations to serve as hip-hop's reigning "teacher" with the essence of Malcolm X, the organic intellectual and cultural revolutionary. This is most evident in BDP's overt decision to compose and perform music that was more politically conscious and empowering in nature following the tragic loss of Scott La Rock. From 1989 onward, KRS-One and BDP penned songs that attempted to advance the general level of discourse within rap music beyond thoughts about cars, clothes, jewelry, dance moves, and other trendy topics that had dominated rap music during its early years.

By the start of the 1990s, this expression of black nationalist/Afrocentric rap was on the verge of becoming a nationwide force. This is best represented by the solo work of the rapper Ice Cube during this period. Through *Death Certificate,* Ice Cube infused his social commentary about racial and class inequality during the Reagan-Bush era with the imagery and ideological tenets of Louis Farrakhan. Designed as a concept album, Ice Cube divided the songs equally between "Death" and "Life." The "Death" side is intended to expose the internalized pathology and nihilism that fomented the self-destructive tendencies that surfaced in poor/working-class African American youth culture during the 1980s and 1990s. Conversely, the "Life" side focused on generating a rebirth of consciousness by using incisive social critique to target problems, generate intra-communal dialogue, and ultimately work toward a concrete agenda for racial uplift. In many regards, Ice Cube's *Death Certificate* represented the musical transliteration of Farrakhan and the NOI's ideological platform. From the outset, the album marked a considerable departure from standard hip-hop fare, serving more as political polemic than party record.

By embracing Farrakhan's teachings within his musical purview, Ice Cube merged the moral authority of the NOI with his street credibility as a pioneering gangsta rapper in order to scrutinize black people's complicity in their own devastation. It was only after his adoption of NOI beliefs, no matter how cursory, that Ice Cube assumed the quasi-religious/quasi-political position of a "prophet of rage." I do not want to give the impression that such a gesture was intellectual posturing or some sort of career move. Instead, this move was a serious confrontation with spiritual malaise and social injustice by a young Black man, in the rhetoric of the NOI, "no longer deaf, dumb, and blind." At a moment when gangsta rap was making steady and lucrative inroads into mainstream America, Ice Cube complicated his image as hip-hop's "Nigga You Love to Hate" by asking (and in some instances forcing) his listeners to do something they had never done before—take a deep breath, muster courage, and dive into the most confused, dissonant recesses of the black psyche.

The jihad of words once promised by NOI-influenced rap music of the late 1980s and early 1990s met its untimely end through the renaissance of Malcolm X as pop culture icon. In 1992, director Spike Lee mounted a dizzying publicity campaign to advertise the long-awaited film adaptation of *The Autobiography of Malcolm X.* The hype surrounding the motion picture soon spawned a proliferation of posters, baseball caps, clothing, and various other forms of merchandising bearing an "X" logo which began surfacing across the United States and overseas. This gross reduction of Malcolm X and his jihad to a letter "X" emblazoned on all kinds of cheaply manufactured goods sold by countless bootleggers helped dilute and ultimately diminish the intellectual and moral gravitas that Malcolm had personified at the zenith of his public notoriety. Even as artists like Public Enemy, KRS-One, and Ice Cube tried to imbue rap with the fiery spirit of the "jihad of words," the commercial and media feeding frenzy inspired by Lee's cinematic homage to the fallen black Muslim leader ironically led to the evisceration of Malcolm's life and beliefs. As the late Joe Woods states:

> To understand the reemergence of Malcolm we begin by considering his iconic power. In these hostile times, many African Americans are hungry for an honorable sanctuary, and Black spirit fits the bill. ... But are the buyers, African American or not, angry or not, Black believers? Not necessarily, because Black spirit has never meant one thing ... which is its great power *and* failure. Spirit has no spine; it bends easily to the will of the buyer.[8]

Journalist Greg Tate elaborates on this problem by stating that the murder of Malcolm X left African Americans with "their first revolutionary pop icon ... We celebrate the death of Malcolm X for what it is—the birth of a new black god ... He's like the Elvis of black pop politics-a real piece of Afro-Americana. That's why Spike's X logo is branded with an real piece of Afro-Americana. That's why Spike's X logo is branded with an American flag. Malcolm couldn't have happened anywhere else."[9] One need not share Tate's satiric outlook to appreciate the implicit crisis of transforming one of postwar America's most profound political voices into a fashion accessory. Furthermore, the commodification of black America's "shining prince;" to borrow from Ossie Davis's eulogy, left many African Americans with cognitive dissonance about the revolutionary potential of black nationalism and Afrocentrism.

Jihad of Words, II: The Five Percent Nation and Rap Music

African American Islam and rap music underwent major transitions during the early nineties. From the early heyday of Ice T and NWA (Niggaz With Attitude) to the crossover appeal of Dr. Dre and Snoop Dogg, the preponderance of West Coast rap emphasized musical postulations of "life in the ghetto" that were deeply apolitical, predatory, and nihilistic in nature. Though the artists were neither the first nor only purveyors of this more ruthless edge of African American popular culture, this trend hit its apex during the early 1990s largely due to the fact that white middle-class teenagers in suburbia were buying gangsta rap music at a phenomenal rate. Also, whereas the urban black communities along the eastern seaboard of the United States certainly had their own indigenous gang subcultures, those gangs never achieved the same essential function or cultural relevance for urban black youth on the East Coast during the 1980s as gang culture had out West.

This geographic displacement also marked the diminution of the strong black nationalist/ Afrocentric fervor that once dominated rap. In the matter of a few years, the politicized school of East Coast rap soon gave way to the increasingly shallow and virulent gangsta consciousness that served as West Coast rap's stock-in-trade. Through a process of signification—the process of naming and subsequent identity formation as a means of self-definition—Dr. Dre's renunciation of "medallions, dreadlocks, and black fists" in "Dre Day" marked those symbols of the hip-hop generation's pro-black militancy as archaic and useless relics.[10] As Todd Boyd notes, "The emergence of gangsta rap has seen an open rejection of politics by those involved."[11]

The East Coast hard-core scene responded to the prevalence of West Coast gangsta rap by emphasizing its most esoteric and exclusive collective, namely the Five Percent Nation of Islam (also known alternatively as the Five Percenters and the Nation of the Gods and Earths).[12] The

Five Percent Nation was founded by Clarence 13X. After joining the NOI, Clarence 13X was assigned to Temple No. 7 in Harlem in the early 1950s and subsequently became a lieutenant in the Fruit of Islam (the NOI security force) and a youth minister. During this period, Clarence 13X worked closely with Malcolm X and found much inspiration in his de facto mentor's direct challenges to the NOI's hierarchy and dogma. There were several concepts that were central to the NOI that Clarence 13X later canonized within the teachings of the Five Percent Nation: black people were the "original" people in the world and emanated from Asia; Christianity was an integral tool used by white slave masters to control the minds of black people; white people were a devilish and grossly inferior race created by a mad scientist named Dr. Yacub some six thousand years ago as the living embodiment of evil on earth; and the only hope for black people in America is total separation from whites and self-reliance.

In the early 1960s, Clarence 13X began to question the NOI doctrine that God had appeared in Detroit in 1930 in the person of Master Fard Muhammad. He reportedly began to question whether or not Fard was actually God, since the NOI taught that the Original Man qua Asiatic Black man was Allah. This seemed contradictory to Clarence 13X since Fard Muhammad looked white. Clarence 13X began to teach that every black man was the physical manifestation of God. He was reprimanded in 1963, left the NOI along with a few followers, changed his name to Allah, and began preaching to the youth on the streets of Harlem. In emulation of the Middle Eastern sites made legendary within historic Islam, Clarence 13X and his growing cadre of followers changed the names of Harlem, the Bronx, and New Jersey to "Mecca," "Medina," and "New Jerusalem," respectively.

Father Allah, as his followers came to call him, taught that the Five Percenters are black men who have acquired "knowledge of self" and use this knowledge to release the hidden resources of the black man. Once a man has tapped his hidden talents, he is a God. In fact, most members refer to themselves as Gods rather than Five Percenters, reserving the latter term for those who have only begun studying the knowledge. The general premise is that 85 percent of the black population is manipulated and otherwise victimized by the 10 percent who are the "bloodsuckers of the poor." According to the teaching of Fard Muhammad, as later disseminated by Father Allah, the 10 percent includes the grafted, blue-eyed white devil and those, such as those in the Nation of Islam, who have knowledge and power but who use it to mystify and abuse the 85 percent. The Five Percenters are the poor righteous teachers who preach the divinity of the (black) man-the god who is "manifest" in living flesh (not a spook, not a mystery god). They also believe they, through their teachings, will save the 85 percent from destruction.

In its orientation, the belief system of the Five Percenters represents a form of African American gnosticism. Generally speaking, gnosticism refers to the mystical perception of transcendent spiritual knowledge that is disseminated and interpreted only by spiritually mature adherents and initiates.[13] For example, within the Judea-Christian experience, the gnostics of the ancient world viewed Jesus as a great teacher rather than as divine messiah and believed that the ultimate essence of Jesus' real teaching was that the kingdom of Heaven was a present, corporeal reality to be experienced through personal comprehension of sacred truth.[14] Therefore, inasmuch as the Five Percenters developed an integrated system of mythology and metaphysical teachings intended to explain the creation of the world, the genesis of humankind, and the perfectibility of the human soul, the Five Percent Nation operates in a fashion similar to classic gnosticism. In keeping with gnosticism as an esoteric school of thought, the Five Percent Nation philosophy revolves around fundamental principles such as the divine origins of the cosmos; the presence of evil that corrupted humanity; and recovery of humanity by nurturing the inner life of true believers.

Father Allah willfully spread Fard Muhammad's secret teachings, known as the "Lost-Found Muslim Lessons" to black youth who were outsiders to the NOI.[15] (During the 1960s, NOI members were not allowed to discuss the tradition with outsiders, maintaining a great deal of secrecy about their core beliefs, rituals, and practices.) Father Allah also developed his own system of teachings, known as the Supreme Mathematics and the Supreme Alphabet. The "divine sciences" of Supreme Mathematics and Alphabet are sets of principles and an evolving system of analysis, attached to numerals as well as the letters of the alphabet, which serve as the keys to divine knowledge. For Five Percenters, the "science of Supreme Mathematics is the key to understanding man's relationship to the universe." Islam, for them, is a mathematics-based science, a way of life and not a traditional religion. For Five Percenters, "the science of Supreme Mathematics is the key to understanding man's relationship to the universe."

The Supreme Alphabet of the Five Percenters has been instrumental in making members extremely adept at the "breaking down" of words, in order to arrive at their true, esoteric meaning, in accordance with the lessons provided by Master Fard and Father Allah. "Knowledge is the Foundation of all in Existence;" according to Father Allah's Supreme Alphabet, "It is the Original [Asiatic Black] Man, who 'knows the ledge' or the boundaries of himself and knows that there is 'no ledge' or no ending to his circumference. ... Wisdom is your Wise Words, Ways and Actions ... Wisdom is developed from the knowledge of Self, which allow[s] One to be Wise or Speak Intelligently from the Dome or the Mind." For instance, rap artists Pete Rock and CL Smooth's "Anger in the Nation" illustrates this theme: "Libraries, broken down as lies buried/Television tell a lie vision."[16] In addition, the hip-hop group Brand Nubian's song "All for One" asserts "You got to know the ledge of wise and dome/And understand your culture of freedom."[17]

When using the Supreme Alphabet to ascertain the true meaning of Allah, the Five Percenter visualizes each letter of the Arabic term for "God" to be part of the following acronym: "Arm, Leg, Leg, Arm, and Head." By depicting God in this very anthropomorphic fashion, the Five Percenter equates this use of word play with the fundamental belief that black men are the living embodiment of divinity in the world. Likewise, using the Supreme Alphabet to decode the meaning of Islam, the Five Percenters transform the term, which means "submission" in Arabic, into the following statement: "I Self Lord and Master." In doing so, this alternative definition of Islam by the Five Percenters directly contradicts the historic interpretation of the word from its Arabic origins. But the Five Percenters do so in order to advance a more personal and empowering theology that places black people as well as their desire for human dignity and self-governance squarely at its center.

There is also a noteworthy material culture that coincides with the ideology of the Five Percent Nation. For example, the Book of Life, also known as the "Power Papers" by the Five Percenters, is circulated in the form of photocopied pamphlets that are passed hand-to-hand from initiated members of the group to new recruits. The Book of Life represents the amassed teachings of Father Allah and serves as the main source for the Five Percenters' "lessons." In addition, the Book of Life was central to the bitter feud between the NOI and the Five Percent Nation. As a former youth minister for the Nation of Islam's fabled Mosque No. 7 in Harlem, Father Allah was privy to numerous doctrines that were handed down by Fard Muhammad himself and were closely guarded secrets of the NOI's leadership. With Father Allah's departure from the NOI, he incorporated these secrets into the Five Percenters' Book of Life.[18] In addition, the "Power Flags" used by the Five Percenters have an eight-pointed star with an encircled number 7 in the center of it with the motto "In the Name of Allah" imprinted above it.[19]

Of great significance to the gods is the number 7. It stands for the seventh letter of the alphabet, G, and, by extension, for God.[20] According to Fard Muhammad's *Lost-Found Muslim Lesson* no. 2, the Original Man has 7-1/2 ounces of brain when compared to the white devil, whose brains weighs only 6 ounces. This symbolism is extended further: the flag of the Five Percenters, also known as the Universal Flag of Islam, contains a 7 (symbol of God) surrounded by a crescent moon (signifying the black woman) and a star (signifying the child). Rappers who embrace the teachings of the Five Percent Nation note the significance of this number. Famed rapper Rakim, for example, has produced lyrics such as those in the song "No Competition" which declare "I'm God/G is the seventh letter made," reflecting the centrality of seven as the number of divine perfection.[21]

Anyone who is remotely aware of Five Percent jargon is cognizant of the racial essentialism that fuels believers' assault on white supremacy. As for the subject of the white people, Five Percent lyrics often refer to them variously as "snakes," "serpents," "the Yacub crew," "skunks," "cave dwellers," and so on. Poor Righteous Teachers and Gang Starr, for example, represent the most adamant position. In the song "Word from the Wise," Wise Intelligent of Poor Righteous Teachers asserts, "Most definitely Poor Righteous Teachers never be down/We're with the kings and crowns not clowns/No blue eyes and blonde hair is over here."[22] Guru, the rapper from Gang Starr, expounds, "And yo, the devil's got assassination squads/Want to kill niggaz cuz they're scared of God" in the song "Tonz 0' Gunz."[23] In both instances, the lyrics illustrate the level of racial antagonism and mistrust that emanate from the belief that any contact with whites will result in the downfall and subsequent demise of blacks.

It must be noted that the Five Percent rappers grapple with this issue of race in a very complex and varied manner. Taken at face value, Rakim's classic lyric from the song "In the Ghetto"—"It ain't where you're from, it's where you're at"—appears to summarize a postmodern or antiessentialist argument that political identity and geographic location are what really matter more than biological origin and cultural heritage.[24] Yet most observers generally pay no attention to other lines within the same song that arguably denote the racial essentialism and ethnic absolutism at the core of Five Percenter thought. For instance, in keeping with the classic iteration of NOI/Five Percenter racial theory, Rakim mentions those who "lived in the caves" (the white men) and "they couldn't cave me in/cause I'm the Asian" (the Original Asiatic Black man). Furthermore, while repeatedly emphasizing the power of his "third eye," a direct reference to the mind used in Five Percent terminology, Rakim states, "From knowledge to born back to knowledge precise." This serves as another Five Percenter allusion indicating the constant personal and spiritual evolution that came from the acquisition of self-knowledge.

Central to the mission of the Five Percent Nation has been an attempt to move beyond a critique of nihilism into a mode of empowerment for poor and working-class African Americans who are otherwise disenfranchised, disaffected, and desperate. When considered in light of Cornel West's definition of nihilism as an all-encompassing specter of "psychological depression, personal worthlessness, and social despair,"[25] the song "Life's a Bitch" by rappers Nas and AZ vividly illustrates the manner in which the beliefs of the Five Percent Nation can be perverted. The duo provides a fascinating insight into this fundamental crisis by re-creating the ghetto mentality of New York City's underside through the pensive, albeit frustrated, voices of those who have to contend with the harsh realities of the "mean streets." The song begins with the two rappers discussing how to split money that the listener assumes they have gotten through nefarious means. After they expound on the relative merits of fifty, twenty, and one dollar bills, respectively, Nas says, "That's what this is all about right ... /

Clothes, bankrolls, and hoes …" From that starting point, AZ's initial verse sets the stage for an exploration of how this materialistic zeal is embraced in spite of their best intentions: "Visualizin' the realism of life in actuality/ … A person's status depends on salary/And my mentality is money orientated/I'm destined to live the dream for all my peeps who never made it/ … we were beginners in the hood as five percenters." Furthermore, AZ insists that "Even though we know somehow we all gotta go/ … as long as we leavin' thievin' we'll be leavin' with some kind of dough/ … to that day we expire … /Me and my capers will be somewhere stackin' plenty papers/ … Cause life's a bitch and then you die!"[26]

Nas and AZ's exchange declares their intent to satisfy a desire for goods, wealth, and sensual pleasure as the definitive interests that give life meaning and substance. Their song reflects Cornel West's warning that the nihilistic tendencies for urban black youth can be summarized as "fortuitous and fleeting moments preoccupied with getting over—with acquiring pleasure, property, and power by any means necessary."[27] Rap music inherited the fearless audacity and racial empowerment that was central to the examples of Malcolm X and Louis Farrakhan as noteworthy Black Muslims in recent memory, but the Five Percenters were largely bereft of the NOI's political sensibility as well as its moral compass.

Young black men have been drawn to the Five Percent Nation because, for example, of the movement's emphasis on male leadership. Much like the NOI had done previously, the Five Percenter teachings were able to criticize black men for abdicating their "rightful" place as leaders both in the public and private spheres while affirming their role. Thus Five Percenters' beliefs challenged African American men to assume control over their destinies, and they responded in kind. Black women within the Nation of the Gods and Earths—referred to as Earths or Queens—are taught to respect themselves, to submit to the will and authority of men, and to manage the affairs of family and home. Ironically, a growing number of young black women are attracted to the Five Percenter movement because they appreciate the strength of the men and the protective posture toward them in a society that either denigrates or ignores black femininity. Moreover, according to Five Percent beliefs, only a man can achieve the level of perfection symbolized by a 7, whereas a woman can only reach a 6. In the song "Can I Start This," the Poor Righteous Teachers illustrate this gender dynamic by proclaiming, "Peace to all the Queens/Submitting to the sevens."[28] Women are to subordinate themselves to men just as the Earth revolves around the Sun. Furthermore each woman, or "Earth," must cover three-quarters of her body by wearing head coverings and long, loose-fitting garments, just as three-quarters of the Earth is covered by water. While this is often dismissed as symbolic gesture or ritualistic code of dress, one must note that this practice is deeply imbued with concerns over male concepts about and control over the black female body.

As becomes clear, much of what is taught within the Five Percent Nation has served to reify modes of patriarchy that are insidious and regressive. For instance, it is important to note that there are only a handful of female Five Percenters in the entertainment industry.[29] Also, unlike her male counterpart, a female Five Percenter is known as a "Muslim;" because she bears witness to the fact that her man is Allah and willingly submits herself to the black man.[30] In the song "Love Me or Leave Me Alone," the members of Brand Nubian declare, "I ain't down for a honey who don't wanna submit/See I'm not the kind to let a woman run it."[31] To a generation of urban black youth who are unaccustomed to the security of a strong nuclear family with traditional gender roles, the Five Percent Nation provides a welcome social structure. The underlying message of the Five Percenters is that the disorder they had experienced up until then had been caused by outside forces beyond their control, evil influences they were now able to overcome through self-mastery. Although the Five Percenter movement proclaims empowerment for the entire black community and tends to treat black women with respect, their sexist orientation provides little space for female Five Percent rappers or the unrestricted articulation of women's issues.

Jihad of Words, III: Sunni Islam and Rap Music

The NOI underwent several dramatic changes following the death of the Honorable Elijah Muhammad in 1975.[32] Under the brief leadership of Warith Deen Muhammad, one of the Honorable Elijah Muhammad's sons, the original Nation of Islam was transformed. The name of the organization was changed to the Bililian Community, and later to the World Community Al-Islam in the West (WCIW). To this day, members continue to be known as Bililians, in tribute to Bilal ibn Rabah, an Ethiopian Muslim who was born and lived during the seventh century A.D. and served as the first muezzin, the one who calls Muslims to prayer.

Although Warith made membership and participation in the WCIW open to people of all races, its membership remained predominantly black. Nonetheless, expansion of the organization marked a profound move from a black separatist movement with quasi-Islamic traditions to a black Sunni Muslim collective that aligned itself with global Islamic orthodoxy. Warith Muhammad restructured the NOI, not only to give the organization an orthodox Islamic sensibility but also to integrate black Muslims more fully into mainstream America. Over the past three decades, Imam Warith D. Muhammad made greater attempts to foster better relations with the United States government and foreign Islamic governments. More than that, the changes made by Warith Deen Muhammad were important because they brought the WCIW in line with other Islamic nationalist movements around the world.

Warith D. Muhammad sought to align the doctrine of the organization with the Qur'an. He boldly did away with Elijah Muhammad's doctrine of racial separation. He struggled to dismantle the overly secretive and hierarchical structure of the former NOI. After nearly a decade of his vilification by top-ranking NOI ministers, Warith made a deliberate effort to restore Malcolm X to a position of honor within the WCIW, most notably by renaming Mosque No. 7 in Harlem after his fallen friend. Also in direct contradiction to his father's teachings on racial separatism, Warith began honoring the U.S. Constitution and encouraging his members to participate in the political process. In another drastic move, Warith made certain that most of the organization's real estate holdings were quickly sold off. He also redefined W. D. Fard as a "wise man" and began to teach the five pillars of orthodox Islam.

Meanwhile, due to intense differences with Warith Deen Muhammad concerning the political and economic perspectives of the parent organization, Louis Farrakhan separated from the WCIW in 1977 yet retained the organizational name "Nation of Islam." As Edward Curtis notes, Farrakhan's attacks deemed Warith Deen Muhammad's efforts to reform the NOI into a Sunni Islamic entity as "a misguided departure from Elijah Muhammad's teachings" and subsequently charged Warith with establishing new policies that "ignored the issue of racism."[33] This newly formed NOI was clearly intended to be a political, as opposed to religious, enterprise. It is crucial to note how, under Louis Farrakhan's leadership, the NOI has actually constricted rather than expanded discourses on race, religion, and politics in the minds of the American public.

There has been resurgence in scholarly and popular interest about the NOI in general and its chief spokesperson, Minister Louis Farrakhan, in particular, largely based on the media attention generated by the Million Man March. On October 16, 1995, the NOI brought about one million African American men together to the National Mall in Washington, D.C., in support of what Louis Farrakhan called a "Day of Atonement," an event that garnered Farrakhan a great deal of publicity and influence within American politics. Despite this media visibility and overtures to the American mainstream, the future of the NOI is a matter of great debate. Like Elijah Muhammad and Malcolm X before him, Farrakhan is radical in his racial outlook, yet quite conservative in his political and economic views. Yet, unlike his predecessors, the inflammatory rhetoric of Louis Farrakhan has brought the NOI into the American sociopolitical mainstream. Mattias Gardell notes that "it is difficult to determine where on a political scale Farrakhan and the NOI should be placed. As a religio-political ideologist, Farrakhan moves in a different universe than secular politicians, making the left-right scale an inadequate tool of classification."[34] Even though the NOI has held a fairly prominent position within American society, the organization is losing ground because of its long-standing unwillingness to either embrace Sunni Islam or assimilate itself into American life by denouncing its race-based theology. In either case, the ideological tensions that once ensured the significance of Farrakhan and the NOI—racial separatism, black cultural pride, economic self-help, and political neutrality—now cause the man and the organization to become increasingly questionable to blacks and whites alike.

At the turn of the century, Minister Louis Farrakhan proclaimed a new direction for his organization. On February 26, 2000, a day the NOI designated as "Savior's Day," the NOI leader declared that he and his followers would accept orthodox Islam as the basis of their faith. After decades of eschewing any attempts to enter the larger Islamic community worldwide, this was an implicit shift away from the racialized mythology that epitomized the NOI's theology and religious practice under the Honorable Elijah Muhammad's leadership. In turn, this act greatly assuaged the prolonged ill-will that existed between Farrakhan and Warith Deen Muhammad.

This public acceptance of orthodox Islam by the NOI also represented a transition from the race-based theology and black nationalist ideology it embodied toward a worldview that still awaits true definition. Nevertheless, it is evident that the future of the NOI seeks to embrace the multiracial, multiethnic dimensions of the Muslim world yet retain its own core doctrines and definitive organizational structure. With the broad scope and great diversity of Islamic traditions and communities within the United States, the NOI led by Louis Farrakhan has actually been overshadowed and now stands as one of the smallest expressions of African American Islam in the nation. There are nearly twenty subgroups of Black Muslims within the United States today, ranging from Imam Warith Deen Muhammad's American Muslim Mission, to the Anser Auset (Nubian Islamic Hebrews of Brooklyn), to the Tijaniyah Sufis from Africa, to the Dar al-Islam Tabligh movement of Sunni Muslims.

The influence of African American Sunni Islam within rap music is neither a coincidence nor a marginal cultural phenomenon. Mos Def, Talib Kweli, Common, A Tribe Called Quest, Everlast, the Intelligent Hoodlum, Encore, Divine Styler, and the Roots are among a select constellation of hip-hop artists who have emerged as the musical vanguard of rap artists who are either Muslims or who have pro-Islamic tendencies. Two members of the critically respected hip-hop group A Tribe Called Quest, Q-Tip (who has since changed his name to Fareed Kamal) and Ali Shaheed Muhammad, whose last two albums are *Beats, Rhymes and Life* and *The Love Movement*, are Sunni (orthodox) Muslims. The Roots, a hip-hop group whose renowned use of live instrumentation and lengthy improvisational jams have garnered favorable praise by fans and critics alike, is a unique collaboration among members who are both Sunnis and Five Percenters.[35]

While they still constitute a minority presence in hip-hop, Sunni Muslim rappers have gained much respect in media and industry circles for their stylized depiction as "conscious rappers." This recent manifestation of the black Muslim presence in hip-hop has been positioned and marketed as a bulwark against the more facile, materialistic, and thuggish elements that tend to mark the current state of mainstream rap music. In the song "Fear Not of Man," the rapper Mos Def provides a stark contrast to the prevalent trend in hip-hop during the late 1990s. The song begins with Mos Def uttering the *Basmala*, a solemn Arabic invocation, *Bismallah ir Rahman ir Raheem*, which means "In the Name of God the Most Merciful, the Most Compassionate." The *Basmala* is traditionally done without musical accompaniment in a tone akin to a reverent whisper. By offering the *Basmala* as the first words on his album/CD, Mos Def performs *dhikr*, a brief yet poignant prayer intended to assert one's full awareness of the union between God and the faithful believer and to purify the Muslim of all that is bad. Thus, Mos Def expresses an intention to commit himself and his musical work to divine will by repeating the name and attributes of God in the hopes of drawing himself closer to God. This deceptively modest gesture can be seen as a profound shift in the articulation of African American Islam in contemporary rap music.

In many ways, the rapper Common has emerged to represent a conscious effort to raise moral and artistic reflection within black youth culture in general and rap music in particular. Common raps in the song "The Sixth Sense:' "Some say I'm too deep, I'm in too deep to sleep/Through me, Muhammad will forever speak:'[36] In the song "G.O.D. (Gaining One's Definition)," Common explores the possibility of a truly ecumenical expression of black religiosity by stating: "Who am I or they to say to whom you pray ain't right/That's who got you doing right and got you this far/Whether you say 'in Jesus's name' or 'Al urn du'Allah'/Long as you know it's a being that's supreme to you/You let that show towards others in the things you do."[37] In his lyric, Common indicates that religion, for him, transcended concerns about its functional (what it does) and substantive (what it is) dimensions and must focus on its definitive (what it means) aspects.

Aside from his strictly religious overtures, the greatest controversy in Common's musical career arose from his first ode to rap music entitled "I Used to Love H.E.R." As the rapper has stated, the H.E.R. in the song's title stood for "Hip Hop, in its essence, and real." In the song, Common provides an allegorical history of hip-hop's evolutionary migration from an underground East Coast subculture to a mainstream West Coast phenomenon in terms of his romance that had gone awry with a female lover. For Common, the disintegration of his love affair with rap music was keenly reflected in his fiery comments in the song. By way of illustration, he comments: "Talkin' about poppin' glocks, servin' rocks, and hittin' switches/Now she's a gangsta, rollin' with gangsta bitches/Always smokin' blunts and getting' drunk/Tellin' me sad stories, now she only fucks with the funk/Stressin' how hard core and real she is/She was really the realest, before she got into showbiz."[38]

In 1996, prominent West Coast rapper Ice Cube verbally attacked Common in a guest verse on "Westside Slaughterhouse" for Common's negative depiction of gangsta rap as a flawed expression of hip-hop culture. In turn, Common responded by producing an independent underground record called "The Bitch in You" in which he levels a contentious musical reproach of Ice Cube. In that song Common criticizes Ice Cube for going after quick cash in his Hollywood and later recording career, which glamorized everything that violated his staunch beliefs as a Muslim. Common delivered clever albeit scathing lines to highlight Ice Cube's many transgressions, such as: "Hypocrite, I'm filling out your death certificate/Slanging bean pies and St. Ide's in the same sentence/Shoulda repented on [the] 16th of October/Get some beats besides George Clinton to rock over."[39] In this one rhyme, Common brought to public attention how Ice Cube's present activities diverged greatly from *Death Certificate*, the musical testament to the rapper's conversion to the NOI. Moreover, Common argues that

Ice Cube's decision to participate in the NOI's brand of self-help capitalism (the reference to "bean pies") while also serving as an advertising spokesman for a leading alcoholic beverage that was ravaging urban black America (the mention of "St. Ide's") is incongruous as well as contemptible. By arguing that Ice Cube "shoulda repented" during the Million Man March, Common is calling into question Ice Cube's moral commitment to the collective welfare of black people in the United States. This point is finally leveled as an indictment of Ice Cube's banal choice of recycling musical samples from George Clinton and other 1970s funk musicians, a move that simply followed the dominant trend within gangsta rap rather than making musical or aesthetic choices that might either challenge listeners or bring forth innovations within rap music in general.

With the intense schism between the East Coast and West Coast leading to the violence that might have contributed to the murders of Tupac Shakur and the Notorious B.I.G. during that period, there was much concern that a battle between Common and Ice Cube, whether lyrical or otherwise, might result in unwanted bloodshed and further public disgrace for the hip-hop community. As a result, Minister Farrakhan called a summit in which both parties were called to NOI headquarters in Chicago to parlay and work out their grievances amicably. As much as the Million Man March promoted a sense of personal responsibility and moral atonement for black men of all ages across the nation, Farrakhan's direct mediation of this potential feud helped establish a paradigm for crisis management and peaceful negotiations for the hip-hop generation.

Final Thoughts

To summarize, this chapter has analyzed how the evolution of African American Islam in the postwar era coincided with the growth and development of hip-hop. Rather than simply illustrating a unilateral imposition of Islamic influences upon this African American art form, I have argued that a heightened concern about black consciousness, adherence to complex rhetorical/ideological codes, and establishing a diverse system of aural/lyrical/visual aesthetics affected African American Islam and hip-hop to equal degrees from the 1960s to the present.

By using the "jihad of words" as an analytical rubric, it is vital to reconsider the ways in which African American Islam and rap music revise dominant notions of the relationship between religiosity and artistic creativity. As historic analogues, both African American Islam and hip-hop exposed codified as well as unwritten myths, ideologies, and stereotypes. They rejected the normative logic and realities of dominant society, creating alternative formulations that were far more relevant to the lives and experiences of black people. While black Muslims have provided the vision for new levels of social critique and spiritual renewal, the creative work of rap artists provided the means and rationale for the transformation of daily reality. By the coevolution of Islam and rap music within the African American experience, it is possible to contemplate how religion and popular culture operate in tandem to provoke many people to consider evil and strive toward social justice.

It is interesting to note that the development of a more "orthodox" turn in rap's Islamic sensibilities mirrors the general shift in the Islamic orientation within the larger black community. As demonstrated herein, the various manifestations of the black Muslim presence in hip-hop has been positioned and marketed as a bulwark against the more facile, materialistic, and thuggish elements that tend to mark the current state of mainstream rap music. While we have a sense of what this turn in hip-hop and the larger community means in terms of the diversity of both cultural production and religious sensibilities in black America, it remains to be seen how this complexity will ultimately manifest itself in years to come.

Study Questions

1. How is Malcolm X's role and influence in the NOI used to develop the conceptual framework of "jihad of words?" How is this framework further expanded to analyze varied Islamic expressions in rap music throughout?
2. What are some examples of African American Islamic themes and ideas in rap music and hip hop used within this article?
3. How would you classify and chart the similarities and differences between various Islamic worldviews and ideas expressed in rap music?

Notes

1. Malcolm X, *The Autobiography of Malcolm X* (New York: Ballantine, 1973).
2. Steven Barboza, "Allah's Will in America," in Steven Barboza, ed., *American jihad: Islam after Malcolm X* (New York: Doubleday, 1993), 14.
3. Ibid., 18.
4. Richard Brent Turner, *Islam in the African American Experience* (Bloomington and Indianapolis: Indiana University Press, 1997), 185.
5. Barboza, "Allah's Will in America:" 17.
6. William L. Van Deburg, *New Day in Babylon: The Black Power Movement and American Culture, 1965–1975* (Chicago and London: University of Chicago Press, 1992), 2.
7. Public Enemy, "Party for Your Right to Fight," on *It Takes a Nation of Millions to Hold Us Back*, Def Jam, 1988.
8. Joe Wood, "Malcolm X and the New Blackness," in Joe Wood, ed., *Malcolm X: In Our Own Image* (New York: St. Martin's Press, 1992), 6–7.
9. Greg Tate, "Can This Be the End of Cyclops and Professor X?" in Joe Wood, ed., *Malcolm X: In Our Own Image* (New York: St. Martin's Press, 1992), 185.
10. Dr. Dre, "Dre Day," on The Chronic, Death Row/Interscope/Priority Records, 1992.
11. Todd Boyd, *Am I Black Enough for You?: Popular Culture from the 'Hood and Beyond* (Bloomington and Indianapolis: Indiana University Press, 1997), 39.
12. Among the commercially successful and critically hailed rappers who belong to the Nation of Gods and Earths are Rakim Allah of Eric B and Rakim, MC Ren, Shorty from Da Lench Mob, K-Solo, Daddy 0 from Stetsasonic, Big Daddy Kane, Poor Righteous Teachers, Busta Rhymes, Guru of the group Gang Starr, Pete Rock and CL Smooth, Brand Nubian, Digable Planets, and Mobb Deep. *All* members of the hip-hop collective Wu Tang Clan such as the RZA, Method Man, 01' *Dirty* Bastard, the GZA, Raekwon, and Ghost Face Killah belong to the Five Percent Nation.
13. The author is aware that gnosticism has been viewed historically as the designation given to certain heretical sects among the early Christians who claimed to have superior knowledge of things spiritual, and interpreted the sacred writings by a mystic philosophy. It is my attempt herein to utilize a broader, more contemporary connotation of this term.
14. Mary Pat Fisher, *Religion Today: An Introduction* (London: Routledge, 2002), 187.
15. There has been speculation that the format of the NOI lessons, which are arranged in question-and-answer format, might have been modeled after the Freemasons' catechism.
16. Pete Rock and CL Smooth, "Anger in the Nation," on *Mecca and the Soul Brother*, Elektra/Asylum, 1992.
17. Brand Nubian, "All For One," on *One for All*, Elektra/Asylum, 1990.
18. There are allegations that Father Allah's disclosure of the NOI secrets motivated the organization to have him condemned to death. Father Allah was found murdered in 1969 under mysterious circumstances.
19. The Five Percent Nation has been condemned by various state and federal law enforcement agencies as nothing more than a criminal "gang;" citing the group's involvement with the burgeoning

underground drug economy and other illicit activities. In addition, critics from across the American political and social spectrum have denounced the Five Percenters as an assembly of criminals and thugs who use Arabic sayings and Islamic aesthetics as a means of justifying their unlawful activities and self-indulgent practices. There has been an increasing number of complaints from incarcerated Five Percenters in recent years against the Departments of Corrections in New Jersey, South Carolina, and other states about the violation of their civil liberties. Many of the members of the Five Percent Nation have had their constitutional right to religious freedom curtailed by prison authorities because of their unwillingness to view the Nation of the Gods and Earths as a legitimate community of faith. I want to suggest, however, that this treatment of the Five Percenters is both unbalanced and over-simplified. It disregards the significance of the group's beliefs, practices, and value system for individual members. Additionally, such pejorative views of the Five Percent Nation deny the exigent circumstances that gave rise to the Five Percenter phenomena.

20. Five Percenters originated the salutatory expression, "What's up, G?" whereby "G" originally stood for "God," not "gangsta," as has been stated recently.
21. Eric B. and Rakim, "No Competition," on *Follow the Leader*, Universal, 1988.
22. Poor Righteous Teachers, "Words from the Wise," on *Holy Intellect*, Profile Records, 1990.
23. Gang Starr, "Tons O' Gunz," on *Hard to Earn*, Capitol, 1994.
24. Eric B. and Rakim, "In the Ghetto," on *Let the Rhythm Hit 'Em*, MCA, 1990.
25. Cornel West, *Race Matters* (Boston: Beacon Press, 1993), 13.
26. Nas, "Life's a Bitch," on *Illmatic*, Sony Music, 1994.
27. West, *Race Matters*, 5.
28. Poor Righteous Teachers, "Can I Start This," on *Holy Intellect*, Profile Records, 1990.
29. Female adherents of the Five Percent Nation who have gained recognition in the past few years are Erykah Badu, Lady Mecca of the Digable Planets, and Blue Raspberry, a female member of the Wu Tang roster.
30. Yusuf Nuruddin, "The Five Percenters: A Teenage Nation of Gods and Earths," in Yvonne Y. Haddad and Jane L. Smith, eds., *Muslim Communities in North America* (Albany: State University of New York Press, 1994), 128.
31. Brand Nubian, "Love Me or Leave Me Alone," on *In God We Trust*, Elektra/Asylum, 1993.
32. Due to his advanced Qur'anic education and extensive travels through the Middle East and North Africa, Wallace Muhammad (later renamed Warith Deen Muhammad) had a profound effect on Malcolm X's theological views during the late 1950s and early 1960s. Prior to Malcolm's controversial rift with the Honorable Elijah Muhammad and the NOI hierarchy in 1963, it was Warith who initially distanced himself from the organization for what he deemed to be false Islamic teachings. By most accounts, it was evident that the more Warith read the writings of W. D. Fard, the more he questioned his father's claim to be the "messenger of Allah," Although they were going through their own respective crises of faith regarding their affiliations with the NOI, both Warith and Malcolm eventually concluded that it was unreasonable to believe that Fard was Allah himself. In spite of being separated by considerable amounts of time and space, both men came to similar conclusions and hence began to lean more toward orthodox Islam.
33. Edward E. Curtis IV, *Islam in Black America: Identity, Liberation, and Difference in African-American Islamic Thought* (Albany: State University of New York Press, 2002), 130.
34. Mattias Gardell, *In the Name of Elijah Muhammad: Louis Farrakhan and the Nation of Islam* (Durham, NC: Duke University Press, 1996), 283.
35. Furthermore, in addition to Islamic doctrine in rap music, the resurgence of Middle Eastern musical textures within today's rap music has been noteworthy. Most recently, songs such as Missy Elliott and Timbaland's "Get Ur Freak On," Norega's "Nothing," Erick Sermon and Redman's "React," and Truth Hurts's "So Addictive" have been major R & B/hip-hop hits that use Middle Eastern rhythms and melodic structures to give their recordings some exotic flourishes. The latter song was further accentuated in this regard not only by the stellar production by West Coast rap legends Dr. Dre and DJ Quik, but also with the lyrical assault by the penultimate hip-hop lyricist and Five Percenter,

Rakim Allah. If we think that some of these doctrines are problematic or heretical, we need to try to understand them, to engage them, and to try to work to change conditions that produce them.

36. Common, "The Sixth Sense," on *Like Water for Chocolate*, MCA Records, 2000.
37. Common featuring Cee-Lo, "G.O.D. (Gaining One's Definition)," on *One Day it'll All Make Sense*, Relativity, 1997.
38. Common, "I Used to Love H.E.R.," on *Resurrection*, Relativity, 1994.
39. Common, "The Bitch in You," on *Relativity Urban Assault*, Loud Records, 1996.

14
Re-inventing Islam with Unique Modern Tones
Muslim Hip Hop Artists as Verbal Mujahidin

Alim charts the relationship between the global hip hop nation and the Islamic faith whereby artists are understood to participate in a sort of "verbal mujahidin." But despite the impact of the Islamic faith on hip hop, Alim queries why we still know little about these intentional and implicit connections. Practitioners of verbal mujahidin use valiant speech acts to communicate collective and individual beliefs about nation, America, oppression and suffering. Alim presents the possibility of Islams' influence on/in hip hop as a means by which to create a powerful and durable counterhegemonic movement in America. Conceiving of hip hop's lyrical mujahidin as "weapons of mass culture," Alim concludes that Muslims in hip hop hold immense power for change, and that such an Islamicized Hip Hop Nation continues to influence the "unique tones" re-inventing the Islam faith today.

Re-inventing Islam with Unique Modern Tones: Muslim Hip Hop Artists as Verbal Mujahidin*

H. Samy Alim

What happens when Beanie Sigel, one of the hardest rappers in the United Streets of America, clenches his jaws and spits in that South Philly Black street speech, "I fear *nu'in* ['nothing'] but Allah"?[1] What has attracted such a large number of rappers to seek Islam as a means of establishing their faith claims? More generally, how much do we know about the relationship between "Hip Hop" and "Islam"? This article explores aspects of the complex relationship between two entities—Hip Hop Culture and the Islamic Faith—which have both been separately constructed by dominating discourses as "threats to American civilization." To some practitioners, Hip Hop Culture represents a counterdiscourse that is not only mass-based, but also mass-mediated, circulated, and communicated to millions of youth. Like the Muslim *umma*, the Global Hip Hop Nation functions a world-wide network of "believers" around the world who have created "nationhood" through cultural, ideological and imaginary means. In this article, I view Hip Hop artists—particularly those engaged in what I have called the "transglobal Hip Hop *umma*[2]—as "verbal *mujahidin*," with their speech activities serving as alternative media sources narrating the beliefs and experiences of a "nation." Their very experiences, when verbalized, represent a discursive struggle against oppression. As Dyson has noted:

> The rap artist, as Cornel West has indicated, is a bridge figure, who combines the two potent traditions in black culture, preaching and music: the rapper appeals to the rhetorical practices honed in African American religious experiences and the cultural potency of black singing/musical traditions to produce an engaging hybrid. In a sense rappers are truly urban griots dispensing social and cultural critiques, verbal shamans exorcising the demons of hiphopcrisy and a laissez faire orality that refuses to participate in the media of cultural exploration and social provocation.[3]

Initial Questions and Concerns

In this article, I am raising questions from multiple perspectives. From a historical perspective, can an exploration of the histories of Black American Muslim Movements, and their contemporary presence in the Hip Hop Nation (HHN), move us towards a more in-depth understanding of the social, political, and cultural consciousness that is central to the philosophy of the Hip Hop Cultural Movement?[4] Through ethnographic research, I explore issues of central concern to Religious Studies and anthropologers of religion, namely issues of *praxis* and *consciousness* in the believing subject. How has Islam served as a transformative force both in the personal lives and in the public roles of many Hip Hop artists as community conscious agents? How has Islam helped to shape their identities and ideologies as human beings in process and practice, and their actions as socially and politically conscious Hip Hop beings involved in a movement for change in the world? Throughout this article, I will be highlighting the potential of Muslims in the Hip Hop Cultural Movement to create a counterhegemonic discourse that "threatens" the ruling class, and their ideas. In other words, we'll see how the Muslim verbal *jihad,* the discursive struggle against oppression, "threatens," as Chuck D and Flava Flav rapped years ago, "the powers that be."[5]

Despite journalist Harry Allen's description of Islam as Hip Hop's "official religion,"[6] Islam's dynamic presence and central role in the HHN have been largely unexplored. I will be raising a number of issues and questions for further exploration in our on-going attempt to gain an increased understanding of the Global Hip Hop Nation and how it functions within a borderless Islamic nation. That is, Prophet Muhammad of Arabia did not speak of an "Islamic Iran" or of a "Muslim Malaysia"; he imagined a transglobal Muslim community, an *umma* where citizenship was predicated upon faith rather than contemporary nation-state distinctions, or rather, on how colonizing cartographers cut up the global landscape.

My use of "Islam" in this article is broadly conceived, encompassing a spectrum of ideologies and schools of thought. I will address the three most dominant forms of Islam in the HHN in the U.S. (the Nation of Islam, the Nation of Gods and Earths, or the Five Percent Nation of Islam, and the Sunni Muslim community) paying particular attention to the Nation of Islam which has had and continues to have the most profound impact upon the HHN. While there are theological and terminological differences between these communities, all view Islam as a transformative force in the lives of its practitioners, and the data reveal similarities among the views of their adherents. These similarities are revealed through conversations with Hip Hop artists about the various creative processes involved in their craft.

It is useful to note that as Islam was having such a powerful effect on the HHN in the U.S., Islamic Studies itself was experiencing significant changes. One scholar observed, "Islamic Studies—or the study of Muslim groups and their religion Islam—has been changing dramatically in the last decades. Until recently, Islamic Studies was largely the exotic focus of a relatively small group of academics who wrote books about it mainly for one another's consumption."[7] These significant changes in Islamic Studies are happening in an Islamic world that is itself experiencing dramatic changes and challenges. "The contemporary Muslim world is facing internal and external challenges. Entering the twenty first century, Muslim societies are struggling in their confrontation with enormous cultural dilemmas as they are rethinking, renegotiating and in some instances re-inventing traditional society but with unique modern tones."[8]

The first study of Hip Hop Culture to highlight the widespread practice of Islam in the HHN, its "unique modern tones," and how it has impacted the philosophy of key players within the Hip Hop Cultural Movement, was *Nation Conscious Rap: The Hip Hop Vision,*[9] which spawned the unique, French language film by Algerian filmmaker Bernard Zekri, *Rap et Islam.*[10] In preparing *Nation Conscious Rap*, the Black History Museum Committee consulted with some 57 representatives of the Hip Hop Cultural Movement—which they referred to as a "major cultural transformation of Western Civilization"—including Chuck D, Flavor Flav, Big Daddy Kane, Q-Tip, Sister Souljah, Poor Righteous Teachers, X-Clan, KRS-One, Sister Harmony, and many others. Conversations with artists ranged from 1 hour to 9 1/2 hours in a single session. The results were 227 hours of taped interviews, 1279 transcribed pages (some singlespaced), and invaluable insights into the histories and ideologies of the HHN.[11] This current research continues the work begun by the Black History Museum and is part of a larger project that includes dozens of interviews with Muslim Hip Hop artists.[12]

A number of interesting articles on Hip Hop and Islam were published in the early 1990s. The British publication, *The Face,* carried this headline on its cover page "Louis Farrakhan and Muslim Rap."[13] The author writes, "Rakim, Lakim Shabazz, Isis, Hakeem X, Professor Griff, Brand Nubian, Poor Righteous Teachers, X-Clan, KRS-1, Afrika Bambaataa, Jungle Brothers, King Sun, Movement Ex, Big Daddy Kane, Gang Starr, 2 Black 2 Strong, The Jaz, Queen Mother Rage, Paris, Two Kings In A Cipher, Public Enemy, all of these rap artists have introduced some version of Afrocentrism, Black nationalism or Islam to Pop Culture." He continues, pointing to what he saw as an Islamic shift in Black American music, "African American singers used to dedicate their albums to God or their attorneys, now they give album sleeve credit to Minister Louis Farrakhan, the Honorable Elijah Muhammad, Malcolm X, Marcus Garvey, Clarence 13 X, Khalid Muhammad, the Five Percent Nation, The Nubian Islamic Hebrews, and the Moorish Holy Temple of Science. The best popular music has always concealed a sense of mystery behind its open heart, but a growing section of rap is plunging into deep realms, that the inventors of rock 'n' roll could never have dreamed of."

The first rapper the author mentions is Rakim, one of the most influential rappers in the history of Hip Hop. Rakim testified to the power of Islam in his life: "I had a crazy childhood. I needed something to pick me up. I used to go to church but that was like looking up to something I couldn't see. The Nation of Islam taught me about myself, my history and everything under the Sun. I took the name Rakim Allah. Ra means Sun God. Kim [as in Kemet] was another word for Egypt, meaning 'land of the burned-faced people.' Once I got into Islam I had to speak on it. We reveal rather than conceal." In a widely distributed article, one Hip Hop journalist writes plainly, "Rap's got religion and that religion is Islam."[14] The journalist, a Euro-American who was vexed that "certain white teens across America seem to be craving contact with the metallic powers of Satan while their black brethren are busy digging the prophets of ancient scriptures," continued to show the influence of Islam on Hip Hop artists, "On his track called, 'The Universal Flag,' King Sun flows with the funk while 'elevating' on Five Percent doctrine. The video for Brand Nubian's 'Wake Up' shows lead rapper Puba 'rolling up on a cipher' before a massive posse of 'gods' in front of Five Percent Headquarters—the School of Allah on 125th Street in Harlem. Another video, this time for 'The Lost Tribe of Shabazz' finds Lakim Shabazz journeying to the Motherland and lip synching in front of the pyramids along the Nile."

Hip Hop music, from its inception, has been an active vehicle for social protest in the U.S. and around the world. As Tricia Rose wrote in *Black Noise,* its targets have been racism, discrimination, police brutality, miseducation, and other social ills.[15] When Hip Hop pioneer Afrika Bambaataa launched the Muslim-influenced Zulu Nation in the U.S. in the 1970s, and expanded the movement globally in places like France in the early 1980s, he was networking to help spread socially and politically conscious ideas and ideals, to build a community of people who would actively resist social, political, and economic subordination.[16] Bambaataa, inspired by Michael Caine's *Zulu,* formed the Universal Zulu Nation as a postcolonial resistance force in the streets of Black America and later the world.[17] As a child, he had been influenced by the NOI and continues to be influenced by them throughout his adulthood. As he recalled:

> I first heard the Honorable Elijah Muhammad when I was real little. A lot of my family was a part of the Nation of Islam. Some uncles and aunts and cousins. I began hearing the speeches of Malcolm X and the Honorable Elijah Muhammad. I

was there in 1975 when Wallace D. Muhammad took over and there was a shift in power. Mr. Muhammad [Elijah] wasn't the kind of speaker Minister Farrakhan and Malcolm were, but you heard everything that you needed to hear and he got right to the point. A lot of times now when I get lazy, like I've got to fix something in the house. ... It's not that I hear Minister Farrakhan's voice or Malcolm's voice speaking to me. I hear Elijah saying, 'Brother, you better get up and do something for self.' Sometimes his voice comes to me like an angel in the night ...[18]

Other researchers mention the impact of the NOI on the ideologies of the HHN, but few are in direct conversation with the Hip Hop artists themselves.[19] Recent work has focused on the Five Percent Nation of Islam[20] and on the diverse spiritual sensibilities of Hip Hop Culture, the latter which contains a particularly relevant article that examines the co-evolution of Black American Muslim Movements and Hip Hop Culture.[21] In this article, I build upon Floyd-Thomas' description of Malcolm X's "jihad of words" by going beyond lyrical production and engaging artists in ethnographic interviews in order to uncover the *jihad* of their lived experiences.

Hip Hop Lyrical Production as an Extension of Central Islamic Texts

In response to the dominant discursive construction of Hip Hop and Islam, many Hip Hop artists have constructed Hip Hop lyrical production as a creative, artistic extension of central Islamic texts. Just as Mecca remains the metaphoric center of the global Muslim *umma,* so do the concepts of the *Qur'an* and its revelation to Prophet Muhammad remain at the core of Muslim beliefs. Diverse Muslim members of the HHN have independently observed that the very means by which the *Qur'an* was revealed to the Prophet—that is, orally and, in large part, through rhymed prose—exhibits parallels to the linguistic and literary mode of delivery found in Hip Hop lyrical production. The Black American oral tradition has rarely been interpreted in this way, yet Muslim artists have creatively conceptualized links between their mode of production and their Islamic faith. Muslim Hip Hop artists are forging new connections between Hip Hop lyrical production and the method and means by which *Allah* revealed the *Qur'an* to The Prophet. An important methodological point is that these connections unfolded during the course of ethnographic interviews about Hip Hop Culture generally, *not* Islam, underscoring the need for direct engagement with Hip Hop artists in order to uncover layers of meaning.

Engaged in a conversation about how Black youth, often as early as pre-school, are familiar with "rap language," rapper Wise Intelligent (a member of the Nation of Gods and Earths, and representing the rap group Poor Righteous Teachers), in a case of strategic essentialism, claimed: "You have to understand that the potency of the melanin in the black man makes him naturally rhythmic. So when he hears anything that has that rhythm he's going to become a part of that instantly. Anything that rhymes. Many of our ancestors were poets. Imhotep, who built the first step pyramid. The pharoah Akhenton, he was a poet. The Prophet Mohammed even wrote poetry. This is our blood."[22] Rapper Mos Def, who is a member of the Sunni Muslim community, discussed the reasons why he believes Hip Hop lyrics can be an effective medium in educational practice. In the midst of his animated description, he drew a bridge between Hip Hop poetics and the *Qur'anic* text as forms of poetry, each possessing a rhyme scheme and an ability to transmit "'vital information" in a relatively short amount of time. His knowledge of the *Qur'an* and the Arabic language through which it was revealed were evident in his comments:

Alim: What do you feel the larger relationship between hip hop and education could be? Mos Def: I mean, hip hop could be *phenomenal*. Hip hop's relationship to education could be phenomenal. It could be 'extremely phenomenal in the sense that hip hop is a medium where you can get a lot of information into a very small space. And make it hold fast to people's memory. It's *just* a very radical form of information transferal.

A: So, you see it as being a vehicle for transferring information?

M: Oh, hell, yeah! I mean, do you know how much information—vital information—you could get across in three minutes?! You know, and make it so that … I mean, the *Qur'an* is like that. The reason that people are able to be *hafiz* [one who memorizes the entire *Qur'an* through constant repetition and study] is because the entire *Qur'an* rhymes. [Mos Def begins reciting Islamic verses from the *Qur'an*.] "*Bismillah Al-Rahman Al-Rahim. Al-hamdulillahi Rabb Al-Alameen.*" Like everything … Like, you see what I'm saying? I mean, it's any *surah* that I could name. "*Qul huwa Allahu ahad, Allahu samud. Lam yalid wa lam yulad wa lam yakun lahu kufwan ahad.*" It's all like that. Like, you don't even notice it. "*Idha ja'a nasru Allahi wal fath. Wa ra'aita al-nas yadkhuluna fi dini Allahi afwajan. Fa sabbih bi hamdi rabbika wa istaghfirhu innahu kana tawwab.*" Like, there's a rhyme scheme in all of it. You see what I'm saying? And it holds fast to your memory. And then you start to have a deeper relationship with it on recitation. Like, you know, you learn *Surat Al-Ikhlas*, right. You learn *Al-Fatiha*. And you learn it and you recite it. And you learn it and you recite it. Then one day you're reciting it, and you start to understand! You really have a deeper relationship with what you're reciting. "*A'udhu billahi min al-shaitan al-rajim.* …" You be like, "Wow!" You understand what I'm saying? Hip Hop has the ability to do that—on a poetic level.[23]

Bay Area rapper JT the Bigga Figga also refers to the literary similarities between what young Black Americans are doing with language (what I refer to as Hip Hop Nation Language[24]) and the purposeful use of creative language by Allah as a pedagogical tool to reach the hearts and minds of mankind. In a discussion of the relationship between the "language of the streets," and the "language of Hip Hop," JT draws on his knowledge of the *Qur'an* and links it to his Bay Area comrade rapper E-40's inventive and metaphorical use of language:

Alim: How does he [E-40] come up with all this different stuff, man?

JT: Just hangin out and just different people talkin. And, you know, "fo sheezy, off da heezy!" Me and you, what we doin right now, to him, it's called marinatin.

A: Yeah, I hear him say that.

J: Marinatin. We marinatin right now. We goin over … Like, it's almost like with *Allah* how he'll describe his prophets as moonlight. He'll describe his word that he speaks in a metaphoric phrasing. Where he'll say the clouds and when they swell up heavy and the water goes back to the earth, distilling back to the earth. The water's heavier than gravity so it distills back to the earth on dry land, producing vegetation and herbs comin up out the ground, you feel me? And results is happening, you feel me? And the Disbelievers, how they dry land and the sun's scorching it. … [JT is paraphrasing well-known verses about *jihad* in the *Qur'an*, 25: 45–60. In verses 48–52, it reads:

> 48 *And He it is Who sends the winds as good news before His mercy; and We send down pure water from the clouds,*

49 That we may give life thereby to a dead land, and give it for drink to cattle and many people that We have created.

50 And certainly We repeat this to them that they may be mindful, but most men consent to naught but denying.

51 And if We pleased, We could raise a warner in every town.

52 So obey not the disbelievers, and strive against them with a mighty striving with it.

[A footnote to verse 49 reads: "The mercy of Allah, which appears in the form of rain in physical nature, comes spiritually in the form of revelation. As the pure water from the clouds gives life to a dead land, so does the pure water of revelation from Him raise the spiritually dead to life."]

A: So he's describing the Believers when things start growing, right.

J: Yeah, yeah. He describe the different conditions, you know what I'm saying? And it can be related to nature, you feel me? *Nature.* And what we see, how we conduct ourself, can be related to some aspect of nature. … And that's kinda like what E-40 do when he take something and take a word and apply it, you feel me?[25]

Whether engaged in conversations about young Black children's familiarity with "rap language," or the pedagogical potential of Hip Hop music, or the inventive and innovative use of language by specific artists within the HHN, Muslim Hip Hop artists' descriptions of their craft often recall the function of the *Qur'an.* In many of my interviews, I heard Islamic knowledge being invoked spontaneously in the flow of conversation (as often occurs in Muslim–Muslim conversations), pointing to the fact that members of the HHN are studying and applying Islam in their everyday lives as well as casting Hip Hop Culture and lyrical production in a uniquely Islamic light.

Nation-Conscious Narratives from the Members of the Transglobal Hip Hop *Umma*

Many of the artists involved in the global manifestations of the Hip Hop Cultural Movement—in places like France, Brazil, Japan, Italy, South Africa, Cuba, and Palestine—resist the multifarious forms of oppression in global societies. Exploring what he refers to as the "transglobal Islamic underground," and writing in particular about England's Fun-Da-Mental and France's IAM, Ted Swedenburg states: "In both countries Muslims are attempting to construct cultural, social and political spaces for themselves as ethnic groups (of sorts), and are massively involved in anti-racist mobilizations against white supremacy. Hip Hop activism has been an important arena for anti-Islamophobic mobilization for both French and British Muslims."[26]

Many Hip Hop artists in the U.S., as we heard from pioneer Afrika Bambaataa, became acquainted with the NOI as a direct result of the Nation's work in Black communities. Once introduced to Islam through the Nation, many artists speak of reclaiming their Black identity and of regaining a "knowledge of self" that was stripped from their ancestors by European slavemasters. Once that identity is reclaimed, an ideology of nation-consciousness and nation-building shapes the actions of those involved in the HHCM. They can no longer see themselves as merely "artists," but as active laborers in the rebuilding of their Nation. How do the members of the HHCM become acquainted with Islam? What is that process like? What do they see as their role within the HHCM? What are their stories?

The next generation of Hip Hoppers grew up listening to rappers like Public Enemy and Ice Cube, and many of them became acquainted with Islam through their lyrics. In addition, many Hip Hop artists have direct contact with the NOI and their narratives of spiritual transformation and moral responsibility are riveting. DJ Hi-Tek, hailing from Cincinnati, and one half of Reflection Eternal with his Muslim rhyme partner Talib Kweli, takes the mic and describes how he became a "next generation soldier":

Hi-Tek: I went to the Mosque, you know what I'm saying? I wanted to be a Muslim … I was a Muslim, you know what I mean? … I went to Mosque No. 5 at Avondale, at the firehouse, you know what I'm saying? That was real. That's really what got me to being the next generation soldier, you know what I'm saying? You know … Farrakhan and Malcolm X, you know, that's what I was into. And that's really what kept me focused, man. Knowing the realities of who I am as a Black youth, you know what I mean?

A: If you had to take away maybe one or two of the most important points of Minister Farrakhan, what would they be for you?

H: At the time when I got into Farrakhan it was around the time when a lot of my peoples was dying and getting shot. You know. dying from crack, you know what I'm saying? He was just saying, "'Stop killing ourselves! Stop killing," you know what I'm saying? [Minister Farrakhan launched a nationwide "Stop the Killing" tour in 1993–94] And "Uplift the young Black youth." And that's what I was into. I kinda seen it. When I was young, everybody used to say I was a old man. I just kinda seen it like, "Yo … " You know, I wasn't no preacher, but I was living it, too. It was like, it was real, man, you know what I mean? Still, it ain't over yet, you know what I'm saying? It's still out here. … Man, just the depression of my people, man, you know especially being from Cincinnati. I feel a lot of depression when I go back home … [Muslim rapper Common enters the backstage area and begins playing a mellow tune on the piano] … A lot of people just talk a lot of depression talk, you know what I'm saying? I just want my people to see what they can do, you know what I'm saying? … That's my job, man. I wasn't given this position for no reason. So, I'ma take advantage of it, man … I was blessed to make good music that people like that stands out, so I'ma take advantage of that. If I don't, God might punish me if I don't. So, you know, All Praises and Thanks to the Most High All the Time, man.[27]

There are many "next generation soldiers" with stories to tell, including Philadelphia's Ced Synatra who became involved with Mosque No. 12 in Philadelphia and Soldierz At War who are members of Mosque No. 2 in Chicago. Both groups heavily supported the NOI's efforts at the Million Family March on October 16, 2000.

Another next generation soldier, who attended the March suited up as a member of the NOI is the Bay Area's JT the Bigga Figga. While conducting a hiphopography of the Bay Area, we have interviewed JT on six separate occasions resulting in over ten hours of audio and videotape. Like many who come to the Nation, JT tells of being caught up "livin that life" and then making the transformation into a righteous way of living. His transformation, once again is not only manifested through moral change, but also through an ideology of nation-consciousness and an active involvement in the nation-building process. We join the conversation backstage in San Francisco's Maritime Hall as JT discusses when, where, why and how he entered the Nation:

A: How long have you been a member?
J: I been a member since January 4, 1995.

A: What made you become a member?

J: What made me become a member of the Nation of Islam? Following and reading the *Final Call* newspaper, number one. The *Final Call* newspaper is a paper that the Brothers from the Nation of Islam, the FOI, go out to the communities and deliver the paper. And the Brothers was delivering the paper in my community, where I was involved in crime and, you know, a lot of evil things, basically. In San Francisco, the Fillmore District. And, you know, being out there livin that life, it really wasn't what I was looking for, you know what I'm saying? It really wasn't. … Well, actually, it *was* what I was looking for, let me change this. … It was what I was *looking* for, but it was the wrong path. I was on the wrong path. And the *Final Call* newspaper was like a light in the community for brothers like us who were getting the paper. Buying it for a dollar from the brothers, supporting them, who just was out there doing what we was doing. And now they coming back as a savior, you know what I'm saying? They coming back to do a *work*. Sacrificing. You could see the work, you know what I'm saying? So, that inspired me to know, "Man, you was just stealing cars with me! Now you come selling a paper to me," you feel me? And they're like, 'Brother, you know, I'm changing my life.'"

A: You knew *something* happened.

J: It *had* to be something, and I wanted to get it. I wanted to see what that was about. What caused that, you know what I'm saying? "I want to learn about what you learning that helped you get like this. Because I'm not strong enough to do that right now. I gotta sell you rocks, I gotta steal these cars," you know what I'm saying? So, getting them papers, that was the first thing. Then one day, Allah (God) just must have guided me to the Mosque. Because one of my potnas was like, "Man, I'ma go see what these Mooozlims talkin about."

A: [Laughter]

J: You feel me?! Because they was right on our turf, you feel me? Brother Christopher Muhammad in San Francisco, Mosque No. 26. You know, it was at the Community Center. This is like '92, you know what I'm saying? So, '91, that whole year I'm buying the papers. And '92, right after the riots had happened [The LA riots], I go into a Mosque meeting and he was talking about the whole thing about the riots and how the FBI and the government allowed it to happen to paint a picture of the Black Man, you know what I'm saying? So, all of that is going on; you know what I'm saying? I'm going through that. I'm hearing these new teachings about God and Allah and Muslims …[28]

JT's initial involvement with the NOI leads him to reconsider his real purpose in life. Later in the same conversation, he states:

Eventually, I see myself being a Minister in the Nation of Islam in helping Minister Farrakhan take this message throughout the country, taking it throughout the world, you know. Being the first major rap artist to be a Minister, you know what I'm saying, for Minister Farrakhan. And to really do it, though, you know what I'm saying? And to inspire more people to come closer to the Nation of Islam. And one thing that he's teaching us is that even if you a Christian, if you white, if you Black, it don't even matter. It's about the human family coming together and getting the truth of these spiritual keys that Allah blessed the Honorable Elijah Muhammad with and now the Honorable Elijah Muhammad blessed *him* with it. And now he's carrying it on, you feel me, continuing the work. And I want to participate in that.[29]

Five months later in the same year, we resume the conversation on the corner of 3rd Street and Revere in the Bay View/Hunter's Point district. Now we're driving in JT's mobb (vehicle). We join the narrative and witness JT's evolving ideology and his evolving view of his role within the HHN. Like DJ Hi-Tek and Public Enemy before him, JT learns to view his position within the HHCM as one of increased responsibility and duty to himself, his people, and Allah:

Alim: You were saying that, you know, you feel that you were put in a certain position …

JT: Oh, yeah, I really was just talking about how, you know, how my whole life in terms of the life of crime and, you know, like every other young brother out there trying to do it your own way first and going through all the trials and tribulations. But I never would've thought I would've been in no position where I'm probably the number one artist. … Maybe Maybe not because I rap the best, but just because of how I conduct myself, you know. I'm not just a regular rap artist. I got something positive to say, you feel me? The hardcore brothas respect me. A lot of people respect me for my business ethic, how I conduct myself in the business. I put it out there real heavy about being independent. All these different principles in the way that I conduct myself I'm learning at the Mosque, though. So, maybe how I was naturally really got brought up out of me *fully* by coming to the Mosque. Islam bring that up out of you, whatever's in you. So, over time I start seeing that, you know, Allah put me in this unique position to address the parents, to address the children. The parents is at me about doing these songs. … So, I look at it that I'm not supposed to be in this rap game like everybody else, just trying to please myself. I'm thinking about the impact it's having on my community, the impact it's having on the Nation, the impact that it just has on me, you know. I really started realizing it when I first started coming to the Mosque in '92. Now, it's 2000 and it's like now I can see it even more clearer that I got a bigger work to do through this music. And Minister Farrakhan confirmed it even more, too, when we was at his home on April 3, 1997—about who the rappers are, you know. … He said the rappers are the leaders, you know what I'm saying? He said we're like the "pied pipers." He didn't want to use that word, but the people respond to our tune. They listening to what we saying. White boys trying to imitate us, you feel me? They parents is mad at them! But they don't care; they want to be like us, you feel me? So, he was really just letting us know that we're put in this position for God's purpose, though, you know what I'm saying? So, it's really like, you know, to realize that maybe I was born to do *this,* you know … Because I could sit here and talk to you and tell you what I think I'm seeing, but to really know that in your heart mean you gon *act* on it now, even in a bigger way, you feel me? And have faith in yourself and in the God who brought you into existence to know that, "I'm behind you. Do the inspiring thing." Like what Minister [Christopher Muhammad] was saying how Minister Farrakhan act on inspiration, you feel me? I feel that sometime in the music I be inspired to try to do positive things. I see these visions of how I'ma help my people some kinda way. I don't know it all the way, but I know that dudes out here risking they life over a thousand dollars. Maaan, I could show all these dudes how to make a thousand dollars. I could show people how to make a hundred thousand dollars, you feel me? I don't want nothing for it. It's just that our people is caught up in selling dope, want to just get high everyday, want to just chase women everyday, you feel me? The different things that give us pleasure. The lowest things that's giving us pleasure—we at the bottom of the scale now. The real pleasure, the number one pleasure come from pleasing Allah, or God as you know him, you know what I'm saying? But we all caught up in going the other way. So, you know, now that my album is out, I tried to design my album according to … I kinda tried to design it as best I could to whereas Minister Farrakhan would be happy how I put it together.[30]

These brief but remarkable examples of nation-consciousness offer a range of sites for us to explore a fundamental question: How do the Muslim members of the HHCM make the move from practical to discursive consciousness? In other words, how do these agents go from, as some heads would say, "*talkin* about it, to *bein* about it"? What is it that makes Public Enemy's Chuck D "try to do some of the things that he talks about"?[31] When San Francisco's JT the Bigga Figga states, "'Because I could sit here and talk to you and tell you what I think I'm seeing, but to really know that in your heart mean you gon *act* on it now, even in a bigger way, you feel me?" what is mediating the move to an active, discursive nation-consciousness? Clearly, from these narratives, these moves are predicated upon faith. JT continues: "And have faith in yourself and in the God who brought you into existence to know that, I'm behind you. Do the inspiring thing."

As verbal *mujahidin*, artists also engage in *jihad* of the hand and fight in the way of Allah (*jihad fi sabil Allah*) to help improve their local communities. My research reveals that not only are these artists studying Islam (as demonstrated by their ability to quote and vividly describe *Qur'anic* passages) and applying it to their everyday lives, but they are also operationalizing Islam, that is, acting upon what they have learned in order to help build a nation. Mos Def does not only rap about issues like consciousness and justice, he lives them. His Islamic consciousness moves him and partner Talib Kweli to rescue Nkiru Bookstore, a Black-owned bookstore in his home community of Brooklyn, from shutting down. It guides him to actively participate in the creation of a Hip Hop album (*Hip Hop for Respect*) dedicated to obtaining justice for police brutality victims and the immoral murder of Amadou Diallo, a Muslim immigrant from Guinea who was murdered by the NYPD in 1999. Mos paraphrases the *Qur'an* and expresses his faith in Allah at a public rally against the acquittal of the officers who fired 41 shots at the brother: "To people who seek justice, to the Amadou Diallo family, and to everyone who speaks against oppression, I say, FEAR NOT, Allah is the best of judges."[32]

Similarly, Public Enemy front man, Chuck D's Islamic consciousness moved him from giving live performances in concert halls to giving talks about nation-building in the streets, prisons, and schools of Black communities. It is what moved him to become perhaps the most well-known advocate for "cutting out the middle man" in the Hip Hop record industry by circumventing major record labels and distributors and building independent labels and engaging in e-commerce. JT the Bigga Figga not only realized that he "had a bigger work to do through this music," but he has also helped to revitalize his local communities of Fillmore and Bay's View/Hunter's Point through speaking engagements and providing business classes to youth. He did not only actively support and attend the Million Man March and Million Family March, and the many NOI-sponsored Hip Hop Summits since 1997, he has also assembled a group of young Blacks, Latinos, and Pacific Islanders into a national cooperative business venture named Black Wall Street (in commemoration of the Tulsa Police Department's bombing of Oklahoma's Black Wall Street in 1921), thereby providing networking opportunities and economic growth to those traditionally excluded from such enterprises. JT's *jihad fi sabil Allah* is a prime example of how artists have become more than verbal *mujahidin* (fighting with their lyrics, speaking engagements, interviews, and other opportunities to dialogue). Although talk is itself a form of social action, Muslim Hip Hop artists are not only "speaking out against evil," but they are actively engaged in "community development" in a direct effort to "stop that evil with their hands."

I am currently conducting research to uncover more of these Islamic nation-building activities within the HHN. More attention needs to be directed at uncovering the role of Muslim female artists who are covering in the name of Allah. What do we know about Philadelphia rapper Eve's struggle and search for inner peace in a male-dominated recording industry? As she reminds us, "Heaven Only Knows." But we can start by engaging Eve, and other Muslim female artists, in familial conversation. Eve, who opened up the liner notes on her album *Eve of Destruction* with "All Praise Is Due To Allah," speaks on her relationship with Islam: "'It's not strong like it should be. I'm striving. When I get to the point where I'm stable I definitely want to cover and go to the *masjid*. But now it's hard. It is really hard. But it definitely has a grip on me. I pray to Allah every night, every morning, all during the day, know what I'm saying? If it wasn't for Him I wouldn't be blessed."[33] What do we know about NYC's Egyptian female rapper Mutamassik (meaning "tenacious" in Arabic)? What are her personal struggles, and how has she contributed to nation-building activities through and beyond her music?[34]

The *Jihad* Continues …

This article has shown that Hip Hop artists are creating, as Iron Sheik says, "new poems" for a new day. As verbal *mujahidin* engaged in the "transglobal Hip Hop *umma*," their speech activities function as "weapons of mass culture" that narrate the marginalized experiences of a "nation." Their experiences, when verbalized, represent a discursive struggle against oppression and Hip Hop's engagement in a battle over the manipulation and control of discourse. Throughout the article, I have highlighted the potential of Muslims in the HHCM to create counterhegemonic discourses that threaten to overturn existing power relations. Hip Hop Culture, as textual evidence of Black American youth's agency, provides global youth culture with incredible resistive potential in what has become an uncertain and unsettling geopolitical landscape. At the same time, Hip Hop artists continue to be central figures in the continued reinvention of Islam with unique modern tones.

Study Questions

1. How does Alim describe the hip hop *umma*?
2. What has been the impact of the Islamic faith on hip hop culture? What varieties of Islam have been used and how have these uses assisted in hip hop in crafting messages of social justice?
3. How does Alim blend anthropological and religious studies concerns in this essay to chart the impact of the black American Muslim movement within and influence upon the HHN?

Notes

* Due to copyright permissions, photos have been excluded from this chapter.

1. Full interview appears in James Spady, H. Samy Alim, & Samir Meghelli. *Tha Global Cipha: Hip Hop Culture and Conciousness*. Philadelphia: Black History Museum Press, 2006.
2. H. Samy Alim. Exploring the transglobal Hip Hop Umma. In Miriam Cooke and Bruce Lawrence (eds.), *Muslim Networks: From Hajj to Hip Hop*. (Chapel Hill, NC: UNC Press, 2005).
3. Michael Eric Dyson. Performance, protest and prophesy in the culture of Hip Hop. *Black Sacred Music: A Journal of Theomusicology* 5(1), (Spring, 1991), see p. 22.
4. Jeff Chang. *Can't Stop Won't Stop: A History of the Hip Hop Generation* (New York: St. Martin's Press, 2005).
5. Public Enemy. "Fight the Power." *Fear of a Black Planet* (Def Jam, 1990).
6. Harry Allen. Righteous indignation: Rappers talk about the strength of Hip Hop and Islam. *The Source* 48 (March/April, 1991): pp. 48–53.

7. Akbar S. Ahmed and Donnan Hastings, eds. 1994. *Islam, Globalization and Postmodernity* (London: Routledge, 1994).

8. Anita M. Weiss. Challenges for Muslim women in a postmodern world. In Akbar S. Ahmed and Hastings Donnan, eds., *Islam, Globalization and Postmodernity* (London and New York: Routledge, 1994), pp. 127–140.

9. James G. Spady and Joseph Eure. *Nation Conscious Rap: The Hip Hop Vision.* (New York/Philadelphia: PC International Press/Black History Museum, 1991). This book is the first part in the Umum Hip Hop Trilogy. The other two parts are: James G. Spady, Stefan Dupres, and Charles Lee. *Twisted Tales in the Hip Hop Streets of Philly* (Philadelphia: Black History Museum Press, 1995) and James G. Spady, H. Samy Alim, and Charles Lee (Art Director). 1999. *Street Conscious Rap* (Philadelphia: Black History Museum Press, 1999).

10. Bernard Zekri. Rap et Islam (Documentary film, 1992).

11. James Spady. 1994. Living in America where the brother got to get esoterica: The Philly Hip Hop Language and philosophy of Schooly D. *Fourth Dimension* 4(1): pp. 26–27.

12. J. Spady, H. S. Alim, & S. Meghelli. *Tha Global Cipha: Hip Hop Culture and Conciousness* (Philadelphia: Black History Museum Press, 2006).

13. David Toop. 1991. Prince Akeem: Coming down like Babylon. *The Face* (UK), (October 1991).

14. Charlie Ahearn. The Five Percent Solution. *Spin* 6(11) (February, 1991): pp. 54–57, 76.

15. Tricia Rose. 1994. *Black Noise: Rap Music and Black Culture in Contemporary America* (Middletown, CT: Wesleyan University Press).

16. Andre J. M. Prevos. Postcolonial popular music in France. In Tony Mitchell, ed., *Global Noise: Rap and Hip Hop Outside the USA* (Middletown, CT: Wesleyan University Press, 2001). See also: Samir Meghelli. Returning to The Source, En Diaspora: Historicizing the emergence of the Hip Hop Cultural Movement in France. *Proud Flesh* (3) (2004).

17. David Toop. *Rap Attack: From African Jive to New York Hip Hop* (London: Pluto Press, 1984,1994, 1999).

18. James G Spady. 2004. The Hip Hop Nation as a site of African-American cultural and historical memory. *Dumvoices Revue*, pp. 154–166.

19. Havelock Nelson and Michael Gonzales. *Bring the Noise: A Guide to Rap Music and Hip Hop Culture* (New York: Harmony Books, 1991). See also: William Eric Perkins. Nation of Islam ideology in the Rap of Public Enemy. *Black Sacred Music: A Journal of Theomusiology* 5(1): pp. 41–50 and Ronald Jamal Stephens. 1991. The three waves of contemporary rap music. The emergency of black and emergence of rap. *Black Sacred Music: A Journal of Theomusiology* 5(1) (1991): pp. 25–40.

20. Felicia M. Miyakawa. 2005. *Five Percent Rap: God Hop's Music, Message, and Black Muslim Mission* (Bloomington, IN: Indiana University Press, 2005). See also: Kathleen O'Connor. Alternative to "Religion" in an African American Islamic Community: The Five Percent Nation of Gods and Earths. In Eugene V. Gallagher and William M. Ashcraft (eds.), *Introduction to New and Alternative Religions in America: Volume 5, African Diaspora Traditions and Other American Innovations.* (Greenwood, 2006).

21. Anthony B. Pinn, ed. 2003. *The Religious and Spiritual Sensibilities of Rap Music* (New York: New York University Press, 2003). See especially Juan Floyd-Thomas' chapter, A jihad of words: The evolution of African American Islam and contemporary Hip Hop, pp. 49–72.

22. In Spady, and Eure, p. 74.

23. Personal interview with author, October 2000.

24. H. Samy Alim. Hip Hop Nation Language. In Edward Finegan and John Rickford, (eds.), *Language in the USA: Perspectives for the 21st Century* (Cambridge: Cambridge University Press, 2004). See also: H. Samy Alim. 2004b. *You Know My Steez: An Ethnographic and Sociolinguistic Study of a Black American Speech Community* (Durham, NC: Duke University Press, 2004) and H. Samy Alim; *Roc the Mic Right: The Language of Hip Hop Culture* (New York & London: Routledge, 2006).

25. Personal interview with author, November 2000.

26. Ted Swedenburg. 2002. Hip Hop music in the transglobal Islamic underground. In H. Samy Alim, ed., *Black Culture's Global Impact. Special issue of The Black Arts Quarterly* 6(3) (Stanford, CA: Stanford University, Committee on Black Performing Arts, 2002), see p. 16.

27. Personal interview with author, December 2001.

28. Personal interview with author, November 2001.
29. Personal interview with author, March 2002.
30. Personal interview with author, July 2002.
31. In Spady and Eure, p. 91.
32. In the archives of www.daveyd.com
33. Full interview to appear in Spady. Alim, & Meghelli.
34. Ted Swedenburg. 2001. Islamic Hip Hop versus Islamophobia. In Tony Mitchell, ed., *Global Noise: Rap and Hip Hop Outside the USA* (Middletown, CT: Wesleyan University Press, 2001).

The Five Percenter "Way of Life"

Miyakawa dissects the varied dimensions of the eclectic and esoteric Five Percent theology, taking into account original sources such as Clarence 13X's lessons. Using the life experiences of Five Percenters as primary data, Miyakawa holds tightly to the Five Percent doctrine of "way of life" rather than "religion" as a primary trope for her study. By extensively analyzing the Five Percent lessons, which include the supreme mathematics and alphabet among other areas, to carefully analyzing the differentiations between Five Percent as a scientific "way of life" versus a "religion," Miyakawa highlights the core building blocks that sustain the ideological positions within the group. Yet, Miyakawa holds in creative tension the group dynamics and individuality promoted by this approach. She concludes that despite the declining significance of a "conscious" bent, hip hop has and continues to play a major role in communicating and persuading younger generations of the Five Percent "way."

The Five Percenter "Way of Life"*

Felicia Miyakawa

The Five Percent Nation may be unknown to most Americans, yet within hip-hop culture, Five Percenters have long been an active presence. Any "old-school hip-hop head" (long-time fan of hip-hop music and culture) will speak knowingly of the "Gods" and may even have passing familiarity with basic Five Percenter doctrines, yet the details of Five Percenter theology—an idiosyncratic mix of black nationalist rhetoric, Kemetic (ancient Egyptian) symbolism, Gnosticism, Masonic mysticism, and esoteric numerology—are not widely understood. In this chapter I examine Five Percenter theology in depth, taking into account the lessons Clarence 13X inherited from his forerunners and brought with him from the Nation of Islam, as well as the new lessons Father Allah devised for his new Nation. Because Five Percenters believe that what they practice is not a religion but a "way of life," the second half of this chapter considers the impact of Five Percenter theology on daily life. The chapter concludes with a consideration of the Nation's most effective methods for bringing their message to the masses, including hip-hop music and culture.

Readers should be aware that as an outsider, an "etic" observer, my perspective is limited, subject to the availability of sources, and influenced no doubt by my own theological upbringing and the specific consultants whose views inform this book. I quote liberally from consultants, Five Percenters who generously shared their experiences and opinions with me. I am deeply grateful to these consultants for enriching my understanding of their way of life. Quotations from my consultants should be read as authoritative personal opinions and not as representative of an entire body of thought; as I will explain in the following pages, Five Percenter theology is a highly individualized matter.

I also draw extensively from Five Percenter lessons, which I have gathered from a number of printed and on-line sources. As far as I know, the lessons have not been compiled in a single place and published for study.[1] In the early stages of this project, I envisioned including the complete lessons as an appendix. One of my consultants strongly suggested, however, that doing so would be a disservice both to the Five Percent Nation and to my readers. In the Five Percent Nation the lessons are not considered secret rites; they are tools. In their proper cultural context the tools are handed down as part of an enculturation process that includes mentoring by older Gods and Earths. If not accompanied by the cultural knowledge of how to interpret them, the lessons are simply words ripe for misunderstanding. In my consultant's opinion, printing the lessons in full would rob readers of the opportunity to encounter them within their cultural context and could also open the Nation to an even greater number of harmful attacks. To honor my consultant's advice, in the following discussion, I quote complete lessons only when necessary to clarify specific theological points.

Lessons

Clarence 13X and his followers may have split from the Nation of Islam for theological reasons, yet doctrinal differences between the two groups are few. Initiates in the Nation of Islam—known as "Lost-Founds"—learn doctrine through a series of lessons that use a question-and-answer format, like a catechism. Initiates must know both questions and answers by rote and be able to explain each lesson in order to complete a stage.[2] The series begins with the "Student Enrollment Lesson," ten questions and answers concerning the population of various ethnic groups, the measurements of the earth, and the origins of mankind; completion of this stage earns the student his X. (The letter X replaces the initiate's last name, considered to be his slave name. X is used because it mathematically represents the unknown: in this case, the unknown original family name of the initiate. In the Nation of Islam's early days, an initiate could choose to retain his or her X through future stages, or petition Elijah Muhammad for a new, "original" name.) Initiates then move on to "Actual Facts," eighteen questions and answers concerning the features and measurements of the earth. "Actual Facts" are followed by "English Lesson no. C1," a series of thirty-six questions detailing Master Fard Muhammad's mission. Finally, initiates move to the two-part "Lost-Found Moslem Lessons." Part one consists of fourteen questions, and part two of forty questions; together they concentrate on geography, the history of the races, and the coming Armageddon.[3]

Five Percenters use many of the same lessons in a different order, with additional lessons of their own devising (see figure 15.1 for a comparison). They begin with two lessons not included in the Nation of Islam's instruction: the "Science of Supreme Mathematics," and the "Supreme Alphabet."[4] Initiates then move on to the same "Student Enrollment Lesson" used in the Nation of Islam, followed by "English Lesson no. C1" and the "Lost-Found Lessons." The "Lost-Found Lessons" are followed by two final lessons: "Actual Facts" (also borrowed from the Nation of Islam) and "Solar Facts" (original with the Five Percent Nation). Five Percenters thus learn the same history, geography, origin theories, and eschatology as the Nation of Islam, but the re-ordering of lessons and the addition of new lessons suggest different spiritual priorities in the Five Percent Nation. Specifically, by beginning their training with the "Science of Supreme Mathematics" and the "Supreme Alphabet" and ending with "Solar Facts," Five Percenters underscore the significance of science and numbers in their theology.

Clarence 13X and his right-hand man, Justice, began the Five Percent Nation's emphasis on numbers with their invention of the Science of Supreme Mathematics and of its counterpart,

Nation of Islam Lessons	Five Percent Nation Lessons
Student Enrollment Lesson	Supreme Mathematics
Actual Facts	Supreme Alphabet
English Lesson No. C1	Student Enrollment Lesson
Lost-Found Lessons (parts 1 and 2)	English Lesson No. C1
	Lost-Found Lessons (parts 1 and 2)
	Actual Facts
	Solar Facts

Figure 15.1 Nation of Islam and Five Percent Nation Lessons

the Supreme Alphabet. At some point in the history of the Nation of Gods and Earths, symbolic significance was attached to specific numbers (see figure 15.2).[5] According to Beloved Allah, Father Allah and Justice devised the Supreme Mathematics and Supreme Alphabet in order to teach the youth "how to break down and form profound relationships between significant experiences within life," including "the meaning of their names, age (degree), why life was so hard and cold for the blackman and other significant facts of life."[6] As a result, Five Percenters believe that the Science of Supreme Mathematics is the key to understanding man's relationship to the universe. Indeed, the ultimate way to prove that something does not make sense in Five Percenter logic is to proclaim—as does Lord Jamar in Brand Nubian's song "Ain't No Mystery"—"Mathematically that just don't go."

Once Gods and Earths (Five Percenter men and women) have committed the numbers and their meanings to memory, they use the numbers to creatively "show and prove" facts and ideas. For example, in an interview with social scientist Yusef Nuruddin, Five Percenter Sincere Allah gives the following explanation of Degree Five of the Student Enrollment Lesson:

1 = Knowledge
2 = Wisdom
3 = Understanding
4 = Culture of Freedom
5 = Power of Refinement
6 = Equality
7 = God
8 = Build-Destroy
9 = Born
0 = Cipher

Then the fifth degree says, "What is the area in square miles of the planet earth?" The area in square miles of the planet earth is 196,940,000 square miles. Now, the way I see that right, only showing and proving right, like, you give me a piece of paper I could show you, like, years in it. In the 196,940,000 square miles, you've got the year 1960 in there; you've got the year 1964 and 1969. Now, the way I see it is when Allah—knowledge was born by equality, born back to the culture, to the cipher [this is the numerological analysis according to the Supreme Mathematics; knowledge = 1, equality = 6, born = 9, culture = 4, cipher = 0, i.e., 1960 = knowledge–born–equality–cipher] only showing and proving that year 1964 when Almighty God Allah (Clarence 13X) when he left the temple, you know, in 1964 he showed and proved that the black man was God'.[7]

Figure 15.2 Science of Supreme Mathematics

What Sincere Allah does here in casual conversation with his interviewer is standard practice in Five Percenter circles (or "ciphers"). He methodically applies the meanings he has learned from the Science of Supreme Mathematics to the fifth Student Enrollment lesson. For outsiders, the lesson has no obvious bearing on Clarence 13X's life, but for Five Percenters, numbers reveal hidden relationships between all levels of existence.

Every stage of Five Percenter training emphasizes the relationship between numbers and cosmology. Initiates learn by rote the distance between the earth and the sun, the circumference of the earth, and the amount of water and land on the earth (among many other measurements). Each initiate should be able to "show and prove" these scientific facts through the manipulation of numbers. The lessons known as "Solar Facts," which simply state the distances of the planets from the sun (see figure 15.3), are particularly ripe for manipulation.

Mercury is 36,000,000 miles from the Sun.

Venus is 67,000,000 miles from the Sun.

Earth is 93,000,000 miles from the Sun.

Mars is 142,000,000 miles from the Sun.

Jupiter is 483,000,000 miles from the Sun.

Saturn is 886,000,000 miles from the Sun.

Uranus is 1,783,000,000 miles from the Sun.

Neptune is 2,793,000,000 miles from the Sun.

Pluto (platoon) is 3,680,000,000 miles from the Sun.

Figure 15.3 Solar Facts

Like all lessons, "Solar Facts" are merely a starting point for the revelation of higher truths, as a Five Percenter scholar named Divine Ruler Equality Allah illustrates on the Five Percent Nation's Website.[8] He begins by finding the internal sums of each planet's distance from the sun: for instance, Mercury's distance from the sun is 36,000,000 miles, and when the digits are added they produce 9 (born). Similarly, Venus's distance from the sun produces 4 (culture or freedom); Earth's distance from the sun produces 3 (understanding); Mars's distance from the sun produces 7 (God); Jupiter's distance from the sun produces 6 (equality); Saturn's distance from the sun produces 4 (culture or freedom); Uranus's distance from the sun produces 1 (knowledge); Neptune's distance from the sun produces 3 (understanding); and Pluto's distance from the sun produces 8 (build-destroy). He then adds these internal sums again ($9 + 4 + 3 + 7 + 6 + 4 + 1 + 3 + 8 = 45$; $4 + 5 = 9$) and produces 9 (born). This final internal sum of 9 holds symbolic significance for Divine Ruler Equality Allah because, as he points out, "this is also equivalent to the Sum of the Mathematics" ($1 + 2 + 3 + 4 + 5 + 6 + 7 + 8 + 9 = 45$; $4 + 5 = 9$). Divine Ruler Equality Allah's point here is that the Science of Supreme Mathematics must be a valid system because it is perfectly aligned with the workings of the universe. He goes on to justify why there is life only on Earth by explaining that the Earth is the only planet to have a distance from the sun that "borns" (produces) the same number as its relative position from the sun. That is, Earth is the third planet from the sun, and its distance from the sun reveals understanding, or three, through internal sums.

Icons of the Nation of Gods and Earths capitalize on the relationship between numerology and cosmology. The Universal Flag of the Nation of Gods and Earths, for example, features a number 7, as well as the sun, the moon, and a star: here, the number 7 indicates both God and man, while the combination of the sun, moon, and star represents the basic building block of the nation, the family unit of man, woman, and child (see figure 15.4).[9] Thus the harmony of celestial bodies is mirrored in the harmony of the family.

The flag and its meaning are ready symbols for use in lyrics. Poor Righteous Teachers make use of this symbol in "Strictly Ghetto": "The sun, the seven, the moon, and the star/Supremely shows and *proves* who we are." A more complete treatment is found in King Sun's song "Universal Flag," which "breaks down" the flag's symbolic significance, devoting a verse each to the sun (man), moon (woman), and star (child). "Universal Flag" ends with a rousing didactic challenge: "are you able to show and prove on this flag that you bear?" In keeping with Clarence 13X's emphasis on mathematical truths, the Five Percent Nation draws both its name and its identity from mathematical percentages found in Lost-Found Lesson no. 2, questions 14 through 16:

Figure 15.4 Universal Flag of the Five Percent Nation

14. Who are the 85 percent? The uncivilized people; poison animal eaters; slaves from mental death and power; people who do not know who the Living God is, or their origin in this world and who worship that direction but are hard to lead in the right direction.

15. Who are the 10 percent? The rich slave-makers of the poor, who teach the poor lies to believe: that the Almighty, True and Living God is a spook and cannot be seen by the physical eye; otherwise known as the bloodsuckers of the poor.

16. Who are the 5 percent? They are the poor righteous teachers who do not believe in the teachings of the 10 percent and are all-wise and know who the Living God is and teach that the Living God is the Son of Man, the Supreme Being, or the Black Man of Asia, and teach Freedom, Justice and Equality to all the human family of the planet Earth; otherwise known as civilized people, also as Muslims and Muslim Sons.[10] Five Percenters are thus those who have knowledge of self and are charged with sharing that knowledge with the 85 percent. In their own words, Five Percenters must "civilize the uncivilized."

For Gods and Earths, numbers not only unlock the mysterious scientific workings of the universe, but also provide a way to understand the "true" meanings of words. The Science of Supreme Mathematics is typically used in conjunction with an alphabetic system known as the Supreme Alphabet, in which every letter of the alphabet is assigned a mystical meaning,

A	Allah	B	Be; Born
C	Cee or understanding	D	Divine
E	Equality	F	Father
G	God	H	He; Her
I	I or Islam	J	Justice
K	King; kingdom	L	Love, Hell, or Right
M	Master	N	Now; Nation; or End
O	Cipher	P	Power
Q	Queen	R	Ruler
S	Self; Savior	T	Truth; Square
U	You or Universe	V	Victory
W	Wise or Wisdom	X	Unknown
Y	Why	Z	Zig-Zag-Zig

Figure 15.5 The Supreme Alphabet

or sometimes several (see figure 15.5). The meaning of individual words can therefore be determined by treating words as acronyms and "adding" together the meaning of each letter to find the "true" meaning of the word. As Nuruddin demonstrates, "Five Percenters illustrate that the black man is divine by unfolding the secret meaning of the word 'man': My Almighty Name. This human/divine relationship is further corroborated by unveiling the name of Allah which means *Arm Leg Leg Arm* Head."[11] In other words, in "breaking down" the word "Allah" to mean "Arm Leg Leg Arm Head," Allah is given human form, described by making a transit of the body. Describing Allah in human form is consistent with the Five Percenter belief that each black man is divine. Five Percenters do not limit themselves only to the original meanings ascribed to each letter but instead creatively apply the spirit of the system to find meaning.

Although the Science of Supreme Mathematics and the Supreme Alphabet are new systems, Clarence 13X's interest in numerology finds a precedent in an ancient Muslim interest in cosmology and numerology.[12] The Supreme Alphabet takes as its model the spiritual science *Hurufa-i-jay-Hurufa-Ab-jay*, an Arabic science of interpreting mystical meanings from each letter of the Arabic alphabet; the Five Percent Nation's version simply uses the Roman alphabet.[13] Since the late 1970s, the Nation of Islam has also shown interest in numerology, although it does not seem to have been influenced by the Five Percent Nation's brand of numerology. In 1975, Rashad Khalifa, an American Sufi mystic, used his computer to uncover a mathematical code in the Qur'an and claimed that it contains hidden messages based on the number 19. His findings encouraged leading Nation of Islam theologians to uncover hidden Qur'anic meanings for themselves. Mother Tynetta Muhammad, one of the Nation of Islam's leading theologians, adopted Khalifa's revelation that the number 19 is the key to the Qur'an. According to Mattias Gardell, the Nation of Islam has also adopted an Arabic practice of assigning numerical values to letters, known as the Abjad scheme.[14] Unlike the system in the Supreme Alphabet, which assigns numbers to letters according to their position in the alphabet, the Abjad scheme assigns numbers to letters according to symbolic values.[15] But whereas the Nation of Islam uses numbers to uncover hidden Qur'anic mysteries, Five Percenters call on the power of numbers in their everyday lives. For the Five Percent Nation numbers are a flexible way to find and create meaning; numerology is used creatively to "show and prove" ideas that otherwise would be matters of faith.

The Five Percenter "Way of Life"

Five Percenters take care to distinguish between Islam as a science or "way of life" and Islam as a religion, and maintain that they are, above all, scientists, investigating Islam in a mathematical manner. Indeed, the Nation of Islam refers to Five Percenters as "philosophers" or "scientists," evidence of the Five Percenter emphasis on metaphysics and esoterica.[16] Using the spirit of the Supreme Alphabet, Five Percenters "break down" the word "Islam" to mean *I Self Lord Am Master*," emphasizing the divine essence of each black man. In an article entitled "Why We Are Not Muslims," Sincere Allah Merciful God explains that Islam as a religion is based on the idea of submission to Allah—the word "Islam" itself means "submission"—but for Five Percenters submission to Allah has no meaning since each (black) man is Allah incarnate. As Sincere Allah Merciful God puts it, "God is not a Muslim. God does not submit."[17] In other words, instead of seeing Islam as a set of practices intended to give reverence to a Supreme Being, Five Percenters see Islam as a flexible way of life, a mode of encountering the world in their own self-deified orbit.

Furthermore, Five Percenters argue that whereas religions have clear moments of beginning, the Islamic "way of life" does not. As taught by Elijah Muhammad, the original state of the universe was a triple blackness of space, water, and divinity.[18] If blackness is original, blackness has no birth record. Rap MC Wise Intelligent explains,

> People consider us a religion. This does not have anything to do with religion. This has nothing to do with something which was started up in the past. This has no said birth record. That blackness that was there at the beginning that created all things in the universe was that of Islam. That's what we're dealing with. When you're saying Islam you're saying I-Self-Lord-Am-Master, or an Independent Source of Life and Matter. For that's showing and proving the ability to create.[19]

Wise Intelligent's statement attests to a foundational belief shared by both the Nation of Islam and the Five Percent Nation: that Islam—equated with blackness—is the natural state of the Original Man, that is, the black man. "Lost-Founds" have found the "natural" way of life—Islam—lost to them through the centuries. Adherence to Islam is thus not a conversion for the black man, but a return to his original self.

Five Percenters take pride in their ability to "show and prove" the naturalness of their way of life, instead of allowing useless rules to determine their daily practices. As Islamic scholar Yusef Nuruddin points out, "because Five Percenters view Islam as just a natural 'way of life' rather than a religion, they 'break down' the term *Sunni Muslim* to mean 'Soon to be Muslim,' (i.e., not yet Muslim and still hung up in the useless performance of a lot of rituals)."[20] One of my consultants explained this in a similar way: "what makes the Nation of Gods and Earths so great is its absence of structure. There have been people who try to add more structure, but it never works, it's not supposed to, and it couldn't."[21] Unlike members of the Nation of Islam, Five Percenters tend to ignore the five pillars of mainstream (Sunni) Islamic faith: declaring there is no God but Allah, daily prayer, fasting, giving alms to the poor, and making the *hajj* to Mecca.[22] Five Percenters value their freedom from strict rules, and their belief that each black man is a God allows for a looser moral code than is allowed in other Black Muslim sects. In the words of Lord Jamar of the rap group Brand Nubian, "See, in the Five Percent Nation, each man is the sole controller of his own universe. If you're the god of your universe, you set up your own laws."[23] As members of the 5 percent who know and understand the identity of the true God, they believe they have self-knowledge hidden from the rest of the 95 percent, rendering their individual decisions beyond reproach.[24]

Much of Five Percent doctrine hinges on the identity of God, or Allah. Five Percenters believe that each black man is divine and is in fact a god. They stress, however, the connections between divinity and humanity. As mentioned above, Gods "break down" the meaning of the word "Allah" to indicate that the black man is indeed divine: "*Arm Leg Leg Arm Head.*" Throughout history Allah has taken a variety of incarnations. According to the Nation of Islam, W. D. Fard was the latest incarnation, but the Five Percent Nation counters that Clarence 13X was also Allah in the flesh. The essential idea of Allah incarnate begins, then, not with the Five Percent Nation, but with the Nation of Islam. In a 1959 interview with African American journalist Louis Lomax, Elijah Muhammad was asked about this idea:

Mr. Lomax:	Now if I have understood your teachings correctly, you teach that all of the members of Islam are God, and that one among you is supreme, and that one is Allah. Now have I understood you correctly?
Mr. Elijah Muhammed:	That's right.[25]

Five Percenters stress two fundamentals when "showing and proving" that the black man is God. First, in both the Nation of Islam and the Five Percent Nation it is believed that all humanity is descended from the black race. According to their theology it is genetically impossible for a race of beings to progressively add color to their skin, but it is possible, through inbreeding with inferior races, to lighten skin color. The Nation of Islam holds that black skin is the progenitor of all other skin colors, and is therefore the purest; all other variations are corrupted and thus cannot realize divinity. According to one of my consultants, however, the Nation of Gods and Earths approaches this doctrine with more flexibility:

lighter skin is not a hindrance, or weaker according to NGE theology ... the eight rays of the Sun each contain two elements, one yellow and one black, signifying the "16 shades" of the original man, from black, "dark skinned," to "[yellow]." ... So the darkest pur[e]st "African" Blackman is not necessarily closer to being God, just like the lightest "mixed" Blackman is not necessarily further from being God. But as far as a whiteman being God, that's starting from a complete contradiction in terms.[26]

Second, both the Nation of Islam and the Five Percent Nation believe that God is not a spirit (a "spook"), but is a man. Elijah Muhammad spends the first chapter of his *Message to the Blackman in America* discussing the identity of God and uses both the Bible and the Qur'an to prove that God is not a spirit. Five Percenters further categorize anyone who teaches the masses that the Living God is a "spook" as part of the 10 percent, the "bloodsuckers" of the poor.

Because each black man is a God in his own right, each man has the ability to make his own decisions about clothing, use of drugs and alcohol consumption of particular foods, and roles in relationships. Nevertheless, many Five Percenters do advocate healthy living: most eschew pork and some are strict vegetarians. Clarence 13X continued the Islamic ban on eating pork on the grounds that the pig is "one-third dog, one-third rat, and one-third cat," and no one in his right mind would eat any one of these animals.[27] Five Percenters recognize that heart disease, diabetes, high blood pressure, and other ailments rampant in the black community are greatly affected by food choice.[28] Wise Intelligent articulates this idea:

You have to understand, you being what you eat, when you eat the food becomes a part of your way of thinking. Eating foods that are not fit for a living man, that will cause the brain to gain fat, and when you get fat on the brain, you get lies on the mind, and when you get lies on the mind you get poison in the body, and when you get poison in the body you are dead.[29]

Earths (women) are therefore encouraged to select and prepare wholesome, nutritious foods for their Gods (men) and seeds (children).

Furthermore, unlike the Nation of Islam and other Black Muslim groups such as the Ansaaru Allah Community—another black Islamic sect active primarily in the United States, especially in New York City—the Five Percent Nation follows no strict dress code.[30] Indeed, as rap MC Lakim Shabazz suggests, the lack of a dress code indicates a major difference between the Five Percent Nation and the Nation of Islam: "The only difference between the Five Percent Nation and the brothers who follow Farrakhan is that they have a dress code. They are always dressed nicely with a suit and tie, where the Five Percent Nation, we figure you can wear any garment you want as long as you're dressed."[31]

Such free individualism inevitably leads to charges of hypocrisy and inconsistency. Wise Intelligent himself points out that not all self-proclaimed Five Percenters are true believers: "In the 5% you have your hypocrites. You have your brothers who are not 5%ers, but jive pretenders. They are fronting [pretending] like they are Gods, but they are not Gods they are god damn fools."[32] Wise Intelligent is not the only Five Percenter MC to charge his brethren with hypocrisy. In an interview with journalist Charlie Ahearn, rapper King Sun accused all Five Percenter MCs (excepting himself) of being "phony," but singled out Big Daddy Kane for a specific allegation: "like Big Daddy Kane is supposed to be Five Percent—his name is King Asiatic Allah. But he made a record, *Pimping Ain't Easy*. Doesn't sound very righteous, does it?"[33]

Five Percenters value the foundational role of the family, and maintain the patriarchal family model set forth by Elijah Muhammad for the Nation of Islam. Gods (men) should provide for their families financially and emotionally and are responsible for teaching their mates, called Earths, the "knowledge of self." The family unit of man, woman, and children is often spoken of in a celestial metaphor of sun, moon, and stars; just as the moon receives its light from the sun, so, too, the Earth receives the light of knowledge from her God. According to one Earth, the relationship between a man and a woman "is that of equality," illustrated metaphorically in the solar system:

> There exists a homeostasis between the Sun and the Earth, a natural systematic relationship governed by the laws of mathematics. The Sun can exist without relationship governed by the laws of mathematics. The Sun can exist without the Earth, however she complements his greatness and radiance by taking that light and turning it into life. … He provides her with that environment that is conducive to the growth and development of life on her [planet] as she submits herself to him and endlessly revolves around him, bearing witness that he is the foundation for her existence.[34]

While Gods are free to choose their own paths in life, the role of Earths is somewhat more restricted. A woman's body should be at least three-fourths covered with clothing, just as the earth is three-fourths covered by water. Like orthodox Muslim women, Earths often wear head coverings.[35] The main goal for an Earth is reproduction, because through reproduction a woman symbolizes the life-giving forces of the earth.[36]

A family unit of "sun, moon, and stars" is theoretically the goal, yet Earths in the inner city often find themselves with multiple stars fathered by multiple suns. In her study of the role of females in gangs, Anne Campbell traced one young girl, Sun Africa, from her involvement with a minor gang called the Puma Crew through her subsequent initiation into the Five Percent Nation. Sun Africa rejoices in her role as an Earth and submits willingly to her God. By age seventeen she has dropped out of high school, is seven months pregnant, and is living with a new God, his first Earth, and his Earth's children.[37] Gottehrer, too, was struck by the high rate of teenage pregnancy in the early days of the Nation: "I couldn't get used to the young Five Percenters, the girls who had children while they themselves were still children of thirteen or fourteen."[38] By mainstream American standards, Sun Africa's situation (and that of other Five Percenter girls) would be seen as another sad tale of an unwed teenage mother. Yet from a Five Percenter worldview, Sun Africa is fulfilling her intended role in the universe, which is a cause for rejoicing. Furthermore, Five Percenters are at best ambivalent about "marriage under the government." Sources close to Father Allah in the early days of the Nation maintain that he did not recognize state-sanctioned marriages, and the relevancy of marriage under the government continues to be debated.[39]

For many Gods and Earths, the Five Percenter "way of life" is severely tested on a daily basis by the high incarceration rates among Five Percenters. Like the Nation of Islam, the Five Percent Nation recruits heavily among prison populations. The Five Percent Nation's homepage includes links to letters and essays written by Five Percenter inmates, contacts for prisoner outreach, and reproductions of penal codes concerning prisoner civil rights. Because most law enforcement agencies still consider the Five Percent Nation to be a gang, state corrections systems routinely deny Five Percenter prisoners access to Five Percenter literature and materials. One God in the "injustice," Lord Natural Self Allah, included the following testimonial in an essay titled "The Five Percent Dilemma" now posted to the Nation's Website:

> In 1996, the New York State Department of Correctional Services began confiscating 5%'er literature and emblems under the guise that the 5% were an unauthorized organization i.e., gang. This stigma began in the southeastern states of the country, more specifically North and South Carolina, and has now spread to Ohio, New Jersey, Massachusetts, and Georgia. South Carolina and New Jersey have gone so far as to create "indoctrination programs" where known 5%'ers and other "gang members" are placed in a special unit where they remain locked in cells for 23 hours per day with one hour of recreation (most often chained and shackled), no contact visits, and limited telephone [calls] and showers until they renounce their affiliation as being 5%'ers.[40]

Five Percenter inmates in New York State have only recently been granted the right to worship as they please.[41]

"Each One, Teach One"

To instruct new believers, Five Percenters rely primarily on the pedagogical technique of "each one, teach one," passing each lesson down to younger members through oral teaching, and more recently through photocopies.[42] The Nation has also taken advantage of various printed media to spread its ideology. In 1987, *The WORD*, a short-lived, bimonthly newspaper limited primarily to the boroughs of New York City, made its debut. On the last page of every issue, the following list, entitled "What We Teach," appeared:

1. We teach that Black People are the Original People of the Planet Earth.
2. We teach that Black People are the Mothers and Fathers of Civilization.
3. We teach that the Science of Supreme Mathematics is the key to understanding man's relationship to the universe.
4. We teach Islam as a natural way of life: not a religion.
5. We teach that education should be fashioned to enable us to be self-sufficient as a people.

6. We teach that each one should teach one according to their knowledge.
7. We teach that the Blackman is God and his proper name is Allah.
8. We teach that our children are our link to the future and they must be nurtured: respected, loved, protected, and educated.
9. We teach that the unified Black Family is the vital building block of the Nation.[43]

In recent years, the Nation has found new, effective ways to spread doctrine widely. "What We Teach" is now available on the World Wide Web, another media source appropriated by the Five Percent Nation for proselytizing. The Five Percent Nation's homepage includes links to "What We Teach," as well as to the following list of goals entitled "What We Will Achieve":[44]

1. National Consciousness: National Consciousness is the consciousness of our origin in this world, which is divine. As a nation of people we are the first in existence and all other peoples derived from us. National Consciousness is the awareness of the unique history and culture of Black people and the unequaled contributions we have made to world civilization, by being the fathers and mothers of civilization. National Consciousness is the awareness that we are all one people regardless to our geographical origins and that we must work and struggle as one if we are to liberate ourselves from the domination of outside forces and bring into existence a Universal Government of Love, Peace, and Happiness for all the people of the planet.
2. Community Control: Community Control of the educational, economic, political, media, and health institutions on our community. Our demand for Community Control flows naturally out of our science of life, which teaches that we are the Supreme Being in person and the sole controllers of our own destiny; thus we must have same control on the collective level that we strive to attain on the individual level. It is prerequisite to our survival that we take control of the life sustaining goods and services that every community needs in order to maintain and advance itself and advance civilization. Only when we have achieved complete Community Control will we be able to prove to the world the greatness and majesty of our Divine Culture, which is Freedom.
3. Peace. Peace is the absence of confusion (chaos) and the absence of confusion is Order. Law and Order is the very foundation upon which our Science of Life rests. Supreme Mathematics is the Law and Order of the Universe, this is the Science of Islam, which is Peace. Peace is Supreme Understanding between people for the benefit of the whole. We will achieve Peace, in ourselves, in our communities, in our nation and in the world. This is our ultimate goal.[45]

In addition to "What We Teach" and "What We Will Achieve," twelve key concepts known as "The Twelve Jewels" appear frequently in Five Percenter teachings, including their music.[46] In order, the "Twelve Jewels" are Knowledge, Wisdom, Understanding, Freedom, Justice, Equality, Food, Clothing, Shelter, Love, Peace and Happiness.[47] The Five Percent Nation has produced no document that gathers its doctrine in a single place, but "What We Teach," "What We Will Achieve," "The Twelve Jewels," and the lessons learned during indoctrination together outline the essential teachings and goals of the Five Percent Nation. These lessons all appear regularly in Five Percenter lyrics.

Originally a movement confined to the boroughs of New York City, today the Five Percent Nation is a national and increasingly international phenomenon, thanks to the wide availability of Five Percenter doctrine.[48] Rap music has played an important role in spreading this doctrine. As Gardell rightly suggests, "the hip-hop movement's role in popularizing the message of black militant Islam cannot be overestimated. What reggae was to the expansion of the Rastafarian movement in the 1970s, so hip-hop is to the spread of black Islam in the 1980s and 1990s."[49] The Five Percent Nation's Website gives a good deal of space to "God Hop"— rap produced and performed by Gods and Earths—illustrating the importance rap holds for the Nation.[50] Five Percenter MCs and DJs include such major figures as Rakim Allah, the Wu-Tang Clan, Poor Righteous Teachers, Brand Nubian, Capone and Noreaga, Queen Latifah (a former member), Guru (of Gang Starr), DJ Pete Rock, Mobb Deep, Doodlebug (and perhaps also Ladybug Mecca) of Digable Planets, Leaders of the New School (featuring Busta Rhymes), and Black Thought of The Roots.[51] Many of these artists perform regularly on world tours, thus influencing hip-hop music and culture in other nations. The Five Percent Nation continues to grow, adding members throughout the United States and abroad. And where the Five Percent Nation takes root, God Hop is sure to follow.

Rap is a perfect medium for spreading the Nation's doctrine. Rap not only captures the attention of an international audience, but also capitalizes on the Nation's emphasis on verbal ability. God Hop musicians have many tools at their disposal. They quote and paraphrase Five Percenter lessons in lyrics; craft infectious grooves in order to capture the attention of their intended audience; make use of particular digital sound samples in order to create multiple levels of meaning; and give careful attention to album organization and packaging. Together these tools help Five Percenter musicians spread their message of redemption, a task eloquently outlined by Wise Intelligent of the rap group Poor Righteous Teachers: "Rap is [a] gardening tool. Get the brains right and exact so we can drop the seed. Drop that seed, fertilize it, and it's bound to grow to infinity."[52]

Study Questions

1. How does Miyakawa distinguish between Five Percent theology, way of life, and religion and what sources does she use to support claims?
2. What comprises the Five Percent Nation lessons and how does she identify these aspects in rap music?
3. How is "nation" and "consciousness" understood among Five Percent group members? Have these themes in rap music changed over time according to Miyakawa's study?

Notes

* Portions of this chapter from the text Five Percenter Rap: God Hop's Music, Message, and Black Muslim Mission (Miyakawa, 2005) have been omitted and/or altered for style, consistency and flow.

1. The full set of lessons is available in Felicia M. Miyakawa, "God Hop: The Music and Message of Five Percenter Rap" (PhD. diss., Indiana University, 2003).
2. The catechism-styled lessons of the Nation of Islam and the Five Percent Nation bear a striking resemblance to lessons fashioned by Noble Drew Ali for his followers. A list of 101 lessons he drew up, entitled "Koran Questions for Moorish Children," includes questions pertaining to Noble Drew Ali's background, the founding of the Moorish Science Temple of America, the paternity of Jesus and his status as a prophet, the nature of the self, and definitions of words such as "Black," "Colored," "Negro," and "Ethiopia." Like the lessons later fashioned by Elijah Muhammad, Noble Drew Ali's lessons include both question and answer (Noble Drew Ali "Koran Questions for Moorish Americans," folder 4 of 7, special collection on the Moorish Science Temple of America, Schomburg Center for Research in Black Culture, New York).

3. Clegg, An Original Man, 27. "Actual Facts," the "Student Enrollment Lessons," the "Lost-Found Lessons," and "English Lesson no. C1" are all available in Master Fard Muhammad, "The Supreme Wisdom Lessons."

4. See "The Eight Planes of Study to Be Born as Revealed to Us by Allah," available at http://www.angel fire.com/ga/9thJeWel/8planesofstudy.html, accessed July 8, 2004.

5. Aklem Allah Ellsra (DJ Kool Akiem) corrected my original placement of 0 (cipher) before 1 (knowledge) with the following explanation: "Cipher comes after Born [9], it represents completeness. The decimal system, base ten, uses the '0' as a place holder, meaning as a Written indicator—there is no value, but the number to the left is multiplied … So in the decimal system It represents the completion of the cycle through all the numbers 1–9" (personal communication, June 24, 2003).

6. Beloved Allah, "The Bomb."

7. Nuruddin, "The Five Percenters," 127; the bracketed explanation is by Nuruddin.

8. Divine Ruler Equality Allah, "Solar Factorization," available at http://www.ibiblio.org/nge/ under the "Plus lnfo" link, accessed July 8, 2004. Divine Ruler Equality Allah holds a master's of science in physics from Purdue University (personal communication, October 14, 2003).

9. The flag was designed by Universal Shaamgaud Ailah, one of Father Allah's "First Born." See "Universal Flag of Islam," available at http://www.ibiblio.org/nge/ under the "Plus Info" link, accessed July 12, 2004.

10. Nuruddin, "The Five Percenters," 11S-16. See also Master Fard Muhammad, "The Supreme Wisdom Lessons."

11. Nuruddin, "The Five Percenters," 117.

12. In the early stages of the development of Islam, Islamic mystics codified a system of cosmology and numerology based on the Writings of Greek philosophers, particularly Ptolemy. See John David North, The Norton History of Astronomy and Cosmology (New York: Norton, 1994), 179.

13. Nuruddin also suggests that the Supreme Alphabet finds a parallel in the Kabbalistic science of the Path of Letters and notes that the Science of Supreme Mathematics shares common concepts with Sufism, Kabbala, and Pythagorean numerology. See Nuruddin, "The Five Percenters," 122–23.

14. Gardell, Countdown to Armageddon, 176–81. Gardell also offers examples of numerology at work in Nation of Islam theology.

15. This is also true of Hurufa-Hay-Hurufa-Abjaia' for example, the third letter of the Arabic alphabet, (transliterated as "ta"), is associated with the number 400. See Gabriel Mandel Khan, Arabic Script: Styles, Variants, and Call/graphic Adaptations, trans. Rosanna IVI. Giammanco Frongia (New York: Abbeville Press Publishers, 2001).

16. See Gardell, Countdown to Armageddon, 225.

17. Sincere Allah Merciful God, "Why We Are Not Muslims," available at http://www.ibiblio.org/nge/ under the "Pius Info" link, accessed July 8, 2004.

18. Gardell, Countdown to Armageddon, 144.

19. Quoted in Eure and Spady, Nation Conscious Rap, 65–66.

20. Nuruddìn, "The Five Percenters," 129.

21. Akiem Allah Elisra (Kool Akiem), personal communication, May 29, 2003.

22. Gardell, Countdown to Armageddon, 225.

23. Quoted in Ahearn, "The Five Percent Solution," 57.

24. Nuruddìn, "The Five Percenters," 117.

25. Lincoln, The Black Muslims in America, 75.

26. Akiem Allah Elisra (Kool Akiem), personal communication, June 24, 2003.

27. Gottehrer, The Mayor's Man, 97.

28. The Nation of Islam is also concerned with proper eating. Elijah Muhammad published two books on healthy eating, and Minister Farrakhan has declared a "war on obesity" and advocates exercise and a vegetarian diet. See Louis Farrakhan, "Declare War on Obesity (Fat)," Final Call, July 22, 1991, and "Exercise to Stay Alive," Final Call, August 19, 1991. See also Abdul Allah Muhammad, "Eat to Live-Or Else!" Final Call, August 13, 2002, http://www.finalcall.com/columns/eleven.html, accessed August 16, 2002 (page no longer available).

29. Quoted in Eure and Spady, Nation Conscious Rap, 72.

30. For the history and theology of the Ansaaru Allah Community, see Gardell, Countdown to Armageddon, 225–31.

31. Quoted in Charlie Ahearn, "Lakim Gets Busy Dropping Science," *New York City Sun* 6, no. 17 (April 26, 1989): 19.

32. Quoted in Eure and Spady, *Nation Conscious Rap*, 65.

33. Quoted in Ahearn, "The Five Percent Solution," 76.

34. Sha-King Ceh' um Allah, "Social Equality?" National Statement, http://www.nationalstatement.com/e/sha-kingAllah_pg1.htm, accessed October 14, 2001 (page no longer available).

35. Nuruddin, "The Five Percenters," 128. See also Beloved Allah, "The Bomb."

36. Gottehrer suggests another reason for the heavy emphasis on reproduction: "Allah [Clarence 13X] believed that one way for Five Percenters to inherit the earth was to produce more children than any other group and out populate the competition" (*The Mayor's Man*, 96).

37. Anne Campbell, *The Girls in the Gang*, 2nd edn. (Cambridge, Mass.: Basil Blackwell, 1991), 191 and passim.

38. Gottehrer, *The Mayor's Man*, 104.

39. Born Allah, "The Undisputable Truth." National Statement, http://www.national statement.com/e/AllahB-tUT_pg1.htm, accessed October 14, 2001 (page no longer available).

40. Lord Natural Self Allah, "The Five Percent Dilemma." available at http://www.ibiblio.org/nge/ under the "Prison Outreach" link; accessed July 8, 2004.

41. See Paul von Zielbauer, "Inmates Are Free to Practice Black Supremacist Religion, Judge Rules," *New York Times*, August 18, 2003, available at http://www.nytimes.com/2003/08/18/nyregion/18PRIS.html, accessed July 8, 2004. I wish to thank Travis Jackson for bringing this article to my attention.

42. Akiem Allah Elisra (Kool Akiem) explained that photocopies play an integral role in passing down lessons: "I was given my Lessons by going to Kinkos and copying them. First I was given the Math and Alphabet orally to Write down and memorize. Later, I was given photocopies of Math and Alphabet that went along with all the rest of the Lessons. Now I have several different photocopied versions, including versions photocopied directly from NOI sources. Photocopying is routine, usually lesson by lesson starting with the Math and ending with Solar Facts" (personal communication, July 30, 2003).

43. "What We Teach," *Word* 1, no 2 (July 1987), 12, quoted in Nuruddin, "The Five Percenters," 113.

44. In the interest of keeping the text uncluttered with editorial brackets, I have silently corrected spelling and punctuation in documents taken from the Internet.

45. "What We Teach" and "What We Will Achieve" are linked off the Five Percent Nation's homepage at http://www.ibiblio.org/nge/, accessed July 8, 2004. (The link for "What We Will Achieve" is labeled "What We Achieve.") "What We Teach" and "What We Will Achieve" (here titled "What We Achieve" and omitting "Peace") are also included in *All Eye Seeing*, a Five Percenter Web journal, volume 4, pp. 11–12 (available at http:// www.ibiblio.org/nge/thealleyeseeing/volume4/page11.html and http://www.ibiblio.org/ nge/thealleyeseeing/volume4/page12.html, accessed July 8, 2004).

46. See for example, the Gravediggaz' song "Twelve Jewelz" from their album *The Pick, the Sickle and the Shovel*.

47. The Five Percenter Web journal *All Eye Seeing* includes narrative explanations of all of the "Twelve Jewels" except Happiness. Knowledge "is to know, look, listen observe and respect. To retrieve information based on fact and record that which is true." Wisdom "is wise words based on facts, to speak what you know. Wisdom is wise ways, actions and thoughts used to educate others on what is true." Understanding "is to comprehend what one hears and sees. Understanding is to have insight as well as eye sight." Freedom is "to release from obligation and control. To have the ability to progress without hindrance." Justice "is to reward the good and correct the Wrong." Equality "is to have equal opportunity to express ones thoughts and or ideas; Whether wrong or right. One must take that which is of quality (good) to aid in the development and growth of ones self (Nation)." Food "is that which nourishes the body, physically as well as mentally." Clothing "is the garments one wears on the outside to show what one sees on the inside. The moral and decent coverings [one] wears to protect them from shame." Shelter "is a place of refuge in the wilderness to protect one from the elements of the jungle." Love "is to desire for your brother or sister what you want for yourself. And Peace "is the absence of confusion. Peace is the goal of the righteous and the Way of life of the civilized man." See

"Twelve Jewels," http://www.ibiblio.org/nge/thealleyeseeing/volume4/page10.html, accessed July 8, 2004.

48. World Wide Web sources suggest that the Nation has also begun to spread internationally. For example, Blackseven.com, an online magazine devoted to Five Percenters and their teachings, was based in the United Kingdom.

49. Gardell, *Countdown to Armageddon*, 295.

50. The Five Percent Website at http://www.ibíblío.org/nge/, under "Other Links," offers information on and links to both commercial and underground acts.

51. The Five Percent Nation is also heavily represented in the "underground" hip-hop scene (that is, hip-hop that is not generally available through mainstream commercial outlets), but since underground rap is very difficult to track, it is beyond the scope of the present study.

52. Quoted in Eure and Spady, *Nation Conscious Rap*, 69.

16

Rap on 'L'avenue
Islam, Aesthetics, Authenticity and Masculinities in the Tunisian Rap Scene

Based on ethnographic fieldwork (2008–2009) in Tunis's small but growing rap scene, Shannahan and Hussain explore the impact of (Sunni) Islam on rap artists lives, lyrics, and identities. Making initial contact through *Myspace*, 'snowballing' methods (where subjects of a study recruit future subjects based on their social networks) were used to contact other Tunisian rappers for this study, which produced intense participant observation in a wide variety of places in Tunisia. Although religion plays a contested role in Tunisia, they suggest attention to Islam in rap music provides insight into the changing articulations of Islam informing the global aspects and connections among a transglobal hip hop *umma* (which they note as articulated by H. Samy Alim). Too close a focus on The Nation of Islam or The Nation of Gods and Earths, according to Shannahan and Hussain, offers little understanding of Muslim hip hop around the globe. Opening the discussion to issues such as gender and social conditions, they argue distinctions in terms of meaning are important because they are felt among Islamic group members. Thus, parsing out the connections and dissonances between Islamic sensibilities is vital for understanding Islam's wide impact on the global hip hop *umma*. They conclude that rap music remains a powerful mode of self-expression both locally and globally.

Rap on 'L'avenue': Islam, Aesthetics, Authenticity and Masculinities in the Tunisian Rap Scene

Dervla Sara Shannahan and Qurra Hussain

I see my life like a desert in bad weather,
son of the Saharah, Arab, Muslim, head to toe.
I take my pen,
raise it up like a katana [sword].
I speak Tunisian, going to Tunisians, just let me speak Tunisian.[1]

('Just a question of time,' T Men)

Introduction

Rap emerged as a child of hip-hop culture in New York's African-American and Afro-Caribbean communities in the mid-1970s. It has been described as a form of 'black cultural expression that prioritizes black voices from the margins of urban America … [through] a form of rhymed storytelling' (Rose 1994: 2). These stories initially told of the environments in which the hip-hop movement began, and served to articulate protest against conditions on the 'street' where the artists lived. In the last 40 years US rap artists have reached dizzy commercial heights (Rose 1994: 58) which have spread across the globe, 'prompting some artists and fans to proclaim the emergence of a "global hip-hop nation"' (Condry 2007: 638). Now its beats vibrate through urban streets as far apart as Sydney, Palestine, Cuba City, Tokyo and Rome, and its expression in diverse contexts takes on both global and local elements, a fusion that has been termed 'glocal' (Mitchell 2001: 11). As a transnational subculture, rap has proven to be a powerful vehicle for young people as 'the entire expressive culture of hip-hop … resonate[s] not only with the anxiety of youthful social rebellion, but extant global socio-political inequalities as well' (Osumare 2005: 268). Further, studies of rap and hip-hop culture have definitely made it into the academy.[2] The focus is usually upon the US context; that is where the loudest, biggest and most economically successful rap is taking place. Endeavours to explore rap outside the US (such as Mitchell 2001; Kahf 2007; Condry 2007; Orlando 2003) suggest that it takes both globalised and internationalised forms yet remains 'rooted in the local' (Mitchell 2001: 10).

In this paper we discuss research findings from fieldwork conducted in Tunis in late 2008–early 2009 where the rap scene is small yet rapidly expanding. We seek to explore the ways that (Sunni) Islam influences the lives and lyrics of the rap artists that we met there, and the ways that their particular locations shape their positions within what Alim terms the 'transglobal hip-hop *ummah*' (Alim 2005: 264). Although Allen may be correct in positing Islam as 'hip-hop's official religion' (Allen in Alim 2005: 264), the majority of references to Islam in US hip-hop respond to the legacy of The Five Percenters and The Nation of Islam (Aidi 2004: 111), an inheritance which is not necessarily intentionally reproduced by Muslim rappers in other locations. Orthodox Muslims (taken here as Sunni and Shia) and the Five Percenters may produce lyrics which share identical terminology and symbols, yet they are imbued with starkly differing meanings, a nuance which is not always perceptible when listening to the raps of 'Muslim artists.' In other words, the Islam that is spoken of by artists who are influenced by, or are members of, more heterodox forms of Islam (such as Eric B and Rakim, Brand Nubian, Busta Rhymes, Nas, Daddy Kane and Ice Cube), can easily be understood to be Sunni Islam although the implied frames of reference differ dramatically. This distinction is not automatically understood by listeners, particularly outside of the US. In contrast, US rappers whose lyrics are inspired by, and take their religious landscape from orthodox Islam (such as Native Deen, Mos Def, Q Tip/Fareed Kamel and Ali Shaheed Muhammad, from A Tribe Called Quest), are not so widely known outside the US, or at least that is what we found in Tunisia.

In Tunisia, as in much of the regional area, rap and hip-hop culture more broadly has propagated primarily through channels which downplay these differences—or elide them all together—whilst promoting a very particular form of what rap is (such as MTV/MTV Arabia, and Hollywood films). Thus the differences between rap being produced in a Muslim-majority culture such as Tunisia and the more religiously heterodox counterparts in the US deserve attention, particularly when considering just how Islam (as an umbrella term for multiple traditions) can function to inform the music itself. A question that then arises is which (interpretations of) Islam is articulated within different raps, and how do they intersect with the artists' identities? This difference is significant when considering the interplay of global and local that the 'glocalisation' of hip-hop embodies, and the ways that a particular form of art or cultural practice can intersect with religious identities and take on highly different meanings in diverse contexts.[3] Indeed, during our stay in Tunis it seemed that the majority of the artists find rap as an extension and elaboration on their identities as Muslim men. For them, the two cannot be separated (which takes either positive/transformative forms or negative ones, as shall be discussed below), through the lens of theory, in listening to and analyzing lyrics, or on the streets where they are performed. For this reason it is vital to look at both aspects of the artists' self-definitions; as Muslims, but also as men within particular situated geographies.

A further impetus to exploring Tunisian rap is the aspiration to add to existing research on gender in the Middle East, which as an area of study is currently heavily weighted towards women's studies. As Connell suggests, in 'discussions of politics, 'gender' is often a code-word for women' (Connell 2009: 122); this is particularly true within the context of Islamic studies and Muslim cultures, where 'much of the literature ... has been written and read with Muslim men as an unmarked category' (Ouzgane 2006: 6). The Tunisian rap scene is currently small (especially when compared to neighbouring Algeria, see Bouzine 2000) and the artists discussed in this paper share similarities and differences with their non-rapping counterparts. However, Tunisian rap is created, produced and dispersed through locations which are predominantly male domains, and the processes which it takes encapsulates the intersections of contemporary Islam, modernity, globalisation and constructions of masculinities. To this aim, consideration of the Tunisian scene can add to contemporary studies of masculinity, and also to the place of Tunisian rap in the 'glocalised' hip-hop nation.[4]

The Research

The data for this discussion comes from research conducted in late 2008–early 2009, primarily in the capital of Tunisia, Tunis.[5] Following initial contact through online networking tool *Myspace*, we used snowballing methodology in order to meet other rappers. Overall, we spoke to thirty eight men connected with the rap movement, and twelve self-identified rappers.[6] The remaining twenty six were involved in the scene in various ways, either in production, music engineering, promotion, dj-ing or graf artists. We also met women during our stay, yet their place within the movement seemed less central, a point which will be discussed further later in this discussion. The research consisted of fieldwork, or just 'hanging out' on the scene and getting to know the artists and the men they refer to in American hip-hop slang as 'homies,' and also eleven in-depth interviews. These interviews ranged from 40 min to 3 h each and were semi-structured. Whilst we would begin the interviews with just one or two artists, often other men would appear and contribute to the discussion, frequently interspersed with freestyling or playing particular raps from mobile phones or MP3 players. These took place in a variety of settings, including studios, family houses and cafes along the main street of central Tunis, 'L'Avenue Bourguiba.' Fieldwork was conducted in similar locations, and involved many informal, group discussions, predominantly about rap, religion and global politics. We also had the opportunity to travel to Hammamet to a nightclub where one of the interviewees was performing; a large group of Tunisian artists and supporters also attended en masse.

This paper initially focuses upon Tunisian rappers in relation to their social and geographical locations and explores the various ways that rap can serve as a forum for protest, both locally and internationally. It then looks at issues of authenticity and self-censorship when freedom of expression is delineated by the state, and the significance of staged performances for the artists' self-perceptions. The second section of this paper turns to Islam as a source of inspiration and motivation within the artists' lives and lyrics. It discusses the ways that artists' interpretations of Islam are articulated through rap and also their understandings of the place of music within Islam. It explores how the aesthetics of hip-hop culture are negotiated in the public sphere by Tunisian artists and finally turns to the multiple ways that gender interacts with the Tunisian hip-hop scene and is expressed therein. Throughout this discussion the concept of double consciousness is relevant, as in the multiple ways the artists' have to negotiate between distinct ways of being. Gilroy explains double consciousness as a 'double vision,' one which 'allows people to be in two places at once and maintain a double perspective on reality' (Tate 2001: 211). Gilroy's definition will be used in this paper and thus the terms 'double vision' and 'double consciousness' may be read as interchangeable.

Following Hip-Hop to Tunis

A history of the rap movement in Tunisia is beyond the scope of this paper, but a brief excursion backwards is necessary to set the stage for the following discussion. There is a clear division between what the artists refer to as the 'old school' and the 'younger generation' of rappers on the scene, and relationships of mentoring and mutual support are common. Our initial introduction to the scene was through an 'old school' producer and writer, Kamel, who quickly introduced us to younger artists, commenting on their talent.[7] Almost every old school artist we spoke to claimed to have started the movement—claims which obviously require caution—yet we found wide consensus that the first wave of rap in Tunis began in the early 1990s, when US rappers (Wu Tan Clan emerged as a common influence) first gained popularity amongst young Tunisians. As T Men, (a group of four 30–40 year olds) told us, the group they call their 'clan' formed on the rooftop of a member's family home, and was propelled forward by a shared love of rap. They see their clan as distinctly located in Tunis, as Mac of T Men explained;

> We are old men, from the old medina, you know it? We began this so long ago, right there in the medina. Outside of Tunis it is not the same, cannot be the same. The music comes from the street, the small ones of the medina, from between the houses, on the rooftops, in the small spaces between the walls.

By linking his own lyrical inspiration to the very bricks of the old medina, Mac firmly situates his music within his own autobiography, claims authenticity is geographically located and hints at potential differences of context between what the artists broadly term the 'street.' All the artists we met display a strong sense of connectivity with their national identity (even whilst remaining critical of the actions of the state itself), and local struggles are articulated in their music through distinctly male experiences. The way that clans are named encapsulates this; T Men stands for Tunisian men, and their logo (designed by D'Ali's wife) is of five men. There are four clan members and the fifth, as Jamal explained carefully, symbolizes the Tunisian man, 'all the other men not talking.' Not dissimilarly, the name Gangstas Wanted is understood by clan member Hossam 'in the positive way. A Gangsta means being a man going out for work, for family, for his children, and being wanted by the people.' Many of the raps reiterate the situatedness of the rappers; in 'Arabi,' for example, the central theme is Arab unity, which is presented as entwined with the land and the history of the artists.

> I am Arab proud and simple,
> but proud of my land and the land of my ancestors
> and proud of my Arab brothers.[8]

This shared connectivity is reflected within the wider scope of the music; in response to the question 'what do you write about?' the artists unanimously agreed that the social problems of the Tunisian people provide a main thread to their rap. Issues of poverty, unemployment,[9] job insecurity, state repression (overt and covert), curfews, harsh behaviours of security forces, political hypocrisy (national and international), European imperialism and political strife are recurring themes. In this sense, Tunisian rap can 'be understood not so much as an individualist obsession with the self but rather as a dialogical engagement with community' (Pennycook 2007: 103), an engagement which firmly situates itself within local geographies. It also seems that the authenticity of their raps (as measured by other artists) is directly related to their experiences as located within the nation state and social setting of Tunisia, where Arab, Muslim and male identities intersect and are consolidated collectively through music.

Keeping It Real

A recurring theme in hip-hop culture and its observers is the importance of keeping it real, of authenticity, of artistic integrity (Basu 1998). The intersections between integrity as an artist and authenticity as a lyricist have been cited as key aspects of being successful in hip-hop, and reflecting upon rap beyond the US, Pennycook (2007: 103) asks 'the question, then, is what is real talk on the global stage?' In Tunis, it seems, real talk has to resonate with contemporary social realities. Solo artist Ahmed commented on how the general population of Tunis is slowly changing their attitudes towards the music, as the lyrics increasingly respond to local realities; when non-rappers listen, he explains, 'they hear their problems in this music, you understand? It is their lives in our tongues.' The long-term outcome of such recognition obviously remains to be seen, yet the artists that we met seem confident that rap is a more effective vessel for articulating these realities than other, more traditional forms of music. Similarly, Kahf argues that for Palestinian rappers, the elevation of the 'uniqueness of hip-hop as a form of expression and resistance' is a crucial part of validating their authenticity as Muslim, Palestinian rappers (2007: 362). Writer/producer Kamel explained how 'popular music here is *taboukah* … and some R'n'B. Traditional music is all tak tak, *habibi, habibi*, but life is not all *habibi habibi* [my love, my love]!' This comment is met with much laughter, nods and agreement.

Approaching rap as resistance begs the question, what is being resisted and how? It seems that the resistive-elements of Tunisian rap take two broad forms, with starkly different political consequences. First, resistance to local and national conditions is a highly controversial trope and, whilst a recurring one, is potentially dangerous for artists. Envisioning rap as a sophisticated form of social critique demands a correspondence between local context and the speakability of it, which finds a particular intersection in Tunisia, where the realities that inspire the lyrics cannot simply be challenged or critiqued. It is necessary to mention at this stage the limits placed upon rap artists in Tunisia by strict regulations on freedom of speech, association and expression.[10] Government enforced restrictions on internet access, state actions against journalists and violent security responses to incidents of social unrest and protest are common, adding to an environment of insecurity and social frustration. A recent Amnesty International report stated that:

> authorities continue to use their 'security and counter-terrorism' concerns to justify arrests and other repression of Islamists, and political dissent in general—including the rights to freedom of expression, association and assembly—and arrests and harassment of alleged Islamist youth are common.
>
> (2009: 6)

Limits on freedom of speech are subtle yet ever present, and the artists that we spoke to displayed a deep awareness of how their music is created within and against this backdrop. Whilst we were told that things have improved (the clampdowns on public concerts and seemingly random closure of rap events which were common in 2004/5 are less frequent at the time of writing, 2009) a culture of self-censorship is evident within lyrics and everyday discussions of anything that could have political undertones. Gangstas Wanted 'One-by-One' evinces such indirect self-censorship and simultaneously provides a critique of everyday conditions through metaphor:

> On the street I say oh my people jump in the palaces of the inferior, they turned you into plastic people/It is the underground revolution! Magically I talk about what's happening in my town, using my music.[11]

A kind of utopian justice is promoted here; for 'the people' who are described as 'plastic' (stripped of dignity, self-worth and individual power) 'jumping in the palaces' is presented as a metaphorical move to claim back power from the wealthy, and hip-hop is placed at the 'underground' centre of this move. Raps such as this one mention 'bad conditions' yet do not go into specific details about them, instead using metaphor and allegory (which are commonly understood by Tunisian listeners) to avoid potential critique, yet there is a sense that much is held back. When we asked an older artist 'what would you say about if you could rap about anything at all?' he laughingly responded; 'all the things I cannot say to you now, I would say it then.' In practical terms the lengthy bureaucratic processes and need for official permission to act in the public spaces renders production, performance and distribution precariously challenging. To make a music video, for example, it is necessary to be granted permission to record anything in public spaces, and as a film student explained, subject areas that can be explored in film are severely limited. Returning to the question of authenticity, it is tempting to ask just how relevant it remains when exploring contexts where real talk is restrained before the lyricist's pen is even picked up.

Artists are also keen to point out the 'bad conditions' around the world. This second form of resistance, the critique of bad conditions beyond Tunisia, is less likely to put the artists at risk and in some cases, (especially pro-Palestinian raps) is actively encouraged by the state. Our second visit to Tunis coincided with the Israeli offensive in Gaza, an event that shadowed our visit and was at the forefront of the artists' discussions, emotions, and lyrics. There was a tangible sense of frustration amongst the men, which is not simply a reaction to gross political and military injustices, but also a frustration at their inability to help change the situation in Palestine in direct ways. Hossam expressed his frustration in painfully eloquent terms, displaying unshakable links between the Palestinian struggle, shared membership of the *ummah*, and gendered roles.

> Their children are our children, their sisters are our sisters; 1,000 dead in 1 day, did you see it? Did you? … But they don't do anything. No one does anything … I cry, you cry, he cries … and will all our tears rain into Israel and flood [them]?

Palestine is repeatedly evoked as a symbol of continuing injustice in the world, one which has particular poignancy for Muslims everywhere and reverberates through Tunisian rap. Swedenburg makes a similar point in discussing the significance of the Palestinian struggle in the lyrics of UK group Fun-Da-Mental (2001: 60). Also, links between oil, wealth and international politics were raised on multiple occasions, with the current international power balance cited as an obstacle to Arab unity and economic progress. The artists expressed skeptical views of the 'wars' in Afghanistan and Iraq, which accord with Zoubir and Aït-hamadouche's observation that

> the overwhelming majority of the populations in MENA believe that the main objective of the Anglo-American operation was to control Iraqi oil wealth, consolidate Israel's security and guarantee oil supplies to Israel.
>
> (Zoubir and Aït-hamadouche 2006: 44)

In this sense, rap can provide a forum for protest; against national, international and transnational political events and trends, yet as a form of resistance it remains within the limits set by the nation state. Gross et al. observe how World Beat discourses about Raï 'are essentially based on a projection of a white, Eurocentric model of the culture wars onto Algeria,' a projection which elevates the whole genre as a resistance movement whilst glossing over issues such as complicated relationships to the nation state (Gross et al. 2002: 203). Thus it is clearly necessary to avoid romanticising all rap as resistance (which in itself ignores the diversity and locatedness of different artists and productions), yet within Tunisian rap, there are notable elements of political resistance taking place. These are nuanced and multifaceted; rap may be used as a vehicle for expressing frustrations against political climates, yet simultaneously it may display sophisticated use of metaphor as self-censorship, in order to protect the same artists from political ramifications.

Staged Selves

Nowhere is the potential for rap as action in itself more visible than in the artists' relationship(s) to their stage performances, and their stage selves.[12] Significantly, the artists who are usually modest about their music and talent often describe their live performances in boastful terms, urge us to return in the summer to see them on stage, and on many occasions, show us DVDs of their past concerts, animatedly pointing out themselves, their clothes and their crews. The divergence in autobiographical attitudes and self-expressions that these stage performances evoke is striking; in such recollections, reference to their (own and others') stage names is common, and the English term AKA ('also known as') is widely used. Yet in everyday social situations, they use their first names. Is it possible to read such performative elements of the artists' dual identities as expressions and affirmations of double consciousnesses? When asked the question 'who are you?' on stage, Hossam answered, 'me, I am me, and I am Achille. A different me!' This 'different' or 'other' self appears closer to Hossam's ideal(ised) hip-hop identity, where enactment and embodiment of the perceived roles of a hip-hop artist (such as aesthetics, body language, use of language and attitude) frees him to engage in a performativity that reflects a (self-perceived) truer self. This different self is there already, before the stage, even partially, propelling the artist onto the stage itself, yet depends on the public space within, and yet outside of the constraints of, the regulated public sphere. The performative aspects of double consciousness which emerges on stage/in staged spaces (arguably extendable also to coffee shops and the imagined listeners of all lyrical productions) are at once personal, individual and self-affirming and simultaneously, public, shared, collective and identity binding. The effectiveness of the performance rests upon the shared awareness of the framework of public performance—of the rap artist and persona—in contrast to the restrictions and shared reality of everyday, off-stage life. Ibrahim's description of being on stage is typical; 'I want to show myself to the world; I play by my feelings.' Such reported experiences include personal, collective, and public elements, which blend together into a particular freedom of being, and indicate the power of rap 'to call into being through performance new identities and subject positions' (Rose 1994: 21–22). The artists' relationships with their staged selves and their everyday selves is thus negotiated in a performativity that takes a deeper resonance when on stage, and infuses the same lyrics with a stronger political, transformative potential than when they are free-styled in coffee shops. Hythem recounts how on stage

> There I am free. People are interested in me, in myself. It is like being president, my ideas matter, they care, everybody listens. I hope, one day, if we keep speaking, others will want to speak to.

The power that comes with performing on stage and having the chance to use a voice that is rarely heard outside close circles of friends is infused with political power, with the aspiration of location, national and international transformation, with hip-hop providing the vehicle towards desired change. Small venues 'dramatically enable performances that question authority and challenge audience members to act for social change, even as they entertain' (Dowdy 2007: 77). Through being on stage, the transformative potential of hip-hop's performativity is transferred from the artists' lyrics to the audience which is where, as Hythem's account above indicates, the possibility of real change lies. This possibility is rendered more precarious and precious because of the particular environment of rap concerts in Tunisia, where freedom of speech and expression are not necessarily guaranteed, and where the concerts themselves have frequently been closed down by local authorities.

Interpretations of Islam

Tunisia is often described as the most liberal of Maghrebi countries, especially in terms of family law (Brand 1998: 201). Like its regional neighbours it has struggled to achieve a balancing act between diverse, and often conflicting, trends within its society, a balancing act which has been contained, or some may argue, resolved, by carefully propagating a particular interpretation of Islam. As Lee explains, 'the Tunisian government now sees Islamism as its principal opposition and takes pains, as do so many Muslim governments, to clothe itself in an official, conventional Islam' (Lee 2008: 159). The dramatic reinterpretation project begun by Bourguiba in 1956 was presented as a modern reading of Islam, which aimed to

> undermine any independent base of Islamist or traditionalist opposition ... not elimi-
> nating, but rather bringing under state control, all forms of civil society organization.
> (Brand 1998: 178–179)

Whilst Ben Ali's government has elaborated upon Bourguiba's reinterpretations of theology and at times engaged in an 'Islamization of official discourse' (Brand 1998: 192), the shift towards political and economic liberalization that Bourguiba's reign effected remain in place (Charrad 2001: 214). It is this reinterpretation which has facilitated the enactment of theology-inflected legislations, such as the dismantling of *shariah* courts and centres of Islamic studies and the prohibition of polygamy. Further, it has effectively recast public displays of religiosity as incompatible with the trajectory towards liberalism. If 'for Bourguiba, Islam represented the past, the West is Tunisia's only hope for a modern future' (Esposito and Voll 2001: 92), Islamic practice in the public sphere as a route to Tunisian modernity is rendered potentially precarious.

In this context the way that rap (a distinctly modern form of music and art) is used as a vehicle for interpreting and expressing religion offers an alternative route to locating religion in the public sphere. Interpretations of Islam are not something separate from the Tunisian rap scene; rather they are an integral part of the scene's identity. Religion holds a central, relevant and vital part of the movement's core in Tunis and by showing that religion remains relevant to their music and to their very existences, artists could be seen as adding to existing interpretative discourses on the meaning and place of Islam in the public sphere. Though all the artists we met subscribed to Sunni Islam, theological differences were notably downplayed; for example in 'One-by-One,' Gangstas Wanted rap 'God willing I will end with the people of heaven/with your hand on white Shi'ah or Sunni,' with white being used as a symbol of spiritual purity.[13] Mac, who describes himself lyrically in 'Just a Question of Time' as a 'son of the Sahara, Arab, Muslim, head to toe,' positions Islam at the 'beginning and the end' of his relationship to music. When we asked him how Islam affects his rap, he explained that

> Islam is my roots; I cannot move [away from] my roots. We do not talk about Islam
> exactly it is just there in every verse and ... you know, we are Muslims and we are artists.

Although Mac says that they do not talk about Islam explicitly, the omnipresence of Islam is central to their lyrical frame of reference; it is found in between verses dealing with all sorts of other subjects. Gangstas Wanted rap 'Arabi' became almost like a theme tune to our stay in Tunisia because it was played, freestyled and hummed so often by various artists. Amongst content rejoicing in (an almost utopian) Arab unity and Muslim brotherhood, we find the verse:

> I'm happy I am Muslim walking on the (straight) path,
> the finger of testimony always up;
> *There is no god but Allah.*
> The word Muslim unites us all ...
> This is what the Prophet said;
> The Qur'an is the source, its the law,
> its the distinction between good and bad,
> between oppressor and oppressed.[14]

Appealing to Muslim unity, the transcendental character of religion and the traditions that form the roots of all other interpretations of Islam, the track returns its listeners to the key sources of Islam. Whilst the religious phrases chosen are not uncommon in everyday speech and interactions in Tunisia, the centrality of the sources to the rap is striking. As an interpretation of religion and its place in contemporary lives, it is one that effectively bypasses political debate over who can interpret Islam in Tunisia, and how. Considering how official interpretations may appear to refute the authority of the *sunnah* in certain areas (such as the prohibition of beards), 'Arabi' is a striking testimony to the prevailing importance and centrality of the *sunnah* and *sirah* in the rappers' lives, consciousnesses, identities and frames of reference. Religion is the force that unites the rappers here, and the Qur'an is the primary framework for social and ethical behaviour. Again, by appealing to the Qur'an as the highest authority, they are effectively returning to age old definitions of what Islam means, and doing so through undeniably modern routes.

Islam also functions in the rap scene as a connecting force. 'Arabi' draws heavily on themes of pan-Arab unity, and this rap elevates the potential of Muslim identity to transcend all other identity positions and affinities. Although later in the track Hossam raps; 'there is no black and white, no difference between origins, in Islam,' race is notably not discussed as a significant factor in this intereptation. The chorus states, in French, English and Arabic, a vivid aspiration of pan-Arabism and a celebration of the locatedness of Tunisian rap:

> Brother I'm so happy I'm an Arab.
> We speak together, one language Arabic. We pray
> together, we fight together. Forever ever, I'm still Arab.[15]

If the rap movement expresses pan-Arabism and international Muslim solidarity (particularly evinced in their unified concern for the Palestinian struggle) it is most vitally a vessel for brotherhood amongst Tunisian artists. The spaces where rap is written, produced, distributed, exchanged and listened to facilitate relationships centred around the music itself. Membership in a clan creates different modes of relating and identifying, modes which may, or may not, elaborate upon more traditional forms of belonging. Rap can thus serve to work out and consolidate individual and collective identities, whilst offering escape from the struggles of everyday life. Mac writes in 'Just a Question of Time,'

> Satisfaction with my crew and with my section [area]. Despite the bad mentality and
> the bad conditions, Brother Mac gets called the scorpion.[16]

In this rap it is precisely the 'bad conditions' that strengthen the locatedness and sense of belonging to a 'crew,' and it is the potential for being named that inspires the satisfaction within the section (geographical area), that is the focus of this rap. Although clan membership in itself does not overtly challenge the political system or nation state, 'these musical forms fracture unity and promote a new model of heterological subjectivity that is not rooted in the political status quo' (Orlando 2003: 402). Significantly, it is individual talent that allows entry to clans, and in this sense at least, Tunisian rap provides artists with a space for community within the wider community. Like Raï, Potter suggests, hip-hop culture can function to create a 'new vernacular' of 'insurrectionary knowledges' that are juxtaposed with traditional 'historical societal forces' (Potter in Orlando 2003: 402)

Halal vs. Haraam?

Many artists spoke of the negative images attributed to hip-hop in Tunisian society, blaming both the national media and American films which glorify 'gangsta' violence. Considering the relationship of Islam to rap, it is worth remembering that 'the issue of music and singing has always been surrounded by controversy' (Dien 2004: 138) in Islam, and the 1994 assassination of the Algerian Raï artist Cheb Hasni evinces the contemporaneousness of the issue.[17] We were interested in how artists in Tunis, as Muslims, interpreted and articulated this relationship. When the issue was raised in discussion, the artists were divided; either they emphasized the potential to spread Islamic values through music, or they were adamant that rap is *haraam*, and that their involvement as artists is incompatible with their Muslim identities.

The first perspective focused on what may be termed the transformative potential of music; the artists' answers were cautious, yet generally well thought through. At a table with five artists, the eldest stated unambiguously 'it is not for you or for me to say it is *haraam*, only Allah can know,' and proceeded to cite a beautiful *hadith*; 'the distance between you and a decision is the distance between you and the [hell] fire.' The other men nodded in agreement, and talked animatedly for a while, before the one seemingly acting as spokesman for the clan cites the elements of American hip-hop which strike him as evidently *haraam*, such as the use of female sexuality and bodies, the consumerism and the violence of the culture.[18] He concludes carefully:

> It is like a knife, for me, music. You can use it to kill someone or to cut meat to eat. For me it is like this. Look at D'Ali … he is a discotheque manager and he just been to make his *jummah* [prayers].

Other interviews echoed this sense of context, the importance of *niyat* (intention), and the way that music can actually bring listeners and artists closer to Allah. Hythem, a well-read and articulate 25 year old, talked about global (mis)perceptions of Muslims, and laughed dismissively over how 'they think Muslim equals terrorist; its not true!' He continued to stress that music can be a form of da'wa (spreading Islam), in that it can bring knowledge to non-Muslims about what Islam really is, taking the form of a revolutionary message, hearkening back to what he termed 'the original heart' of Islam. 'In the music we will change the condition. We can use it to tell people about Islam—how it is here, and how it can be.' From this perspective, the transformative potential of rap can bring about positive change and is inherently tied up with the artists' own intentions and aspirations.

In contrast, a slightly older artist, Ibrahim, cast rap as a more negative force in his understanding of Islam and social conditions. He started rapping 12 years ago, is relatively successful and co-owns a recording studio. Ibrahim welcomed us to the studio in a suburb of Tunis, apologizing for the club-style display of alcohol. With all the trappings of a fully functional studio, the walls are painted graffiti style with prayer beads hanging over the multiple computers. He often chooses to stay overnight at the studio to work (rather than returning to his family home), and rents out the equipment to other musicians of all kinds. Unlike the younger artists, Ibrahim is cynical about the potential of rap to change anything in Tunisia, saying he 'can't do a revolution by rap' and is now focusing on diverse musical genres. He played us his current project of classical style piano, he is involved in a soft rock band, and self-describes as a musician, not a rapper. Although Ibrahim is one of the most successful artists in Tunis (a position confirmed by others' admiration for his work, and desire to 'make it' like he has) he presents a very different understanding of the relationship between Islam and rap.

> I believe it is *haraam*. Allah did not put two hearts in one human.[19] I cannot love music and Islam. It is shame on me. I lost three prayers yesterday, and my prayers are so late. Always. Yes, it is *haraam*.

The tension within Ibrahim's account cannot simply be understood as conflicting identities, although his perception of Muslim identity creates a debt-of-meaning which informs his artistic choices. Perhaps it is better seen as the way that the particular pulls towards action(s) and lifestyle choices play out in his self-consciousness, affecting his own self-perception as a precarious subject. Instead of positing rap as a transformative and positive sphere of expression, he views it as touching a weak point within himself, one inherently implicating his own spiritual struggles between right and wrong actions as a Muslim man. Although respectful of different opinions, Ibrahim is adamant that the music that he loves is keeping him away from his practice, that he 'loses' his focus when he is producing and that his inability to stop when he hears the *adhan* (call to prayer) is the work of *shaitan* (the devil).[20]

DuBois's concept of double consciousness may be relevant at this point. In DuBois's account the focus is on skin colour, yet the concept can usefully be applied to other experiences of a nuanced multiplicity of identities. Pattillo explains how DuBois's double consciousness

> is not half of this plus half of that, but a full part of each; not this or that, but both. There is no middle in this formulation—no transitional point in a journey of migration, hybridization, and later-generation assimilation; no central actor linking organizational nodes.
>
> (Pattillo 2007: 115)

Within Ibrahim's account of himself as a Muslim who is also a musician (within the hip-hop scene), the struggle for self-identity is very much entwined with the locatedness of both sides of his consciousness. He describes rap as 'like addiction, but I don't smoke [grass] or drink, *alhamdulillah* [all praise belong to God].' He admits that many artists who come to his studio do drink, immediately locating the context of rap as part of the perceived problem, and cites the tendency towards un-Islamic lifestyles as one of the problems of the genre. Pattillo (2007: 115) renders double consciousness as not a 'split' between two parts of an individual identity, it is not about 'liminality, but simultaneity.' In Ibrahim's case, the simultaneity of the environments that his double consciousness evokes is the difficult point; for him, the environment that rap exists within is a key obstacle to fuller realisation of Muslim consciousness. As a very talented musician who seems tormented by his love of hip-hop and his interpretation of

Islamic practice, Ibrahim states, 'I am fighting with myself, over music.' Such negotiations of consciousness require a never-ending chain of choices and modes of affiliation, modes which are at once responsive and self-determined. As Clifford writes on the pressures of maintaining a double vision within ones self-perception,

> this hooking-up and unhooking, remembering and forgetting, gathering and excluding of cultural elements—processes crucial to the maintenance of an 'identity'—must be seen as both materially constrained and inventive. Of course it is difficult, analytically and politically, to sustain this double vision.
>
> (Clifford 2000: 97)

Aside from Ibrahim, three interviewees insisted that music in general and rap in particular is haraam, or at least *mukrouh* (reprehensible), and indicated challenging dual affinities towards their talent and their interpretation of their faith. The new generation artists gave brief answers such as 'yes, it is *haraam*, only *daff* [a kind of drum] is really allowed,' and two further suggested that women's voices are completely *awra* (not to be exposed in public), a view that proves particularly problematic for artists when production entails sampling female vocals, or having them in their videos. Aladdin, who we spoke to on many occasions, had his twenty-fourth birthday whilst we were there, and announced how he intends to 'start my *deen* [religion] now,' seeing it as a pivotal age. He takes his religion very seriously, echoes Ibrahim's views about the incompatibility of hip-hop with his interpretation of Islam, yet appears to currently have less trouble maintaining this double consciousness within himself.

Disciplined Aesthetics vs. Streetwear

Aesthetics are central to hip-hop culture across the world, most visibly in streetwear, which plays a central role in hop-hop culture and is often 'virulently masculine' (Fleetwood 2005: 332). As Fleetwood writes, if 'the relationship between hip-hop music, specifically its lyrics, and fashion is mimetic … clothing acts as the visual identifier of the sound' (Fleetwood 2005: 329). The artists in Tunis reported that the aesthetics of rap are met with widespread negativity from Tunisian officials and wider society because of the image propagated by (American) films and perceived links between the music and gangster and/or Mafioso aggression. To dress as they perceive rappers should, could prove to be a barrier to employment, not dissimilarly to overtly Islamic apparel.

Tunisia's 1990 official ban on *hijab* in civil buildings is enforced to varying degrees in different areas,[21] and it seemingly functions to remove particular forms of religious observance from public domains. Restrictions on male aesthetics are less often commented upon. The government frowns upon male expressions of religiosity in the public sphere and wearing a beard and religious adornments can be a barrier to employment. The rules of public aesthetics may be understood as a disciplining of the visual, which takes a particular form for religiously observant members of the rap scene. One young artist exclaimed; '*Hijab* and *barb* is in the *sunnah*, but here, everything is forbidden ['*ala ici, tout interdemit*']. Where are we, Beirut or something?' The intentionally flippant rendering of the situation is enjoined with frustration at the divergences between official interpretations of Islam (and the selectivity of their applications), the Islam of traditional sources (such as the Prophet's *sirah* and *ahadith* collections), and their own quests for individual and collective identity as Muslim men.

Hythem, who works as an administrator for a university, explained how he once, when he was 'more religious,' had a beard, but was pressured to remove it when looking for work, a pressure he once again met when he started wearing street wear. As he explained, 'I like to look as is not okay now, no. If I wear like this [motions to baggies] I cannot work.' For Hythem, the need to belong is inherently entwined with appearances, or external regulation of aesthetics; the aspects of his identity expressed through how he dresses, walks, or wears his beard demand constant negotiation. This is not a unique account. In interviews at the end of the artists' working day, for example, it was not unusual for them to turn up at the cafe in formal workwear, and before sitting down, pull on a t-shirt over their day clothes, add shades and lower a cap over their eyes. Further, at discotheques the artists wore American style baggies, caps and t-shirts, visibly and aesthetically embodying the music that they play and dance to (perhaps testifying to the globalising aesthetics of hip-hop culture).

Here the concept of double-vision resonates with the artists' attitudes to the aesthetics of streetwear which they juggle in the Tunisian public sphere. We observed a clear discrepancy between the artists' aesthetic image—what they feel they should/would/could wear to be rappers—and the way they dressed on a daily basis. Returning to the lens of double vision, the artists' management of their dual identities appears to be heavily entwined with aesthetics through a sophisticated juggling of appearances and performances. Tate suggests that conceptualisations of double vision need to 'include the possibility for agency in the construction of identities in talk' (Tate 2001: 211); what emerges here is the centrality of aesthetics for constructing and confirming identities which contain elements of double vision. If the artists display double perspectives of their selves, these positions yield nuanced relationships between external actions, choices of appearance and aesthetics, and expressions of agency, and its control, in the public sphere. The aesthetic changes that they embody, and undergo on a daily basis, hint at the performativity of aesthetics and the disciplining of appearances in public spaces. In Tunisia this aesthetic performativity could be interpreted as being similar to the guidelines for Islamic apparel; either can prove to hinder the individuals' employability and general acceptance in wider social spheres, yet both make demands on the artists' identity constructions. It seems that the very real need to be accepted in the public sphere requires the artists' understanding of hip-hop culture, rapper identity and Islam to be negotiated along already set lines.

Located Masculinities

Hip-hop cultural sites in Tunis are predominantly male. The scene is located in mixed venues, such as coffee shops and discotheques, yet the women who are involved in production seem to be either girlfriends or transient members, but not individual rappers or relatives of male artists (during our experiences at least). We were told that there are a few, 'maybe two or three,' female rappers on the scene, but were frustratingly unable to obtain any reliable information about them.[22]

Whilst the younger artists expressed frustration about the expenses involved in marriage, they also displayed surprisingly conservative views on gender roles for married couples. (Surprising because such views stand in contrast to the attitudes shown in everyday mixed interactions).[23] One artist, who'd been married for a year, laughed that he tells his wife he's going to listen to rap and drink coffee 'for my head.' When we asked his clan members about this, we were told that his wife 'stays at home, he doesn't like her to come here or there, she doesn't go for coffee and he stays home more now [that he's married].' Although perhaps an unusually conservative example, Ibrahim explained that his dream is to take his (future) wife and mother to live in Saudi, and practice what he called 'real Islam.'

Women are also conspicuously absent in their lyrics, which stands in sharp contrast to US rap where 'the representation of women as sexual objects for men's use is a common trope'

(Crossley 2005: 506). When we asked a large group of artists how their music differs from their American counterparts, the lyrical placing of women was immediately raised. Following much animated discussion, Jamel explained,

> it is not the same image, women here is different, she is the inspiration beside you in struggle, she is … she is not the subject, we don't treat them like subject of music … we don't need to talk about them too much.

Such responses emerged as common and are certainly refreshing to hear against the oft-objectifying backdrop of mainstream US rap. In this regard the artists appear to differentiate between a conscious and commodifying depiction of women, and interpretations of gender-roles in Islam play a central role in this differentiation. Arguably this differentiation is in line with the artists' overall critical approach to the dominant values of mainstream US rap, and is less about feminism in any form; more, it reflects contextually-specific conceptions of gender difference articulated against those purported by American artists. Whilst the quote above shows that women are not 'the subject' of raps, it also shows that gender is not an overt theme in the overwhelmingly male domain of Tunisian hip-hop.

Kamel explained that 'our sisters come to the concerts, our mothers, [so] we're not permitted to swear or say bad words about women,' yet many of the tracks that we were played did contain words and terminology closer to misogyny than respect. Inclusion of female-derogatory terminology and slang in Tunisian rap could arguably be seen as less about mainstream hip-hop values, and more as reflective of traditional Tunisian patriarchal Arab attitudes towards women, and male unease with the speed at which gender roles are changing in Tunisia. This unease also emerged in discussions of female involvement in hip-hop production; the younger generation of artists were completely comfortable discussing rap with female friends and dancing together in nightclubs yet simultaneously displayed unease around the use of female voices, samples and bodies in music videos.

Such answers placed us (as consumers of rap, as feminists and as Muslim women), in an interpretative dilemma; it would be impossible to gauge just how much of the artists' responses were affected by our gendered presence, and by the multiple different ways of relating which our locations as researchers produced. It is clear, however, that the ways in which attitudes towards gender intersect with the Tunisian hip-hop scene are nuanced and multifaceted. The artists' hopes for their own futures contrast with their unmarried behaviour in mixed settings, for example, and whilst they insist that their music is more respectful to women than that of their US counterparts, the inclusion of some female-derogatory terms curiously contradicts that. Is this an example of how double consciousnesses can play out against social and cultural backdrops? If the self-perception of rap artists requires a certain kind of embodiment of action and attitude, do the misogynistic frameworks of reference so embedded within mainstream hip-hop culture cast a particular light upon the gendered sides of rappers' double consciousnesses? At the very least the gendered attitudes of the artists contain a selective adoption and creative criticism of US rap which is continued into their music. In conversation they would frequently speak scathingly of the egotism and materialistic lifestyles promoted therein, and we were intrigued by how the artists' own lyrical content is negotiated alongside the hip-hop culture broadcast by MTV Arabia and similar medias.

> I am sorry to say this to you but most of it is bullshit. Everything bling bling, women, cars, money, clothes; this is what they do. If you look at any of them … [like] 50 Cent … this is their life. They think this is life?

Whilst Kamel states he has a lot of respect for the production industry and musical talent of many American artists, he takes a selective approaches to what is included in his own music. The raps discussed here use diverse music samples. For example, in 'One-by-One' the sound is incredibly Arabic; synthesised samples of Arabic flute and oud-like string instruments are interspersed with a standard rap beat. However, there is also a continuous return to reggae chants in the background, and a heavily patois accent is used throughout the chorus. In contrast, 'Arabi' is much closer in style to a West coast/LA sound and contains no Arabic style samples. Instead it is a composition of different melodies with a distinctively (Western) classical tone, clustered around orchestral strings and piano-orientated crescendos. Amongst the artists who identify as 'new generation' there is a distinctive reggae influence on the composition, words and samples used; for example, young solo artist Weld 15 raps about Islam in a track entitled 'Soldiers of Jah's army.' Such attitudes of critical consumption and sample selections indicate that the rhizomic globalization of rap is not a simple instance of the appropriation of a U.S./African-American cultural form; rather, it is a linguistically, socially, and politically dynamic process which results in complex modes of indigenization and syncreticism (Pennycook 2007: 107).

Clearly, far from a neat admiration of all things western, artists such as Kamel are responding critically to the superficiality and ethical framework which mainstream American rap can reproduce. D'Ali elucidates on his own relationship to US rap as 'we are not obligated to take all parts, we don't imitate. I like the clean rappers, not the dirty parts of it, like Common.' In this sense, mainstream rap is like much of American culture which 'is imitated and admired … yet at the same time it is contested' across the world (Zoubir and Aït-hamadouche 2006: 51).

Between the Ink and the Feather: Conclusion

This paper has discussed rap in Tunisia from a variety of angles, including gender, aesthetics, authenticity and censorship, social conditions, external restraints and interpretations of Islam. The concept of double consciousness has been a useful lens through which to view some of the apparent contradictions within the artists' identities and we have suggested that a degree of 'double vision' is forced, to a certain extent, by restraints on agency in the public sphere. Social and structural constraints render the current hip-hop scene in Tunis challenging and frustrating; to be an artist is not to expect financial or even public rewards, and, as we heard in numerous variations, rap 'is not a life' in Tunisia. However, there are some exceedingly talented artists whose devotion to the genre is enabling the scene to grow, if slowly. Opportunities provided by cyber networking resources and advances in production technologies[24] are increasingly rendering auto-production a more feasible option, which will surely diversify the future of the scene. In terms of religion, the Tunisian rap scene testifies to the power of 'Islamic hip-hop … [which] has emerged as a powerful internationalist subculture for disaffected youth around the world (Aidi 2004: 124). The interpretations of Islam found within the artists' lyrics are absolutely situated within the Tunisian context, and the employment of a framework informed by Sunni Islam is strikingly different to the ones used by the Muslim artists that they admire in the American context. This fidelity to Muslim identity intersects, as we have seen, with rappers identity construction in diverse ways in Tunisia. The majority of artists interviewed cite the transformative, positive potential of rap to bring listeners closer to Islam. However, the synthesis of identity affiliations is far from simple. Attitudes towards women, for example, and Ibrahim's summary 'I am fighting with myself' testify to the dual-vision which artists may express in synthesising these different aspects of being Tunisian, Muslim rappers.

Tunisian rap emerges as a powerful vehicle for self-expression, one which is firmly situated within the artists' geographies and biographies, whilst simultaneously looking beyond national boundaries. By focusing on Palestine as a site of gross injustice the artists also strengthen transnational connectivities as Muslim men and as Arabs, and offer support for a cause that unites and mobilises emotional responses. Rap is posited by the artists as a form of resistance; by articulating what they see as the 'bad conditions' that surround them (both locally and globally), the artists at once draw attention to their own streets and the multiple politics embedded therein. In the track 'Just a Question of Time,' T Men say 'lyrics are like 25 bullets; hip-hop is the foundation of the revolution.'[25] Here the pen is adorned with the power to resist, as a weapon to be employed in the defence of Tunisians,[26] and in depicting himself as an Arab Tunisian warrior,[27] Mac's lyrics point towards the potential for change that rap as a genre can predict, articulate, and even help effect.

> I take my pen, raise it up
> like a katana [sword].
> I speak Tunisian,
> going to Tunisians,
> just let me speak Tunisian.[28]

It must be noted, however, that for all the revolutionary potential hinted at within the lyrics, the artists are less clear about the transition from rap as performative resistance to solid political change. We have suggested that the stage allows the artists to perform their other selves, embody their ideal/ised understandings of rapper masculinity and aesthetics, and move towards desired social change. Remembering Hythem's statement about being on stage, 'I hope, one day, if we keep speaking, others will want to speak too,' indicates the potentiality within rap as a form of communication and political mobilisation. Yet as the lyrics above suggest, the desire to be allowed to speak freely is omnipresent; even on stage the constraints on freedom of speech limit just how far 'keeping it real' can take this mobilisation.

Whilst it is necessary to avoid romanticising rap as resistance, it is clear that Tunisian rap does contain political potentialities; simultaneously, it may also function to reinforce dominant notions of the nation state and interpretations of religion. Further, the way that gender roles and performativity interact with the rappers' self-identities is far from a neat genealogy. Though artists display critical attitudes to the materialism promoted by mainstream American rap and claim that women have a different place within their culture and thus their music, their lyrics were not completely clean. Rather, they do include female-derogatory phrases and terminology, which could be seen as a reflection of the rappers' propagation of situated patriarchal attitudes. This is also suggested by the duality that the men display in terms of everyday gender relations; whilst they are comfortable in mixed social settings, conservative views of gender roles emerge when the issue of marriage is raised, and this is as significant for considering gender in their music as the place of women in mainstream American rap. In this sense rap can be seen as perpetuating dominant attitudes and social frameworks as much as it provides spaces for their contestation. As female rappers carve out their own place within the Tunisian hip-hop scene this will invariably change. The self-censorship that the Tunisian context demands is another area that is at once (arguably necessarily) perpetuated and contested.

Overall, the scene facilitates relationships and a sense of belonging where identities can be worked out and consolidated. In this sense, Tunisian rap can be seen as 'serving to establish and contribute towards the formation of ethnic and geographic identities, while carving out 'spaces of freedom' (Whiteley 2005: 8). Tunisian rap is firmly located in the streets that inspire it, yet it also turns beyond Tunisia; within such spaces of freedom, there is much potential. The artists' lyrics indicate that desire for social change is widespread; yet rap is also, for these artists, an intensely personal and spiritual endeavour, one where conflicts of religious inter-pretation, globalisation, masculinity, nationality and belonging can be worked out. As Arab Muslim Tunisian men, rap is a central aspect of the artists' identities and is further a route to discovering identity; as Mac freestyles in a busy street cafe, 'I find myself between the ink and the feather, and on one piece of paper I started to express myself.'[29]

Study Questions

1. What role does the internet play in the ethnographic method employed in the study? How does the virtual space, according to Shannahan and Hussain, contribute to the accessibility and growth of a global hip hop *umma*?
2. How do these authors view the connections and differences between heterodox Islamic sensibilities in rap music in the US and abroad? Are there necessary distinctions that must be made between location and geography?
3. Based on their data, what do the authors suggest about the role and function of double consciousness and vision of rap music in the Tunisian world?

Notes

1. 'Ça fait ma vie comme un désert dans les mal temps/fils de Sahara, Arabi wa Muslim hau a bot/Je tire mon stylo il fouq, comme un katana. Kalami Toonsi, meshi il Toonsi, khaleni net kalem Toonsi.' All the lyrics here have been translated with the artists in the hope of reaching the most meaning-faith-ful English translation. Raps frequently involve code switches and mix (Tunisian) Arabic, French and English; lyrics are presented here are as they are spoken. For more information on the groups discussed here and some tracks, see http://www.myspace.com/gangstarwanted (Gangstas Wanted); http://www.myspace.com/weld15 (Weld 15); http://www.al-fann.com/path/Tunisia/Rap/T_Men/(T Men); and http://www.myspace.com/daly_blaze216 (Daly Blaze of T Men).
2. This is shown not only by the variety and diversity of approaches to be found in academic works on rap, but also in the interdisciplinary reach of hip-hop studies. Alim reminds us that many US universities are now offering 'hip-hop courses in departments as diverse as linguistics, religious studies, philoso-phy, and African American studies' (Alim 2005: 272), a variety which will inevitably increase in time.
3. Whilst many of the rappers that we met in Tunis were quick to point out that Nas and Busta Rhymes are Muslims, they were less certain of the format that their Islam takes; the routes that their (hetero-dox) Islam provides in bringing them to, and articulating as, Islam, are surely very different to the Sunni, Maliki Islam that the Tunisian artists practice.
4. For further information on Arab/ic hip-hop a good place to start is the forum of *Hip-hop Arabia*, http://hiphoparabia.ning.com/forum. (accessed July 10, 2009)
5. We were told that the hip-hop scene is primarily located in Tunis (although there are artists working in other places such as Sfax and Sousse) and summer concerts take place in diverse coastal resorts.
6. This may seem a small sample group but the number of people considered rap artists with the scene is relatively small; as producer Kamel told me, 'there are maybe fourteen or fifteen artists in Tunisia.' This reflects surely his distinction between artists who are producing and recording, and 'wannabes,' a quick search on Myspace casts doubt onto this figure, and also indicates that there are many more of the latter.
7. Two more commercially successful Tunisian rappers are Balti Hiroshima and Sincero. The majority of artists we spoke to were rather doubtful about their status within the holistic movement, particu-larly emphasising the (perceived) trajectory towards R 'n' B that Balti appears to have taken. We did

travel to see Balti in concert but, due to a low turnout, it ended early, and unfortunately we were unable to interview him during our stay.

8. 'Ena Arabe fakhour baseet, la khin fakhour bi ardi ow ardh ajdaadi bil Arab ikhwaani.'

9. 2008 figures put the official unemployment figure at 14.1%, though unofficial figures place it much higher. Due to the seasonal nature of much of the work in Tunisia,(most notably tourism and agriculture) figures are estimates at best.

10. For more information, see Amnesty International 2009 and Ben Mhenni 2009.

11. 'Fi sharah akhi ah sha'bi nukuz fil abrage mteera ithul/khalowkum people plastic/underground tra revolution!/Bi saher mnit kelim aley sigher fi hum bil musica mtayeh.'

12. The artists perform in public at least twice a year in a variety of venues, such as summer festivals, nightclubs and self-organised concerts. Balti (who is more commercially successful) was said to perform a few times a month.

13. 'Insh'allah wil khatma min ahl Jehnah / min yiddek alla ubayid Shi'a wala Sunni.'

14. 'Muslim farhan nimshey ala as sirat/subah shahada deyma il fouq; la illaha illah allah / tajmana kilmit Muslimeen … hadah she wasa Rasul, kitab il Qur'an whoah il mem bah, whoah el kahnoon, whoa iley ey faruk bayn il haqh wil batil, nayn addalim wa al mathloom.'

15. 'Arabe, fière de l'être frero I'm Arab / We speak together, one language Arabi/We pray together, we fight together / Forever ever, I'm still Arab.'

16. 'Satisfaction with my crew and with my section/malgré la mentalité mauvaise / and the bad conditions / MAK frère nomé le scorpion.'

17. For an in-depth discussion of Raï in Algeria and France see Gross et al. 2002.

18. This perspective is similar to that presented by the popular site Muslim hip-hop, where music from, and information on, Muslim artists is offered online, supporting the argument that some music, if the focus is halal, can bring listeners closer to Islam, rather than further away. See for example 'Music in Islam,' Muslim hip-hop (MHH), http://www.Muslimhiphop.com. (accessed 10th of July 2009)

19. This is a reference to the Qur'an; 33:4.

20. Discussing raï artists in Algeria Schade-Poulsen noted as similar tension; whilst artists reported spiritual elements within the musical process, some also felt it kept them from complete religious observance (1999: 140).

21. During a visit to a large university in the suburbs of Tunis, a senior Professor estimated that one third of university students wear *hijab* on campus, despite the official ban. As *hijabis*, we didn't encounter any problems. However, many women confided to us of frequent, unpredictable harassment and refused entry by security forces at the gates to campus, the most extreme case being the actual pulling off of a woman's scarf. They were keen to stress that enforcement is as much the whims of the particular officers as it was higher directives. (Interestingly, in towns in southern Tunisia the ban was more strictly enforced, with many women choosing between the scarf or employment in civic offices and universities.)

22. This stands in contrast to raï's gendered spaces and roles, where *sheikhat* (female artists) have been fundamental to the history and development of the genre. Virolle suggests that in Algeria female performers open up spaces 'whereby masculine and feminine signs are superimposed, inverted, corresponding, and mutually nullifying' (Virolle 2003: 226).

23. For example, as the research progressed we faced the experience of being offered 'hugs' by some of the artists, something completely novel to us within a mixed Muslim context.

24. Programmes such as *Cubase* and *Fruity Loops* are dramatically changing the landscapes of production, enabling artists to create and auto-produce their raps at home. Copies of such programmes are widely available in Tunis's markets for as little as 1 Dinar, (50 pence) at the time of writing.

25. 'Lyrics comme les balles, revolution hip-hop sas.'

26. Lyrically linking the potential of the pen with weaponry is of course nothing new in rap, hearkening back to Tupac's words 'so I fight with my pen' (*To Live & Die in L.A.*, 1996).

27. 'Harbi Toonsi Arbi.'

28. 'Je tire mon stylo il fouq comme un katana. Kalami Toonsi, meshi il Toonsi, khaleni net kalem Toonsi.'

29. 'Nelga rouhi bayn el blouma will habar, wa'al eh wargah bdeet na'buur, jaar.'

References

Aidi, H. (2004). 'Verily, there is only one hip-hop Umma': Islam, cultural protest and urban marginality. *Socialism and Democracy*, 18(2), 107–126.

Alim, H. S. (2005). A new research agenda: Exploring the transglobal hip-hop Umma. In M. Cooke & B.B. Lawrence (Eds.), *Muslim networks, from Hajj to Hip-Hop* (pp. 264–274). Chapel Hill: University of North Carolina Press.

Amnesty International. (2009). *Tunisia: Continuing abuses in the name of security.* London: Amnesty International Publications.

Basu, D. (1998). What is real about 'keeping it real'? *Postcolonial Studies*, 1(3), 371–387.

Ben Mhenni, L. (2009). Tunisia: attacks on freedom of expression. *Global Voices Online*. http://globalvoicesonline.org/2009/02/01/56217/. Accessed July 19, 2009.

Bouzine, D. (2000). Algerian rappers Sing the Blues. *Unesco Courier*, 34–35, July–August. Brand, L. A. (1998). *Women, the state, and political liberalization: Middle Eastern and North African experiences.* New York: Columbia University Press.

Charrad, M. M. (2001). *States and women's rights: The making of postcolonial Tunisia, Algeria, and Morocco.* California: University of California Press.

Clifford, J. (2000). Taking identity politics seriously: 'The Contradictory, Stony Ground …' In Hall, S. Gilroy, P. Grossberg, L., & McRobbie, A (Eds.), *Without guarantees: in honour of Stuart Hall* (pp. 94–113). London: Verso.

Condry, I. (2007). Yellow B-Boys, Black Culture, and Hip-Hop in Japan: Toward a transnational cultural politics of race. *Positions*, 7(15), 637–671.

Connell, R. (2009). *Gender.* Cambridge: Polity.

Crossley, S. (2005). Metaphorical conceptions in hip-hop music. *African American Review*, 39(4), 501–522.

Dien, M. I. (2004). *Islamic law, from historical foundations to contemporary practice.* Edinburgh: Edinburgh University Press.

Dowdy, M. (2007). Live hip-hop, collective agency, and 'acting in concert.' *Popular Music and Society*, 30(1), 75–91.

Esposito, J. L., & Voll, J. O. (Eds.), (2001). *Makers of contemporary Islam.* New York: Oxford University Press US.

Fleetwood, N. R. (2005). Hip-hop fashion, masculine anxiety, and the discourse of Americana. In H. J. Elam & K. A. Jackson (Eds.), *Black cultural traffic: Crossroads in global performance and popular culture* (pp. 326–345). Michigan: University of Michigan Press.

Gross, J., McMurray, D., & Swedenburg, T. (2002). Arab noise and ramadan nights: Raï, Rap, and Franco-Maghrebi identities. In J. Xavier Inda & R. Rosaldo (Eds.), *The anthropology of globalization: A reader* (pp. 198–231). Oxford: Wiley-Blackwell.

Hip-Hop Arabia. http://hiphoparabia.ning.com/forum. Accessed July 10, 2009.

Kahf, U. (2007). Arabic hip-hop: claims of authenticity and identity of a new genre. *Journal of Popular Music Studies*, 19(4), 359–385.

Lee, R. D. (2008). Tunisian intellectuals: Responses to Islamism. *The Journal of North African Studies*, 13(2), 157–173.

Mitchell, T. (Ed.), (2001). Global noise: *Rap and hip-hop outside the USA.* Middletown: Wesleyan University Press.

Muslim Hip-Hop. http://www.muslimhiphop.com/index.php?p=What_is_MHH/Music_in_Islam. Accessed 10 July.

Orlando, V. (2003). From rap to raï in the mixing bowl: Beur hip-hop culture and Banlieue cinema in urban France. *Journal of Popular Culture*, 36(3), 395–415.

Osumare, H. (2005). Global hip-hop and the African diaspora. In H. J. Elam & K. A. Jackson (Eds.), *Black cultural traffic: Crossroads in global performance and popular culture* (pp. 266–288). Michigan: University of Michigan Press.

Ouzgane, L. (Ed.), (2006). *Islamic masculinities.* London: Zed Books.

Pattillo, M. E. (2007). *Black on the block: The politics of race and class in the city.* Chicago: University of Chicago Press.

Pennycook, A. (2007). Language, localization, and the real: hip-hop and the global spread of authenticity. *Journal of Language, Identity & Education*, 6(2), 101–115.

Rose, T. (1994). *Black noise: Rap music and black culture in contemporary America.* Middletown: Wesleyan University Press.

Schade-Poulsen, M. (1999). *Men and popular music in Algeria: The social significance of raï.* Texas: University of Texas Press.

Swedenburg, T. (2001). Islamic hip-hop vs. islamophobia: Aki Nawaz, Natacha Atlas, Akhenaton. In T. Mitchell (Ed.), *Global noise: Rap and hip-hop outside the USA* (pp. 57–85). Middletown: Wesleyan University Press.

Tate, S. (2001). 'That is my Star of David': Skin, abjection and hybridity. In S. Ahmed & J. Stacey (Eds.), *Thinking through the skin* (pp. 209–222). London: Routledge.

Virolle, M. (2003). Representations and female roles in the raï song. In T. Magrini (Ed.), *Music and gender: Perspectives from the Mediterranean* (pp. 215–232). Chicago: University of Chicago Press.

Whiteley, S. (2005). Rap and hip-hop: Community and cultural identity. In S. Whiteley, A. Bennett, & S. Hakins (Eds.), *Music, space and place: Popular music and cultural identity* (pp. 8–15). Aldershot: Ashgate Publishing Ltd.

Zoubir, Y. H., & Aït-hamadouche, L. (2006). Anti-Americanism in North Africa: could state relations overcome popular resentment? *The Journal of North African Studies*, 11(1), 35–54.

Discography

T Men. (2007). *Just a Question of Time*, Unsigned. Gangstas Wanted. (2006). *One-by-One*, Unsigned. Gangstas Wanted. (2008). *Arabi*, Unsigned. Aladdin. (2009). *Soldiers of Jah's Army*, Unsigned.

Tupac Shakur. (1996). *To Live & Die in L.A.*, Death Row/Interscope Records.

17

Believe Me, This Pimp Game is Very Religious
Toward a Religious History of Hip Hop

Sorett begins his study by considering the hybrid-like responses to white supremacy and suffering within black culture. He uses this as a way to explore a heterodox collection of "post-soul" spiritualties—giving considerable attention to KRS ONE's religious and spiritual influences on hip hop culture. He moves into an examination of uses of the religious in Kanye West's 2003 release of "Jesus Walks" and then examines religion and power in the work of rappers Ja Rule and female artist, Remy "Remy Ma" Smith. Furthermore, he argues shifts in religious references and spiritual commitments in hip hop and rap music reflect the larger shifts within the reconfigurations of American religion in the latter end of the twenty-first century. He concludes that hip hop artists draw on religious references and language for a wide variety of reasons, some superficial and others as a strategy to secure/promote the artist's ulterior motives. Yet, such messy and convoluted uses of religion in rap music also speak to, among other things, mundanity, altered notions of the sacred and societal shifts impacting African American religion.

Believe Me, This Pimp Game Is Very Religious: Toward a Religious History of Hip Hop

Josef Sorett

In his important book, *The Black Atlantic: Modernity and Double-Consciousness*, Gilroy (1993) asserts that black diasporic musics are

> facilitated by a common fund of urban experiences, by the effect of similar but by no means identical forms of racial segregation, as well as by the memory of slavery, a legacy of Africanisms, and a stock of religious experiences.

> (1993, 80)

This stew of cultural and political experiences – a hybrid blend of responses to the experience of white supremacy and inheritances of African cultures – also defines what Hall identifies as the 'cultural repertoires' that constitute the 'black' in black popular cultures (Wallace 1992). While the subject of religion has not been a top priority in the field of cultural studies, there is indeed much in the realm of popular cultures which has captured the interest of scholars of religion.[1] Thinking more specifically in the direction of a religious history of hip hop, the most obvious ingredient in this stock has been Islam, which in various forms – Sunni, Nation of Islam and Five Percenter – has been ubiquitous in the music and culture since its emergence roughly 30 years ago.[2]

Too many rappers have expressed allegiance to this multiform tradition to provide a comprehensive list here, but a litany of artists from Rakim to Lupe Fiasco could be quickly compiled. Alongside Islam, Christianity was a fixture in hip hop as far back as 1987 when MC Hammer's first record included 'Son of the King', a track that showed up again on his second and more popular album, *Let's Get it Started*.[3] While A Tribe Called Quest is most commonly associated with the eclectic Afrocentric spirituality posited by the Native Tongues collective and Afrika Bambaataa's Zulu Nation, the group featured two Muslims (Ali Shaheed Muhammad and Q-tip) and Fife, who on the group's ever popular 1991 album, *The Low End Theory*, cited his own Christian upbringing.[4] The five-foot tall assassin exclaimed, 'I was raised as a Christian, so to God I give thanks'. Of course, biblical imagery has suffused the lyrics of many artists who did not necessarily self-identify with any particular religious tradition. One thinks of the reference to John 3:16 which appeared on the CD cover of Notorious B.I.G.'s posthumously released *Life After Death* album, Bone Thugs and Harmony's invitation for listeners to meet them at the 'Crossroads', Lauryn Hill's remixing of the church hymn 'Marching to Zion', and Tupac's prophetic ruminations, including the song 'I Wonder if

235

Heaven Got a Ghetto'. While this brief survey provides an oversimplified account of hip hop's religious milieu, it serves my purposes to suggest that religious diversity has more often than not been the rule of rap music.[5] Additionally, what appeared to bind these artists together was not a particular religious orthodoxy, be it Christian, Islamic or otherwise. Rather than specific confessional claims, by locating these religious significations within the cultural repertoires of the African Diaspora, one is able to offer some analytical coherence to otherwise multifarious musical musings. Specifically, they reflect the particular experiences of primarily black youth living in the United States' post-industrial urban centers. In short, this otherwise heterodox collection of post-soul spiritualities bore witness to the lived (and imagined) realities of black youth reluctant to align themselves with the religious institutions of their elders.[6]

KRS-ONE: Religious Significations and Cultural Repertoires

The famous American philosopher Ralph Waldo Emerson once argued that all history is in fact biography. By this he meant that the stories humans tell say just as much about a particular author as they do about any actual historical record that an author documents. A quick look at KRS-ONE, the famous MC and hip hop theorist, provides an opportune contemporary case to test out Emerson's claim in the inverse. That is to say, in KRS-ONE's biography one is able to discern the same developments that have defined hip hop's religious history, more generally. By paying attention to the spiritual evolution of KRS-ONE, one can map a preliminary history of the religious dimensions of hip hop as it has evolved from the 1980s to the present. While he has consistently attempted to critically situate himself in opposition to mainstream rap music, KRS-ONE's own religious biography pairs well with the shifting religious sensibilities articulated by several hip hop artists who have been most popular during the span of these same years. KRS-ONE, real name Lawrence Parker, began rapping in the mid-1980s as part of the group Boogie Down Productions (BDP). As a member of BDP, his recordings included the albums *Criminal Minded* and *By All Means Necessary*, with the latter being a clear reference to Malcolm X. In fact, on the album cover of By All Means Necessary, KRS appeared holding an Uzi while gazing out of the window in a manner reminiscent of the classic photograph of Malcolm X, with a shotgun in tow, leaning on the window sill. In more recent years, however, KRS-ONE has released music, most obviously his 2002 *Spiritual Minded* album, which displays an employment of more explicitly Christian lyrics. The songs on *Spiritual Minded* continued KRS-ONE's earlier critique of the American mainstream; but they also specifically addressed such issues as the sacredness of virginity, the importance of cultivating a 'Christ consciousness', and the necessity of being 'born again'.[7] In the years between these albums, Parker moved from an affiliation with New York's Riverside Church, a bastion of liberal Protestantism, to Barbara L. King's Hillside International Truth Center in Atlanta (a Unity Church grounded in American New Thought traditions), and on to Clarence McClendon's Full Harvest International Church, a multi-cultural congregation in California grounded in the contemporary charismatic Christian movement.[8] Like KRS-ONE, who moved from drawing on the iconography of Malcolm X to an appropriation of Christian categories (and affiliations with increasingly more evangelical idioms of Christianity), as rap music moved to the centre of mainstream popular culture its most prominent religious sensibilities also shifted from Islam to Christianity. In the case of KRS-ONE, his use of shifting religious rhetorics evinced his commitment to hip hop serving as a consciousness-raising resource, which he calls 'edutainment', as he voices various criticisms of American society.[9] Through an appeal to Malcolm X, he offered an analysis of white supremacy and in evangelical Christianity KRS-ONE finds a critique of mainstream hip hop's celebration of capitalism and crude displays of sexuality.

KRS-ONE's personal evolution reads as a rich religious narrative on its own terms, and it is surely worthy of further attention. However, his biography also provides an excellent starting point for thinking towards a religious history of hip hop music more broadly. Consider the following narrative. Amidst the public resurgence of black nationalist sensibilities during the late 1980s and 1990s, most visible in events like the Million Man March and Spike Lee's biopic Malcolm X, a sort of 'blacker the better' rationale ordered the religious indices of hip hop culture. More specifically, within this framework Islam represented a greater degree of alterity and perceived authenticity, and numerous scholars have documented the appeal of Islam within black popular culture during these years.[10] If you were wise enough to 'know the ledge' you would swagger straight to the store and purchase your X hat and Africa medallion to secure your salvation.[11] Hip hop historians will recall the countless rappers – most notably, Guru of the group GangStarr in the video 'I Manifest' in 1989 – who attempted to perform Malcolm X by standing behind podiums with kufis adorning their heads. Of course, such performances speak to the role of the market in mediating identities, religious, racial or otherwise, clarifying that the commercialisation, commodification and consumption of blackness in popular culture is a quintessentially American phenomenon. Still, reflective of the hegemonic place afforded to Christianity within the United States, Islam played the most overt role in the formation of rap music, and thus helped to shore up early definitions of hip hop as an oppositional discursive practice in relation to the American cultural mainstream (Dyson 1998). However, in the historical development of rap music into hip hop culture, and its subsequent triumph as arguably the most fashionable force in global pop culture, Christianity has emerged as the primary religious sensibility of new millennium MCs, including such disparate figures as West, Cassidy and Elliott.[12]

Making the Shift

Significantly, the progression of hip hop's most evident spiritual commitments, from Islam to Christianity, has reflected shifts within black popular culture, as well as reconfigurations in American religion at the end of the twenty-first century.[13] The religious dimensions of hip hop have evolved from a neo-nationalist, 'black' spirituality associated with the Nation of Islam to an embrace of Christianity. Certainly, this shifting of allegiances from Islam to Christianity allowed for the expression of a range of differences within each of these respective traditions. However, the version of Christianity most frequently visualised is an idiom largely made accessible over the airwaves by televangelists and marketed by megachurch pastors. It often also includes the celebration of a gospel of 'Bling' evidenced in the affinity of many rappers for prosperity preachers. Additionally, in today's scene Islam is no longer perceived to be a necessarily oppositional religious discourse. Talk of black 'gods' has moved from the mouths of black Muslims to the tongues of hip hop moguls like Jay-Z, for whom the 5% lexicon figures as but one religious constellation in a universe of words. In fact, even Lupe Fiasco, hip hop's most recent Muslim MC of choice, nods his head in the direction of Christianity, giving praise to two gospel music stars (Yolanda Adams and Smokie Norful) and an Atlanta-based megachurch pastor (Creflo Dollar) on his most religious song. On the chorus to his underground single, 'Muhammad Walks', a remix of the famous West track that he has released over the internet, Lupe raps, '*I'm not trying to profit off the prophet, so this one's for free*'. While Fiasco does not forego his own religious commitments as a Muslim, he articulates his faith in relationship to Christian figures who have achieved semi-celebrity status in the American religious landscape.

More significantly, references to Creflo Dollar, who is arguably the most popular black prosperity preacher of the day, have become a fixture in hip hop music. They include a cameo appearance in Ludacris and Jermaine Dupri's 'Welcome to Atlanta' video, an acknowledgment in verse by 50 Cent, and a professed affiliation by the rapper-turned-pastor Mason Betha.[14] Within hip hop, Christianity has become as much a signifier of wealth and power as it is evidence of any specific theological vision. Rather, more accurately, many rappers bear witness to a theology that valorises wealth as divine blessing – a notion that is, to quote Dead Prez, much 'bigger than hip hop'.[15] Pastor Dollar, for whom wealth is indeed a core spiritual value, seems to embody for many rappers the essence of hip hop's hustle doused in holy water. Of note, Dollar has his own music video in the works, performed by a group of rappers who belong to his church and record label. Not surprisingly, the song's refrain is simply, 'Money, money, coming down!'[16]

Kanye West: Walking with Jesus

Hip hop's rising Christendom culminated in 2003 with the release of Kanye West's 'Jesus Walks', a popular single that was, perhaps, the major exception to the rule of conflating Christianity with capital. On the one hand, the rapper preached a deeply personal piety. West explains:

> I ain't here to argue about his facial features;
> or here to convert atheists into believers.
> I'm just saying the way school need teachers, the way Kathy Lee needed Regis,
> that's the way I need Jesus.[17]

In this brief verse, West accomplishes at least four specific tasks. First, he offers a critique of Black Theology's preoccupation with God's racial identity ('I ain't here to argue about his facial features'). Second, West distances himself from the religious impulse to convert unbelievers ('or to convert atheists into believers'). Third, he draws on mainstream American popular culture ('the way Kathy Lee needed Regis'). And fourth, West endorses a brand of spirituality popular in contemporary society which caters directly to personal desires ('that's the way I need Jesus').[18] Yet, in the song's chorus West also proclaims a theology of the oppressed and outcast, as he insists that Jesus walks most closely with murderers, strippers and drug dealers. Surprisingly, West provided a rather nuanced vision of contemporary American Christianity; so much so that he felt the song required three separate music videos.[19] True to the post-modern moment in which he became a celebrity, in the three videos West de-centres any one normative account of African American religion in favour of elevating several religious visions. Yet he simultaneously taps into spiritual sensibilities that remain influential across a significant portion of society. However, despite the complexities captured in each video, West also appeared to bow to prosperity pressures. On the remix to 'Jesus Walks', he invited the ex-rapper Minister Mase, a protégé of Creflo Dollar, to offer a prayer in which Mase proclaims, 'I'm healed, I'm delivered, I'm rich'.[20] West had also planned to design a line of diamond-encrusted Jesus-pieces with hip hop's favourite jeweller, Jacob 'The Jeweler' Arabo.[21] West's appearance on the 8 February 2006 cover of *Rolling Stone* magazine, adorned with his own crown of thorns, suggested to some that his invocation of Jesus might not be much more than an effort to generate cash-flow by creating controversy. At a minimum, it raised the question of whether West's vision of religious complexity was a mere mask for what Lofton (2006, 39) has referred to as 'spiritual capitalism'. But a cynical reading that reduces West's engagement with Jesus to mere market motives must be held at bay in light of a larger tradition of hip hop artists who have featured themselves on the cross. To this I will return soon.

Ja Rule: Religion and Power

By contrast with the complexities of American Christianities portrayed by West, the ideal entry-point into the religious aesthetic of rap music, wherein Christianity functions as a form of social, cultural and financial capital, is through the career of Jeffrey Atkins, also known as Ja Rule. Raised as a Jehovah Witness, Ja Rule frequently worked religious references throughout his music when he topped the charts at the turn of the twenty-first century. He did this most obviously when he named his triple-platinum-selling second album *Rule 3:36* – a not so subtle signification on Christian scripture. The cover of the CD creatively re-imagined the biblical passage (John 3:36) by substituting Ja Rule in Jesus' place: 'He who believes in Ja shall have everlasting life. He who does not shall not see life, but the wrath of my vengeance … Pain is love'.[22] A song that Ja Rule recorded with Ashanti in 2002, entitled 'Always On Time', best captures the way Christianity has often functioned in rap music. As the song moved towards its end, Rule's passionate plea is simply this: 'Believe me, this pimp game is very religious'.[23] Throughout the song, Rule's lyrics celebrated his professed sexual powers, but its title and chorus signified the familiar black Christian adage, 'He (God) may not come when you want him, but He's *always on time*' (italics mine). The chorus to Rule's version, sung by Ashanti, went as follows: 'I'm not always there when you call, but I'm always on time …' In utilising the term 'religious', Ja Rule seemed intent on convincing his listeners just how seriously he takes the business of dominating women. While the pimp figure has occupied a prominent place in American popular culture, here Ja Rule elevates pimping to an 'ultimate concern'.[24]

Before examining the song's overt misogyny and sexism, it is important to address Ja Rule's general pairing of religion and power, which subtly supports the social privileging of Christianity in hip hop music. Probing his use of the term 'pimp' helps to unveil power dynamics that put Christianity in the place of religious authority even when it is not explicitly invoked. And while there has been abundant evidence of black religious diversity – including Judaism, Islam and African-derived religious traditions – across the terrain of hip hop culture, Christianity comes with the most ready-made capital (Verter 2003). To invoke Christianity, whether or not one expresses an exclusive allegiance to its theological tenets, has been to avail oneself of rhetorical, cultural and financial capital. Additionally, with regards to gender, it is equally important to point out at the same time that Ja Rule employs the black Christian vernacular, it is Ashanti's voice that made possible his very profitable 'cross-over' career. More generally, while male rappers have inscribed, performed and consumed their masculinity via black women's bodies, they have often participated in the presentation of those bodies for public consumption and their own profit. To make this claim does not serve to deprive Ashanti, and the scores of other women in the industry, of agency in hip hop music and culture. Nor does it deny the degree to which such performances of manhood are premised upon the female other (Hill-Collins 2004). Rather, it reveals the way in which Christianity serves as a symbolic resource in support of the very gender and sexual politics that has contributed to hip hop being perceived as irreligious if not profane. Testifying to the power of these norms, Ja Rule's cross-over success quickly faded as he was deemed a 'sell-out' for mainstream acclaim, arguably because he performed one-too-many duets, thus blurring his identity with Ashanti's and crossing the boundaries of hip hop's proscribed gender roles.

'Shesus Khryst': Another Approach

Returning now to the controversy surrounding West's appearance on the cover of *Rolling Stone* with a crown of thorns, as a final example of hip hop's religious ethic and aesthetics, one can turn to the tradition of artists who have imagined themselves in the image of Jesus on the cross. Before West, rappers such as Tupac, Diddy (then Puff Daddy) and Nas all experimented with such iconography.[25] Additionally, this tradition also provides an opportunity to avoid the trap of painting a picture that re-inscribes male privilege by rendering women MCs invisible. Countless women rappers have critiqued and countered the gendered representations proffered by all too many male MCs.[26] The most recent installation in hip hop's stations of the cross introduces the first female rapper, Remy 'Remy Ma' (formerly Remy Martin) Smith, to take up the cross, as well as it provides an image that further complicates the interplay between religion and gender in hip hop.[27] In her short video 'Shesus Khryst', also the title of her most recent album, Remy explains her understanding of the cross in relationship to male rappers who have adopted religious names. She raps:

> If Jay Z's J-Hova, and Nas is God Son
> and I was spitting crack so the people would die, son …
> I'm the BX savior, Shesus Khryst!
> See Pun told them, she's so nice …
> some of the greatest of men the way she would write …[28]

In its earlier incarnations, the image of the crucified rapper was meant to conjure memories of the lynching tree, wherein black men were cast as crucified by the exploitative corporate forces of recording labels. However, in a peculiar synthesis of hip hop's gender politics, Remy usurps masculine power (by citing her endorsement from Big Pun), while her posture on the cross capitalises upon her curvaceous 'feminine' figure. Rapping 'like some of the greatest of men' while draping her body across the cross, she both seduces male listeners and seizes power typically perceived to belong to male rappers. By the song's end, Remy Ma makes her point abundantly clear. For many hip hop artists, male and female, God-talk (Muslim and Christian) has represented a readily available avenue for articulating one's lyrical authority. In short, hip hop's range of religious sensibilities confirms the genre's preoccupation with power, both spiritual and social.

Concluding Thoughts

In this article I have attempted to outline a preliminary history of hip hop's religious dimensions by providing brief encounters with how several of the music's most iconic figures have treated religion in their music. This short litany of artists, from KRS-ONE to Remy Ma, provides fans and scholars alike with a rather rich vision of the multiple ways rappers have engaged (and been shaped by) the American religious landscape. More specifically, in looking for change over time, one is able to discern a pattern in which Christianity gradually supplanted Islam as the most prominent religious tradition in contemporary hip hop music. At the same time, hip hop moved from being understood as an oppositional discourse to the lingua franca of popular culture around the world. Significantly, I have attempted to track this shift by focusing on those figures who have found 'mainstream' success and have received promotion on major radio and television networks. As such, one might argue that this shift in religious sensibilities was abetted by the same corporate entities that kept artists who glamorised violence, unbridled capitalism and no-strings-attached sex on the airwaves. True enough, but to concede this point does not mean one can reduce these spiritual musings to nothing more than rhetorical strategies employed to sign record deals, secure media airtime or improve profit margins. To the contrary, it demonstrates the degree to which rap lyrics are more than simply literary or musical representations, but they reflect (and offer a view of) the historical particularities of American religious culture in time and space. Specifically, this preliminary narrative of hip hop's religious history directs critical attention to the ways in which the market and new technologies mediate religious identities (alongside race and gender) in the twenty-first century.

Hip hop artists, like all human beings, draw on religious language for myriad reasons and to varying degrees of depth. Some of the examples addressed in this essay reveal superficial references (i.e., Jay-Z's use of Five Percenter terminology), others perhaps illumine proof texts used to confirm an artist's modus operandi (i.e., 50 Cent's shout out to Creflo Dollar), and some surely expose religion to be a resource for asserting one's own ambition (i.e., Remy Ma's 'Shesus Khryst'). Yet all of this could also be said of the scores of religious persons who populate everything from Pentecostal revivals to Buddhist pilgrimages. Still, other songs reflect deep, messy and meaningful engagements with religion. For instance, the questions of where KRS-ONE's spiritual evolution will lead him next, and of which version of Jesus Kanye West claims to walk with, are taller tasks than this essay is able to tackle; but they are important inquiries nonetheless. All of these examples affirm that one's ultimate concerns cannot be divorced from the more mundane, and sometimes seemingly sacrilegious, elements of our cultural worlds. More generally, hip hop confirms religion to be always historically contingent (if not wholly reducible to historical context), and the ways that rappers invoke religion bears witness to what's happening on the ground in black communities, in American society, and around the globe. To be sure, hip hop, and popular culture more generally, presents scholars of religion with a veritable treasure trove of materials, and my hope in this essay was to contribute to efforts to more critically map out this terrain. While I have suggested that religious diversity has been the rule of rap music, highlighting the gradual shift from Islam to Christianity reveals the ways in which black popular culture does not exist in a cultural vacuum or outside of history. Additionally, it also accents the fact that both of these traditions – as well as the very categories of religion and popular culture – are implicated in a broader field of power relations.

While hip hop's early roots drew on the oppositional legacies of 'Black Power' from the 1960s, especially through appeals to Malcolm X and variations of Islam, in its move towards the mainstream Christianity became more central. Moreover, more often than not the images of Christianity invoked in hip hop are not those of the civil rights clerics of the 1960s. Rather, it is the twenty-first century televangelist and megachurch preacher who emerges as exemplary, the very same figure who is providing cues to much of the contemporary American religious landscape. Perhaps, as a dose of postmodern irony, at a moment when multiculturalism and religious diversity are being realised, hip hop reveals that Christianity has maintained its centrality in American popular culture. In fact, many rappers prove the persistent appeal of a version of Christianity that posits a particular set of narrow gender and sexuality norms and celebrates the acquisition of cultural capital, social power and financial prosperity as spiritual virtues. As an important afterthought, it is important to note that it is these same qualities that have more often than not led hip hop music to be described as certainly not religious, typically secular, and quite often profane.

Study Questions

1. If early hip hop drew inspiration from the legacies of Black Power in the 1960s and variations of black Islam as represented by figures such as Malcom X, what sources, movements, and figures does rap music use to draw motivation today? How has a shift in sources likewise altered the message?
2. How does Sorett use the work of KRS-One to suggest something of the shift from religious signification to cultural repertories?
3. What depictions and ideas of religion are represented in the work of rappers Kanye West, Ja Rule and Remy Ma according to Sorett's study?

Notes

1. For two works that explore the efforts of scholars of theology and religion to engage the field of cultural studies see Davaney 1996, and Brown et al. 2001.
2. For a sample of writing on the place of Islam in Hip Hop, see Cheney 2001, Floyd-Thomas 2003, Miyakawa 2005 and Knight 2008.
3. MC Hammer. 'Son of the King', *Feel My Power*. Capitol Records, 1987.
4. A Tribe Called Quest. 'Jazz (We've Got)', *The Low End Theory*. Jive, 1991.
5. By now the reader would have realised that I am using the terms 'rap' and 'hip hop' interchangeably, and I will continue to do so throughout this essay. While I recognise the different definitions that continue to circulate regarding the purported differences between rap and hip hop, I am less interested in engaging this normative debate than I am with examining the ways in which religion figures in the music which both of these terms are used to reference. Additionally, that I use these terms interchangeably also reflects that my interests in this essay centre on the lyrics of the song performed by rappers.
6. The term 'post-soul' is generally used to refer to the generation that came of age during the 1970s and 1980s. For a more detail explanation of the term see Neal 2002, and Nelson 2004. Additionally, here I am inverting the argument of Wilfred Cantwell Smith, who argues that all religions (cumulative traditions) share a common theological and ethical core (faith). In contrast, I am suggesting that it is the experience of racial subjectivity (not as an essence but a historical reality) that provides shared core of religious sensibilities that suffuse hip hop music. See Smith 1991.
7. KRS-ONE. Spiritual Minded. Koch, 2002.
8. I gathered this sketch of KRS-ONE's spiritual biography through an interview I conducted with his former personal assistant, Saideh Browne (3 March 2008).
9. KRS-ONE used the term 'edutainment' to argue that hip hop should both educate and entertain. His fourth album with the group BDP took its title from this philosophy. See Boogie Down Productions 1990.
10. Two of the most significant of these works include Wood (1992) and Dyson (1995).
11. Eric B. and Rakim. 'Know the Ledge', *Don't Sweat the Technique* (MCA, 1992).
12. See West 2003; Cassidy, *Leaning on the Lord*; and Elliott 1999.
13. According to Robert Wuthnow, in the years since World War II American religious culture is more defined by the divide between right and left than it is by doctrinal differences and denominational affiliations. KRS-ONE's evolution from Islam to Christianity, and within Christian from Liberal Protestantism to Charismatic circles, seems to reflect the developments that Wuthnow delineates.
14. Creflo Dollar makes a cameo appearance in a music video: Ludacris and Jermaine Dupri. 'Welcome to Atlanta', So So Def, 2002. In a song recorded with G-Unit, 50 Cent raps, 'I preach the sermon 'bout the paper like Creflo Dollar.' See G-Unit. 'Poppin' Them Thangs', *Beg for Mercy*. G-Unit/Interscope, 2003.
15. For a discussion of the prosperity gospel, and its appeal within African American communities, see Harrison 2005.

16. See 'Money Coming' at http://www.youtube.com/watch?v¼dFyMEnXDG4g and 'Make it Rain' at http://www.youtube.com/watch?v¼GerKpRw2nkE. The images in the Dollar's video – of dollar bills flying across the screen – mirror those of Fat Joe and Lil' Wayne. Noticeably absent in the Christian version are half-naked black women's bodies.

17. West 2003. West is among many mainstream hip hop artists who have included religious themes throughout their music. While West clearly works within Christian tradition, many other artists have drawn on variations of Islam (Sunni, Nation of Islam and Five Percent Nation of Gods and Earths) and African-based religious traditions. Also, I use the language of 'mainstream hip hop artists' to distinguish such artists from the sub-genre of gospel hip hop.

18. See Wuthnow 1998a, 1998b.

19. West 2005. See 'Jesus Walks' videos. In Video One (the Church Version), West imagined himself inheriting the mantle of the Civil Rights Movement version of black Christianity, as he rapped while jumping around the pulpit, donning a black suit and thin black tie in the image of Martin Luther King, Jr. In Video Two (the Chris Milk Version) West made connections between the history of white supremacy in America and contemporary race politics, featuring images of chain-gangs of shackled black men, the Ku Klux Klan and burning crosses, and desert border crossings negotiating by white police officers and presumably Latino drug-runners. Meanwhile, dressed in all white slacks and a blazer, West rapped over a backdrop engulfed in flames. Finally, in Video Three (the Street Version), he seemed to poke fun at the Prosperity Gospel, while also performing the personal piety professed in the song's lyrics. Dressed shabbily in dusty jeans and a T-shirt, West is followed around by a stereotypical white Jesus, who puts money in his pockets, food in the refrigerator and provides physical healing for a friend on crutches. Yet this white Jesus is also contrasted with two black Christ figures, each adorned with a crown of thorns: the first an overweight, humorous character with permed hair, who playfully dances on the front lawn with neighbourhood children; the second, a thin and tall man with dreadlocks, who stands on the sidewalk, surrounded by gangsters, and stares with a sober demeanour into the camera. At the end of the video Kanye enters a storefront church, prays quietly in the pews and finally approaches the pulpit, to proclaim his own testimony ('that's the way I need Jesus').

20. Kanye West featuring Mase, 'Jesus Walks: The Remix'. Roc-A-Fella Records, 2004.

21. West and Arabo's jewellery line was temporarily suspended when Arabo was indicted for money laundering. See Nancy Jo Sales. 'Is Hip Hop's Jeweler on the Rocks?' Vanity Fair, November 2006. http://www.vanityfair.com/fame/features/2006/11/jacob200611.

22. Paul B. Raushenbush. 'Double Crossed By Religion: Ja Rule's new album "Rule 3:36" asks a harder question about "What If God Were One of Us?"' on www.beliefnet.com/story/45/story_4551_1.html.

23. Ja Rule, featuring Ashanti. 'Always On Time', *Pain Is Love*. Def Jam Recordings, 2002.

24. Big Daddy Kane, 'Pimpin' Ain't Easy'. *It's a Big Daddy Thing*. Cold Chillin'/Reprise/WarnerBros. Records, 1989.

25. Nas carried the cross in the video to the song 'Hate Me Now' (Columbia, 1999), which he recorded with Puff Daddy. Tupac appeared on a cross on the cover of his final album, *Makaveli* (Death Row/Interscope/MCA, 1996).

26. For one of the first academic discussions of gender and sexuality in hip hop, see Rose (1994).

27. More recent scholarship has complicated the ways in which women rappers engage questions of gender and sexuality in hip hop. See Perry 2004 and Sharpley 2007.

28. Remy Ma. Video Trailer for 'Shesus Khryst'. See http://www.youtube.com/watch?v¼ LcNBP4DpR7c.

References

Boogie Down Productions. 1990. Edutainment. Jive/RCA Records.

Brown, D., S.G. Davaney, and Kathryn Tanner, eds. 2001. *Converging on culture: Theologians in dialogue with cultural analysis and criticism*. New York: Oxford University Press.

Cassidy. Leaning on the Lord, B.A.R.S. The Barry Adrian Reese story. J Records.

Cheney, C. 2001. Representin' God: Rap, religion and the politics of culture. *The North Star: A Journal of African American Religious History* 5, no. 1. http://northstar.vassar.edu/volume3/cheney.html.

Collins, P.H. 2004. *Black sexual politics: African Americans, gender and the new racism*. New York: Routledge.

Davaney, S., ed. 1996. *Changing conversations: Cultural analysis and religious reflection*. New York: Routledge.

Dyson, M. 1995. *Making Malcolm: The myth and meaning of Malcolm X*. New York: Oxford University Press.

Dyson, M. 1998. Ethical leadership in Black America: Malcolm X, urban youth culture, and the resurgence of nationalism. In *The Stones that the builder rejected: The development of ethical leadership from the black church tradition*, ed. Walter E. Fluker. Harrisburg, PA: Trinity Press International.

Elliott, M. 1999. 'Religious Blessings', *Da Real World*. Goldmind/Elektra.

Floyd-Thomas, J. 2003. A Jihad of words: The evolution of African American Islam and contemporary hip hop. In *Noise and spirit: The religious and spiritual sensibilities of rap music*, ed. Anthony B. Pinn. New York: New York University Press.

Gilroy, P. 1993. *The black Atlantic: Modernity and double-consciousness*. Cambridge, MA: Harvard University Press.

Hall, S. 1992. What is this 'black' in black popular culture? In *Black popular culture: A project by Michele Wallace*, ed. Gina Dent, 21–33. Seattle, WA: Bay Press.

Harrison, M. 2005. *Righteous riches: The word of faith movement in contemporary African American religion*. New York: Oxford University Press.

Knight, M.M. 2008. Holy intellect: The story and impact of the five percent nation. *Vibe*: 88–93.

Lofton, K. 2006. Practicing Oprah; Or, the prescriptive compulsion of a spiritual capitalism. *The Journal of Popular Culture* 39, no. 4: 599–621.

Miyakawa, F.M. 2005. *Five percenter rap: God hop's music, message and black Muslim mission*. Bloomington, IN: Indiana University Press.

Neal, M. 2002. *Soul babies: Black popular culture and the post-soul aesthetic*. New York: Routledge.

Nelson, G. 2004. *Post-soul nation: The explosive, contradictory, triumphant, and tragic 1980s as experienced by African Americans* (previously known as blacks and before that Negroes). New York: Viking Books.

Perry, I. 2004. *Prophets of the hood: Politics and poetics in hip hop*. Durham, NC: Duke University Press.

Rose, T. 1994. *Black noise: Rap music and black culture in contemporary America*. Middletown, CT: Wesleyan University Press.

Sharpley, W.T. 2007. *Pimps up, ho's down: Hip hop's hold on young black women*. New York: New York University Press.

Smith, W.C. 1991. *The meaning and end of religion*. Minneapolis, MN: Fortress Press.

Verter, B. 2003. Spiritual capital: Theorizing religion with Bourdieu against Bourdieu. *Sociological Theory* 21, no. 2: 150–74.

West, K. 2003. 'Jesus walks', *The College Dropout*. Roc-a-Fella Records.

——. 2005. *The College Dropout* video anthology. Roc-A-Fella Records.

Wood, J., ed. 1992. *Malcolm X: In our own image*. New York: St Martin's Press.

Wuthnow, R. 1998a. *After heaven: Spirituality in America since the 1950s*. Berkeley, CA: University of California Press.

——. 1998b. *The restructuring of American religion: Society and faith since World War II*. Princeton, NJ: Princeton University Press.

18

Put Down the Pimp Stick to Pick Up the Pulpit
The Impact of Hip Hop on the Black Church

Kirk-Duggan forges a conversation between the black church and the hip hop generation, suggesting that, when it comes to hip hop, the black church need not be "… a pimp or pusher of punishment." With a concern for "reaching" the youth of the hip hop generation, Kirk-Duggan explores the effects of hip hop on the black church as well as the church's conflicted response to and silence around pressing social issues faced by marginalized youth. Kirk-Duggan explores ways Christian ministries from a black church perspective might be more hospitable to and understanding of hip hop culture. By reminding gospel music of its "secular" and paradoxical inheritance of the blues, she forcefully suggests a blurring between the "awkward" and the "awesome" as proxies for the sacred and the profane. Moreover, Kirk-Duggan encourages a rethinking of the church's mission from a framework of resistance, adding that the space of the church should not be shielded from that which is seen as dirty and deviant but rather, should be a space of flourishing, possibility and opportunity. Likening "good" missionaries to "good anthropologists," Kirk-Duggan concludes that churches ought to be open to using hip hop culture to advance contemporary missions, practices, and activities of the meaning and doing of the black church today.

Put Down the Pimp Stick to Pick Up the Pulpit*

Cheryl Kirk-Duggan and Marlon F. Hall

Communication, attitude, and relationships affect everything we do. These three elements affect our experience of God, our lives, and ourselves. Communication pertains to how we make contact, interact, and how we grasp the message or stories. Attitude concerns our approach, outlook, feelings, opinions, and ways of thinking. Relationships pertain to associations and dealings with God, self, and others. When done with honesty, integrity, love, and mutual respect, relationships can be powerful; we can communicate out of empathy toward understanding, with openness and hope.

But too often abuse arises in our relationships, particularly in our homes. Statistics show that one in four people are victims of domestic violence. That means if a congregation or organization has one hundred members, twenty-five of them have experienced abuse. Abusers may use belts, switches, sticks. Some pinch. Some abuse because their parents did the same. Some well-meaning parents spank and punish their children out of love and out of their understanding of scripture, particularly Proverbs 13:24: "Those who spare the rod hate their children, / but those who love them are diligent to discipline them."

Sparing the rod and spoiling the child is not about punishment. The rod was not a kind of "board of education"; rather, in the Bible, the rod is the staff a shepherd used to bring the sheep to him. Sheep are dumb animals that will drown if left in a watering hole. First, we need to understand the use and meaning of a rod, then we can move to the second part where the proverb tells us to spend time with our children, to hold them close. The latest toys and gadgets, no matter how expensive, can never take the place of time with loved ones and having ongoing support by a "village" of people, like the church. But we have become nomadic people, in that many of us do not live in the communities in which we were born. So now, it is even more important for the church to reach out to the young people in its congregation and in communities surrounding the church.

In order to reach the Hip Hop generation, the church needs to put down all sticks and not be a pimp or pusher of punishment. Rather the church needs to fill itself with love for our youth; a love with acceptance, not condemnation; a gift of compassion, not a font of fear. "Put down the pimp stick to pick up the pulpit" is the church's invitation to be relevant.[1] Here I explore the dynamics and effects of Hip Hop on the black church. After examining the Church's response (or nonresponse) to youth reality, youth ministries, and prophetic understandings, the chapter reflects on power and intricacies of liturgy, music, and evangelism and explores the implications of paradoxes, challenges, and problems. This essay also addresses wrestling with tensions when doing ministry in dialogue with Hip Hop culture and concludes by deconstructing the dynamics of judgment and pondering Paul's use of syncretism.

What effect does Hip Hop have on the church? Hip Hop makes the church face its commission to reach the unreached and connect with the disconnected. In a changing world, the church is learning that it must deal with Hip Hop in a way that allows the church to discover a new sense of what the Great Commission of Jesus (Matt. 28:19–20) is for itself, in the service of others. Hip Hop challenges the church to look risque when reaching out to such people as former pimps, the way that Jesus and the apostle Paul reached out to sinners two thousand years ago.

Don "Magic" Juan (born Donald Campbell) is known in Hip Hop as a mentor and elder who is celebrated for his sensitivity and trusted leadership among Hip Hop artists and celebrities alike. Juan met West Coast rapper Snoop Dogg backstage at one of his concerts, and Snoop adopted him as an uncle and spiritual advisor. Campbell was formerly a pimp in Chicago and was known for his decadent lifestyle and charismatic flair. In 1985, he had what he calls "a moment of clarity" inspired by God during which he received a vision from the "Most High" that led him to retire from the "pimpin' game" and plant a church and a community assistance program in Chicago. He literally "put down the pimp stick to pick up the pulpit." His approach to the movement of Jesus is interesting because he uses resources as risque as Christian pornography for married couples and the International Players Ball featuring women in bathing suits competing for the title of "The Best of the Best."[2]

Many leaders in the Christian community have challenged Juan's methods and theology since he appointed himself Archbishop Don "Magic" Juan, but what is unchallenged is his paternal leadership in a community of mostly young men who grew up in homes without fathers and very few positive male influences. The greatest travesty is not who Don Juan is, but what the church is not in the lives of impressionable young people seeking fathers, reconciliation with God, and leadership. The travesty is that the church is not an impressive source of innovation, inspiration, and interest. Although the church has access to the most relevant and creative resource known to humanity, the Holy Spirit it nevertheless refuses to allow the Spirit to lead us in a sensitivity training that equips us to reach innovatively those who are reaching a nation through their music.

The church's unwillingness to risk being seen with and connecting with a wayward generation is the real travesty, not a former pimp's risque approach to evangelism. Juan is immersed in Hip Hop culture and has found a way to intrigue, inspire, and innovate where most people are traditionally irritated, insulted, and repulsed. Though he dresses like a person who quantum-leaped out of the 1970s and into the present, he turns irresponsibility into innovation through his affirmation to a community that many others have rejected. To tum irresponsibility into innovation means to use what frustrates you about the world as a cue to do something about it. This concept is a response to Mahatma Gandhi's words when he challenged the world to "be the change you want to see." Don Juan may be a bad model for discipleship and a nuisance to the church, but he is also a motivation for the church, which must get past its fears to reach younger generations. Juan may irresponsibly represent the gospel of Jesus, but he also has the ears of thousands of young people the church is unable to reach for lack of sensitivity.

Sensitivity (or Not) to Youth Reality

The Awkward and the Awesome

The church's call is to be in mission for Jesus. It is called to put its finger on the pulse of the world and sensitively listen for God's heartbeat. The Matthew 28:19 commission to go into the world and make disciples of all nations is directive. This commission is bold enough to touch, sensitive enough to feel, and quiet enough to hear the heart of God pulsating underneath our world's pain.

Georgia Tom and Christ

"Unintelligible" wiles of young folk unnerve traditional communities. The differences between the generations often leave a bad taste in the mouths of the young and old. For example, gospel music is the standard for modern and traditional music in the black church today, but it was once rejected as music that lacked taste. Gospel music was considered a nuisance to the traditional worship services led with tasteful and holy hymns. But today, gospel songs are known as the hallowed standards from heaven that bless worship experiences, despite the fact they were once known as bar tunes that came from the bowels of society.

Thomas Dorsey, a young blues musician, introduced gospel music to the church. Dorsey used blues arrangements to chart a new course for spiritual music. Before being known as Thomas Dorsey, the founder of gospel, he was "Georgia Tom," the blues artist. When he first played his neohymns set to the rhythm of blues music, he was deemed a demon of sound; but today he is known as a deliverer of souls. A musical genre once known as morally awkward for the church is now considered awesome. Likewise, there are youth in our midst who may appear to be awkward demons, who will eventually become deliverers when given the right support and sensitivity.

To be sensitive to the reality of youth, we must be willing to embrace what is awkward at first and to provide a safe environment for it to become awesome and even anointed. We must help them know what is appropriate and affirm their lived experience. We must help them think critically about what they do, sing, and engage in when exploring their creativity. Hip Hop is like a teenager learning to navigate his or her way around. It is like a clumsy teen learning to redefine space and distance with growing limbs. The differences between development of the mind and the body make some youth clumsy. Misjudging steps and boundaries are part of their natural development. In response, adults can provide a safe and consistent environment of encouragement where youth can grow more sure and confident in themselves and in their faith. This is the work of the church with respect to Hip Hop. The language, ideology, and trends of the Hip Hop movement may seem socially, politically, and spiritually clumsy to an onlooking establishment such as the church, but the church must be sensitive to this developing movement, for this is the future.

Jesus did not put down a pimp stick to minister to others, but he did leave his lofty place in heaven to deal sensitively with human folk who were clumsy, irritating, insulting, and totally irresponsible with the life and purpose that God had given them. Creating a nurturing space for youth to become awesome means following the way of Jesus. Here is John 3:16 rearticulated, "The ancient God so loved an immature and irritating humanity that God sent this phenomenal son to create a space for the clumsy to find clarity." That was Jesus' "missio," his mission, and it is ours. God sends us to those around us to touch, feel, and listen for the pulse and possibility of life everlasting.

Resistance from the Establishment, Grandma's Couch, and Mission

The church is an ancient and beautiful establishment: the bride of a regal and dynamic groom (Jesus) who wants to save the world. But Jesus wants an outdoorsy kind of bride, not one who is staid or artificial. We often misunderstand the kind of beauty that the bride is. We treat her (the church) like grandmother's plastic-wrapped white (now kind of pearl) couch that no one can sit on. As a teenager, you dare not even set foot in the room where the couch is, let alone attempt to sit on those plastic seat cushions. The church is not that kind of beauty. The church is that rugged kind of beauty who can take the dirt, grime, accidents, and mistakes of a young person and wipe them clean.

The church should create a space in which those who are in between awkward and awesome can experiment with the love and grace of God. The beauty of the church is not to be protected from the socially, politically, and even spiritually clumsy, because it can handle any stain or smudge or damage. God designed the church to be a place where the people have opportunities to choose and make mistakes. Allowing and forgiving mistakes are parts of making disciples for Jesus.

We do not have the right to use our personal irritations as motivation to promote a plastic-covered faith. As missionaries, God calls us to respond to who and what irritates us with the love and grace of a grit-proof God. A missionary is one who knows that he or she is uniquely responsible to influence what irritates them about a culture in which they live. At the core, a missionary is an anthropologist and an archeologist. Like an anthropologist, the missionary becomes a participant observer of the culture he or she wants to connect with in order to learn the practices, language, and music of that culture. Missionaries are also like archeologists in that they excavate what is ancient and precious when it is buried beneath the dirt of the present. They do not bring God to people; missionaries, like archeologists, discover and excavate God wherever God can be found because God is already there through prevenient grace.

Acts 17 tells the story of how Paul was left alone in the city of Athens. Athens was a cultured, educated city that had a rich political tradition. It was an intellectual mecca, where innovative thought and expansive philosophy found expression, much like Kemet or ancient Egypt. Similarly, Hip Hop is a foreign culture few missionaries dare to explore for redemptive potential. The daring missionaries who do explore Hip Hop are usually demonized for their interest; the music is teeming with divine potential and possibilities masked in heretical and irreverent trends that seem countersacred.

Sunlight and Insecurity

Missiology is practical theology that processes the mandate, message, and work of Christian mission. This process must not exclude anthropology for fear of rejection. The truth may be that Hip Hop practitioners are not as countersacred as the church is "plain old scared." Approaching what is different with an already different message can be scary, but putting our personal feelings before the prophetic power of the message that sets us free from our insecurities is harmful. Like a person standing in the sunlight, we stand in the way of Jesus (the Son of God), and the shadows of our insecurities get projected onto the folks we deem irreverent and disreputable. We must get our insecurities and fears out of the way of Jesus' light and let his light shine on the secular while we gaze in awe at the human beauty and divine possibility his light reveals. Our irritation is an indication that we are in the way of the light.

Paul was more called than scared. He not only explored the missiological commission to share the good news of Jesus but also knew how to reach God in the persons to whom he evangelized. Jesus was the Divine wrapped in the flesh. He was flesh and divine on the outside and on the inside. He was a complete package of divinity and humanity. This is true of those whom the church seeks to reach as well; they live completely human and divine, but we allow what is human and flawed to impair our sight of what is divine. The flesh we inhabit externally and the soul, or spirit, on the inside are both divinely made. Sometimes our negative views of the external and our ungodly behavior keep us from seeing God's glory inside and out.

Strawberry Blow Pop Dropped in the Dirt

Strawberry Charms Blow Pops are my favorite childhood candy. Blow Pops are lollipops with bubble gum centers surrounded by a hard candy shell. I love the fact that what you see is not all you get. Eating a strawberry Blow Pop is not about what the lollipop is as much as it is about what the sweet treat is becoming. The Blow Pop becomes chewing gum with a sweet and sour crunch! Once opened, a one-dimensional lollipop becomes a multisensory explosion of fun with a bubble-gum center you can blow with your mouth until the pop is heard with your ears and a strawberry scent can be smelled with your nose.

Question: What happens to a strawberry Blow Pop when it is dropped in the dirt while no one is looking? Answer: It is eaten! One sensitively and patiently takes it to the nearest source of water to wash it off. What a travesty of all things sweet and savory, if one has to destroy it just because of a mishap. One can look past an irritating dirty patch to discover an intriguing way to redeem the pop. The focus is not about what the strawberry delight is when it is dirty; the focus is on all that it can become when it is clean. Seeing the possibility of a taste, sound, and smell beyond the dirt is akin to the goal of an anthropologist. The anthropologist must become more intrigued with what a culture is becoming for her or him and the world than be personally irritated by what the culture appears to be now. She or he must see an opportunity to bring a larger truth to the world through what is uniquely human and special about the taste, sound, and sight of a people.

Good missionaries are also good cultural anthropologists. They become participant-observers of the people they want to serve and share Jesus with. As anthropologists, missionaries stand with the people to observe what is meaningful about their culture. They look for trends that communicate deeper human trends that they are exploring. In essence, anthropologists look for what human trends they can identify.

What do the trends in music, dress, and language say about the humanity of a people? While in Decin, Czech Republic, a small city outside of Prague, I (Marlon) did an anthropological study on a segregated ethnic group in central Europe known popularly as "the Gypsies." Some believe they are an immigrant ethnic group living mostly in Europe, who trace their origins to medieval India. Others believe they are Balkans who originated in Egypt and, in one narrative, were exiled as punishment for allegedly harboring the infant Jesus. When I asked one of the so-called Gypsies he said, "We are from where we are, so deal with it." His coarse response communicated the general disposition of this fringe people who are treated like black folk in a 1950s United States: segregated, discredited, and identified as criminal derelicts. Popular society tells them their best contributions to a society are their low-paying vocations that require minimum intellect and discipline. Dominant society calls them the dregs of the community, and they are, not surprisingly, angry because of it.

They openly accepted me as a brother because they believed I was a disenfranchised African American survivor of a journey they were still moving through—from oppression to opportunity. Because I was young and a black male, I soon became known as the Hip Hop ambassador from a liberated people in America. My interpreter, Marco, however, was the whitest Czech in the whole town, which made it hard for him to move fluidly with me through the ghettos of what was called Gypsy Town. Some of the places in Gypsy Town where my new friends hung out were threatening for Marco, so we did as much interviewing and observing in the day-time as possible. I had to spend thirty minutes communicating that he was "cool" before every single interview.

Marco insisted every day that the Gypsies were "bad ... very bad people," and from their trends and surface behavior, you might have said the same. The young men and women were excessive cursers, drinkers, and tobacco and marijuana smokers who listened to Tupac non-stop. This was annoying mostly because they acted like *All Eyes on Me* was Tupac's only album. Most of them could not speak much English, but they knew the English in that album from start to finish. They played it all day while I was around, and it kind of insulted me because they assumed I liked Tupac because I was young, black, and from the United States. The fact that I did like that album did not matter. They did not know that, and I was subtly offended; but what should have completely turned me off intrigued me instead.

By moving through my irritation, I discovered intrigue, brothers, and friendship. Their weed-smoking was a self-medicating behavior used to mask the true rejection that was their way of life. Their cursing was a reflection of the true curse they felt in their hearts as a disenfranchised people. All the Tupac music was a way to connect with the deep longing for freedom, and the hunger for meaning they sensed in Shakur's voice was deeper than language. I was given an audience of the biggest dope-dealing pimp of the region. He had heard about me and wanted to meet me. This made me scared and excited. He wanted to meet at an after-hours club that he owned that opened at 2 A.M. Marco and I walked through the doors of the club and saw a few friends who escorted me to my host's table. As I walked toward the table, my heart began to beat so fast, I could hear it. Looking in the direction of the table, all I saw were strobe lights reflecting erratic beams of light through the thick, blue smoke. The smoke cleared as I approached the table, and I was able to see my heavyset host who had a woman underneath each arm and who wore a button-down shirt exposing chest hairs and several gold chains.

He removed his arm from the neck of one of the women and extended his hand toward me. When I looked in his hand, I saw the biggest bag of marijuana I had ever seen. This irritated my religious sense because I am a former drug abuser, and my deliverance is a daily walk. That night made it a hard walk. I sat down, and he motioned to one of the women to sit next to me. She smiled, as did I, but I was embarrassed, wondering what in the world my pastor would say if he saw me sitting next to a known prostitute in a club. I wore an uncomfortable grin that may have looked like a satisfied smile depending on where one was sitting in the club. After all, men have gone to war for mistaking uncomfortable grins for satisfied smiles.

After politely letting him know that I was not interested in the drugs or the women, he asked why I was in Europe. I asked Marco to let him know that I had traveled thousands of miles around the world to learn more about the Gypsy culture. He asked why I would do a thing like that, considering the Gypsy culture is not that important. I told him that I stand with the Creator of the world, and through God's eyes, there is beauty and power in what some see as "meaningless." He then asked who this creator was, and I almost jumped out of my seat. A bigwig in the culture I had come to love was asking me about Jesus!

I leaned forward, stared him in the eye, and responded to his question by saying, "Jesus, the Son of God who sees beauty in what others call ugly, calls us all to live a life of purpose." Then this scary-looking man asked me a precious and timeless question, "Can you introduce him to me, and may I live for him?"

That drug-dealing pimp accepted Jesus that night and asked for a round of drink from the bar afterward to celebrate. We talked about what the "new life" looked like until the sun came up. By my digging beneath the surface of the dirt around a drug dealer who insulted my religious sensibilities, together we discovered God anew. By pushing through my irritation, I learned to love a rowdy bunch of the most innovative, fun-loving, funny, and sincere people I have ever met. They were a mess, but the Messiah was at work in that mess; and as a missionary anthropologist, I had to change my perspective and join forces with people to help them see what I sensed: the Divine at work.

The irritation that turned into intrigue led to my discovering God in new ways. We must be daring enough to go where others dare not go and be present for the lost who others dare not be around; we must be missionaries who turn insult into inspiration.

Liturgy, Music, and Evangelism

Hip Hop in Worship

On a recent humid summer evening, I (Cheryl) participated in a Hip Hop worship event unfolded to a packed intergenerational house. The MC, or presiding liturgist, for the event, Rev. Phil Brickle—who operates a homeless ministry and feeding program in Raleigh, North Carolina—set the context for our time together: we had come to praise and worship. As Brickle announced the performing groups for the evening's program, he used the language of offering. All were clear that this was not entertainment or performance but worship. Throughout the evening, the worshipful expressions by youth from early teens to early twenties were powerful outpourings of praise as they offered their gifts to the Lord. A variety of performers praised God with honesty, integrity, and exuberance. The youth ministries included spoken word, Hip Hop, liturgical dance, and step.

The themes of the music, spoken word, and lyrics that accompanied the liturgical dance were words of encouragement *and* critique. The songs told people's life stories and how success often requires sacrifice, and they offered critique of a dead gospel and personal connection with scripture, saying that one knows the world is full of crime and evil, yet one can still identify with Peter walking on the water and Jonah being swallowed by the big fish.

One performer, doing a gospel rap sermon, shared his experience of the Christian walk, and he admonished listeners to read the Word, focus on exposing hypocrisy, and remember that God is not pleased when we misbehave. Other songs focused on family issues, living with disabilities, the importance of keeping it real, and understanding the reality that if persons cannot find heaven on earth, it is hard for them to maintain hope. He went on to say that despite this reality, one must try not to be pessimistic, recognizing that life is complex and offers many important opportunities for forgiveness. Other offerings focused on the need to be kind even when this experience is not reciprocated, over a background beat, while inviting the audience to create additional rhythm by chanting, "Jesus, Jesus, Jesus." A sister and brother team noted that their vocation is to compel young people to live for Christ. They signified about the presence of the devil as intruder. The step team used a type of dancing that involved clapping, stomping, and using their hands to slap their bodies to make a beat. Sometimes the highly coordinated movements involved one stepper connecting with another by slapping each other's hands in precision movement. An intergenerational vocal quartet sang a few contemporary gospel/praise songs. The last group to perform prior to the featured artists was an ensemble of teens who signed the words of the music and used gentle liturgical dance movements. Their dance signified faith and inspiration.

All of the Hip Hop music and spoken word had an accompanying sound track. Some of the sounds were more lyrical, while others were mostly percussive beat. The culminating act was an inspirational Hip Hop quartet, Leviticus. This group comes out of the Young Missionary Temple Christian Methodist Church in Raleigh, North Carolina. The members of this group have grown up together in Sunday school, church choir, the youth mentoring program, and usher board.

In just seven years, the members of Leviticus (Timothy Caldwell, Jared Caldwell, Joseph Ragland, and Ashton Howard) have grown in wisdom and faith. They began working together in 2003; and in addition to offering praise at the church I (Cheryl) minister, they have made numerous regional appearances. They made their Apollo Theater debut in August 2010 on Amateur Night.[3] Their performance was dynamic, with great energy, high praise, and a passion for worship. Their articulation was sharp, and their dance movements had the audience up on their feet. Leviticus took the house down with their Hip Hop version of "Now I Lay Me Down to Sleep." Just as youth are participants in Hip Hop ministries, there are adults working with them and offering guidance. In Leviticus's case, their mentor is Reginald Caldwell, father of two singers and father-mentor to countless young people.

In Austin, Texas, a man who grew up with Hip Hop uses this music in teen ministries. Reverend Kevin White, pastor for youth ministries at Greater Mount Zion Baptist Church, finds Hip Hop music a powerful tool when used appropriately and with balance. Reading material related to Hip Hop, knowing the culture, and hanging out with youth, he brought Hip Hop music to Greater Mount Zion. His interest in Hip Hop emerged as he was growing up when it was coming on the scene from the East Coast. He knows the power of music. So when Hip Hop came around, it emerged as a voice for the voiceless; it tells stories on the street. He knows how Hip Hop allows people to bond and "kick it" with one another. This is how culture operates. We can use the same kind of feel and put the gospel into it.

Hip Hop, as a tool for ministry, is another vehicle to communicate the gospel, the Word of God. In fact, some rappers who are really walking with Jesus and studying the Word are now going to seminary. When they come out, they will be modem-day street preachers, communicating in everyday language. People connect with the beat and the gospel. This music and culture can be used together instead of them pushing each other away.

Reverend White posits that kids are listening to Hip Hop and that we may as well use it and change the message. The music has beats kids recognize, but the message is changed.White noted that to him, as Tommy Kyllonen says, Hip Hop is like the new Roman road. When the apostles set out to communicate the gospel, the Roman Empire already had established a vast network of roads; this allowed the gospel to flow. Culture is at a point at which Hip Hop crosses gender, race, and geographical areas; it is another road on which the good news of Jesus can be proclaimed.[4] Using liturgy and music to engage and educate provides an opportunity for evangelism. Before reviewing the use of Hip Hop as a tool of evangelism, first we turn to the function of music.

Music, Sounds, and Spirituality

Music provides the appropriate mystery and silence to human language, gestures, and sounds required by prayers offered to God. Music—made of sounds and silence by nature, the human voice, and instruments—exudes "vitality and ... doxology. This natural language of praise is found in the fusion of ordered sound, ruled kinetic participation, and a communal sense of shared narrative. ... The body remembers shared music making long after the mind may be dimmed."[5]

Music has the tremendous capacity to instruct and communicate memory with influential connections. The experience of music has a deep relationship with our spiritual selves, our temperaments, wants, and desires. Music helps us tell our human, experiential stories, as we deal with symbols through time. It is also a means to elicit bodily, sensory memory. All of our senses, as well as our entire body, can be engaged when making music. When we worship and sing praise songs, sorrow songs, words of thanksgiving, and intercession to God, that experience of singing can confer special esteem and dignity upon our own human needs and desires. The experience of music engages our senses, particularly as we experience spiritual, divine presence. The role of the spirit allows our experience to transcend what we hear with melody and lyrics. As we embrace the experience of making music, the movement of sound connects with beliefs, attitudes, and sustained ways of seeing the world, because music expresses what cannot be stated verbally. Making music is phenomenal and dynamic: it is a practice, a living practice that involves our physical reality and the world in which we live; its powers resonate within our bodies; and music's deep connection with us moves our soul.[6]

Music, Worship, and Empowerment

From Genesis to Revelation, scripture requires us to worship, to make a joyful noise unto the Lord, but we see this especially in the psalms. Psalm 150 commands that everything that has breath praise the Lord. The psalm tells us where, when, and how to praise God, and it closes with specific instrumentation regarding corporate praise and worship: with trumpet sound; lute and harp; tambourine and dance; strings and pipe; and loud, clanging cymbals.

The New Testament is also full of worship references. In Luke 1 Mary's Magnificat reflects personal worship, as she petitions the Lord for God's divine favor. In the passion narratives of all four Gospels, Jesus commands the disciples to remember him. While he did not tell them (or us) to remember his death per se, he admonished them to remember him for who he is, for all that he has done, and his edict to them: to heal the sick, raise the dead, and preach good news to the captives. Worship as praise involves music to honor and adore God, as Trinity: Creator, Son, and Holy Spirit.

Over the years, the church has developed a means to celebrate and worship throughout the year using a liturgical calendar. The liturgical calendar begins with Advent, during which time we prepare for Christmas, for the birth of the Christ Child, and prepare to receive Jesus as he comes again, the *parousia,* symbolized by the color violet (or sometimes now, blue). The third Sunday in Advent, termed *Gaudete* Sunday (rose color) signals to us to rejoice in the Lord always. Christmastide, symbolized by the color white (Joy and purity), is the celebration of the Word made flesh, the birth of the incarnated Jesus, who emptied himself to come into the world (Phil. 2:6). Lent, a time of penance, begins with Ash Wednesday and lasts for forty weekdays, in recognition of the forty days and nights that Christ fasted in the desert while being tempted by Satan. (When counting the forty days, skip all Sundays.) Lent ends with Holy Week, which begins with Palm Sunday. The week also includes Holy Thursday, Good Friday, and Holy Saturday, and it ends with Easter Sunday. The color of Lent is violet, and the color for Easter is white. Fifty days following Easter is Pentecost, symbolized by the color red, which celebrates the outpouring of the Holy Spirit (Acts 2). After Pentecost is ordinary time, also known as Kingdomtide. This season pertains to God's rule over us. The color is green.

Although many Protestant churches are not liturgical churches, an awareness of the different senses of time in the Christian life can help give us a better sense of spiritual seasons. Having an awareness of spiritual seasons offers a different focus on the type of music that we use, as well as offering a variety of scriptures for proclamation. Worship is a dynamic event during which we honor and adore God as a corporate community.

Music is essential for such a powerful celebration and witness. Music is part of an energetic, moving witness in the church, particularly in worship. Following the New Testament church, African American liturgical traditions center on how we live the life that God calls us to embrace, how we desire and prayerfully engage in ultimate intimacy with God, recognizing the importance of personal and corporate worship, confessing wrongdoing, receiving forgiveness or pardon, and experiencing transforming renewal. In gathering together for the worship event, we can experience empowerment. Melva Costen, specialist in liturgy and music, reminds us that when gathered in such empowerment events, we remember the importance of us going out into the world to serve and love, even if the world and people in the world are hostile and abusive.

Songs, sermons, and prayer provide opportunities for empowerment and engagement that can be life changing. Singing communicates our faith experience. The preaching event is a celebratory affirmation, during which the preacher has the authority to proclaim the good news in a way that both listener and preacher can experience the Word. The preacher challenges the congregation to embody the testimony in a holy manner toward transcendent transformation, nurturing the total individual and communal self.

The congregation utters prayers of gratitude, thanksgiving, and joy because God affords us the freedom to do so. God saves us so that the church can worship and be Jesus in the world. In worship, the church comes forth regardless of life circumstances and even amid systemic, heinous oppression. Such salvific freedom to respond, framed by creativity, spontaneity, openness, and vulnerability to *diakonia*, service, and proclamation, undergirds all forms of African American worship.[7] Such salvific freedom gives opportunities for improvisation, creativity, and joy in trying new things and exercising God's gifts to celebrate and honor God. This is also the desire of the Hip Hop generation, as they praise God in dance, spoken word, and song.

Such gifts, graces, and offerings are tools for the service of God. Serving God includes participating in evangelism, making disciples of all generations, including children of the Hip Hop culture who are outside of the church. Ralph C. Watkins reminds us that the call to evangelize will yield intergenerational churches. We need churches with all age groups to give us balance. Diversity is not to be feared but to be embraced. For the same folk who are in the world are also in the church. To evangelize those steeped in Hip Hop culture, we must be mindful of their need to self-express and to have meaningful dialogue. The church needs to engage them well rather than just preach at them.

Preachers must be creative, be able to tell stories and create word pictures, and be versatile and socially relevant; sermon delivery must have flow—cadence and syncopation. Pastors must discover their own unique voice, have a vocal presence, and use story, metaphor, or simile when talking about the text. Hip Hop participants want to be free, to know what Jesus has to offer, to be allowed to come to Jesus in their own way, and to be able to ask questions, where the church community is loving but firm, real and relational. With evangelism, we are to meet people where they are, let culture be our friend, not our enemy. As we build community within the church, we will find that we all need our Hip Hop sisters and brothers, just as we need our infants and retirees. God calls us to help the Hip Hop generation release emptiness and stuff and embrace love. God calls us to go out into the highways and the byways to praise God.

Paradoxes, Challenges, Problems, Opportunities

The gift of life is blessing. Some days the blessedness seems to be dwarfed because of the stuff of life, the challenges, problems, and paradoxes that unfold at home, at work, in the community, or at the church. There are many things we do not understand. Sometimes we misread a situation and fail to grasp fully what is transpiring. Much of the African diasporan history of abuse and oppression colors who we are today, how we process information, what we value, and how we contribute in the world. Perhaps paradoxically, the music and culture of Hip Hop is more about a mindset than a particular locale.

Traditional African philosophy did not envision a separation of secular and sacred, for all is part of the sacred. But in today's world, the separation is very apparent, even in the church. So while the church becomes more secular, the church must, like Jesus, speak the language that modern people can understand. In worship, the congregation reflects on God's acts of grace and mercy, as God responds to sociocultural, theological, and political concerns. Then the congregation responds in word, act, and song.[8] But just as many black congregations rejected gospel music early on, we find ourselves again at a crossroads where some churches embrace Hip Hop and others are adamant that there is nothing redemptive about Hip Hop culture, including its music.

Kevin White says that if it is allowed, Hip Hop can have an effect. His congregation, for which he serves as a youth minister, welcomes rappers and even changes in the music beat. The challenge with many black churches is that they are not ready to embrace Hip Hop, because it is viewed in such a negative light in the secular arena. White says that when his congregation first started worship services with students, they used Hip Hop heavily. But he soon recognized that there is a generational gap even in Hip Hop; there is old-school and new-school Hip Hop. Themes—messsages they communicate are totally different.

For some parents, including Hip Hop in worship means perpetuating something that they disapprove of because they do not understand that the church is trying to communicate a different message to youth. Parents really have to understand the context and culture of town (society), gown (academy), and church and then seek a balance. In the church or in the world; on Wall Street (big business), or Main Street (everyday folk), if we cannot talk in the same language, we cannot communicate. If we cannot communicate, we will lose our integrity, our values, and our souls. There has never been a time in these United States when we have not had drugs, guns, and gang warfare. Just as a rose by any other name is still a rose, whether we call it heroin, Mrs. Pinkham's Laudanum, crack cocaine, or ju-ju dust, drugs are drugs. All individuals have the potential to become thugs, whether we dub them Mafia, gangsters, militia, or a crew given an intent to do harm. The challenge of working with youth doing Hip Hop is getting out of our comfort zones and remembering the church's reason for being-to bring Jesus' salvation to the world. With prayerful communication, open doors, and open hearts, the church can learn to let go and let God.

In White's church, they use Hip Hop videos, or they may use a DJ during praise and worship. Even the preacher's message is delivered differently. Messages or sermons are shorter, with a lot of interaction and, for example, group discussion. This Hip Hop generation likes to talk, so everyone has an opportunity to use the mike. Back in the day, only the preacher had a mike; now you have to understand and incorporate students. After the sermon, students are given a chance to dialogue and to act out what they heard through rap, skit, song, and poetry. But many black churches are still hesitant to use Christian Hip Hop, which is about Jesus and getting connected to Jesus, the one who can help those who are oppressed in the community.[9]

Hip Hop Meets a Need

Hip Hop is good for reaching the younger crowd, although it is not fully embraced because of the negative stereotypes surrounding this genre. Although the church needs to use this music, it must be used with wisdom. A challenge is not letting Hip Hop become just another gimmick. Kevin White notes that if the church tries to use Hip Hop as a gimmick, then people will always look for the next trick, just like in the music industry. Understanding that it is a culture, the church needs to engage by letting people be and share themselves in a loving way.[10]

This is the import of speaking the language of the youthful souls of black folk in the twenty-first century. Everyone in the church needs God, not only the adults. In addition to youth, young adults and even forty-somethings can relate to Hip Hop. One of the challenges that the church faces is that many in the twenty-to-forty age group are unchurched. If the church wants to create disciples as Jesus taught, then the church needs to be able to communicate to people wherever they are. People do not always mature at the same rate, nor do they tend to change their style in music to appease someone else. Tommy Kyllonen, like the apostle Paul, reminds us that the church must meet the needs of others. In meeting these needs, it is also important that the Great Commission is central to daily Christian living. If the church is to meet the challenge of engaging Hip Hop aficionados, it must be prayerful, open, and authentic in its approach and witness.[11]

Tensions and Messages Given and Received

If we do not take seriously the needs and cares of our youth, the church will continue to experience loss, unbearable pain, grief, angst, and confusion. The church cannot continue to be the church if it has no children, youth, and young adults. Perhaps if the church had been a better witness, Tupac Shakur, one of Hip Hop's icons, would not have met such a tragic death. Leona Welch, author and minister, views Tupac Shakur as emblematic of many young black males whose nurture is stymied through great pain and deprivation.

For all of his success, Shakur was failed by the church and society. Somehow, the church did not provide access, programming, or mentoring that would or could reach out to a young, bright black male child before his life was so disconnected and dysfunctional, to a point of no return. The church and society at large created a system that forced him and his mother to move eleven times by the time he was nine. This contributed to him feeling alienated and broken in spirit, heart, and soul. Welch sees in him a hard, street-language outer self and a softer, gentle true self who cried out for help. Shakur's cries paralleled those of any persons sick and tired of being sick and tired. Some of his work even shows incredible similarities to the prayers of King David recorded in the Psalms. That he was a street prophet who could call us on our hypocrisy, that he could pray in one moment and blast our hypocrisy in another, makes his case even more tragic. He indicted us with our sins of omission, such as not taking time out to help another parent's child who may be lost.[12] How many more Tupac Shakurs must die in the streets before the church is willing to be disciples and invite "who so ever will, let them come"? Can the church work to make those who find Hip Hop persuasive feel like they belong? Beyond the graphic sexism and heterosexism in Hip Hop and rap songs, can the church see other issues of race, class, and ability emerging?

Some do not see a lot of tension in society. Rather, they see a lack of respect and self-love and Hip Hop as just another vehicle that allows one to disrespect others: men and women disrespecting one another, women not respecting themselves, and men not respecting other men. Hip Hop too often measures the pulse of access, acquisition, and accumulation. What you drive, how many people you sleep with, and how hard you appear to be are key values. Hip Hop culture tends to be antiauthority, so an opportunity emerges for the church when Hip Hop can be used to talk about submission to the ultimate authority of God.[13]

Insult into Inspiration: Archeology and Mission

Archeology is the scientific study of ancient cultures through the examination of their material remains. These remains include buildings, graves, tools, and other artifacts, usually dug up with careful methods and sensitive processes that involve instruments as small as a toothbrush to exhume sites buried as deep as twenty feet. The archaeologist digs up the ruins in order to excavate precious antiquity lying beneath. The work of a missionary is like the work of an archeologist. Archeologists do not bring what is ancient to an archeological dig with the hope of putting it in the ground; they discover it where it already is. To be sensitive to youth reality, the church must mobilize missionaries who refuse to bring God to people, but who passionately discover God where God already is and has been in the lives of those they want to reach for Christ.

Missionaries realize that being sensitive to those they want to reach means journeying with people to reveal the divine. These life-sensitive missionaries work with indigenous people slowly and patiently, to excavate the ancient, knowing that mission is a process and not an event. There is a process for pulling precious artifacts of God's love (God's prevenient grace) that is at work beneath the ruins of present pain.

Missionaries do not bring God to the mission field any more than archeologists bring artifacts to a dig; such an act would be unprofessional and insane. It is not productive or helpful to force dogma, doctrine, or theological ideals down a person's throat under the assumption that mission means thrusting Jesus on others. Missionaries do not begin a work of God in people's lives. They partner with people to help them discover where God has been at work. They do not begin conversations about God; they continue conversations that God has already been having in the events and experiences of a person's life.

Because Athens was a progressive city with some of the foremost philosophers living there, some threw insults Paul's way, declaring that his message was weird and ignorant. A well-educated and cultured man himself, Paul used the slanderous insults directed toward him as inspiration. The apostle Paul did not strike the people of Athens who insulted his intelligence with a proverbial shovel. He listened to the people, experienced the culture, and then continued a conversation that God was already having in the lives of those he called "extremely religious" people (Acts 17:22).

Speaking to people about God does not activate God's work, for God has already been speaking through their lives. God is already in conversation with the "Godless." The church must simply join the conversation. Some may say that the Athenians' conversation with God lacked some key communication dynamics. Although they did not know God's name or know much about God, they did have a relationship with God. They had a divine reality that Paul could not ignore. God was at work in the lives of Athenians, and Paul decided to see God's work as a process and not an event, a journey and not a destination.

Jerome's Journey

Be patient my son for the Journey will be more clear. I was like, can you be clearer?
—Jerome Washington[14]

Mission is not a destination but a journey. It does not happen in a day; it happens daily. Overestimating the event of transformation and underestimating the process of planting seeds of change is easy. Mission work is not like a stagnant pond where mosquitoes breed but more like a stream that flows out of the river waters of God's plan.

I (Marlon) learned this lesson through my relationship with Jerome Washington, a prolific poet in Houston. Through poetry, I was able to hear the cries and queries in a new way. Jerome's words ask real questions that are often silenced by the church. Jerome's poems felt like sermons that had a finger on the pulse of the culture. A sea of head-nods and a symphony of finger-snaps were the choreography and sound track that affirmed his intuitive wisdom.

The blue lines resembled a cross, I was afraid of the cross 'Cause positive equals accountability and responsibility.

—Jerome Washington

One day Jerome joined me for catfish and conversation. During our lunch, I asked him about his story, and he openly shared. As I listened, his story reminded me of the story of the prophet Jeremiah. I told Jerome that like Jeremiah, he was consecrated before being formed in his mother's womb, to speak his words to the nations. Trying to stop the tears in my eyes, I saw a vision of Jerome's unique ability to infuse uncommon and absolute poetic truth. I gripped my napkin and told him his journey as a poet and prophet was stuck in the womb of his potential. I invited him into a discipleship relationship and a journey to be birthed into God's purpose.

I knew this was to be his dramatic soul-saving event. He was going to cry with me as I led him in the Sinner's Prayer, but Jerome took another bite, furrowed his brow, and with a blank stare said, "Hmm." I was hurt and a bit insulted. How is this dude going to eat the fish I paid for and not acknowledge my tear-stained "Jesus speech"?

It was the eleventh day when I found out I will soon be a father Not only a father, but a follower, walking into the unknown blind Like three mice; me, myself, and I.

—Jerome Washington

Months of silence passed; then Jerome called out of the blue to tell me he and his girlfriend were having a baby. He wanted to begin a journey with God and did not know where to start. He had already named their unborn child Journey. Our discipleship relationship began that night on the phone. His commitment would soon be tested though, and after a series of hard times, Jerome grew distant.

I held my daughter Journey close and held my faith closer. We both were born that day, to fulfill God's purpose

—Jerome Washington

I tried to keep in touch with Jerome, but sometimes he would not answer my calls, so I just prayed and talked when he did. A year went by, and he reappeared. He wanted to tell me something important, that he wanted to receive the life and way of Christ. He asked if I would help him finally come out of the womb, and I could not believe he remembered our conversation about Jeremiah. For this great prophet, it was always about the influent stream of God's plan. Today Jerome and his group, The Global Movement, are leaders in a musical community of artists we call Influent Stream Artists. Among others, Jerome tours the city sharing his original written and arranged words of freedom and truth that mirror the heart of Christ.

The Unreligious Are Not Always Irreligious

Religious people are sometimes so insulted by the unreligious that they cannot see a divine stream flowing in the lives of the so-called secular. This attitude devalues and secludes potential followers of Jesus from the sacred places of our minds, daily schedules, and buildings. Just because someone is not religious does not mean that they are irreligious or antireligious.

Detroit underground rapper MosEL on a recently released song said, "I don't find God and peace in organized religions so I find God in other visions … follow me."[15] This emerging artist responds to the rejection he experienced in established religion by finding his own way and then challenging his listeners to follow him in doing the same. Rapper Jay Electronica on his 2009 mix tape, *Victory*, says rappers "Tupac and Biggie Smalls were the last pastors." In that one sentence, he says that there is no pastor alive who can lead him with sensitivity. Electronica also underscores the Church's irrelevance by giving pastoral authority to two men who were in no way sanctioned or ordained by the church.

Paul was different because he embraced culture in order to transform it. He never forgot that although God found him guilty, he was blinded, not as a punishment, but as an act of God's grace (see Acts 9 and Acts 7:57–8:3).

After embracing the people who insulted him, Paul began to preach the good news of Jesus. He moved from insult to inspiration by deciding to love the people who insulted him. The insults were only a surface response to what he believed was lying dormant beneath their hunger for "the unknown God." Their resistance to the gospel authenticated their need for Christ. Paul knew that he could not authentically share the good news with an attitude, so first he had to love those very ones who hurt him. Through Paul's action, we can see the core of the gospel message. The ones who inflicted the wounds are now the ones healed, as we are healed by the stripes of Jesus that our sins caused.

Paul reoriented the syncretism of a polytheistic Roman Empire by communicating good news about the heart of the true and living God revealed in Jesus. Using Paul's example, we must meet the syncretism of our time. Syncretism in the twenty-first century may seem like a nuisance to the established church, but it is quite the opposite. As a nation we have shifted from being mostly Christian to many being not Christian or other-than-Christian, and syncretism drives much of the spiritual reality of the day. But for the church, our time in history can be an opportunity.

Human 2.0 and Youth Ministry

The Hip Hop generation is a great place to begin to understand the needs of the future church better; they are the 2.0 version of human life. The term 2.0 is computer speak for a version of a product. Likewise, we have new versions of the Bible, including the NIV (New International Version), NKJV (New King James Version), and NRSV (New Revised Standard Version), among many others.

Hardware is the mainframe of a computer. The motherboard, the keyboard, and the monitor are all components of the computer's hardware. Software drives the programs that a computer uses. Microsoft Word, PowerPoint, and iTunes are all software programs that work inside the hardware of a computer. When a computer is in need of a newer version of the software, the maker of the existing program usually presents an opportunity for computer users to receive the newer version. It typically goes from a 1.0 version to a 2.0 version. If the church is sensitive to God, it will not be content to create some other place for youth to experience God in new buildings, gymnasiums, and summer camps. A church sensitive to the spirit of God will see youth as a community of consultants for framing and shaping the future of the church, because this generation is a newer version of humanity.

God is the master programmer who provides hardware and software for human life. Human hardware is the human body. God includes the human body and all of its natural senses of touch, taste, and sound in a relationship with God as hardware, amidst divine compassion and love. Practices such as communion and rituals such as prayer invite hands, mouths, and minds to participate with God to be at work in the world. Part of our human software is the soul. This soul is the way we experience the grace of salvation and the love of God. God is the master programmer, and God is giving humanity a genuine opportunity through our youth and their perspectives to upgrade our capacity to reach the lost. Their experiences and grassroots knowledge can equip the church to do more than youth ministry; they can equip the church to do ministry, period, in a new human context.

Peter Drucker, a 2002 Presidential Medal of Freedom honoree, declares that, "Every few hundred years in Western history there occurs a sharp transformation. ... Within a few decades, society rearranges itself, its worldview, values, and its arts."[16] We are experiencing this transformation in these times. The context of life as we know is changing. In this transition, Gen Yers and the church should not miss a great opportunity. Currently, the vast majority of Generation-Y culture is missing an opportunity to maximize potential in life through the mission of Jesus Christ. The church (as an institution), however, is missing an opportunity for Gen Yers to assist it in maximizing its potential.

Just as this generation is younger, they are also newer. They are the newest version of human beings equipped with many upgrades. As with downloading new software into an old processing unit, there are bound to be glitches, and the older hardware may not be able to process the newer software; the computer may freeze and shut down. This is the metaphor that drives the relationship between the church as a representative of an older culture and young culture (human 2.0). While there are some nonnegotiable practices and spiritual disciplines that are a must in the church, the "hardware" structures of the church that we give preference must be updated constantly to process the new "software" that comes with human 2.0.

Japanese cultural anthropologists have a great understanding of this new generation's identity. The Japanese term for Generation Y is *Shin fin Rui*, which means a new kind of human being raised in a new world. We must collaborate with this new generation that has an understanding of the new sense of life. The church must let its irritation, defenses, and resistances go. Hip Hop has unveiled a new human reality that the church can explore. This is not a generation that the church *has to* deal with; it is a generation that the church *gets to* partner with to bring the power and love of Christ into a fuller reality.

This is a *got to* moment in the history of a church if it is to survive. This is a moment in human history in which the church can live out its mandate to be a community of faithful followers of Jesus Christ.

Study Questions

1. How does Kirk-Duggan use the tropes of "awkward" and "awesome" (of hip hop and youth culture) as a way into rethinking the sacred and the profane?
2. What does she suggest about the role hip hop and youth culture ought to play in the future of black churches' structure and practices?
3. How does she connect music and spirituality and what suggestions does she make for the ways in which rap music should be handled in churches today?

Notes

* Portions of this chapter from the text *Wake Up: Hip Hop Christianity and the Black Church* (Cheryl Kirk-Duggan and Marlon F. Hall, 2011) have been omitted and/or altered for style, consistency and flow.

1. Quotation from Bishop Don Juan, known as the spiritual guide for many Hip Hop recording artists.
2. Bishop Don Juan's Best of the Best Contest is found on his website: http://www.thebishop.us/default.html

3. See http://www.apollotheater.org/artists/leviticus.htm (viewed August 1, 2010).

4. Kevin White, phone interview, July 31, 2010. The Reverend Kevin White is the youth pastor at Greater Mount Zion Baptist Church in Houston, Texas.

5. Don E. Saliers, *Music and Theology, Horizons in Theology* (Nashville: Abingdon Press, 2007), 5.

6. Ibid., 7–14.

7. Melva Costen, *African American Christian Worship*, 2nd edn. (Nashville: Abingdon Press, 2007), 105–19.

8. J. Wendell Mapson, *The Ministry of Music in the Black Church* (Valley Forge, Penn.: Judson Press, 1984), 19–21.

9. White interview.

10. Ibid.

11. Tommy Kyllonen, *Unorthodox: Church, Hip Hop, Culture* (Grand Rapids, Mich.: Zondervan, 2007), 109–23.

12. Leona Nicholas Welch, Tupac, *Rahab and Them: A Call to Compassion and Commitment Toward Those Often Unheard, Untouched, and Unsung; Ultimately, Unloved* (Columbus, Ga.: Brentwood Christian Press, 2005), 10–16, 19, 20, 27.

13. White interview.

14. This and the following epigraphs in this section are taken from a personal interview with Jerome Washington in August 2005.

15. MosEL, "Vent." *Just Thinkin Out Loud.* MosElmusic, 2010.

16. Peter Drucker, *Post-capitalist Society* (New York: HarperBusiness, 1993).

19

Rhetorical Synthesis through a (Rap)Prochement of Identities

Hip-Hop and the Gospel According to the Gospel Gangstaz

Hatch explores the intersections of the gospel and hip hop by giving attention to the group, Gospel Gangstaz (GGz). Hatch carefully charts the historical emergence of hip hop and then gospel rap music with full attention to the work of GGz. He then moves into a close rhetorical synthesis of GGz's song, *I Can See Clearly Now*. He argues attention to the lyrics found in this album points to the ways in which gospel rap is tied to a recovery rhetoric rooted in redemption and reconciliation. Beginning with the contradistinction between "gospel" and "gangstaz," Hatch argues that GGz resolves the two and in doing so, alters traditional religious meanings and norms—and pushes against the ways in which some scholars privilege notions of cognition, literary and "proper" reflection.

Rhetorical Synthesis through a (Rap)Prochement of Identities: Hip-Hop and the Gospel According to the Gospel Gangstaz

John B. Hatch

> I'm genuine, not a copy, and you bustaz can't stop me,
> All you can do [is] follow the rules, take notes and watch me. […]
> Look, I keeps it, Gospel and Gangsta, at the same time:
> You get sick, I pray [for you]. You disrespect, and I'm
> [gonn]a take mine—
> 'Cuzz God and this West Coast Ganglish made me famous.
> Gospel Gangstaz, *I Can Now*

In 1999, an album entitled *I Can See Clearly Now* was nominated for a Grammy in the Best Rock Gospel Album category. The album's musical style, however, belied the category, being West Coast hip-hop (except for strains of gospel in a few of the refrains and the final cut). The name of the rap trio, likewise, defied traditional categories, fusing together two highly incongruous terms: "Gospel" and "Gangstaz." Such a blatant jarring of accepted usage has become, ironically, rather normal in a postmodern age of popular music that revels in ironic reversals of meaning (e.g., a singer named Judas Priest and a "Madonna" who performs in seductive attire). In the case of the Gospel Gangstaz, however, the attack on established meanings invites further consideration, for it goes far deeper than mere sensationalism or youthful rebellion. Rather, their avowed intent is to carry out a spiritual and social rescue mission among their peers. The "gospel" in the group's name is meant quite seriously, but it represents a gospel somewhat veiled to the traditional religious listener, obscured within stories of past gang life and boasts of present success in the rap game. More importantly, the meaning of this "gospel" is problematized by its baptism into the aggressive realism inherited from gangsta rap and the materialistic self-aggrandizement and self-gratification current in hip-hop while the meaning of "gangsta," likewise, is problematized by its association with gospel ministry. In the rhetoric of the Gospel Gangstaz, the traditional gospel and hip-hop undergo a rhetorical synthesis that transforms the meanings of both.

The term "rhetorical synthesis," as set forth by Gage Chapel, denotes a "rhetorical response to situations in which differing ideas, values or policies are in conflict," which "functions to resolve conflict while at the same time constructing a larger encompassing vision that does not alienate individuals on either side of the controversy" ("Rhetorical Synthesis" 344). Although largely synonymous with Black's notion of "argumentative synthesis" and Rushing and Frentz's "dialectical synthesis," Chapel's construct is more explicitly analyzed into discursive constituents. Chapel also goes farther than the others in pinpointing the limitations of rhetorical synthesis, suggesting that it appears to be "largely intellectual discourse appealing to a literate and reflective audience" ("Rhetorical Synthesis" 358).

The Gospel Gangstaz' rhetoric, however, clearly contradicts the Chapel's view as it offers a street-level response to the exigency of urban Black youths fight for survival.[1] Although *I Can See Clearly Now* did not go on to win the Grammy award or achieve blockbuster sales,[2] it merits rhetorical analysis because it exemplifies the elements of rhetorical synthesis in a unique and arresting manner, reflecting the influence not only of medium (music, which favors emotional experience over rational argument), but also culture (a vigorous African-American tradition of self-definition, self-assertion, and group identification through oral discourse), both converging potently within the hip-hop genre. Indeed, this piece of discourse challenges us to round out Chapel's model with other critical concepts to explain how rhetorical synthesis can operate via a popular musical form for a culturally marginalized audience that is oriented toward orality and involvement rather than "literate and reflective" modes of cognition. Moreover, hip-hop music in itself deserves serious scholarly attention, as Michael Dyson contends:

> Rap is a form of profound musical, cultural, and social creativity [...] Besides being the most powerful form of black music today, rap projects a style of self onto the world that disciplines ultimate social despair into forms of cultural resistance, and transforms the ugly terrain of ghetto existence into a searing portrait of life as it is lived by millions of voiceless people. For this reason alone, rap deserves attention and should be taken seriously.[3]

("Performance" 24)

The purpose of the present essay is to bring an analysis of the Gospel Gangstaz' latest album to bear on Chapel's model of rhetorical synthesis. I argue that the model should be conceived within a broader framework that acknowledges the centrality of identity construction, identification, and narrative to some expressions of synthesis, particularly within the African-American community. Besides reflecting the influence of dramaturgical/narrative perspectives (particularly those of Kenneth Burke and Walter Fisher), this contention is in keeping with Ronald Jackson's call to recognize how culture conditions both rhetorical practice and theory building. While the musical nature of the Gospel Gangstaz' rhetoric certainly exerts a significant influence on their synthesis, I have chosen to focus on the role of their Black experience and sensibilities, believing these to be the dominant force both in the rhetorical situation and the rhetors' response to it.[4]

My analysis begins by discussing Chapel's model of rhetorical synthesis and its applications in the literature to date. I then sketch the development of hip-hop in the historical context of changes within the Black community, the crack epidemic, and alienation from the church, relating this rhetorical situation to Aaron Gresson's notions of racial recovery and Black apocalypse. Next, I briefly address the emergence of gospel hip-hop as a response to that apocalypse and the Gospel Gangstaz as radical standard-bearers for this genre. I then proceed to analyze their rhetorical synthesis in the lyrics on *I Can See Clearly Now,* using the categories within Chapel's model while emphasizing the dominance of the rhetors' identity construction and audience identification over thematic development, thus reversing Chapel's emphasis. Fisher's motive view of communication provides the rubric by which I explicate the Gospel Gangstaz' thematic development of their rhetorical synthesis. The discussion at the end of this essay considers the Gospel Gangstaz' identity-oriented approach to rhetorical synthesis as a manifestation of interpositionality, a stance favored by Blacks and others on the margins of society, and it considers the implications of my analysis for our understanding of how rhetorical synthesis works and why it often fails to attain widespread appeal.

Rhetorical Synthesis

According to Chapel and Jensen, rhetorical synthesis is "the process of unifying ideas (arguments, policies, themes, narratives, visions), that appear disparate or contradictory, into a coherent whole [...] often providing a third alternative to conflicting points of view:" (98). In Chapel's model, a rhetorical synthesis is primarily embodied in three discursive elements: (1) An *encompassing conception* that pulls together disparate ideas or attitiudes into a coherent whole—"the central rationale which makes the synthesis viable, justifiable, and understandable [...] [and] tells an audience *how* the synthesis is synthesized;" (2) a *collapsed statement* of the encompassing conception "that serves as a useful shorthand term for the conception;" and (3) the *thematic development* of the encompassing conception, with supporting arguments and "sanctioning and legitimizing agents or agencies" ("Rhetorical Synthesis" 345). Chapel's article on Jack Kemp, includes a fourth element (or cluster of elements): *reinforcing strategies of style, emotion, ethos, and delivery*. Chapel suggests that the linkage between rhetoric and rhetor, as expressed in these elements, is particularly salient to the audience in rhetorical synthesis because "rhetorical synthesis, in effect, creates something new, [...] a new social reality grounded in yet different from the elements he or she synthesizes" (345).[5] Yet Chapel tends to privilege rational argument over ethos, emotion, style, and delivery, as indicated by their complete omission in his most recent explication of the model ("Synthesizing").[6] In the published literature to date, Chapel has applied his model to three different instances of rhetorical synthesis: Japan's Seicho-No-Ie movement (a. synthesis of Eastern and Western religious beliefs), Jack Kemp's political discourse of progressive conservatism, and Mary Baker Eddy's Christian Science. Given these examples, his conclusion that rhetorical synthesis is "largely intellectual discourse appealing to a literate and reflective audience" is not surprising.[7]

In contrast to the bodies of discourse studied by Chapel, the Gospel Gangstaz' rhetoric of survival on the urban streets and in the rap game breaks the mold of intellectualism, appealing much more to the physical and emotional needs that dominate daily existence in a fractured urban community. As young Black men who have lived the violence and nihilism of gang life, the Gospel Gangstaz relate their experiences to their own racial and generational community, sharing a story of redemption and reconnection with the higher source and purpose of reality. Furthermore, in their rhetorical synthesis, it is the creation of identity and ethos, more than thematic development, that predominates in the fleshing out of the encompassing conception. In fact, it is probably more accurate to speak of an "encompassing image" at the heart of the Gospel Gangstaz' synthesis, the image they project of gospel hip-hop as a way of life and of themselves as its embodiment.[8] Their rhetoric thus illustrates the importance of defining one's social identity, a delicate task that has dominated Blacks' existence in White America but has been complicated by the fragmentation of the African-American community since the civil rights era.

The Black Urban Community: A House Divided

The traditional role of the Black church as the spiritual, social, and economic center of the African-American community is well attested.[9] However, during the 1960s, the disparity between the hopes kindled by the civil rights movement and the cold facts of persistent racism began to rend the fabric of this community. Many young Blacks found the messages of Malcolm X and Black Power more compelling than the nonviolent approach of the church, as epitomized by Martin Luther King, Jr. Moreover, as African-Americans gained the freedom to live wherever they chose, middle-class and ambitious working-class city dwellers began moving out to the suburbs, leaving behind a vacuum of leadership and economic stability in the ghetto. Into this vacuum rushed the trade in heroin and other drugs. By the early 1980s, crack cocaine had become the drug of choice, fueling an explosion of gangs, violence, and prison experience for young Black males.[10] The relative cohesiveness of urban Black neighborhoods was shattered by gang warfare, and the church was not able to stem the tide of bloodshed.

Meanwhile, in the late 1970s, a new constellation of musical and visual art forms had appeared in the ghetto. Youths in the South Bronx (mostly Afro-American and Afro-Caribbean) developed four strands of creative self-expression: tagging or bombing (graffiti artwork); b-boying or breaking (break dancing); DJ-ing (mixing selected musical passages from older records using two turntables); and MC-ing, better known as rapping.[11] Interwoven together through the social experiences of young urban Blacks, these strands evolved into a form of pop culture known as hip-hop. At first, hip-hop was primarily light-hearted entertainment, the latest metamorphosis of African-Americans' penchant for appropriating technologies, reinventing them in their own image, and developing art that reflected their distinct cultural experiences and sensibilities. Like the blues, jazz, and rock-'n'-roll before it, hip-hop provided a venue for Blacks (especially men) to create identities of their own choosing and to vie for status through demonstrations of technical skill combined with personal style. Predictably, this new worldly diversion drew the ire of some ministers and churchgoers. Nelson George relates how the Reverend Calvin Butts, minister of Harlem's prestigious Abyssinian Baptist Church, campaigned against a purveyor of local hip-hop parties, seeing these gatherings as a "catalyst for drug taking, teen fornication, and general licentiousness" (28).

In time, however, the circumstances in the ghetto pushed this new musical genre in a more ominous direction that would only increase its alienation from the church. Hip-hop artists responded to the crack epidemic and its effects by subsuming them into their portrayal of urban Black experience, beginning notably with "The Message" by Grandmaster Flash & the Furious Five in 1982. While such early examples of "reality rap" communicated a moral sense of alarm, by the late-80s, some rappers seemed to be portraying the gangster mentality and violence as normative, and "gangsta rap" gained nationwide) notoriety.[12] The church, for its part, proved ill-equipped to deal with the urban crisis that gangsta rap reflected; while ministers decried the influx of drugs and violence (and the outflow of young men to prison), they generally offered little in the way of relevant alternatives for the generation growing up in such conditions.[13] By and large, the church's response to the gritty new realism in rap was to condemn it.[14]

Undaunted, hip-hop continued to develop its own values. Where gospel music tended to deflect congregants' attention from present disappointments to dreams of a better world in the hereafter, the hip-hop nation chose to face the brutal realities of everyday life squarely and broadcast them bluntly in their ghetto poetry. This refusal to whitewash their world, expressed in the phrase "keepin' it real," became a cardinal virtue for hip-hop culture, and with it came a particular disdain for religious hypocrisy.[15] Hip-hop artists also made themselves odious to the church by using profanity with abandon while often exhibiting what appeared to be a calloused, amoral attitude toward sex and violence. The hip-hop nation defended these expressions as keepin' it real to the street, however. Hip-hop also reflected males' self-assertion and self-determination in the face of a world (and church) that offered them few opportunities to obtain power or status as men. It mirrored their socialization into gangs as an alternative source of solidarity, power, and economic advancement. In terms of Elijah Anderson's ethnographic categories of "decent" and "street" orientation, hip-hop (particularly gangsta rap) rhetorically embodied the street code in opposition to the decent orientation as encouraged by the church.[16]

Aaron Gresson's notions of "recovery rhetoric" and the "Black apocalypse" shed light on this division and the exigency it presents for a rhetorical synthesis. Gresson accepts Joseph Campbell's thesis that the loss of unifying myths in the contemporary world has shifted the onus to the individual both to "make meaning for the self and convince others of its integrity." Thus, "people must recover ways of being related and connected to something and someone larger than 'I' and 'me'" (3). In various ways, individuals try to reclaim "an original or ideal state of being" in the spiritual, psychological, and/or social domains, and they engage in "conversation about self-Other liberation" (4). According to Gresson, the rhetoric of recovery uses narratives to legitimize one's chosen recovery strategy in the eyes of the self and the Other simultaneously, implicitly inviting the audience to identify with that strategy and accept its liberative power (5).[17] Applying this concept to our case, both rappers' monologues of ghetto survival and gospel singers' testimonies of redemption may act as recovery rhetoric,[18] though they represent opposing approaches to regaining personal and racial integrity.

Gresson's primary interest is how the rhetoric of recovery has been applied to the problem of race in America since the 1960s. Now that the myth of a united Black race struggling against monolithic White oppression no longer universally resonates with individual experience, African-Americans face what he calls the "Black apocalypse"—"the split of Blacks into camps over their recovery visions" (16). While Gresson's main concern here is the emergence of "Black privatization" (an individualistic, postmodern orientation toward race, marked by a rhetoric of personal choice in opposition to the demands of racial loyalty), many African-American youths' identification with the "hip-hop nation" as opposed to the church arguably constitutes a form of Black apocalypse. Where the church once embodied Blacks' unity of faith and hope in ultimate deliverance from racial discrimination and poverty, its rhetoric no longer resonates with many younger members of the African-American community, who find their hopes and fears expressed more compellingly by the likes of Tupac Shakur and Jay-Z. In sermons and gospel music, the church continues to tell its "old, old story" of finding comfort in Jesus and deliverance through faith in God, a faith rooted in the stories of the Old and New Testaments, the slave songs and the spirituals. The hip-hop nation's rap artists, however, tell a different story-narratives of aggressive self-assertion and self-promotion in the face of a world that denies wealth and status to Blacks yet yields these rewards to those who are strong, skillful and fearless enough to wrest them from its tight fists. Hip-hop's preeminence as the top selling genre in the music industry today indicates the extent to which this type of recovery narrative resonates, not only with Black youth, but also with American youth as a whole.[19] To the extent that the church opposes the recovery vision represented in hip-hop, it appears to be losing the battle.

The Evolution of Gospel Hip-Hop and the Gospel Gangstaz

I argue that the Gospel Gangstaz' rhetoric constitutes an attempt to transform this rhetorical battle by reuniting the Black urban community—the church and the street—in a recovery vision that synthesizes the strengths of both, making these foes allies in the fight against the common evils that plague their community. The Gospel Gangstaz are not the first gospel musicians to move in this direction. In the 1980s, a few gospel artists on the fringe of the burgeoning Contemporary Christian musical genre began trying to reach out across the widening crevasse between the church and the hip-hop nation. Michael Peace, PID (Preachers in Disguise), DC Talk, and others pioneered "gospel hip-hop" as an attempt to express the core beliefs and values of the church in an evangelistic format tailored to a generation growing up on hip-hop (Marriott).[20] For the most part, however, early gospel hip-hop musicians' work lacked the artistic quality to compete with secular hip-hop, and some artists' approach laminated a veneer of rap style on top of a thoroughly traditional form of gospel message (e.g., Gooch 237).

In the beginning of the 1990s, the Gospel Gangstaz emerged as the first notable exception to this characterization.[21] Comprised of two former members of the Crips gang and a former Blood from Los Angeles (who call themselves Mr. Solo, Chille' Baby, and TikTokk, respectively), the Gospel Gangstaz ("GGz" or "2Gz" for short) began performing during the heyday of gangsta rap, and their sounds and lyrics reflected its influences. While they straightforwardly expressed some traditional gospel themes, the GGz also unapologetically embraced the culture and mindset of the mean streets from which they came. The Gospel Gangstaz made two critically acclaimed albums in the mid-90s (*Gang Affiliated* and *Do or Die*) and, after a four-year hiatus, recorded *I Can See Clearly Now* in 1999. More than the first two, this third album aimed to break out of the confines of the Contemporary Christian market into mainstream hip-hop venues, utilizing secular producers on some of the tracks and being marketed to the mainstream through an arrangement with Interscope. Although the album did not attain hoped-for blockbuster sales—only about 200,000 copies sold in the first year—it did make inroads into the mainstream, receiving video airplay on MTV and BET and scoring the Grammy nomination mentioned earlier. Having joined the same gospel label (B-Rite) on which Kirk Franklin's hip-hop-flavored urban gospel sound had achieved notable success,[22] the Gospel Gangstaz apparently aimed to ride on Franklin's coattails to reach a wider audience with their much grittier sound and message. Indeed, they made an appearance with Franklin on Jay Lena's Tonight Show, and the second single on *I Can See Clearly Now* is a Franklin-flavored track backed by his Nu Nation gospel choir (*Real Gz*).

Despite their unorthodox approach, the Gospel Gangstaz' promotional literature indicates that they see themselves as an extension of the church. Upon his conversion from a drug-running thug to a devout Christian, Mr. Solo, the leader of the trio, embraced the church and gave up rapping as "wicked"—until his brother-in-law told him, God gave you the gift; use it for Him" ("About Gospel Gangstaz" 2). Bandmate Tik Tokk declares, "We don't consider ourselves above anybody. But God has given us insight to see the truth. We understand their pain, and they know we know the real. I gotta make music for my homies. I believe in bringing the church to people, not just bringing people to church" (*Real Gz*). A leaflet from B-Rite asserts, "Mr. Solo, Chille' Baby, and Tik Tokk are deeply committed to accountability, to each other, their families, and their pastors and church families" ("About Gospel Gangstaz" 2). Yet their lyrics paint a much different picture than one would expect from gospel ministers. More than just bringing the church to the street, as earlier gospel hip-hop artists did, the Gospel Gangstaz seem to hew out a new niche and weld together a new Christian ethos out of elements from both the church and the street, gospel and hip-hop, particularly on their latest album.

Rhetorical Synthesis in *I Can See Clearly Now*

The following analysis largely follows the pattern set forth by Chapel, identifying an encompassing conception, a collapsed statement of that conception, and its thematic development in the lyrics.[23] However, since the elements of ethos and image—which have received less emphasis in Chapel's work—generate most of the energy welding together the Gospel Gangstaz' rhetorical synthesis, I discuss thematic development *after* analyzing how *I Can See Clearly Now* works at the level of identity, identification, and image to draw Black urban youth into its rhetorical synthesis of recovery visions. The following analysis reveals a group seeking to identify with the hip-hop nation—while retaining ties to the church—and working to reaffirm and purify the images of both gospel and hip-hop, with the underlying goal of reconciling or uniting these images in their own identity as rhetors.

The encompassing conception

Insinuated through the lyrics of *I Can See Clearly Now* are five related claims that hold together the disparate recovery visions of gospel and hip-hop and provide a rationale for the synthesis. These claims largely implicit, though some of them are made explicit by the rhetors' statements in interviews or promotional literature:

1. *The true gospel does not ignore or reject reality but redeems it.* This claim is implied in the assertion that one cannot (or should not) reject one's past, and that to do so is to be unreal or inauthentic. Moreover, the GGz insist on applying the gospel to the real problems of the ghetto.

2. In redeeming human reality, *the gospel promises not only spiritual salvation but also material success to believers* (thereby reversing the economic deprivations that drive many urban youth to sin). This claim is made quite explicit in certain lyrics.

3. *Hip-hop does not run counter to spiritual truth but rather keeps its application real and relevant to the street.* Hip-hop's honest reflection of the ghetto's harsh reality is an ally of the gospel; only its excesses (reveling in graphic sexuality, profane language, violence, greed, and substance abuse) are to be shunned.

4. Thus, *hip-hop is a spiritually sound means to achieve prosperity and bring holistic redemption to the ghetto.* The GGz reject churchgoers' blanket criticisms of rap.

5. *As redeemed gangstas who excel in hip-hop as ministry, the Gospel Gangstaz embody and thus substantiate these claims.* Using their own violent past and their mastery of hip-hop as a platform to identify with their audience, the GGz put themselves forward as a model for urban Black youths' recovery of lost spiritual and material well-being.

Collapsed Statement of the encompassing conception

The group's name, "GospelGangstaz," captures the essence of their rhetorical synthesis. Nowhere on the album do they use the term "gospel hip-hop" or "gospel rap." This apparent oxymoron challenges traditional, oppositional understandings of "gospel" and "gangsta," much as Christian Science redefined "Christianity" and "science" in such a way as to eliminate the perceived antipathy between them. However whereas the latter summed up the synthesis of two worldviews or philosophies, the shorthand term "Gospel Gangstaz" encapsulates the rhetors' integration of two *identities* within themselves, with the personal narratives they use to persuade themselves and others of the integrity and viability of that paradoxical fusion.

Therefore, we will examine the role and character of the identity they construct for themselves before considering the thematic development of the synthesis.

Projecting a Credible Identity

For the listener accustomed to gospel music in both its traditional and contemporary forms, perhaps the most striking feature of the Gospel Gangstaz' lyrics on *I Can See Clearly Now* is their fixation with establishing their own identity and credibility. In this venue, one expects the gospel to be couched in street lingo over "phat" beats, but the gospel themes on this album are overshadowed by the prominence and sheer volume of verbiage devoted to self-assertion, self-definition, posturing, bragging, and challenging all comers. This obsession with the rhetors' self-image relative to their peers is par for the course in hip-hop, which is the latest and most strident permutation of a long tradition of African-American self-assertion through verbal sparring.[24] Gospel music, by contrast, usually emphasizes the comfort and strength found in depending on God as the mighty and caring Deliverer. While that theme is present on much of *I Can See Clearly Now* (in contrast to mainstream hip-hop), it is mostly reduced to a supporting role within a concerted effort by the Gangstaz to define themselves and establish their credibility. Both the placement and the amount of gospel material relative to ethos-building material manifest this unorthodox arrangement.

First, the two singles released from the album clearly tilt the balance in favor of self-assertion over gospel exhortation or praise. The title cut, "I Can See Clearly Now," which received airplay on MTV and BET, constitutes their self-introduction to the hip-hop world as real (though enlightened) gangstas who now excel in the rap game.[25] The second single, "I'll Be Good," is the aforementioned collaboration with Kirk Franklin's Nu Nation gospel choir, which musically aims to appeal to both gospel and mainstream audiences via a hook (refrain) sampled from a Top 10 R&B hit by Angela Winbush. The verse sung by the choir is a generic expression of hope found in God amid life's trials, but the rap verses reveal the GGz' decision to focus more on their own credibility instead. While the lyrics printed in the liner notes emphasize what God has done for each member of the trio, the lyrics they actually recorded for "I'll Be Good" emphasize their own identity and ability as a hip-hop act.

It might be expected that the singles would emphasize hip-hop credibility rather than gospel themes, since these comprise the Gospel Gangstaz' introduction to the mainstream audience via radio and video airplay. However, the album as a whole is thoroughly saturated with the group's self-assertions, to the extent that the rhetors' identity becomes the album's primary message. Thus, the first cut—"Amazin' Grace"—reveals a revision similar to that in "I'll Be Good." While the liner notes contain a hook and rap lyrics that clearly express the theme of the redeemed sinner's gratitude for God's grace, the track we hear on the CD is just a snippet in which R&B singers croon the phrase "It's your amazing grace" a few times. Thus, the Gospel Gangstaz merely tip their hats to divine grace before launching into their primary message in the second (title) cut: We're real Gz (gangstaz) and superior rappers who happen to be redeemed by God. The lyrics of the third and fourth tracks, likewise, center around the rhetors' ethos, although they increasingly weave in the themes of their past redemption from sin and present calling to gospel ministry. The fourth cut, "Once Was Blind," threads their salvation testimony through more statements of ethos, this time emphasizing the spiritual side of that ethos as men on a mission to open the eyes of their peers on the street. Not until the fifth track do the GGz apparently leave behind their focus on ethos as they address their "Questions" to God about the cruelties of life in the ghetto and the difficulty of living right.

However, "Questions" does not, as one might expect, signal a transition away from the ethos emphasis for the remainder of the album. Rather, of the remaining ten cuts, six devote almost all their lyrics to establishing the rhetors' identity, mission, and credibility (while addressing gospel themes along the way), two others are divided evenly between ethos and non-ethos statements, and only two can be characterized as clearly gospel-oriented tracks, where the focus is on God and how much the GGz and the ghetto need his help.

Having established that their ethos or credibility is the main focus of the Gospel Gangstaz' rhetoric, let us now consider the content of this ethos. Aristotle's *Rhetoric* identifies three dimensions in ethos: (apparent) intelligence, character, and goodwill toward the audience. The GGz' rhetoric works primarily on creating impressions of intelligence and goodwill.

Intelligence. For this term, some scholars substitute the more comprehensive *competence*, as associated with "qualification, expertness, intelligence, authoritativeness" (McCroskey and Teven 90). I will adopt this broader term. The Gospel Gangstaz project competence in terms of their street knowledge, hip-hop skills, and spiritual enlightenment. They also reinforce this image of competence through projections of success in the music industry and power in the spiritual realm. Let us consider each in turn.

The GGz make much of their life experience, portraying themselves as street-wise, battle-hardened veterans of the ghetto. In the first verse of the title cut, Mr. Solo projects this worldly-wise image when he says to those in the 'hood, "Ain't nothin' you can tell me, or dream you can sell me," and then proceeds to dispense wisdom about handling money (and gold-digging women). In "I Call Your Name," he tells where he got his education: "My grant is canceled and I don't play sports, I'll never see college/[so] I hung in my 'hood, and I got a little street knowledge." In "One Way," Mr. Solo draws out a cleverly rhymed lyrical sketch of his younger self in full gangsta uniform, running cocaine and dodging the police. Chille' Baby in particular paints himself as the super-sociopath: "Westside G-boy—had no love in my fetal stages/Bust gauges from a pee-wee to BG to teenage rampages/Outrageous, I ain't the one to step to/I'll sting you like a killer Bee and swarm like the Wu." With such experience and expertise as soldiers of the street, they can credibly say, "I ain't tellin' what I heard, I'm tellin' what I know."

Having abandoned the practices (if not the mentality) of "thug living," the Gospel Gangstaz proclaim and parade their prowess on another level: mastery of the lyrical, vocal, and musical skills of hip-hop. In the hook of the title track, Mr. Solo declares that he's got the hip-hop game "down to a science." Chille' Baby quips, "Like Orville Reddinbocker, I keep it poppin', baby. […]/My lyrics got hang time/Beat so tight, if you could see it/It'd be throwin' up gang signs." In "One Way," he threatens rap rivals with verbal destruction, and Tik Tokk gets his boasts in: "I arise from the boon docks, consume blocks when my tune knocks/Blow the speakers out [of] ya boom box." The final rap track, "Interlude #2," is just Mr. Solo's soliloquy of self-congratulation, a tour-de-force of rhymed gloating about the album's lyrical achievements and his presumed defeat of rival MCs.[26]

To listeners unaccustomed to hip-hop, the Gospel Gangstaz may seem to leave behind any semblance of Christian humility in their zeal to establish an ethos of expertise. Nevertheless, they lay claim to Christian knowledge as well, and the way they describe having received this knowledge puts their boasting in perspective. The source of the GGz' spiritual awareness, as they portray it, is divine enlightenment that broke through when they were still blindly bent on sinning: "I saw the light, He shined on me/I once was blind but now I see" ("Once Was Blind"). In "One Way," Mr. Solo tells how, after he was nearly shot to death by a rival gang, God revealed his grace to him and showed him "a vision of how life was/and could be, should be in the 'hood/If we show some love." In tandem with these spiritual revelations, the GGz refer to the Bible or "Word" as the source of their spiritual understanding. To defend his unorthodox ministry to critics in the church, Mr. Solo says, "Found out what it means to be a Christian, broke away from tradition" because "Traditions of man make the Word of God to no effect." The GGz claim to interpret the sacred text better than their critics; even though many of these critics "went to college," they "perish for a lack of knowledge," because they have not been spiritually enlightened by God. The importance of claimed enlightenment to the GGz' ethos is indicated by the title of the album and first single. In fact, the video for "I Can See Clearly Now" features a shot in which the Gospel Gangstaz appear (ironically) as Asians, seated in a Buddhist-like meditative posture and floating in mid-air; in another shot, Mr. Solo's eyes turn to flaming beams of light.

Closely linked with the GGz' projections of intelligence are their presumptions of success in the hip-hop industry and spiritual power in the face of evil. Some of the lyrics cited above reflect the claim of hip-hop success. Other lyrics speak forth the GGz' expectation of platinum album sales, lavish living, and world fame as if these were already realized. In one hook they gloat, "Could it be the way the track was laid? [...] Could it be how frequently the video's played? [...] Could it be the way they playa hate [= envy] 'cause I'm paid? [...] Could it be the way I bump-bump-bump all day? They don't even believe that I'm saved!" The Gospel Gangstaz depict the nation's clubs as "movin' to my beat" and the dance floors of the world as packed with fans partying to their music. Mr. Solo taunts the womanizing preachers (or MC rivals?) who criticize his ministry: "Line lobbin', rhyme throbbin', mind bogglin'/Got your concubines bobbin' while the rhymes lodgin'."

Images of spiritual power may seem strange bedfellows for the life-of-the-party image described above, but the Gospel Gangstaz don't skip a beat in declaring the power of their ministry to combat evil and effect spiritual blessing. In "They Don't Believe," Chille' Baby explains, "Got demons on the run, like Bruce Jenner/They all drop like Niagara Falls when the Spirit enters. [...] My agenda is to infiltrate hmm, let me see/Put out a platinum album and watch it penetrate/See sin disintegrate." Such proclamations may not appeal to the party crowd, but they would strike a chord with the young gospel audience that I enjoyed songs such as "Demon Killa" on the GGz' earlier albums.[27] Their purported spiritual power has a positive side as well: Mr. Solo says he has "compassion to heal the ill and faith to move mountains," and through the GGz' ministry, victims of demonic bondage become enlightened, "born again," "saved," and "blessed."

Goodwill (identification). In addition to creating an image of competence, the Gospel Gangstaz' discourse works to construct an impression of goodwill or "perceived caring" toward their audience (McCroskey). The concept of goodwill overlaps considerably with that of identification.[28] In A *Rhetoric of Motives,* Kenneth Burke writes, "You persuade a man only insofar as you can talk his language by speech, gesture, tonality, order, image, attitude, idea, *identifying* your ways with his" (55). Although one may consciously and superficially manipulate such factors in order to persuade by "flattery," Burke believes that identification as "consubstantiality" more often operates subconsciously, being the persuasive essence of all communication. Such is certainly the case in popular music, which favors emotional connection over rational argument. Therefore, I will discuss the Gospel Gangstaz' goodwill in terms of this more fundamental notion. Through both intention and the substance of who they are, the GGz' music works to identify with their target audience(s) on several levels. Stylistically, their music reflects the influence of major rappers such as Tupac Shakur, Snoop Doggy Dogg, E-40, W C., Busta Rhymes, and Master P Qohnson, Bush). Furthermore, the GGz speak "ganglish" like the natives that they are, with a full compliment of gang-sign gestures, hip clothing, and break dancing to round out their identification with the street non-verbally.

Beyond these stylistic elements, the lyrical content of the Gospel Gangstaz' music identifies with the hip-hop nation in many of the themes, values, attitudes, and concerns conveyed. Mostly, their rhetoric depicts the struggle to survive in the ghetto or thrive in the music industry. True to gangsta rap and post-gangsta hip-hop, the struggle they portray entails drug running and gang violence (in their past), confronting rivals with their purported hip-hop prowess (in the present), and celebrating the material rewards of their success (speaking forth their projected future as though already realized). Thus, the GGz exemplify the rhetoric of recovery, using narrative to show how they have discovered a superior way to recover their losses as Blacks born and raised in the ghetto. By telling this story, they implicitly (and sometimes explicitly) invite their peers to identify with and experience the liberative vision it contains.[29] Throughout their narratives, the Gospel Gangstaz make clear their continued identification with the homies and thugs on the streets, sharing their attitudes, concerns, pains, disappointments, and hopes. Mr. Solo confesses, "My outlook on this world is from a G's perspective" ("Once Was Blind"), and Tik Tokk punningly asserts, "When a thug comes off the street/He can never really shake his rap sheet" ("I Call Your Name"). In "Once Was Blind," Mr. Solo laments the death of his fellow gangsta in a shootout, and in "Questions," Chille' Baby says, "I know banging was wrong, but it was real." In a poignant description of the ghetto's violence and despair, he pleads, "All we know how to do is play the cards we was dealt […] Hear my cry, I need a quick reply/Ain't nothin' proper 'bout seein' my homiez die!" ("Let Us Pray"). These statements of strong identification with the ghetto contribute to an image of goodwill toward the hip-hop audience. It is crucial to recognize that the Gospel Gangstaz do not identify with the hip-hop nation only, for they also wish to represent the gospel that has been preserved (if sometimes fossilized) by the church, identifying with its core meaning and values as they understand them. For many of their target listeners, this secondary yet essential identification is problematic, in that it seemingly contradicts their identification with the hip-hop community. For instance, a reviewer in *Vibe* expresses respect for the GGz' sincere effort to bring a redemptive message to the ears of the "Saturday night club crowd/sinners" but I confesses, "it's hard not to label the album as slightly corny, a little too preachy, and plain old soft" (Miguel Burke). Another reviewer, who does give them credit for achieving a credible gangsta rap sound, identifies the source of the problem: "if the Gospel Gangstaz really wanted to 'get over,' they should've been a bit more subtle than their hooks, song titles, and unfortunately corny name, affords them. The only rap fans that could enjoy this would be those already in line with GG's agenda and, as expected, that's just preaching to the converted" (Patel).[30] Such sentiments are not shared by all reviewers, but they certainly illustrate the challenge of identifying with the core of an established audience when attempting to gain acceptance for a new rhetorical synthesis.

Thematic Development

Having established that the Gospel Gangstaz' fundamental rhetorical project on *I Can See Clearly Now* is the construction of a credible and persuasive ethos, we are ready to consider how they develop their rhetorical synthesis thematically in accordance with that ethos. My primary argument is that this African-American manifestation of rhetorical synthesis revolves around the impulse to creatively define oneself in defiance of existing categories and, by implication, to redefine or reform those categories in light of one's own identity and experience. Counter to Chapel's perception of rhetorical synthesis as intellectual discourse appealing to a literate and reflective audience, the Gospel Gangstaz demonstrate an approach to rhetorical synthesis that works *primarily* by constructing a credible fusion within the image of the rhetors and thus challenging the existing, apparently incompatible images of gospel and hip-hop in society. This they do by identifying themselves with ostensibly compatible aspects of both images while separating themselves from mutually objectionable, corrupt elements of each.

Walter Fisher (1970) extended Kenneth Burke's idea that rhetorical discourse carries out its persuasive function by creating images with implicit instructions on how the audience is to think, feel, and act. Fisher posited that rhetors are guided by one of four possible motives regarding audience perception of the image at hand: *affirmation* (to birth a new image), *reaffirmation* (to renew an existing image), *purification* (to correct the image), and *subversion* (to undermine the image). Fisher noted a complementary relationship between affirmation and subversion: "to affirm an image is, in effect, to subvert an old one; to subvert an old one is, in effect, to affirm a new one" (138–139). In line with Burke's view of rhetoric as infused with a Cycle of Order requiring repeated redemption,[31] I suggest that reaffirmation and purification likewise are complementary motives with respect to a single rhetorical image. It may be necessary to purify the existing image of corrupting elements in order to revitalize it for the audience. This is what the Gospel Gangstaz attempt to do with the images of *both* gospel and hip-hop in their rhetorical synthesis. In effect, they bring the (traditionally) antithetical images together by displaying a fundamental underlying unity between them that has been obscured by the corruption of both but is now brought to light in the credible identity of the rhetors, who have been enlightened and "can see clearly now."

My explication of the thematic development in the GGz' rhetorical synthesis is organized to show the reaffirmation and purification of pairs of commensurate aspects within the images of both gospel and hip-hop. The following pairs of themes and values came to the fore in my close reading of the lyrics on *I Can See Clearly Now*: (1) *embracing the truth of God* and *facing the reality of the street*; (2) *spiritual salvation* and *material survival/success*; (3) *respect for God* and *respect for the individual*; (4) *bonds of Christian communion* and *bonds of community*; and (5) *fighting sin/the devil* and *fighting the social ills of the ghetto*. While these do not exhaust the thematic content of the album or represent the only defensible way to categorize it, they bring to light the kind of image redemption and reconciliation that fleshes out the rhetors' construction of a "gospel gangsta" identity for their audience to identify with.

Approach to truth. The Gospel Gangstaz affirm the value both of embracing God's truth and facing the ghetto's realities. They reaffirm the truth of the Bible, calling it the text "that can answer every question." They appeal to the Word as the legitimizing agency for their ministry and their message, and they echo its themes of impending judgment on sinners and salvation for all who repent and believe in Christ. At the same time, the GGz repeatedly affirm the cardinal credo of hip-hop: "keepin' it real." They both state this credo and practice it in their music. In "Questions," Mr. Solo and Chille' Baby are brutally honest with God about the realities in the world that seem to contradict His goodness (as Chille' Baby says, "you ain't walked in my shoes [...] I know banging was wrong, but it was real"). By staying true to themselves, their blackness, and the streets, the GGz keep it real, as the phrase is understood in the hip-hop nation.[32]

While the Gospel Gangstaz reaffirm the Bible's truth and hip-hop's realism, they also purify their own gospel truth and hip-hop realism of elements that are mutually incompatible. On the one hand, the Bible and the church proscribe lewd desires, language, and acts. Not surprisingly, then, the Gospel Gangstaz' music is purged of the sensuality, profanity, and (to some extent) gratuitous violence typically found m hip-hop. In fact, while praising his own verbal accomplishments in "Interlude #2," Mr. Solo boasts, "I didn't curse." Thus, the GGz bring forth a different image of "keepin' it real" in hip-hop, one that arguably faces evil but doesn't glorify it by flaunting behaviors that Christianity traditionally considers unclean. On the other hand, they rehabilitate the image of gospel truth for the hip-hop audience. Rap's commitment to harsh realism renders abstract or sentimental religious messages out of place and irrelevant. Thus, the Gospel Gangstaz restrict their gospel almost exclusively to those concepts that would meet the felt needs of the hip-hop nation. For example, their songs are devoid of biblical stories and examples from long ago, instead using their own story of deliverance from spiritual and physical danger and themselves as examples of Christian living. The world of their gospel is the world of street survival and hip-hop music. The God they present is a God of the streets—strong, worthy of respect, able to punish wrongdoing, willing to extend mercy through the death of Christ, and giving material success to the faithful. He is not, however, presented as a God of love, for soft or abstract notions of spiritual love may appear irrelevant to the harshness of daily survival.[33]

Concept of the Good. The Gospel Gangstaz unite two views of human good in their lyrics: spiritual salvation and material survival/ success. The gospel tells of spiritual (eternal) salvation that is accomplished through God's Word and grace. Hip-hop emphasizes temporal survival and economic success achieved through the clever words and charisma of the MC or musician. In reality, however, African-Americans' understanding of the gospel has traditionally interwoven the material and spiritual, emphasizing God's earthly liberation of the oppressed as much or more than the joys of heaven. It is ghetto youths' disillusionment or impatience with the church's more peaceable approach to earthly liberation that has partly contributed to their disaffection with the gospel message in recent decades. In response to this exigence, the Gospel Gangstaz offer a renewed (reaffirmed and purified) synthesis of heavenly salvation and earthly success. They talk about themselves being saved from their sins and hell and exhort their peers to turn to God before it's too late, but beyond that their spiritual vision of salvation is sketchy at best. On the other hand, they develop an image of the prospering Christian—themselves as hard-working, savvy, successful artists—that is right in line with the hip-hop nation's fixation on making it big financially.[34] A sampling of their lyrics shows how they reaffirm and knit together both spiritual destiny and economic prosperity in tandem: "My whole purpose is bein' right and makin' cheese [money];" "I take time to holler at the Father, what y'all call prayin'/Tryin' to ball [= work] all day, and while y'all playin'/You can catch me on the grind, tryin' to make cash money/Checks from execs, y'all can have the fast money" ("I Call;" "Whatcha Gonna Do"). As the last line shows, the Gospel Gangstaz denigrate the pursuit of "fast money" through drug running and other illegal activities, and they describe their own experiences with that way of life as too insecure and stressful. Furthermore, they speak against greed, saying in effect, "Make all the money you can, but don't sell your soul to get it." In this way, they both reaffirm and purify hip-hop's image as a means to big success for those disadvantaged by their race and environment.

Likewise, the Gospel Gangstaz reaffirm and purify the Black Christian image of salvation as a spiritually grounded liberation in the present world. On the one hand, they use the Bible to justify their assertion that God promises prosperity to the faithful in this life. In "Live It Up," Chille' Baby quotes from the Proverbs, "The wealth of the wicked is laid up for the righteous, partner, watch me get it/Lifestyles of the rich and saved, homie, watch me live it," and Tik Tokk explains, "His resurrection made us qualify [...] Read through the text that can answer every question why. [...] The end is near, but closer is the life at hand, the right to stand/Wallow in poverty was not the plan/Since a man died for the cherished promise." On the other hand, they criticize the spiritual mentality that seems to advocate the poverty of the oppressed, and they mock their critics in the church for adopting this attitude. As Mr. Solo says in "Operation Liquidation," "I'm just trying to see paper [= money], bless the world over beats and be at peace with the Maker/And y'all don't like this, 'cause I'm righteous/Wanna see me broke, while the world roll the tightest!" They also accuse the church critics of laziness and "hating," which in hip-hop parlance signifies badmouthing an MC out of envy for his/her success. The GGz try to shame the preachers who judge them by boasting about the big tithes they are giving to the church as a result of their success in the hip-hop game. The result of these rhetorical motives working together is that the GGz' image of Christian salvation is purged of associations with passivity and poverty, their image of hip-hop arguably is distanced from associations with outright greed, and a newly integrated vision emerges of Christian salvation as materially practical and hip-hop as a spiritually respectable profession.[35]

Respect. In accordance with the street code it reflects, hip-hop places a premium on respect. Rappers demand respect from others and challenge those who enviously "playa hate" (bad-mouth) or "fade" (downplay) their ability and status. The Gospel Gangstaz are no exception. Not only do they talk up their own verbal prowess and success, they also go on the offensive against the "playa haters," trying to teach them a little respect. As Chille' Baby says in the first "Interlude," his goal is to be "loved by few, hated by many, but respected by all." The GGz have two contrasting sets of playa haters to deal with: rival MCs who try to steal their glory, and preachers or churchgoers who criticize them for making rap music. The former are guilty of not respecting the individual's accomplishments, while the latter are guilty of not respect-ing a credible, God-anointed minister of the gospel who mixes with the sinners like Jesus did. Both are charged with trying to puff up their own importance by tearing down someone who really has the importance they lack. Thus, the GGz mock the "playa haters" as people who have a "P.H. Degree," and they pull no punches when it comes to putting others in their place. In "They Don't Believe I'm Saved," Mr. Solo tries to talk some sense to the impudent: "You ain't even got a passport. You ain't even in the union. You're still trying to be a player. See, I'm the Coach. I done played the game [...] and I'm coming back to teach you." Chille' Baby takes a more menacing tack: "Don't get out of line. [...] I smell the blood of a petty MC, step up if you want some. [...] I'm a veteran, don't gamble off your soul big spender. [...] It's brawl time, you small time; we the heavyweights." By the same token, the Gospel Gangstaz go on the offensive against hypocrites in the church who judge them. In "Operation Liquidation," Mr. Solo echoes Christ's answer to the legalistic critics of his day: "You may not like the way I mob, but show respect/Traditions of man make the Word of God to no effect." With a veiled threat, he warns, "your P.H.-ing don't even move me/Saying you would do me?/But truly you'd be quiet if you knew me." In this way, the Gospel Gangstaz' discourse reaffirms the images of the hip-hop MC and the Christian prophet who demand respect by their actions and attitudes. It also works to purify their gospel image of any association with meek church-goers who bow to tradition and let the preacher lord it over them.

Sense of Community. The church (especially the Black church) has traditionally been a community, a place of *koinonia* or close fellowship and support. However, it also has been accused at times of exclusivity, of being a pharisaical fellowship. Hip-hop, on the other hand, reflects the high value placed on local loyalty in the ghetto and gangs. Alums by rappers from different parts of the country record protracted regional rivalries and express their loyalties to their hood or gang. Gangsta rap reflected the lengths of hatred and violence to which these rivalries could go, as in the shooting deaths of Tupac Shakur and the Notorious B.I.G.[36] In the case of both the church and the hip-hop nation, the Gospel Gangstaz reaffirm the value of tight community and eschew the extremes of excluding and feuding. Their expression of Christian fellowship is largely subsumed into connections that the hip-hop audience would relate to: their circle of musicians and business associates. The GGz make only one direct reference to attending church and several oblique references (mainly about giving tithes);

their overt expression of Christian love is to each other and the "Committee," a small circle of like-minded Christian hip-hop ministers. Mr. Solo says that when he goes to minister in the ghetto, "Committee got my back," and Tik Tokk pledges, "2Gz for life, Committee ride, we all tight."

At the same time, the GGz do not exhibit the kind of pious isolation that the church is accused of: they perform with mainstream artists, seek a platform in the clubs, and frequently express their allegiance to their region and their peers on the streets. In the title cut, Mr. Solo has himself arriving to address the locals in his hometown of L.A., and in "Once Was Blind," he declares, "I'm West Coast Cali, tried and tested." Even in the gospel version of this song, their background singer (Twenty/20) sings," "These Gz, they made me everything I am." In "Live It Up," Chille' Baby interjects, "Much love to my homie, Untouchable, that's in the pen," and in "Once Was Blind," he prays, "God bless all the Gz, and open up they eyes [...] just like He did me." Nowhere do the Gospel Gangstaz put down another region, record label, or rival gang, as some rappers do. They portray rigidly narrow loyalties (such that provoke violence) as a destructive dead-end for the ghetto, and they occasionally speak of themselves as representing a love that would transcend these loyalties and benefit all their people. Indeed, they validate such statements by the very fact that these former members of rival gangs (two Crips and a Blood) are now one team with a common cause. They even affirm love toward the Christians who "hate" them.[37] Thus, the GGz' ethos embodies a redeemed Christian love and a redeemed sense of ghetto community in tandem.

Warfare. Gangsta rap portrays the ghetto as a war zone in which life is brutal and short and young "soldiers" (gangstas) are killed in their prime. This was the flavor of the Gospel Gangstaz' first two albums, which sublimated the battle theme to a spiritual level and cast demons as the real enemies who must be destroyed. Post-gangsta hip-hop retains its sense of the brutality and brevity of life, as do the GGz on *I Can See Clearly Now*. In fact, this theme dovetails very well into their street-oriented gospel message. But, as with the other themes in their music, their project of creating a credible rhetorical synthesis requires them to separate their gospel hip-hop image from corrupt, incompatible forms of Christian warfare and ghetto warfare.

To reaffirm hip-hop's sense of life as war, the Gospel Gangstaz depict the ghetto as a battle zone and identify with its sufferings. In "Let Us Pray," Chille' Baby paints a grim scene: "Picture a 'hood full of 64s, 'lacs and Regals/Westside riders, strapped with Tees and Desert Eagles/Lethal, caught up in crime, making fedi illegal/Contaminated minds drenched with the thoughts of evil/Killing off our own kind, not knowin' who's plottin'/Ghetto birds in the air 'cause the pistols is poppin'/Bodies is droppin', the numbers in the morgue ain't droppin'." In light of such a scenario, one of Mr. Solo's "rules of the game" is "Always be prepared to die, 'cause you never know when it's your turn to say goodbye" ("Operation Liquidation"). He also relates the violence on a personal level "My dogg took 2 [bullets] to the back of the dome/ Left in the back of a Brougham, with his brain splattered." While empathizing with their peers caught up in this war, they also dissociate themselves from the hate and illegal activity that fuel the violence. For example, the references above to "contaminated minds" and Black-on-Black violence clearly cast gang activity in a negative light. On several cuts, Mr. Solo tells the "playa haters" that he is not angry with them (and hence will not retaliate), though he has the right to. In "Let Us Pray," he confesses to God that, as a thug from the streets, his greatest weakness is anger, but he resolves to love his enemies anyway "'cause they know not what they doin'."

In addition to using their own experiences as a model of redemption from the gang life, on a few occasions the GGz directly exhort their listeners to forsake the drug trade and violence in view of coming death and eternal judgment. Thus, they go on the offensive against the roots of war in the ghetto—poverty, drugs, and hatred—and they simultaneously integrate this offensive into their spiritual mission, reaffirming the Christian imagery of spiritual warfare against Satan's evil principalities and demons. In "Questions" and "Let Us Pray," they reveal their personal struggle with besetting sins of the flesh and pray for strength to overcome the devil's temptations: In other songs, some of which have been cited above, they assert their authority over the demons that blind and bind their listeners, and they claim to have the devil's minions on the run. Yet the mission is not without peril for these soldiers; in "Once Was Blind," Mr. Solo describes himself as a potential martyr for the cause: "I'm livin' life on the run; will I end up in jail or die by a gun?/Can't hide when they come, y'all know where I'm from, I ride with the Son./My outlook on this world is from a G's perspective/Find those in a life of sin, get 'em born again is my objective." Despite the spiritual warfare imagery, the Gospel Gangstaz clearly distance themselves from the way the church misuses that imagery to attack the sinners themselves. In the hip-hop magazine *XXL*, Mr. Solo echoes Ice Cube's advice to ministers: "It ain't wise to chastise and preach/just open the eyes of each" (Everett 54). Clearly, then, the GGz reaffirm the image of Christians in a spiritual war against sin but attack the church's judgmentalism against "sinners" (their fellow gangstas).

At the end of "Let Us Pray," Chille' Baby laments the plague of violence among urban Blacks and raps with intense emotion, "God, I stand in the gap for the ghetto/Please give us this day/As we bow down our heads, repent, and pray." The phrase "stand in the gap" is an allusion to the prophet Ezekiel, where God speaks of the need for someone to intercede for humanity. However, the phrase aptly describes the Gospel Gangstaz' rhetorical effort to claim the middle ground between the gospel community and the hip-hop nation. As the analysis above shows, they refuse to allow the traditions of the church or of hip-hop to define their identity completely. Occupying the marginal space between the borders of each, they contest those borders by presenting redeemed images of the two domains, images that converge in their own identity as gospel gangstas. Their self-identification abounds in paradoxical unions: Tik Tokk proudly refers to himself as the "Holy Hoodlum;" Chille' Baby boasts, "Look, I keeps it, Gospel and Gangsta, at the same time," and Mr. Solo aspires to "be a thug, plus blessed." By reaffirming ostensibly compatible aspects of the gospel and hip-hop, they redraw the borders of the two images so that the domains they represent overlap. And by marginalizing the polluted regions within gospel and hip-hop, they identify themselves with the presumably pure common ground—where "gospel" suggests a message of real, relevant help from above and "gangsta" or "thug" means one who is loyal to his peer group, aggressive enough to thrive in a dangerous world, and committed enough to die for what he believes in.[38] Thus, through redemptive rhetoric they give birth to one new identity out of the two.

Discussion

My analysis of the Gospel Gangstaz' lyrics demonstrates that Fisher's motive view of communication can offer insight into the thematic development of a rhetorical synthesis, particularly when social identity and identification are most salient in the rhetorical situation. Furthermore, this analysis suggests that the Gospel Gangstaz are carrying on an African-American heritage of contesting the borders of imposed identity through interpositionality.[39] As defined by Brooks and Jacobs, *interpositionality* is a strategy for symbolic emancipation that "moves back and forth between [...] two communities in a quest to facilitate the construction of anti-essentialist identities for members of both communities" (292). While the GGz explicitly identify with the hip-hop nation in their music, they also retain their ties to the church-financially, spiritually, and accountably. Thus, they challenge traditional images of how a churchgoer carries out Christian ministry even as they contradict hip-hop's typical image of vulgarity and misogyny. In the process, they face criticism from both camps. While conservative church members regard them as too worldly, Burke's and Patel's reviews indicate that the Gospel Gangstaz' lyrics still come across as "corny" or "preachy" to those outside the church. From a theological standpoint, the GGz certainly leave themselves open to charges of "soft-pedaling the gospel for profit" or even "syncretism." Thus, they confirm Brooks and Jacobs' assertion that interposers will experience dual backlash from the groups they represent because, from their marginal position, they appear as a threat (or misfit) to both sides.[40]

By circumscribing (and staking their own claim on) a new commons within the African American community, the Gospel Gangstaz implicitly invite listeners to embrace a re-synthesized recovery vision that is purportedly big enough to encompass the core visions of the church and the hip-hop nation and powerful enough to heal the Black ghetto. Such a rapprochement may be a long way off, however, given I the difficulty of gaining a wide following for a rhetorical synthesis. Unlike Kirk Franklin, who has added the spice of urban sounds to what is essentially a gospel act, the Gospel Gangstaz have not achieved platinum or even gold record sales, despite their substantial effort and outlay of cash to achieve a mainstream breakthrough with *I Can See Clearly Now*. While Franklin's music still appeals squarely to the gospel audience (albeit its younger members), the GGz have attempted a much more radical and difficult task by taking their stand in the no-man's-land between gospel and the hard-core hip-hop audience, attempting to construct a rhetorical synthesis that the hip-hop audience can strongly identify with. Judging by album sales and mixed reviews, their synthesis still has limited appeal-at least in part because of the nature of rhetorical synthesis.

Chapel suggests that rhetorical synthesis, although intrinsically attractive as a means of healing a controversy, "may have limited popular appeal because it is an intellectual, conceptual articulation that may not necessarily resonate with the popular mind" ("Rhetorical Synthesis" 358). However, the case of the Gospel Gangstaz contradicts Chapel's explanation, converging instead on interpositionality as a locus of limitation. It is easier to adopt scripted identities than to create one's own identity between the lines; it is doubly difficult to identify with both sides of a controversy to the point that they can be lured out of their comfort zone into a transcendent, socially transformative identity and vision. Like a peace initiative between warring countries, a rhetorical synthesis represents a departure from entrenched and familiar oppositions to the unstable, mine-ridden middle ground of dialogue and rapprochement. Even the most credible and skilled rhetors may not be able to convince many listeners to join them on such a middle ground.

Marginality, Culture, and Rhetorical Synthesis

The foregoing study of the Gospel Gangstaz' rhetoric indicates that Chapel's conception of rhetorical synthesis should be broadened to reflect the role of culture (as well as medium) in establishing its conditions and manifestations. While it may be true that literate intellectuals are more likely to contest received thought systems and create or embrace a rhetorical synthesis that transcends two systems, it is also evident that marginalized groups, such as African-Americans, have learned well how to challenge rigid categories and find creative ways to transcend oppressive social divisions, and often these ways are not abstractly intellectual. Given the salience of identity management for Blacks—as exemplified in the Gospel Gangstaz' rhetorical synthesis—the role of the rhetor's identity should, perhaps, be given greater weight in Chapel's theory, at least for some situations or cultural groups. As noted in the beginning of this essay, Chapel does recognize the importance of ethos as a *reinforcing* factor, particularly in the case of Jack Kemp. However, like Aristotle, Chapel's work as a whole still places greater emphasis on *logos*.

The Gospel Gangstaz' rhetorical synthesis in *I Can See Clearly Now* turns Chapel's approach on its head; their synthesis springs from the all-important exigence of creating a credible and viable social identity in an excruciatingly fractured society, maintaining a sense of self-respect and meaning in a degrading and often nihilistic environment. Their rhetorical synthesis manifests Gresson's recovery project, telling stories of how the gospel they have discovered is working to save them *as gangstas*, spiritually and economically. They count on the power of these narratives to effect their own economic redemption (by selling albums) and, in the process, to influence their peers to embrace the liberative powers of this gangsta gospel.

My analysis of an African-American rhetorical artifact indicates that the study of rhetorical synthesis has much to gain from considering the contributions of non-Eurocentric rhetorics. Indeed, beyond their experience of marginality, Blacks are the heirs to a richly oral African rhetorical tradition that features the rhythmic counterpoint between the inventive skill of the rhetor and the active participation of the audience, creating a sense of community, harmonizing opposites, and balancing dynamic forces through the power of the spoken word. So central are these features that Molefi Asante has defined rhetoric from an Afrocentric standpoint as "the productive thrust of language into the unknown in an attempt to create harmony and balance in the midst of disharmony and indecision" (35). Blacks' experience in White America has forced them to draw upon the depths of their faith in God and their native rhetorical resources to maintain harmony and balance. W. E. B. DuBois eloquently characterized the tensions within Black identity: "an American, a Negro, two souls, two thoughts, two unreconciled strivings; two warring ideals in one dark body, whose dogged strength alone keeps it from being torn asunder" (215). As the economics and rhetoric of post-civil-rights America have worked to pull apart the African-American community, rhetors such as the Gospel Gangstaz have been striving valiantly to hold it together and re-harmonize its dissonant elements through the power of the spoken word. Such efforts epitomize rhetorical synthesis and challenge us to see it in a new light.

Study Questions

1. How does Hatch use the work of Gospel Gangstaz to challenge and advance Chapel's concept of "rhetorical synthesis?" What specific role does "interpositionality" in black cultural realities play in this reworking?

2. How are the oppositional parallels, realities and resolution (in the work of GGz) between "gospel" and "gangstaz" used in this essay? For what means, purposes and ends?

3. What does the close rhetorical synthesis of the song *I Can See Clearly Now* reveal about the inner-workings of rhetorical synthesis in black culture and life?

Notes

1. In this essay, I have chosen to use the labels "Black" and "African American" interchangeably, in part for aesthetic reasons, but also because polls show the majority of African Americans see either term

as appropriate, and scholars do not agree on a preference for one over the other (e.g., see Orbe and Harris 57–58).

2. According to Duffie, a little over 200,000 copies were sold.

3. The communication literature has shown a burgeoning interest in hip-hop in the past decade. McLeod's study of authenticity ("keepin' it real"), Watts' article on gangsta rap as cultural commodity, and Aldridge and Carlin's rhetorical analysis of KRS-One's anti-violence rap lyrics are especially germane to the present study. In addition, scholarly books on hip-hop have begun to appear, such as Dimitriadis' ethnography of youths and hip-hop culture.

4. Space does not allow me to do justice to a rhetoric-of-music framework (e.g., that of Chesebro, et al. or Sellnow) in addition to the other theoretical concepts and cultural factors that inform my analysis. African-American experiences, traditions, and sensibilities have powerfully shaped popular music in many of its twentieth-century forms: the blues, jazz, rock, and above all, hip-hop (even when adopted by white performers, such as Eminem). In addition, the Gospel Gangstaz' lyrics are clearly directed toward their own cultural community with its unique exigencies. Therefore, I have chosen to emphasize culture over medium in my approach to this analysis. However, the literature on the rhetoric of music (e.g., Irvine and Kirkpatrick; Booth; Chesebro et al.; Rein and Springer; Sellnow) offers insight into the ways that the GGz' rhetorical synthesis contradicts Chapel's approach. For one, music nondiscursively conveys emotional messages that interact with, significantly shape, or even overshadow the discursive communication in song lyrics. Additionally, songs' rhetorical function tends to work at the level of identification rather than overt persuasion. Hence, hip-hop, being a musical form, would favor a persuasive strategy that relies on the emotional power of images and identification. Indeed, such is the case with the Gospel Gangstaz' rhetorical synthesis.

5. In Chapel's study of Jack Kemp, he writes, "Because rhetorical synthesis, in effect, creates something new, more attention is often paid to the creator of the message than would be paid to one mouthing cliches or mundane messages. [...] the synthesis is vulnerable because it can be weakened by the lack of credibility of the rhetor or by attacks on the credibility of the rhetor. This being the case, it is useful for the rhetor to build credibility-enhancing strategies into the message" (350). The author also observes that "Kemp's rhetorical synthesis is not just an intellectual endeavor. His character, personality, physical presence, and temperament come together to make him, in an important sense, the embodiment of his synthesis; he is idea and attitude in action" (353).

6. This focus on *logos* is not surprising, since Chapel's model clearly builds on the Aristotelian tradition.

7. Eddy's Christian Science discourse resonated with an "audience of literate middle- and upper-middle class Americans" who were educated enough to be seriously troubled by the growing contradictions between science and the Bible (Chapel and Jensen 104). Masaharu Taniguchi's Seicho-No-Ie religious movement was most influential among Japanese intellectuals. And Jack Kemp's political synthesis of liberal and conservative agendas "gained favorable notice with important elites: the media, think tanks, special interest groups, and Washington insiders," with little impact on the national electorate ("Rhetorical Synthesis" 354).

8. Martha Solomon refers to embodiment, "wherein a rhetor enacts the principle or argument s/he is discussing," as an "especially powerful strategy that bridges ethos and logical argument" (190). Chapel recognizes the vital role of embodiment in Jack Kemp's rhetorical synthesis. However, I argue that, in the Gospel Gangstaz' case, embodiment does not just support, but rather controls thematic development of the rhetorical synthesis.

9. See Bennett 124–26, 310–311; Henderson 21–23; Frazier; Lincoln and Mamiya.

10. See George 34–44 for a lucid explanation of these developments in the Black ghetto.

11. For more detail on the origin and nature of these art forms, see George 11–21. As hip-hop music evolved from live performance to studio recording, the function of DJ-ing was taken over and expanded by "sampling," the technique of electronically storing, manipulating, and combining sounds from various older recordings into a hip-hop track (89–96).

12. George asserts, "Gangsta rap [...] is a direct by-product of the crack explosion. [...] [It] first appeared in the mid-'80s. It exploded at the end of that decade and has leveled off—just like crack use—in

the 90s" (42). Explaining the complexity of gangsta rap, George writes, "Not all rappers who write violent lyrics have lived the words. Most exercise the same artistic license to write violent tales as do the makers of Hollywood flicks" (46).

13. Eugene Rivers, an African-American pastor and the founder of Boston's Ten-Point Coalition, addresses the shortcomings of the Black church: "In many cities it is easier for a homeless black teenage girl to find sanctuary in a crack house or a bar on a Friday night than it is for her to find refuge behind the locked doors of many established black churches" (26). He goes on: "With rare exceptions, the black church's pastoral vision does not speak to the experience of intense alienation of the colonized in the urban metropolitan centers in the country." Michael Eric Dyson writes, "Gangster rap IS largely an indictment of bourgeois black cultural and political institutions by young people who do not find conventional methods of addressing personal and social calamity useful" ("Bum Rap").

14. For example, the Reverend Butts, who had earlier opposed hip-hop as a source of carnal tempta-tions, now crushed rap records in front of his Harlem church to protest their increasingly dark messages.

15. Dyson avers, "Gangster raps' greatest sin, in the eyes of many of its critics, is that it tells the truth about practices and beliefs that rappers hold in common with the black elite. This music has embar-rassed black bourgeois culture and exposed its polite sexism" ("Bum Rap").

16. Anderson derived these categories ("decent" and "street") from Black urban residents' own usage. The decent orientation more or less aligns itself with mainstream, middle-class American values, such as hard work, moral rectitude, self-reliance politeness, making sacrifices for the future, and having faith that justice will prevail: Anderson notes that many decent families are churchgoers who "see their difficult situation as a test from God and derive great support from their faith and from the church community" (83). The street orientation, on the other hand, reflects "a profound lack of faith in the police and the judicial system" and thus throws off traditional norms and hopes as oppressive and futile. The code of the street is rooted in an obsession with "juice" or respect, "viewed as almost an external entity that is hard-won but easily lost, and so must be constantly guarded." The attainment of juice depends on displaying a predisposition to violence as well as acquiring valued objects (e.g., fash-ionable clothing, jewelry, cars, and women), often by taking them from others. While some gangsta rap artists (e.g., NWA) seem to celebrate the ruthlessness of the street code, Dyson reminds us that a number of hard-core rappers, such as KRS-One, have clearly spoken out against violence in their music ("Performance"). Indeed, much of the time the harsh demeanor presented in much hip-hop is more presentation than lifestyle. As Anderson explains, "many less alienated young blacks have assumed a street-oriented demeanor as a way of expressing their blackness while really embracing a much more moderate way of life; they, too, want a nonviolent setting in which to live and raise a family" (94).

17. While Gresson scarcely makes reference to Fisher's narrative paradigm, his project clearly mirrors Fisher's belief in the centrality of narrative rationality and identification in rhetoric, as expressed in the latter's seminal work *Human Communication as Narration*.

18. Being musical forms, gospel and rap are especially conducive to recovery rhetoric since the rheto-ric of music works through audience identification and self-persuasion. As Irvine and Kirkpatrick explain, "the amplificative meaning generated by music. [...] is participatory to the extent that the auditor contributes elements of interpretation to complete the event. Because of this, the new [...] meaning generated includes identification and commitment from the auditor. The new meaning is personalized and, therefore, self-persuasive" (278).

19. According to Farley, since 1998 rap has been the top-selling musical format in the U.S., and white buyers account for more than 70% of its album sales.

20. As early as 1992, scholars such as Jon Spencer were taking note of this new musical movement and its potential to break through the barriers of irrelevance, otherworldliness, and "whiteness" that had kept more traditional forms of Black gospel music from speaking to the needs of the ghetto poor. Interestingly enough, Rev. Butts, who crushed gangsta rap records in front of his Harlem church, has given gospel rap his stamp of approval (Marriott).

21. Since then, other artistically respectable gospel hip-hop groups have emerged, such as the Cross Movement, Prime Minister, GRITS, etc.

22. According to McCain & Company, Franklin's 1998 Nu Nation Project went platinum.
23. A rhetorical analysis of their musical form (as outlined by Sellnow or Irvine and Kirkpatrick) would exceed the scope of this essay. Furthermore, there is little in the way of a gospel sound on *I Can See Clearly Now*. In contrast to Kirk Franklin's fusion of rap and gospel music, the GGz' rhetorical synthesis does not hinge on a synthesis of musical styles.
24. As Thomas Kochman observes, Black communication style leans toward being "high-keyed"—animated, interpersonal, and confrontational—as manifested in the conventions of exaggerated boasting, serious bragging, showboating (showing off individual flair while accomplishing a task), woofing (fighting through verbal threats rather than physical altercation), and "playing the dozens" (trading cleverly worded and increasingly devastating insults). See also Hecht, Collier and Ribeau; and Daniel and Smitherman.
25. For example, Tik Tokk brags about traveling "around the world in a day 'cause we in demand" and Chille' Baby says, "When Interscope want a bomb hit, they page me." Tucked in among these boasts are a few passing references to the spiritual side of their conquest of the music business. The following few lines illustrate how: "The D. J's play us, yelling 'Jesus saved us,'/Rockin' with the majors, vacate in Vegas/Gone till November, if you need us, you can page us/B-Rite paid us, now millions await us/To get the crowd moving to a track Meech made us."
26. In the pursuit of excellence, the GGz certainly put their money where their mouth is: they went $300,000 in debt in order to procure top-notch producers and promotion for *I Can See Clearly Now* (Johnson). Furthermore, their lyrical flow and delivery have gained respect from some mainstream hip-hop artists and reviewers (e.g., Everett, Bush, Shawn Campbell).
27. The theme of conquering demons comes up on several tracks in *I Can See Clearly Now*. For example, in "Operation Liquidation," Mr. Solo says, "I shine the light of Christ and watch them scatter like roaches. [...] Spot those that turn they back and get to flashing on those busters I Escalade sideways and get to smashin' on them suckers." In "Live It Up," he compares the GGz to Batman and Robin "fightin' goblins [...] in Gotham City."
28. For example, Rybacki and Rybacki define goodwill as "the extent to which a rhetor is identified with the audience and their concerns" (42).
29. The GGz stake the viability of this recovery vision on their own claims of success, striving to make these claims compelling enough, lyrically and musically, to actually effect that success. This effort illustrates Cresson's assertion that recovery rhetoric works to persuade both the self and Other simultaneously.
30. Indeed, my perusal of visitor responses on the GGz' web site indicated that their fans already share their religious vision (Real Gz; Message Board). Approximately 60% of their albums are sold through mainstream outlets (Aviles), but it is quite possible that many of these are purchased by listeners who already share their religious views.
31. See Burke's *The Rhetoric of Religion*.
32. McLeod has identified six different semantic dimensions according to which "keepin' it real" is variously understood within the hip-hop community: (1) staying true to oneself (versus following mass trends), (2) being Black instead of White, (3) making music underground (rather than going commercial), (4) being hard, not soft, (5) maintaining close ties to the streets (versus selling out to the suburbs), and (6) respecting the pure hip-hop created "back in the day" before the genre became mainstream. As McLeod's study revealed, "Keepin' it real is a floating signifier in that its meaning changes depending on the context in which it is invoked" (139).
33. The absence of divine love as a theme on this album stands in stark contrast with almost any other contemporary Christian (or crossover) recording, where divine or human love is often the dominant theme (e.g., the music of Amy Grant).
34. Eric Watts sheds light on the link between hip-hop and materialism: "there exists a spectacularly symbiotic relationship between the dictates of the street code and an energetic American consumerism," in that "the street code legitimates aggression in the pursuit of juice [respect] and manifests it in material possession [...] Gangsta rap artistry vivifies harsh imagery and its consumption establishes a set of exchange relations among public culture, rap music, and the rap industrial complex" (50).

35. Closely related to the themes of spiritual salvation and material success are faith in God and confidence in oneself as the bases for appropriating these benefits. As the discussion of their ethos demonstrated, the GGz exude self-confidence in almost every line. Yet this self-confidence is wedded to occasional expressions of faith in God, such as the following: "Now faith in God and paying tithes got me living well." The assertive and sometimes boastful attitude with which the GGz express their faith in heaven's blessing is strikingly similar to the bravado that hip-hop exudes in the name of respect. In his early analysis of gospel hip-hop, Spencer noted the emergence of this self-assertive attitude and contrasted it with the "fanatical self-effacement of individual identity and human personhood" in old-style gospel, where "Jesus is 'everything' and 'all,' and human beings and human life are *nothing*" (450). Spencer went on to observe the racial overtones of this theological shift: "The Jesus of old-style gospel is 'white' because the message that black people are *nothing* coincides with what long has been told them by white America. In gospel hip-hop, however, this tradition is being radically overturned" (451).

36. George (129–143) traces the development of the East-West conflict that culminated in Tupac's death.

37. Mr. Solo expresses a sort of tough love toward the church in "Operation Liquidation:" "You haters, the outcome of a hater and a fool's the same/But out of love I give you five rules to the game." He then imparts five guidelines of Christian ministry-free nuggets of wisdom for the misguided.

38. In an article in *Contemporary Christian Music Magazine*, Mr. Solo is quoted as saying, "A gangsta is someone who's willing to live as well as die for what he believes in. We're laying our lives down for the gospel. We never forget where he came from. But we understand that our weapons are not Tec-9s or 9mm Uzis or AK-47 rifles, but our weapons are 'mighty through God for the pulling down of strongholds'" (DeBarros).

39. For example, Frederick Douglass challenged the separate categories of "White" and "Negro" by asserting himself as biracial. Douglass' abolitionist rhetoric also transcended existing dichotomies (Stephens). The mature Malcolm X also arguably exemplified interpositionality. In a speech that he gave near the end of his life, Malcolm explored the limitations and possibilities of both domestic and international perspectives for black identity, repeatedly stepping across the border between the two and thereby challenging his audience to "reject the definition imposed upon them by the dominant culture and to remake themselves" (Terrill 67).

40. Brooks and Jacobs explain, "While traveling through disparate communities, interposers must anticipate attempts to shore up borders at the intersections of those communities: they are informed (subtly and not so subtly) about the 'correct' identities within and are subjected to efforts to enforce the performance of those identities. Interposers challenge these assertions [...] [and] pursue flexible identities, ones that are informed by traditional understandings but that are not scripted to mimic those realities closely" (292).

Works Cited

"About Gospel Gangstaz." Promotional Leaflet. Inglewood, CA: B-Rite Music.

Aldridge, Heather, and Diana B. Carlin. "The Rap on Violence: A Rhetorical Analysis of Rapper KRS-One." *Communication Studies* 44 (1993): 102–16.

Anderson, Elijah. "The Code of the Streets." *The Atlantic Monthly* May 1994: 80+. Asante, Molefl Kete. *The Afrocentric Idea*. Philadelphia: Temple UP, 1987.

Aviles, Gabriel. "Re: Gospel Gangstaz." E-mail to the author. March 23, 2000. Bennett, Lerone, Jr. *The Shaping of Black America*. New York: Penguin, 1993.

Booth, Mark W "The Art of Words in Songs." *Quarterly Journal of Speech* 62 (1976): 242–49.

Brooks, Dwight E., and Walter R. Jacobs. "Black Men in the Margins: *Space Traders* and the Interpositional Strategy Against B(l)acklash." *Communication Studies* 47 (1996): 289–302.

Burke, Kenneth. *A Rhetoric of Motives*. 1950. Berkeley: U of California Press, 1969.

——. *The Rhetoric of Religion: Studies in Logology*. Berkeley: U of California Press, 1961. Burke, Miguel. Rev. of *I Can See Clearly Now*, by Gospel Gangstaz. *Vibe* Sep. 1999: 268.

Bush, John. Rev. of *I Can See Clearly Now*, by Gospel Gangstaz. *All Music Guide*. March 9, 2000 <http://www.allmusic.com>.

Campbell, Joseph. *The Hero with a Thousand Faces*. 2d edn. Princeton, NJ: Princeton University Press, 1968.

Campbell, Shawn (Hip-hop producer). Telephone interview. April 14, 2000.

Chapel, Gage. "Rhetorical Synthesis and the Discourse of Jack Kemp." *Southern Communication Journal* 61 (1996): 342–62.

Chapel, Gage. "Synthesizing Eastern and Western Religious Traditions: The Rhetoric of Japan's Seicho-No-le Movement." *The Journal of Communication and Religion* 12:1 (March 1989): 14–21.

——, and Richard Jensen. "Synthesizing Jamesian Pragmatism and Platonic Idealism in Nineteenth Century America: The Discourse of Mary Baker Eddy's Christian Science." *The Journal of Communication and Religion* 23 (2000): 95–122.

Chesebro, James W, Foulger, Davis A., Nachman, Jay E., and Andrew Yannelli. "Popular Music as a Mode of Communication, 1955–1982." *Critical Studies in Mass Communication* 2 (1985): 115–35.

Daniel, Jack, and Geneva Smitherman. "How I Got Over: Communication Dynamics in the Black Community." *Quarterly Journal of Speech* 62 (1976): 28–39.

Dimitriadis, Greg. *Performing Identity/Performing Culture: Hip Hop as Text, Pedagogy, and Lived Practice*. New York: Peter Lang, 2001.

DuBois, W E. B. *The Souls of Black Folk. Three Negro Classics*. New York: Avon, 1965. 207–389.

Duffie, Michelle. "Gospel Gangstaz Sales History." E-mail to the author. March 28, 2000.

Dyson, Michael Eric. "Bum Rap: It's Too Easy to Bash Gangster Lyrics from the Pulpit." *The New York Times* 3 Feb. 1994: A21.

—— "Performance, Protest, and Prophecy in the Culture of Hip-Hop." *Black Sacred Music* 5 (1991): 12–24.

Everett, Vic. "Nuthin' But a 'G' Thang." *XXL* Dec. 1999: 54.

Farley, Christopher J. "Hip-Hop Nation." *Time* February 8, 1999: 54–64.

Fisher, Walter R. "A Motive View of Communication." *Quarterly Journal of Speech* 56 (1970): 131–39.

——. *Human Communication as Narration: Toward a Philosophy of Reason, Value, and Action*. Columbia: U of South Carolina Press, 1987.

Frazier, E. Franklin. *The Negro Church in America*. C. Eric Lincoln. *The Black Church Since Frazier*. New York: Schocken, 1974.

George, Nelson. *Hip Hop America*. New York: Penguin, 1998.

Gooch, Cheryl Renee. "Rappin' for the Lord: The Uses of Gospel Rap and Contemporary Music in Black Religious Communities." *Religion and Mass Media: Audiences and Adaptations*. Ed. Daniel A. Stout and Judith M. Buddenbaum. Thousand Oaks: Sage, 1996, 228–42.

Gospel Gangstaz. *Do or Die*. Holy Terra, 1995.

—— *Gang Affiliated*. MYX, 1995.

—— *I Can See Clearly Now*. B-Rite Music, 1999.

Gresson, Aaron D. III. *The Recovery of Race in America*. Minneapolis: U of Minnesota P, 1995.

Hecht, Michael L., Collier, Mary Jane, and Sidney A. Ribeau. *African American Communication: Ethnic Identity and Cultural Interpretation*. Language and Language Behaviors 2. Newbury Park, CA: Sage, 1993.

Henderson, George. *Our Souls to Keep: Black/White Relations in America*. Yarmouth, ME: Intercultural, 1999.

Irvine, James R., and Walter J. Kirkpatrick. "The Musical Form in Rhetorical Exchange: Theoretical Considerations." *Quarterly Journal of Speech* 58 (1972) 272–84.

Jackson, Ronald L. II. "Africalogical Theory Building: Positioning the Discourse." *Rhetoric in Intercultural Contexts*. Ed. Alberto Gonzalez and Dolores V. Tanno. International and Intercultural Communication Annual 22. Thousand Oaks, CA: Sage, 2000. 31–40.

Johnson, Billy Jr. "Taking Gospel Rap Mainstream." *Launch*. March 9, 2000. <http://www.launch.com>.

Kochman, Thomas. *Black and Whzte Styles in Conflict*. Chicago: U of Chicago Press, 1981.

Lincoln, C. Eric, and Lawrence H. Mamiya. *The Black Church in the African-American Experience*. Durham, NC: Duke U P, 1990.

Marriott, Michel. "Rhymes of Redemption." *Newsweek* November 28, 1994: 64–65.

McCain & Company Public Relations. *Gospel Gangstaz Receives First Stellar Award Nomination*. Press Release. October 22, 1999.

McCroskey, James C. *An Introduction to Communication in the Classroom*. Edina, MN: Burgess, 1992.

McCroskey, James C. and Jason J. Teven. "Goodwill: A Reexamination of the Construct and Its Measurement." *Communication Monographs* 66 (1999): 90–103.

McLeod, Kembrew. "Authenticity within Hip-Hop and Other Cultures Threatened with Assimilation." *Journal of Communication* 49 (1999): 134–50.

Message Board. Gospel Gangstaz. 1 May 2000 <http://www.gospel-gangstaz.com/guestlog.htm>.

Orbe, Mark P., and Tina M. Harris. *Interracial Communication: Theory into Practice*. Toronto: Wadsworth, 2001.

Patel, Joseph. Rev. of *I Can See Clearly Now*, by Gospel Gangstaz. *CDNOW*. March 9, 2000 <http5:// www.cdnow.com>.

Real Gz-Who Are. Gospel Gangstaz. March 9, 2000. <http://www.gospel-gangstaz.com/whoweare.htmb

Rein, Irving J., and Craig M. Springer. "Where's the Music? The Problems of Lyric Analysis." *Critical Studies in Mass Communication* 3 (1986): 252–256.

Rivers, Eugene F. III. "Challenge from Within."*Sojourners* January–February 1996: 25–28.

Rushing, Janice Hocker, and Thomas S. Frentz. "The Rhetoric of 'Rocky': A Social Value Model of Criticism." *Stern Journal of Speech Communication* 42 (1978): 63–72.

Rybacki, Karyn, and Donald Rybacki. *Communication Criticism: Approaches and Genres*. Belmont, CA: Wadsworth, 1991.

Sellnow, Deanna D. "Rhetorical Strategies of Continuity and Change in the Music of Popular Artists over Time." *Communication Studies* 47 (1996): 46–61.

Solomon, Martha. "Ideology as Rhetorical Constraint: The Anarchist Agitation of 'Red Emma' Goldman." *Quarterly Journal of Speech* 74 (1988): 184–200.

Spencer, Jon Michael. "Rapsody in Black: Utopian Aspirations." *Theology Today* 48 (1992): 444–51.

Stephens, Gregory. "Frederick Douglass' Multiracial Abolitionism: 'Antagonistic Cooperation' and 'Redeemable Ideals' in the July 5 Speech." *Communication Studies* 48 (1997): 175–194.

Terrill, Robert E. "Colonizing the Borderlands: Shifting Circumference in the Rhetoric of Malcolm X." *Quarterly Journal of Speech* 86 (2000): 67–85.

Watts, Eric K. "An Exploration of Spectacular Consumption: Gangsta Rap as Cultural Commodity." *Communication Studies* 48 (1997): 42–58.

Where Are My Dawgs At?
A Theology of Community

Beginning in personal reflection about the importance of hip hop during his youth, Hodge notes an ongoing tension between his "crew" and his "church community." The latter viewed Hodge's cultural associations with hip hop and his commitment to the church as antithetical. Noting community meaning and identity as central to hip hop culture, Hodge argues that theologically speaking, community is, above all, everything. From Jesus's birth to hip hop cyphers, community is central and Hodge relies upon this claim to challenge churches to reconsider the context of community and presence of God in broader and more relevant ways. Using space, place and identity as lenses of analysis, Hodge broadens the parameters of sacrality and where it can be found and encountered. Mapping the linguistic differentiations and distinct experiences between the "soul era of the 'hood" to the "post-soul hip hop world" one is able to see the changing nature of black orality and meaning of words such as God, pimp, and hustle, among other notable hip hop terms. Hodge concludes that, with strong emphases on "meaningful relationship," hip hop is more relational in its organic theology than is the theology/theologies of churches today.

Where Are My Dawgs At?: A Theology of Community

Daniel White Hodge

When I was in high school, my mom and I lived in a cramped one-bedroom apartment. The place was just large enough to accommodate my twenty-two pound cat, Milo, and us. It was one of those apartments you had to go through the bedroom to get to the bathroom; and we shared the one bedroom, so I would often wake her up.

If I had more than three people over, there was simply no room for them to sit down. We were the last apartment on the west side of the building, so we could make some noise and not have to worry about neighbors complaining, but they did anyway. Because my friends had to take the stairs to get to the apartment, everyone would know when they were coming; they had the uncanny habit of stomping up every stair to notify me of their arrival.

Saturday nights were the time to connect with friends and extended family. We would reflect together on the previous week, social conditions, politics, relationships, economics and, of course, Hip Hop. We were an eclectic, multiracial group: my friend Sam was Filipino; my friend Ali was Black mixed with some Caribbean and Native American; my friend Kavicka was a mix of Irish and Scottish; Nancy was Korean and White; Wha King was Nigerian and Black; Rob was Korean and Black; Cherie was Black and Chinese; Shawn was Black. And I was, and still am, Black and Mexican. Saturday nights were a time of community for all of us.

For three years it was a day that we would all rarely miss. We would meet at my place soon after sunset. If the mood was right, we would just chill out and watch movies or listen to music. But often we would pile into Sam's GMC Astra van and take a ride down to the boardwalk. Sometimes we would terrorize tourists.

The boardwalk in the Monterey Bay was not your typical multicultural fair. It was quite often filled with people who looked at us as lowlifes. So one day Sam decided that we should play into that stereotype. He suggested that while walking down the street as a group, we should all simultaneously and aggressively reach into our jacket pockets when passing tourists to give them "something to talk about." This worked like a charm. As we passed unsuspecting tourists in a group, we would all reach into our jacket pockets and give them quite a fright. We would then, of course, walk away laughing as if to say, "See, not all of us are criminals."

I know, I know. We could have spent our time a lot better, but hey, I was a teenager. A lot of us do crazy things when we are that age. One of the biggest opponents to my hanging with this community was my church community. At the time I was attending a church youth group, and the people in the group called my friends "bad influences," "bad seeds" and "sinners." Why would a Christian hang out with such people?

At first, I tried to hide the fact that I was hanging around my friends. But when I blew off youth group to go with my friends on Saturday night, I would typically get caught at the bowling alley or boardwalk. My church community did not understand my relationship with my friends. It was rare that my friends would negatively talk about my church community, but my church saw my relationship with them as not "glorifying God." My church community even tried an intervention with me to "cast out" the spirit of the world. When I would go through rough times, my church community would often blame my friends as the cause of those problems; meanwhile, my friends would provide communal support for me.

My church group would constantly talk with my mom, trying to get her to make me leave my friends. That did not work either. Saturday nights would come, and we would do our same routine much to the disapproval of my church community. Sure, my friends were not perfect. Sure, my friends and I did some things that bent one or two laws. And sure, my friends and I were not always "pure." My friends and I would also get into arguments; it was not as if our relationships were perfect. But that is what you do in community: live life together. And more important, they were more church to me than my church was.

The number one argument that my church community had about my friends and I was the fact we all listened to rap music. Rap, in the church's eyes, was evil and needed to be avoided at all costs. It was of the world and had no part in the church. At the time, Ice Cube's first solo album, *AmeriKKKa's Most Wanted*, had dropped. The language alone was enough to convict me of sin in my church's eyes.

I wish there could have been more congruity between my church community and my friends. I think there were a lot of opportunities for both groups to learn from each other. Moreover: from a youth pastor's perspective, there was a huge opportunity to minister to not only one student but a whole tight-knit group. Instead, the church decided to build walls between us and God. God was made out, by the church, to not care for us unless we were all dressed up, spoke right, never used foul language and followed every commandment in the Bible—including some Levitical codes.

Those were the days though. It was. The late 1980s and early 1990s were a great time for Hip Hop. Hip Hop was in its teens and having fun. Hip Hop was being defined and redefined, including its understanding of community. Space and place are fundamental elements for Hip Hop. Street names, area codes and city names provide the Hip Hop community meaning, identity and community in an environment that has vastly left them unknown. Theologically speaking, community is everything. Most Bible stories happen in the context of community. Even Jesus' birth even took place in a communal setting. Salvation happens in community and with people. Western Eurocentric theology has given us a more individualistic view of salvation and community,[1] but the idea that we can "do it by ourselves" and "pull ourselves up by our own bootstraps" not only undermines the gospel, it is practically impossible. Yet many churches continue to insist that we can go at salvation, missions, evangelism and our personal walk with Jesus without a supporting community.

For Hip Hoppers, life is done in community. Whether those communities are small, large, medium, one or two people, sixty or one hundred, community is still occurring. Church happens in that community; the presence of God is not only felt but experienced.

Space, Place, and Identity within Hip Hop

Community happens in spaces. Spaces have places. And within those spaces and places there is a thing called identity.

Identity helps to shape who we are. Identity refers to the reflective self-conception or self-image that we derive from family, gender, cultural, ethnic and individual experiences during multiple and complex socialization processes. There are several forms of identity, including

- social identity
- personal identity
- ethnic identity
- cultural identity.

Identity in community therefore takes on many different shapes. How our social construction of identity is realized will influence how we interact with different spaces and the people within those spaces. For example, if we were brought up in a conservative evangelical Christian home, our parents may have taught us that the world outside the house is "sinful" and "wicked." Our friends may have reinforced that belief, as did the media outlets we used. Our pastor may have confirmed that the "world" is in fact scary and should be avoided; our educational systems may also have supported that conviction. Our social construction of identity would thus tend toward social anxiety. We might avoid conflict at all costs, have passive-aggressive tendencies, see the world through only one or two lenses, restrict our socialization to people of "our own kind," will see "the world" as needing "salvation," and view "strangers" as potential enemies and or threats.

Meanwhile theologians such as Harvey Cox or Ray Bakke would argue that "for the urban Christian and pastor there can be no throw-away real estate because 'The earth is the Lord's, and everything in it' (Ps 24:1), and that includes every 'hood."[2] Any number of places are rendered sacred for Hip Hoppers—places where Jesus "shows up"—including

- concerts
- spoken-word event venues
- recorded rap music
- dancing
- small groups
- battle raps.

Murray Forman observes that in Hip Hop "space is a dominant concern, occupying a central role in the definition of value, meaning, and practice."

A highly detailed and consciously defined spatial awareness is one of the key factors distinguishing rap music and hip-hop from the many other cultural and subcultural youth formations currently vying for popular attention.[3]

When I lived in the Monterey Bay area, many of my friends had t-shirts featuring the area code "408" as well as having it tattooed on their arms, legs, neck, stomach and other body parts. When the silicon revolution hit during the early 1990s and everyone began getting multiple phone lines, the area code for our area changed from 408 to 831. But even when those area codes changed, people were still identifying themselves with 408. It was not about the "change" or even the physical numerical code. It was about space and place and the identity that ensues with that. Geraldine Pratt writes, however, that identity is also created by crossing boundaries into different spaces, producing a sharpened sense of consciousness; social inequalities become "visible through travel," as when one goes from the 'hood into a suburban space.[4] Imani Perry contends that "good music often has a beauty identifiable across the boundaries of nation and culture. And yet a musical composition, and musical forms in general, have identities rooted in community."[5]

Space in the 'hood is very important. Gangs set their territory by space. Families relegate themselves to a certain square mile and never leave that space. Urban neighborhoods are "sectioned" off by city officials, and rap artists identify themselves with the "space" they are from.[6] In the film *8 Mile*, characters were distinguished and categorized by which area code they were from. B-Rabbit (played by Eminem) calls out Papa Doc by showing that he was from an area code that had nothing to do with the 'hood. Tupac was known for his upbringing in Marin City, California, an area known for being "hard" and "mean." Compton became an important identifier in the West Coast rap scene with recordings by DJ Quick ("Jus Lyke Compton") and N.W.A. (the album *Straight Outta Compton*).[7]

Anderson contends that respect, a strong part of the code of the streets, has a role in the identity formation of teens within their space.

> Typically in the inner-city poor neighborhood, by the age of ten, children from decent and street oriented families alike are mingling on the neighborhood streets and figuring out their identities. Here they try out roles and scripts in a process that challenges their talents.[8]

Street corners thus become spatial corners in which not only identity formation is taking place, but also socialization skills.[9] It can then be assessed that one becomes a "product of their environment" and the socialization within that environment helps to shape the over-all person's identity. With identity so important to the genre, and the genre so conducive to identity formation, Hip Hoppers are often able to identify one another with very little interaction.[10]

Church, therefore, can happen in the unorthodox spaces where Hip Hoppers find themselves and one another: concerts, spoken word venues, street corners, malls, battle raps or face-to-face conversations become sacred ground, in contrast to the contrived settings of churches using Hip Hop as "bait" or as a novelty act for special events. We can begin to see the postmodern in this concept.[11]

People form their collective identity in a four-rung process I call the spatial identity formation model (see Figure 20.1).

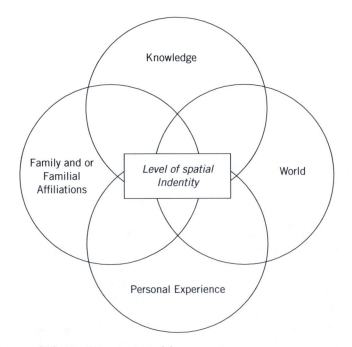

Figure 20.1 The Spatial Identity Formation Model

Each sphere represents a different culture, context or social construction, and comes with its own set of cultural patterns and history. There is much overlap in the different spheres. From the center comes our level of spatial identity for whichever social group we are a part of. Several factors influence our level of spatial awareness:

- family dynamics
- family communication
- education
- worldview/take on life
- personal origins
- personal sense of spatiality
- theological training.

Total strangers can go to a concert and connect with each other in a way that outsiders will not be able to understand. Spatial identity is why the actor Martin Lawrence coined the now famous term "It's a Black thang, you wouldn't understand!" People in that spatial arena "understand" the statement, while outsiders remain confounded.

Identity and the Self in the Post-Soul Hip Hop World

Identity in the soul era of the 'hood was embedded in public figures such as Martin Luther King, Cesar Chavez, the Black Panther Party, Malcolm X, and Angela Davis. They came to define for the soul era what a public figure "should" be. For the post-soul urbanite, however, identity takes on different dimensions. Todd Boyd argues that Hip Hop culture is this current generation's Civil Rights Movement, their voice and vehicle to the public sphere. "Hip-hop has always placed great worth on making connections to a larger historical sense of the culture, thus the lofty status accorded to the idea of an 'old school.'"[12]

If the city was the catapult of modernism, as suggested by Scott Lash, then the city has been the catapult for the postmodern, post-soul era.[13] Ghetto values continue to be marketed to the masses. Baggy pants, initially a ghetto style, originated when released prisoners would keep their oversized prison outfits, because they could store a great deal of concealed objects. Baggy pants made their way into stores like the Gap and the Limited. Now, almost anyone can identify themselves with the "Loose Fit."

Drive down Slauson or Vernon Avenue in L.A. You will see a mural of graffiti art that identifies one's name, ranking, talent and position in society. In the film *Wild Style*, artists would sit in a certain corner of the Bronx just to watch the subway train go by so that they could see their name, art, and new artists pass them by on the train.[14] Graffiti was introduced to Los Angeles through the movies *Wild Style, Beat Street* and *Style Wars*. Lacking the New York subways, the L.A. answer was to "bomb" or paint freeways and use empty lots as outdoor studios with rotating exhibits of wildstyle pieces.[15]

The modern mind saw "broken English" as deviant and "bad." But with the rise of Hip Hop culture and music, the language of the ghetto has made its way into everyday conversation.[16] Twenty years ago it was uncommon for a White man to say, "You go girl!" But in postmodern America, it is common. Table 20.1 shows the evolution of terms from the modern to postmodern era.[17] Similarly, the Blaxploitation films of the 1970s helped make it possible for vulgarities to be mainstreamed into general society.

Soulists like Delores Tucker, Jesse Jackson and Bob Dole had so much trouble with Hip Hop lyrics because they did not understand the revised root meaning of such words and could not comprehend the cultural significance. The postmodern Hip Hopper utilizes micronarratives,

Table 20.1 Post-soul Urban Language Differentiations

Word	Soul Context	Post-soul Context
God	Deity	Person (New York context)
Down	Literal sense	Are you with me?
Love	Marriage/Family	Sexual
Dub	To make a copy of	Two vowel sounds together or two letters back to back. J-Dub would be Jason Double.
Hood	Head covering	Community/Ghetto
Freak	A weird person	Someone who is not only open with sexuality, but is open to the public about it as well
Pimp	Street thug	Someone who dresses nice, got it going on, and has nice things
Pimpin	Street thugs with prostitutes	Living large with money
Jackin	Messing up, using a person	Taking someone else's stuff
22's	Guns	Rims
Hustle	Street thugs	To make money and survive

not a macronarrative, to make sense of their world.[18] Hip Hop and the post-soul worldview gives voice to the voiceless, demands justice and gives way to micronarratives for the people; the individual urban youth responds to this with open arms.[19] The tribal narrative of the urban post-soul era has the wind at its back and is dominating the contemporary landscape.

Within the soulist worldview, the self then becomes what Stanley Grenz calls "The Self-Focused Self,"[20] a derivative of the Enlightenment that has engulfed parts of the Hip Hop community.

> The elevation of individual autonomy in the Enlightenment led to an atomistic understanding of the social realm that viewed the individual as the source of social institutions as well as of society itself. Society, therefore, was a collection of autonomous, independent selves, each of whom pursues his (and sometimes her) own ends, albeit within the context of some overarching wider harmony. ... The modern self is the self-created and self-sufficient above the vacillations and shifting relationships that characterize day-to-day living.[21]

Some Hip Hoppers feel that in order to "make it" in the business realm, one must be "self-sufficient" and "self-reliant." While part of that is true—to a degree to which if someone has a dream, then they are typically responsible in seeing that dream come true—there is a part of that worldview which leaves out authentic community and separates that individual from societal interactions despite being, as Grenz contended, still in pursuit of the overarching "wider harmony." Thus, though your neighbor might be eight inches away from you, you will not know him or her, because in the city we are to remain anonymous. This is what Zygmunt Bauman describes as strangerdom.

> Strangers are likely to meet in their capacity of strangers, and likely to emerge as strangers from the chance encounter which ends as abruptly as it started. Strangers meet in a fashion that befits strangers; a meeting of strangers is unlike the meetings of kin, friends, or acquaintances—it is, by comparison, a mismeeting. In the meeting of strangers there is no picking up at the point where the last encounter stopped, no filling in on the interim trials and tribulations or joys and delights, no

shared recollections: nothing to fall back on and go by in the course of the present encounter.[22]

In such an environment, Bauman recognizes, "loving your neighbor" is made difficult.[23]

Bauman also illustrates the kind of conversation that characterizes urban postmodern industrial community—the talk is small, usually centered on self-autonomous achievement and typically about sex, some new monetary conquest, lifestyle, and or sports. The conversation is shallow, brief and forgetful: "How are you?" and other American idioms have no substantial meaning. Rap songs are no different: commercial Hip Hop has grown untamed in this consumerist environment.

The commercialization of the Hip Hop community roughly began during the mid to late 1990s when media moguls such as Warner Music Group, NBC and Fox realized that they could make money off urban struggle. Television shows like *New York Undercover, The Marin Lawrence Show, The Fresh Prince of Bel Air,* and even *The Cosby Show* made Black culture popular and paved the way to a post-soul industrial community, in which capitalism and globalization have made an impact on the vitality of urban space.[24] There is not a corner in South Central L.A. that does not have some type of transglobal trademark. Herbert Schiller suggests that corporate logos are being distributed to youth and teens all around the world, consequently squelching the individual opinion.[25] Production companies in fact manipulate individual opinion in order to make a buck. Community forums are made available for most television shows, films and even rap groups. "Ordinary" people are there free to complain, voice concern, comment on programming and give a piece of their mind to anyone happens by the site. Ricky Ross, former drug dealer turned community activist, observes that in such an environment, talent and thoughtfulness take a back seat.

> It's all about packaging and marketing. Talent is no longer a requirement. Sources like BET, MTV, MySpace, and others dictate who will make it and who will fail. … Now, being the most talented rapper or MC, or even the best producer is no longer important.[26]

Rappers like 50 Cent, Snoop Dogg, Jay Z, Nelly and The Game, by celebrating hedonism rather than exploring the serious sociopolitical trends covered by their predecessors, embody a certain element of this cultural trend. But many Hip Hop moguls, such as Eminem, Ice Cube, Tupac, Dead Prez, Common, KRS-One and Queen Latifah, have continued to cultivate space for authenticity and depth. The Hip Hop soul singer Gina Rae produces a climate at her concerts that evokes a surreal, spiritual experience for the participant and listener. Gina connects with God through song, dance and spoken word, and the spatial identity brings in people that connect not only with Gina but with the larger community of soul Hip Hop and find a Christ transcended in this communal experience.

Even within commercial rap, Jesus is still present. He might be packaged up, blinged out, and rolling in an Escalade to be sold to the highest bidder, but nonetheless, he is still present within the industry of Hip Hop community.

The Jesus of Community in Hip Hop

Commercialization aside, Hip Hop continues to connect with the poor, downtrodden and marginalized of society. Christologically speaking, this was what Jesus did too. It is what Jürgen Moltmann describes as "the messianic mission of Christ" where Jesus was a person in social relationships.

> As we have seen, Jesus lived in mutual relationships with the poor and the sick, sinners, and the men and women who had been thrust out of society. It was in his reciprocal relationships with the faith of the people concerned that the miracles of the messianic era came about. It was in his reciprocal relationships with the men and women disciples who followed him that Jesus discovered his messianic secret. We have to look more closely at his life in the context of these social relationships, for we can only understand the life-histories of men and women in the light of their relations with other people, and the communities to which they belong.[27]

I find it interesting that Moltmann discusses how we need to get to know Jesus in the context of social relationships. This is a stark difference from the Western individualist gospel message we receive in many of our churches. For Jesus, it was about, as Jack Seymour has put it, finding the "God in the peoples of God."[28] Jesus looked beyond people's flaws and imperfections, entrusting his message to people who would not always get it right, who in fact changed the world in which we live today.

Jesus' social relationships were some of his most important interactions. Many of the valuable lessons Jesus taught were learned in community. For Hip Hop, it is no different; Hip Hoppers learn, grow, worship, love, argue and see Jesus through social relationships. In Mark 3:34 we find Jesus telling his people that whoever does "his will" is part of his community: "Whoever does God's will is my brother and sister and mother." In Matthew 12:46 the word *family* is replaced by *disciples*, but even the process of discipleship was done in community and among others; the root of the word means "pupil" or "learner." Further, the word *brothers* in verse 33 can connote connectivity. For Jesus, it meant being connected to him not just in spirit but in community as well.

Jesus became space, place, and identity for many who did not have that nor could not have it. In Mark 6:33–44 we find Jesus feeding the multitudes. "When Jesus landed and saw a large crowd, he had compassion on them, because they were like sheep without a shepherd. So he began teaching them many things." Moltmann asserts that "the 'multitude' are the poor, the homeless, the 'non-persons.' They have no identity, no voice, no power and no representative."[29] Jesus became hope and vision for people that had none. It is no surprise when Hip Hop also becomes this type of christological incubator for many who are also "harassed," who have been displaced, marginalized or broken by hardships in life.

In Mark 8:34–38, Jesus calls the community to discipleship, encouraging the crowd to follow him and giving the basic plan of salvation. Jesus becomes our representative as we represent him. For Hip Hop, a simple rap song or video can be such a representative: the listener or viewer is able to see in the images or lyrics not just him- or herself but the community of which he or she is a part. Through this newfound community in Hip Hop, the struggle of our lives is given greater meaning. "His [Jesus'] 'compassion' is not charitable condescension. It is the form which the divine justice takes in an unjust world."[30]

Moltmann observes Jesus' "reciprocal" relationship with his people. Jesus' life was constructed around that reciprocity. He was not concerned with making himself look good; he was about the other person—not just building them up but building his gospel in them. While Hip Hop is not an end to salvation, it does provide a similar reciprocity that builds people up, helps its members out and points to Jesus through creative forms within its art. Hence, Hip Hop is like Jesus to many urban post-soulists. So those of us who want urban post-soulists to know Jesus, need to know Hip Hop.

What becomes problematic for some Christians is the notion that Jesus would even be in places like a club, rap concert, and or event that was not centered around some church. Some Christians cannot see beyond the four church walls and the programs that run it. So, finding

Jesus in these irregular and nontraditional places will be hard to understand. Still, even in these nontraditional spaces, community is happening. And, if we really believe that God is Alpha and Omega, omnipresent, "all-seeing," might Jesus be in that smoke-filled strip club trying to talk to the inhabitants there?

Jesus did not avoid these tough problems engaging community. He knew that within community nothing is perfect. Community within Hip Hop is not some utopian place where everyone gets along and hugs each other until they are blue in the face. The Hip Hop community has arguments, fights, loves, hates, despises, embraces, encourages and lifts up. The Hip Hop community is real and transparent, but in that community there exists the ability to grow with others and learn from others. Jesus' community during his time was no different. Jesus' world was not utopian either, but many Christians are simply unable to see that aspect of Jesus' community. We continue to want a G-rated savior in an NC-17 world.

Being able to interpret, comprehend, analyze, and then digest messages is all part of the ever-important skill of listening. It is not always easy—particularly when certain elements of Hip Hop are loud, vulgar and oversexualized, of when they tear down people and exhibit extreme pride or lust. I can understand why so many "church folk" find rap offensive and just ugly to listen. I really do. Listening in those types of situations is not an easy task. Still, when I find myself offended and or my own levels of indignation rising, I ask myself, *Am I missing anything here? Could God be speaking in the midst of all of this?* More important, I ask how I can engage this community that seems to think, feel, believe, and act this way in which I do not approve of. That, for me at least, is the basis for listening to the very important messages given within the Hip Hop community. Often I find myself coming away with newfound knowledge.

Many parts of Hip Hop's community are infused with spirituality. Dance, a great social connector in Hip Hop, can relieve stress, tell a story, detail people's struggles and open minds to new understandings of life. In the 1980s, crews would come together at community centers to battle out their differences on linoleum dance floors. Each crew member would take turns trying to show the other crew out. A winner would be determined and granted bragging rights. Rarely did the issues go beyond the dance floor. After spending three to four hours dancing, you are too tired to fight. Most members would simply go home to prepare for the next day's battle.

Many Hip Hoppers, thanks to cultural factors such as the latchkey revolution and the urban crisis generated during the Reagan presidency, come from less than ideal living situations and need a lot of support; the communities they discover in Hip Hop do that for them. For about 75 percent of my interviewees, the community they found in Hip Hop culture provided them with

- shelter from the elements of life
- companionship for life's daily struggles
- comedic relief chiefly in times of dire problems
- familial bonds, especially for those who were living without strong parental figures
- rich and deep historical context
- a social map when times got a little confusing
- sounding boards for life decisions.

Interviewees who reported this type of communal support were more focused, better able to deal with life's problems, had a better ability to integrate their lives into other social situations, could better articulate their needs and indicated that they felt connected, respected, and grounded, which left them with an overall better self-esteem and self-efficacy.

The remaining 25 percent of interview subjects, who did not have strong experiences of community, displayed the following characteristics:

- were less focused
- often felt friendless, left out, forgotten by the world
- indicated feelings of hostility, anger and hatred
- could not articulate their needs as well
- were not able to deal well with sudden change.

The importance of meaningful relationship is obvious. And with its emphasis on space, place and identity, Hip Hop culture has shown itself to be more relational in its theology than the conventional church. Carter Heyward suggests:

> Relational theology should be understood as a metaphysics that is built not merely on speculation but on *experiencing* one another, including the earth and other creatures in the course of our daily lives, work, and love. At the same time, relational theology must be a theo-ethics of *liberation*. It is about *noticing* the real world—our loveliness and pathos, our interconnectedness and fragmentation—and it is about *changing* this world. [31]

Heyward's observations here are central to Hip Hop's theology of community: This is where Jesus shows up. This is where growth in Christ is gained. This is where all of life intersects— the good, the bad, and the ugly. A community of experiencing one another is a community that is not only biblical but christological.

Martin Buber asserts that true communication is "experiencing the other side."[32] We must experience someone else to truly commune. We do not experience Hip Hop in order to conquer it, we encounter Hip Hop as we enter into relationship with Hip Hop people.

In the film *8 Mile*, the main focus of community for everyone living in the cold, miserable, dejected part of inner-city Detroit was a place called the Shelter. Established in the basement of a church, the Shelter nevertheless wasn't populated by "nice," smooth and charming Christians. By the end of the film, infused with profanity and featuring gratuitous partial nudity from Eminem, we learn that in the end, you really are what you are. Eminem's self-acceptance, and the crowd's embrace of his true self, took place within the sacred place of the Shelter.

Most Christians find the authenticity so prized in the Hip Hop community hard to swallow. Many ministries doing work with Hip Hoppers thus enter into a process of "pookizing" the people they work with—telling a sanitized version of their story for an outside (and funding) audience, thus capitalizing on their identity and profiting from the caricature. Pookizing destroys authentic community, highlighting the "salvation" reel while downplaying the larger context of a life, and showcasing the ministry rather than building up the person. If we are to listen to the communal story of Hip Hop, then we must be ready to, as Buber suggests, "seek to understand what people are saying through the culture before we critique the culture."[33] Community can begin once we lay down our righteousness spears. I remember when I would go to my church youth group when I was in high school. I was always made to feel bad about the music I listened to. Rap music was seen as "worldly" and something that we all needed to "give up" for the Lord. Fast forward years later and now I was that youth pastor, doing the same thing with the young people I was working with. I would constantly call out artists like Tupac for being "unholy" and "lost." I would have arguments with teens about their use of "Hip Hop idols" and condemn any type of Hip Hop community. One night I looked in the mirror and had a hard reality check. I sat down with several students, and I said, "I really don't understand this, help me!" For the first time I was able to really commune with them, learn from them. But I had to get my ego out of the way for this type of community to be developed.

Fast forward many years later. I was at the Urban Youth Workers national conference, doing my first workshop on the theology of Tupac Shakur. I saw one of my former students. She and I had gone back and forth about the "evil" in the music she had in her CD-player; I even questioned her salvation at one point because of the music she was listening to. This was the first time she had seen me in a teaching capacity for many years. I could tell she thought I was still "judging" artists like Pac. I told her that our conversation many years prior had sparked in me a desire to look beyond the obvious profanity of artists like Pac, and move into what Pac could actually teach us. I let her know that my workshop was actually admonishing and uplifting Pac and I was letting people know that we had to get on board with certain theologies regarding Pac. The moment I told her that, it was as if her entire countenance was changed. She smiled and we began talking about her life, my workshop, and just how far both of us had come since those early youth group days. That was community. But it did not happen overnight, it was not pretty. And it involved many more arguments and frustrating moments. But in that moment, she and I knew we had grown and because we had the history behind us, we were able to commune together, and our relationship was not only strengthened, but also deepened as a result of it.

In order to engage the Hip Hop community and really listen to it, we must first be willing to embrace the hostility that lies within that community. Jesus did. Jesus still does. More important, he does that with all of us, every day.

Study Questions

1. How does Hodge examine space, place, identity and community among hip hop culture and practice? How is this connected to Hodge's alternative depiction of Jesus's mission and the presence of hip hop culture today?
2. What cultural similarities and differences exist among changing rhetorical meanings between the "Soul Context" and "Post-Soul Context?"
3. Does Hodge propose a way forward for a better understanding between the church and hip hop culture?

Notes

1. See John William Drane, *The McDonaldization of the Church: Consumer Culture and the Church's Future* (Macon, Ga.: Smyth & Helwys 2001); Zygmunt Bauman, *Liquid Modernity* (Malden, Mass.: Polity Press, 2000).
2. Ray Bakke, *The Urban Christian* (Downers Grove, Ill.: InterVarsity Press, 1987), p. 63.
3. Murray Forman, *The 'Hood Comes First: Race, Space, and Place in Rap and Hip-Hop, Music/Culture* (Middletown, Conn.: Wesleyan University Press, 2002), p. 3. The dimensions of this book restrain me from going deeper into the complex, multifaceted, yet intriguing conversation regard spatial awareness. Forman argues that space takes on several elements including apparatus domination, hegemonic order and the bounding of subjects within that space (pp. 1–34). For further insight see Henri Lefebvre (*The Production of Space* [Oxford: Basil Blackwell,1991], pp. 24–26) as he discusses how space is "produced." David Harvey ("From Space to Place and Back Again: Reflections on the

Condition of Postmodernity," in *Mapping the Futures: Local Cultures, Global Change*, ed. J. Bird, B. Curtis, T. Putnam, G. Robertson and L. Tickner [New York: Routledge, 1993]) concludes that spaces can be used for power and manipulation, and Harvey Cox (*The Secular City: A Celebration of Its Liberties and an Invitation to Its Discipline* [New York: Macmillan, 1965]) details the complexity of urban space and how spirituality exists in many of those places.

4. Geraldine Pratt, "Grids of Difference," in *Cultural Studies: An Anthology*, ed. M. Ryan and H. Musiol (Malden, Mass.: Blackwell, 2008), p. 158. Bell hooks (*Yearning: Race, Gender, and Cultural Politics* [Toronto: Between The Lines, 1990]) agrees with Pratt's assessment.

5. Cf. Imani Perry, *Prophets of the Hood: Politics and Poetics in Hip Hop* (Durham, N.C.: Duke University Press, 2004), pp. 11, 38–57.

6. Davarian Baldwin, "Black Empires, White Desires: The Spatial Politics of Identity in the Age of Hip-Hop," in *That's the Joint! The Hip-Hop Studies Reader*, ed. M. Forman and M. A. Neal (New York: Routledge, 2004), p. 160.

7. Forman, *Hood Comes First*, pp. 193–98.

8. Elijah Anderson, *Code of the Street: Decency, Violence, and the Moral Life of the Inner City* (New York: W. W. Norton, 1999), p. 68.

9. Ibid., pp. 69–72.

10. See Melissa August, Leslie E. Brice, Laird Harrison, Todd Murphy and David Thigpen, "Hip-Hop Nation: There's More to Rap Than Just Rhythms & Rhymes," in *Common Culture: Reading & Writing About American Popular Culture*, ed. M. Petracca and M. Sorapure (Upper Saddle River, N.J.: Prentice Hall, 2001); Raymond D. S. Anderson, *Black Beats for One People; Causes and Effects of Identification with Hip-Hop Culture*, Ph.D. dissertation, (Virginia Beach: Regent University, 2003). For Hip Hoppers, these means of reorganization can be broken down into several categories—relevance, respectful and authentic—as a way of identifying each other within the community of Hip Hop.

11. Murray Forman discusses that spatial discourse coheres around the concept of the hood; this concept is manifested in what is called "Gangsta Rap" or "West Coast" rap. This is an important special element that Forman argues is a pivotal point for Hip Hoppers (*Hood Comes First*, pp. 191–92).

12. Todd Boyd, *The H.N.I.C.: The Death of Civil Rights and the Reign of Hip Hop* (New York: New York University Press, 2003), p. 124.

13. Scott Lash, "Postmodernism as Humanism? Urban Space and Social Theory," in *Theories of Modernity and Postmodernity*, ed. B. S. Turner (Thousand Oaks, Calif.: Sage Publications, 1990), p. 31.

14. Tricia Rose, "A Style Nobody Can Deal With: Politics, Style, and the Postindustrial City in Hip Hop," in *Microphone Friends: Youth Music and Youth Culture*, ed. A. Ross and T. Rose (New York: Routledge, 1994), p. 101. Often, Graffiti artists use nicknames and or aliases because public graffiti is illegal and no one really wants to be caught. Urban pseudonyms such as Snoop Dogg, Ice Cube, Ice T, and even Dr. Dre cover up formal names such as Clarence, Calvin, and Andreas.

15. Ruben Martinez, "Going Up in L.A.," *LA Weekly*, February 5, 1998 <www.laweekly. com/1998-02-05/news/going-up-in-l-a/>.

16. Cf. Russell Potter's discussion about Hip-Hop vernacular and the postmodern revolution in speech (*Spectacular Vernaculars: Hip-Hop and the Politics of Postmodernism* [New York: State University of New York Press, 1995], pp. 55–79).

17. Language is a primary source of identity in any society. For postmodern urban youth, how you talk and present that verbal tone, will dictate to them exactly how authentic you are, and "real" you are about their life and with life in general.

18. Jean-François Lyotard, *The Postmodern Condition: A Report on Knowledge* (Minneapolis: University of Minnesota Press, 1984), pp. 32–34.

19. Christopher Tyson explores the generation gap between the Civil Rights Generation and the Hip Hop generation, suggesting new ideologies of Hip Hop culture and music and how the two generations can mend (*Exploring the Generation Gap and Its Implications on African American Consciousness* [New York: Urban Think Tank, 2001]).

20. Stanley Grenz, *The Social God and the Relational Self: A Trinitarian Theology of the Imago Dei* (Louisville, Ky.: Westminster John Knox, 2001), p. 99.

21. Ibid., p. 99.

22. Zygmunt Bauman, *Liquid Modernity* (Malden, Mass.: Polity Press, 2000), p. 95. "Strangerdom" refers to the element of unknown human bodies. Your neighbor is eight inches from your head, but you will never know them, because it is the city, and in the city, you must maintain that anonymity.

23. Zygmunt Bauman, *Liquid Love* (Malden, Mass.: Polity Press, 2003), pp. 77–84.

24. On another level, such television shows also gave White America front row seats into the lives of Blacks and the urban community. It is part of the many reasons why White kids love Hip Hop (Bakari Kitwana, *Why White Kids Love Hip-Hop: Wankstas, Wiggers, Wannabes, and the New Reality of Race in America* [New York: Basic Civitas Books, 2005]).

25. Herbert Schiller, *Culture Inc.: The Corporate Takeover of Public Expression* (New York: Oxford University Press, 1989), p. 124.

26. Ricky Ross, "The Rise & Fall of the Rapper & Rap Music" <http://freewayenterprise.ning.com/forum/topics/2417957:Topic:144>

27. Moltmann, *Way of Jesus Christ* (Minneapolis, MN: Fortress Press, 1993), pp. 145–46.

28. Jack Seymour, "Meeting God in the Peoples of God," *Religious Education* 96, no. 3 (2001): 267–69.

29. Moltmann, *Way of Jesus Christ* (Minneapolis, MN: Fortress Press, 1993), p. 148.

30. Ibid., p. 149.

31. Carter Heyward, *Saving Jesus from Those Who Are Right: Rethinking What It Means to Be a Christian* (Minneapolis: Fortress Press, 1999), p. 64.

32. Martin Buber, *I and Thou* (New York: Scribner's, 1958).

33. Ralph Watkins, *The Gospel Remix: Reaching the Hip Hop Generation* (Valley Forge, Penn.: Judson Press, 2007), p. 3.

21

Hip-Hop Judaica
The Politics of Representin' Heebster Heritage

Focusing on masculinity and the American Jewish hipster scene from 1986 to 2006, Cohen examines the means by which musical evolution and change become vital for the religious and ethnic transmission and preservation of this hipster community. Using a December 2003 *Time Out New York* cover story entitled "The New Super Jews," Cohen notes the emerging new and edgy sensibility among Jewish culture, dubbed radical by outsiders, in spaces such as discos and clubs. These "cool Jews," as they are called, make use of rap and hip hop cultural conventions to challenge and advance notions of creativity and gender among the ever-changing cultural geography of hip hop. This "newish Jewish" group uses transgressive themes in black culture to situate themselves on the margins of traditional Jewish culture, whose limitations they forcefully critique. Yet, Cohen suggests this critique and reshaping speak to a contested Jewish identity and experience that seeks to both transform and preserve Jewish tradition through cultural contestation. He concludes that the Jewish hip hop scene of 1986–2006 provided a powerful space for Jewish youth to explore masculinity, preserve and re-present Jewish identity and tradition for the future, among a host of others.

Hip-Hop Judaica: The Politics of Representin' Heebster Heritage

Judah Cohen

Introduction

In December 2003, *Time Out New York* ran a cover story entitled 'The New Super Jews' (Rakoff 2003). Timed to coincide with the upcoming winter-season 'Jewsploitation' film entitled *The Hebrew Hammer* (D'Addario 2003), the *Time Out* story highlighted a number of New York figures and organisations whose work trumpeted what they called a 'new', edgy sensibility to the Jewish condition. This 'new' Jewish culture aimed specifically at instilling a sense of Judaism where such expression had traditionally been seen as absent – such as the disco, the jazz club, and the fashion world. Often using the term 'radical' to describe their activities, concerns such as *HEEB* magazine, Jewcy.com and John Zorn's Radical Jewish Culture record sub-label projected images, attitudes and sounds that simultaneously celebrated and subverted popular Jewish stereotypes. Urban-dwelling Jews in their twenties and thirties served as the main target: those seen to base less of their identity on the Holocaust, who married later in life, and who portrayed a sense of alienation from both denominational life and the existing Jewish infrastructure.

Discussions about the 'coolness' of these initiatives had made the rounds for several years previously. John Zorn had helped found the Radical Jewish Culture movement in 1992, more than a decade before the *Time Out New York* article highlighted them, and had been involved in the thriving, semi-underground 'downtown' scene promoting such a philosophy ever since (Barzel 2004, esp. pp. 116–65). Jonathan Schorsch's ruminations on the subject in the March/April 2000 issue of *Commentary*, meanwhile, offered a view of the emerging generation of artists that offered both artistic nuance and intellectual vigour. With the *Time Out New York* story, however, the 'cool Jews' theme gained its broadest audience. As if picking up on the topic, a slew of popular journalistic articles and television segments began to appear in both mainstream and Jewish spheres trying to chronicle the phenomenon, giving exposure to the participants, and offering basic theories on the place of such activities within both contemporary Jewish life and the historical American Jewish trajectory (Keys 2004; Waletzky 2004 *inter alia*). Most of these articles hyped the novelty of such seemingly unlikely hybrids as rapper 50Shekel, performance artist Vanessa Hidary ('The Hebrew Mamita') and performance group Storahtelling, describing their cultural productions as youthful reactions to what they perceived as an ossified, even self-effacing, Jewish agenda. Thus did *Time Out New York* frame the story:

'The neurotic nebbish is out; the swaggering ass-kicker is in. From music and film to comedy and fashion, Jewish artists and performers are exploring edgy new personas'.
(Rakoff 2003, p. 13)

The Jewish artists and groups featured in the *Time Out New York* profiles, moreover, actively underscored their own agendas with speculative manifesti, employing literature and philosophical discourses used in institutionalised academic discussion to proclaim their own newness within the narrative of Jewish history. Albums released under John Zorn's Radical Jewish Culture sub-label, for example, would occasionally cite such thinkers as Walter Benjamin, Edmond Jabès, and Alain Finkielkraut in their liner inserts to invoke a specific strand of progressive Jewish intellectualism and imply the modes of creativity associated with the artists' visions.[1] 2002's editor-in-chief of *HEEB* magazine, meanwhile, took on his leadership position with a masters degree from Harvard Divinity School, taught courses at New York University, and routinely talked to at least one of the publication's interns about the magazine's unprecedented coverage and attitude.[2] Releasing their messages through both existing and emerging mass media pipelines, these individuals and organisations promoted a narrative of meaningful deviation from what they perceived as the staid Jewish norms of previous decades, gaining attention and cultural capital in the process.

I do not aim, in this essay, to contribute to that matrix of voices; for they can describe themselves far better than I can describe them. Rather, here I will look at the American Jewish 'hipster' culture phenomenon through a significantly more limited forum – the disjointed but publicly grouped series of artists who express themselves using rap and hip-hop conventions – in order to understand broader issues of creativity and gender within this burgeoning and ever-changing scene. These artists represent the larger radical Jewish music scene in that they are predominantly male, they are conversant with musical genres commonly associated with blackness, and they take pains to situate themselves on the margins of Jewish expression under claims of challenging a complacent Jewish tradition and the society in which it dwells. Yet their practices, as I will suggest, also evidence deeper aspects of cultural activity attributed specifically to the Jewish experience: most notably a publicly negotiated, bipolar sense of Jewish masculinity, as well as an often overt agenda aimed at transforming perceptions of Jewish tradition in order to preserve them.[3]

Portrayals of Jewish Masculinity

According to Daniel Boyarin, Jews, like other marginal minorities, have often been treated as a kind of shuttlecock amid higher-level political and scholarly discussions of gender (1997); and many of these discussions, perhaps based on the male dominated fora propagating them, tended to employ discourses on Jewish masculinity to influence public opinion and legislation toward the Jews as a community. Particularly in the pre-modern period, European social scientists often gave Jewish men feminine identities, claiming they did not embody so-called defining signs of European maleness such as physical or sexual aggressiveness. Boyarin suggests that Jews endorsed such differences in response as a way to assert a separate parallel scale of masculinity. Starting in the late eighteenth century, however – once emancipation began to allow Jews increased latitude within the hegemonic society – a combination of newly granted access to centralised power structures and the emergence of what Boyarin calls a 'homophobic heterosexuality' led to revised conflicts of gender identity. Male Jews remained 'different' and frequently continued to hold a feminised status within the context of secular society; but this time their concerns for social advancement within that society made their feminised status a liability. Governing perceptions of male Jewish physical inferiority, such as the hooked nose, circumcised penis, and flat feet, further eroded Jewish masculinity, and led both medical and social scientists to classify them in less-than-virile terms (Gilman 1991).

The rise of Zionism in the late nineteenth century helped promote a strong counter-discourse aimed at dispelling Euro-American stereotypes of Jewish meekness. Perhaps most famously represented in Paul Newman's 1960 portrayal of Ari Ben Canaan in the film adaptation of *Exodus*, the male Jew, in this rendering, became a handsome and strong – if not musclebound – heart-throb, ready to take swift and decisive action when the times called for it. Paul Breines codified this image within the academic literature in 1990; and in 2001, Warren Rosenberg re-inscribed discourses of the raging Jewish man into Biblical and Euro-American social history. Jewish men, according to such readings, were refashioned as heroes who would not be victimised, even in the face of insurmountable odds.

These two counter-images of the Jewish male co-existed throughout twentieth century America. As the twenty-first century approached, however, academic discourses tended to tilt the dynamic toward the weaker, more feminised, male-based heavily on media images. Harry Brod's 1988 edited collection of 'Explorations in Jewish Masculinity' entitled *A Mensch among Men*, for example, evoked the parallel between so-called 'secular' masculinity and 'Jewish' masculinity while keeping the two in separate spheres. Maurice Berger, meanwhile, entitled his 1996 study of male Jewish depictions on television, 'The mouse that never roars'. Often portrayed as denizens of New York City or its suburbs, Jewish men took on a certain iconicity as particular, neurotic, unathletic, and overshadowed by strong if not overbearing women. Even Jewish 'tough' organisations such as the Jewish Defense League seemed to situate themselves in *reaction* to the idea of the meek Jewish male, propagating reputations of aggressive sentience by remaining always marginal to the 'meek Jew' formation (sometimes by using the social space of radicalism; see Porter & Dreier 1973).

It thus was in some ways appropriate that culturally savvy American Jewish young people would turn to hip hop in the 1980s as a way of actively tipping the scale in the other direction – both to assert their identity to the public at large and to doctor their own self-esteem as Jews. The parallels with the broader hip-hop scene, as portrayed through a growing scholarly literature on the field, were quite strong: although the media companies selling rap for universal consumption would come to advertise it as a music of protest and anomie (a portrayal consumed effectively by many parents, Jewish and otherwise), an intimate knowledge of the music would often reveal it to be a forum for airing minority anxieties about gender roles, associations with national and international power structures, and self-identity.[4] The music's outward connection with a particularly masculine symbolism, moreover, allowed Jewish practitioners to relate directly to pervading discourses of Jewish masculinity.

The First Years of Jewish Rapping: Mimetic Inclusion

Although individuals who could be identified as Jewish, such as Def Jam Records founder Rick Rubin, would play important roles in promoting and commercialising early hip hop, the use of hip-hop stylings to *explore* Jewish identity emerged ostensibly after such commercialisation had taken place, as a reflection of hip hop's new presence within mainstream American culture. While songs such as The Sugar Hill Gang's 1979 'Rapper's Delight' and Newcleus's 1983 'Jam On It' heralded a new sound, it was not until 1984 that hip hop rose to the top of the American record charts with Run-DMC's first eponymous album (which, in addition to receiving radio play, gained wide visual exposure on the recently created MTV cable channel). Within two years, Run-DMC's broadly distributed sound had effected seismic change to the nation's sonic landscape, asserting itself as an inextricable part of the greater cultural scene. The group's popularity, complemented by the emergence and promotion of other rap/hip-hop artists, would inspire numerous Jewish children to begin emulating rap's delivery, rhythm, and beatboxing techniques in their own performances, whether private or public.[5]

Jewish artists and communal organisations from across the religious spectrum embraced the rap style from its earliest years as well; yet they did so mainly as part of a broad (and frequently humourous) parallel production of the American music scene. Some of the earliest 'Jewish' raps took place during *Purimspils*, appearing as part of the historically carnival-like pastiche of musical and dramatic styles exemplifying the spirit of the holiday (Sandrow 1977; Kirshenblatt-Gimblett 1980; Baumgarten 1992; Epstein 1995; Slobin 2003; *et al.*). Though many of these inclusions have disappeared due to the *Purimspil's* often spontaneous and transient nature, those that survive show the genre's usage either outside the Esther narrative, or as a way to present its own self-contained account of the story. Composer and dramatist Elizabeth Swados, for example, included a selection titled 'The Haman Rap' in her 1988 work *Esther: A Vaudeville Megillah* (Swados 1996 [1988], pp. 46–7).[6] Included among selections in various other genres – including rock ballad, gospel, reggae, waltz and tango – 'The Haman Rap' appeared during a halftime-style break in the retelling, as a way to explain when and how to blot out the name of the story's villain throughout the rest of the show (as per common Jewish practice).[7] Swados's particular interpretation of this genre emphasised rap's heavy rhythmic grooves and exclamatory delivery. One cast member led into the song by encouraging those in the audience to use the graggers (noisemakers) passed out by the other cast members in order to make noise at the appropriate times. The rap itself consisted of little more than exhortations to 'beat', 'obliterate', 'stamp … out', 'bash out', and 'drown out' Haman's name. Such an interpretation of the style as one that incites others to (controlled) simulated violence via an outspoken and amplified-rhythmic delivery offered a multi-layered reflection on rap's place in the contemporary Jewish musical environment in its early years, particularly as modulated through the lens of composed music for the Jewish theatre.

Rap similarly filtered into the Orthodox Jewish recording industry during this time through its own humour-tinged venues. Mark Kligman (1996) has noted the tendency of the Orthodox music world to foster its own versions of popular musical genres from the 1960s onward, in part to allow its adherents a less threatening way to experience allowable elements of mainstream culture. Frequently created for young audiences, the mimetic tendencies of such music often involved pairing devotional lyrics or words descriptive of Orthodox Jewish life with genre-based instrumental arrangements and/or familiar tunes. Such techniques had been successful in the past: artists such as Shlomo Carlebach and The Rabbis' Sons brought acoustic folk styles into Orthodox Judaism during the 1960s and 1970s in this way, and Avraham Fried and Mordecai Ben David brought in rock music in a similar manner during the 1980s.

Rap, once established on the American cultural sonic map, faced a similar, and often rapid, incorporation in Orthodox circles. Modern Orthodox musical parody artists Lenny Solomon and Shlock Rock, for example, issued a parody of one of rap's first chart hits – Newcleus's 1983 'Jam On It/Boogie in the Club' – on its first album in 1986, with the title 'Bless On It/Boogie in the Shul [Synagogue]'. In 1987, moreover, Shlock Rock parodised rap's first 'crossover' megahit – Aerosmith and Run-DMC's 1986 collaboration 'Walk This Way' – into a lesson about the Hebrew pre-meal handwashing blessing entitled 'Wash This Way'. Both cuts, while incorporating the new lyrics, nonetheless retained much of the vocal inflection, instrumental accompaniment, attitude, and even stereo imaging of the original.[8] Shlock Rock would record additional rap parodies every one to two years afterward from then on, as well as occasional original raps focusing on such topics as Jewish pride and Jewish history. These additional efforts again mirrored the mainstream rap scene, even if comparatively amateurish: Run-DMC, for example, concluded its 1987 album *Raising Hell* with the track 'Proud to be Black', offering a similar paean to identity via history, role models, political philosophies, and straight out exhortations. That same year, Lenny Solomon's 'Rappin' Jewish' track held as a chorus: 'Jewish pride keeps you going strong/Makes our people last real long/So don't ignore what comes from inside/Let it grow, 'cause it's Jewish pride' (1987).

The most public-forum trajectory of rap in the Jewish imagination, however, involved Jews using rap and hip-hop styles to create a masked, self-consciously humourous reality in the broader music scene. These artists' religious identities never figured overtly into their music; yet just as with Rick Rubin and others in the rap/hip-hop industry, their 'Jewish' identities seemed to travel with them in certain fan circles. The Beastie Boys and MC Serch of 3rd Bass – the most famous of these figures – used self-parody and their unlikely image as early white rappers to confound listeners' expectations about rap and race; and Jon Stratton has gone further to suggest that the Beastie Boys' Jewish identification played a key role in their own ability to negotiate the early commercial rap/hip-hop scene (Stratton, 2008). Mainstream white audiences, which included Jews, clearly resonated with the different sound, perspective, reputation, and vocal delivery of these artists, perhaps feeling them more accessible or similar to their fantasies and situations. Thus, to young Jews growing up during the 1980s, the Beastie Boys and 3rd Bass offered one tacit model for representing a musical style widely discussed as 'black': one that emphasised difference within the rap scene, while offering a means for self-deprecating enfranchisement effected by the very people often marginalised by rap's image of black-dominated authenticity.

These areas of convergence between Jews and rap/hip hop – education, parody, mimesis, and mainstream contribution – continued to develop into the 1990s. Hip hop's increasingly ubiquitous place on the American popular music charts caused authorities in religious circles of the American Jewish community to utilise the style in attempts to educate youth. Among religious Jewish groups, a collective calling itself The Radical Rappin' Rebbes used rap aesthetics to instruct young people in Jewish religious and moral values (Koskoff 2001, pp. 188–9). In addition to telling the story of the Book of Esther, rap became a medium for instruction in other educational settings as well (often propagated by students themselves). Within Reform Jewish circles, for example, Cantor Wally Schachet-Briskin created what he called 'The Debbie Friedman Rap' to introduce young Jews to the musical works of prominent Jewish liturgical composer Debbie Friedman. Performed to some acclaim at Jewish education and youth and conferences in the mid 1990s, the song also appeared on Schachet Briskin's 1997 eponymous solo album: first in a standard version, and then in a 'karaoke' version that allowed others to perform the rap to a pre-recorded groove. Such efforts continued to turn rap into a vessel for communicating religious values and information to youth.

Within the realm of humour, openly Jewish-identified groups such as Miami's 2 Live Jews (formed in 1990 by Eric Lambert, Joe Stone and Danny Paul) and Los Angeles' M.O.T. ('Members of the Tribe' – created by Hillel Tigay and Andrew Rosenthal) continued to merge Jewish stereotypes and rap aesthetics in ways that both exploited and empowered Jewish consciousness. In a sense, these artists' creations, when classified as comedy, represented to many the continued safe appropriation of a music deemed 'dangerous' by marketers and media, yet consumed avidly by an emerging generation of Jews. The 2 Live Jews' 1991 track 'Kosher as They Wanna Be' provides an evocative illustration. Modelled after the Miami-based 2 Live Crew's notorious 1989 album *Nasty as They Wanna Be*, the 2 Live Jews track includes its own stereotyped depictions of Jewish Miami, albeit as imagined by Jewish geriatric retirees. Easy

Irving and Moishe MC, the unlikely rappers on the album, represented two elderly Jewish men, replete with verbal tics and a stereotyped, avuncular cultural knowledge. Their rhyming styles and language play made light of rap conventions (Moishe MC: '… my homeboy Easy Irving, he's as de[a]f as can be'/Easy Irving: 'Wha?'), even as they portrayed the performance as a coming together of two highly dissonant sonic worlds. The song's title riff, moreover, epitomises this uncomfortable meeting ground by foregrounding an expectorating sound referencing both old age and emblematic 'Hebrew' pronunciation for non-speakers, layered over a sample from the epitome of Jewish song, 'Hava Nagila'. Yet amid all the elements of play and Jewish stereotypes, the song's final message turned out to have its own twist: '2 Live Jews has made you see/That you'll lead a better life if you're as kosher as we wanna be!'. Under all the clowning and surface attitude lay a clear, hegemonic articulation of what constituted a 'good' Jewish life, along with an exhortation for Jewish listeners to take such steps.

Though often treated (and treating themselves) as kitschy novelty acts, these artists also opened up new approaches for negotiating Jewish masculinity and Jewishness in general. 2 Live Jews, for example, included on their first album a more serious-themed track entitled 'Young Jews Be Proud', which re-inscribed Jewish history in part through the use of a vocal idiom much more consistent with mainstream hip-hop conventions. The Jewish press, however, tended to dismiss these productions wholesale, making few attempts to go beyond the material's novelty status; and the mainstream press and music industry hardly noticed these artists at all. A case in point is M.O.T.'s album 19.99 (1998): released through the Sire record label (a major label at the time), 19.99 frequently inspired critical amusement through the artists' perceived attempts to clothe themselves in stereotypical Italian, Hispanic and Black trappings of masculinity, even as they consciously undercut such symbolism with Jewish stereotypes. Song titles such as 'Kosher Nostra' and 'Havana Nagilla' complemented a track entitled 'Oh God, Get a Job', which featured one of the musicians' mothers groaning the title during the chorus as well as a punked-out section of a 'traditional' Jewish song (commonly known as 'Chiri Bim').[9] Although the album's liner notes included what may be the first mention of the term 'Hebe-Hop', 19.99 gained publicity almost exclusively as a comedy/novelty album despite its creators' intentions, leading to dismal sales and only passing interest; *The Onion's A.V. Club*, for example, gave it the ignominious distinction of being named on its 'Least Essential Albums of the '90s' list.

Brooklyn-based Yeshiva-educated duo Black Hattitude, meanwhile, took a different tack, using the values associated with rap as a means for championing a passionate, right-wing, religious Jewish agenda to a largely Jewish audience. Performing under pseudonyms 'The Scholar' and 'The Force', the members of Black Hattitude broadcast unapologetic, controversial stances on recent anti-Jewish actions (on the 1991 Crown Heights riots, for example: 'The mayor wasn't trying, to keep it all quiet/Because he was one of theirs [i.e., black], so he couldn't defy it'), Israel's liberal government, the dangers of secular education, and the determinants of meaningful Jewish life. Their 1995 album, *R.E.L.I.G.I.O.N.*,[10] explicitly addressed Jewish youth, came from a first-person perspective, included tracks about Yeshiva boys preparing for the Sabbath and going on shidduch [arranged] dates, and overall presented a nuanced portrait of Yeshiva life, language and ideology. Black Hattitude's delivery, however, fell somewhat more in line with recognised mainstream rap conventions. As opposed to humour-based artists such as 2 Live Jews, the group rarely used 'Jewish' humour or overt self-parody, avoided invoking Jewish stereotypes, employed samples from classic musical artists Led Zeppelin and Peter Gabriel (rather than using typically 'Jewish' tunes),[11] experimented with interpolated spoken tracks, offered cover art evincing an intimacy with hip-hop aesthetics (including a graffiti motif and a red/yellow/green palette), and took unflinching points of view at the (self-described) risk of stirring controversy. Though never marketing themselves to hip-hop enthusiasts, Black Hattitude nonetheless offered a different strategy for incorporating rap into Jewish life, using its stylings to address issues of *Jewish* concern in a manner parallel to the ways their African-American neighbours addressed African-American concerns. The Los Angeles-based duo Blood of Abraham, in contrast, offered a self consciously Jewish but explicitly non-religious alternative that grew out of, and addressed, the greater hip-hop scene. Protégés of rapper/producer Eazy-E, group members Benyad (Ben Mor) and Mazik (David Saevitz) operated and performed entirely outside the Jewish communal realm, incorporating their own diverse Jewish experiences and backgrounds into tracks exploring more expansive rap discourses ('E & Blood of Abraham' [n.d.]; Kanter 1994). Their 1993 CD *Future Profits*, moreover, received a positive reception among rap/hip-hop fans and artists. With provocative tracks such as 'Niggaz & Jewz (Some Say Kikes)', the duo's work effectively addressed larger issues of racism and bigotry that occupied the Los Angeles rap scene, yet offered a different perspective respected by the scene as an honest airing of personal epistemology (Levine 1994). Wu Tang Clan member Remedy followed in this path with his Holocaust-referencing track 'Never Again', which first appeared on the collective's album *Killa Beez Vol. 1*: *The Swarm* and included samples from both *Schindler's List* and the Israeli national anthem. With the rise of hipster Jewish culture organisations a few years later, these artists and works would gain an important context: as American Jewish communal agencies throughout the 1990s gave more attention to Jews in their twenties and thirties due to ominous reports of their increasing ambivalence toward religious life (Dershowitz 1997; *et al.*), the cultural capital of that target population rose accordingly. Just as had happened in the 1970s with such organisations as the Institute for Jewish Life and Jewish Student Projects, new philanthropic initiatives aimed at this population began to transform the public discourse from desperate handwringing and harangues about the young generation's cultural bankruptcy into a more meaningful attempt to promote and cultivate young people's own potential for Jewish leadership.[12] As the twentieth century carried over into the twenty-first, therefore, the status of hip hop within the Jewish community underwent a significant shift: the older authority figures and culture brokers who used hip hop as a somewhat awkward educational tool gave way to younger artists who saw the style as an important part of their own musical language; and the younger artists saw themselves in the spotlight as political figures who could contribute to the future of Judaism.[13] The network created by the rise of the diverse, Jewish philanthropy-funded, interconnected renewed Jewish culture scene in New York, moreover, provided the resources and venues these artists needed to develop both as individuals and as a musical sub-genre. Alliances between artists, publishers and philanthropic organisations thus commonly provided fora for young people to contextualise the music they heard into their own lives; and thus did hip hop gain a new sense of meaning in the Jewish world.

Owning the Groove: Hip Hop and Hipster Jews

The scene that resulted from this shift, if one could call it that, relied heavily on a doubly encoded complex of strategies that simultaneously aimed to critique the Jewish establishment and invite the disenfranchised to participate in alternate forms of Jewish expression, all while maintaining an aesthetic associated with hip-hop culture. Among other issues, the combination of these components opened a space for public, almost carnivalesque, negotiation of masculinity that fell in many ways along the same lines as previous discussions of Jewish masculinity: in one sense, artists aimed at emulating (and consequently embodying) societally sanctioned notions of being male; yet almost paradoxically, they also promoted an image of the Jewish male as a highly desirable 'other' that did *not* conform to society's images of masculinity. Some entered this space using pre-existing material: rapper Etan G's first solo album, *South Side of the Synagogue*, included remakes of earlier Shlock Rock songs such as 'Yo Yo Yo Yamulke' and 'Recognize the Miracles'. Canadian remix artist SoCalled based his creations on the texts or proceedings of Jewish ceremonies and celebrations (SoCalled 2001; 2004; 2005; Solomon & SoCalled 2002). Here, I offer a portrait of that space by focusing on two other artists: Matisyahu, the 'Hasidic Reggae Superstar', and the Latino-Jewish collective called the Hip-Hop Hoodíos. Matisyahu, born Matthew Miller in 1979, began performing professionally some time after his decision to become a religious Jew around 2001.[14] Brought up in a liberal Jewish home in White Plains, New York, Miller became interested in reggae music, and developed a talent for beatboxing. Late in his high-school career, after taking time off to follow the touring group Phish, he embarked on a spiritual path that after several years led him to the Hassidic dynasty of Chabad Lubavitch. One evening, in response to a suggestion from his rabbinic mentor, he gathered a couple of musicians together, and played a reggae set at a Chabad Lubavitch-sponsored public Chanukah candle lighting in New York's Union Square. Several opportunities arose from that performance, eventually leading him to sign on as the premiere artist for the recently founded non-profit JDub Records – a company devoted to developing new Jewish acts initially funded by Jewish philanthropic start-up grants. With his first album release in mid-October 2004 and several television appearances – including spots on Jimmy Kimmel Live!, Steve Harvey's Big Time, and The Late Show with David Letterman – Matisyahu developed both a devoted following and a religious mission. Merging Rastafarian reliance upon Hebrew Bible texts and the conventions of the reggae genre with Hassidic philosophies and the sound world of niggunim (religious melodies; see Koskoff 2001), he fashioned himself as an outreach figure for Lubavitch, performing at clubs in the hopes that listeners could, through the music, consider leading a more religious Jewish lifestyle. During a 29 June 2004 interview on CNN's feature 'The Music Room', for example, Matisyahu, upon being asked by the host to freestyle (i.e. improvise a rap), began by singing the first lines of a Chabad *niggun* to Yiddish words, broke it down into a beatbox version of the melody, and then transitioned into the first couple of lines of one of his original songs before being cut off by the highly entertained host. Similarly, by performing in public venues, Matisyahu opened up a fascinating place for gender negotiation. As a male performer with an intentionally all-male band, he dwelt in a meeting space between reggae and Orthodox Jewish aesthetics. At a 23 October 2004 club concert in Brooklyn, for example, his audience proved to be overwhelmingly Jewish and about sixty to seventy per cent male, with comparatively few single women present; and the semicircle of the most active fans at the front of the stage consisted exclusively of men. Matisyahu's dancehall-tinged delivery and many of his motions were reminiscent of reggae performances. Yet the trappings of masculinity he represented gave clear indications of a specific, Jewish Orthodox form of maleness at variance with societal expectations: those who followed his career knew clearly of his engagement and marriage just a couple of months earlier to a woman who had also joined the Lubavitch community in recent years. Twice during the concert he grabbed arms with other men and danced in close circles with them, the latter time after jumping to the ground to join the rest of the crowd. And perhaps most noticeably, Matisyahu's performance costume comprised the black hat, coat, vest, white shirt and black pants standard to Lubavitch Judaism (personal observation). The audience, meanwhile, provided multiple interpretations of Matisyahu's show. In addition to the modern Orthodox Jewish men and at least four Hasidic men, Orthodox teenage girls in long sleeves and long skirts danced together quietly off to the side of the stage, receiving little attention from the performer. About halfway back, both religious and non-religious couples held each other closely and swayed back and forth in uncharacteristically public intimacy; and a lesbian Jewish couple in their fifties danced in the crowd as their younger friend watched from the bar and called the show pretentious. Another group of Hassidic Jews brought audio and video recording equipment to the show and taped it as part of a documentary on Ba'alei Tshuvah (Jews who become religiously observant). I, meanwhile, sat in the bleacher-like seats at the back of the space next to a middle-aged Orthodox couple who came because the wife loved reggae music. To Matisyahu's manager, the difference between the performer's message on-stage and the happenings in the crowd constituted an important conversation: for him, and for the Jewish philanthropies that funded his company, the concert aimed to create that space where Jewish identity could be displayed, disputed and formed, particularly among young adults. That space, moreover, was the message: informing Jews that a flexible site existed where they were free to explore, respond to, or even take for granted their own senses of Jewish identity. The Hip-Hop Hoodíos aimed to do similarly. Their songs, however, took another tactic, endowing Jewish men with prodigious sexual and social prowess precisely due to the qualities by which broader society had previously feminised them. Composed of two Latin American-identifying Jews and an 'honorary' Jew with a Jewish sister-in-law, the Hoodíos first gained significant media exposure in 2002 with their EP *Raza Hoodía* (or 'Jewish Race'). Basing their music and message on an agenda of invoking and then subverting Jewish stereotypes to spur ethnic and religious pride (including a distancing from the Yiddish/ Eastern European-associated musical sound that had become a signifier for Jewish authenticity in parts of the industry),[15] they provided a particularly androcentric view of the world in their performances in ways that connected with Daniel Boyarin's discourses of marginalisation: songs such as 'Dicks and Noses' highlighted the Hoodíos's active re-encoding of male Jewish iconic signs into symbols of power and hyper-masculinity, with lines such as 'You like our dicks and you like our noses/You see a Jewish guy and you forget where your clothes is/*Venga mami*, take a little sip from my ladle/Take you back to my room and you can play with my dreidel' clearly aimed toward Jewish women – or as their t-shirts label them on their website, 'Hoodia Honeys'. Similarly, in their song 'Kike on the Mic', lead singer Josue Noriega (the stage name of Joshua Norek) burned through several Jewish stereotypes, and then in the following verse evoked consistently thorny issues of Jewish racial and social identity – all while a Spanish guitar played the Yiddish song *Choson Kale Mazel Tov* ('Congratulations to the Bride and Groom') in the background. Such moments presented a Jewish masculinity that not only asserted itself within the broader rhetorical social order, but also critiqued the very boundaries of the Jewish identity being trumpeted.[16] Songs on the group's follow-up album criticising nose jobs and asserting the hidden Jewish heritage of 'millions of Latinos' continued their agenda.

These critiques also provided a space for women, several of whom appeared to be active participants in producing the masculine image and rhetorical schema called for by the genre. In the Hoodíos' video for their cover of Flory Jagoda's song 'Ocho Kandelikas', for example, women appeared as simultaneously objectified and confounded sex-symbols: on the one hand as self-titled Hoodia Honeys in t-shirts and (frequently) long denim skirts, and on the other hand as bikini-clad, bagel-bra-wearing arm candy during a simulation of a seedy Latino rooftop pool party during the video's mid-section (the video appears in full on the group's website, along with other videos for 'Gorrito Cosmico' and 'Kike on the Mic', at www.hoodíos.com). Especially the latter images corresponded superficially with tropes of female exploitation and fetishisation popularly invoked when describing the rap industry (Neal 2004, p. 247). Yet I would suggest that in this case, as with *HEEB* magazine's recent sex issue (#9, 2005), such imagery was the very point: the whole video – directed, filmed and edited by female director Lori Grossman – contributed to a more broadly reinvented system of Jewish symbolism that gained its power by forcing a reconsideration of what would acceptably fit into a Jewish framework. Likewise, as reported to me by a student, and seen personally to a lesser extent, several women who attended a Matisyahu concert squealed when the performer took off his outer coat in the middle of a set, replicating a gender stereotype in a nearly absurdly reframed, yet self-consciously Jewish, situation. Carefully constructing their public actions, women involved in these images appeared to collaborate carefully and consciously with this system of signification to forge a symbolic gender dynamic that simultaneously emulated and challenged the very idea of what it meant to be Jewish.

The Ever-breaking Frame

Throughout 2004, the sounds Matisyahu, the Hip-Hop Hoodíos and others created continued to bear such dissonance with conventional expectations of 'Jewish music' that reviewers still often portrayed their albums as comedy or novelty recordings – framing such activity as paradoxical and light-heartedly using the artists' music to highlight a sense of Jews' well-intentioned *inability* to produce effective hip hop. Yet as the steadily growing number of (predominantly male) Jewish hip-hop artists suggested, the discounting of such Jewish artisanship may have indicated an important process at work in understanding how young people negotiate inherited traditions. To those familiar with the Jewish hip-hop aesthetic, it appears, the approach provided a musical ideology virtually untouched by expectations associated with Judaism; by wrapping themselves in a hip-hop musical language, therefore, Jewish artists could find a nearly undisturbed forum for actively exchanging and testing agendas of gender, ideology, exclusivity and knowledge, handed down to them by their elders. To those unfamiliar with hip hop, the pairing was so unlikely as not to be taken seriously – and thus became rendered radical enough to provide a safe space for young people to make individual choices about their religious identities.

It is important to recognise that this space continues to change, buffeted about by different concepts of what it means to be a Jewish hip-hop artist. The Los Angeles based release of a compilation of Jewish hip-hop tracks entitled *Celebrate Hip-Hop* in October 2004, for example, retained the exclusively androcentric representation of the genre, but almost completely eliminated any mention of nebbishy Jewish 'stereotypes' in favour of a more muscular, internationalised, and to some extent Israel-centred symbolic language. The album's producer, Jeremy Goldscheider, consciously eliminated the term Hebe-Hop from the album due to its kitsch value, avoided artists such as 50Shekel based on a preference for artistry over perceived pedagogy, and added several more recognised mainstream hip-hop artists, such as Wu-Tang Clan member Remedy and harder core Jewish rappers Blood of Abraham, who explored Jewish identity with a less self-conscious subversion of racial or ethnic stereotypes (Khazzoom 2004; Goldscheider, personal communication). The New York-centric basis of the scene I have up to now described disappeared as well, replaced by a view of hip hop as a global Jewish sonic language on the album: the Hip-Hop Hoodíos became a South American group; and Goldscheider also brought in tracks from self-consciously Jewish rap artists in Israel, Russia and Great Britain (though, notably, the album provided no translations, again suggesting the novelty of the 'world' classification). Such changes provide further evidence of hip hop's space as a mutable site of negotiation among the young – with gender as only one of a number of important fronts for negotiating Jewish identity. Since *Celebrate* Hip-Hop's appearance, the fates of the various artists described here have moved and diversified into still newer territory. Matisyahu, whose producer probably never considered him a hip-hop artist despite his use of beatbox, his early journalistic framings with other Jewish rap artists, and his description in a December 2005 issue of *Billboard Magazine* as a 'Hassidic reggae rapper', began playing to growing audiences in Europe, Israel and the United States-Outside-New York City, while gaining his own reputation within the significantly larger reggae scene; his second album, 2005's *Live at Stubbs*, peaked at #30 on the *Billboard 200* chart on 18 March 2006. Headlining both the 2005 Legendary Records 8th Annual Carifest and the Chabad of Washington Square Jewish Life Festival, and singing guest tracks for Christian Heavy Metal group P.O.D. within the course of six months, his multivalent performance identity appeared to rely less and less upon the Jewish cultural scene, and more on his own (increasingly less surprising) merits as a songwriter, performer and recording artist ('Rock of Ages', 2006). In early March, Matisyahu's third album – evocatively entitled *Youth* – came out as a joint release between his original label JDub Records, Or Music, and major label EPIC (a division of Sony BMG which first picked up *Live at Stubbs* several months after its release); and shortly afterward, he broke his contract with JDub Records, opting instead for more experienced and mainstream representation (Sisario 2006).

In contrast, 50Shekel, one of the first rappers to capitalise on the public upsurge of Jewish hipster culture, went in a completely different direction. As the Jewish rap scene developed after 2003, he became progressively disenfranchised: enthusiasts of the rap genre derided him as untalented, derivative and preachy; and he became the target of an attack rap by upstart Minneapolis-based parody group the Ju-Tang Clan.[17] Shekel's own album release, described as imminent for over a year, became more and more delayed. Finally, in May 2005, the artist known as Shekel reinvented himself as a Messianic Jew, eventually changing his stage name to his birth name, Aviad Cohen. Shunned by the Jewish community, he claimed, Shek reached a moment of epiphany after watching Mel Gibson's *The Passion of the Christ* and thereafter began to explore and broadcast a new message of Jesus as Lord: at first still doin' it 'True Jew', and then, by January 2006, reorienting himself under a rubric of 'Hebrew'. His CD, meanwhile, eternally nearing completion, shifted names from the spoken-word *Banned from da Shul*, to a continuation of his 50 Cent motif in *Get Righteous or Die Tryin'*, to the more overtly messianic *For His Glory*, and then to *Hooked on the Truth* when the album finally came out in fall 2006.[18] As one of the first to leave the Jewish hip-hop scene, 50Shekel's dramatic transformation offers an important paradigm in its nearly complete effacement of his previous identity: Cohen's first music 'hits' and his early web announcements are no longer available; his network of 'True Jews' evaporated; and his place within the Jewish culture-producing community almost forgotten.

Other Jewish hip-hop artists have increasingly allied with other genres, shifting public identities to appeal to other markets. Yiddish-tinged hip-hop artist SoCalled, who gained broad attention with his 2002 album *Hiphopkhasene* ('Hip-Hop Jewish wedding') began playing more un-remixed Yiddish songs at his appearances, accompanied by his accordion – perhaps in a nod toward greater alignment with the progressive yet somewhat more academically oriented Yiddish music scene.[19] Remedy, seemingly in concert with the Jewish hipster phenomenon, gained a great deal of attention as a serious Jewish rapper, conducted performances for pro-Jewish and pro-Zionist organisations, toured Israel, and recorded songs with Israeli rightwing rapper Subliminal (Moore 2003; Galdi 2005). The Hoodíos, meanwhile, worked closely with the Latin music industry (their lead singer, after many years as a marketing executive with several Latin music labels and groups, became an entertainment lawyer for the industry, and founded the Latin Alternative Music Conference), opened for Latin Alternative music acts, and were as quick to defend Latino heritage and identity as they were to address Jewish organisations and concerns;[20] at the same time, the group also appeared in

New York City's May 2005 Salute to Israel Parade, though having to honour specific requests *not* to perform songs such as 'Kike on the Mic' or 'Dicks and Noses'.[21]

Humour and Education: The Same Lessons, in New Bottles

While the groups discussed above attempted to bring Jewish discourse to a new level through hip-hop conventions, sub-discourses focusing on humour and education remained consistent if somewhat understated throughout this period. Comedians MC Paul Barman and Eric Schwartz (aka Smooth E) created their own Jewish-themed hip-hop parodies, specifically aimed at stand-up audiences. More significant was Sacha Baron Cohen, who, as faux-gangsta Ali G, used hip-hop culture as a foil for cultural critique; while Ali G made little reference to Judaism himself, Cohen's identity as an 'observant Jew' received frequent mention in discussions of his HBO show.[22] Propagated on the whole separately from the 'radical' Jewish hip-hop scene, these figures and their works continued to explore the relationship of Jews with hip-hop in the United States, replete with the racial, gendered, and cultural implications such relationships outlined. Schwartz, for example, performed his 'Suburban Homeboy' routine in front of a predominantly African-American audience on a BET special; his 'Chanukah Hey-Ya' parody (of OutKast's 2004 hit 'Hey Ya'), with flash animation added by a different person, became a popular download among Jewish interest e-mail listservs in Winter 2004; and a flash animated setting of his original song 'Matzah' became one of the 'classics' on the JibJab website (known for its politically satirical flash animation works) in Winter and Spring 2006.[23]

The use of hip hop for Jewish educational purposes, meanwhile, continued to exist in a somewhat lower profile world. Away from the publicity, Jonathan Gutstadt and others at the University of Oregon combined to create Dr. J$ and the OJGs, whose somewhat didactic *Hip Hop Shabbat* album comprised in large part rap interpretations of the various Sabbath prayers and rituals. Etan G, in contrast, continued to perform, though as part of the same Shlock Rock collective that had supported him originally.

And the circle would continue to turn. In November 2005, Los Angeles-based rap collective Chutzpah released its first album, *Eponymous*. A project of veteran actor George Segal (who featured prominently as Dr. Dreck), entertainment industry insider Tor Hyams, and others, the album and its related DVD covered much of the same territory covered collectively by 2 Live Jews, Shlock Rock, and M.O.T.: Jewish guilt, ambivalence over non-Jewish women, Jewish pride, Jewish mothers, the importance of Ashkenazic signifiers such as Yiddish and the shtetl, and the diaspora – always with a basic pedagogical message of self-preservation and Jewish cultural maintenance. The 'old Jewish man' voice, the play on Dr. Dre's name, expectorations, and songs translating Jewish/Yiddish words into English, all made their reappearance. Nonetheless, the group commenced the album by once calling attention to itself as an unprecedented:

> Yo check it: this album is dedicated to all the Jews and gentiles that have been down since Day One. Welcome to Diaspora Records. We got Dr. Dreck, MC Meshugena [Yiddish for 'crazy'], Jew-Dah, and myself, Master Tav [last letter of the Hebrew alphabet] representin': twelve tribes – and the one that got lost. We wish you peace, to decrease the diaspora – makin' it one tribe: right here, right now, and for all eternity. We're Jews on a mission, unitin' all people; representin' West Coast to East and back again. Cause you're hearing the new sounds – the positively novel rappin' Jew sounds – of Chutzpah: the world's first ever Jewish hip-hop super group.
>
> (Chutzpah 2005; track 1)

The moment offered a paradoxical glimpse into the discourses of 'Jewish' sound, and of Jewish cultural expression more generally. Media outlets across the country framed Chutzpah in much the same way as they had initially approached Matisyahu or the Hip-Hop Hoodíos: as a special-interest guest bringing a Jewish point of view to a broader audience, in this case during the winter holiday season. To those familiar with the scene, Chutzpah appeared to offer little new (Weiss 2005); yet its conscious erasure of the numerous Jewish hip-hop groups preceding it also spoke to a crucial process of novelty that might once again pave the way for a new population to emerge from under the now-dominant 'Heebster' culture, again to inscribe its own sense of Jewish identity onto the American scene.

Once again, the Jewish gender discourses sustained themselves: using Jewish icons to subvert a perceived attenuating image of Judaism amid the skilful employment of key iconic Jewish referents, all in an ambivalent space that alternately slid between humour, kitsch, offensiveness and didacticism.

Conclusion: the Mutability of Jewish Identity

While the language of hip hop offers a particularly evocative, well-populated and well-documented vessel for exploring the convergence of Jewish cultural activity that took place at the turn of the twenty-first century (the cover of *HEEB* magazine's first issue, after all, featured a round *shmura* [hand-baked] matzah situated on a DJ turntable), this essay could have covered similar patterns in a number of different styles, whether punk (Abraham 2006), reggae (Levay 2005), klezmer (Slobin 2000; Svigals 2002), or gospel (Ross *et al.* 2000). On one level, the Jewish-oriented hip-hop scene between 1986 and 2006 offered a vivid index of empowerment among young Jews, particularly in its commentary on historical discourses of masculinity (and the historic tendency to use masculinity to represent the public Jewish image, particularly in the musical realm [see Wagner 1894]). At the same time, although masculinity served an important stake in this scene, on another level masculinity served largely as a vessel for Jews to reassert a sense of self into a conversation from which they had previously been largely absent: one of several strategies used both to unmoor and to redefine what it meant to be a 'new' Jew during this time. That specific male-centred cultural norms formed a crucial part of Jewish hip-hop musicians' musical output, moreover, suggests a method of understanding tradition that requires change in order to instil a sense of meaning. Discussions about the transmission of Jewish tradition often treat as unproblematic (or perhaps automatic) the expectation that successive generations should wish to preserve the traditions of their elders; deviations from that process thus become grounds for crisis (and, in the public realm, questions of preservation). Yet this example, I suggest, implies exactly the opposite. Musical (and by extension cultural) change is not just an option for maintaining religious identity for this population: mirroring the work of Sunaina Marr Maira on Indian American youth (2002), and other studies of youth culture (Boynton and Kok 2006; Cohen 2006), change in this context becomes a crucial part of the religious and ethnic transmission and preservation process. Hip hop, once established as a common language among (or in some cases, for) young people, thus became a prime site for the performance of competing discourses of Jewish 'authenticity' (see Cheng 2004, pp. 84–124). Particularly for a population constantly and publicly identified by its elders as a source of anxiety and ambivalence for the future of their 'people', such spaces served as culturally bounded laboratories for expression – places to play out these inherited anxieties both individually and as a group, while forging a new/old language of authenticity, heritage and identity. Within the Jewish cultural circles inscribed by the Heebster and hip-hop phenomena, interestingly enough, the aim of such activity remained remarkably conservative: for in creating or appropriating this carnival-like forum, artists and organisations maintained the basic defining frame as a 'Jewish' one. Acting inside that frame, young Jews defined and redefined their own terms, celebrating their triumphs over the struggles of the past while forging an agenda for the *mensches* of the future.

Study Questions

1. Why were young urban-dwelling Jews in their twenties and thirties often the main target of movements and campaigns such as 'The New Super Jews' cover story in *Time Out New York*?
2. What is the role of gender (masculinity more specifically) among the burgeoning scene of America Jewish 'hipster' culture? What is the role of blackness in the ways in which many Jewish youth think of marginality?
3. What is the relationship between and among the emergence of Jewish rap and traditional and reimagined ideas of Jewish life, culture, and religion?

Notes

1. See liner inserts to Jewlia Eisenberg, *Trilectic* (Tzaddik: TZ7155, 2001); John Zorn, *Kristallnacht* (Tzaddik: TZ7301, 1992/3); Kletka Red, *Hijacking* (Tzaddik: TZ7111, 1996).
2. Personal communication, Lake Serrins.
3. This study emerges from ethnographic research conducted during three years of postdoctoral work at New York University (Fall 2003 to Spring 2006), a time when several of the artists described in this essay were coming into their own. I have attempted to broaden this material by adding a critical consideration of the larger Jewish hipster scene, based in part on conversations held at the Working Group for Jews and Media at New York University's Center for Religion and Media. Thus, in this article I look at the relationship of Jews and hip hop through a decidedly New York-centric (and more broadly United States-centric) lens, yet I do so with the recognition that New York arguably held an international reputation as a major hub for 'Heebster' activity at the time through its sheer density of events and available resources; some of the figures described here, as I note, have since gone on to foster national and international reputations. It is interesting to consider that scholars from outside the United States (primarily in Great Britain) have fashioned their own 'local-global' discourses on this phenomenon, usually under the rubric of 'Kewl Jewz' (or some variant spelling). Hopefully, by examining their publications side-by-side with those now being produced by US-based scholars, we can gain a fuller sense of the larger local, transnational, historical, religious, ethnic, and gender-based implications of this theoretically rich activity. I add that this essay does not examine the hip-hop scene in Israel, which, save the connections I describe toward the end, is the subject of a different study entirely.
4. See Rose (1994) for a particularly compelling early framing of this issue, and Forman and Neal (2004) for a sense of how that literature has developed.
5. Such was the story of rapper Etan G, who included in his 2004 album *South Side of the Synagogue* a recording of himself rapping at a Jewish youth convention in the mid-1980s (on track: 'Hava Na Wha?').
6. A Megillah is the name of a scroll containing one of five documents in the Hebrew biblical canon: The Books of Esther, Ecclesiastes, Ruth, and Lamentations, and the Song of Songs. In recent usage, the term has come to gain a more general meaning of any story, usually recounted during personal interaction (such as in the phrase 'the whole megillah').
7. Haman, according to this account, begins the story as the egotistical chief advisor to the King of Persia. Upon discovering that a Jewish man will not bow down to him, he sets up a scheme to exterminate all Jews; but the man's relative, Esther, who has secretly insinuated her way into the queenship, thwarts the plot and has Haman and his family killed instead. Many Jewish traditions therefore

frame Haman as the prototypical anti-Jewish villain, and tend to describe other anti-Jewish figures in history as his descendants.

8. The recording truly came into its own at the end, however, when Solomon and Shlock Rock over-dubbed a parody of a Jewish youth group Friday-night hand-washing experience, complete with an adult calling out table numbers for people to attend washing stations, antagonistic comments from young people, an Eastern European-accented 'sage' chosen to lead the blessing over the bread, and a chorus of hums (the only form of vocal communication sanctioned after hand-washing and before the blessing over bread in many observant circles).

9. Also known as 'Az Ikh vil Zingen'.

10. According to the album, the acronym stood for 'Rap Enforcing Large Intense Geshmak [Religious pleasure/enjoyment] In Our [Jewish] Nation': a message aimed at revitalising what the duo saw as a crisis state among Jewish young people.

11. Among the samples Black Hattitude used were the introductory instrumental licks from Led Zeppelin's 'Whole Lotta Love' and Peter Gabriel's 'Sledgehammer'.

12. For more on the 1970s initiatives, see Siegel, Strassfeld & Strassfeld (1973, p. 6).

13. Such was the case with DJs Aaron Bisman and Dan Sieradski: the former a founder of JDub Records, and the latter the creator of jewschool.com and other Jewish web initiatives.

14. The biographical information supplied here is based on interview with Matisyahu, 19 October 2004.

15. The Hip-Hop Hoodíos' personification of 'difference' in the Jewish music world offers a rich area for discussion that plays off numerous layers of 'Jewish' identity and could well occupy its own essay. On one hand, the Hoodíos' assertion of a Latin-American voice in Jewish music – and its repression in the American Jewish music scene up to that point – indicates to many North-American and European Jews an identification with Sephardic (Spanish-Portuguese derived Jewish) identity. Indeed, the Hoodíos' fronting of the invented Ladino (JudeoSpanish) Hanukkah song 'Ocho Kandelikas', and their song '1492' (which chronicles the 1492 expulsion of the Jews from Spain, their eventual migration and integration into the New World, and their presence in the 'blood' of much of the Latin-American population), offer such imagery. Yet this association is in many ways imagined by North-American and European listeners through the 'mystique' of Latin America, the common linguistic associations with Spanish, and the tendency to label Jewish activity according to a Sephardic/Ashkenazic (Eastern European-derived) dichotomy. More than evoking 'Sephardicness', the Hoodíos reflect the complex nature of the present-day Latin-American Jewish population, which uses Spanish as its home language, yet is itself largely Eastern European derived (thus the entirely appropriate inclusion of a riff on Hava Nagilah, Yiddish folk tunes, and references to such Eastern European Jewish cultural icons as bagels and lox). The broader population, meanwhile, retains a knowledge of the earlier 'crypto-Jewish' Sephardic groups that lived there centuries earlier as a part of its heritage. For more, on larger discussions of 'Judeolatinidad' see Cohen (2008).

16. A second version of 'Kike on the Mic', released on the group's 2004 album *Agua Pa' La Gente*, either removes or obscures the guitar introduction in favour of a more raucous sound punctuated by riffs from Klezmatics trumpeter Frank London.

17. 'Schindler's Fist (50 Shekels of Shame)', <http://www.ju-tangclan.com>

18. <http://www.50shekel.com>, accessed periodically between January 2004 and June 2006.

19. Personal observation, SoCalled performance, 30 October 2005 (Toronto, Canada).

20. Note the Hoodíos' publicised brush-up with HEEB magazine regarding an off-hand comment deemed insensitive to Latinos, <http://www.jewlicious.com/?p=1102>

21. Informal conversation, Gloria Kaufman, 26 May 2005. The Hip Hop Hoodíos, notably, did not appear in the parade the following year.

22. Although Ali G appeared on British television as early as 1998, and became a considerable cultural phenomenon in the UK, he remained relatively unknown in the United States until the American version of his show aired on HBO in 2003–2004. Even then, because of his lack of geographical and cultural connection to the American Jewish hipster scene, Ali G came up only rarely, generally as an outside cultural referent for understanding the American scene. The *Time Out New York* 'New Super Jews' features, for example, offered no mention of Ali G.

23. <http://www.jibjab.com>, accessed 15 December 2005; also see <http://www. suburbanhomeboy.com>

References

Abraham, I. 2006. 'Punk pulpit: religion, punk rock, and counter-(sub)cultures', paper given at *Annual Conference of the American Academy of Religion*, Washington, DC, 19 November.

Barzel, T. 2004. *'Radical Jewish Culture': Composer/Improvisers on New York City's 1990s Downtown Scene*, Ph.D. diss., University of Michigan.

Baumgarten, J. 1992. 'Le "Purim-Shpil" et la Tradition Carnivalesque Juive', *Pardès*, 15, 37–62.

Berger, M. 1996. 'The mouse that never roars: Jewish masculinity on American television', in *Too Jewish?: Challenging Jewish Identities*, ed. N. Kleeblatt (New Brunswick, Rutgers University Press), 93–107.

Boyarin, D. 1997. *Unheroic Conduct: The Rise of Heterosexuality and the Invention of the Jewish Man* (Berkeley, University of California Press).

Boynton, S., and Kok, R. (eds.) 2006. *Musical Childhoods and the Cultures of Youth* (Middletown, Wesleyan University Press).

Breines, P. 1990. *Tough Jews: Political Fantasies and the Moral Dilemma of American Jewry* (New York, Basic Books).

Brod, H. (ed.) 1990. *A Mensch Among Men: Explorations in Jewish Masculinity* (Freedom, CA, The Crossing Press).

Cheng, V. 2004. *Inauthentic: The Anxiety Over Culture and Identity* (New Brunswick, Rutgers University Press).

Cohen, J. 2006. '"And the youth shall see visions …": summer camps, songleading and musical identity among American reform Jewish teenagers', in *Musical Childhoods and the Cultures of Youth*, ed. S. Boynton and R. kok (Middletown, Wesleyan University Press), 187–207.

—— 2008. 'The ethnic dilemmas of Latin-American Jewry', in *Rethinking Jewish-Latin Americans*, ed. J. Lesser and R. Rein (Albuquerque, University of New Mexico Press), pp. 266–84.

D'Addario, D. 2003. 'Private Oy', *Time Out New York*, 427 (4–11 December), pp. 26, 28. Dershowitz, A. 1997. *The Vanishing American Jew* (New York, Little, Brown).

Epstein, S. 1995. 'The Bobover Hasidim Piremshpiyl: from folk drama for Purim to a ritual of transcending the Holocaust', in *New World Hasidim: Ethnographic Studies of Hasidic Jews in America*, ed. J. BelcoveShalin (Albany, SUNY Press), pp. 237–55.

'Eric Wright: E. & Blood of Abraham' [n.d.] <http://www.eazy-e.com/eazy-e-boa.html>, 23 January 2006.

Galdi, D.S. 2005. 'The Orange Party', *The College Zionist* <http://www.thecollegezionist.org/2005issue/orange.html> , 31 December 2006.

Gilman, S. 1991. *The Jew's Body* (New York, Routledge). Goldscheider, J. 2004. Telephone communication, 15 November.

Kanter, L. 1994. 'Jewish rap: not an oxymoron anymore', *Jewish Bulletin of Northern California*, 6 May, p. 40.

Keys, L. 2004. 'Hasid trip'. *New York Post*, 7 May, p. 56.

Khazzoom, L. 2004. 'Hip-Hop's Jew Crew takes center stage', *The Jewish Journal of Greater Los Angeles*, 10 December.

Kirshenblatt-Gimblett, B. 1980. '"Contraband": performance, text and analysis of a "Purim Shpil"', *The Drama Review*, 24/3, pp. 5–16.

Kligman, M. 1996. 'On the creators and consumers of Orthodox popular music in Brooklyn', *YIVO Annual*, 23, pp. 259–94.

Koskoff, E. 2001. *Music in Lubavitcher Life* (Urbana, University of Illinois Press).

Leibovitz, L. 2005. '"Latino-Jewish peacemongers" on parade', *New York Jewish Week*, June, p. 3.

Levay, W. 2005. 'Roots, Rock, Rebbe: Matisyahu and the cultural version', *Anamesa: an Interdisciplinary Journal*, 3/2, pp. 20–38, <http://www.nyu.edu/pubs/anamesa/archive/03_2_culture/05_levay.pdf>

Levine, R. 1994. 'Pop music review: Blood of Abraham goes beyond shtick', *Los Angeles Times*, 6 June, p. 8.

Maira, S. 2002. *Desis in the House: Indian American Youth Culture in New York City* (Philadelphia, Temple University Press).

Marcus, S., et al. [n.d.] 'Stars of David', *Time Out New York*, 427 (4–11 December), pp. 20–22, 24.

Miller, M. 2004. Personal interview, 23 October.

Moore, M. 2003. 'Remedy, Killah Priest perform in Israel', *AllHipHop News*, 21 May, <http://www.allhiphop.com/hiphopnews/?ID=1919>, 31 December 2006.

Neal, M. 2004. 'Part IV: I'll be Nina Simone defecating on your microphone: hip-hop and gender', in *That's the Joint! The Hip-Hop Studies Reader*, ed. M. Forman and M. Neal (Middletown, Wesleyan University Press), pp. 247–50.

Porter, J., and Dreier, P. (eds.) 1973. *Jewish Radicalism: A Selected Anthology* (New York, Grove).

Rakoff, J. 2003. 'The new Super Jews', *Time Out New York*, 427 (4–11 December), pp. 13–14, 16, 18.

'Rock of Ages'. 2006. *Billboard Magazine Online*, 23 January, <http://www.billboard.com/bbcom/search/google/article_display.jsp?vnu_content_id=1001883061>

Rosenberg, W. 2001. *Legacy of Rage: Jewish Masculinity, Violence and Culture* (Amherst, University of Massachusetts Press).

Ross, T., Sorensen, J., Vuijst, F., and Winding, V. (dirs.) 2000. *Keep On Walking: Joshua Nelson, the Jewish Gospel Singer* (Filmmakers Library).

Sandrow, N. 1977. *Vagabond Stars: A World History of Yiddish Theater* (New York, Harper & Row).

Schorsch, J. 2000. 'Making Judaism cool', *Tikkun Magazine*, 15/2, pp. 33–6.

Siegel, R., Strassfeld, M., and Strassfeld, S. (ed.) 1973. *The Jewish Catalog* (Philadelphia, Jewish Publication Society of America).

Sisario, B. 2006. 'Hasidic reggae singer surprises his managers', *New York Times*, 14 March.

Slobin, M. 2003. 'On Beregovsky's work on Purim Shpil', *YIVO-Bleter*, NS 4.

——. 2000. *Fiddler on the Move: Exploring the Klezmer World* (New York, Oxford University Press).

Stratton, J. (2008). 'The Beastie Boys: Jews in whiteface', *Popular Music*, 27/3.

Svigals, A. 2002. 'Why we do this anyway: Klezmer as Jewish youth subculture', in *American Klezmer: Its Roots and Offshoots*, ed. M. Slobin (Berkeley, University of California Press), pp. 211–19.

Swados, E. 1996 [1988]. 'Esther, a vaudeville Megillah', in *Fruitful & Multiplying: 9 Contemporary Plays from the American Jewish Repertoire*, ed. E. Schiff (New York, Mentor), pp. 1–82.

Wagner, R. 1894. 'Judaism in music', In *Richard Wagner's Prose Works*, trans. W. Ellis (London; reprint, St. Clair Shores, MI, Scholarly Press), vol. iii, pp. 75–122.

Waletzky, D.J. 2004. 'One love: meet Matisyahu', *HEEB: The New Jew Review*, 5, p. 60.

Weiss, A. 2005. 'More Jewish rap? That's Chutzpah', *Forward On-Line*, 9 December, <http:///www.forward.com/articles/7006>

Discography

2 Live Jews, *As Kosher As They Wanna Be*. Kosher Records, HTCD 3328. 1990.

Black Hatitude, *R.E.L.I.G.I.O.N.* Black Hatitude, CDBH101. 1995.

Blood of Abraham, *Future Profits*. Ruthless Records. 1993.

—— *Eyedollartree*. Basement Records, 1151, 2005 with DVD; original CD release attempt by Mastergrip Records. 1999/2000.

Cantor Wally Schachet-Briskin, 'The Debbie Friedman Rap', *Cantor Wally*. Wally Schachet-Briskin. 1997.

Chutzpah, (*Eponymous*). Jewish Music Group, 18005. 2005.

—— This Is …? [Mockumentary DVD]. Diaspora Records/Jewish Music Group, JMG 18006–9. 2005.

Dr. J$ and the OJGs, *Hip Hop Shabbat*. 2003.

Etan G., *South Side of the Synagogue*. 2002.

Hip-Hop Hoodíos, *Raza Hoodía EP*. 2002.

—— *Agua Pa' la Gente*. Jazzheads Records, 1147. 2005.

Ju-Tang Clan, *The New Testament*. http://web.archive.org/web/20070526011742/www.jutangclan.com/mp3s.html">http://web.archive.org/web/20070526011742/www.jutangclan.com/mp3s.html, 2001. 7 July 2008.

Matisyahu, *Shake Off the Dust … ARISE*. JDub Records. 2004.

—— *Live at Stubbs*. [JDub]/EPIC/Or Music, EK 96464. 2005.

—— *Youth*. [JDub]/Or/EPIC Records, 97695. 2006.

M.O.T., *19.99*. Sire Records, 9 47101–2. 1998.

—— *Merkava* MK-4, <http://web.archive.org/web/20041207034601/membersofthetribe.com/themu sic.htm>. [n.d.]

Remedy, *Code:Red*. Musicrama, CREC7002. 2002.

—— *The Genuine Article*. Fifth Angel Recordings. 2001.

—— 'Never Again', on Wu Tang Clan, *Killa Beez Vol. 1: The Swarm*. Priority Records. 1998

Shlock Rock, *J Rap City*. Shlock Rock, SHL 8613. 2005.

Smooth-E, *Kosher Kutz*. 2004.

SoCalled, *Electranukah EP*. 2004.

—— *The SoCalled Seder*. JDub Records, 302. 2005 [completion of an earlier work by the same name from c. 2001].

—— *Ghettoblaster*. Label Bleu, LBLC 4011. 2006.

Solomon, Sophie, and SoCalled. *Hiphopkhasene*. Pirhana Records, CDPIR1789. 2002.

Various, *Celebrate Hip-Hop*. Sweet Louise Music, 2004.

22

'RaGap'
Music and Identity Among Young Ethiopians in Israel

Focusing on the "Beta Israel" community of Ethiopian Jews who migrated to Israel beginning in the 1980s, this essay explores reggae and rap music among young Ethiopians in Israel and the realities of an emerging Afro-Israeli identity. Against a geopolitical backdrop of crisis and disaffection, Israeli youth often identify with the experience of suffering among the black Diaspora. Shabtay exposes the manner in which the "Beta Israel" community's troubled classification as Jews remains contested and controversial on a variety of fronts. Shabtay argues that growing tensions over color difference and ethnocentrism have pushed Ethiopian adolescents toward the margins of Israeli society, and have helped to create an Afro-Jamaican/American-Israeli subculture which has a close affinity to black music, such as rap and reggae. These black and diasporic musical productions are used to reimagine and renegotiate identity. The emergence of "special nightclubs" and the ways in which they cater to this demographic speaks to the role of music and durability of newly adopted identities among young Ethiopians. Using the musical styles of reggae, rap, and ragamuffin (a bridge between reggae and rap in Jamaica), Shabtay presents ethnographic findings for the practice and meaning of each musical genre among Ethiopian youth identity and suggests there's something symbolic about the common struggle with and among the black diaspora, shared through music as a space of dialogue, that creates a sense of identity, belonging and boundary crossing.

'RaGap': Music and Identity Among Young Ethiopians in Israel

Malka Shabtay

The Collective Experience of a Threatened Community

The young people to be discussed here are members of the 'Beta Israel' community—as they called themselves in Ethiopia—who became known as Ethiopian Jews after their immigration to Israel.[1] The origins of Ethiopian Jews are still controversial: The academic view is that the crystallisation of Beta Israel as a distinct group began in the 14th century and that it formed an integral part of Ethiopian society. The popular Jewish-Israeli version sees the Beta Israel as a tribe from beyond the river Cush that has been Jewish since time immemorial, whose members therefore have the right to immigrate to Israel as Jews (Kaplan, 1993). All agree that the Beta Israel are a religious-Jewish group distinct from their neighbours, even if their cultural characteristics are similar to those of many other groups in the surrounding area. The Beta Israel emphasise these differences through ritual and everyday behaviour, and have successfully maintained their beliefs and separateness (Shelemay, 1989; Quirin, 1977; Kaplan, 1992; Salamon, 1993).

The community has undergone enormous changes since the visits of Jacques Faitlovitch (the most influential European figure to have been in contact with Ethiopian Jews) early in the 20th century. Delegations and missions began to arrive in Ethiopia following the establishment of the State of Israel to strengthen their Jewish group identity by means of Hebrew education and modifications in lifestyle designed to bring them into line with modern Judaism and *halakhah*. The yearning of Ethiopian Jews to immigrate to Israel soon flourished. There were disputes prior to 1975 about the right of Beta Israel to immigrate. American Jewish organisations, as well as pioneering Ethiopian Jews who had reached Israel, pressurised the government of Israel until, in 1973, the Sephardi Chief Rabbi Ovadia Yosef declared the Ethiopian Jews to be the offspring of the Ten Tribes, and they should therefore be seen as Jews who needed to be saved from assimilation. It followed that their immigration to Israel must be hastened. Two years later, it was finally decided to consider their immigration in accordance with the 'Law of Return', in other words as Jews (Corinaldi, 1988). Following this decision, the desire to immigrate spread and strengthened. This culminated when, with the Communist revolution in Ethiopia in 1974, conditions in Ethiopia became more difficult for Jews and economic constraints further encouraged young people to look for ways of leaving the country. Calls on the Israeli government to organise the immediate transfer of Ethiopian Jews became still stronger (Winston, 1980).

The exodus from Ethiopia to Jerusalem began during the 1980s although the 'Sudanese Route' cost the lives of about 4,000 Jews and traumatised many of those who survived to reach Sudan. Large numbers of individuals were separated from their families. The first wave of immigrants was airlifted from Sudan to Israel in 'Operation Moses' during the winter of 1984. Nearly all Ethiopia's Jews had left by the end of 'Operation Solomon' in 1991.

Following their arrival in Israel (Shabtay, l995a; 1995b; 1999; 2000) the most significant hindrance to successful absorption was the doubt cast on their Jewishness by the Rabbinate and the demand that they undergo formal conversion to mainstream Judaism through ritual immersion before they could be granted full Jewish status or permitted to marry religiously. This issue still remains open and plays a major role in the process of identity reformulation (Corinaldi, 1988). Another problem relates to skin-colour which in Ethiopia had determined the social hierarchy. Light-skinned Ethiopians (including Jews) were considered 'red', while slaves, originally from Negroid tribes in the south, were 'black' and Europeans 'white'. On the white/black scale in Israel, however, Ethiopian Jews were regarded as falling into the same category as their slaves, with consequent lowering of self-esteem.

A more recent event—the 'blood scandal' of January 1996—appeared to offer evidence of an ethnocentric and even racist approach toward the Ethiopian community (Weil, 1997). It was discovered that blood donations taken from Ethiopian people (including soldiers) were being thrown away, in the belief that this group was at high risk of carrying HIV. The news evoked deep feelings of frustration among the community, and led to protests that were occasionally violent. This generated public debate about other aspects of Ethiopian integration into Israeli society. Stigmatising the community by disregarding the importance of blood in Ethiopian culture and deception of Ethiopian blood donors were seen as major humiliations and became symbols of the threat to their identity and of the tenuousness of their integration into Israeli society.

Many of those involved with facilitating or studying this integration predicted that Ethiopian children would undergo identity crises because of the magnitude of the changes they would experience, the doubts raised about their Jewishness, and the low status awarded them in Israeli society (Haiman & Tabechnik, 1985; Varon, 1985; Shabtay, 1985; Zima, 1987; Barrett, 1987).

These factors have indeed had a deep impact on the lives of young members of the community and, together with other external forces, explain why a phenomenon such as 'black' music has come to influence the social identity and lifestyles of Ethiopian young people today.

Colour Difference and Ethnocentrism Among Young People

Alienated Ethiopian adolescents have, over the last few years, been moving in growing numbers towards the margins of society (Shabtay 1996b; l998b; 1998c; 2001, Shabtay & Flex, 1999). This has resulted, for instance, in a dramatic rise in crime among young Ethiopians since 1994, a higher school dropout rate than the rest of Israeli society, and a large number of young people at risk and in distress (Ufshits & Noami, 1998; Fishbain, 1998; Shemesh, 1998; Shabtay, 1998a). At the same time, however, an Afro-Jamaican/American-Israeli sub-culture has emerged which identifies with black music such as reggae and rap. There is growing participation in exclusively Ethiopian clubs as a channel for identity reformulation and as an expression of their present identifications.

The appropriation of musical genres such as reggae and rap and the emergence of special nightclubs to cater for these tastes, together with other external markers of a newly adopted identity, cause much concern in the community and among the authorities and organisations involved with the integration of Ethiopian youth into Israeli society. As an applied anthropologist who has been involved for over 16 years both in research and projects on their behalf,[2] I decided in 1997 to study these developments and to identify the relationship between music, identity, and integration or alienation among young Ethiopians.

By 1999 my research had included participant-observation in nightclubs, 70 in-depth interviews conducted with young Ethiopians and other participants in their social scene such as disc jockeys and nightclub owners, and trips to Jamaica, Trinidad, Cameroon and Nigeria to refine my understanding of the musical genres and of the role of music and problems of identity among young people in general. The research participants were 60 adolescents aged between 13 to 18. Thirty-two were female and 28 male. Eight were born in Israel, 28 arrived as babies or small children and had been more than 10 years in the country. Twenty-four had immigrated over the previous 10 years, mainly during 1991. Eighty percent are clubbers, and 20 percent not—five rejecting such music and seven listening to it but not going clubbing. Out of the 55 who either go clubbing or listen to the music, 15 prefer reggae, 14 rap and 26 reggae-rap. Fourteen of them studied in rehabilitation institutes, 13 in elite educational institutions. Six were out of education, 18 in religion schools and 36 in secular schools.

The final results of this research are outlined in a book entitled *Between reggae and rap— the integration challenge of Ethiopian youth in Israel* (Shabtay, 2001a). It is an account of the ideas, experiences and views on black music and the sense of alienation among young Ethiopians living in Israel. Before highlighting some of the findings of this research, I will briefly introduce reggae-ragamuffin-rap, the musical genres that are the heart of the phenomenon under study.

Reggae-Ragamuffin-Rap: Black Musical Genres

'Reggae, rap and raga originated in a complex ideological space in which identities are continually contested. Profound issues of race, class and gender are re-presented in the noisy discourse of African diasporic popular music.'

(Cooper, 1998, p. 166)

Reggae

'Reggae is a philosophy which heals', say Davis Stephen, and Peter Simon, (1983: 181) in their book on reggae international. Reggae is a musical genre combining traditional African rhythm, American blues and Caribbean Jamaican popular music. The main themes are the Rastafarian movement, political protest and social and humanistic messages of equality, brotherhood and peace (Stephen & Simon, 1983; Hebidge, 1987; Jones, 1988; Lewis, 1993; Chang & Chen, 1998).

Reggae developed in Jamaica and was associated with Bob Marley[3] who made it world famous. It is linked to the Rastafarian movement that emerged in Jamaica after Haile Selassie became the King of Ethiopia in 1930. External markers of the followers of this movement include an independent lifestyle, vegetarianism, ritual smoking of ganja (marijuana), and growing their hair in a dreadlock style. They resist 'Babylon', the Western world, and they dream and long for Africa, which is called 'Zion'.

Ethiopia is a central motif in Bob Marley's songs, and the 'return' to Ethiopia—Zion—is a prominent theme. Reggae became internationally popular and influenced artists and listeners from all societies (Cashmore, 987; Jones, 1988; Mitchell, 1996; Lull, 1987).

Rap

'Rap is now a worldwide phenomenon, rap is the CNN for young people all over the world', claims Chuck D. (the founder of and lead rapper for 'Public Enemy') in his book (1997, p. 256). It is considered a musical and social invention, both a medium and a message; it is an alternative communication (Morley, 1992).

Rap, developed by Jamaican immigrants from the South Bronx in New York, has become popular since the mid-1970s and a whole 'hip-hop' culture has evolved around it, including characteristics such as large, loose clothes, big cassette players and special language. When MTV (Music Television) begun broadcasting rap in 1989 it became popular among white young people as well, but rap remains a voice of the black community in the United States, allowing participation and identification with a worldwide population. Rap has been appropriated and integrated by musicians and fans from Japan, New Zealand. South Africa, Porto-Rico and Algeria as well as Israel and many other places (Mitchell, 1996; Weintraub, 1993). It is often controversial because of its vulgar language and seeming approval of violence, but its legitimacy and unique contribution are acknowledged (Morley, 1992; Rose, 1994). Tricia Rose, suggests that rap has transcended its original local context to become a medium of youth protest all over the world (1994), while Dick Hebidge adds that rap has made available a sense of pride to those who listen to it (1999), or even a master narrative, a universal language that allows a sense *of* symbolic participation through music (Mitchell, 1996).

Ragamuffin

Ragamuffin developed recently in Jamaica and is considered a bridge between reggae and rap (Cooper, 1995; 1998). The 1997 movie *Dancehall Queen*, which promoted this genre, tells the story of a hard-working woman trying to care for her daughters and being exploited by a family member. She decides to compete in a dance competition in order to win prize money that would allow her to buy her freedom and improve their life. She practices secretly, designs her own costume and competes against other well-known dancers to emerge victorious. Carolyn Cooper describes the film as "'a celebration of self awareness of female power." Chris Salewicz adds that the film reflects both the ideals of escaping social ghettoisation and poverty, and of attaining female empowerment (Salewicz, 1998).

The genre of ragamuffin, which includes sexual body language and minimal dressing, was emulated by many young people (especially women) all over the world. The musical genres featured here developed in specific socio-cultural contexts with their own specific styles of language, dress and other external markers that their fans emulate. Music and lifestyles have spread throughout the world and have been appropriated by innumerable young people (Jones, 1988; Mitchel, 1996; Bennet 1998; 2000; Willis, 1974, 1978; Weintraub, 1993; Liechty, 1995; Schade-Poulsen, 1995; Ullestad, 2000).

Young Ethiopians and the Reggae and Hip-Hop Scene in Israel

Reggae and rap reached Israel before the Ethiopians. An individual who encountered reggae in Paris and returned to Israel to start the first nightclub[4] (later travelling to Jamaica where he became more involved with reggae artists) increased his promotion of reggae in Israel and organised annual festivals. His club was small and at first attended by only a limited group of Israeli enthusiasts.

Today the reggae scene in Israel includes several nightclubs and bands, two radio shows, a reggae festival to which reggae artists are invited from Jamaica and elsewhere, and an Internet site. One popular Israeli rap group, Shabak Samech, performs nationwide. Hip-hop has become part of Israeli youth culture in general, having been popularised through MTV which enables young people to imitate the clothes and language or their peers throughout the world.

The local reggae scene has been transformed, however by the overwhelming presence of Ethiopian youth in the nightclubs. In the specific nightclubs where young Ethiopians go clubbing reggae, ragamuffin and rap form part of a mixed repertoire.

From 1997 the initial reggae nightclub began to see more and more Ethiopians among its customers. When the majority became Ethiopian, other Israelis and African foreign workers began to leave and the club became almost exclusively Ethiopian, with a preference for MTV music and a mixture of reggae-ragamuffin-rap. Violence became a regular part of the nightclub experience, together with heavy drinking and other problems. Following the success of this venue, more nightclubs opened to cater specifically for Ethiopians. The greatest number of participants came on Friday night.

As a result of the violence there was debate in the media and among those involved with the Ethiopian community, especially in the field of education. It was clearly necessary to explore the relationship between these genres of music and young Ethiopians' sense of identity, alienation and involvement in violence.

Although nightclubs are the most significant element in the Ethiopian appropriation of these musical genres, they are not the only one. Reggae-rap involvement includes identification, listening and dancing among fans, as well as the emergence of Ethiopian artists in these genres. One reggae and one rap singer perform in the nightclubs, and are broadcast on radio and television."[5]

'Ragamuffin style': Findings

Many young Ethiopians consider this phenomenon of identification and appropriation of black musical genres as universal among their peers in Israel. 'I can't sleep when reggae is playing out there, I want to be up all night,' said one young person.

Most claim that the appeal is in the rhythm more than the words, since few understand the patois. Their identification with reggae is reinforced by what are seen as coded allusions to Ethiopia, while rap is felt to reflect their social experiences. One person commented: 'Rap talks about racism and reggae about Ethiopia, and I am attached to both of them.' This relationship is backed up by imaginary links such as the claim that: 'Bob Marley's mother was Ethiopian, so he was half Ethiopian.'

Ethiopian identity is merged with that of other blacks not only by skin colour and common African origin, but also by the shared experiences of marginality and alienation. 'They are my real brothers,' said one, 'they are like us.' While another added: 'We are black, so we are part of them; this population feels different all over the world from the rest of society, so we stay together all the time.'

This sense of common struggle with the black diaspora has been appropriated through the shared music, symbolically generating a sense of belonging to a larger people. One of them explained, 'What they have been through is similar to what we have been through here. They lived in a poor social environment; they face racism everywhere they go. Now they have progressed ... I believe that we shall progress as well, in spite of our skin colour.'

Young Ethiopians living in Israel have in this way transformed their collective and personal experiences of alienation, both real and imagined, into an ideology identifying themselves as the blacks in Israeli society and attributing the relatively poor achievements of Ethiopians and their sense of inferiority and failure to racism. Their language of disappointment, disillusionment and hostility is addressed to those they hold responsible for their situation. They believe Israelis to be prejudiced towards them and see in them the reason that their chances of achieving integration are low: 'You feel betrayed and are called "nigger". You made it to Israel and it doesn't work.'

They are able to discuss openly the humiliation and alienation that attracts them to the community of other blacks and the way that their music appears to offer this kinship. One young Ethiopian explained, 'I think we listen to the music and feel we belong here less. We see ourselves as different and seek refuge. The music is the place of Ethiopians in Israel.' Another young person admitted, 'We are influenced more and more by the music, and as we become more involved in learning who makes the music and how they live, we identify with them. The music creates the difference.' The tendency among young Ethiopians to doubt their accept-ance in Israeli society is reinforced by the music, which in this way becomes a mechanism for moving away from Israeli society and approaching other alternatives. As one of them remarked: 'I hope it will be good, but as far as I can see I don't believe it will be.'

Although the Jewish elements of their identity persist, many Ethiopians define themselves as black Jews in the first instance rather than as Israelis. Black identity is adopted since it seems to relate to their alienation. Israeli identity appears to have been missed out on the way, or at least to have been appropriated to a much lesser extent.

The nightclub, so central to the lives of many young Ethiopians that they are prepared to run away from school and home to be there, especially on Friday, forms a micro-world to which they feel they belong. There they meet, listen to music, develop common ideas and generate Ethiopian youth sub-culture, amidst heavy drinking, violence, drugs and sexual experiences, worlds of temptation that simultaneously provide relief and generate new ten-sions. Clubs are repeatedly closed because of violence and even murder, making young people feel free and happy, but also scared. Girls in particular are regarded by their elders as having 'crossed all barriers and lost their dignity', overturning their expectations in Ethiopian culture and it is feared, damaging the identity of the community in general.

The complex alternative home offered by the nightclub, both as a place of belonging and of creating a world of their own, offers a symbolic identification that seems to resolve their crisis of identity in Israeli society. But this solution creates new conflicts, which contribute to their sense of alienation and further distance them not only from Israeli society, but also from their own homes and families. These experiences serve to emphasise their 'otherness', and could lead to the creation of a potentially hostile sub-culture should the means for return and reintegration not emerge. Reggae and rap are the locus for a dialogue between Ethiopian youth and black musical genres in which the search for belonging is being conducted. Black music is a powerful cultural resource in the processes by which Ethiopian young people seek identity and belonging.

The fact that young Ethiopians wish for true and full integration is clear from their enthu-siastic adoption of *an* affiliation that they feel is open to them without qualification. Their search for a home is temporarily satisfied by reggae and rap, which I have termed 'ragap' and their ragamuffin cultural style. This encounter with black musical genres is a matter not only of musical taste, but of self-image and image in the eyes of others. Whether they will secure integration into Israeli society or instead seek to belong to an imagined black community that seems to invite them through the pull of music, will be seen in the near future. Efforts directed at reducing alienation while increasing positive experiences of integration will be critical in this juncture. Their forefathers' dream of returning to Jerusalem still remains to be realised.

Conclusion

Black music is a communication space (Lull, 1978) where dialogue on belonging and identity takes place, both allowing boundaries to be crossed and defining affiliations (Frith, 1996a).

Black music links people all round the world, but simultaneously increases local sensitivities and serves as a vehicle for young people to establish their identities and the boundaries with others (Mitchell, 1996; Kurkela, 1992). For young Ethiopians it is a tool for placing themselves historically, politically and stylistically (Frith, 1992; Malbon, 1999), through interpreting and identifying with the music (Lewis, 1992; Lull, 1978; Frith, 1996a) and enabling them to share a sense of partnership in a common struggle (Mitchell, 1996; Weintraub, 1993). 'We feel that we are not the only black ones, so we feel more comfortable,' said one girl. Some young Ethiopians consciously reject this pattern and disapprove both of this mode of identification and the ideology of alienation that underpins it.

But the future participation—symbolic or active—of Ethiopian youth in a black Diaspora identity and common struggle, depends on whether they are successful in attaining full integration in Israeli society, or whether they give up on it.

As Bob Marley himself sang:

> *Oh children Zion train is coming our way get on board now*
> *You got a ticket so thank the Lord.*
>
> (Zion Train)

Study Questions

1. What is the historical context of an Afro-Israeli identity among Ethiopians in Israel and why does Shabtay find the movement among this group significant in her study?
2. What are the connections between black culture and the youth culture that emerges within the subcultures of Afro-Isreali identity?
3. What role do black musical styles play in the search for identity among Ethiopian youth? How does this data advance and support the shared struggle within the black diaspora?

Notes

1. On their different collective designations, see Weil, 1995, pp. 25–40.
2. See Shabtay, 1985; 1995a; 1995b; 1996a; 1996b; 1998a; 1998b; 1998c; 1999; 2000; 2001a; 2001b; 2003; Shabtay & Flex, 1999.
3. Bob Marley's biography was written by his mother, Cedela Booker, called *Bob Marley: An intimate portrait by his mother*, 1996.
4. Personal communication with Gil Bonshtein, who has an impressive collection of documentation of reggae development in Israel. The Israeli reggae web site is:www.irielion.com/Israel
5. The reggae singer is part of a mixed group, called *Roots Africa*, singing 'roots reggae' in English. While the rap singer sings in Amharic and Hebrew and mostly writes his own songs on issues relevant to the Ethiopian community in Israel.

References

Barret, D. 1987. Going Home: Problems of Acculturation and Identity Experienced by Ethiopian Jews. *Journal of Intercultural Studies*, 8.1, 27–37.

Bennet, A. 1998. The Frankfurt Rock Mobile: A New Insight into the Significance of Music Making for Young People. *Youth and Policy*, 60, 16–29.

Bennet, A. 2000. *Popular Music and Youth Culture: Music, Identity, and Place*. London: Macmillan Press Ltd.

Booker, C. 1996. *Bob Marley: An Intimate Portrait by His Mother.* London: Penguin Books.

Cashmore, E.E. 1987. Shades of Black, Shades of White. In J. Lull (ed.), *Popular Music and Communication* 245–26. London: Sage.

Chang, K. et al. 1988. *Reggae Roots: The Story of Jamaican Music.* Jamaica: Ian Randle Publishers.

Cooper, C. 1998. Ragamuffin Sounds: Crossing Over from Reggae to Rap and Back. *Caribbean Quarterly,* 44, 153–168.

Corinaldi, M. 1988. *Ethiopian Jewry: Identity and tradition.* Jerusalem: Reuven Mass.

Chuck D. 1997. *Fight the Power: Rap, Race and Reality.* Edinburgh: Payback Press.

Fishbain, Y. 1998. *Youth in Between Cultures.* Jerusalem: Center for Information for the Ethiopian Youth, Israeli Association for Ethiopian Jews.

Frith, S. 1992. The Cultural Study of Popular Music. In L. Grossberg et al. (eds.), *Cultural Studies,* 174–86. London: Routledge.

Frith, S. 1996a. Music and Identity. In S. Hall, & P. du Gay (eds.), *Questions of Cultural Identity.* London: Sage Publications.

Frith, S. 1996b. *Performing Rites.* Oxford: Oxford University Press.

Haiman, A. & Tabechnik, E. 1985. *Coping and Identification Difficulties, and the Identity Crisis among Ethiopian Students in Youth Aliya Villages.* Unpublished Report. Tel Aviv: Youth Aliya, the Clinical Unit.

Hebidge, D. 1979. *Subculture: The Meaning of Style.* London: Routledge.

Hebidge, D. 1987. *Cut n Mix: Culture, Identity and Caribbean Music.* London: Routledge.

Jones, S. 1988. *Black Culture, White Youth: The Reggae Tradition from JA to UK.* London: Macmillan Education.

Kaplan, S. 1992. *The Beta Israel in Ethiopia.* New York: New York University Press.

Kaplan, S. 1993. The Invention of Ethiopian Jews: Three Models. *Cahiers D'etudes Africaines,* 132 (xxx-iii), 645–658.

Kurkela, V. 1992. Music as Collage: The End of National Music. In A. Opekar (ed.), Central European Popular Music Proceedings from the International Conference, 112. Prague: ISAPM.

Lewis, G. H. 1992. Who Do You Love?: The Dimensions of Musical Taste. In J. Lull (ed.), *Popular Music and Communication, 2nd Edition.* London: Sage.

Lewis, W. F. 1993. *Soul Rebels: The Rastafari.* Illinois: Waveland Press.

Liechty, M. 1995. Media, Markets and Modernisation: Youth Identities and the Experience of Modernity in Kathmandu, Nepal. In V. Amit-Talai & H. Wulff (eds.), *Youth Cultures: A Cross-Cultural Perspective,* 166–201. London: Routledge.

Lifshits, H., & Noam, G. 1998. *Research on the Integration of Ethiopian Youth: A Multidimensional Survey.* Jerusalem: JDC—Brookdale Institute of Gerontology and Human Development.

Lull, J. 1987. Listener's Communicative Uses of Popular Music. In J. Lull (ed.), *Popular Music and Communication,* 140–74. London: Sage.

Lull, J. 1992. Introduction in J. Lull (ed.) *Popular Music and Communication,* Second Edition. London: Sage.

Lull, J. 2000. *Media, Communication, Culture: A Global Approach, Second Edition.* Cambridge: Polity Press.

Malbon, B. 1998. The Club: Clubbing, Consumption, Identity and Spatial Practices of everynight Life. In T. Skelton & V. Gil (eds.), *Cool Places: Geographies of Youth Cultures,* 266–286. London: Routledge.

Malbon, B. 1999. *Clubbing: Dancing, Ecstasy and Vitality.* London: Routledge.

Morley, J. 1992. Rap Music as American History. In L. Stanley (ed.), *Rap: The Lyrics,* xv–xxxi. New York: Penguin Books.

Mitchel, T. 1996. *Popular Music and Local Identity: Rock, Pop and Rap in Eurpoe and Oceania.* London: Leicester University Press.

Quirin, J. 1977. *The Beta Israel (Falasha) in Ethiopian History: Caste Formation and Cultural Change 1270–1868.* University of Minnesota: Ph.D. Dissertation.

Rose, T. 1994. *Black Noise: Rap Music and Black Culture in Contemporary America.* London: Wesleyan University Press.

Salamon, H. 1993. *Beta Israel and their Christian Neighbors in Ethiopia.* Hebrew University of Jerusalem: Ph.D. Dissertation.

Salewicz, C. 1998, September–October. Dancehall Queen. *Beat Culture,* 38–45.

Schade-Poulsen, M. 1995. The Power of Love: Rap Music and Youth in Algeria. In Amit-Talai & H. Wulff (eds.), *Youth Cultures: A Cross Cultural Perspective,* 82–113. London: Routledge.

Shabtay, M. 1985. *A Baby in One Hand and a Book in the Other: Immigration and Absorption Experiences among Ethiopian Children*. Haifa University. MA Thesis.

Shabtay, M. 1995a. The Experience of Ethiopian Jewish Soldiers in the Israeli Army: The Process of Identity Formulation within the Military Context. *Israel Social Science Research*, 10(2), 69–80.

Shabtay, M. 1995b. *Identity Reformulation among Ethiopian Soldiers: Processes of Interpretation and Struggle*. Ben-Gurion University of the Negev, Beer-Sheva: Ph.D. Dissertation.

Shabtay, M. 1996a. The Melting Pot Works from Outside: The Dynamics of Identification with Ethiopian Culture. *Society and Welfare*, 16(2), 199–216.

Shabtay, M. 1996b. *Ethiopian Adolescents in Familial, Educational and Social Contexts: A Pilot Study*. Beer-Sheva: Ben-Gurion University of the Negev, Department of Education.

Shabtay, M. 1998a. Identity Reformulation among Ethiopian Immigrant Soldiers: Processes of Interpretation and Struggle. In T. Parfitt & E. Trevisan Semi (eds.), *The Beta Israel in Ethiopia and Israel: Studies on Ethiopian Jews*. The University of London, London: Curzon Press Ltd.

Shabtay, M. 1998b. *Invention Project with Ethiopian Adolescent Girls in Distress: Evaluation Report for the First Year*. Tel-Aviv University, Tel-Aviv: The Forum for Youth and Children Affairs, School of Social Work.

Shabtay, M. 1998c. *Ethiopian Adolescents in Familial, Educational and Social Contexts: Youth Immigrated in 'Operation Solomon.' A Pilot Study*. Ben-Gurion University of the Negev, Beer-Sheva: Department of Education.

Shabtay, M. 1999. *Achi Achi [Best Brother]: The Identity Journey of Ethiopian Immigrant Soldiers*. Tel-Aviv: Tcherikover.

Shabtay, M. 2000. Identity Reformulation among Ethiopian Immigrants in Israel: The Case of Ethiopian-Israeli Soldiers. In E. Olshtein & G. Horenczyk (eds), *Language, Identity and Immigration*. The Hebrew University, Jerusalem: The Magness Press.

Shabtay, M. 2001a. *Ben Reggae Le Rap [Between Reggae and Rap]: The Integration Challenge of Ethiopian Youth in Israel*. Tel-Aviv: Tcherikover.

Shabtay, M. 2001b. *Living with threatened Identities: The Experrience of Living with Color Differene Among Young Adult and Adolescent Ethiopian Youth in Israel* (1988–1999). *Megamot* (Hebrew).

Shabtay, M. 2003. From Jerusalem to Ethiopia and Back: From Identity Confusion to Committed Identity. *Adult Education in Israel*, 7, 141–167.

Shabtay, M., & Flex, T. 1999. *Ethiopian Adolescents in Familial, Educational and Social Contexts: Israeli Born Ethiopians—A Pilot Study*. Ben-Gurion University of the Negev, Beer-Sheva: Department of Education.

Shelemay, K. K. 1989. *Music, Ritual and Ialasha History*. East Lansing: Michigan State University Press.

Shemesh, A. 1998. *A Survey on the Drop-out Characteristics among Ethiopian Youth in Distress*. Tel-Aviv: The National School for Education and Youth Workers, The Institute for the Advancement of Youth, Ministry of Education, Culture and Sport.

Shepherd, J. 1986. Music Consumption and Cultural Self-Identities: Some Theoretical and Methodological Reflections. *Media, Culture and Society*, 8, 305–30.

Stephen, D & Simon, P. 1983. *Reggae International*. London: Thames and Hudson.

Ullestad, N. 2000, January. American Indians Rap. *Popular Music and Society*.

Weil, S. 1995. Collective Designations and Collective Identity among Ethiopian Jews. *Israel Social Science Research*, 10(2), 25–40.

Weil, S. 1997. Religion, Blood and the Equality of Rights: The Case of Ethiopian Jews in Israel. *International Journal on Minority and Group Rights*, 4, 497–512.

Weintraub, A. 1993. Jawaiian and Local Cultural Identity in Hawaii. *Perfect Beat*, 1(2), 78.

Willis, P. 1974. *Symbolism and Practice: A Theory for the Social Meaning of Pop Music*. Stenciled Occasional Paper, Birmingham Center for Contemporary Cultural Studies, Sub and Popular Culture Series, 13.

Willis, P. 1978. *Profane Culture*. London: Routledge & Kegan Paul.

Winston, D. 1980. The Falashas: History and Analysis of Policy Toward a Beleaguered Community. *Perspectives*, 1–24.

Yaron, U. 1985. On the Identity Crisis and the Threat to Self-Esteem among Ethiopian Immigrant Youth. *Alim*, Youth Aliya, 9–19.

Zima, S. 1987, July-August. Forty-Two Ethiopian Boys: Observations of their First Year in Israel. *Social Work*, 359–60.

23

Hip-Hop Hinduism
The Spiritual Journey of MC Yogi

Mixing sacred acumen with rap artist abilities, this interview uncovers the artist who has " ... a penchant for Hip-Hop Hinduism." Meet MC Yogi, born Nicholas Giacomini in the Bay area of California, whose technique animates and emulates a New York urban style and message is deeply rooted in a Vedic archetype. Incanting divinities, MC Yogi is an international artist who sees himself as seeking and performing truth. In this interview conducted in 2008, the author/interviewer places MC Yogi in the tradition of other spiritually and politically minded hip hop greats such as Afrika Bambaataa and NWA in addition to a lineage of well-known and inspirational yogic poets. Throughout this interview, MC Yogi speaks to a wide range of topics including his childhood, mysticism, spirituality, yoga, and race.

Hip-Hop Hinduism: The Spiritual Journey of MC Yogi*

Steven J. Rosen

MC Yogi is a phenomenon. The next big thing in sacred chant, he's a rap artist with profound social awareness (check out his songs about Obama and Gandhi) and a penchant for Hip-Hop Hinduism (*à la* Ganesh, Hanuman, Rama, Krishna, and others).

Born Nicholas Giacomini in the Bay Area, California, MC is a musical navigator who takes his listeners to the Bronx by way of Bengal. Though his style is steeped in rap and the urban grooves of New York Hip-hop, his message comes from India's sages of old—his is the Vedic paradigm with a little bit of Big City rhyme.

Giacomini's incarnation as MC Yogi sets the world alight with his passion for truth. Not preachy truth, mind you. Just down home, simple, "the way it is." Irresistible and irrepressible logic. The divinities in his songs are neither vouched for nor denied. They are not presented as literal aspects of reality, nor are mere metaphors. In a sense, he presents them as both, and as neither. His point: learn what you can from them, because they are here to stay.

Some background: hip-hop music, also referred to as rap, is a musical genre that makes prodigious use of spoken word lyrics highlighted by deep, in-the-pocket grooves, with rhythms over backing beats. The style originated in the Bronx in the 1970s, predominately among African-Americans and Latinos. Break-dancing, turntablism and graffiti are also parts of hip-hop culture. Rap usually incorporates portions of other songs, which is called "sampling," as well as synthesizers, drum machines, and, sometimes, live musicians.

MC Yogi uses all of these, along with Indian instruments and exotic chants, but especially noteworthy are Obama and Gandhi's sampled voices, overlaid like beautiful crystal on a fine chandelier. Still greater light comes through the agency of famous contemporary *kirtan* singers, Krishna Das and others who lend a helping hand, or, more precisely, a helping voice.

Rapping is also referred to as "MCing" or "emceeing," which is where MC Yogi gets the first part of his name. The second part comes from the fact that he and his wife own their own yoga school, the Yoga Toes Studio in Point Reyes Station, California. Yoga is also a big theme in his rap music. That is why he likes to call himself an "un-rapper." Whereas most rappers talk about contemporary life and love, and usually with a heavily materialistic message, MC is about something else. He's about Yoga and spirituality, about positivity and change. Hence the name: MC Yogi.

He thus follows in the footsteps not only of predecessor rap artists, like Grandmaster Flash, Afrika Bambaataa, the Beastie Boys, Public Enemy, NWA, Run-DMC, Missy "Misdemeanor" Elliot, and Queen Latifah, but also of predecessor yogic poets, like Jayadeva, Tulsidas, Tukaram, and Mirabai. As these latter Indic saints wrote *kavyas, champus, stotras,* and *stutis*—various forms of devotional poetry—so, too, is MC contributing a modern-day facsimile.

His chosen art form, it must be admitted, partakes of poetic and musical devices that are centuries old, and he uses them much in the same way that the Sanskrit, Bengali, Braja-bhasha, and Marathi poets did. Rap incorporates alliteration, allusion, assonance, denotation, connotation, metaphor, repetition, rhythm, figurative language, free verse, hypebole, imagery, irony, refrain, simile, and so on. MC is merely adapting these techniques to a relatively new musical form.

True, there have been numerous "Hindu" rappers already: BlaaZe, Ranidu Lankage, Yogi B, Natchatra, Princeten, Kadhalviruz, Krishan Maheson, Dr. Burn, and Suresh da Wun. But none have approached the genre quite in the way MC does. Bringing his listeners to hip-hop heaven, he raps the entire story of Hanuman, for example, with so much detail you would think he was a properly trained *Brahmin,* with years of Sanskrit learning. He presents legitimate Vedic knowledge with style and passion.

Moreover, he doesn't seem to subscribe to the idea of "Hinduism" as a sectarian religion. Rather, his well thought-out tunes show that the motifs and deities of "Hindu" philosophy are meant to represent non-sectarian, overarching truths, as real to Christianity as they are to Hinduism, as applicable to the life of an atheist as they are to those who are deeply religious. He uses "Hindu images" to convey everyday reality, which is how they were used in ancient India, and how, amongst the well-informed, they are used in India today.

Of course, traditional Hindus might see MC's methods as somewhat irreverent, or perhaps as respectfully irreverent. But this is missing the point. For example, when he refers to Ganesh as his "homie" or as having a face "only a mother could love," or when he sings of Hanuman's victories as a comparable to those found in the movie *Rocky,* he is not being even slightly irreverent. Rather, he is using the slang and jargon of hip-hop to tell a story, to bring Ganesh and Hanuman within the purview and understanding of his chosen audience. He is speaking the language of his people.

While it's true that hip-hop is a revolutionary culture that revels in rebellion, with little regard for tradition, MC Yogi is taking it in a different direction. He is using the forms and language of hip-hop to convey the universal love and overwhelming spirituality found in sanatana dharma. Though most people today identify this tradition with Hinduism, MC is taking it out of this preconceived valley of misinformation and placing it squarely where it belongs: in the blissful, rolling mountains of truth, and in the hearts of all sincere souls.

What follows is an interview that I conducted with MC in 2008.

Rosen: **So let's begin with the beginning: Western name, year of birth, geographic setting, things of that nature.**

MC: I was born Nicholas Giacomini in San Francisco, California, August 26, 1979. My mom was in labor on the Golden Gate Bridge. We almost didn't make it to the hospital. They thought she was going to give birth on the bridge.

Rosen: **Maybe that's why your music is about bridge building and the harmony of religions. [laughter]**

MC: [laughter] Maybe. Maybe not.

Rosen: **Siblings?**

MC: A brother and a sister, yes.

Rosen: **Did you grow up with both music and religion?**

MC: Yes, I grew up as a Catholic, first of all. Very religious. My grandmother taught Catechism. I'd consider her one of my first religious teachers. No doubt.

Rosen: **Catholic School?**

MC: Yep. Baptized, confirmed—the works. I've always been an innately religious person. But the Church got to be a bit much. There were always things in the Church that I didn't like …

Rosen: **Some Examples?**

MC: The idea of eternal damnation—of a compassionate God sending flawed practitioners to Hell, forever. You know, that just never made sense to me. Or Christian exclusivity—that Jesus was the only way. What about all the people that came before Jesus? Or what about other sincere devotees in other religious traditions?

Rosen: **So, it seemed to defy logic and to be unfair.**

MC: Definitely. And so even though so much good comes out of religion, I could see another side, a down side, and that was discouraging. I knew at a young age that these things just didn't make sense.

Rosen: **Right. That aspect of religion can be frustrating for thinking people. It's the external, fundamentalist aspect of religion, where people interpret the religion in the most superficial of ways. That's what leads to religious wars as such. But let's get into your musical influences. Where does that begin?**

MC: I must have been about seven years old when I got my first two hip-hop albums: The Beastie Boys and Run-D.M.C., which revolutionized my consciousness. Before that, I was a quiet kid, into comic books, *Star Wars* action figures. But that hip-hop stuff opened me up. That's when I got into graffiti and breakdancing and stuff like that.

Rosen: **What was it all about through records?**

MC: Well, this was the late '80s, when MTV was really popular and hip-hop was having a hard time breaking into the mainstream. These two records were produced by Rick Rubin, and the albums had wide appeal, on a number of levels. They were like crossover albums, with rock and hip-hop. So it was able to get me, and so many others like me, into hip-hop, to appreciate it as an art form.

Rosen: **Every generation seems to have its share of transformative music—special albums that open people up to new forms of artistic expression. And there are pivotal albums that undeniably have that affect on people. In my generation, there was stuff by Dylan, the Beatles, the Stones, Jimi Hendrix. All breakthrough material.**

MC: Right. Although I wasn't around when it first came out, the *Sgt. Pepper* album seems to capture what I'm talking about. That must have been for your generation what these rap albums were for mine.

Rosen: **Sgt. Pepper. That was a big one, certainly. But that music often had an overtly spiritual message. How did you go from hip-hop to Eastern spirituality?**

MC: Oddly enough, the first time I heard the words *namas te*, which is a standard Indian greeting of respect, as you know, was on a beastie Boys album called *Check Your Head*. Remember, I was into East Coast hip-hop, which is very different from West Coast hip-hop, and they often had Muslim MCs. This was a foreign, exotic faith, at least for me; so this turned me on to new ideas about religion and spirituality. That's how it started.

   Also, I do have to say that *Sgt. Pepper* was a special record in my own spiritual journey, even though I got it long after the fact, many years after its initial release. My dad also got me Bob Marley's album *Legend*. Both of those records changed my life in a big way. *Sgt. Pepper* was the first time I heard Indian instruments, and that really struck a chord. It resonated deeply …

Rosen: **And this led to an interest in Eastern mysticism and yoga practice?**

MC: Well, when I was about 18, my dad got me into yoga, *Ashtanga-yoga*. He was doing it with some friends and it seemed like the logical next step for me. He was doing Mysore style, without a teacher. He and his friends knew the sequence and they practiced on their own. It was a vigorous method, without doubt. And his meditation practice flowed from the *Siddha-yoga* tradition, Gurumayi, and her approach to meditative techniques. So, initially that was the lineage I was introduced to.

Rosen: **And how did the interest in yoga and hip-hop coalesce?**

MC: Well, initially, when I got into yoga, I suppressed the hip-hop side. I let it drop for a while. I stopped listening to rap, and I got into a one-pointed pursuit of the spirit—excellent yoga practice was all I wanted. That was my focus. But gradually, all of the things I loved before getting into yoga started to seep back in, and that's natural, I think. You set them aside, for a while. But your natural interests and inclinations come out again in due course. They start to blend.

Rosen: **That's a natural occurrence, yes, and quite common in the lives of spiritual practitioners with artistic interests. You assimilate. You make your spiritual path your own, and then you incorporate the things that are close to your heart. It's quite natural.**

MC: So my love for rap and my love for yoga naturally came together.

Rosen: **But I want to know how you learned the Vedic literature, and why you seem to have a certain expertise when it comes to Vedic deities. When you rap, you tell the stories so well! You are clearly not a Sanskrit scholar, and I don't think you've pored over the traditional literature …**

MC: Well, I went to India and got into the comic books … [laughter]

Rosen: **[laughter] You mean like *Amar Chitra Katha*?**

MC: That's them. Of course, I'd get the basic ideas from there and then check back with the sacred texts, just to make sure that I was getting the stories right. Also, I guess I just really absorbed them along the way, hearing different parts of the stories from various teachers, in yoga classes, and so on. These myths—some people call them myths, which is a loaded word, I know—are just embedded in my consciousness. I think they go beyond the "Hindu" connotations and their surface associations. They speak to something fundamental and raw within each of us.

And there's the hip-hop beats, too, which are very hypnotic. They're like a drum loop. And when you get into that zone, they bring out all these inner feelings and thoughts and realizations. So whatever I had learned from the Indian comics, and teachers, and so on, it all becomes enhanced when I try to express it through hip-hop. When I rap, I go into a kind of trance, and I'll free-style, I'll start reciting spontaneous poetry. That's when it all comes out. So I write it down and then repeat it over and over, and then newer stuff comes out. That's how it works.

Rosen: **And it sure does work. I'm so impressed with the CD. Joel Davis, the Label manager at White Swan Records, told me the story of your signing with the label. In his own words:**

As co-owner (along w/his wife) of Yoga Toes Studio in Point Reyes Station, California, Nick (MC Yogi) has been a longtime customer of White Swan Music Distribution and knew Parmita Pushman, White Swan co-founder and president. He approached her in early '08 about his yoga hip-hop project and gave her an early demo copy of the track "Ganesh Is Fresh." She dug it and shared it with me. I flipped for it as well. We kept in touch with Nick, who continued feeding us tracks as the recording progressed … We weren't sure how the yoga community would respond to *Elephant Power* [MC's first CD] but felt that that quality of the music, and Nick's charm and energy in creating as well as promoting it, made this project worth the gamble, and with little hesitation, we jumped on board. The response so far has exceeded our early expectations, and we're all feeling great after the great vibes shared at the *Jivamukti* CD release party. That party also showed us that there's a lot of work ahead as we strive to garner MC Yogi the success he so richly deserves.

Rosen: **So that's how Joel sees your origins with the label, and he's obviously excited about your project. But I'm curious about another aspect of all this: how did you get the big *kirtan* guys, like Krishna Das and Jai Uttal, on the record?**

MC: That's quite a story in itself. The short version: Jai lives close by, and we've been friends for a while. He's been like a mentor, providing a lot of guidance and instruction. I'm also friends with his wife, Nubia, who is also a yoga instructor in my area. So that just worked. It was natural. KD happened to be playing California, and I'm a huge fan, so I went to see him. Interestingly, he was staying in the apartment complex where I grew up, and I was visiting a friend of mine, who was living there. So we hooked up. I did some of my rap stuff for KD and he loved it. He was floored. It kind of worked like that for all of the celebrities or well-known musicians and artists that are on my CD. And I'm so grateful that they're there.

Rosen: **Well, you're certainly unique. It's seem odd, in a sense, a white guy doing rap, though I know that many white guys are in fact rapping these days …**

MC: Some people compare me to Eminem, since he's a white rapper. But I focus on yoga deities. That's the difference. In that sense, I'm an un-rapper! I'm the antithesis of the usual rapper. Like the first album focuses a bit on Ganesh, who has an elephant head. He's the lord of overcoming obstacles. I like to make this joke when people compare me to Eminem. Since I am rapping about a divine elephant, they can think of me like this: I'm M&M with peanuts.

Study Questions

1. What factors shape MC Yogi's fusion and approach to music and religion? What influences his thinking about hip hop and spirituality?
2. How is yoga thought about in relation to hip hop culture and how does MC Yogi's thinking about the two change over time?
3. How does the interviewer/author (Rosen) situate the person and work of MC Yogi in terms of religion and hip hop? What other questions would you have asked MC Yogi and why?

Note

* See MC Yogi's website, here: http://mcyogi.com/

24

Battling Hip-Hop Samurai

Outside of a racial categorization, how are we to classify the ways in which Japanese emcees battle and compete for authority? This essay considers the history of hip hop in Japan, and why this scene must be understood beyond terms of global homogenization and localization. In an effort to explain the diversity within and among Japan's hip hop scene, Condry makes use of "battling samurai" as a working and culturally specific metaphor to understand and unpack the historical processes of hip hop culture in Japan. The use of hip hop Samurai extends beyond metaphorical import and suggests that Japanese emcees are often clothed in battle clothing, emulating hip hop samurais seen in the rituals of posing with swords (*katana*), the wearing of a topknot hairstyle (*chonemage*) and conceiving of the mic as a sword—elements drawn from the show—and the battle like nature of US born hip hop culture. Examining works from albums such as the 2002 group King Giddra, Condry explores themes of the contemporary articulations of historical Japanese events such as the Meji Restoration of 1868 as ways in which Japanese hip hop samurais negotiate their Japanese culture and popular Americanized images, such as gangstas. Here, Condry suggests a both/and tug and use of the processes of global standardization and local indigenization. Extensively taking into account imagery, fashion, history of music and Japanese cultural developments, historic hip hop elements such as battle, the influence of the US music scene, and traditionally used Japanese instruments, Condry examines Japanese hip hop's complicated relationship to the local and global. He concludes that the typology of the battling hip hop samurai within the Japanese context represents the desire to retain an edge of distinction among fans and record companies alike—that is, the ideals that drive hip hop culture over time are ever expanding and changing. Commonly seen as disparate processes, here the global and the local represent "symbolic crystallizations" of fluid and ongoing processes over time. Sites of performance offer solid moments by which to examine the interactions and exchange between the local and the global. Hip hop samurais do not represent a Japanese cultural homogeneity; rather, they embody a hip hop culture of battle.

Battling Hip-Hop Samurai*

Ian Condry

Black clouds, rain and lightning	*Kuroi kumo ame ni rakudai*
Wandering in wind, today's samurai	*Kaze ni sasurai aruku genzai no samurai*
If I grab my rhyme sword, look out!	*In no katana tsukandaraba abunai!*
	—King Giddra, "Heisei ishin"

If Japanese hip-hop cannot be explained in terms of racial dynamics, what are the terms in which emcees compete for authority and fame? I consider in more detail the history of hip-hop in Japan to explore why neither the term *global homogenization* nor *localization* accurately describes the scene's evolution. The challenge is to explain a widening diversity within Japan's scene amid a deepening global connectedness. I argue that "battling samurai" offer a metaphor for this dynamic historical process.

Perhaps it should come as no surprise that Japanese emcees often clothe themselves in images of samurai toughness. The idea that hip-hop artists must prove themselves in public battle encourages artists to pose for photos with *katana* (samurai swords) to assert that "the mic is my sword" and to describe a ponytail hairstyle as a *chonmage* (topknot). On their 2002 album, the group King Giddra (Zeebra, K Dub Shine, and DJ Oasis) even uses images of samurai to call for a Heisei restoration *(Heisei ishin)*, that is, a present-day version of the Meiji restoration of 1868, when the military shogunate was overthrown to restore the Meiji emperor to power. However, Zeebra's goal of restoration does not involve the emperor, nor even the government, but rather suggests that a youthful generation inspired by hip-hop should lead Japan. What kind of globalization is this?

At first listen, "Heisei Restoration" seems to be evidence that hip-hop samurai are attempting to legitimate their styles by emphasizing their Japaneseness. Yet one of the striking developments in Japan's hip-hop scene in the first years of the twenty-first century has been the increase of this kind of traditionalist imagery of samurai alongside a more pronounced use of the "Americanized" imagery of gangstas, platinum chains, and expensive cars. Although one might expect a somewhat linear process of domestication in Japanese hip-hop over time, we instead see both global standardization and local indigenization becoming more pronounced simultaneously. Standardization is evident in the ways that, in comparison to novice rappers a decade ago, young rappers today show a more subtle understanding of lyrical flow, rhyming, the ideals of self-emphasis *(jibun shuchō)*, and the historical origins of hip-hop in African American culture. At the same time, Japanese hip-hop artists in recent years increasingly use traditional instruments (koto, *shamisen* [a three-string, banjo-like instrument], and *taiko* drums) in sampling, adopt vocal styles mimicking traditional voice performers of kabuki or bunraku puppet-play narrators, and promote imagery of samurai, ninja, geisha, and so on. Some songs even liken club performances to town festivals where groups noisily transport portable shrines (*mikoshi*) on their shoulders.[1] Sometimes the same artist can seem to be pulled in two directions at once, as when Uzi also posed for a magazine photo spread waving a samurai sword while wearing a Los Angeles Raiders hat and jersey. If neither more global nor more local characterizes the trends in hip-hop, what can we say about the processes that extend global connectedness while also multiplying the diversity of local, individual outcomes?

The idea of battles between groups and families of groups provides a dynamic perspective on the music's unfolding history in Japan. To battle means to work within certain rules of engagement and to acknowledge that not everyone will prevail. The idea of battling hip-hop samurai suggests a way of conceptualizing the somewhat paradoxical features of deepening connectedness and widening plurality. Hip-hop in Japan shows connectedness across national boundaries: rappers around the world grasp the aesthetics of rap flow, of sampling in music production, and of a playfully brash, in-your-face attitude. We see a widening plurality globally in the multitude of languages and settings, diverse intersections with race, and different kinds of integration with commercial, governmental, and social forces.[2] There is no simple flow from more powerful to less powerful elements of society (or vice versa), but rather improvisatory, expanding networks of links, often fueled by competition among groups. We have already seen some contours of this connectedness and plurality. I put the idea of shifting contexts and transformative *genba* into motion by looking at the historical unfolding of Japanese hip-hop dance, rapping, and music production.

How Japanese Are Samurai?

The idea of battling samurai offers a way of thinking about Japaneseness and a transnational imaginary. We might draw some lessons from films. From an American perspective, a recognizable exotic—samurai, geisha, sushi, anime—often comes to stand for a Japanese authenticity. When Tom Cruise (*The Last Samurai*, 2003) and Uma Thurman (*Kill Bill*, Vol. 1, 2003) pick up swords, we see how the samurai—with their skill at handling the *katana*, their commitment to death with honor, and their unwavering loyalty—often stand for a narrow range of Japanese ideals in the Western mind. I would not deny the entertainment value of these films, but as tools for teaching about culture, they err by essentializing samurai ideals while underplaying the conflicts that arose among samurai themselves. Yet what makes these American visions of samurai instructive is not so much what they get wrong, but what they deem essential to get right.

A somewhat similar essentializing conceptual move occurs when the Japanese are characterized as "good at borrowing." Such depictions mistakenly suggest that transnational flows can be explained in terms of the country's national character. Roland Robertson (1992, 177–78), for example, argues that the syncretism of Japanese religion, namely, the importation of Buddhism and its linkage with indigenous Shinto forms, has given the Japanese a privileged role in the current round of globalization because they are well suited to glocalizing foreign cultural elements. Arjun Appadurai (1996, 37) uses Japan as a way of contrasting "ideoscapes" with "ethnoscapes" to show how flows along one dimension (ideas) are not necessarily matched by flows along another (people): "The Japanese are notoriously hospitable to ideas and are stereotyped as inclined to export (all) and import (some) goods, but they are also notoriously closed to immigration." Such portrayals can reinforce the notion that cultural borrowing is a matter of national essence, when it can more accurately be described as fraught processes of learning, adaptation, and transformation, processes that unfold unevenly because they are always caught up in shifting relations of inequality. Indeed, it is the unevenness of American samurai movies—what they portray and what they do not—that provides the most insight into the processes of global flows.

In Japan, while the samurai still offer a model of a courageous Japanese spirit, they also evoke an exceedingly troubled past. The Japanese film *Twilight Samurai (Tasogare seibei,* dir. Yamada Yōji, 2002), for example, depicts class differences among and conflicts between samurai themselves.[3] Some samurai were chivalrous noblemen, but others were murderous vagabonds, while yet others were insensitive members of elites, living off the efforts of starving peasants. In Japan, samurai do not stand for a singular image of "us versus the West." Rather, samurai are widely acknowledged to be important, while their actual meaning, a relative concept to begin with, has always been very much contested. Thus battling samurai can be seen as evoking a contest over the meaning of Japaneseness, more than a particular national character. This is analogous, I would argue, to the kind of conceptual move required to understand hip-hop in Japan in that its meaning does not come down to one monolithic form vis-à-vis the US scene, but rather is animated by an unfolding series of debates about what hip-hop means, a debate that attends to hit trends and counter-movements in both the United States and Japan. The battles unfolding in Japanese hip-hop offer a way of grasping the relationship between the widening global reach of hip-hop and the increasing diversity of styles in different social and geographic locations.

This essay is more about battles than samurai per se. But given the way samurai themselves changed dramatically over the course of Japan's history, we can learn from the analogy. Hip-hop in japan has changed the ways we view youth culture, musical creativity, and the meaning of political engagement through expressive culture. Why do Japan's hip-hoppers battle, and for what do they battle? If today's samurai really are hip-hoppers, what does this suggest about the loyalties of youth in contemporary Japan?

A brief overview of Japanese popular music history gives a sense of the dynamic interaction between imported Western music styles and social changes within Japan during the postwar period. *Genba,* as networked performance spaces and sites of production, provide a way of conceptualizing broader shifts in the practices of media and record companies as the music business developed. I then discuss the history of hip-hop in Japan, which I divide into three eras. The first era, circa 1984 to 1994, might be characterized as the period of discovering the nature of hip-hop. The second era, circa 1994 to 1999, is characterized by an ongoing debate over what makes *Japanese* hip-hop, that is, a concern over whether more commercially successful party-rap (or J-rap) artists were more Japanese, or whether more oppositional and underground styles were better examples of Japanese hip-hop. I will also consider why this middle era differed from the development of hip-hop in the United States in that it offered few examples of songs that drew on famous music samples. A third era, from 2000 to the present, might be characterized in terms of widening diversity without a center. That is, we see a shift toward a wider range of hip-hop styles in terms of region, class, and gender, alongside a growing indifference to other approaches to Japanese hip-hop. That is, in comparison to the previous era, when both party rappers and underground hip-hoppers attended to and criticized each other, the later-era hip-hop artists tended not to care about contrasting approaches to hip-hop style. Dividing Japanese hip-hop into these different eras risks overgeneralizing, but it also gives us some guides for thinking about the ways in which families of rap groups organized around different aesthetic commitments and managed to build excitement around their styles. Over time, as the Japanese hip-hop scene expanded, we can imagine it as a kind of pyramid, featuring more stars reaching higher sales at the top, along with a widening at the base to include a variety of artists throughout Japan and on all rungs of the socioeconomic ladder.

A Brief History of Popular Music in Japan

A brief look at the history of popular music in twentieth-century Japan gives some perspective on what is particular about hip-hop, as well as on the variety of mixing between global and local forms. The tension between borrowed and indigenous is in no way unique to rap music. Depending on the era and the genre, music globalization emerges from processes driven from above and below. Changes in business practices and structures of fandom alter the meanings of the popular. We can see this, for example, in the contrasts between the centralized control and marketing of idol singers and the more grassroots development of singer-songwriters in folk music. A *genba* perspective draws attention to the contexts of performance, the businesses that support them, the audiences that come together, and the media that circulate musical trends.

Western music in Japan is closely associated with the country's modernization. During the Tokugawa period (1600–1868), the military rulers largely closed off Japan to the outside world, prohibiting foreigners from coming to the country and Japanese from leaving. In1853, US Commodore Matthew Perry brought his "black ships" into Edo (now Tokyo) harbor to forcibly open the country to foreign trade. Shortly thereafter, several feudal clans introduced military marching bands along with European military education. The establishment of the Meiji government in 1868 inaugurated Japan's modern era, and for many Japanese music scholars, this moment marks the beginning of popular music (*popyuraa ongaku*) as well (Hosokawa, Matsumura, and Shiba 1991, 1).[4]

Popular music in early-twentieth-century Japan emerged in diverse ways. Military songs celebrated Japan's wars with China (1894–95) and with Russia (1904–5). Opera in the Asakusa district of Tokyo, with Western costumes and scenery, proved a sensation among fashionable youth until the devastating Kantō earthquake of 1923 drove the opera musicians to other parts of Japan. The first Japanese jazz group got its start when it traveled to San Francisco in 1912 as a ship band and brought back sheet music. Before World War II, the term *jazz* encompassed a wide range of foreign music, including tango, rumba, foxtrot, and Tin Pan Alley jazz (Atkins 2001). In 1929, the song "Tokyo March" ("Tokyo kōshinkyoku") had great success, celebrating the lifestyle of jazz and dance halls in Tokyo's upscale Ginza shopping district, the new center of evening entertainment after Asakusa's decline.

Popular music's meanings shifted with the introduction of broadcasting, publishing, and recording. The 1920s saw Japan's first music copyright law go into effect (1920), the start of radio broadcasts (1925), and the establishment of three of Japan's major record companies (1927). In 1930, French films popularized chanson and imbued this romantic music style with Parisian artiness. Dance promoted the spread of Western music as well, with a tango boom in 1937 (Savigliano 1995). By the late 1930s, the effects of war in China were being felt in the music world. The number of patriotic songs about Manchuria and South China increased, while songs about love were prohibited by the government. In 1940 and throughout the Pacific War, tango and other "degenerate" styles of music were forbidden. As the war went on, the Japanese government took a more active role in censoring popular song and in promoting patriotic compositions (Tonoshita 1993).

According to Shuhei Hosokawa, Hiroshi Matsumura, and Shun'ichi Shiba (1991, 11), after World War II, the history of *kayōkyoku,* a broad term for Japanese popular song, was animated by a battle between native and American elements. While this might be the case in terms of the sound of the music, I would draw attention as well to the ways different contexts, especially different *genba,* provide a way of seeing how these battles also reflected broader changes within Japan. The immediate postwar period was marked by Japan's embrace of a new, peaceful, and democratic national identity (Dower 1999). The soundscape reflected these new borrowings as well. Shuffle rhythms appeared in popular songs, and even traditional instruments like the three-stringed *shamisen* were used to grind out boogie-woogie. Japan's defeat by the Allied forces also led to a wide-ranging adulation of things American, symbolized especially by the growing popularity of jazz brought by and played for the occupying forces. By 1953, jazz was more popular than any other kind of music in Japan (Hosokawa, Matsumura, and Shiba 1991, 13).

In the postwar period, we can see how the associations Americans make between social class and musical genres in the United States can be turned upside down in Japan. The Japanese who formed country-and-western bands were often sons of the aristocracy. This seeming incongruity, however, has a simple explanation: they were the ones with sufficient leisure and education to develop an interest in new foreign music and to understand, if only partially, the language in which it was sung (14). In Japan, hillbilly music, as it was sometimes called, was for the elite.

Jazz and Questions of Japaneseness

Sites of performance and the character of the audience clearly played a role in defining the limits of creativity in popular music. In E. Taylor Atkins's (2001) examination of the history of jazz in Japan, we see how Japanese musicians catering to American troops during the Occupation played in self-consciously American styles, reproducing as accurately as possible the sounds they heard on records. Later, interest in jazz deepened with the visits of Art Blakey (1961) and John Coltrane (1965). Jazz coffee shops (*jazu kissaten*), where patrons could listen to records being played on expensive audio equipment and where talking was prohibited, also appeared on the scene. In the 1960s, more avant-garde approaches to so-called yellow jazz emerged, attempting to define a Japanese jazz distinct from America's. This included efforts to create a hipster culture of renegade Japanese who met regularly to experiment with improvisatory jazz in Ginza performance spaces. Atkins (2001, 226) calls this period the most prodigious flowering of Japanese jazz creativity. Here we can see the centrality of a kind of social, networked *genba* where creative artists could perform, and, perhaps as important, could find knowledgeable and engaged audiences who provided the necessary support and criticism. Atkins notes that the discourse surrounding authenticity in Japanese jazz reflected a desire for exclusivity, for example, in regard to the importance of a unique sense of space, or *ma,* between notes. The artists sought to produce a jazz that only Japanese could play and that foreigners could not imitate. Some other jazz musicians attempted to formulate a linkage with American black nationalist discourse by drawing on *min'yo* (traditional folk songs) to mimic a historically indigenous, vernacular culture that paralleled the blues. Such efforts make sense, however, if we think of jazz not as a single style of music (either universal or particular), but as a diverse collection of competing artists. Interestingly, some of the challenges Japanese jazz artists faced in trying to authenticate their music played out differently than they would with Japanese rap musicians later in the century. Because Japanese rappers wrote Japanese language lyrics, which is something they shared with other Japanese musicians who sang in their native tongue, they had less trouble defending their Japaneseness.

A Musical Generation Gap Develops

After 1955, Japan experienced two decades of dramatic economic growth, and the 1960s saw rapid changes in the music world as well. Although Japan's popular music scene is known more for importing songs and styles than exporting them, Sakamoto Kyū's "Ue o muite arukō" (Walking Along, Looking Up) proved a major exception to that pattern. Sung in Japanese, the light jazz tune reached number one on a 1963 US Billboard chart, an unequalled accomplishment for a Japanese musician. In the United States, the song became known as "Sukiyaki," the word for a sweet beef noodle soup, which is somewhat ironic given that no food is mentioned in the Japanese original. We might also note that Kyū symbolized a certain style of popular music production that relied on in-house musicians and songwriters. The song's longevity is such that Snoop Dogg made a parody of it on his debut album *Doggystyle* (1993).

As the 1960s progressed and the trappings of middle-class lifestyles spread to broader segments of the population, hints of a global youth culture expressed through music and closely allied with urbanization and the rise of consumer culture in Japan emerged. Economic growth also generated income for the recording industry. With the release of more music, generation gaps appeared in the kinds of music that people consumed. A range of upbeat variety groups appeared, such as the Crazy Cats who borrowed the style of Spike Jones. Their management company adopted the epoch-making strategy, also borrowed from American business, of using television to create hit songs. Visiting foreign groups like the Ventures, the Animals (both in 1965), and the Beatles (1966) sparked a wide range of similar bands, collectively categorized as "group sounds" or simply GS. Given that no equivalent category of group sounds exists in the United States or the United Kingdom, one wonders how Western it is. More critical than the Westernness of this new genre was the way it expressed a youthful resistance to older traditions. Before long, electric guitars and long hair had become so popular they were banned in high schools.

The late 1960s also saw a folk (*fuōku*) boom, which refers not to indigenous folk music, but to performers who imitated American groups like the Kingston Trio and Peter, Paul and Mary. In a split that replays itself generation after generation, at first many cover bands appeared, mouthing the English words of imported hits (college folk). Later, people who sang serious protest songs in Japanese (underground folk) came to the fore. Some of these latter folk singers performed in the outdoor *genba* of the Shinjuku train station's west gate, drawing the ire of police who tried to break up these self-identified folk guerillas. The folk-music ethic of self-made, self-performed songs was somewhat new to the music business in Japan, which, prior to this, had relied almost exclusively on in-house producers and lyricists (Aso 1997). After the folk boom, a Japanese style of folk rock came to be known as "new music." One of its main characteristics was its emphasis on the singer-songwriter expressing self-written lyrics.

Coincidentally, the mid-1960s were also a time of Japan's asserting its return to the international scene as a powerful country. In 1964, Tokyo hosted the summer Olympics. In 1968, Japan's GNP was second only to that of the United States, and a year later Japan became the world's leading manufacturer of television sets (Allinson 1997, xii). The nation's recording industry was maturing as well. From 1945 onward, Western music had consistently dominated sales in Japan, but in 1967, sales of Japanese music (*hōban*) overtook sales of Western music (*yōban*) for the first time in the postwar era (Kawabata 1991, 335).[5] In addition, the volume of music sales grew tenfold during the 1960s.

At the same time as locally produced music was coming to dominate the market, there was a growing debate among Japanese rock bands about whether one should sing lyrics in English or in Japanese (Uchida et al. 1990, 84–85). The debate hinged on two factors. Should artists aim for a global (i.e., American) audience or cultivate the local scene? Is the Japanese language suitable to the rock rhythm, or is English better? It is worth noting that this debate emerged in the context of Japan's growing economic power, an expanding national market, and the appearance of a new style of music journalism. According to the music scholar Shuhei Hosokawa, music magazine reporting on GS-type bands tended to focus on trivia like the lead singer's blood type and favorite color. But in the late 1960s, he told me in a personal communication, *New Music Magazine* introduced the tone of a critic (*hyōronka*), so that questions of authenticity in music, social background, and so on became common topics for reporting. In each case, we witness a kind of feedback loop among the networks of artists, *genba,* record companies, fans, and media that reinforces particular aesthetic and business approaches, both of which shift depending on the era and the genre of music.

The 1970s witnessed a growing generation gap in musical tastes among the Japanese. *Enka* offers a key example. With its wavering melodies and melancholy themes, the music echoes earlier *min'yō,* or indigenous folk music. Although sometimes likened to country and western because of its association with rural Japan and blue-collar audiences and themes, *enka* differs in that it generally appeals to an older generation. The anthropologist Christine Yano (2002) presents a compelling story of the ways *enka* stood for a disappearing past and thus the "soul of the Japanese" (*nihonjin no kokoro*). It depicted—through songs of love and loss, harbors and tears, and above all sake—a rural, harborside Japan upstaged by a young, urban, postwar generation. Yano shows how the emotionality of *enka* provided a sentimental way to imagine an enduring nation in the midst of such rapid change. *Enka* also heralded a new era in which popular culture would become increasingly segregated along generational lines.

Rock, folk, new music, and Japanese pop all appealed to a younger generation of listeners. These genres brought new ways of looking at youth, not as the bearers of an older tradition, but as the people imagining a new social order under the collective banner of the new middle-class Japan. As a result, the "kind of song that was sung by both young and old became extremely rare" (Hosokawa, Matsumura, and Shiba 1991, 11–12). This phenomenon highlights one outgrowth of diversifying media industries as well. Although *enka* remains largely absent from prime-time television (except for public TV) and FM, it endures, firmly rooted in karaoke, AM, and wire broadcasting. Although today *enka* is viewed as a more traditional style of music, certainly when compared to J-pop, it is worth recognizing that *enka* was viewed as pop music, not traditional music, in its early days. The use of Western instruments, especially the violin, created a newfangled music that only later was seen to represent a traditional past. In this, *enka* parallels the performance genres discussed by Marilyn Ivy (1995), who examines discourses of vanishing cultural forms in the face of modernity.

Idol Singers Drive Television Hits, YMO Starts Sampling

In the late 1970s, good-looking teenage singers of Japanese pops (*poppusu*), as it is called, appeared in rapid succession and ushered in the age of idols (*aidoru*). These performers sang pop songs with guitars, bass, drums, and keyboards. They closely mimicked Western styles, but in many ways there was also an equally noticeable localization of idol music, despite the performers' imitative qualities. Idol singers gained their authenticity from reaching out to an ever widening crowd, localizing the music through its wide consumption. Idols were linked very strongly with advertising and the public-relations industry. Talent counted for much less than the ability to appeal as a cult object on TV and radio. Music magazines, too, proliferated and diversified, becoming an increasingly important medium to promote artists (Skov and Moeran 1995). The burgeoning teenage consumer culture can be credited for the popularity of these idols (Hosokawa, Matsumura, and Shiba 1991, 19). The slick packaging of singers with a notable lack of musicality continues unabated and has even been taken to a further extreme recently (Aoyagi 2000). In 1995, the idol style entered the Internet era with the debut of three female virtual idols, whose computer-generated images appeared on magazine covers. They released CDS as well, with the identity of the actual singers kept secret. It appears to have been a short-lived (and failed) experiment.

In the 1980s, Japanese pop music grew by using the marketing insights of idols, but it kept diversifying in terms of performance spaces. Large venues like the Budokan (literally, Martial Arts Hall) featured leading pop stars from Japan and from the United States. Small clubs and discos supported a solid underground scene that followed Western trends in punk, new wave, and by the mid-1980s, rap music as well. One group worth noting is YMO (Yellow Magic Orchestra), which included the composer Sakamoto Ryūichi. The group's synthesizer-based music was a precursor to the style of constructing music (i.e., not playing instruments) by cutting fragments of sounds and looping them using computer technology.

Even in this brief sketch of popular music history in Japan, we can see how genres more or less borrowed from the West gained their meaning not only from their points of origin also but from the context of Japan's shifting popular music scene amid broad social and economic changes. While the sounds of different music styles could be distinguished by a conflict between indigenous and foreign elements, it was more generally the changes in Japanese society that gave meaning to the contrasts between Japanese and Western. During the postwar period, Japan witnessed large internal migration from rural areas to cities, as well as a shift in employment from agriculture to manufacturing and, later, to service-industry jobs. Economic growth also encouraged the rise of a consumer culture that became not only more widely shared but more finely tuned to distinctions of taste and status in various social groups and age cohorts. Social classes and generations came to be distinguished by their consumption patterns. To reduce the logic of popular music in Japan to localization would give the wrong impression if we concluded that there was some inherent aptitude for syncretism on the part of all Japanese people, or simply a linear trend toward domestication.

During the 1980s, when the bubble economy was booming, the new breed (*shinjinrui*) of twenty-something consumers flocking to expensive restaurants and then dancing at glitzy discos provided the dominant image of nightlife. In the music business, the success of idols reflected the marketing prowess of record companies, but for many Japanese it was symbolic of a consumerism devoid of value or deeper meaning. For those youth seeking more of an edge, rock music was getting old, and even punk was losing its radical chic. By the mid-1980s, some young people—and even somewhat established musicians—found inspiration in their first encounters with hip-hop.

Given Japan's continuous importation and adaptation of Western music styles, it is hardly surprising that hip-hop came too. Indeed, the more intriguing question is why the flow of foreign music styles to the United States is so limited compared to the abundant flows of Euro-American musical styles to Asia.[6] For now, let us consider how the distinctiveness of hip-hop in Japan emerged less from an interplay between foreign hip-hop and Japanese culture than from the shifting character of hip-hop battles as they unfolded.

The Early Era: What Is Hip-Hop?

Japanese hip-hop offers an intriguing example of cultural globalization in part because it expanded despite skepticism on the part of record companies and major media outlets. In addition, the history of hip-hop in Japan shows that certain kinds of cultural exchange begin not from complete understanding, but rather from some interaction that can incite a desire to learn more, to participate, and to contribute something of one's own. From the mid-1980s to the early 1990s, hip-hop in Japan was rather informal, smaller scale, experimental, and often, truth be told, not very good, at least by today's standards. It was a time during which performers asked, "What is hip-hop?" Given the relative lack of information, in some ways they had to make up the answers themselves. The early days of hip-hop in Japan are also notable because neither economic forces nor powerful national leaders can explain the emergence of this cultural form in Japan.[7] Instead, we must examine the particular youth drawn to the style, as well as their own efforts to participate in a globalizing process that had little to offer in terms of economic incentives. In this regard, breakdancing offers an example of globalization through body movement that can hardly be explained by the imposition of some outside force.

On the other hand, the early days provide some clues regarding the character of crossovers and the motivations that keep cultural movements alive. What provided the first sparks? What resonances provoked some people to take up hip-hop? Early hip-hop was clearly not led by corporate interests; indeed, it was largely ignored by large record companies and performance venues. This was partly because, in Japan, breakdancing was one of the leading edges of hip-hop, and one would be a fool to get into that art form for the money.

Crazy-A and the First Sparks from Breakdancing

Although the American rap records of Grandmaster Flash and the Sugar Hill Gang could be heard in Tokyo discos earlier, an important spark for hip-hop in Japan came in 1983, not through music alone, but when breakdancing appeared in Tokyo through film and live performances. While breakdancers may have become less visible in the United States in recent years, in Japan the movement continues more than two decades after its initial appearances in film. World breakdancing festivals exist, and multitudes of small groups practice and perform to this day, not only in Japan but around the world. How did breakdancing develop in Japan? What explains its persistence in spite of what some observers dismiss as its faddish and ephemeral character? It is easier to imagine how ballet becomes a globally recognizable form, supported by elite communities, institutionally secure performance venues, and a network of schools enrolling hopefuls at the youngest ages. But that break-dancing became a worldwide phenomenon shows that paths of globalization do not flow only from the most powerful segments of society. Robert Farris Thompson (1996) describes the diverse cultural mixtures of the Bronx that gave rise to hip-hop, a history that reaches back to African rhythms and resistance to slavery, passing through Congo Square in New Orleans and moving a language of the body across centuries and national boundaries. From original New York breakdance groups, such as Rock Steady Crew (RSC), the phenomenon spread around the world through informal channels, honed on the cardboard ground of public battle.

Films and traveling performers prompted the initial crossover. Crazy-A, one of the forefathers of Japanese hip-hop, was nineteen years old and on a blind date when he went to see the movie *Flashdance* in July 1983. As he told me in an interview in December 1996, the scene featuring Rock Steady Crew so mesmerized him that when he got home, he tried to moonwalk and spin on his back. Yet at first he was skeptical about the idea of dancing. "I always thought dance is something that only women do," he said. Although he occasionally went to discos, "I only went to drink and to get into fights" (Krush et al. 1998, 10). In October 1983, *Wild Style* (dir. Charlie Ahearn, 1982), a low-budget film featuring the first generation of American rappers, deejays, and breakdancers was shown in Tokyo theaters.[8] At the time, many of the performers also came to Tokyo to promote the film, performing in an Ikebukuro department store and also in a couple of clubs (Pitekan Toroposu and Tsubaki House). The hip-hop writer Egaitsu Hiroshi (aka Egaluzee) describes the events of the era: "Of course, in 1983, it was huge that the cast and crew came to Japan to promote the classic hip-hop film *Wild Style*. Futura, Cold Crush Brothers, Fab Five Freddie, all the important old school players came to Japan. It was a complete shock, but maybe one that only those people who actually saw it can fully understand" (Egaitsu 2002). What did this shock convey? Takagi Kan, another of the first generation of emcees, says, "I couldn't tell what was what with the rap and the deejaying ... but with the breakdancing and graffiti art, you could understand it visually. Or rather, it wasn't understanding so much as, 'Whoa, that's cool' [*kakkoii*]. With rap and deejaying, I couldn't imagine what could be cool about it" (Goto 1997, 27).

When breakdancing appeared in Japan, the people initially influenced did not fully understand the movement's roots in New York City and African American culture, but they were nonetheless attracted by its newness. For breakdancing, the body was a medium of globalization, but it was also carried importantly through film. Interestingly, it seems that breakdancing in New York City owes a debt to movies from East Asia. According to Crazy Legs, a leader of RSC, "The only place I'd say we learned moves from, which was universal for a lot of dancers, was karate flicks on Forty-Second street, 'cause those movies are filmed the best, you could see the movement of the whole body" (Fernando 1994, 18). Dance, movement of the body, and the visual language of graffiti can move easily across linguistic and cultural boundaries. Movies and videos were clearly an important channel for this exchange. It is also clear, however, that a flow begins not from complete understanding, but rather from some interaction that can incite curiosity and a desire to participate.

What were some of the early resonances? Dilapidated urban backdrops and the idea of battle proved key. When Crazy-A saw *Wild Style,* he could relate to the bombed-out look of inner-city New York, with the trains rolling by overhead and people hanging around on street corners. It reminded him of where he grew up near the San'ya section of Tokyo, a place where many of the people who have fallen through the cracks in society come to pick up day-laborer jobs (Fowler 1996). Crazy-A even produced a dance-centered music video that, although set in Tokyo, mirrors the *Wild Style* setting. The video highlights train tracks, empty lots, and unemployed men as Crazy-A's brother Naoya, wearing Japanese construction-worker clothes, breakdances among the down-and-out.

Crazy-A described himself as a gangster boy (*gyangusutaa* shonen) and offers oblique references in his songs to fighting in back alleys. Yet breakdancing, he found, offered a more satisfying focus for his energies. As he explained in a December 1996 interview with me,

> Hip-hop after all is battle. So, instead of fighting, I quit the violence and started doing hip-hop. You can fight and get stronger, but—how can I put it—in the end, nothing of substance remains [*katachi ga nokoranai*]. It's not as if there are brawling tournaments or anything, so nothing lasts. But with dance, there are competitions and a sense of form stays with you. You can say, I'm number one, and appeal to an audience. That gives you something that lasts.

Although not all of the early participants in Japanese hip-hop had a *furyō* (bad boy) background, some did. Intriguingly, the ones who allegedly had the most experience with gangs were, at least in the early days, the ones least likely to talk about it, especially in their music.

This may have something to do with the somewhat different connotations of gang member-ship in Japan and the United States. In Japan, the Yakuza are notoriously hierarchical, and the hazing of subordinates is a finely tuned art of humiliation (Hill 2003). Being young and in the Yakuza is not particularly cool.

DJ Krush tells of working for the Yakuza when he was young (Krush and Sekiguchi 1995). In one case, he ran an errand to pick up a package, delivered it to one of the bosses, and then saw that what he had been carrying held a severed finger (a self-inflicted sign of loyalty). Krush credits the film *Wild Style* with saving him from a life in a gang. He says that the day after he saw the film, he went to buy turntables and turned his attention away from crime and toward deejaying, a career that would allow him to support a family. MC Bell also acknowledges a gang background, but in his lyrics with B-Fresh he always tended toward lighter visions of youth culture. Bell also says that the hip-hop dance forms he learned from American service-men at discos in Yokohama gave him a way to stand out. The stories of these early encounters with hip-hop emphasize the genre's newness and the ways it provided alternative paths to status and pleasure for its adopters.

Hokoten as an Outdoor Genba

Sites of performance where groups and individuals could compete and others could watch nurtured early hip-hop. Yoyogi Park, located between the youth shopping districts of Shibuya and Harajuku in Tokyo, has for decades served as a gathering point for all manner of youthful fans and performers (Stanlaw 1990). Every Sunday until the late nineties, traffic was stopped and diverse bands and dancers would gather to perform outdoors along the street, which became known as "Hokoten," short for *hokōsha tengoku*, "pedestrian paradise."[9] Not long after the film *Wild Style* was shown in Tokyo, Crazy-A heard that breakers were gathering in Yoyogi Park on Sundays. When he went to see the action, however, "there was only this older guy who had a big Disco Robo [boom box] playing rap music," he said in the December 1996 interview. Crazy-A described the scene where he and other late-teen enthusiasts hung out:

> But as time went on, people like me gradually gathered there to listen to the music. Once there were about three or four of us, we gradually started to adopt the pos-ture [soburi], and move to the rhythm. More people would come by, and I'd ask if anyone knew where there was dancing going on, but no one was doing it. Then I suggested that maybe *we* start. From the next week on, four of us started dancing. At first, with a radio cassette and cardboard laid out on the ground. Sometimes we had turntables and a PA system. It was like a block party, a natural phenomenon [*shizen genshō*]. And then people like B-Fresh started to show up too.

With that practice and exposure, by 1984 Crazy-A was dancing on a television show (*Dance kōshien*). He also toured Japan as a backup dancer for the teen idol Kazami Shingō. Meanwhile, other US films (*Breakdance, Breakin' 2*) were shown in Tokyo in 1984. Other groups of Japanese breakdancers came to perform in Harajuku as well (Krush et al. 1998, 20). There was a kind of feedback loop between practice, performance, media spotlights, and widening influence that initiated a break-dancing boom. Groups met, competed, and split up, drawing audiences and honing their skills. DJ Krush, MC Bell, and Cake-K (of B-Fresh), Crazy-A, and others were all there and helped define this early movement.

Crazy-A says it was an American woman working as a model in Tokyo who told them during one of their Sunday performances that "in New York they would call you 'b-boys.'"

That was when Crazy-A started calling his group the Tokyo B-Boys. This collective later was tapped by Crazy Legs of the New York City-based Rock Steady Crew to join their world network of groups, and thus was born Rock Steady Crew Japan.

Breakdancing illustrates that *genba* need not be built around business interests but can develop from a kind of performative sociability that draws people into a universe of shared interests. From the beginning, breakdancing was clearly more than just a new kind of dance. The dance involves the appropriation of public space, not unlike graffiti. Sidewalks, public parks, and underground shopping mall hallways are transformed into a public stage, sometimes marked by cardboard or linoleum being rolled out, but often simply created by the dancers themselves. We also see in these youths' fancy footwork, gymnastic spins, and coordinated steps a reminder of the fact that the body is not only an empty hanger on which to display one's consumer choices but an active site of performative identity. Thus the body and the street take on meanings outside the realm of consumerism and give some concrete meaning to the ideal of street culture. A different notion of street fashion is widely circulated through teen fashion magazines, with roving photographers capturing the fractured styles of hip Tokyo youth with impromptu street snaps. Thus youth wandering the trendy districts of Shibuya, Takeshita Street in Harajuku, or the back alleys of Ura-Harajuku perform in a parade of fashion to see and be seen. Unlike school uniforms or the salary-man's blue suit, street fashion speaks to more flexible institutions of status and power. Meanwhile, breakdancers' street battles take competition in a different direction, relying on physical prowess and style within certain rules of engagement. Breakdancing is a public assertion of the central place of performance in social life.

Yet if breakdancing highlights certain ideals, it also goes through changes. What attracts young breakdancers to hip-hop, and the contexts in which they can perform, has shifted. In 1996, when I first interviewed Crazy-A, he was thirty-two years old and could no longer compete as he had before. The younger members of Rock Steady Crew Japan were between twenty-two and twenty-five years of age; they dearly represented a different generation drawn to b-boying. Hyaku, one of the dancers, recalled being attracted to hip-hop after seeing Crazy-A on television. Gori, another dancer and a former soccer player, appreciated the physical challenge of b-boy dancing. In a December 1996 interview, Katsu said, "When I first saw it, I thought it was awful. But I started because I wanted to pick up women. Then I saw Crazy-A and others doing it seriously, so I took it more seriously. It was when they said, 'It's not that kind of thing,' that I began learning about hip-hop and really wanted to do it." In 1996, several of the members of RSC Japan came from Sōka Daigaku, a Buddhist university that boasts one of the largest and most successful breakdancing teams in Japan, D-Crew. In 1996, D-Crew had over one hundred members, quite a contrast to Crazy-A going to Yoyogi Park with a few friends.

We can see hints of a generation gap appearing when one of New York City's pioneers judged a breakdancing contest in Tokyo. Starting in 1999, Crazy-A began organizing an annual hip-hop festival in Yoyogi Park called B-Boy Park, a four-day event that included contests in freestyle rapping, deejaying, and breakdancing. At B-Boy Park 2001, Crazy Legs, one of the New York City break-dancers seen by Crazy-A during his fateful viewing of *Flashdance,* served as a judge of the breakdancing contest in a performance space called Liquid Room. The dark room on the tenth floor of a Shinjuku building was packed on a Thursday afternoon with upward of a thousand people. A boxing ring-style stage was set up in the middle, and dancers competed head to head in single elimination rounds. Interestingly, there was no separate women's category; the women competed directly against male groups (and lost). Crazy Legs judged and performed with the dance group Tribal during a break in the competition, while his four-year-old son fidgeted. At the end of the day's events, Crazy Legs offered a critical response to the battles through an interpreter. He was not completely happy with what he had seen.

Crazy Legs thought there had been too many "power moves" and not enough attention to footwork: "People have to remember, it's a dance." He sounded a little like an old-timer complaining that the kids were doing it all wrong because it was also clear that if you wanted to win a competition in front of a thousand people, you would need big power moves to wow the crowd, not subtle, fancy footwork. The audience gave its most enthusiastic response to gymnastic tricks, wildly gyrating legs, flips, and handstands. Here, respecting the pioneers was trumped by what it takes to win in the *genba*. A history of breakdancing around the world deserves its own book, but at least we can note that distinctions between generations are appearing in the global scene. This suggests that the key dynamic may not be a rivalry between foreign and local hip-hop but between factions and generations across international lines.

Rap Starts in Classy Clubs

There was another and somewhat separate stream out of which hip-hop in Japan emerged, and it flowed from those who performed in the discos and clubs. Key artists included Itō Seikō and Tinnie Punx, whose hip, irreverent, and oppositional stance becomes evident on one of their album covers, *Kensetsuteki* (*Constructive [Criticism]*), which features three musicians looking upward and giving the finger (reissued in 1991, Pony Canyon, PCCA-00807). This early era of experimental rap is documented by Gotō Akio (1997), who provides a series of interviews with some of the forerunners of the Japanese hip-hop scene in a collection describing "the birth of hip-hop culture" in Japan. Itō Seikō tells of introducing rap as a kind of "standing talk" in a club called Pitekan Tropos in Harajuku. A number of musicians reported struggling to educate audiences who could not understand why there was no band, and why the "singer" was not singing. And what was that scratching noise coming from the records? Takagi Kan points out that although *Wild Style* was important, the hip-hop scene took years to develop (44–47). He started as a punk-rock musician before becoming entranced by the music of Afrika Bambaataa, who performed in Japan in 1985. Chikada Haruo took the name President BPM and rapped with the band Vibrastone. He says he felt a connection with the South Bronx, the outsider style, and the emphasis on direct communication (36–37). Tinnie Punx (pronounced "tiny punks") included Takagi Kan and Fujihara Hiroshi. Their playfully critical stance on Tokyo society and government planted the seeds of an oppositional perspective through rap.

MC Bell (of B-Fresh) felt a closer kinship to street dancing and calls this club stream the classy (*oshare*) style (Bell and Cake-K 1998, 112). The idea of *oshare*, which means "stylish," "trendy," and "hip," suggests alternative measures of value. *Oshare* can be distinguished not only by these groups' interest in musical performance (rather than the street) but by the kind of audience they could draw. The image of clubs as classy locales also refers to the new breed of conspicuous consumers known as the *shinjinrui*, twenty-something urbanites enamored of brand-name items. They were the see-and-be-seen type of consumers who contrasted with a darker, more isolated version of fan communities called the *otaku*. Early Japanese rap aimed to provide audiences of late-night clubs with a certain urbane hipness. I would like to focus on the competition among performers as a way of grasping the evolution of the scene. These early days had only a few artists recording at the independent level, and yet these artists are the ones that others defined themselves against.

Ironically, the early *oshare* rap performers never mention the breakdancing scene in Yoyogi Park, but the break-dancers did come to check out the club rappers. The book *Japanese Hip-Hop History* (Krush 1998) includes the stories of some of the Yoyogi Park performers including B-Fresh, Crazy-A, and DJ Krush. They all acknowledge their awakening to the greater attention being paid to the rappers. One show in particular loomed large.

In December 1986, Run-DMC, riding a wave of attention accompanying their hit remake of the Aerosmith song "Walk This Way," performed two shows at NHK Hall in Shibuya. Itō Seikō, Tinnie Punx, and President BPM performed as the opening acts. When MC Bell, Cake-K, Crazy-A, and other Hokoten performers discuss this event, they offer two conclusions: while rap drew a larger, more excited crowd than breakdancing, the Japanese acts lacked style. In the words of Rhymester's Utamaru, "When I first saw Japanese rappers opening for an American group, I thought to myself, 'It wouldn't take much to be the best rapper in Japan'" (Rhymester 1999). This is an interesting moment because it shows that witnessing a lackluster performance in a favored genre can ignite the desire to become an artist as much as can a virtuosic performance. In other words, a driving force in hip-hop appears to come not so much from a feeling of admiration as from one of self-confidence. This internal battling dynamic has proven central to the style. Succeeding generations of Japanese rappers, some of whom cut their teeth with performances in Yoyogi Park, worked to define their contributions to the genre often in terms of a deeper lyrical engagement with hip-hop core ideals. The battles centered around quality and skill. Even though there was plenty of disagreement about what counted as skill, I was always struck by how well rappers knew other rappers' lyrics, by how carefully and critically they measured their own sound against the sound of others. The fact of artists attending to artists marks another important dimension of the battles surrounding the early scene.

Many streams broke off, dried up, or joined tributaries to build the scene in Japan. From 1988 to 1992, the scene picked up energy in part from a growing number of club events that featured contests for rappers, DJS, and breakdancers. Some were sponsored by companies selling DJ equipment (e.g., Vestax). The DJ Underground Contest, begun in 1988, featured many of the prominent artists of the mid-1990s. ECD started the Check Your Mic contest in 1989, which continued off and on for five years, even producing a live album. Many of the second generation of performers such as Scha Dara Parr, You the Rock, B-Fresh, and others competed in these events. Years later, these groups would rarely appear together, but back in the early days, the different families competed directly, face to face.

The first club devoted to the genre, aptly and succinctly called Hip-Hop, opened in Shibuya in 1986. A regular there, DJ Yutaka is now a member of Zulu Nation (Bambaataa's organization) and splits his time between Tokyo and Los Angeles. Zeebra says he, too, started as a DJ at that club when he was still under the legal drinking age of twenty. From the mid-to late-1980s, rap gained more airplay on the radio as well. A Yokohama radio station began airing the "scratch mix" of the hip-hop DJ collective MID (Egaitsu 1997b). In 1987, a TV comedy show featured rappers giving the weather report. Specialty magazines began covering hip-hop in greater detail, and this meant that there was also a deepening compartmentalization of the hip-hop scene as more and more media options became available. Major Force, a hip-hop and dance-music label founded by Takagi Kan and others, began producing albums in 1988.

In 1989, a flood of American artists traveled to Japan to perform, including the Jungle Brothers, the 45 King, and De La Soul. After Public Enemy's show, which featured armed security pretending to spray the audience with machine-gun fire, Japanese rap groups began to include motionless, silent, brooding "security" in their onstage shows, a practice laughed about today. A second breakdancing boom appeared in 1990, after Bobby Brown visited Japan. On the whole, however, the rap scene was rather small compared to the larger world of Japanese pop music. Record companies, mainstream music magazines, radio, and television largely ignored this burgeoning group of hip-hop musicians. The period up to 1994 is generally regarded as a winter (*fuyu*) or ice age when few record labels, including indies, were willing to release hip-hop.

The Second Era: What Is *Japanese* Hip-Hop?

Things changed in 1994, when the rap trio Scha Dara Parr teamed up with the guitarist-song-writer Ozawa Kenji to produce the first million-selling rap hit. The mellow funk song called "Kon'ya wa būgi bakku" ("Boogie Back Tonight") was an anthem to hanging out with friends and flirting with women in clubs.[10] Music magazines heralded the song's success as evidence of the arrival of a Japanese rap scene because it was now capable of producing hits. Some reported that rap had finally earned its citizenship (*shiminken*). Then, in the summer of 1995, two songs by the group East End X Yuri climbed the charts, eventually selling around a million copies each. The songs "Da.Yo.Ne." and "Maicca" both capitalized on teenage slang to portray a carefree attitude toward everything from school to love affairs.[11] These commercial successes prompted a wave of publicity in music magazines, and the term J-rap was coined to represent the new, up-and-coming genre. Major record labels began to show interest in a variety of hip-hop groups that had been languishing on independent labels, particularly groups that emphasized a more playful approach, generally referred to as party rap (*paateii rappu*).

Not all emcees were enthusiastic about the J-rap boom. In the free paper *Rugged,* Zeebra and others lamented that these "sellouts" could be mistakenly seen as representing hip-hop culture (*Rugged* 1995, 7) In the clubs, groups like Rhymester would talk about respecting hip-hop as a culture (*bunka*), which meant understanding the history, recognizing the four elements, and speaking for oneself. East End, with Gaku and DJ Yoggy (along with producer Rock-Tee, initially), had at least been performing for a few years in the club scene, but Yuri had worked as part of a revolving-door pop group called Tokyo Performance Doll. Unsurprisingly, some viewed Yuri as a poser who ignored hip-hop culture and produced just pop (*tada* no *kayōkyoku*). The sappy music video produced by Epic/Sony, with corny illustrated backdrops, reinforced this impression.

One response from the underground hip-hop scene can be seen in a song by the group Lamp Eye. In 1995, Lamp Eye (a short-lived unit including Rino, Twigy, and Gama) titled their mini album *Gekokujō*, meaning literally, a samurai retainer overcoming his master. By using a term that referred back to the warring states period of the 1300s, the group explicitly drew attention to the ways that hip-hop offered a space for contesting the hierarchical certainties of the pop world. For them, the master was the mainstream entertainment industry, which they contrasted with their underground scene of lyrical skill. One song that gives a sense of the underground response to the J-rap boom is Lamp Eye's "Shōgen," a title that means "testimonial" or "speaking the truth." The track features other central emcees of the Kaminari family at the time, namely, You the Rock, G. K. Maryan, and Zeebra. Each verse offered a different attack on J-rap and an assertion about what made the underground scene different. For example, You the Rock uses wordplay to ridicule the party-rap group Dassen Trio (literally, "derailed trio") (Zeebra 1996b, 89).

> Psychotic rules, sucked in by a fad   *kurutta ruuru hamatta buumu hazureta reeru*
> running on broken rails, an empty "real"   *no ue hashiru chippoke na kiipu riaru*
> get out of our way, you can't cut in   *jama sasen warikomi wa ikemasen*
> this is our culture, burning ...   *oretachi no bunka chakka ...*
> ......
> with the strength of words   *kotoba no chikara*
> my verbal word spirit spreads power   *ore no kotodama kara minageru pawaa*
>   —Lamp Eye (1996) Shōgen (Polystar, Japan, PSCR-5547)

These lyrics capture the language of the time, emphasizing a culture of overflowing words, personal expression, the rejection of fads, and scorn for the J-rap boom. A video of "Shōgen" was produced by the graphic designer Ben List, an American living and working in Tokyo who followed the hip-hop scene closely, even producing an online free paper called *Elebugi*. The rough-hewn video is dark, mostly black-and-white, and gives a visual sense of the street image that Lamp Eye and their Kaminari collaborators expressed. Given that the video was edited without a digital time code, matching the visuals to the song also expressed a do-it-yourself ethic. The discourse of toughness was echoed by Zeebra and K Dub Shine in an April 1996 interview with me after the release of the debut King Giddra album the same year. They cited Public Enemy, Rakim, and Big Daddy Kane as gauges of realness, and they talked about the oppositionality at the core of the style arising out of the experiences of African Americans. If lyrics offered no opposition to mainstream society's injustices, they argued, there could be no realness.

From the perspective of some of the so-called party rappers, the street-toughness stance of underground groups is simply an adopted pose. In November 1995, I interviewed Dassen Trio, who use comedy and the regional Kansai dialect in their raps. The trio of rappers hails from Osaka and includes Robo-chu, MC Boo, and King 3K. They argued that lighthearted rap was more appropriate to Japanese teens than the preachy, self-important boasting of underground groups. MC Boo and King 3K expressed doubts about the suitability of the keep-it-real slogan in Japan.

MC Boo: If "keep it real" means "good things should be fun," I think that's OK. Being "real" is fine if you are real (laughs). But we don't want to say things like that.

King 3K: If we said, "keep it real," we'd have no idea which direction to head in to make an album. And to say, "keep it real" in Japan, well—

MC Boo: I think we don't have the kind of personality to do things that way.

King 3K: When overseas rappers say "keep it real," I think I know what they mean. But to say that this is the god of hip-hop, well, it may be cool sometimes, but we can't really say that. To tell the truth, I get a little embarrassed when Japanese rappers say, "Reality!"

They would argue that the measure of being real is whether the lyrics speak to one's audience; therefore, the larger the audience, the more real the music.

It is too simple, of course, to suggest that hip-hop in Japan can be explained by two competing camps, party rap versus underground hip-hop. Factions (*habatsu*) existed within each camp, and all camps followed closely, and shared a musical inspiration from, the latest US underground and commercially successful hip-hop. Nevertheless, the party rap/underground hip-hop dichotomy does serve to highlight alternative orientations in some of the different styles. More lighthearted groups like Dassen Trio, Scha Dara Parr, EDU, and East End X Yuri tended to draw audiences with a greater proportion of young women fans. They were more likely to have major-label contracts and to appear on radio and television. In 1995, East End X Yuri even performed in NHK's year-end musical extravaganza Kohaku Gassen (Battle of Red vs. White). Meanwhile, the underground hip-hop collective Kaminari held to a tougher, more abrasive ethic. They performed to packed clubs, for example, in an event called Anettai Urin (Tropical Rain Forest). When I attended one of these events at club Yellow in Nishiazabu, the sweat-soaked air, virtually all-male audience, and screaming emcees all moved in a zone of abrasive energy. Interestingly, at this time, there were not clear age or class distinctions that determined whether artists tended toward the party or underground ends of the spectrum.

Magazines are also notable for their role in developing the distinctions that came to guide Japanese hip-hop categories. In my discussions with artists, I found they tended to react with distaste to questions of their own style, but for magazine writers, making such distinctions constituted a full-time job. In particular, the hip-hop magazine *Front,* later renamed *Blast,* helped nurture the underground scene. The magazine usually opens with reports from live shows (again, the *genba*) that are then followed by long interviews with American artists, sometimes translated from American interviews (the magazine has a relationship with the US hip-hop and R& B magazine *Vibe),* more often done directly by their staff. In contrast to US hip-hop magazines, *Blast* gives relatively equal coverage to both commercial, mainstream American artists and lesser-known underground US artists. A US hip-hop magazine like the *Source* is more heavily weighted toward commercially successful groups. One of the striking characteristics of hip-hop fans in Japan is their knowledge and understanding of the US underground scene. Groups like Jurassic 5 or emcees 7L and Esoteric toured in Japan, drawing crowds that might not be smaller, at least in Jurassic 5's early days, than the ones they would attract in the United States. Japan's music magazines cover the US underground scene more than some of the leading American hip-hop magazines (the *Source* and *Vibe* especially). This speaks to differences in advertising revenue as well, because the specialty record shops in Tokyo that advertise in *Blast* carry selections from underground artists regularly.

As part of my fieldwork, I attended monthly editorial meetings in Tokyo for *Remix,* a "street and club sounds magazine," from 1996 to 1997. The magazine was published monthly and covered a variety of genres, including hip-hop, techno, house, dance jazz, and rock. The most contentious debates among the editors revolved around which artist or genre to represent on the magazine's cover. Each editor could make a pitch for a particular cover, and in 1996 Japanese rap struggled to make an appearance. DJ Krush, a crossover artist bridging hip-hop and electronica, was a favorite, that is, he was featured on covers when releasing new albums, but rappers themselves seldom appeared. Although questions of who would be advertising in the issue could play a role, the editors and writers felt responsible for vetting the quality of the music with their own ears first. Nevertheless, the group featured on the front cover was, more often than not, also featured in a paid-for advertisement, and few of the rap artists in this middle era received support for expensive magazine ads.

The artists selected for coverage inside the magazine were those with new releases (singles, albums, remixes, etc.) and those performing live that month. In this way, we, can see how magazines focus their attention on clubs and the output of recording studios as well. In other words, *genba* are important because they produce something (a show, a CD) and because this production sets in motion media and fan responses to the performance. The networks themselves are performative, that is, they emerge around hit songs, hit albums, and big stars—just as well as they emerge in the realms of mini-media, word of mouth, underground club events, and amateur contests. Once hip-hop went more pop in Japan, the underground did not disappear. If anything, more groups emerged, and some members of the younger generation emerge with a style more deeply trained in the widening range of hip-hop's history and present.

Families Define Artistic Stakes through Moriagaru

In the midst of the competition between individual groups, so-called families (*famirii*) of rap groups emerged as well, providing a social organization to the scene that helped define evolving artistic stakes. For example, over the years, the Funky Grammar Unit has included Rhymester, East End, Kick the Can Crew (and their precursor groups By Phar the Dopest/ Radical Freaks), Mellow Yellow, Inosence, DJ Kiyo, and others. Little Bird Nation includes Scha Dara Parr, Dassen Trio, Tokyo #1 Soul Set, Kaseki Cider, and others. Zeebra broke off from King Giddra in late 1996 to form Future Shock and led UBG (Urbarian Gym), which included Uzi, Tak the Rhymehead, and later Soul Scream. K Dub Shine began Atomic Bomb Productions, including the talented emcee Dohji-T. The large crews provided support and helped define aesthetic approaches generally shared within families and contrasting with other families' approaches. Occasionally, families collaborated on recordings or live shows, but otherwise, the group affiliations remain somewhat fluid. In general, being in a family means that one supports the others' projects when possible. Families also lend to draw at least some regulars who follow the particular family's events over a period of time. From October 1995 through February 1997, I attended the Kitchens family's events almost every week, first Thursday nights at Grass in Harajuku, then Saturday nights at Rowdy in Roppongi. Kitchens was led by Umedy of EDU and also included Now (later Now Now, a three-woman group), Cake-K, Moon Trap, DJ Etsu, DJ Cool-K, and Climax. In the fall of 1995, Co-Key used to attend the nights at Grass to participate in freestyle sessions, but then he moved on to work with other families. Groups with similar aesthetic tastes tended to gravitate toward each other. In so doing, families would gather energy for their particular aesthetic approaches by attracting a fan base, staying active enough to keep in the news, and working toward recording projects, and, ideally, ever larger recording contracts and performance venues.

If families were battling for attention, how can we understand what it takes to win? A key word for understanding how families build energy in the scene through club events is the term *moriagaru*. When the audience gets hyped, excited, energized, that's *moriagaru*. The term suggests a piling on (*mori*) and rising up (*agaru*) of energy and emotion. It describes the energy in the audience when a show is going well. When families hold successful events, the experience of *moriagaru* can make a lasting impression on audience members. Contrary to the idea that musical taste is all subjective, when a club act falls flat, everyone in the audience and onstage can feel it. Even if you do not appreciate a particular genre of music, or even if you do not understand the language of the performers, I would argue that you would be able to recognize, literally feel on your skin, whether a show is going well or falling flat. In this sense, the battles between groups and between families are waged in the *genba* with *moriagaru* as the prize. This *genba* realization echoes a recent manifesto from several key cultural studies scholars who call for more attention to be paid to "culture that sticks to your skin" (Jenkins, McPherson, and Shattuc 2002). Their vision of the political recognizes that "any viable politics must begin in the spaces people already inhabit" (22). In this they encourage a study of hip-hop in Japan, not as recorded texts but in terms of sweat, pulsating beats through giant speakers, and the pendulum swing between fan adoration and fan skepticism.

Thus families in effect organize groups of fans as well, hardening people's notion of what they do and do not like in hip-hop music. In the late 1980s, many second-generation groups— Rhymester, Scha Dara Parr, You the Rock—would compete against one another in late-night contests. By 1997, each of these groups had developed its own fan following, its own family of like-minded groups. Groups seldom performed with different families, but rather held their own regular or semi-regular events. In a sense, each family was working to define a certain approach to answering the questions, "What is *Japanese* hip-hop? How can we make this our thing?" The underground–party divide seemed at the time a potent struggle for the soul of hip-hop in Japan. Would it go the commercial J-pop route? Or would audiences in Japan awaken to the street-battle ideologies of underground hip-hop, even if it was less suitable to television and karaoke?

Rhymester's "B-Boyism" as a Watershed

One of the elements in the debate over making hip-hop Japanese involved developing a new language that would express both a Japanese and a hip-hop sensibility. If we look at

Rhymester's efforts of the mid-to late 1990s to develop Japanese catch-phrases, we can see a notable example of the shifts in aesthetics. In songs like "Mimi o kasu beki" ("You Better Listen Up"), released in 1996, one can hear Rhymester's knack for hooks that encapsulate a generation's yearnings. The rapper Mummy-D focuses on the importance of practice—"washing dishes" for little money, that is, practicing as a DJ (because "plates" is a pun on "vinyl records")—in order to hone one's skills. The group's other emcee, Utamaru, challenges young people to find something they believe in or risk becoming losers in life's game. Above all, they say the people who should "listen up" are the older generation who blithely comment on youth's shortcomings while failing to understand their aspirations.

In 1998, Rhymester created an anthem to Japanese hip-hop ideals. Released that year as a single (and in 1999 on the album *Respect*), the song took its name, "B-Boyism," from Utamaru's monthly column in *Front* magazine. The column reflected on the connections among old movies, old toys, old games, a traditional storytelling performance called *rakugo* which became materials for meditating on the links between hip-hop ideals and aspects of Japan's popular heritage. In Utamaru's worldview, hip-hop made perfect sense. He did not belabor the stark difference between the reality of the streets in US hip-hop and its supposed absence in Japanese youth culture. Rather, he focused on B movies, underground fads, and forgotten individualists (from Japan) who characterized a b-boy ethic even before the term *b-boy* was known.

Rhymester brought together many of these themes in the song "B-Boyism." To set up the chorus in one part of the song, Utamaru asks his fellow rapper Mummy-D to "define the 'B' in "B-Boy."

> I'm not surrendering this aesthetic *keshite yuzurenai ze kono bigaku*
> Flattering no one, I improve myself *nanimono ni mo kobizu onore o migaku*
> only the wonderful, useless people *subarshiki roku de nashi tachi dake ni*
> get it, and roar, at the edge of the bass *todoku todoroku beesu no hate ni*
> —Rhymester (1999) "B-Boyism" *Respect*
> (Next Level/File Records, Japan, NLCD-026)

The lyrics use dense rhyming to emphasize the personal ethic of improving oneself ("onore o migaku") by holding fast to "my aesthetic" ("ore no bigaku"). There is also a double meaning in the *B* of *b-boy* and the identically pronounced *bi* (beauty) of *bigaku* (aesthetics, literally, the "study of beauty"), such that beauty and the *B* of *b-boy* become one and the same in the song's universe. Yet the rootedness of Rhymester's aesthetic lies less in the serendipitous homonyms of Japanese and English than in the group's fans. As Utamaru explained in a personal communication to me in 2001, Japan's b-boys are "wonderful" (*subarashiki*) and "useless" in the sense of not pursuing society's arbitrary goals, focusing instead on finding their own way. In one part of the song, Utamaru likens the toughness of Japan's b-boys to Barefoot Gen (Hadashi no Gen). A child character in the comic book by the same name, Gen survives the bombing of Hiroshima, but must struggle to get by emotionally and physically after watching his mother die in the flames of their crushed home. The idea that hip-hop in Japan produces a kind of Americanization fits uneasily with the particulars of many lyrics. Viewing the song "B-Boyism" as a performative event shows how cultural flows are actualized at specific moments in the development of the scene.

Rhymester's "B-Boyism" music video brought Japan's hip-hop scene full circle. Rhymester hired Rock Steady Crew Japan to battle on a linoleum mat set out in front of the stage in Yoyogi Park. The videotaping was advertised as a block party on flyers handed out at club events. A veritable who's who of Japanese hip-hop showed up for their cameos, including Zeebra, K Dub Shine, Kreva, MC U, Gaku, Uzi, and numerous others. Crazy-A himself danced for the video in the park where breakdancing in Japan began a decade and a half before. Although Rhymester says they never intended the song to become a watershed in Japan's scene, looking back on the moment brings with it a certain feeling of nostalgia. At that time, groups associated with Kaminari argued that Japan's hip-hop scene should aim for a harder edge. Scha Dara Parr and the groups associated with Little Bird Nation focused on wordplay and more ludic criticisms of Japanese society. Regardless of the particular stance, there was a sense that everyone was focused on "the scene." In contrast to the first era, when people questioned what hip-hop was, the second era was characterized by a shared debate, though not shared understandings, about the proper basis of the scene.

Before turning to these developments, let us consider a back story of hip-hop with regard to battles among Japanese hip-hoppers, namely, conflicts over sampling and copyright. Given that a key crossover hit in the United States, Run-DMC's "Walk This Way," brought rap to rock audiences by sampling a hit Aerosmith song, one wonders why similar big sample (ōneta) songs did not appear in Japan. Why did not any Japanese artists sample famous Japanese pop songs to try for a crossover? The answer lies in copyright laws and practices, market size, and particular histories in the US and Japanese hip-hop scenes.

Sampling and Copyright in the United States and Japan

In hip-hop, one of the striking features of the ideologies of artistic creativity is the sharp divergence between rappers and DJs. If you are a rapper, the idea is that you must express something about yourself in your own words, with your own rhymes and flow. In contrast, the track-makers generally create the music using samples from other people's recordings. Here, personal expression is not virtuosic performance, but rather programming the mix. Of course, borrowing styles from other artists is nothing new in music history. What is different about the current hip-hop moment is that incorporation is done directly from already recorded material through digital sampling and DJ scratch solos. This entails consequences regarding originality and ownership in music that deserve a brief exploration.

A difference between the United States and Japan in the ways samples are used points to a gray area of intellectual property in digital-age musical production. In the United States, rap songs that sample well-known songs arguably have been very influential in creating crossover hits that eventually helped move hip-hop from underground into the mainstream. Run-DMC used Aerosmith's "Walk This Way," Public Enemy used all sorts of James Brown material, A Tribe Called Quest used Lou Reed's "Walk on the Wild Side," Jay-Z sampled from the Broadway show *Annie* the tune "It's a Hard Knock Life," and so on. Yet sampling practices developed unevenly, as we can see from several key moments in US hip-hop history (Baran 2002). In 1992, the rapper Biz Markie used a Gilbert O'Sullivan sample, "Alone Again (Naturally)." Biz Markie's record company had been unable to clear the sample (i.e., pay for permission to use it), but released the album anyway. The company was sued, lost the court case, and was forced to remove the records from store shelves and then deliver them to O'Sullivan's representatives to be destroyed. This event is often credited with a shift in the United States to more conscientious efforts to clear recognizable musical samples and led to the establishment of clearance warehouses, businesses who manage the payments between record companies. One legal case involving sampling even made it to the US Supreme Court. The raunchy, Miami-based 2 Live Crew sampled without permission Roy Orbison's "Pretty Woman," over which they rapped "Big Fat Hairy Woman." The Supreme Court ruled that because the new version was a parody, the use of the sample was permitted under the copyright law's fair-use provision. An overview of some of these musical copyright wars is available through the online exhibition illegal-art.org, which also makes many of the songs available for download.

More recently, a public debate occurred surrounding DJ Danger Mouse's *Grey Album,* a remix album of 2004 that used the a cappella vocals from Jay-Z's *The Black Album* (2003), remixed with samples from the Beatles' *White Album* (1968). Since the Beatles' copyright holder EMI never permits the sampling of Beatles' songs, Danger Mouse's album became a symbol of how copyright laws were limiting the kind of artistic creativity that new technologies make possible. How much control should original artists (or, more accurately, the companies that manage the downstream monetization of intellectual property) have in determining what kinds of artistic production can and cannot occur? Some might argue that stealing the talent of the Beatles to piggyback on their celebrity cannot be condoned, but what about the (sometimes unknown) African American artists whose songs, such as "Money (That's What I Want)," were covered by the Beatles and formed the basis of some of their early works? Does that not constitute a similar kind of borrowing, drawing on cultural heritage to make something new? Clearly, we are witnessing an evolving interplay between ethics and law that as yet is not fully resolved (Schloss 2004).

In Japan, there are far fewer examples of musicians using famous song samples. Why the difference? In the mid- to late 1990s, gossip about a scandal involving Sony was commonly cited by musicians and record-company representatives as the main reason why Japanese hip-hoppers do not sample famous songs. In one recording studio session I observed, a musician brought a demo tape with some new songs. He asked the record-company director whether they might be included on the compilation that the company was producing. The director said no, giving the example of "Da.Yo.Ne." as a reason. End of discussion. As it turned out, it was because the demo-tape songs were too obvious about the origins of the music sampled. Later, when I asked the musician about the exchange, he was reluctant to talk about it because it was gossip and also made Sony look bad. As he put it, "I'll tell you, but this is from 'Mr. X,' OK?"

The story goes like this. Like most rap songs, East End X Yuri's single "Da.Yo.Ne." included a sample from recorded material, in this case a song by George Benson. As the song began climbing the charts, George Benson happened to be in Tokyo for a show at the Blue Note. Apparently, he was riding in a taxi with his manager when they heard "Da.Yo.Ne." on the radio. Benson turned to his manager, asked if they had some deal going on in Japan, to which the manager replied no. And so one thing lead to another. Epic/Sony, which released the single, allegedly ended up paying Benson around $100,000 (¥1.5 million at exchange rates then). It was even rumored that someone at Sony was fired for the mistake. (Another musician later commented that although the payment was likely ten times higher than the normal fee had the sample been cleared, the song was such a hit that Sony still made plenty of money.) As a result, most record companies became very circumspect about the samples they used, requiring artists to change samples if they were famous or recognizable. This also discouraged the use of Japanese samples because they would be more readily caught.

This event highlights part of the relationship between sampling and popularity. Sampling is OK, if no one, at least no one who might sue, hears it. It is noteworthy too, however, that it is not actual lawsuits or court cases that circulate as defining rumors regarding sampling in Japan. Instead, the standard procedure appears to be negotiation and settlement between record companies. Record companies have little incentive for going after small fish-indie labels, mixtape DJs, and so on—but rather attend to releases of those with deep pockets. While artists at the lowest echelons are safest, and those at the upper echelons can get company support to pay for samples, the greatest risk in using sampling arises for those in the middle.

The magazine writer Innami Atsushi found himself challenged by the rapper ECD, however, for participating in a book that revealed the origins of different samples in a variety of Japanese songs (Murata 1997). Innami said he initially questioned the project, but was incensed when the publisher accused everyone in hip-hop of wanting to hide something. After the book's publication ECD attacked Innami for his naïveté:

> We [the musicians] are the one's taking the risk. If word gets out that sampling is going on, it's dangerous. But it's part of hip-hop as an art form. If a sample is found out, and money taken, I'm telling you that's like a train wreck. Given that's the case, I think what you did was like putting a rock on the track. … It's not that we've decided to hide something. We're the ones taking the risk, so I wonder how much cowardice is involved when you're talking about a risk someone takes to do business. If some problems arose because of that book, they [the publishers] wouldn't be taking any responsibility. The only people who would lose would be us. … Since the substance of hip-hop itself is illegal, I can't think of what you did as anything other than a betrayal.
>
> (ECD 1997, 63)

ECD recognized that sampling is technically illegal, but asserted that the style of musical production is also the substance of hip-hop. He is willing to take the risk. Besides, it takes a certain kind of skill and knowledge to recognize obscure musical samples. A published book fed a desire on the part of many hip-hop artists and fans, though perhaps especially of DJs, to see which rare grooves were plundered for the melodies and beats, but such a book also made it easy for music publishers to put pressure on record companies to clear samples.

As the market for Japanese hip-hop has grown, groups and their record companies are clearing samples on a more regular basis. For his song "Lonely Girl," ECD, who above defended the illegality of sampling as part of hip-hop, presumably cleared the prominent sample of Marvin Gaye's "Sexual Healing." When Rhymester recorded the song "Uwasa no shinsō" (Truth behind the rumors), they produced two versions. One track featured synthesized horns playing Cream's "Sunshine of My Life," while a second version used a different track. It was only days before the CD went into production that Rhymester's A & R director Okada Makiko was able to clear the sample through a personal contact who spoke directly to Eric Clapton. Major-label record companies sometimes use live bands to reproduce the sound of the sample to avoid directly sampling and to shield themselves from legal challenge. In one case I learned that an American track-maker hired to make a song for a Japanese hip-hop artist actually used a sample from a Japanese pop artist, Matsuda Seiko. Since the major label had also produced the Matsuda track years before, it was a simple, internal process to clear the sample. What becomes clear is that there is no simple rule of thumb for determining what samples can and cannot be used. Indeed, when I asked a record-company rep about trying to get some Japanese hip-hop sold through the US iTunes Music Store, he answered that the potential increase in sales would not be worth the danger of having sampled songs discovered. He used the phrase *yabuhebi,* basically meaning, "don't wake the snake sleeping in the bush." It turns out that "the more popular, the better" is not true of all music, at least when sampling is involved.

The battles involving sampling and copyright point to a gray area in recording-studio practices. In terms of the law, there is no gray area; every sampled sound should be cleared. In practice, however, the calculus of risk depends on a wide variety of factors, such as the fame of the sample, its ownership, the likelihood of the record company being sued, and so on. Because the market for Japanese hip-hop, with few exceptions, stayed relatively small until the late 1990s, there was not enough income from hip-hop albums to justify the expense and trouble of clearing samples. The common philosophy in the studios was simply, don't ask, don't tell. It may be that an era of mainstream samples will yet appear in Japanese hip-hop, and indeed, we are already beginning to see some examples. But the fact that songs with cross-over samples, such as Run-DMC's "Walk This Way," have not become prime movers in the history of hip-hop in Japan serves as a reminder that different legal, business, and cultural settings produce alternative histories of genres and that the American experience is not reproduced in every respect overseas.

The Third Era: Widening Diversity, No Center

Although one cannot point to the song "B-Boyism" as the cause of a shift in Japan's hip-hop scene, at least one can note that the idea of a single hip-hop scene has disappeared in the first years of the twenty-first century. Instead, we see scenes among scenes that the party-underground divide can no longer come close to capturing. We find a broad spectrum including rock rap to hard core to gangsta, spoken word/poetry, to conscious, old school, techno rap, antigovernment, pro-marijuana, heavy metal-sampled rap, and so on. Alongside the widening diversity within the hip-hop scene, we also see the disappearance of any orientation toward a center. In the years that followed the release of the song "B-Boyism," regional scenes became more active in Nagoya, Osaka, Sapporo, and Okinawa. For example, Yokohama rappers, living only a half hour from Tokyo, became more aggressive in asserting their "045" (area code) style. Diversity without a center became the order of the clay. The era in which underground hip-hoppers debated with party rappers has given way to more personal conflicts between rappers. These conflicts gesture toward ideas of what hip-hop should be about, but the question of what makes hip-hop *Japanese* seems but a shining artifact of the past.

Among the key developments was the arrival of more popular rap groups such as M-Flo, who entered the mainstream market without passing through years of performances in clubs. The rock band Dragon Ash started rapping, included a DJ, and sang a song called "I Love Hip-Hop" (1999), but was it hip-hop? Few commentators seemed overly excited about trying to police the boundaries, certainly not in the way that East End X Yuri's songs provoked. Meanwhile, underground rappers such as Zeebra broke into mainstream consciousness in part by teaming up with Japanese R & B singers like Sugar Soul and Utada Hikaru. Such widening heterogeneity did not eliminate the importance of the *genba,* but many rappers reported that the clubs were no longer the only places people could learn about hip-hop. Club imagery was appearing in television dramas, thus mainstreaming the club experience. It also became easier to find Japanese rap in record stores and karaoke establishments. Zeebra and Rhymester began making music videos. As DJ Jin of Rhymester put it during a conversation at Club Web in June 1999, "What's different today is that when I say to old grandma-types [*obaasantachi*] that I'm a DJ, they nod and say, 'Oh yeah, l know what that is.'" Intriguingly, the mainstreaming of hip-hop as a recognizable Japanese style also entailed an increasingly niche orientation, with different families of groups attracting distinct types of fans.

In addition, different regions of Japan are producing their own scenes, some of them led to some extent by dominant groups, but even here the notion of a leader seems out of date. A duo called Tha Blue Herb (MC Boss and DJ Ono) put Sapporo on the hip-hop map, particularly because of Boss's poetic lyrics. He is also notable for his general indifference to making his lines rhyme. Nor does he add stress accents to make his lyrics sound English in their rhythmic flow. But newcomers like Mic Jack Production and Shuren the Fire, also from the capital city of Japan's northernmost island, illustrate that there is no single Sapporo style. In the mid-1990s, it seemed unlikely that Japanese rappers would brag about doing cocaine, but after the turn of the millennium, Nagoya rappers M.O.S.A.D. produced several songs depicting their love of white lines. Tokona-X, the lead emcee with M.O.S.A.D., died at a young age, and many in the scene suspect that drugs were involved. Meanwhile, Ozrosaurus represents for Yokohama, Gagle for Sendai (in northeast Japan), Gaki Ranger for Kumamoto (on the island of Kyushu). Even Tokyo rappers now talk about what area of Tokyo they represent. K Dub Shine sees himself as the "Don of Shibuya," while a female rapper named Hime represents for Hachioji. Chiba, a bedroom suburb that is generally looked down on as a second-tier industrial zone, now boasts its own rappers who pride themselves on the "big-hair-smelling-of-shampoo funk" that the group Chiba Craziest Channel provides, a reference to the yankee (i.e., biker bad boy) love of big hair.

At the same time, some rap groups have catapulted into mainstream, pop-music-world success. Ketsumeishi, Kick the Can Crew, Rip Slyme, and M-Flo all count themselves as rap groups, yet their primary competition comes from other pop groups rather than from others within the hip-hop scene. Meanwhile, the underground scene continues to try various approaches to develop its own, competing standards of value. For example, the Tokyo-based group Suika performs with a live band and produces lyrics that cross over with the spoken word/poetry slam scene developing in Tokyo. In this sense, battling hip-hop samurai evoke different reference points to locate themselves and defend their personal aesthetics.

The widening use of samurai imagery with swords on album covers and in music videos proceeds in tandem with the increased use of gangsta imagery with guns. Pop rap, conscious rap, Korean Japanese rap, *burakumin* rap—all slide fluidly past one another rather than combining into a single, overarching Japanese scene. When the writer Innami Atsushi contributed a monthly column called "Represent Nippon" to the magazine *Black Music Review,* he referred to what now seems a distinct era when writers and rappers sought to lay claim to the Japaneseness of hip-hop for their own ends. One of the more intriguing recent examples of hip-hop samurai involves an anime television series called *Samurai Champloo.* The director, Watanabe Shin'ichirō, also made *Cowboy Bebop,* a TV series (1998) and film (2001) about futuristic bounty hunters that features jazz and blues artists from Japan. *Samurai Champloo,* a twenty-six-episode series, mixes a Tokugawa-era samurai story with hip-hop music by the Japanese artists Nujabes, along with DJ Tsutchie, Force of Nature, and the American expat artist Fat Jon. In a March 2005 interview, Watanabe pointed to the concept of representing to demonstrate that hip-hop complies perfectly with certain aspects of the samurai warrior ethic: "Nowadays, people think of the Japanese as reserved, shy, unable or unwilling to express their individuality, but in the past, samurai understood the importance of representing who they were. They devoted themselves to battling through their skills." The weekly, half-hour series, which aired from the summer of 2004 to March 2005, explored cultural remixing within Japan. Even the title uses the Okinawan word for stew, *champloo,* to refer to a mixing of everything to see what comes out. Different episodes explored discrimination against Christians, foreigners, Ainu peoples, and so on in ways that ultimately questioned the oneness of the Japanese people. Again, identity emerges from battling, not from some primordial essence; in this, Watanabe may be onto something. If Japaneseness is not something timeless, or something encoded in one's genes, then performances that represent Japan through hip-hop are not paradoxical at all. Rather, performance becomes a way of understanding identity in its location, among specific audiences, and occurring at specific historical junctures.

Conclusion

The image of battling hip-hop samurai highlights the processes of competition that drove the development of hip-hop in Japan. Hip-hoppers are samurai in the sense that they draw on histories, language, their own lives, and the setting of Japan not primarily to make the music local in a way that combats global homogenization, but rather to make it original, interesting, and noteworthy—both to their fans and to the record companies seeking new talent. It is struggles between factions, and the ways these factional battles changed over time, that give the clearest sense of how abstract global ideals become enacted in Japan. Yet the history of hip-hop in Japan also shows that the sense of what ideals drive hip-hop also changes over time. The uncertainty about what hip-hop meant in the early days due to a lack of information and understanding has been transformed today into an uncertainty about what hip-hop means because there are so many examples to consider. In this way, widening battles, diversifying scenes, and far-flung regional developments point to processes that suggest a way of thinking beyond localization or domestication.

Part of the challenge of understanding cultural globalization involves recognizing that the global and the local are not so much matched pairs as they are symbolic crystallizations of more fluid, ongoing processes unfolding over time. Does the spread of such popular culture forms ultimately produce cultural homogenization or increasing diversity? Evidence can be amassed to support either claims of global convergence or of local diversity, yet I doubt that we can ever establish, once and for all, a scale of analysis that can legitimately give one interpretation priority over the other. What seems most likely is that we are witnessing both convergence and divergence, albeit in different dimensions and with contradictory effects. The idea of *genba*—actual sites of performance—helps us see how the global is refracted through particular actors and contexts, but what we can also see from the example of the samurai is that the local, too, is refracted through performance. Samurai do not stand for any single Japaneseness, and in this they accurately represent hip-hop and its battles.

Study Questions

1. How do Japanese MCs compete for authority in hip hop culture in Japan?
2. How does Condry use the typology of the battling hip hop samurai to explore the role of Japanese culture in hip hop?
3. What role do sites of performance play in examining the interactions and exchange between the "symbolic crystallizations" of the global and local in Japanese hip hop?

Notes

* Due to copyright permissions, photos have been excluded from this chapter.

1. See Kick the Can Crew, "Mikoshi Rockers (feat. Rhymester)," on *Vitalizer* (Warner Music Japan, 2002, HDCA-10084).
2. The character of the battles in Japan unfolds in *genba* that contrast in diverse ways with hip-hop in other countries. See for comparison a growing number of studies examining hip-hop in other countries (Durand 2002; Fernandes 2003; Japan-Foundation 2005; Maxwell 2003; Mitchell 2001a; Mitchell 2001b; Perullo and Fenn 2003; Prevos 1996; Urla 2001; Weiss 2002).
3. Yamada Yōji gained fame for his Tora-san series of films. *Twilight Samurai* revolves around a group of samurai who tally the substantial holdings of their regional lord. These samurai entertain

themselves with geisha at night and ridicule a fellow samurai they call "Twilight" because, as a poor widower, he must go home at dusk to care for his young daughters. Meanwhile, the townspeople are struggling through poverty and famine. In one of the film's most affecting motifs, dead children float by on the river. When their bodies get caught on the reeds by the riverbank, farmers matter-of-factly push them along. Thus we see the limits of assertions of a singular way of the samurai.

4. This narrative draws heavily on Hosokawa, Matsumura, and Shiba 1991.

5. What is Western? What is Japanese? Kawabata (1991) states, "The current standard for classifying *hōban* [Japanese records] and *yōban* [Western records] is three-fold: first the nationality of the original record; second, the performers' nationality; and third, the language of the song's lyrics. There is really no strict distinction." It is worth noting that the distinction between domestic and import is determined by where the CD is manufactured, not by the nationality of the artist or group. Most so-called Western music sold in Japan is *kokuban* (pressed in Japan). This domestic press usually includes a bonus track and translations of the lyrics and liner notes into Japanese, but costs about twice as much as an import ($25–30 for the domestic press versus $15 for an import). One would imagine sharp competition, but imports are seldom available except at the enormous Tokyo retailers like Tower Records, HMV, and Wave. The rapid growth of the mail-order business of record and CD sales in the 1990s may mean more listeners are benefiting from the import prices.

6. One could argue that language differences, a relatively closed media market in the United States, and the sheer dominance of American popular culture globally precludes Americans from wide experimentation with foreign popular culture, but none of that explains why manga and anime have managed to become major business in the United States, while Japanese music has not. There are already some important studies of Japanese popular culture success outside of Japan (Allison 2003; Belson and Bremner 2004; Iwabuchi 2002; Tobin 2004), but the question of the slow flow of J-pop music to the United States is a subject for another project.

7. As Cornel West (2004, 22) says, globalization is inescapable; the question is whether it will be an American-led corporate globalization or a democratic globalization. The answer, of course, is that globalization is and will be both corporate led and potentially democratic. This points us toward what is perhaps the more important question, namely, what kinds of social structures and motivations can drive democratic globalization? What kinds of organizing principles besides corporate capitalism can encourage transnational cultural movements? The early years of hip-hop in Japan offer some lessons.

8. A video of *Wild Style* with Japanese subtitles was rereleased in September 1996 through the record company Vortex (MLK-001). It also had a brief run as a midnight show at the Parco Department store in Shibuya around the same time.

9. In the winter of 1997, live bands were banned from playing at Hokoten. However, the area continues to provide a gathering place for fan groups, but there are fewer musicians than in the past. The so-called rock 'n' rollers still come every Sunday wearing jeans, leather jackets, and boots, and sporting greased-back Elvis hairdos, to do a kind of twist to American rock of the 1950s and 1960s. Female fans of various bands also gather nearby and engage in costume play (*kosu pure*) wearing lacy bridal-style gowns (white, black, or red), black lipstick and eye makeup, and colored, tormented hair. We see here the links between street-parade fashion (as *genba*) and street stages (as *genba* as well).

10. Ozawa Kenji, "Kon'ya wa boogie back feat. Scha Dara Parr" on *Life* (Toshiba-EMI, 1994, TOCT-8495).

11. Both songs appear on the album East End X Yuri, *Denim-ed Soul II* (Epic/Sony, 1995 ESCB-1590).

25

Western Style, Chinese Pop
Jay Chou's Rap and Hip-Hop in China

Based on ethnographic data drawn from fans, fan clubs, and performances, this essay discusses the career of Chinese singer Jay Chou (Zhou Jielun), and considers the cultural strategies of his quick and impressive commercial sweep of authoritarian China. Fung argues Jay Chou's style, image, and personae drawn against historical backdrop of China–Taiwan tensions over independence and the structural realities and political expectations of popular culture account for much of his success. Jay Chou's mode of popular expression—"Western-Style, Chinese-Pop"—is able to cut across geopolitical space, transgress barriers, and strategically market products. Fung explores Chou's ability to please local and national cultural demands through his products, and suggests this speaks in some ways to evolving ideological positions in China. Fung concludes that, despite popular opinion, and strict control, "foreign cultural forms" such as hip hop are not "unacceptable" in China. In fact, the use and incorporation of such western styles are encouraged so long as they "help" the state and maintain elements of traditional Chinese culture. Thus, such Sino-Western cultural products express both dissent within society as a form of compromised confrontation, a strategic globalized use of Western products, as well as celebration of the very society and culture from within which its contestation takes place.

Western Style, Chinese Pop: Jay Chou's Rap and Hip-Hop in China*

Anthony Y. H. Fung

Jay Chou or in Chinese Zhou Jielun, is undeniably the most popular Chinese singer in a number of Chinese communities. His glittering career is reflected by his record sales and by the popularity of his concerts. In 2004, his album *Qilixiang,* or *Jasmine,* released by Sony Music, excelled in Taiwan, Hong Kong, and the People's Republic of China (PRC). Despite overwhelming piracy in Taiwan—which has reduced the recording industry to 5 to 10 percent from its heyday—as a Taiwan singer, Jay produced an album that sold a record 300,000 copies. In Hong Kong, his album surpassed local albums with sales of 50,000 units. In China the official figure reached 2.6 million units, a stunning figure that no other Chinese artist has attained. In 2005, his album *Chopin of November* continued this record of success with sales of 2.5 million units in Asia. His charismatic vigor, avant-garde image, and mercantile potential are not only recognized in Chinese societies; the World Music Awards in September 2004 held in Las Vegas acknowledged him, based on his high record sales, as the most popular Chinese singer.

The significance of the Jay Chou story lies in its implications as a successful marketing model for China and beyond to the larger Asia market. Why would a Taiwan-born 25-year-old singer—without flaunting a connection to China or the West—culturally and commercially sweep China with his style, persona, and image and do so while China is actively agonizing over the Taiwanese independence issue? What kind of cultural strategies did Jay Chou embrace to surmount the various political, economic, and cultural constraints involved in the Chinese market? Illustrating how Jay Chou navigates these structural limits and the political agenda of popular culture is valuable. Theorizing a framework for how popular culture cuts across geopolitical spaces and surmounts cultural barriers is not only beneficial for marketing of other culture products, but also sheds light on the ideologies of evolving Chinese popular culture.

This paper thus illustrates how Jay Chou's music production has wittingly strategized to construct images and products that can be both locally and nationally assimilated into Chinese culture and nationally accepted as a "prototype" product—a product whose political standard has been authoritatively acknowledged by the state. The study is based on three years of ethnographic study of Jay's fans, fan clubs, and performance in China, as well as on in-depth interviews with the various production agents and media in different Chinese cities. In this paper I describe, from the production side, Jay Chou as an icon and his image-making and marketing strategies. From the audience's point of view, I explore how Jay Chou has been reconstituted from being a "foreign" singer (in the eyes of the PRC) into a Chinese artist.

Strategic Cultural Production

The study of popular music and stardom can be quite murky and some even see it as trivial. Popular Culture is often conceived as the culture of the common people or mass culture functioning only to entertain and lacking in seriousness vis-à-vis critical and political implications in relation to the state and civic society (Modleski 1986). However, contemporary cultural studies (Storey 2003, Cullen 2000) have demonstrated that societies have consistently invented popular culture that reflects not only ideologies of the day, but also in effect manufactures, manipulates, and distorts popular culture politically as a source of nationalism, socially as a representation of daily life, economically as a product of transnational corporations, and through the forces of the political economy of globalization.

As for popular music, melody, rhythm, beat, harmony, lyrics, and timbre are not simply creating form and aesthetic. Each of these elements are actually embedded with a semiotics of meaning that can create a sense of community, crystallize imaginary identities, and create sentimental adventures for the audience (McClary and Walser 1990). While all these reinforcing, complementary or contradictory realms are worth unpacking, understanding these elements in relation to political, economic, and cultural contexts is even more important. Thus, rather than just deconstructing complex musical art forms per se, this paper considers popular music production in relation to the demands of the state.

Popular Culture, Market, and State

The development of any cultural forms—including the popular music of Jay Chou—in a particular cultural setting is closely tied to its relations to the nation-state and market (Caporaso and Levine 1992). For most Western democratic states, under capitalism, the primary consideration for cultural production rests on how the supply and demand will determine the market and yield a maximum profit. Market demands naturally screen popular culture. The state's role in such capitalistic systems is therefore minimal in that it only sets economic policy, or perhaps implements a fair environment for players to operate. However, in many of the closed states, which have a vigilant eye on foreign cultures, compatibility between the ideology of popular culture with the national ideology seems the key to success. Under the nationalistic imperative of closed states, the authorities institutionalize their ideology in practices that dictate the economy and sometimes ignore market demand (Frey 1984). This may well be the case with the PRC: despite the people's desire to consume western goods and the fact that the foreign investment that accompanies this consumption may also benefit the economy, the state would rather defend its ideological agenda than allow alternative and liberal values to infiltrate society. Thus, popular music that is allowed to operate in China first has to meet the regime's political agenda before it is circulated to the public. Jay Chou's and other foreign pop stars' success in marketing in China is possible only after the PRC evaluates the potential impact of popular music and a star's image on its people, considering the revolutionary power and the possibility of popular culture being used to westernize, globalize, and pervert China in some way.

What should be emphasized here is that the leadership of the PRC is not just passively filtering the inflow of foreign popular culture. To fine-tune popular culture they exercise power through different regulations and political censorship and by using rewards or economic sanctions and co-option. Popular culture in modern China, as we have already seen, plays a crucial role in the political formation of the state. For example, Chang-Tai Hung (1996) found that popular culture in China played a major role in galvanizing public support for the

Sino-Japanese war in 1937–1945, and, for the Communists, popular culture was refashioned into a socialist propaganda instrument creating lively symbols of peasant heroes and joyful images of village life under their rule. I also found (2003) that Andy Lau's entry to mother-land China required him to morph into a pan-Chinese icon that was politically acceptable in China. For the PRC, the economic viability of any popular star is always secondary to issues of political stability.

On the other hand, even under the looming presence of political control, corporations should not only be regarded as passive agents bowing to state interests. Transnational corporations, as always, behave and function with a calculative and capitalistic agenda. For these corporations, the solution to the "China challenge" is to self-adjust and conform, to a degree, with the requirements of state ideology. Such corporations must devise an optimal marketing strategy so that their product minimizes potential antagonism with the national culture.

The Cool Youth Icon

To understand how Jay's marketing strategy works, it is essential first to understand the meaning of Jay as an icon. Jay displays quite a complex and paradoxical image for the new "GenY" generation, a group which consumes cultural products, brandnames, and current styles to highlight their unique identity yet continues to need approval from society, parents, and teachers. However, ironically, this "cool" generation is in fact passionate and strong-willed at heart; they value relationships with friends and want to be trusted by parents. But psychologically they desperately need a space of their own to escape parental control and supervision (Fung 2004). Jay provides an image this generation can identify with in their struggle for identity. Often wearing a cap and lowering his head, Jay seemingly possesses a shy, quiet, and introverted character and appears unduly reticent about his own ideas and opinions. Like other successful stars, Jay's songs are full of romance, as in *Shiny Stars* (2000) and *Simply Love* (2001). But, on the one hand, Jay's songs are utterly representative of youth defiance, insolence, and non-compliance. For example, in *Second Class of Year 3* (2003), Jay sings:

> How strong is the champion?
> How many stages I have to go through?
> Can't I let go this award?
> I want to be my own judge
> (lyrics by Feng Wenshan)

In this song, a youngster faces enormous pressure in the competitive environment of public examinations, sports, and even games in Chinese society. The song talks about the young generation's reluctance to fulfill the expectations of the adults who want them to win awards and become champions. This is described as the "void of pride." In another song *Bullfight*, Jay also expresses the kind of dissatisfaction and anger that youth feel. While in the chorus of another song, *In the Name of Father* (2003), Jay sings:

> The Merciful Father, I have already fallen in the abyss of sin.
> Please forgive my obstinacy
> That designates my loneliness,
> (lyrics by Wang Junliang)

As expressed in this song, the cool generation knows that their stubbornness and refusal to abide by rules or traditions will naturally result in their rejection and hence their loneliness. What they call for is not a direct and sturdy resistance and challenge to adulthood, but merely the forgiveness of their "merciful father" or parents for their independent actions.

This last song also hints, on the other hand, to young people's hidden desire to maintain relationships with parents and develop intimacy in friendships. Consumption of popular products, including Jay Chou, is an avenue for the cool generation to crystallize their peer network—a phenomenon also seen in the West (Skelton and Valentine 1997). In a study about the relationship between cool culture and cell phone branding in China, Jing Wang (2005) a researcher and marketer at the Beijing office of a transnational advertising agency, demonstrated that music as entertainment serves to maintain the social and interpersonal network for cool youth in China. Thus, the cool generation embraces new technologies and fashion, not only because psychologically they are curious, creative, and independent, but also because they need to build communities around these products with their peers.

On the whole, Jay's persona serves as a model of this cool image, not being remote enough to alienate parents outright, but distinct enough to appear independent and defiant to young people. This cool image has captured the attention of international corporations who aspire to market their products in China to the new generation. For example, Pepsi uses Jay as their spokesperson in the Chinese market. Both Pepsi and Jay symbolize the desires and individualistic pursuits of this new generation. For the audience, the consumption of such products also enhances the formation of their own communities across China, especially in the form of fan clubs (for example see jaycn.com and jay family, which are Jay's two biggest fan clubs in China).

Syncretization of Western Style

Given his huge popularity among the new generation, the question remains: why would the authorities continue to allow this semi-foreign, Taiwan-born artist to be a popular icon capable of swaying an entire generation? As mentioned earlier, the Chinese authorities prioritize political concern over economic consideration when they make relevant cultural policy. Jay, therefore, must culturally and politically fit into the agenda for the country. His success lies in his capacity to sublimate himself into an icon of Chineseness while maintaining his popular and commercial facade, i.e., his cool image. Paradoxically, his most popular songs trigger the audience's emotions in a celebration of Chinese tradition and values, including conscientiousness, tolerance, and reservedness. His Chineseness can be explicated on two levels.

First, as a cultural icon he sells his cool image in concerts or on MTV. He performs in a rhythm and blues style, but within this western form, he has inserted Chinese melodies, themes, and rhythms. His song *Dong Feng Po* (East Wind, 2003) features a typical Chinese melody performed in R&B style; its instrumentation also creates a Chinese atmosphere with a Chinese *pipa*. In the lyrics, Jay expresses sadness and loneliness subtly, similar to traditional Chinese poetry.

> Who uses Pipa to perform *Dong Feng Po*
> I can see my childhood when paints peel off from the wall
> And remembering those were the old days when we were young
> But now you still haven't heard of the melancholy in my Pipa music
> (Lyrics by Fang Wenshan)

Jay supplies a more overt image of Chinese patriotism by referring to "Shuang Jie Gun" or Nunchakus, a Chinese weapon widely used by Martial Arts Master Bruce Lee against those who would oppress the Chinese. The lyrics of Jay's song *Shuang Jie Gun* (2001) state:

> One footstep forward. Remember one left fist
> and right fist
> Those who incite me will be in danger. It once appeared.
> (Kungfu is like) a cigarette which I have never smoked but is with me. It is always besides me.
>
> (lyrics by Fang Wenshan)

In the song Jay reminisces about legendary Bruce Lee who fought the Japanese and publicly declared in his classic movie *The Chinese Connection* (1972) that Chinese are not the "Sick Men of Asia." To the global Chinese audience and other audiences overseas, the kungfu movies from Shaw Brothers and Bruce Lee's productions in Hollywood epitomize martial arts as a symbol of the Chinese. This symbol is therefore exploited as connecting to a Chineseness. In fact, more than once Jay has indicated publically that his song can be equated with Chinese kungfu.

Jay's performance on stage also connects with a sense of Chineseness. Quite often, without overwhelming the modern, cool image, he hybridizes the cool outlook with Chinese conventionality. In a nasty 3 degree Celsius outdoor concert at the Shanghai Stadium December 12, 2003, for example, while performing *Shuang Jie Gun* and *Dong Feng Po*, Jay slam-dunked a basketball on stage. Though his clothing was wide-sleeved with loose pants in a western hip-hop style at a previous concert, at the Guangzhou concert in December 2003, he was dressed in a Chinese robe bespangled with shinny golden dragons. These performances suggest that while the state is now more receptive to various foreign cultural forms, such as elements of hip-hop or R&B, commercially, a complete adoption of western style would not be wise. Jay, rather, successfully brings western musical forms to the Chinese audience, but also evokes the national culture of the PRC.

The Safe Political Icon

The second level of Jay's Chineseness lies in his construction as a "safe" icon for society. Jay is not heroic, quite the contrary. As an icon of the cool generation, he is obliged to be skeptical and critical. Jay's songs often address a wide range of social issues from macro issues, such as expressing anti-war sentiment (e.g. *The Last Battle,* 2002 and *The Hymn of Anti-War,* 2004) or environmental protection (*Farmland,* 2003) to micro problems, such as domestic violence (*Baba, I Come Back,* 2001) or the generation gap (*Grandma,* 2004). Particularly touching is *The Last Battle* in which the lyrics describe the melancholy of a soldier embracing the dead body of a fellow combatant. *Baba, I Come Back,* on the other hand, depicts a horrible scene of a drunken father beating his wife as in the following:

> Don't beat my mum in this way
> Do you feel pain in your hand?
> I call you dad, but why do you beat my mum.
> Are you blind? Why do you follow your drunken nose? Why don't you listen to me?
> Painful, it is our pain.
>
> (lyrics by Jay Chou)

Challenging social problems is a crucial component of Jay's stardom, but, for the state, all the targets of attack in his songs are channeled to the social rather than to the political. Jay is critical of the relative universal and persistent social problems that have no direct connection to any authorities. Jay is actually benign toward the central political authorities. He particularly avoids direct political issues. As a local-born Taiwanese, he parries questions about the Taiwan independence issue, a taboo for the Chinese authorities. In my interviews with members of his fan clubs, they stated that they were unaware of Jay's political position toward the issue of the unification of China. In fact, quite surprisingly, in 2003, fans in Shanghai and Beijing were in a row online over whether Jay identified more with one city or the other—an issue that the Taiwanese would not understand. Although these fan clubs were not given any legal status by the authorities (in that the government did not provide any formal system for registering such groups), the PRC regards such interactions as impinging on the patriotism of the people. But Jay remained removed from these arguments.

For the state, Jay soothes opposition and the people's sense of relative deprivation in the wake of rapid economic development and broadening social inequality. Jay presented himself as an ordinary person, humbly born without any tertiary education. However, amidst the adversity and chaos, as an exemplary model, he chose not to blame the authorities, question the legitimacy of the state, or publicly censure them over social injustice. Rather, he chose to climb up the social ladder assiduously through his own skills and determination. His image as a non-antagonistic "layman singer" squarely matched the needs of the authorities. In contrast to the official top-down model of the veteran Leifeng, who sacrificed himself for the public, Jay is a bottom-up model for the public. In early 2005, Jay's song *Snail* (2001), a self narrative of his own success story as he climbed up slowly and patiently like a snail, was listed as one of the approved "educational" materials for high school students in Shanghai. This was a public gesture by the government to embrace this non-confrontational youth culture but also a political acknowledgement of Jay's preeminence as a popular icon in China. Once this official status was bestowed on Jay, the political thresholds that normally constrain foreign culture were subsequently removed. At this point a popular culture star was given the unique privilege of further expanding his market with the compliments of and through the state's apparatus.

Capitalizing Cool Culture

It is true that Jay's initial success lay in the strong support of his fans. But the further expansion of his influence could not have been achieved without the support of the state. Given the vast geographical distances involved and differences between regions and cities, marketing an artist requires enormous promotional efforts in China. Even if Jay's management (Sony Music and Alfa Music International) was resourceful enough, launching a performing artist in different cities in China requires the support of the local media and government offices as well as integration with local corporations which are associated with state or public-owned corporations. Prioritizing political concerns over economic gain, the corporate body of the PRC would not support an artist who contradicts state policy and national ideology. Thus, an artist imbued with the qualities that the state requires is ideal.

But given Jay's success at negotiating the needs of his fans and demands of the state, he has been embraced by corporate culture. *It's My Site; It's My Command* (in Chinese, *wo de dipan, wo zuo zhu*), the first song on Jay's album *Qilixiang* (*Jasmine,* 2004), for example, is also the slogan of "M-Zone: the mobile site;' for China Mobile Company, a state owned enterprise. Ogilvy, an international company, created the slogan, breaking a company taboo of using a spokesperson to sell products. The Zone targets youth ages 15 to 25, the same generation who needs to be "cool." Through this relationship, Jay bridged into marketing in China under the guidance of a giant state corporation. China Mobile was also able to extend its arm to a new generation who could afford messaging (SMS) and other special features such as Mobile QQ (equivalent to ICQ in mobile form) to maintain their network.

In Wuhan, a southern province in China, the Hubei branch of China Mobile sponsored an entire show, and, essentially, the sponsored company had full rein on ticket distribution. In order to get a single ticket, fans or parents of fans had to deposit either RMB 420 (around US$50) or RMB600 (around US$75), the equivalent of two years of mobile phone fees. The entire production was therefore guaranteed a profit. By compelling users to lock in mobile packages, China Mobile boosted its market sales. Since the show was primarily a promotional event for China Mobile, the campaign for the concert was different from other typical concert promotions. The focus of the promotion in the local media, mainly in newspapers (*Wuhan Evening Post, Chutan Metropolitan Daily, Chutan Gold Daily,* and *Changjiang Daily*) and a few television and radio stations (*Wubei TV, Wuhan TV, Chutan Music Radio, Radio Wuhan Radio,* and *Radio Hubei*), was mainly on China Mobile and not Jay Chou. Of course, there are drawbacks to this kind of concert promotion. Because of the mismatch between Jay Chou's fans and the mobile users, some of the attendants at the concert were not core fans. In fact, according to my observation, the enthusiasm of the audience at the Xinhualu Stadium in Shanghai was not as intense as it was in other cities.

The Political Economy of Foreign Culture in China

It is a matter of fact that the state has strict control over foreign culture in China. In October 1997, the State Council headed by Primer Li Peng, instated the *Regulation of Management of Performance Operations* for non-state artists, performance organizers, investors, and managers of performance sites. The new regulation aimed to control the technical aspects of the performance to ensure safety, copyright protection, and proper taxation. The regulation also allowed control over content and the management of the shows. The law states clearly that a live performance should not gainsay state policy and social order and delimit values and behaviors (e.g. sex, violence, etc.) that could possibly pervert people's minds. It also declares clearly that no foreign joint venture should be allowed to run concerts or rely on foreign investment. Only government-approved groups could manage the concerts and ensure "security."

There are actually many local rules that foreign companies could not possibly handle, especially the custom of giving tickets away to state, police, and stadium officials. For Jay Chou's concert in Shanghai, for example, out of the 80,000 seats in the Shanghai Stadium only 43,000 bona fide tickets were sold. In addition to space allocated for the complex stage that takes 200 people to assemble, the promoter had to relinquish 10 percent of tickets to sponsors and to the Security Guard, the Fire Department, and related departments. In essence, this practice allowed the government indirect control over the foreign production.

When we look broadly at China's control over popular culture, we see that as late as 2003 there were still barriers for Taiwan artists. A few privileged groups were limited to twelve concerts from Hong Kong-Taiwan artists every year. Investors had to partner with a privileged company to get a license (called a *Piwen*) from the Ministry of Culture before they could promote concerts and sell tickets. Concerts featuring artists from western countries bear an even higher risk. The western artists Wham in the '80s, and Bjork and Ricky Martin in the '90s performed in China, but did so to promote their nations' images. Tickets were given away free and not sold. However, other groups such as Ace of Base and Roxette attempted to have commercially viable concerts but in the end made very little money. The Suede concert organized by Modernsky, an indie record company, also ran into problems over ticket sales.

Given the high risk of marketing foreign artists in China, organizers best promote concerts with corporate sponsorship. However, because of the specific political economy in China, the collaboration must incorporate commercial and state concerns. According to Fanli, the organizer of Jay's concert in Shanghai, they are a huge risk. In October 2003, the investor Zhen Long Performance Company in Shanghai risked RMB8 million (around US$1 million), mainly covering the RMB4 million (around US$500,000) charge for Jay Chou's production company for organizing the concert. However, being a second tier performance company, they had no authority to deal with overseas clients; they had to partner with the first-tier Shanghai East Asia Performance company which could apply for a license.

Besides a commercial partner, the organizer had to rely largely on the Chinese media for promotion. Yet, all the media in Shanghai are de facto state-owned and placed under the Shanghai Media Group (SMG). The concert could enjoy vast publicity, but every performance and entertainer has to get the tacit approval of the state, a condition that only happens when the ideologies of the singers do not contradict with that of the authorities.

The Commercial Viability of Foreign Culture

Upon satisfying the state's need and passing their "standards," entertainment corporations can work on acquiring monetary rewards. Serving as the spokesperson for local products or services, for example, is a major source of revenue for Jay Chou. Besides state-owned enterprises like China Mobile, Jay also serves as spokesperson for many new generations' consumer products, such as Panasonic mobile phone, Japan's DHC cosmetics, Pepsi (for the entire Asia market), and local clothing brand Meters Bonwe.

Meters Bonwe, a local Chinese brand and chain store set up in 1994, markets casual wear to young people in 1,000 retail outlets in China in Beijing, Shanghai, Wenzhou, Hangzhou, Chongqing, Chengdu, Shenyang, and Xi'an. In the early days, Meters Bonwe was famous for its wool clothing and proud to be a Chinese brand. But as it expanded, and produced over 20 million units of casual wear annually in 200 apparel factories all over China, it has aspired to become an international brand, selling franchises that reflect a chic, trendy image. According to the organizer of Jay's concerts, Meter Bonwe covered RMB2 million (around US$250,000) of the expenses for Jay's marketing in Shanghai and sponsored Jay's "Ten perfects Meter Bonwe" concert in Beijing in September 2003.

Maintaining the Integrity of Chineseness

In sum, this paper illustrates that for a cultural product to be marketed in an authoritarian regime that values the political over the economic, a commercial marketing plan devised for the financial gain alone is destined for failure. For the PRC, developing the economy is a priority, but the concerns of the state take precedent. They will avoid any detraction from the political agenda and will risk losing revenue to safeguard this turf. Finally, foreign artists in China can only survive when they meet the political needs and participate in the government's cultural agenda.

This study further illustrates a seminal case in which a state-owned enterprise collaborated with a foreign group, in this case Jay's production team. It demonstrates that foreign cultural forms (such as R&B, hip-hop, and other Western styles) are not unacceptable in

China. The reality is that these Western forms and styles are now encouraged and being used insofar as they can help serve the state. Jay Chou's creation of Western-style-Chinese-pop is a benchmark case where a foreign artist successfully reproduces popular culture that retains its Chineseness while at the same time embracing the West. The music produced, then, is not only a Sino-Western fusion that carries a "Chinese signature," it is also a form of pop culture that recognizes the growing dissent of society as a consequence of social and economic reforms, yet is safe, compromising, and non-confrontational to the state.

Study Questions

1. Why does the influence and popularity of Chou's success and rise to fame mark a unique opportunity to examine popular culture and the structural and political realities of China?
2. Is popular culture (like Chou's work) a reliable source for the study of the geopolitics of Chinese culture? What are the possibilities and challenges of using this type of data to make claims about geopolitical concerns?
3. What interactions does Fung uncover between local and national cultural demands as exemplified within Chou's cultural products?

Note

* This paper was fully supported by a grant from the Research Grant Council of Hong Kong Special Administrative Region. (Project no. CUHK4274/ 03H)

References

Caporaso, James A., and David P. Levine. 1992. *Theories of Political Economy.* Cambridge: Cambridge University Press.

Cullen, Jim. 2000. *Popular Culture in American History.* Malden, MA: Blackwell.

Frey, Bruno. 1984. "Modelling Politico-Economic Relationships." In *What is Political Economy? Eight Perspectives*, ed. David Whynes, 141–61. Oxford: Blackwell.

Fung, Anthony. 2003. "Marketing Popular Culture in China: Andy Lau as a Pan-Chinese Icon." In *Chinese Media, Global Contexts*, ed. Chin-Chuan Lee, 257–69. London: Routledge Curzon.

Fung, Anthony. 2004. "XYZ Generation Series: GenY;" *Ming Pao*, August 22, Hong Kong edition.

Hung, Chang-Tai. 1996. *War and Popular Culture: Resistance in Modern China 1937–1945.* Taipei: SMC Publications/University of California Press.

McClary, Susan, and Robert Walser. 1990. "Start Making Sense! Musicology Wrestles with Rock." In *On Record: Rock, Pop, and the Written Word*, eds. Simon Firth and Andrew Goodwin, 277–92. London: Routledge.

Modleski, Tania. 1986. *Studies of Entertainment: Critical Approaches to Mass Culture.* Bloomington: Indiana University Press.

Skelton, Tracey, and Gill Valentine. 1997. *Cool Places: Geography of Youth Culture.* New York: Routledge.

Storey, John. 2003. *Inventing Popular Culture: From Folklore to Globalization.* Malden, MA: Blackwell.

Wang, Jing. 2005. "Youth Culture, Music, and Cell Phone Branding in China." *Global Media and Communication* 1(2): 185–201.

Videography

East Wind Breaks (Dong Feng Po, 东风破)—Jay Chou. *See:* http://www.youtube.com/watch?v=qrnMb_6jeE0

Shuang Jie Gun—Jay Chou. *See:* http://www.youtube.com/watch?v=PHrq3Ew0T-I

Part V
Hip Hop as Religion

In this last section, we circle back around to the context and sources from which hip hop culture emerged to consider the future study of hip hop in/and/as religion—where the initial concepts and sources vital to the birth of this area of study re-emerge in new and exciting ways. What was once a cultural creation birthed from the street corners of New York's postindustrial city blocks, where art imitated life—where the props and visuals so important to hip hop were raw and organic—forced options and crumbs from the structural inequities of life on the underside of struggle and inequality. As capitalism in America advanced, so too did the contexts, products, and spaces of hip hop production and practice—rugged street corner cyphers were slowly replaced with and by fancy cameras, high profile magazines, and Hollywood-like movie sets. The face-to-face aspect and illusion of hip hop's initial emergence would, over time, become replaced by artists staring down cameras and video crews with forced "homies" and fake "crews" that had to audition and rehearse a (ghetto) life often not lived out in reality. All of that to say, hip hop, since its birth in the 1970s, has changed and evolved much and so too have the intellectual questions of orientation and concern in the area of religion and hip hop thought.

This section begins in the bright lights of a music video by one of hip hop's most powerful contemporary icons—Nasir "Nas" Jones, whose relationship to and with religion is complicated, extensive and ever-changing. Here, Nas reimagines himself as prophet—a figure who comes to challenge the establishment and status quo of society. Hip hop, it is argued, as performed and expressed in and through the figure and work of Nas clearly situates hip hop as, above all, religious. Not religious in a typical or conventional fashion—but rather, as something fundamentally singular and distinct from both hip hop and religion, as such. While searching for the meaning of religion in hip hop can often incite and provoke flattening and making more simple and plain the inchoate and sometimes undecipherable cypering of complexity, here, we are encouraged to maintain hip hop's complexity—staying aware that marginalization, as exemplified in hip hop, has provided both struggle and possibility for meaning making and deep questioning—where life's hurts, pains and struggles are responded in and through this cultural wonder. From Nas, we then move into a theoretically dense and layered exploration of another hip hop great—the late Tupac Shakur who is here figured as and within the pantheon of the African Orishas and deities. Here, we don't have to travel internationally to get global because the local—America—as the said birthplace of hip hop is rightfully situated within—and as—the larger African diaspora. With a focus on race, religion, and black expressive culture, Tupac figured as the deity Ogou assists in troubling traditional American religious ideals, arrangements and values, such as false distinctions between sacred and profane, good and evil. The reconciling of such qualities takes place here in the unsuspecting rugged figures of often demeaned rappers—their oppositional stance to the world in their desire to speak truth to power on behalf of their community and counterparts is here privileged as a productive critique of American colonization and hegemony. Above all, by redescribing and reimaging what some have labeled depraved and beyond salvage in hip hop is here refigured as sacred. Thus, we are forced to see the sacred and divine in the profane (hip hop) and challenged to question that which perpetually claims to be sacred (America, religious institutions, etc.). Most importantly, we are reminded that, above all, at the epicenter of both religion and hip hop, are bodies, people, communities and histories.

Finally, this reader ends with a return to some of hip hop's most influential founders and figures as a way to chart and map the change and shifts in religion and spirituality in the products of rap music. From entertainment music to "truth telling" we are offered a thorough examination of how historical shifts impacted the look, style, sound and content of rap music throughout the years. Like other thinkers in this section, the final essay in this volume returns to the roots of West African and African American cultural traditions and traits in order to unpack a growing "hip hop spirituality" that is highly syncretic and moves and changes with technological innovation. Changes in hip hop, music composition, style, technique and content not only reflect the historical moments in which we find ourselves, but also open up access to fundamentally alter religion and spirituality in unforeseen ways—making variation, bricolage and choice of such things more possible than ever before.

26

"Hate Me Now"
An Instance of NAS as Hip-Hop's Self-proclaimed Prophet and Messiah

Dube uses Nas's video "Hate Me Now" to consider the broad context of Nas's critique of religion in relationship to religious and political leadership that fails to transform circumstances encountered by the misfortunate. In this regard, Nas portrays himself, in some sense, as a prophet providing a Jeremiad—or challenge to the status quo with severe consequences for those who fail to foreground righteousness. In this regard, through prophetic figures such as Nas, hip hop becomes a particular religious sensibility that offers the marginalized life meaning within an absurd world. Dube suggests that Nas's lyrical output is "Other" to both religion and hip hop, and seeks to make the relationship between religion and hip hop more complex, rather than simplistic and reductionistic. Marginalization as religious space of critique and transformation, by extension beyond Nas, becomes a primary lens and means by which hip hop artists as prophets or messiahs view and make sense of the world culturally and religiously (as a response to suffering).

"Hate Me Now": An Instance of NAS as Hip-Hop's Self-proclaimed Prophet and Messiah

Siphiwe Ignatius Dube

Introduction

In light of the broader observation that "a rigorous examination of the religious and theological contours of hip-hop culture, such as rap music, are slowly beginning to take shape" (Pinn and Miller 2009, 1), this article analyses rapper NAS' video entitled "Hate Me Now" as an instance of his broader self-perception/self-construction/self-affirmation/self-proclamation as the Messiah of hip-hop and a rap-prophet making proclamations on American socio-political and religious values. Born Nasir bin Olu Dara Jones on September 14, 1973 and often self-described by names such as "God's Son" or the "Street's Disciple" or "NAStradamus" or "I AM"—all names which are also titles of his albums—NAS often uses religious icons, imagery, and ideas as ways of talking about socio-political issues facing contemporary American society. In particular, this article locates and evaluates the significance of the video "Hate Me Now" within the broader context of the artist s ambiguous negotiation of the relationship between religion(s) and hip-hop—explicitly rap music—that extends beyond the usual blues connection.

By arguing for NAS' clear appropriation of two Christian religious symbols, the Messiah and the prophet, the article makes the claim that through rap music and other aspects of hip-hop culture, certain hip-hop artists see themselves as performing the role that they believe religious leaders and politicians seem to have failed at fulfilling. The particular way through which religious leaders and politicians are deemed to have failed is by minimally affirming hope for a better tomorrow and challenging traditional political and religious institutions on behalf of the oppressed. The theme of marginalization, therefore, figures significantly not only for rap, but also for addressing a paradigmatic religious experience of African Americans. Consequently, the implications of the following analysis require that hip-hop's language (and the experiences described by this language through rap music in particular) be accorded idiosyncratic status from one of simply being derivative. In this sense, NAS' soteriological self-portraiture in the video analysed in this essay, and his musical career in general, is more than simply metaphoric, but enters into the realm of the metonymic, thus opening up space for a reconfiguration of not only hip-hop as another source of a religious sensibility, but also of "religion" as another commodity in the diverse marketplace of worldviews that give meaning to our everyday reality.

Two Points on Context

First, the title of this issue's focus "Film, Frames and Video Games: Religious Insights into Media" assumes a particular relationship between religion and popular culture. In their book, *Religion and Popular Culture in America* (2005), Bruce Forbes and Jeffrey Mahan identify four such relationships, one of which will help frame the analysis of this essay. Forbes and Mahan argue that we can examine the relationship between religion and popular culture, first, by looking at Religion in Popular Culture: where the discussion focuses on the appearance of "traditional" religious themes, language, imagery, and subject matter in elements of popular culture, whether implicitly or explicitly (10–12). Second, we can broach the subject via Popular Culture in Religion: where we can observe the appropriation of aspects of popular culture by "traditional" religious groups and institutions (12–15). Third, we can also look at Popular Culture as Religion: where popular culture serves as religion or functions like religion for many people (14–15). Fourth, scholars can look at Religion and Popular Culture in Dialogue: where it can be observed that the relationships between Religion and Popular Culture are fluid, and if one tends to gravitate towards one (monolingual) direction, the perspectives of the other might be helpful in suggesting additional possibilities (15–17). Crucial to these discussions, however, are questions of definitions of religion, since most arguments about popular culture and religion are based on functionalist and/or formal definitions of religion. Arguably, the title of this special issue of *Religious Studies and Theology*, of which this essay first appeared, assumes the fourth of these relationships, whereby the concern is with how religion appears to be in dialogue with popular culture media, thus both informing and being informed by popular culture. In other words, the important conclusion that should be drawn through this dialogical approach is that popular culture both reflects and shapes us (Forbes and Mahan 2005, 4–5). In light of this vein of argument, the essay will demonstrate how the relationship between rap and religion is more dialogical and dialectical than might seem at face-value.

Second, while it is easy and tempting to conflate hip-hop, the larger cultural phenomenon, with rap, one of its inflections or manifestations, scholars need to be careful to make this distinction. As Adam Krims argues, "'rap' describes only a kind of music, whereas there is also hip-hop dancing (break-dancing), hip-hop visual art (graffiti), hip-hop clothing, and, depending on whom one asks, perhaps other hip-hop things as well ..." (Krims 2000, 10). There is indeed much scholarship that makes the distinction between the two concepts clear,[1] even while admitting that in this essay I will be using NAS' rap music as a way of talking about hip-hop in general. To this end the idea of metonymy, as opposed to metaphor, will play a significant role in framing the discursive claims pursued in this essay about NAS' oeuvre as artist, Messiah, and prophet. In other words, rap, as a specific part of hip-hop that comes to refer to the whole movement, is used metonymically (a definition of metonymy particular to this essay's analysis is proffered later). However, and more significant, rap also comes to signify more than mere affirmation of either traditional religious ideology or the simplistic reduction of hip-hop culture as the reification of American consumer culture. In this sense, we encounter NAS' rap music as the "other" of both religion and hip-hop—as the penumbral shadow of either institution. In the words of Anthony Pinn and Monica Miller, "hip-hop calls, beckons and invites new, creative, (de)constructive ideas of the religious in the face of the radical otherness and alterity of these things we call meaning" (Pinn and Miller 2009, 5). Shying away from any claims of authenticity, the essay problematizes simplistic and reductionist re/presentations of both religion and hip-hop simultaneously, and NAS becomes a most useful tool for articulating such re-inscription.

Religion and Hip-Hop

In addressing the relationship between contemporary hip-hop in North America and religion one might indeed be tempted to point immediately to Kanye West's "Jesus Walks" rap (including the video) as a contemporary paradigmatic example of the marriage of rap and religion. Indeed, Josef Sorett argues that "by paying attention to the shifting religious references of various rap artists one can map a preliminary history of the religious dimensions of hip-hop as it has evolved from the 1980s to the present" (Sorett 2009, 11). Sorett maps this history of the religious dimensions of hip-hop via KRS ONE's (born Lawrence Parker) religious biography as the rapper moves from the iconography of Islam to Christianity during his career. Sorett's argument is that KRS ONE's biography is a perfect mapping of rap's own religious "progression" such that, "Hip hops rising Christendom culminated in 2003 with the release of Kanye West's 'Jesus Walks', a popular single that was, perhaps, the major exception to the rule of conflating Christianity with capital" (Sorett 2009, 15). Sorett is not alone in placing "Jesus Walks" on this pedestal, even while recognizing that there are others who have come before West. *MTV.com* ran an article in the summer (July) of two-thousand and four entitled "Finding My Religion: Hip-Hop Gets the Spirit" (MTV 2004). Despite citing various hip-hop artists who "have the spirit" such as Cam'ron, LL Cool J, Mase, and NAS amongst others, the article places West's "Jesus Walks" at the centre as well. This focus is especially evident in the number of visual references to West that the reader/viewer is exposed to as opposed to the other artists, as well as the fact that a majority of the article focuses on West at the expense of the other artists mentioned.

There is no doubt that West's open profession of his faith in Jesus, and what this means for him in the context of a popular medium such as hip-hop culture, constitutes a challenge to both hip-hop's supposedly secular language and Christian theology's limited understanding of the medium of hip-hop as expressing the experiential truth of most of its performers and listeners. However, before getting too lost in such limited readings, it should be noted that there is a whole genre of Christian hip-hop that recognizes on the one hand the utility of speaking in the vernacular the message of the gospel, such that West's "Jesus Walks" is nothing astounding as such. In fact, in contrast, for performers and listeners of Christian hip-hop, Kanye West might be regarded as a "fraud" in that his Christian beliefs are only showcased in special circumstances and do not define his everyday worldview as much as those of artists whose primary concern is delivering the message first and the medium after. That said, there is a general lack of scholarship on the topic of "holy hip-hop" (Cross Rhythms 2003), and various reasons can be proffered to explain this anomaly. However, even though the particular topic of holy hip-hop is not the focus of this article, I wanted to highlight it as a way of further contextualising my analysis of NAS's video as only a very small part of a larger phenomenon of the intersection of religion and hip-hop, a tradition which has a long history as Sorett's article aptly demonstrates.

Rap and the Idiom of Prophecy

In her book aptly entitled *Prophets of the Hood: Politics and Poetics in Hip Hop* (2004), Imani Perry argues that "Hip hop artists are often self-proclaimed contemporary prophets, their work constructed of truth-revealing parables and pictures. That truth may be spiritual, cultural, personal, beautiful, and it may resonate with inspiration or tragedy" (Perry 2004, 2). Perry's particular construction of hip-hop artists as prophets is premised on an understanding of prophecy as an activity that serves as the moral conscience of the nation; a conscience that throws "into sharp relief how the promises of the nation had been denied" (Perry 2004, 4) for particular kinds of groups in America. This idea of prophets as the bearers of the moral lamp-post of society is also the perspective this essay takes on NAS' self-construction as both a prophet and Messiah of hip-hop through rap.

A further argument supporting the notion of hip-hop artists, and rap artists in particular, as critics of the socio-political conditions under which they live in the sense of conducting prophetic activity as defined above is put forward by Robin Sylvan in his book entitled *Traces of the Spirit: The Religious Dimensions of Popular Music* (2002). Using fieldwork interviews, Sylvan argues at one point that: "the prophetic, Utopian, transcendental element within contemporary rap is not only very strong but, according to the rappers I interviewed, constitutes the core of the hip-hop tradition" (Sylvan 2002, 194). In other words, there is a certain critical edge to rap music that refuses to take refuge into an "other" and "spiritualized" world by facing squarely the harsh reality of oppression and marginalization. It is in this sense that rap artists can be construed as serving a prophetic role—by serving as the moral conscience of the nation via the questions they raise through their lyrics. Granted that the notion of prophecy that the essay draws from is very limited, I believe that it still captures the essence of how rap artists understand their art/work as prophetic in some instances.

Moreover, the above representation is only one side of hip-hop and rap, and perhaps one that some might argue no longer exists. A lost world where "hip hop produced internal and external dialogues that affirmed the experiences and identities of the participants and at the same time offered critiques of larger society that were directed to both the hip hop community and society in general" (Rose 1994, 60). Nevertheless, as Tricia Rose further notes, "Not all rap transcripts directly critique all forms of domination; nonetheless, a large and significant element in rap's discursive territory is engaged in symbolic and ideological warfare with institutions and groups that symbolically, ideologically, and materially oppress African Americans" (Rose 1994, 100–101). This is a point echoed by Charise Cheney in her analysis of what she calls the golden age of rap nationalism. Cheney argues that it is important not to "overstate the case for the existence of seditious thinking within hip-hop culture. While the power of rap music lies in its ability to articulate the hidden script of black cultural expression, not all rap music is counterdiscourse" (Cheney 2005, 5). In actual fact, rap can be a vehicle for the promotion and endorsement of conservative American values such as "conventional gender roles, the rampant heterosexism and homophobia, and the romanticization of capitalist pursuit" (Cheney 2005, 5). This criticism of rap notwithstanding, Rose's conclusion is that "rap's social commentary enacts ideological insubordination" (Rose 1994, 101) despite its troubled relationship with reinforcing certain problematic stereotypes.

Elsewhere, Perry identifies this contradictory character of rap music and hip-hop culture as actually the core discursive make-up of both the content (rap) and the form (hip-hop); whereby, "holy and well-behaved gestures sit next to the rough and funky. Violence, sexuality, spirituality, viciousness, love, and countless other emotions and ideas all form part of the discursive space" (Perry 2004, 6). In this context, rap music videos and lyrics that celebrate rappers' charisma and affluence are not merely imitation of capitalist values, but they also describe and bring attention to what Perry calls "the alienation of the impoverished and the depression of marginalization" (Perry 2004, 1). In this milieu of contradiction is where NAS' video "Hate Me Now" finds illustrative purchase as critical of both the failure of religion to deliver the poor from suffering and rap music for failing to live up to its visionary call of resistance and liberation.

Religion, Rap music, and NAS …

In an article espousing the theological complexity of rap music, Monica Miller notes that, "NAS has definitely been no stranger to invoking religious themes and recasting them with a thugged-out twist" (Miller 2009, 51). In particular, of his nine studio albums, five have titles that directly reference religious symbols, above all the themes of prophecy and the Messiah—and that is not counting the lyrics in the raps themselves. The albums I am referring to are: *It Was Written* (1996); *I AM ...* (1999); *NAStradamus* (1999); *God's Son* (2002); and *Street's Disciple* (2004). While NAS has drawn from both Islam (at least the Five Percent kind) and Christianity, it is the latter from which much of his musical appropriation of traditional and institutional religion has drawn for both inspiration and condemnation. However, as NAS himself admits during an interview with Associated Press in 2005, he does not ascribe to any particular religion. When Sean Couch of the Associated Press asks about his religious background growing up, NAS answers, "I was surrounded by Christians ... my grandmothers, all my family was from the South, Baptist. As I got older I got into the 5 Percent Nation, and then that pushed me toward Islam. But (I'm not any) religion." The interviewer, pressing the question of religion further asks, "would you consider yourself Agnostic?" and NAS replies, "I consider myself (pauses) I know there's a higher power" (Associated Press 2005). NAS' self-proclaimed non-institutional religious affiliation raises an important question regarding his use of blatant religious symbolism in his music. In particular the following question arises: what is the purchase of religious imagery, language, and symbolism in NAS' music if he is not affirming the tradition (s) with which he engages in both the lyrics of the raps and their music video renditions?

Miller, who is one of the few scholars working on the topic of religion and hip-hop that has engaged with NAS' use of religion in some depth, proffers a tentative answer to the question posed above. She notes two things with reference to two songs, "Disciple" from the album *Street's Disciple* (2004) and "Heaven" from the album *God's Son* (2002), which are worth reiterating because they are significant for the argument pursued in this article regarding "Hate Me Now" from the album *I AM ...* (1999). First, Miller discusses how the album cover of *Street's Disciple* is reminiscent of the "Last Supper," with NAS playing different characters. Not only that, the album contains twenty-seven songs, which happens to match the number of books in the New Testament. In response to these observations Miller argues that:

> Although one is hard pressed to make claims about what NAS is doing religiously, what we can say is that NAS makes creative use of religious concepts, stories and histories, and makes them his own, to invariably say something about his journey and struggles through his journey as a rap artist attempting to "keep it real." From his album covers to re-depicting religious stories with him as the main actor, the putting on of religion gives NAS a level of power to make his case that, as he believes, he is the "King of the Streets."
>
> (Miller 2009, 52)

In terms of the observation made earlier regarding the relationship between religion and popular culture, NAS seems to be directly appropriating religious themes in a fairly direct and commodified manner for the sake of controversy. This is part of the reason that I think Miller finds it difficult to figure out what it is that NAS is doing exactly. Is he mocking, re-interpreting, translating, or doing all/or none of the above?

Second, as if in answer to these preceding questions, Miller notes the ambiguity of the signifier "heaven" in the song with the same title, with particular reference to NAS' rhetorical question, if heaven was a mile away, what would you do? She argues,

Interestingly, although Heaven is used as a signifier of escape out of the world, a place whereby NAS can juxtapose the craziness going on in society, one does not get the sense that NAS is advocating a quick escape, rather, I believe he wants to get at the larger issue of social transformation and what would it take for one to wake up to the social sins of this world ...

(Miller 2009, 52)

While Miller does not go much further into this social investment of NAS in religious themes (for example, she argues that NAS' use of religion seems only significant for his personal journey), I would like to suggest that what NAS is doing religiously is to evoke the image of himself as a not only the prophet who is despised at home (read hip-hop culture), but also as the self-sacrificing saviour of hip-hop through rap, even in this music's most fetishistic form as braggadocio "gangsta life." In other words, as I will suggest through the analysis of "Hate Me Now" that follows shortly, NAS' use of both religion and rap is to argue that while both rap and religion are subject to corruption, as evidenced by their failures to respond to the needs of their followers, they still contain within them seeds of an incorruptible truth that lies beyond all corporate manipulation in the case of rap, or theological strangulation in the case of religion. Furthermore, to get at this critical ambiguity of NAS' performance we have to privilege irony rather than direct reading of either rap as purely a medium of resistance or liberation, or religion as an unproblematic transmitter of ageless universal truth(s).

The critique of the failure of Christian institutions to speak to the ills suffered by urban communities in America has a long history within hip-hop culture and rap music in particular. Between the late eighties and the mid-nineties, for example, there was a proliferation of rap music aimed specifically at discrediting Christianity as the slavemaster's religion, and, therefore, a hurdle to black self-consciousness and decolonisation in America. Cheney gives an especially convincing account of this aspect of rap music and the nationalism promoted through this type of music. In particular, Cheney notes that:

In fact, the primary perception that prejudiced the Hip-Hop Nation's critique of black Christianity was the belief that it is the "slavemaster's religion." Among raptivists, African Americans adoption of Christianity was interpreted as a sign of black accommodation and submission to white power, not only in the religious sphere but in the political sphere as well.

This reading of Christianity was appealing to a generation of black youth disillusioned with what they felt was the black church's abandonment of a social agenda ... most rap nationalists argued that the black church lacked relevancy—that it was unable or unwilling to confront white power structure—and that the practice of black Christian theology was incapable of inspiring black liberatory thought among its believers.

(Cheney 2005, 125)

However, despite the purchase of the argument against Christianity raised by Cheney's raptivists, what artists such as NAS, Kanye West, and Mase—amongst many others—do when they invoke Christian themes in their music is to affirm the significance of the Bible for both Christian and non-Christian African American communities. This is a point attested to by Theophus Smith in his book, *Conjuring Culture: Biblical Formations of Black America* (1994).

The significant point to take from Smith's book for the purposes of the current argument is that the Bible is a book used by slaves and their descendants to conjure God for the purpose of black liberation. Therefore, the critique of Christianity by Cheney's raptivists elides this important fact in its monochromatic painting of Christianity as only a "slavemaster's religion" rather than attending to the complex ways in which this religious tradition is negotiated in practice. Granted, of course, the problematic uses of Christianity for colonial and subjugation purposes in the context of America cannot be naively glossed over.

I raise the issue of the critique of Christianity within rap music in order to further contextualize NAS' ambiguous and problematic use of Christian imagery not simply at the level of the discourse privileged by this essay, but to also highlight the broader historical significance of this critique as Cheney's discussion above demonstrates. This discussion of the raptivist critique of Christianity also serves the further purpose of highlighting NAS' use of the prophet and Messiah imageries as ironic, since it is arguable that by emphasising the significance of the Christian symbols within his music he is challenging the meaning and utility of this tradition for today's African American urbanites in light of the claim of Christianity to be a liberatory religion. In other words, NAS conjures up the Christian gospel in a way that questions its utility in light of the power of capitalism to supposedly offer all the answers to the questions of meaning raised by the everyday life experiences of those who live on the margins of American society. His approach, however, is not metaphorical, but metonymic as he aims to proffer critique not only against the religious institutions of Christianity, but also the hip-hop culture which also claims to speak on behalf of the marginalized. That we should interpret "Hate Me Now" as metonymic rather than metaphorical will become clearer later on, but for now it suffices to at least delimit how the term is applied within this analysis.

Metonymy

In distinguishing between metaphor and metonymy, Francisco José Ruiz de Mendoza Ibáñez and Ricardo Mairal Usón argue that, "in Cognitive Linguistics metaphor is generally defined as a cognitive mapping (or set of correspondences) across discrete conceptual domains … while metonymy is seen as a domain-internal mapping where one of the domains involved provides a point of access to the other …" (2007, 33). In particular, as Antonia Barcelona concurs elsewhere, "mapping refers to the fact that the source domain is connected to the target domain by imposing a perspective on it, not by projecting its structure onto it, as in metaphor. The mapping in metonymy is unidirectional and asymmetrical, whereas the one in metaphor is unidirectional and symmetrical" (2007, 53). Other scholars in the field of linguistics have put the distinction as follows: metaphor is a relationship of similarity and metonymy one of contiguity; whereby in metaphor we can substitute one item with another familiar one with similar properties but from a different domain, and in metonymy the items referred to already have a relationship. In delineating metonymy, therefore, we can argue that "metonymical methods of representation are by their very nature related to the symbolic; the concept of symbol, in fact, implies affinity between what symbolizes and what is symbolised" (Maj 2005, 89). If we accept Maj's argument, the conclusion we should draw is that metonymic relations cannot be arbitrary since "metonymy is after all deeply connected to the reality of things and their inner relations" (Maj 2005, 90). The items in metonymy are not logically dispensable since such dispensing with the source or the target would eliminate the relation as well.

Although the above definition is a truncated version of a complex and rich concept, I highlight the above delineation in order to circumscribe a particular way of constructing the metonymic relationship that I argue exists between rap and hip-hop, rap and religion, and, religion and popular culture. In the case of rap and hip-hop the contiguity works as follows: as part of the larger hip-hop culture, rap music can be interpreted as the carrier of both the semantic and pragmatic meaning of what it means to be hip-hop (the clothes, the graffiti, the music, and the language all infer one another). In the case of rap/hip-hop and religion: if we accept the argument put forth by many interlocutors of religion and popular culture that both religion and popular culture are significant arenas for meaning-making—where such meaning-making trumps the usually privileged status assigned just to religion as having to do with issues of ultimate concern—then rap and hip-hop, as part of popular culture, also share in this capacity for meaning-making. To put differently, by using religious symbols, or reinterpreting them, or completely dismissing them, popular culture enters into the realm of meaning-making as well. Therefore, in engaging a dialogical analysis of religion and popular culture we can argue that there is metonymic contiguity implied by the relation of meaning-making.

However, it should be noted that the argument is not that all rap is metonymically religious, but that if we grant rap (as a medium of popular culture) the benefit of the doubt regarding its role as constructing meaning for those who regard it as such, we can extend this meaning-making attribute to certain rap artists who use religious imagery in interesting and provocative ways. To go back to our definition above, the structure imposed by this contiguous association is not symmetrical—rap is not religion, nor religion rap, but both can imply and "signify" each other in very specific ways. This association is not arbitrary since there is a deep concern that both religion and rap music remain connected to the reality of the relationships they *actually* represent; they are both arenas concerned with responding to the conditions of marginality created by the neglect suffered at the hands of either religious institutions or the "secular" institutions of capitalism. To that end, both rap and religion share in the meaning-making process, and are, therefore, metonymically related. The concept of metonymy is not only significant for the analysis of the foregoing themes, but also plays an important role in translating the meaning of rap lyrics into visual images that further purport the message of the artist.

"Hate Me Now" as an Instance of Metonymy

In describing the significant role that music videos play in further purporting the message of the rap artist, Rose argues that: "Music video is a collaboration in the production of popular music; it revises meanings, provides preferred interpretations of lyrics, creates a stylistic and physical context for reception; and valorizes the iconic presence of the artist" (Rose 1994, 9). In other words, music videos in hip-hop (and arguably other genres of popular music in general) are usually complex reinterpretations of the lyrics and they produce their own discursive space that demands attention beyond what the lyrics say. As Rose further argues in light of an interview with famous director Kevin Bray,

> video directors find imaginative ways to engage the musical and lyrical texts and enter into dialogue with the rappers' work. For Bray and other directors, the best videos have the capacity to offer new interpretations after multiple viewings, they have the spontaneity and intertextuality of the music, and most importantly, as Bray describes, the best videos are "sublime visual interpretations of the lyrics … ; the music video is a visual instrument."
>
> (Rose 1994, 13–14)

Therefore, to fully appreciate a rap song and its visual representation in the music video, one must learn how to respond to the artist's artistic expression of the musical idea in all its forms, as lyrics and as video.

In appreciating this whole expression of the musical idea, the rap video comes to stand in for the whole concept of the musical idea in the rap that the artist has produced. To that end, it is possible to read both the lyrics and the video not only as interpretations of each other, but also as parts of a representative whole of the concept of the musical idea; the respective parts represent the whole. NAS uses this metonymic ploy very well in his video "Hate Me Now" to address both the limits of the religious message and hip-hop in dealing with the socio-economic conditions that produce marginalisation; conditions which lead individuals to unquestioningly embrace the hip-hop "thug-life" or proclaim the glory of the traditional "Christian God" despite the fact that their conditions as a whole don't improve much. In other words, for NAS, neither the "street dreams" nor the "heavenly" riches are adequate individually as tools for making sense of the complex everyday reality of the marginal "ghetto" life.

The video, "Hate Me Now," directed by Hype Williams, opens with a statement that seems pre-emptive at face-value, but upon closer analysis actually valorizes the rap artist NAS ironically as the Messiah. The introductory credits read:

> Since the first recorded crucifixion in 600 [B.C.E] many thousands upon thousands of men and women have been crucified for their beliefs, their convictions, their love and their crimes … some have been guilty, some have been innocent. Some were nailed to a cross, others tortured in life. Nas believes in the Lord Jesus Christ and this video is in no way a depiction or portrayal of his life or death …
>
> (change mine)

It may be easy to dismiss this preamble as pre-emptive, especially given the controversy surrounding the initial release of this video. As various sources confirm, including NAS in interviews, a scandal ensued over the video because Sean "Puffy" Combs' minister counselled him against appearing crucified in the video with NAS. "Apparently Puffy's minister counselled him that this image was an immoral self-depiction, so that the artist requested his participation in the crucifixion scene be removed, although the original version aired accidentally, much to Puffy's chagrin" as Perry notes (Perry 2004, 150).[2]

In light of the argument of this essay regarding the ambiguity and irony of NAS's use of religious symbols, I would contend that both Puffy and his minister completely miss the irony of NAS' critique of both traditional religion and hip-hop culture in this video, even as he uses clear Christian religious imagery. Also, the lyrics to the rap further demonstrate the ironic use of religion by NAS in this rap. To put it another way, the preamble actually serves to confirm how, despite the fact that there are many thousands who have been crucified, only one of those crucified innocently matters, Jesus Christ. In a similar vein, while there are many rap artists who claim the status of martyrdom, only a few are actually worthy of such status. Furthermore, the same practice of crucifying the innocent for standing up to the inequalities continues today and NAS will go so far as to sacrifice his image, by being crucified against all admonition, for the sake of the message, like Jesus, but not as Jesus. This argument is made especially clear in the first opening minutes following the preamble where NAS is depicted walking through fire and also being crucified. I would argue that this is an allusion to the idea that only the pure or those purified through fire can be fit enough to be messianic figures, and NAS is clearly such a figure not only for the rap game, but hip-hop in general.

This last point is confirmed by both the first lyrics of the rap as well as the opening scene of the video in which NAS appears in front of enormous flames of fire, as already noted. Almost instantaneously, the video cuts into a scene of NAS carrying a cross and being mocked by a group of "haters" dressed in stereotypical "biblical" garb. The group constitutes *seemingly* different individuals—an indication that those who despise come in many hues of race, gender, and class. I would argue that NAS means for us to read this representation as a reference to the "melting pot" of American society. It is not only the stereotypical "white" America that fears rap that hates NAS, but also elements in the black community, Puerto Rican community, Chinese community—everybody. In the same way that Jesus died on the cross for all, at least according to the traditional interpretation of the Gospel according to Christianity, so it is that NAS (and consequently rap and hip-hop) will die at the hands of many who hate what he (it) represents. Furthermore, in case one is not convinced by the video, the lyrics rapped during this opening scene clearly establish NAS as self-sacrificing. Puffy announces the return of Escobar, one of NAS' former incarnations, by proclaiming that "Escobar season has returned ..." NAS responds by confirming not only his return, but also his destiny: "It's been a long time, been a long time comin / Looks like the death of me now / But you know, there's no turning back now / This is what makes me—this is what I am" ("Hate Me Now," AZLyrics 1999). The ineluctability of his destiny is confirmed by the chorus of the rap, where both NAS and Puffy rap: "You can hate me now ... but I won't stop now ... / Cause I can't stop now ... you can hate me now ..." The chorus affirms NAS' mission as not only inevitable, but also divinely destined.

Keeping in mind that these lyrics are juxtaposed with NAS carrying the cross, it is very clear that the use of the imagery of Jesus' coming as announced by John the Baptist in the New Testament is being evoked in the refrain between NAS and Puffy. This is especially true if one considers that one of the names given to God in the Bible is "I AM." Exodus 3: 14, for example reads: "God said to Moses, I am who I am. This is what you are to say to the Israelites: I AM has sent me to you." Furthermore, Jesus makes this self-reference to his divinity according to the book of John. John 8: 58–59 notes, "'I tell you the truth,' Jesus answered, 'before Abraham was born, I am!' At this, they picked up stones to stone him, but Jesus hid himself, slipping away from the temple grounds." In similar fashion to the biblical narrative, NAS evokes the reference to this interpretation of Jesus' coming and mission by proclaiming in his lyrics that, "this is what I am." In this one scene, along with the lyrics that accompany it, NAS has not only proclaimed his identity as the Messiah, but also as a prophet sent to condemn those who have nothing better to do than criticise the "have-nots" for trying to make the best out of life.

NAS is especially critical of those guilty of this latter transgression in his rap; those who hate him for making it despite all the hurdles to the contrary. NAS mockingly invites his "haters" to take all that he has, because in the end none of it matters as they cannot take away the best thing he has, namely, his "flow." As NAS raps:

> You wanna hate me ... what can I do ...
> Hate on me, I blew but I'm the same ol G
> ... when you're on top there's envy
> Took my niggas out the hood, but you doubt on us ...
> Here's my cars and my house ...
> Criticize when I flow for the streets ...
> Try to make it like you the realest, but who the illest ...?

In making reference to the idealized possessions of the rap "high life" such as name brands products like Fendi and Gucci, NAS subtly condemns the sector of American society that won't accept "niggas" because even in the drab of high society the hood can't be taken out of the "nigga." What is interesting is that in the video NAS raps this verse in the most stereotypical setting for gangsta rap videos, the club. Taken at face value, this aggrandizing of the rap game "high life" in the video might seem to further valorise the significance attached to the status of making it in the rap game; the evidence of which includes obscene consumption of alcohol, hyper-sexualization of the rap artist through being swooned over by a group of women, and the ostentatious display of expensive clothing and cars.

The above notwithstanding, I believe that when juxtaposed with the above-cited lyrics, the representation of the "high life" is being criticized in this video as not enough to give the kind of meaning to life that NAS is after. After all, NAS could have just made a video about the hate he perceives and suffers in the rap game that had no reference to any religious imagery and got the message that he is transmitting across just as efficiently, if not more so. So, one has to wonder what NAS is doing inserting this scene of the video in-between two scenes that directly invoke the cross and him as the crucified Messiah. The answer, I believe, is not only that NAS is making a direct reference to himself as the hated street prophet and Messiah, but also claiming that the message of his "ill" raps cannot be stopped even if all his riches were to disappear. In other words, "cause niggas feel this right" he can be criticized for all people want as he flows for the streets, but that is not going to stop him. He is going to carry the cross, as he raps elsewhere: "I carry the cross, if Virgin Mary had an abortion / I'd still be carried in the chariot by stampeding horses" ("The Cross," AZLyrics 2002). After all, as noted already, NAS sees his mission as ineluctable and already written.

That rap is the medium that best proclaims this message of tenacity in the face of adversity is not a coincidence. Rose notes, for example, that rap music, "more than any other contemporary form of black cultural expression, articulates the chasm between black urban lived experience and dominant, legitimate (e.g., neoliberal) ideologies ..." (Rose 1994, 102). Rap music is counterdiscursive and counterhegemonic, by which I mean rap critiques current forms of social oppression (Rose 1994, 103). Hence the representation of rap "high life" in the video under consideration is more than reification of the gangsta image, but serves to juxtapose the everyday poverty of lived experience with the sporadic and few stories of success. That this critique appears in the context of a video that invokes the Christian symbol of the cross speaks to a multilayered and complex use of this symbol in NAS' work in general, but particularly in "Hate Me Now."

As Miller argues with regards to how NAS adjures the cross in "The Cross" from which lyrics were cited earlier: "Using the symbolic capital and the weight associated with the oppressed Jesus, here, Nas becomes the Jesus of the rap game, the one who went from being 'the old king of the streets' to 'N.A.S. (Niggaz Against Society)' transforming the rap game" (Miller 2009, 51–52). NAS affirms this observation in one of his verses in "Hate Me Now" where he brags about his achievements.

> Don't hate me, hate the money I see, clothes that I buy
> Ice that I wear, clothes that I try, close your eyes ...

What is of interest is that as NAS makes all these claims the video cuts back and forth between him and Puffy rapping from a rooftop as well as NAS walking down the street surrounded by his crew. The implication, I would argue, is that despite all the hatred of the hecklers there are still those who love and follow the prophet and Messiah, and to them is granted the iconic status of being recognized or affirmed by the one with the power. In other words, the braggadocio is not just about NAS as the rapper, but also affirms that through rap, and hip-hop, the least of the citizens are granted counterhegemonic power. NAS uses a traditional religious and theological message that the meek shall inherit the kingdom to critique the culture of American society that then turns around and hates these self-made rap artists who are only using what they have at their disposal to make meaning out of their lives. Ultimately, what the above analyses demonstrate is how easy it is to miss this layer of interpretation if one casts NAS' video as just another instance of gangsta rap bragging.

Demonstrating his self-reflexivity in the rap and the video, NAS reiterates that his bragging is not like any other, because he was chosen to do what he does. NAS raps, "I was destined to come / Predicted, blame God, he blew breath in my lungs / Second to none ... Niggas fear what they don't understand, hate what they can't conquer." As he raps these lyrics NAS is back on the cross, and the camera cuts back to him on the street. I would put forth that this cutting back and forth between the NAS on the cross and the NAS on the street is an evocation of a direct correlation between the "gangsta" NAS with "street cred" and the NAS cum prophet and Messiah who critiques the failure of both traditional theological discourse and American society for failing to live up to the expectation to hold up the cause of the poor. Of course the presence of Christian imagery in both the lyrics and the video can easily be read as a commodified and fetishized appropriation of the Christian tradition, thus achieving nothing more than reifying this tradition within popular culture. However, the fact that alongside these supposedly sanitary sacred images we encounter the problematic glorification of violence and hyper-sexualization of women, calls into question the binary logic of sacred and secular assumed by the argument of commodification.

Conclusions

There are at least two conclusions that can be drawn from the above analysis of NAS's use of religious imagery in his video "Hate Me Now." First, by using two supposedly distinct discourses to call into question the utility of either the language of religion or that of secularism in addressing the messiness of everyday life in America, NAS' video forces academic scholarship on religion to have to consider the role of rap music in particular, and hip-hop culture in general, in the process of re-imagining what counts as religious. Miller affirms this point as well by noting that: "the religious imagination of rap music necessitates a reshaping, reimagining and reconstruction of the category of religion itself, as explored in culture, religion no longer becomes a static discourse to be picked from the tree or observed, rather, it becomes a lived reality, an active process embedded within everyday cultural practices" (Miller 2009, 53). In this sense, my engagement with NAS's rap music puts to task the more traditional approach of merely "looking for expressions of dominant religions (i.e. Christian or Islamic) manifest in the cultural practices, and rather, calls for more attention towards the ways such language is used, practiced, and re-appropriated, the multifarious ways in which life experiences and cultural creativity are combined with religious and theological tropes to produces new forms of religiosity" (Miller 2009, 53–54).

Second, as the argument in this essay has proceeded, NAS' appropriation of two religious symbols, the Messiah and the prophet, is a performance of a role that some rap artists perceive traditional religious leaders to have failed to fulfill, by not affirming hope for a better tomorrow and challenging political and religious institutions on behalf of the oppressed. Consequently, the implications of the preceding analysis points to more than a symbolic re-imagining of rap, but signifies a metonymic shift where space is opened up for a reconfiguration of not only hip-hop as another source of a religious sensibility, but also of "religion" (Christianity in this case) as a another commodity in the marketplace of values. Granted that my own analysis has privileged the expressions of one of the dominant religions, I still hold that it goes far in contributing to the argument that popular culture media have more than entertainment value, although this element still forms "part" of their raison d'être. My examination of NAS' rap video "Hate Me Now" has demonstrated that this video is neither merely a retelling of the Christian gospel narrative, nor an unexamined reification rap as counterdiscourse to the hegemony of marginalization challenged by this genre of music in general. Instead, NAS reappropriates the symbols of prophet and Messiah for the purposes of not only establishing his iconic figure as a rap artist, but also undermining traditional religious discourse by lacing it with the temptations of the rap "high-life." In the same vein, however, the vanity of the rap "high-life" is questioned by the use of religious imagery as counter-discourse to hip-hop's elision of its historical roots in the ghetto and the aim of proclaiming a political message.

Study Questions

1. What is the role of prophet and messiah in the work of Nas? How does this challenge normative American values and concerns?
2. What does the role and use of religion in hip hop say about artist's concern over and critique of politicians and religious leaders?
3. What does Dube gain or lose by privileging metonymy over metaphor in her efforts to make the relationship between religion in hip hop more complex rather than reductionistic and one-dimensional?

Notes

1. See also: Samy H. Alim, Awad Ibrahim, and Alastair Pennycook, eds. 2009. *Global Linguistics Flows: Hip Hop Cultures, Youth Identities, and the Politics of Language*. London: Routledge. Cheryl L. Keyes. 2002. *Rap Music and Street Consciousness*. Urbana and Chicago: University of Illinois Press. Robin Sylvan. 2002. *Traces of the Spirit: The Religious Dimensions of Popular Culture*. New York: New York University Press. Craig S. Watkins. 2005. *Hip Hop Matters: Politics, Pop Culture, and the Struggle for the Soul of a Movement*. Boston, MA: Beacon Press.
2. See also, Evan Serpick. 2001. "Nas' 'Greatest Hits': A Track-By-Track Journey With the Pride of Queens." *Rolling Stone*, http://www.rollingstone.com/news/story/172l604l/nas_greatest_hits_a_trackbytrack_journey_with_thepride_of_queens/3

References

Alim, Samy H. 2006. *Roc the Mic Right: The Language of Hip Hop Culture*. London: Routledge.
Alim, Samy H., Awad Ibrahim, and Alastair Pennycook, eds. 2009. *Global Linguistics Flows: Hip Hop Cultures, Youth Identities, and the Politics of Language*. London: Routledge.
Associated Press. 2005. NAS: The mature voice of hip hop. http://www.msnbc.msn.com/id/6786474/
Barcelona, Antonio. 2007. "The Role of Metonymy in Meaning Construction at Discourse Level: A Case Study." In *Aspects of Meaning Construction*, edited by Günter Radden, Klaus-Michael Kopeke, Thomas Berg, and Peter Siemund, 51–75. Amsterdam and Philadelphia: Johns Benjamins Publishing.
Campbell, Kermit E. 2005. *Gettin Our Groove On: Rhetoric, Language, and Literacy for the Hip Hop Generation*. Detroit, MI: Wayne State University Press.
Cheney, Charise L. 2005. *Brothers Gonna Work It Out: Sexual Politics in the Golden Age of Rap Nationalism*. New York: New York University Press.
Conyers, James L., Jr., ed. 2001. *African American Jazz and Rap: Social and Philosophical Examinations of Black Expressive Behaviour*. Jefferson, NC: McFarland and Company.

Cross Rhythms. 2003. http://www.crossrhythms.co.uk/articles/music/Americas_Holy_HipHop/7033/pl/

de Mendoza Ibáñez, Francisco José Ruiz, and Ricardo Mairal Usón. 2007. "Highlevel Metaphor and Metonymy in Meaning Construction." In *Aspects of Meaning Construction*, edited by Günter Radden, Klaus-Michael Kopeke, Thomas Berg, and Peter Siemund, 33–49. Amsterdam and Philadelphia: Johns Benjamins Publishing.

Forbes, David Bruce, and Jeffrey H. Mahan, eds. 2005. *Religion and Popular Culture in America*. Berkeley, Los Angeles: University of California Press.

Gibbs, Raymond, Jr. 2007. "Experimental Tests of Figurative Meaning Construction." In *Aspects of Meaning Construction*, edited by Günter Radden, Klaus-Michael Kopeke, Thomas Berg, and Peter Siemund, 19–32. Amsterdam and Philadelphia: Johns Benjamins Publishing.

Higgins, Dalton. 2009. *Hip Hop World*. Toronto, Berkeley, CA: Groundwood Books and House of Anansi Press.

Holy Bible, NIV.

Keyes, Cheryl L. 2002. *Rap Music and Street Consciousness*. Urbana and Chicago: University of Illinois Press.

Krims, Adam. 2000. *Rap Music and the Poetics of Identity*. Cambridge: Cambridge University Press.

Maj, Barnaba. 2005. "Allegory, Metonymy, and Creatureliness: Walter Benjamin and the Religious Roots of Modern Art." In *The Early Frankfurt School and Religion*, edited by Margarete Kohlenbach and Raymond Geuss, 85–102. New York: Palgrave Macmillan.

Mazur, Eric Michael and Kate McCarthy, eds. 2001. *God in the Details: American Religion in Popular Culture*. London: Routledge.

MTV. 2004. http://www.mtv.eom/bands/h/hiphop_religion/news_feature_071904/index.jhtml

NAS. 1999. Hate Me Now. *Lyrics*, http://www.azlyrics.com/lyrics/nas/hatemenow.html

—— Hate Me Now. Video featuring Sean "Puffy" Combs, directed by Hype Williams http://www.you tube.com/watch?v=dKSJN3WWR3E

—— 2001. The Cross. *Lyrics*, http://www.azlyrics.com/lyrics/nas/thecross.html

Panther, Klaus-Uwe and Linda L. Thornburg. 2007. Metonymy. *The Oxford Handbook of Cognitive Linguistics*. Eds. Dirk Geeraerts and Hubert Cuyckens. Oxford: Oxford University Press.

Perry, Imani. 2004. *Prophets of the Hood: Politics and Poetics in Hip Hop*. Durham, NC: Duke University Press.

Pinn, Anthony B., and Monica R. Miller. 2009. "Introduction: Intersections of Culture and Religion in African-American Communities." *Culture and Religion*, 10(1): 1–9. doi:10.1080/l47556l0902786270

Polletta, Francesca. 2006. *It Was Like a Fever: Storytelling in Protest and Politics*. Chicago, IL: University of Chicago Press.

Richardson, Elaine. 2006. *Hiphop Literacies*. London: Routledge.

Rose, Tricia. 1994. *Black Noise: Rap Music and Black Culture in Contemporary America*. Hanover: University Press of New England.

Sepick, Evan. 2001. "Nas' 'Greatest Hits': A Track-By-Track Journey With the Pride of Queens." *Rolling Stone*. http://www.rollingstone.com/news/story/17216041/nas_greatest_hits_a_trackby track_journey_with_the_pride_of_queens/3

Smith, Theophus H. 1994. *Conjuring Culture: Biblical Formations of Black America*. Oxford: Oxford University Press.

Sorett, Josef. 2009. "'Believe me, this pimp game is very religious': Toward a religious history of hip hop." *Culture and Religion*, 10(1): 11–22. doi:10.1080/l47556l0902786288

Sylvan, Robin. 2002. *Traces of the Spirit: The Religious Dimensions of Popular Music*. New York: New York University Press.

Watkins, Craig S. 2005. *Hip Hop Matters: Politics, Pop Culture, and the Struggle for the Soul of a Movement*. Boston, MA: Beacon Press.

27

Tupac Shakur as Ogou Achade
Hip Hop Anger and Postcolonial Rancour Read from the Other Side

Beginning with the battle between hip hop and America, Perkinson takes up the concerns and inner dialogues of black life as expressed within hip hop culture. Using the personality of the orisha (i.e., African deity) Ogou as a trope by which to explore anger, rancour, and spiritual discernment of power, Perkinson begins to explore the ways in which hip hop troubles traditional religious ideals by bridging the space between good and evil, for instance. Perkinson taps deep into the colonial certainty of Western Christian roots of keeping divided, the divine and the demonic and the ways in which this has played out in and on black life. Blending this religious sensibility with hip hop, Perkinson's framing of Tupac as Ogou becomes a way to "mark" Tupac's critique of the West without leaving that image of Tupac hanging on a cross, inadvertently reinforcing that which Tupac set out to critique. Through the figuring of Ogou in hip hop, Perkinson is able to bridge the divine and the demonic and move into an examination of late rapper Tupac Shakur as representative of Ogou's contemporary expression in black diasporic culture. Perkinson then moves into an examination of what this pairing means for American society today – arguing that this rethinking of Tupac offers a way for white Americans to rethink themselves and denounce their inflated sense of self by seeing African Americans (through Tupac) as "divine."

Tupac Shakur as Ogou Achade: Hip Hop Anger and Postcolonial Rancour Read from the Other Side

James Perkinson

There is a minor tradition in the history of European thought which runs counter to the scientific mainstream; it diverts from the largest and most enduring of obsessions, the desire to observe, in order to draw attention to the state of being observed …

(Kramer 1993, vii)

Beauvoir removed his eyeglass frames and sighted down one of the earpieces. 'That wasn't what I said. I said you didn't have to worry about it, is all, whether it's a religion or not. It's just a structure. Lets you an' me discuss some things that are happening, otherwise we might not have words for it, concepts' – 'But you talk like these, whatchacallem, lows, are – ' 'Loa,' Beauvoir corrected … 'Plural's same as the singular.'

(Gibson 1986, 76)

This article assays fraught terrain. As the serial debate entitled 'Hip Hop versus America' displayed on BET in the autumn of 2007, the status of the rap game remains raucous and rancorous inside black domains of dialogue. What could a white scholar possibly do more than show a fool's hand in trying to weigh in? In what follows, I do not seek to speak to the stakes being debated, but rather, to figure the ferment for white voyeurs pretending innocence. That 70% of the hip hop product is consumed in vanilla suburbs gives pause. Much of the white student bodies I have taught in Detroit and Denver over recent years wear the hat cocked sideways and mouth the mantras of 50 Cent or Kanye, without a clue as to the stakes or their own parents' part in the take that continues to organise suburban affluence as one of the hidden benefits arising from ghetto poverty.[1]

My thinking about hip hop is ultimately a matter of white confession and responsibility: seeking continually to expose and alter white social 'being' as a historic mode of supremacy, whose violence and promulgation has not ceased to do damage here and abroad since its emergence as an ever-changing, theo-scientific project of conquest and accumulation more than 500 years ago.

The effort here is part of an ongoing hermeneutic – as glossed in one of the epigraphs above – of 'being observed'. Indeed, such a reverse gaze has long been my method: grappling with white supremacy and normativity by first attending at length and in depth to the voices of witness, the groans of suffering, the organisations of resistance and the innovations of beauty of those most intractably 'caught' in the structures of white disciplinary power and exploitation (Perkinson 2004a, b, 3–4). Kramer speaks of 'being seen', 'being known', 'being discovered' – of a regime of knowledge production that allowed for reciprocal recognition – before Enlightenment hubris congealed into a systematised, scientific mode of observation, whose vector of knowing was one way and 'irreversible' (Kramer 1993, vii). But in fact, enforcement of a manner of intelligence gathering that presumes a one-way flow, a power of penetration stereotypically male and monolithic, is probably never actually achieved in history. Human beings are simply too much the creatures of their own reflection in the eyes of their various others to escape, entirely, the negations and phantasmagoria they project. Despite all intentions to the contrary, the very attempt to police purity by positing difference – precisely in that very act – not only creates but incurs, the 'contamination' it seeks to exclude.

Such at least is the intimation offered here. Much as I argued in two related earlier publications in this present endeavour, the argument is also more accurately described as a 'thought experiment'[2] in this case, a probing of the popular culture phenomenon of Tupac Shakur for reverse significations on white 'thuggery and skullduggery' ('economic predation and political manipulation').

Entertaining Ogou in the Event

In May 1992, UCLA professor of African and Caribbean literature and folklore, Donald Cosentino, visited Turey's Spiritual Shop in a mini-mall in Hollywood, to interview proprietor, Ysamur Flores, in preparation for writing an article for Sandra Barnes' project on Ogùn, 'Old World and New' (Cosentino 1997, 292). What he met there was street theology prognosticating the *zeitgeist*. Samy, as Flores is known, is a crossover santero, former Jesuit novice and Jehovah's Witness consort, now initiate of Santeria and priest of Oshun, counsellor to 'The Industry' ('showbiz') and Ph.D. graduate from UCLA. Cosentino's interest was the California presence of Ogou – one of the *Orisha* warriors Samy regularly invoked in caring for his *ile's* godchildren. The setting was post-insurrection LA – burned out buildings on all sides, but with Turey's and the mini-mall presiding, intact, over Payless Shoe Store rubble and the looted remains of Korean–Italian furniture outlets. The upheavals of that month overhung the encounter like smoke.

'It was an Ogou event', Samy explained – a moment in time, out of time, when a fragmented earth drew down the *Orisha* of anger to re-establish unity. Samy offered unremitting exegesis. First, the three earthquakes that year – in the desert, then near Palm Springs and then between Eureka and LA – followed by all hell breaking loose in the uprising. Ogou came out, Samy intimated, and said 'You guys get together, or I get you together' (as if, perhaps, more was being ventriloquised in Rodney King's famous 'Can't we all get along' statement on the event than merely his lawyer's pre-crafted lines, designed to secure the lawyer's career in the upcoming civil suit against the acquitted police officers!; Baker 1993, 45; Cosentino 1997, 293). For the resident *santero*, scanning the land for advents of African *Orisha* in disguise of modern antics, the riots were clearly Ogou's business: 'He doesn't know the limits to anything. Once he's out, you can't control him. He kills on the right, and he kills on the left. Death is on the road. You know that's what the problem was' (Cosentino 1997, 293).

Here is the rub of this writing. A spiritual discernment, offered from the left hand of vernacular, a tradition not willing to bifurcate God and the Devil, good and evil, reality and ideals, when speaking of the ultimate. So much in Western influenced traditions of spiritual discernment and ethical analysis – much less theological prognosis – insists that the domain of divinity, however brought to bear on the arc of history, projects a radical declivity between beauty and frenzy, integrity and violence. Older traditions articulating intuitions of indigenous folk, imbedded in local ecologies and responding to intimate concourse with the interdependence of life and death, eating and being eaten, do not separate out 'the good, the bad, and the ugly' when trying to symbolise ultimacy. Samy's comments implicitly throw down a gauntlet of sorts, from the angle of African codifications of spiritual presence. The Western Christian pretense to be able to identify adequately what is divine and what is demonic has probably itself occasioned more genocide and enslavement than any other single predication in history. Scholarly research like that of David Stannard's *American holocaust* now estimates native 'obliteration' – by a double whammy of disease and genocidal policy – at roughly 95% of an indigenous population of roughly 100,000,000 (from northern-most Canada to the tip of Tierra del Fuego) over the course of five centuries since 1492 and an African 'sacrifice' of some 30–50,000,000 expired captives underwriting the 10–12,000,000 of those enslaved who actually made it through the Middle Passage and Caribbean 'seasoning' to the auction block (Stannard 1992, 11, 305, 317). The ignorant colonial certainty (!) that Native American and African indigenous cultures were serving satanic forces in their ritual intercourses and mythology leveraged the entire enterprise of rabid conquest and militant kleptocracy and manic exploitation of labour and rape of culture and the female body. Serious acknowledgment of that history must occasion at least a willingness to listen afresh, if not actual conversion and redress in the code of those forced to undergo such savagery.

Literary critic Houston Baker supplies a second moment of confrontation – this time from a convinced modernist conviction that is nonetheless willing to challenge the pretense of science and objectivity to the final word on life, or riots. Writing in a text titled *Reading Rodney King: Reading urban uprising* immediately after the 'Ogou event' so-called, Baker barks a harsh heraldry: LA in upheaval is not comprehensible to hastily convened forums of hand-wringing officialdom (Baker 1993, 47–8) or academe. Its real significance – like that of slavery before it – is a matter of soundings and sonorities, groans and phatic utterance. Rap bombast, he argues, had long been auguring the inner-city anguish, returning suffering to the national ear in the form of assault rhythm and word-spit 'diss', whose meaning lay more in timbre and tonal stress than in anything Webster could illuminate (Baker 1993, 45–8). The claim is clairvoyant in the same way as Samy's. Some things cannot be merely said. They must be signified and sounded out. Like a submarine probing a bottom (but with a polyphonic 'ping' registered in a base beat frequency). Ogou dances rather than writes, and sings with drums and lust in his voice, not footnotes. What might it take for an academically trained sensibility to entertain such a performative summary as a mode of spiritual agency? The riot was Ogou, like a ghost of the second (or third or fourth or umpteenth) coming, speaking apocalypse, but without any need to answer to formal doctrine or positivist sanction. A category of spiritual anger, embodied in people, beyond the powers of police, articulating a message to a recalcitrant nation! Maybe akin to Ezekiel – but certainly not to any social-policy commission (Cosentino 1997, 304)!

Such at least is the echo I wish to elaborate here. 'Ogou' as *Orisha* of political upheaval, living emblem of indignation, anchored in the deep memory of the race, African in elocution, a category of interrogation, a basic 'structure' – as cyberpunk author Gibson (1986, 76) explores – allowing us to say things we otherwise could not. Of a type with Isaiah's ancient dowsing for divine apparition in Assyrian aggression[3] – but in a cult code now of Guinea and the Caribbean. An energy figured complexly in relationship to cosmology and society alike, capable of coming to roost in individual bodies exhibiting rhythmic intelligibilities in the regime of possession, but also decipherable in large-scale phenomenon. Or perhaps better – a densely coded cipher, opening a happening of history to local inspection from the angle of a particular set of concerns.

Meaning is after all, not simply something 'there', to be picked, like an apple from a tree, but a construct, assembling eloquence and orientation out of chaos and cacophony, in a manner proving efficacious for a given community. The question is not then is Samy's interpretation right or true, but rather, is it productive of insight and further thinking? And for whom?

Ogou and Afrocentricity

Edward Bynum's *The African unconscious* anchors our analysis in interdisciplinarity as well as history. Ina work culling state ofthe art scholarship from multiple traditions to articulate a basic Afrocentric challenge to varied notions of ancient mysticism as well as modern psychoanalysis, Bynum extrapolates from scientific consensus to the domain of spirituality. The basic agreement that humanity traces its common genetic origins to Africa can be stretched to the realm of epigenesis as well. If physical evolution begins with an African inheritance, then, at some level, so must the genealogy of our spiritual traditions. Case in point, for Bynum, is the hermetic practice of Kundalini, explored in Egypt (long before India) as part of the initiation schools, working with ascetical disciplines, near-death experiences making use of grave clothes and quasi-burial in temple tombs, hypnosis and dream interpretation to push novices towards dissociation and trance experience, 'seeing beyond the five senses' and becoming 'twice born' through contact with the 'great macrocosm of which they were a microcosmic reflection' (Bynum 1999, 81–2, 91, 96–7). Where Freud sought to render the vital energies and traumatic conflicts of the unconscious available for conscious work in service of the individual ego, in this earlier Kemetic practice, the focus was on a more broadly collectivised and cross-generationally temporalised work of sublimation and integration – disciplining the vital forces by means of rhythm and controlled tactile sensation, seeking to facilitate 'travel' between consciousness and more numinous states by working close to the edge of death, breaking through the sheath of ego to gain access to the translocal 'implicate order' enfolded within us (Bynum 1999, 81, 84, 93, 239–40). Bynum draws on everything from neuroscience to cognitive psychology, quantum mechanics to relativity theory, anthropology to medical research on neuromelanin and pineal gland activity, to offer his synthesis. At core, it claims an African substrate for consciousness (a kind of 'all-Black underworld of symbols, animals, forces and dynamics'), showing up in unconscious imagery that is 'peopled with the earliest memories of faces of the Blacks and Browns, or "moros", [who were] the parents of the human race', embedded like archetypes and witnessed 'under extraordinary conditions, in ancestral visions, and in the vision-quest of indigenous peoples' (Bynum 1999, 81, 84).

Within this broad characterisation of an older paradigm for spirituality – referencing notions of a higher-order informational matrix beholden both to Jung's 'collective unconscious' and to the Kemetic myth of Osiris, and roughly found extant among the world's non-Western traditions ranging from the *Tao De Ching* of China to the whirling dervishes of Muslim Zhikr practice, from Dravidian yoga to the Greek and Roman cult of Asclepius – Bynum places special emphasis on the personalist orientations of West African notions of *Orisha or loa* that emerge under conditions of rhythmic entrainment (Bynum 1999, 82–3, 87, 94, 97). This he maps onto more contemporary quantum paradigms of theorising matter itself as 'the localisation of waves and rhythms of probability, superimposed on each other but not absolutely located in one area', that may unfold around a given stimulus at a given time (Bynum 1999, 87, 93). Pattern repetition is the stimulus that he commonly traces across the planet in multiple forms but especially emphasises in African traditions of possession that allow for an ecology of personhood permeable by other personhoods in the interests of a 'relational and resonant affinity' of family consciousness (Bynum 1999, 93, 97, 99).

Bynum's *bricolage* is fundamentally an evolutionary recuperation of spirit inside of matter. He figures Kundalini as 'Ase', a movement and energy of the 'braincore and spine in consciousness', codified in approximations as disparate as the Kemetic eye of Horus myth, and the 'flight folklore' of slaves, the literature of Marquez and Morrison, or Walcott and Soyinka, but touching a developmental line running from early hominids to postmodern savants, mesmerised by light along the tracks of neuromelanin in embryology and superconductivity in biology (Bynum 1999, 96–7, 99, 101–2, 284–5). Obviously, the claims are huge and the leaps prodigious. But large views do allow insights of peripheral vision that more focused concentration necessarily eclipses.

Of note for the argument pursued here, Bynum (1999, 95) links his itinerary of cosmic dance and rhythmic incantation with the possibility of a cognitive change that could issue in a 'revolution in the educational system of America's inner cities'. While 'revolution' is certainly too strong a word for hip hop riffs on the long line of Afro-diasporic struggles to forge survivable life ways in 'New World' death traps (plantation slavery, Jim Crow segregation, postindustrial enghettoisation, neocolonial and neo-liberal developmentalism, etc.), the African unconscious such 'inner city' riffs encode in their rhythmic signatures clearly have global purchase. Undoubtedly, hip hop's planetary resonance is partly a result of transnational marketing – the fetish form of 'dark dangerousness', backlit by urban decay and foregrounded in street argot, sells large, where life experience is more anaemic and enervated in bourgeois trivial pursuits. But Bynum's conjuration of a spiritual code accompanying the genetic spirals coiling back to Africa is worth also entertaining, as part of the evident attraction. 'It is implicit in this perspective', says Bynum,

> that each person, each individual, past and present, regardless of surface phenotype, carries this deep rhythmic signature of an African origin. It is reflected in our genetic structure, our hominid morphology, our shared early Paleolithic adventures, and it is constantly recapitulated anew in our individual embryological unfoldment. These individual wavefronts, like all waves, are interconnected with each other and their hominid signature over time, and their repetition creates a holonomic sea of consciousness and information that sustains on a deep level the African unconscious.
>
> (Bynum 1999, 95)

And this includes, Bynum concludes,

> intuitions about bodily and terrestrial currents and forces that, while not presently accepted in the domain of scientific thought, are nevertheless enduring perceptions of natural occurrences and, therefore, worthy of respect.
>
> (Bynum 1999, 95)

That one such rhythmic current might usefully be caricatured as 'Ogou' merely puts a particular cultural ensemble of codification and signification into the mix of our global battles over ideology and rhetorical control. Brought to this essay as academic provocateur, putting contemporary science in dialogue with a wide range of more humanistic disciplines, Bynum's biospirituality offers Afrocentric counterpoint to more traditional Euro-Enlightenment views on social events.

What Western sociology might want to dispose of as 'urban riot' or 'mob madness', some Afro-diasporic approaches might specify as a collective coherence of *Orisha* anger. The efficacy of the category cannot be decided apart from social location, cultural orientation, political commitment and ritual use.

Ogou and the Demonic Divine

This 'war of the sign' (who names, controls) finds obvious eloquence today – against all odds – in the global efflorescence of a figure like Tupac Shakur, arguably more ambient in his digitalised, posthumous epiphanies in video and soundtrack than ever he was 'in the flesh'. And of course, 'Tupac' here is merely one sign among many – a tattooed incarnation of outraged elocution, rooted certainly in a time and place, a family and a space, identifiable and particular, that now ricochets around the planet inside an ever-faster pace of similarly patterned and packaged figures. The object of this writing is hardly a 'quest for the historical Tupac', but rather an experimental 'messianism of the rhythm', not a synoptic PR campaign, but a Makavelian thematising of Johannine *hubris*. We might riff on that gospel's opening,

> In the beginning was the Beat, and the Beat was with God and the Beat was God, and without its syncopation was not anything made that was made. And the Beat became flesh and dwelt among us full of funk and polyrhythm and into its break stepped a man named Tupac. Tupac was not the Beat, but came to bear witness to its Heat and we have felt the groove of that Repeating Feat, as a Riff on the Real. No one has ever danced its Feel, but the Riff called Ogou has made it appealing. And from that wheeling and dealing have we all received, beat upon beat, meat meeting meat, like manna between the teeth, or hyphie in the feet …

But obviously the scandal of such a rendition is part of the plot here. What if we allow 'Ogou' a categorical standing, as a description of a certain kind of historical patterning of human energy that is simultaneously local and translocal – at once incarnate and metaphysical – alongside the Christian category of 'Christ'? And then interpret the brief epiphany of someone like Tupac Shakur in the 'light' (or 'opacity'?) of its particular umbrage?

Actually the scandal is twofold. Equating a category like 'Ogou' with a title like 'Christ' is already a spiritual head-turner; throwing Tupac into the pot with the Baptizer upends the human side of the equation. Yet, so much of the work of either prophecy or advocacy today must be that of de-familiarising, breaking the somnambulance of categorical certainty! I have made a case for the former equivalence (and difference) between 'Ogou' and 'Christ' in the aforementioned 'Ogu's Iron or Jesus' Irony' piece; here I will only gloss. Ogou is beholden to a tradition of spiritual mapping that refuses any easy bifurcation of good from evil, beauty from violence, the divine from the demonic. Brown (1984, 197) has powerfully summed up the difference in her article, 'Why Women Need the War God'. There she claims a tragic vision of life, and skepticism that war can ever be exorcised from human doing by mere division and rejection (Brown 1984, 198). Rather, she locates the roots of war aggression within herself, and under invitation from *voudou* adepts in Brooklyn, 'marries her anger' in an initiation epiphany that ritualises ongoing negotiation with the energies of such violence under tutelage to a community process of possession-cult dramatisation (Brown 1991, 137–8). Sword-wielding Ogou, the archetype of Anger writ large and of political interdiction whether centralised or in rebellion, directs the anger against the other, against allies and finally even against his own 'horse' (or host), in ritual enactments that come nearly as close to doing real physical damage as they do to tapping wellsprings of real rage and antipathy and reworking such (Brown 1984, 197, 199).

In such a scenario, spirit forces bigger than the individual and invasive energies exceeding psychic control are 'communalised' and brought at least to a stand-off relationship, if not 'to heel'. The experience of 'the Overwhelming' – of that which, in History of Religions parlance, coerces through Terror and Dread – is wrestled into a cult vocabulary and a rhythmic motor expression, in a rite that seeks integration, not exorcism. And this, in pithy shorthand, is the exact premise of this article's polemic, as we shall see below: that the 'demonic', however defined, has perhaps more often and more strategically, in various cultural codifications of human concourse with the other world and the world of alien others, been embraced in an alternative idiom rather than cast out. Shall Ogou be banished … or invited in?

Put in the more familiar terms of theodicy: how do we reconcile the hegemonic white Western idea of a goodness of divinity with the reality of unanswered brutality in our history? One way or the other, there is an irrecusable opacity in our ideas of ultimacy – either as active aggressor or as patient isolationist in the heavenly courts, observing, but not interfering in the ongoing rape and ravagement. We are left with a deity that either grins or grimaces, demonically. Merely insisting by dominant culture fiat – against all evidence to the contrary – that 'God is good!' does not solve the conundrum.

Tupac and Ogou

When we turn to the other side of the question, Tupac clearly is immediately (un)graspable as a mix. In background, Pac embraced both Pantherism and profit, both a legacy of activism and a desire for the dollar. In personal style, he described himself as simultaneously the most sensitive and most severe n … on the street – severe because sensitive! Programmatically, he celebrated thug antics while promoting thug politics, struggling to stay connected to 'the folk' in idiom, vision and party levity, while elaborating the style into a programmatic ethics and an elevated consciousness of the causes behind the criminality. Indeed, for biographer Dyson (2001, 157, 170–1), the dance between drive-bys and DVDs – a gangsta art that begins to command a gangsta life – finally caught Tupac in its dilemma, and destroyed him, tragically. But even here with the paradoxical result that many Makaveli devotees continue to report 'being saved' precisely by the hopelessness of the messenger. And an entire community and country remain queried by the apathy that sanctions the early demise of the likes of thousands of Tupacs, anonymous and literally 'unsung'. In exegeting the prominence of autopsy and elegy in rap poetry, Dyson says bluntly:

> If these youth are cynically viewed as the canary in the coal mine – since we all die, and death really is the mark of life, their actions embody the route we all eventually take to prepare for our demise – the sacrifice of their bodies for spiritual wisdom is a symbol of our inhumanity. Even if our reasons for allowing their suffering are not nearly as callous as that, the culture of death that suffocates black youth is nonetheless damning.
>
> (Dyson 2001, 228)

In lambasting Tupac for his choices, as is so easy to do in hindsight, he is sacrificed yet again. And the paradox of a planetary-wide system of contradiction – yielding vast resources for a luxury-loving few, fawned-over fetishistically by a middle class minority of wannabes, while a global majority struggle with poverty or perish early and a biosphere upends in ballooning extinctions – remains one more time hidden and hailed as 'civilisation'. Whatever we might want to conclude about Tupac as tragic travesty of a corporately manipulated pop culture mentality, the 'real' travesty goes unchecked. Pac himself intoned, after being challenged about his language by his elders at the Malcolm X Grassroots Movement in New York in the early 1990s, 'I'm sorry my language offends you, but it can't offend you more than the world your generation has left me to deal with' (Dyson 2001, 151–2). Tupac, as Dyson (2001, 107, 129) intimates, is a living embodiment of the question of theodicy, incarnate as 'the ghetto everyman'. Looking at this 'zeitgeist in sagging jeans', it is worth wondering if an 'Ogou event' of planetary proportions waits in the dock, ready to rock an entire globe with an apocalyptic knock of anger (2001, 107). Tupac may be just an inkling of a larger and much more serious conundrum – the 5000 year-old legacy of human imperial *hubris* – enjoining a new literacy before it is too late. To what degree can his already-lived life be 'illuminated' by Ogou intimations – for the sake of the rest of us?

While by no means a one-for-one match of traits, the life history of Tupac exhibits numerous characteristics that could be said to resonate with the mandates of an Ogou mission. Paragon of the prerogatives of militancy, hunting and ironworking, historically, Ogou emerges in the diaspora as the quintessential *Orisha* of Afro-urban struggle. Brown (1997, 65) guesses, for instance, that he is probably the major *mèt tet* (head spirit) of Big Apple immigrants. In the refocusing of the explanatory energies of African religious systems occasioned by the experience of slavery, Ogou became a kind of crossing point for the right-hand focus on family protection associated with the Rada pantheon of Nigeria and the left-hand ferocity of the Angolan Petro tradition, bending slaveholding coercions back onto the master (Brown 1997, 67–8). Ogou's power, in this New World adaptation, is rooted in emotion; the complexities of rage made to serve the lost and betrayed (ibid. 1997, 72–3). This Ogou (1997, 72, 81–2) has no children, presides over revolution, unpredictably oscillates between creation and destruction, veers close to suicide, carries the deep loneliness of the orphan as the underside of explosive defiance, fights, interminably, in the face of certain defeat, as both character flaw and endearment. In him, the contradictions of history, especially, become intelligible and palpable (1997, 76). In immigrant exile, he has even uncharacteristically been known to add the tears of despair to his repertoire of resistance (1997, 84). As an 'almost clinical diagnosis of what happens when people internalise anger', for Brown (1997, 86), Ogou-in-the-diaspora models a full range of the possibilities of 'wilfulness and assertion', when trouble abounds.

Patently, there is also much else about Ogou that could be commented upon: his Robin Hood-like zeal in aiding the oppressed; his hot-blooded propensity to do damage unwittingly; his legendary ambivalence, at once heroic and dread; his quick, sharp and exaggerated *ejiká* vocabulary in dance; his self-control in the face of danger; his sex-driven excessiveness, especially in drinking; his knife-like finesse, legendary in scarification and circumcision, or in social intervention in general; his workaholic intensity; his transformation as the reformed felon who returns to society, committed to break addiction (Babalola 1997, 155, 156, 168; Cosentino 1997, 294; J.H. Drewal 1997, 256; M.T. Drewal 1997, 216; Mason 1997, 365–6). And of course – as with any other dynamic force – he morphs, and adapts to different geographies and cultures with different flourishes. His modern advent as driving force of technology has him invoked by citizens of New Orleans in hopes of a street-clearing effect, keeping dope-peddlers and criminals out; by Cubans in New York through adding a Glock to their *caldera* of iron objects; by lawyers in Matamoros, Mexico as a co-conspirator in cult murders; by drivers in Nigeria for protection from accidents on the road; in 1990s Haiti, by *lavellas* as the animus of movement energy, articulating retribution against infamous *tonton macoute* savagery (Cosentino 1997, 298, 303–4). He waxes literary in Rigaud's (1953) work on the *Orisha* as incognito 'African manifestations of a universal mythology', personifying the Divine 'discipline of chaos', directing cosmic traffic with his magic sword stroke, and in Wole Soyinka's corpus, serves as 'totality of Dionysian, Apollonian and Promethean virtu[osity]' as well as muse and master of initiation (at the hands of his grandfather), inspiring everything from Soyinka's Dantesque reworking of Yoruban mythology (in his epic *Idanre*) to his eulogy of Muhammad Ali's butterfly stings in the ring (Cosentino 1997, 304–6). He goes Hollywood as 'divine tough guy' in The Believers and Miami Vice, and even ends up as a commodity in the supermercado in San Francisco (in the form of three nails and three rocks in an army boot, selling for only $1200) (Cosentino 1997, 291). Does he also levitate the lips of rhyme-spitting MCs of the city in hip hop parodies of life in the postindustrial terrordome?

Some of the affinity with the life-trajectory of Tupac is obvious. The refusal of resignation to the cul-de-sac of oppression (Brown 1997, 85; Dyson 2001, 138)! The struggle with rage – meting out vitriol as mettle, translating self-destructive pain into razor-sharp analysis, blacksmithing mineral-hard circumstance into explosive eloquence of comeuppance! The embodiment of amoral energy and excoriation of easy bifurcation – warring lifelong and mightily 'against the essential separation of the cursed and the blessed', of the middle class and the poor, of America itself and thug life, of God and gangstas (Babalola 1997, 168, Dyson 2001, 125, 157, 255, 209–11)! The Robin Hood-like concern for the poor (Pemberton 1997, 155; Dyson 2001, 150). The extremity like Ogou: not knowing any mode other than 'full bore', out of control and still full of finesse – as Tupac once lamented, laughing, after publicly 'dissing' Quincy Jones and Eddie Murphy, 'Me and my big mouth!' (Cosentino 1997, 294, 308; Dyson 2001, 9); the schizophrenia of commitments (Cosentino 1997, 294; Dyson 2001, 157); the embodiment of a hopelessness that saves others (Brown 1997, 78, 82; Cosentino 1997, 293–4; Dyson 2001, 123, 170–1); the tormented macho wounding – a masculinity at once hard and yet capable of tears (Cosentino 1997, 296; Dyson 2001, 193–5); the inability to sustain a committed sexual relationship; the felonious banishment and return to society as a workaholic advocate for the downtrodden; the dance with destruction inside of creativity; becoming indebted to powers that can demand one's life in payment (Brown 1997, 79; Cosentino 1997, 294; Mason 1997, 365; Pemberton 1997, 31; Dyson 2001, 187, 215).

The match is just as obviously not 'perfect'. Indeed – as an identifiable *Orisha* in an ever-adapting pantheon that admits of as many as seven or even 21 (or more) such *Orisha* (or *loa*) – no appearance of Ogou ever is so. In body, Ogou is perhaps more readily imagined as Mike Tyson 'muscle' than the miniature stature of Tupac – but interestingly, Pac's pontification on the thug persona, in Dyson's mind, leads inevitably to reflection on the former, as if Pac's art articulated Tyson's fist, at least as demonstratively as anything the latter accomplished in the ring (Cosentino 1997, 296; Dyson 2001, 163–4). On the other hand, one could also venture that Tupac channels Eshu-like tricksterism and humour as much as Ogou-like rage and id-behaviour (Mason 1997, 365). But then, Ogou in diasporic bearing is prone to compounding his capacities with Chango (Ogou Chango), or elaborating his niches in the social structure his idiom helps interpret by developing recognisable 'shades' of his influence like Feray (Ogou Feray) or Badagri (Ogou Badagri) (Brown 1997, 66, 71, 78). Indeed, Soyinka will speak of Ogou and Eshu in the same breath when using them to represent Muhammad Ali (Cosentino 1997, 305–6). Why not a new santo-thug hybrid called Ogou-Eshu of the city? Perhaps, such has already appeared?

In any case, for this writing it is pre-eminently the capacity to embody paradox as a question mark addressed to the context of desperation that speaks 'Ogou' inside Tupac. What Barnes glosses as the exhibition of 'the realisation that people create the means to destroy themselves', what Pemberton remarks as 'Ogou's inability to control the destruction entailed in his [own] creative power', and Brown as the 'mediat[ion] between two diametrically opposed forces', is surely the core of the cult-grammar Tupac has become (Barnes 1997, 17;

Brown 1997, 66; Pemberton 1997, 131; Dyson 2001, 233). Ogou inhabits and embodies the situation of extremity in the form of contradiction. Tupac lives and dies there. Neither will permit easy resolution, or a simplistic choice of sides for the sake of peace. They demand transformation, at the price of great upheaval. In response to criticism from Stanley Crouch charging a void of self-reflection in hip hop, Dyson proposes Tupac as precisely the figure of panoramic complexity, divining young black experience for explanation of the incoherence of an entire (American) culture (Dyson, 128). Citing Moorish Temple Science minister Everett Dyson-Bey to the effect that social activists and thugs alike can find sustenance in Pac's lyrics, Dyson writes that Tupac

> Constantly questioned his direction by filling his lyrics with characters who were both the victims and perpetrators of crime, characters who were thugs begging God for guidance through minefields of self-destruction, characters leaving the ghetto while others stayed, characters who asked why they suffered even as they imposed suffering. In that haze of morbid contradictions, Tupac shone the light of his dark, brooding, pensive spirit, refusing to close his eyes to the misery he saw, risking everything to bear witness to the pain he pondered and perpetuated ... [an] effort [finally] to square belief in God with the evil that prevails, which is at root an attempt to explain the suffering of those he loved.
>
> (Dyson 2001, 128–9)

Yoruba diviner and Ogou 'horse' John Mason writes,

> Ogùn (Ogou) is the reformed felon (murderer, wife beater, child molester) who reenters society ever more conscious of the high ethical standard we must all strive for. He breaks addictions, putting aside drink/drugs/violence, and thus offers hope to the hopeless.
>
> (Mason 1997, 366)

Before entering jail, Tupac told long-time friend Jada Pinkett Smith, 'I'm going to stop thugging; I'm getting rid of the guns; I'm getting rid of all these n ... s around me. I'm changing, Jada' (Dyson 2001, 215). But by all accounts, jail changed him and one side of the paradox broke (Dyson 2001, 216). Nihilism triumphed. But then ... what if he had lived and met some credible form of Ogou, outside of himself, looking in?

Tupac as Ogou

But already I seem to have slipped in my parody. Tupac read as Ogou prophet, as John the Baptist-like pointer towards the epiphany of Contrariety, the hip hop equivalent of Soyinka as the iron god's literary apostle, is different from Tupac as an incarnation of Ogou. Precisely ... at least for those of us Western trained and convinced! But from the angle of possession cult cultures, no! Prophesy about divinity in older elaborations of spirituality meant exactly to 'host' the spirit towards which one pointed. This is the real challenge of the Makavelian epiphany for white America.

The title of the article specifically proposes to read Tupac through the lens of Ogou Achade, a *bokò*-sorcerer wielding aggressive powers – alongside other Ogou *personas* approximating soldiers or politicians – appropriate to situations of confrontation (Brown 1997, 79). 'The inclusion of a sorcerer spirit in the pantheon of the Ogou', says Brown, 'suggests a situation in which power is unevenly distributed, for sorcery is the weapon of the underdog' (Brown 1997, 79). While Tupac was early on banished from being a foot soldier in the drug trade as too inept, he was also certainly too brash to curry favour in the coin of politics. His power was his frankness, a mind questioning 'whatever line you were riding on', according to *Vibe* editor Danyel Smith, a 'full bore' intensity, refusing to shrink from the aggressive swelling of his thug persona (Dyson 2001, 58, 152). 'Achade' is certainly the right nuance to place on Tupac-Ogou – 'a transcendent force of creative fury' whose 'cultural heft', according to Dyson (2001, 106) is readily qualified as 'shamanistic'.

But the task, as already mentioned, is a matter not simply of reading a person, but rather an archetype – creation as much of Tupac's posthumous following as of his own tortured artistry-in-the-flesh. Dyson argues provocatively for a Tupacalypse resurrection – a body built of rumour and re-runs, reverbs and vibes still echoing a decade into the demise. The subject of Urban Legend to be sure, subject to numerology and illusion, is a signification of the ghetto to sound out the continuing impossibilities of living inside a social absurdity. Underneath the tattooed image, augurs Dyson(2001, 254), lies an abandoned people, creating the conditions of their own survival, by giving 'anonymous social power … a face and motivation'. By investing in – and partly inventing – such a posthumous persona, 'ordinary people are in fact recreating themselves' (2001, 262). The thug icon becomes a charged battle zone: an outcropped idea of globalizing culture, in which white control is summoned and eclipsed, glimpsed like the windmills of (Don) Quixote even as misperceptions abound, at once hated in an eloquent exposure and simultaneously embraced in unthought imitation. But the contradictoriness is hardly more scurrilous than in the precincts of whiteness itself. Indeed, I would argue, whiteness is such inconsistency incarnate – amplified now into a global crisis – intent on securing resource flows from abroad while spreading 'democracy' from the barrel of a gun.

Tupac as Ogou to America

Whatever may be the efficacy – or not – for the black community of interpreting Tupac according to the conventions of a spirituality that imagines divinity in the code of paradox rather than simply as 'good', the issue for white America is paradigmatic. Its name is possession, as opposed to exorcism (indeed, 'possession' as in 'being possessed' – corollary in the body to Kramer's hermeneutic of 'being observed'. The passive voice here is crucial; clearly America and the West in general are quite familiar with the act of possessing – they have been virtual incarnations of that enterprise from their historic beginnings). White Western culture has ever been on a mission of eviction – of bodies from lands, of resources from the ground, of flora and fauna from habitat, of culture from ecology, of languages from their native tongues – in a ruthless interdiction of otherness in the mode of (Christian) religious conviction that heterogeneity is by definition demonic. There are no models, within white normativity and control, for encounter with the other through difference honouring mimesis. (The ones that exist – like Dorothy Day on hunger strike for the right of the poor to eat or John Brown in the dock for unlocking the Harper's Ferry armoury to anti-slavery war – are minority and untaught in the halls of pedagogical formation.) Yet, it is just this that I would argue Tupac in particular, and hip hop in general, enjoins for white American culture.

In the space remaining in this article, I can only suggest. Edward Bynum's limning of an African unconscious, coursing under the surface of history's meanderings as a dangerous, and largely unthought, memory admits of an unfathomable corollary: history represents, among other imponderables, a huge and impossible attempt to exorcise, rather than integrate, ancestry. The politicisation of light over dark – wherever social hierarchy has drafted colour codes into its pathology – seems nearly ubiquitous, and represents the quintessence of repressive intentionality and discipline! The claim is huge: racialisation of the world's peoples in service of white (or any other form of) supremacy is merely its latest wrinkle. But its implication is that 'exorcism' itself – as spiritual tactic, as military strategy, as political policy or economic effect – may be precisely the demonic gesture, par excellence. Older traditions across the planet – indeed, the *longue durée* of the species as a whole, in its manyfold figurings of the meaning behind the matter at hand – have generally embraced the strange under the impulse of masquerade and metabolism – an internalising of the fascinating or overwhelming details of the natural or social 'other' by way of imitation (Kramer 1993, 207). Exorcism, if engaged at all, was first informed by possession. Such was the shaman's travail – to take in and bodily 'trans-mutate' the force that frightened.

Fritz Kramer's *Red Fez* rehearses the ramifications at length. Tracking the multiplex modes of 'enculturating the other' in African societies across the continent as the genesis and motive force for possession-cult elaboration, Kramer distils from the weight of theory a basic differentiation (Kramer 1993, 199, 248). Western ethnographic empathy all to the good, *mimesis*, not poeisis, is the manner of negotiation represented in the motherland; Victor Turner's efforts at honouring possession as 'socio-drama' will draw down a charge of ethnocentrism:

> By submitting even 'performative' ethnography to the programme of slipping 'inside' the skin of the stranger, combined with self-revelation, Turner was working completely under the spell of a specifically modern type of confrontation with the other in which, as Hegel wrote, the European spirit wishes to recognize itself.
>
> (Kramer 1993, 245)

Between 'ritual acknowledgement of the other to one's culture in the African cults' and the 'process of analysis and systematisation in modern ethnography' lies the difference of canon-breaking imitation from creative appropriation – a difference not of art and science, but of 'divergent forms of self-interpretation via the other' (Kramer 1993, 246, 253). Submission to influences from without, rather than a gerrymandering of such in ultimate service of homogeneity, is the issue (1993, 246). Whatever we might think of the reality of 'spirits', possession cults and masking rites alike gave a certain amount of autonomous agency to the incursions of otherness, allowing difference to have its say inside the body of the same (1993, 249, 251). The category of consequence for Kramer is that of the 'overwhelming' (Kramer 1993, 249, 251, 253–4, 256). (And here there is obvious intersection with the work of Long (1986) on Rudolph Otto's *mysterium tremendum et fascinans* that so informed my previous thinking about Ogou; Long's argument that the deep difference articulating modernity's encounter with otherness can be found in an archaeological confrontation with overwhelming Terror visited by the West on indigenous cultures, that only confirmed spurious Western ideas of a fascinated superiority, here finds resonant echo even in intra-African encounters.)[4] Only when the other is allowed or is experienced as an advent that overwhelms the operative codes, does 'penetration' effect possession and a mode of expression capable of incubating genuine birth of the new (Kramer 1993, 257).

And here then is the real bite of my convoluted *hermeneusis* of Tupac as Ogou. Tupac as mere artist, as fascinating spitter of rhyme on prime time, as posthumous appearance in an outlaw epiphany seeking company with Elvis or James Dean, remains captive to the enervating American apotheosis of individual genius. Certainly he is as worthy of such, in his contradictory and tortured eloquence, as any other hero of the screen. But Tupac as Ogou is a left-field evocation of a code not captive to Western ethical ledgers. Here, the opposite and the ugly kiss in base-beat cacophony! This is the Tupac that taps 'the unconscious vein of white fear and fascination' (Dyson 2001, 163). He penetrates. He remains as undigested as black ancestry under white skin. 'Symptom' (!) of a more generic Ogou eruption. And LA in May of 1992 as the kind of broader Ogou advent that gangsta rap in general and Tupac in particular signified and sounded out! But that too may have been mere symptom (repeated as recurrent litany in Cincinnati, or Benton Harbor, or even *the banlieues of gai Paris* in 2005). Perhaps, the anger erupting today all over the precincts of public palaver, shredding civility, leveraging hand-wringing, tearing the nation into incoherent rants of red and blue, is not a mere matter of lost politesse. Perhaps, it is intervention in the form of an ancestor, demanding dues. By other lights – an older god in newer dress, 'sussing out' the nation (or even as world-historical event)! And in this form, he is not containable in a Christian prayer (merely) for peace.

Conclusion

Tupac as Ogou is a divine preview – mirroring the conundrum in 'mercy' by comparison with the consequences of not listening to the tone and reading the figure rightly. In many respects, he convened a theatre of the cult of thug – and invited identification by America at large. But if we refuse the efficacies of the possession therapy so offered and insist merely on more of the same – a scapegoating of the named 'evil' as 'criminal', a rejection of the embodied as 'pollution' of *our* body politic, a grasping one more time for the false mirrors of innocence – the logic of the denials could well take us off the face of the planet (given the kind of weaponry now available with which to express anger). Ogou appeared in the flesh and came to his own people and his own people received him not. The conundrum in a nutshell! And it happens again and again – but perhaps not forever. Is Tupac us? I am speaking largely to my own white homies. Shall we exorcise him? Or confess possession *by* him – recognise 'us' in him and 'him' in us – learn the idiom, and direct the sword, finally, towards our own inflated being?

Study Questions

1. What is the significance of the hip hop verses America trope for the understanding of hip hop culture and race?
2. Who is Ogou and how does Perkinson connect this figure with hip hop culture and late rapper Tupac Shakur?
3. What are the differences between the manner in which a figure like Ogou handles the sacred and profane verses American Christian culture? How does Perkinson use Ogou and hip hop culture to offer a challenge and call to the white American community?

Notes

1. The way many of our institutional processes continue to function as de facto 'transfer payments', accumulating profit in corporate ledgers, filling executive pockets and building better McMansions, in part, by funnelling already meagre resources away from communities of disadvantage, is patent. I have elsewhere outlined the process ranging from Social Security payouts to 'shadow-banking' predation, from gentrifying takeover of core city property to prison industrial complex job incubation, from disparate pay for the same effort to exponential differences in net worth. The focus of the unfolding subprime loan debacle on largely black and Latino mortgagees is just more of the same – a structural interweaving of middle-class prosperity and lower class poverty whose history and intractability remains

definitive of social relations inside this country and a rough parable of US relations with the rest of the globe. Here, I will not further press the point, but rather presume it.

2. See Perkinson (2001, 2005).
3. Hebrew prophets were notorious for their cryptic theatricalisations of political dilemmas facing the nation, whether in the form of Isaiah going naked for three years in the public square as sign of coming exile, Ezekiel baking his barley over dried human dung as portent of Yahweh's impeachment of the nation's unjust prosperity, or Jeremiah as celibate in lifelong disparagement of Israel's false sense of domestic security (Is. 20: 1–6; Ezek. 4: 9–13; Jer. 16; 1–4). Isaiah, in particular, invoked Assyria's arising as a mighty flood soon to inundate Israel's false tranquillity (Is. 8: 5–8).
4. See my 'Ogu's Iron or Jesus' Irony', 570–2, 586; Long, 110, 137–9, 177–8, 193–5.

References

Babalola, A. 1997. A portrait of Ogun as reflected in Ijala chants. In *Africa's Ogùn: Old world and new*, ed. Sandra T. Barnes, 147–72. Bloomington, IN: Indiana University Press.

Baker, H. 1993. Scene … not heard. In *Reading Rodney King, Reading urban uprising*, ed. R. Gooding-Williams, 38–50. New York: Routledge.

Barnes, S. T. 1997. The many faces of Ogùn: Introduction to the first edition. In *Africa's Ogùn: Old world and new*, ed. Sandra T. Barnes, 1–28. Bloomington, IN: Indiana University Press.

Brown, K. M. 1984. Why women need the war God. In *Women's spirit bonding*, ed. J. Kalven and M. Buckley, 190–201. New York: Pilgrim Press.

—— 1991. *Mama Lola: A Vodou priestess in Brooklyn*. Berkeley, CA: University of California Press.

—— 1997. Systematic remembering, systematic forgetting: Ogou in Haiti. In *Africa's Ogùn: Old world and new*, ed. Sandra T. Barnes, 65–89. Bloomington, IN: Indiana University Press.

Bynum, E. B. 1999. *The African unconscious: Roots of ancient mysticism and modern psychology*. New York: Teachers College Press.

Cosentino, D. 1997. Repossession: Ogùn in folklore and literature. In *Africa's Ogùn: Old world and new*, ed. Sandra T. Barnes, 290–314. Bloomington, IN: Indiana University Press.

Drewal, H. 1997. Art or accident: Yoruba body artists and their deity Ogùn. In *Africa's Ogùn: Old world and new*, ed. Sandra T. Barnes, 235–62. Bloomington, IN: Indiana University Press.

Drewal, M. 1997. Dancing for Ogùn in Yorubaland and in Brazil. In *Africa's Ogùn: Old world and new*, ed. Sandra T. Barnes, 199–234. Bloomington, IN: Indiana University Press.

Dyson, M. 2001. *Holler if you hear me: Searching for Tupac Shakur*. New York: Basic Civitas Books.

Gibson, W. 1986. *Count zero*. New York: Ace Books.

Kramer, F. 1993(1987). *The red fez: Art and spirit possession in Africa*. Trans. Malcolm Green. London: Verso.

Long, C. 1986. *Significations: Signs, symbols, and images in the interpretation of religion*. Philadelphia, PA: Fortress Press.

Mason, J. 1997. Ogùn: Builder of the Lùkùmí 's House. In *Africa's Ogùn: Old world and new*, ed. Sandra T. Barnes, 353–68. Bloomington, IN: Indiana University Press.

Pemberton III, J. 1997. The Dreadful God and the Divine King. In *Africa's Ogùn: Old world and new*, ed. Sandra T. Barnes, 105–46. Bloomington, IN: Indiana University Press.

Perkinson, J. W. 2001. Ogu's Iron or Jesus' Irony: Who's zooming who in diasporic possession cult activity? *Journal of Religion* 81, no. 4: 566–94.

—— 2004a. Reversing the gaze: Constructing European race discourse as modern witchcraft practice. *Journal of the American Academy of Religion* 72, no. 3: 603–30.

—— 2004b. *White Theology: Outing Supremacy in Modernity*. New York: Palgrave Macmillan.

—— 2005. Modernity's witchcraft practice. In *Shamanism, racism, and hip-hop culture: Essays on white supremacy and black subversion*, 17–42. New York: Palgrave Macmillan Press.

Rigaud, M. 1985 [1953]. *Secrets of Voodoo*. San Francisco: City Lights.

Stannard, D. E. 1992. *American Holocaust: The Conquest of the New World*. New York: Oxford University Press.

28

Rap Music, Hip-Hop Culture and "the Future Religion of the World"

Sylvan begins this essay with an exploration of the cultural and musical history of "old school" hip hop and rap music—their pioneers and the new street culture that began to emerge in the 1970s. After considering the complicated life worlds of DJ Kool Herc and Africa Bambaataa, two of hip hops' founders, Sylvan argues the early days of rap music (1974–1978) were largely representative of an underground dance party phenomenon which is followed by a more salient musico-religious spirituality of truth telling through artists like KRS-One and Public Enemy. Gangsta rap in the 1980s and 1990s arose alongside chaos and societal fragmentation. With the historical development of these three epochs in place, Sylvan examines the existential, cultural, and religious roots of West African and African American culture through a consideration of poetry, polyrhythms, and the prophetic tradition. Over and against the idea of "priestly function," Sylvan explores what he calls hip hop spirituality through a consideration of a wide variety of artists and songs. He concludes by suggesting that a postmodern "bricolage"-like culture represents future religious articulations rooted in technological advancement, developments and changes in compositional principles of hip hop music. This shift makes available religious choices that bypass narrow and more traditional religious options.

Rap Music, Hip-Hop Culture and "the Future Religion of the World"

Robin Sylvan

When rap music and hip-hop culture first emerged from the South Bronx in the late 1970s, critics dismissed it as a superficial fad that would quickly fade and be relegated to the dustbin of history. Over the course of the past three decades, however, this kind of pejorative assessment has been proved wrong time and time again, as rap has consistently dominated the music industry and hip-hop sensibility has become part and parcel of mainstream American popular culture. A case in point is the enormous success of female rapper Lauryn Hill's album *The Miseducation of Lauryn Hill* (1998), which topped the charts at number one for weeks, sold several million copies, and won numerous Grammies. Or perhaps one might channel surf the television to find rap music and hip-hop styles in commercials for everything from McDonald's hamburgers to Pringles potato chips to Mervyn's department store. This is an extraordinary trajectory for an African-American musical subculture that began in what is arguably the most economically and culturally marginalized neighborhood of the country.

What is even more remarkable about the success of rap and hip-hop is that it still contains a powerful and distinctive African-American religious world view that runs directly counter to the religious world view of the mainstream culture it has come to permeate. Faced with the oppressive historical circumstances of African Americans' marginalized status, this religious world view refuses to take refuge in the hope of otherworldly salvation but, rather, tells the truth about the harsh reality of this oppression and transforms the impulse toward anger and violence into empowerment, creative expression, spirituality, and positive change. Here I will look at the contradictory dynamics of hip-hop's rise to mainstream success – its historical and cultural development, its West African and African-American roots, and its spiritual dimensions – and explore the important implications for the larger landscape of religion in American popular culture.

"Old School": Cultural and Musical History

Rap music emerged as one component of hip-hop, a new street culture that included graffiti and break dancing as important forms of expression. The music for rap was put together by DJs mixing stripped-down, bass-heavy, polyrhythmic beats from turntables and samplers, drawing heavily on roots in soul, funk, and disco. This new style of sonic collage quickly became the soundtrack for street parties and "ghetto blasters" (portable tape players) through-out the Bronx. But the term "rap" actually refers to the rhyming poetry that the lead vocalist would improvise on the microphone in rhythm to the beats. Raps were spoken as well as sung, and they featured the rapper's prowess in turning a phrase. This prowess could take the form of innovative rhyming, rhythmic dexterity, boasting, humor, narrative story-telling, or even preaching. The subjects of the raps reflected the grim reality of young African Americans' life in the ghetto: racism, poverty, broken families, substandard housing, unemployment, violence, drugs, gangs, police brutality, arrests, incarceration, and short life expectancy.

Innovative DJs like Kool Herc and Afrika Bambaataa used their turntable mixing skills to create the first beat-driven sonic collages that form the foundation of rap music. These were originally dance mixes for neighborhood parties in houses, parks, and community centers. These pioneering hip-hop DJs not only drew heavily on soul and funk recordings, but also used the new technologies of the cross-fade mixer, the sampler, and the drum machine. Songs were segued seamlessly into each other for a continuous dance mix. At the same time, the breaks in each song and between songs – those places where the instrumentation would pull back to highlight the rhythm section – were emphasized and extended in a collage of peak dance beats. These became known as "break beats" or "b-beats," and DJ Kool Herc was their acknowledged master. The wild athletic dancing that accompanied these break beats became known as "break dancing," and the male break dancers became known as "break boys" or "b-boys" for short. Hip-hop DJs also developed new skills on the turntables which strongly contributed to the distinctive rap sound. Foremost among these was "scratching," a technique in which the DJ used his hand to quickly spin the record back and forth under the needle, thus producing a quirky staccato rhythm. Another technique was "backspinning," in which the DJ isolated a short verbal or musical phrase on a record, and repeated it by quickly spinning back to the beginning. One of the early creators and masters of both the scratch and the backspin was Grandmaster Flash. Both of these techniques produced cross-rhythms on one turntable while the other supplied the main groove, a clearly polyrhythmic approach to musical composition. Samplers also allowed DJs to bring a wide assortment of sound sources into their eclectic pastiches.

Kool Herc and Afrika Bambaataa each had his own group of neighborhood friends, known as their "crew" or "posse," who hung out with them and accompanied them to all their jams. Thus rap music grew out of specific neighborhoods and local communities, each developing its own distinctive style. Often, there were competitions between DJs and their crews for territory, both physical and sonic, in which DJs would exhibit their mixing prowess and b-boys would display their dance moves. These competitions closely paralleled the territoriality of street gangs, but with one notable difference—there was no violence. Instead, the crews channeled their competitive energies into artistic expression, choosing a creative outlet rather than a destructive one. Afrika Bambaataa was a pioneer in making explicit the connection between these hip-hop crews and a sense of African identity and spiritual pride. Bambaataa, whose name means "affectionate leader" in Zulu, called his crew "Zulu Nation," and created an extended family unified not only by hip-hop expression but also by a positive vision of African-American community.

The raps themselves began with the DJs calling out on microphones over the music to exhort the audience to dance harder, repeating phrases like "rock the house," "get down," or "you don't stop." Because DJ mixing is a demanding task requiring full concentration, however, soon they brought in friends to work the microphone full time. Here again, DJ Kool Herc was an innovator in being among the first to use an MC (microphone controller or master of ceremonies). The MCs not only gave the parties more of a live feel, but they also fulfilled the important task of crowd control, maintaining a positive feeling, and keeping potential violence at bay. Very quickly, the MCs developed their own creative styles, using the latest slang and hippest rhymes to supplant the DJ as the focal point of the music. The competitive aspect shifted over to the rappers as well, as MCs dueled on the microphone trying to show who was the best rhymer.

In these early days of rap, roughly 1974 to 1978, it was still primarily an underground party phenomenon. This changed with the successful release of three seminal rap records – the Sugar Hill Gang's "Rapper's Delight" in 1979, Grandmaster Flash and the Furious Five's "The Message" in 1982, and Afrika Bambaataa's "Planet Rock" in 1983 – which quickly established the commercial viability of rap. In 1986, Run-DMC completed rap's cross-over to mainstream popularity when their single "Walk This Way" hit number one on the charts. Articles on rap began to appear in bastions of mainstream journalism like *The New York Times* and *Time* magazine. Run-DMC's crossover paved the way for the commercial success of other rap artists like LL Cool J, Eric B. and Rahim, Public Enemy, and Salt 'n' Pepa, one of the few prominent women rap groups. At the same time, vibrant local rap subcultures emerged in other urban centers around the country, including Miami, Boston, Houston, Oakland, and Los Angeles, each with its own distinctive sound and style.

Artists like Public Enemy and KRS-One made a strong push toward a more hard-core musical sound and a more militant political message. In combining an unflinching critique of contemporary black oppression with a visionary call to resistance and liberation, Public Enemy and KRS-One continued and updated a long-standing African-American musico-religious tradition of truth telling, an approach hip-hop scholar Angela Spence Nelson has called "combative spirituality" (Nelson 1991, 59).

The hard-core sound was to attain its greatest success, however, with the ascendancy of the Los Angeles area "gangsta" rap subculture in the late 1980s and early 1990s. The word "gangsta" is a reference to the centrality of gang activities among African-American and Hispanic youth in Los Angeles, which includes some of the worst crime and violence in the country and an underground economy largely based on crack cocaine. In areas like South Central Los Angeles, gang violence is commonplace, and the panicked response of white authorities has resulted in the creation of a virtual police state with its own violent excesses. The 1991 brutal beating of Rodney King by Los Angeles police, the acquittal of the responsible officers, and the subsequent riots on the streets gave an indication of the high level of hatred and tension in the area. It was out of this tableau of economic despair, gang violence, the crack epidemic, and police repression that gangsta rap emerged. The seminal gangsta group was N.W.A. (Niggaz With Attitude), whose 1988 album *Straight Outta Compton*, with its in-your-face attitude, funky West Coast sound, and gritty tales of violent gang life, sold more than two million copies. N.W.A.'s stylistic and commercial breakthrough opened the door for a number of other Los Angeles-area gangsta rap artists to attain success, including Ice-T, Snoop Doggy Dogg, and original N.W.A. members Ice Cube and Dr. Dre as solo artists.

The post-gangsta rap era has seen a new generation of rap artists break through to mainstream success as the market share of rap music has more than doubled in the past two decades. In addition to Lauryn Hill, artists like Puff Daddy (Sean Combs), Wu-Tang Clan, DMX, Master P, Jay-Z, Mase, and Eminem, to mention just a few, all had their run at the top of the charts. Far from being a passing fad, rap music has proved its staying power over the course of the past three decades, and has steadily grown in influence to become a permanent fixture in the mainstream world of popular culture. The fact that hip-hop is a primarily African-American subculture with strong roots in West African practices and sensibilities makes its penetration of mainstream popular culture an even more significant development from a religious perspective.

Poetry, Polyrhythms, Possession, and Prophetic Tradition: West African and African-American Roots

> We've been rapping forever. You know, there's nothing new under the sun. The griots were doing the same, the storytellers, oral tradition people … And the drum's also the center of it. You can't have it without the drum. And now hip-hop is experimenting, trying new things, but really the beat is what's always. It's the drums, just like drums in any form. That's definitely African.
>
> (Interview with Malcolm [no last name given], Oakland, July 12, 1997)

In the course of doing research in the San Francisco Bay area in 1997, I had the opportunity to spend some time in the East Bay hip-hop community known as the Oakland Underground, attending musical events and conducting interviews with aficionados. Time and again in these interviews, I was struck by the explicit recognition and conscious acknowledgment of the African roots of rap and hip-hop. These roots can be traced back more specifically to two West African geographical and cultural zones: the coastal forest belt cultures like the Ga, Ewe, Fon, and Yoruba of modern Ghana, Togo, Benin, and Nigeria; and the Sahelian cultures of the Manding, Wolof, and Peul of modern Senegal, Gambia, Guinea, Mali, and Burkina Faso.

One of the primary religious complexes in the coastal forest belt is that of possession dances, sacred ceremonies in which drum ensembles and singers supply beat-driven polyrhythmic music and the initiates dance themselves into ecstatic trance states in which the gods take possession of their bodies, becoming physically present among the community for the purposes of counseling, healing, divination, and so forth. Many of the distinctive elements of this complex made their way to the Americas through the slave trade and became important components of African-American music and religion, albeit in significantly changed forms. Rap displays strong continuities with a number of these elements. Musically, one finds the centrality of rhythm as an organizing principle, with the elements of harmony and melody stripped down almost completely. The groove is generated from interlocking polyrhythms, and even though the constituent parts are sampled or prerecorded, they operate in the same way as live drumming. As one rapper said: "That is what, to me, makes hip-hop. It's got the rhythmic conversation of the drum and the rhythmic conversation of the bass" (interview with Paris King, Oakland, July 3, 1997). Another musician put it this way: "I'm pretty much focusing on the groove. … If it's a great groove, then … that really is the bottom line" (interview with Keith Williams, San Jose, July 4, 1997). And this polyrhythmic groove provides a connection to the ancestors, expressed thus: "Our ancestors are still calling. And the break beats we used in the beginning are still from God, still ally [sic] your soul" (interview with Jorge Guerrero, Berkeley, August 6, 1997).

The interconnection between music and dance is also central, as is evident in the importance of break dancing in the early hip-hop subculture. Many of the hip-hop aficionados I interviewed said that break dancing was their initial entry point into the music: "I was taking the energy of the beat and then just amplifying it through my movement. Like making the music almost seem like it was coming more intensely by seeing what I'm doing, or by me seem like it was coming more intensely by seeing what I'm doing, or by me feeling what I'm doing, it seemed like the music became more intense" (interview with Steve Gaines, Berkeley, July 20, 1997). Some of these intensified states contain strong echoes of the possession experience:

> What I felt as a kid was strictly vibration, rhythm, and that music has a rhythm that just called my soul. It would make my soul jump out of my body, literally, and I'd

> have to move to it … It really calls me, it really does … Sometimes my body does things I can't even control and it's like I'm not even here … It's just a link. Something touches you one day, just sparks your whole consciousness, and shows your body you can. Time and space is all about the rhythm in your body … It's the ancients. It's definitely the ancients.
>
> (Guerrero, interview, August 6, 1997)

Interestingly, the circular form of break dancing, and even some of its dance moves, shows a striking similarity to African-American musico-religious dances like the ring shout, the Afro-Brazilian martial art capoeira, and traditional West African dances. The movements can also take the form of call and response, another classic element of African music, with the rapper's calls to "put your hands in the air" evoking an audience response of enthusiastic hand waving. These interactions demonstrate the participatory nature of the medium as well, another important principle of African music.

What is especially distinctive about rap music's continuities with West African and African-American musical principles, however, is the rap itself and its prominent foregrounding of an oral mode of expression, the roots of which are more closely associated with the Sahelian cultures of West Africa. These cultures have a long and distinguished lineage of men's societies of court poets and musicians called *jalis*, known as griots in the West, who maintained complex oral traditions of praise, lineage, and celebration. Many of the *jalis'* pieces were extremely long and had to be memorized; others were improvised on the spot for the specific occasion. In either case, a high level of oral skill was required. In these West African cultures, the spoken word was seen as potent and sacred, having the power to evoke that which was being spoken. This supernatural power of the spoken word was called *nommo*. This ancient power is something that hip-hop aficionados are able to recognize in today's raps: "Some people I hear, and it sounds like a long time ago … These are words of power, like certain words, like positive suggestions of just certain frequencies of sounds" (Gaines, interview, July 20, 1997).

This emphasis on the potency of the spoken word and the oral tradition was to continue after the slave trade brought many of these West Africans to the Americas. During slave times, in the context of plantations especially, the oral tradition manifested itself in more secular forms such as the work song and the plantation tale (e.g. Brer Rabbit or Stagger Lee), as well as in rhyming jokes and singing games. Yet these secular forms preserved elements of the sacred traditions in a way that allowed them to continue in a transformed way. The Christian church, as the only officially legitimized context for religious expression allowed to the slaves, was also an important repository for the oral tradition. This was particularly evident in the preaching style of African American ministers, who relied heavily on rhythm, rhyme, and the skillful use of other rhetorical techniques to raise energy and to give the message greater potency.

The oral tradition continued to evolve in the post-emancipation era, becoming a significant component in both the major forms of African-American secular music – blues and jazz – not so much in the music itself as in the lingo of the subcultures. As African Americans moved from rural southern areas to northern cities, oral expression took the form of urban street talk, which had a more boastful, aggressive quality. Thus practices like sounding, woofing, jiving, signifying, rapping, and telling toasts were raised to high levels of prowess on the city streets in a friendly but competitive atmosphere. Some highwater marks of this oral artistry include the Harlem Renaissance and the poet Langston Hughes, black radio DJs in the 1940s and 1950s, and the game of ritual insult called "the dozens." The Reverend Martin Luther King Jr. captivated the nation in the 1960s with the visionary fervor of his preaching style. Malcolm X also had a powerful oral style that strongly affected the African-American community in the

1960s. And the flamboyant and controversial boxing champion Muhammad Ali, widely idolized among African Americans, exposed the whole world to his boastful, humorous rhyming.

But perhaps the most important trailblazers for contemporary rap were the poet Gil Scott-Heron and the ensemble the Last Poets. Active during the late 1960s and early 1970s, the Last Poets were a group of black militant storytellers and poets who used the rhythms of conga drums to accompany their spoken political raps. Scott-Heron's brilliant work, including famous pieces like *The Revolution Will Not Be Televised* and *This Is Madness,* was innovative and influential, not only for its marriage of spoken raps with rhythmic grooves, but also for its unabashedly hard-hitting political message. Scott-Heron and the Last Poets were a source of inspiration for many key figures in the first generation of rappers, so much so that some consider them to be "the godfathers of message rap" (Perkins 1991, 42).

There is one more vitally important African-American influence on rap that must be noted, that of the blues, arguably the most quintessential of African-American musics. While there are certainly *musical* continuities among African traditions, the blues, and rap, the continuity of concern here is that of world view or theology, particularly with respect to the oppressive historical circumstances of Africans in the New World. The Christian theology adopted by many African-American churches sought to escape the hardships of suffering in this world by placing its faith in deliverance in the next. In contrast, the blues refused to look away from the suffering experienced as former slaves in the African diaspora, and sought a measure of whatever this-worldly redemption could be achieved through embodied sexuality and solidarity within the African-American community. As theologian James Cone eloquently writes:

> The blues are a lived experience, an encounter with the contradictions of American society, but a refusal to be conquered by it. They are despair only in the sense that there is no attempt to cover up reality. The blues recognize that black people have been hurt and scarred by the brutalities of white society. But there is also hope in what Richard Wright calls the "endemic capacity to live." This hope provided the strength to survive, and also an openness to the intensity of life's pains without being destroyed by them ... That black people could sing the blues, describing their joys and sorrows, meant that they were able to affirm an authentic hope in the essential worth of black humanity.
>
> (Cone 1992, 96–97)

There is such a strong similarity between this blues theology and that of hip-hop that this quote could well be a description of the world view of recent rappers, a continuity that has been noted by hip-hop scholars:

> Contemporary rappers, like early bluespeople, are responding to the "burden of freedom," in part by relaying portrayals of reality to their audiences through their personal experiences. They also relay positive portrayals of themselves as a means of affirming their personhood (and vicariously the personhood of their people) in a world that is constantly telling them they are nobodies.
>
> (Nelson 1991, 56)

> Rap music can be a profound extension of the prophetic or blues tradition and the legacy of heroism within the African-American experience.
>
> (Craddock-Willis 1989, 37)

In addition to theology, there is a strong continuity in the priestly role of the bluesman and the rapper as well, one which also has important religious implications. Ethnomusicologist Charles Keil writes:

> In spite of the fact that blues singing is ostensibly a secular, even profane, form of expression, the role is intimately related to sacred roles in the Negro community … As professions, blues singing and preaching seem to be closely linked in both the rural or small-town setting and in the urban ghettos. We have already noted some of the stylistic common denominators that underlie the performance of both roles, and it is clear that the experiences which prepare one for adequately fulfilling either role overlap extensively.
>
> (Keil 1966)

As I will show in the next section, this priestly function is consciously recognized by rappers and traced back through its African-American articulation to its West African roots. This conscious recognition of the African-American and West African roots of rap and hip-hop is a feature of their considerable religious quality, which demonstrates an extraordinary tenacity and adaptability in not just surviving five centuries of oppressive history, but emerging strong in a vibrant new formulation of these traditions.

Hip-Hop Spirituality

Hip-hop has been represented in mainstream media primarily by the gangsta rap image of dangerous black youth – angry, violent, and destructive. Yet, in my interviews with members of the Oakland Underground, they consistently claimed that hip-hop was exactly the opposite for them – peaceful, loving, inclusive, spiritual, and a force for positive change. This seeming contradiction has been a part of hip-hop culture since its South Bronx origins in the late 1970s, and understanding the dynamics of the dialectical relationship between these two polarities is central to understanding hip-hop's essential nature. To begin with, the situation of young African Americans and Latinos in inner-city ghettos is, as noted at the outset, one of racism, poverty, broken families, substandard housing, unemployment, violence, drugs, gangs, police brutality, arrests, incarceration, and short life expectancy. So, for any form of expression to have credibility, it must address that situation head-on, much as the blues did. In this regard, as Chuck D of Public Enemy has said, rap is black urban youth's CNN, providing information about what's going on in their world. This was a function confirmed in my interviews:

> Hip-hop music is always speaking to me, the lyrics. Especially in the late '80s, there were some real conscious things in hip-hop, and that was what was off-setting high school education, mainstream society, with all the information I was getting from KRS One and Public Enemy and X-Clan, all those groups. So, I just needed it at the time. We all needed it. They were speaking to me and educating me. I know they were. And I felt it. I needed it. It came at the right time.
>
> (Malcolm, interview, July 12, 1997)

In addition to providing information and educating, the raps also serve a crucial function of truth-telling: "It's very important to speak about how you really feel about something … This is one of the first times in music where you can really say what's going on … It's very honest.

There's a lot of references to whatever's happening right now" (Paris King, interview, July 3, 1997). There is a deeper spiritual aspect of this truth telling beyond simply educating and informing:

> One thing about rapping is always that you've got to come with your heart, who you are. And whatever that be, whether it be L.A. gangster music or New York "righteous" music or anti-government music, whatever. It's all about coming from your heart, saying what you believe in. Whether it was Ice Cube or Chuck D, it was just the spirit there. That's what was attractive, beyond the word itself, because you knew it was coming from the heart, for real.
>
> (Malcolm, interview, July 12, 1997)

In coming from the heart and speaking their truth, rappers are also speaking for their larger community. As one aficionado put it: "There is a culture of people who feel the voices of [rappers] represent them" (Paris King, interview, July 3, 1997). "Represent" is a word widely used by rappers to describe their function. Some take the implications of this even further and explicitly make the connection to the role of the priest and the griot:

> MCs are like the priests or the pastors of the people right now because a lot of children don't listen to their parents anymore. A lot of kids don't go to church anymore. So, MCs have been elevated to this recognizable status that's easily accessible. It's our duty as MCs to try to bring morals to the community, just like the griots in Africa brought morals and they try to pass down things that were basic … and that's like the role of MCs today.
>
> (Gaines, interview, July 20, 1997)

It is important to remember that the first South Bronx hip-hop crews of innovators like DJ Kool Herc and Afrika Bambaataa arose as an alternative to gang violence and drugs, channeling the destructive impulse into artistic expression. Awareness of this tradition continues today: "Hip-hop – originally, the dancers, the breaking groups – were this alternative similar to the fighting groups. They were just redirecting that energy. That's what they're still doing right now. You know, the energy's there. It's going to happen, it's going to get out one way or another. Hip-hop culture, to me, is one of the best alternatives that I've seen" (Malcolm, interview, July 12, 1997). This, then, is the source of hip-hop culture's seemingly paradoxical valuing of morality and spirituality at the same time it expresses anger and violent impulses – it alleviates the anger by providing a positive alternative direction to channel that energy:

> What it does for me is it calms my soul and all the struggle. I have a lot of anger in me from my ancestors and expressing it through music really gives me a venue. It's like God gave me a gift and He said, "I know that if I don't give you this gift, you're going to do a lot of crazy stuff." So I accept this gift, and I'm still struggling with it because there's a lot of bad things I want to do still, you know. But the music keeps me centered on what I'm here for.
>
> (Guerrero, interview, August 6, 1997)

And what is it that they are here for? Not anger and violence and destructiveness, but peace and love and spirituality. "One of the basic premises [of hip-hop culture] being based in peace and love for everyone, that also appealed to me. I just got absorbed into it. So, that's one of the messages that you got from hanging out in the scene" (interview with Carlos Mena, San Jose, July 17, 1997).

> Hip-hop's always been a spiritual culture. To me, it's just the mainstream doesn't let that show ... I went to something called the B-Boy Summit in San Diego ... and that was just one of the most spiritual things I've ever been to as far as all young people, all different colors, connected by this culture, hip-hop. All peace and love, you know. I mean, the exact opposite of what they'd have you think ... To me, that's what hip-hop is all about. It always has been, that kind of thread, that spiritual thread running through the culture.
>
> (Malcolm, interview, July 12, 1997)

This peace and love spirituality is not simply superficial sloganeering, but something that must be put into practice amid the difficulties of daily life. As one rapper put it: "It's in my day-to-day everyday ... It's not different from my life. It's what I do. It's just what's in life ... It's just onbeat every day" (Guerrero, interview, August 6, 1997). In this regard, another rapper was strongly affected by an experience he had listening to the advice of KRS-One:

> He said: "These are the practices we need to do. Act like the god that you know. Whatever god you know, act like him. If your god is loving and merciful, be loving and merciful. The things that you want to happen in your life, visualize them in your mind before you go to sleep." And he said something that was profound to me, because after all that attack, he came back with love, saying, "Here's something you can do for yourself regardless of what I'm saying or what you said." I talked to other people afterwards, and they were saying they do something like that every day of their life, and it works.
>
> (Gaines, interview, July 20, 1997)

This theme of hip-hop as spiritual practice emerged time and again in the interviews: "The people that I know, they're really trying to learn some things about themselves and tap into the rest of the spring that we don't use and these spiritual powers ... I've always taken the spiritual power seriously" (Malcolm, interview, July 12, 1997). "I have to be true to, not just the music and the musics that I'm bringing in, but now there's this religious thing ... I'm trying to reach another level of enlightenment" (Mena, interview, July 17, 1997).

> What it means to me to be a rapper is like, I look around at everything, and everything I absorb is God and I can express that, literally ... So it's really an expression. It's like praying. It's like being with God, literally, like being with God. Hip-hop culture is a spirituality. And it's everything that I can think of. Anything I am that I can do, that happens in this world, it's like that music, it's the culture ... It just gives you a purpose. It shows you why you're here ... It knows that I know God every day ... All those values have become part of the music and now it's in me every day.
>
> (Guerrero, interview, August 6, 1997)

As this last quote shows, one aspect of hip-hop spirituality that allows aficionados to achieve this type of integration into everyday life is the fact that it is part of a larger hip-hop culture. "Hip-hop is not the music; hip-hop is the culture. The music is rap music ... And those fuller aspects of hip-hop are grafitti, break dancing, MC-ing, and DJ-ing" (Paris King, interview,

July 3, 1997). "On a spiritual level, I think what now I know as hip-hop culture and respect as such [consists of] the grafitti, the dress, the language, the art, the people, the mindset that's the commonality of thought" (Mena, interview, July 17, 1997). So, immersing oneself in hip-hop culture creates connections and links to many different vital aspects of one's life: "It's just been my link to everything-my own spirituality, my self-knowledge, and music also … Everywhere I go, everywhere I grow, starts with hip-hop" (Malcolm, interview, July 12, 1997). "It linked me to everything-my future, my past, my family" (Guerrero, interview, August 6, 1997). It also creates links among different races, classes, and ethnicities, as one rapper observed earlier how "people" of "all different colors" are "connected by this culture, hip-hop" (Malcolm, interview, July 12, 1997). This inclusivity of hip-hop culture is expressed beautifully in this description of one rapper's experience at a concert:

> Everybody in the place was going back and forth at the same time. I remember look-ing back and seeing a whole moving wave of people. And it occurred to me how music brings people together. White people, Asian, Latino, black, different ages. And there wasn't any difference being noticed. Everybody was one. The music was pulling everyone together.
>
> (Gaines, interview, July 20, 1997)

This inclusivity, when combined with hip-hop's power to be a source of political and spiritual awakening in people's lives, leads to a sense that it can be a vehicle for change in the larger world:

> I see it being one of the major forces in the world bringing about change … Hip-hop culture is worldwide now. It's big in Japan. I know in Germany. And I hear from people all the time in places I would never expect – South Africa. Being one of the major forces bringing about change, new ways, new types of lifestyles, because the old ones, we just can't use them anymore. For young people, that'll be our political party … it's the closest thing we have to that. It includes politics. It includes spiritual-ity. It includes music. It includes having a good time. It's inclusive of so much … So, the hope is there in the spirit again, people are putting their hope in spirit, you know, God. Not God as an abstract form, but God in here and in there, you know. That's what we can use to get out of this mess. Hip-hop is just one of the manifestations. That's what we call it in the physical world … To me, music is the future religion of the world.
>
> (Malcolm, interview, July 12, 1997)

This is an extraordinary statement, not only because it describes a significant new hybrid "manifestation" of nontraditional religiosity emerging within popular culture, but also because its hopeful idealism is firmly grounded in the harsh conditions and contradictions of the real world. In concluding this chapter, I will explore the implications for the larger land-scape of religion in America.

Future Religion of the World: High-Tech Universalist Postmodern Bricolage in Popular Culture

The means of musical production has always been central not only to the music itself, but to the symbolism of the musical culture. For example, the drum can be seen as the instrument that symbolizes African music, the saxophone as the symbolic instrument for jazz, and the electric guitar as the symbolic instrument for rock. But, when it comes to rap music, the symbol is not an instrument at all, but the DJ's deck of two turntables and a cross-fade mixer. This simple contrast underlines an important point – that the means of musical production in rap has shifted away from traditional instruments to a new generation of electronic technologies. Moreover, this shift in musical technology has effected a corresponding shift in compositional principles. This innovative transformation in both musical technology and compositional form is a distinctive feature of rap that allows it to retain its African-American orientation at the same time that it points the way toward an emerging high-tech postmodern universalism in contemporary popular culture.

Many critics of rap music argue that the DJ is not actually creating new compositions, but simply taking already existing compositions via samplers and turntables and combining them through the mixer. However, it is precisely this ability to take music and sound from a variety of sources and combine them into an integrated whole that constitutes the craft and the musicality of the DJ, what one aficionado has called "the art of collage" (Paris King, interview, July 3, 1997). According to one DJ, this art "is all about recombinant potential. ... Each and every source sample is fragmented and bereft of prior meaning ... [and] given meaning only when re-presented in the assemblage of the mix ... A mix, for me, is a way of providing a rare and intimate glimpse into the process of cultural production in the late 20th Century" (Miller 1996). Thus the DJ mix is a truly postmodern act of creativity, in which the traditional structures have broken down and new forms have been stitched together from the deconstructed bits and pieces in a high-tech bricolage. This postmodern cut-and-paste bricolage illustrates the universalist inclusivity of hip-hop at a musical level: "Every music made in our last millennium ... leads up to hip-hop because it uses every aspect of every music completely ... It's a universal way of connecting all these different styles of music into one thing ... Mixing is like the universal language" (Guerrero, interview, August 6, 1997). The technology used in the creation of the music drum machines, cross-fade mixers, samplers, sequencers, computers reflects this postmodern sensibility as well. Originating in the elite, white, corporate world, these technologies were taken by low-income African Americans, used in entirely different ways, and transformed into a new mode of expression.

These new forms of musical technology and composition serve as analogical templates for a distinctively African-American approach to life in postmodern America that can be a useful model for mainstream culture as well. In her insightful musicological analysis of rap music, Tricia Rose identifies three crucial elements in its sonic architecture: flow, layering, and rupture. She goes on to spell out how these musical structures reflect a hip-hop worldview, philosophy, and code for living:

> These effects at the level of style and aesthetics suggest affirmative ways in which profound social dislocation and rupture can be managed and perhaps contested in the social arena. Let us imagine these hip-hop principles as a blueprint for social resistance and affirmation: create sustaining narratives, accumulate them, layer, embellish, and transform them. However, be also prepared for rupture, find pleasure in it, in fact, *plan on* social rupture. When these ruptures occur, use them in creative ways that will prepare you for a future in which survival will demand a sudden shift in ground tactics.

As we begin the twenty-first century, "profound social dislocation and rupture" appears to be an accurate description not only of the situation facing African Americans, but the situation facing all of us. Global communication and political economics have put an overwhelming array of diverse cultures, technologies, and information at our fingertips at the same time it is destroying long-standing traditions and paradigms. In this regard, hip-hop culture's ability to combine broken pieces into a new integrated whole can indeed serve as a blueprint for everyone in the new millennium.

Observers of culture and scholars of religion have said many things about the slow decline of institutional religion and the death of God in Western civilization. Yet, for the members of the Oakland Underground I interviewed, and hip-hop culture in general, religion and God are not dead, but very much alive and well and dancing to a hip-hop beat. The religious impulse has simply migrated to another sector of the culture, that of popular music, a sector in which religious sensibilities have flourished and made an enormous impression on a significant number of people. It is clear that hip-hop culture is a powerful religious phenomenon and just one example of many musical subcultures that function as religions in the lives of their adherents. Moreover, as the other chapters in this book show, popular music is just one example of many different arenas of popular culture that also function as religions in the lives of their adherents. From the micro to the macro – the Oakland Underground, rap and hip-hop in general, popular music, and popular culture – these new religious forms have already irrevocably changed the lives of millions of people, not only in terms of the texture of day-to-day living, but also in the way they see the world and the social forms that have sprung from those epistemologies. They signal the emergence of a significant alternative religious choice that bypasses the narrow opposition between traditional religious institutions and secular humanism. These are important changes with large implications that should not be underestimated. Moreover, the dynamic and innovative creativity of these new forms of expression indicates that one can expect them to be a source of religious vitality and evolution for generations into the future. To repeat the words of a DJ: "To me, music is the future religion of the world … Hip-hop is just one of the manifestations."

Study Questions

1. Why, according to Sylvan, is it vital to take African American and West African cultural roots into account when exploring religion in hip hop culture?
2. What can such a study yield about the changing landscape of religion in American popular culture today?
3. How has the contemporary look and form of religion in hip hop changed from the early days of rap music? Has there been a shift in social concerns? What does the future of religion and spirituality in hip hop look like according to Sylvan?

References

Cone, James. 1992. "Blues: A Secular Spiritual." *Black Sacred Music: A Journal of Theomusicology* 6, I (Spring): 68–97.

Craddock-Willis, Andre. 1989. "Rap Music and the Black Musical Tradition: A Critical Assessment." *Radical America* 23, 4 (October/December): 29–37.

Keil, Charles. 1966. *Urban Blues*. Chicago: University of Chicago Press.

Miller, Paul D. (a.k.a. DJ Spooky). 1996. Brochure notes from *Songs of a Dead Dreamer* (Asphodel 1961). CD.

Nelson, Angela Spence. 1991. "Theology in the Hip-Hop of Public Enemy and Kool Moe Dee." *Black Sacred Music: A Journal of Theomusicology* 5, I (Spring): 51–59.

Perkins, William Eric. 1991. "Nation of Islam Ideology in the Rap of Public Enemy." *Black Sacred Music: A Journal of Theomusicology* 5, 1 (Spring): 41–50.

Rose, Tricia. 1994. *Black Noise: Rap Music and Black Culture in Contemporary America*. Middletown, CT: Wesleyan University Press.

Conclusion
Hip Hop *and* or *in* Religion and Other Questions
Monica R. Miller and Anthony B. Pinn

Through this reader the editors provide a working sense of the topic, questions, issues, and conversations that mark what we are calling religion and hip hop studies. Certainly, there are other articles that could have been included, and we encourage readers to take this as an opportunity and invitation to read widely and gain a complex sense of the interaction and, in some cases, synergies between religion and hip hop culture.

All in all, these articles were selected because as a whole they point out some of the basic dimensions of the study of religion and hip hop culture and provide an intellectual trajectory of some of the most pressing issues taken up in this area of study, over time. They highlight issues around what we mean by religion and hip hop and how both function in the world and that are at the core of this area of study. Furthermore, they point to the emergence, content and concerns of a growing area of study—that is, the study of religion and hip hop. It is an area of study connected to both hip hop studies and religious studies, and it shares many of the other's concerns, theories and methodologies. Yet, it has an agenda not captured by either of those fields of study alone. What this volume represents is an area of study that draws from both hip hop studies and religious studies, but exceeds what either can say alone about the intersections of religion and hip hop culture.

Religion and hip hop studies is marked by five primary motivations all informed by sensitivity to the historical development of religion and hip hop:

1. Description of hip hop culture as representing traditional modes of religion;
2. Description of hip hop culture as critiquing traditional modes of religion;
3. Description of hip hop culture as transforming traditional modes of religion;
4. Description of hip hop culture as a form of religion;
5. Description of hip hop culture *and* religion as talk of the self, world, society grounded in social and cultural interests.

This descriptive dimension of this area of study naturally lends itself to analytical work related to the following:

1. New theorizing of the nature and meaning of religion and hip hop;
2. Theorization of the intersections between hip hop culture and religion;

3. Development of new academic vocabulary and grammar sufficient for the theoretical work needed;
4. Exploration of methodologies—i.e., multidisciplinary work—that will allow for the most fruitful analysis of religion and hip hop culture.

Religion and/in Hip Hop Culture

It is clear that this collection raises a variety of definitional speculations. For example, based on the full range of discussions housed in this volume, what exactly is religion? Without a doubt, the authors have varying perspectives and opinions on this question. Such considerations are approached directly and indirectly in these essays, and speak to the manner in which hip hop as a cultural development influences and affects the religious cultures and language of religion present prior to its emergence. For instance, many of the pieces speak about easily recognized traditions within institutions, doctrines, and creeds—e.g., Christianity, Islam, Judaism, Hinduism, and so on. For others, religion is replaced by and in and through other frameworks such as way of life or spirituality—or in the form of understudied and underexplored religious sensibilities, such as Yoruba spirituality. In some instances, religion, as traditionally understood, isn't explicit within the work, yet what is evident is a new cultural cosmology guiding basic hip hop practices, such as battling, DJing and even performance. That is to say, the ways in which the essays in this volume handle such terms with great diversity and range speak to the manner in which discourse on religion and/in hip hop culture highlights a wide variety of understandings and approaches. Here we use and/in to highlight the complex relationship, to present the manner in which there are clear intersections and commonalities between religion and hip hop, but also noteworthy distinctions that speak to methodological and theoretical distinctions in approach to each category. That is to say, "and/in" is meant to highlight the synergies and point of divergence—we recognize that such lines of demarcation are not self-evidently apparent, rather, have been constructed in and through human interests and manufactured divides.

In bringing these "world" religions and hip hop culture together, authors in this volume wrestle with the ways in which hip hop culture in general and rap artists in particular either challenge or affirm the sensibilities advanced by these traditions. For example, is a Christian sense of sin or redemption consistent with the workings of the world as hip hop artists encounter it? Does a particular religious tradition provide a useful way of moving through the world? Are there ways in which hip hop culture modifies these traditions—brings these traditions more in line with the needs and perspectives of the socio-cultural contexts "home" to hip hop? Do hip hop artists represent contemporary advocates for these particular traditions, and in this way offer the hip hop generation(s) avenues for entering and embracing traditional religious communities? Or might hip hop culture have other social interests and means and ends in mind when making use of religious rhetoric beyond traditional notions of belief and apologia? Or does the treatment of hip hop as extraordinary and distinct from other cultural expressions to have come before it suggest anything about how the sacred, "God" or religion might be understood? Just what do we make of how scholars approach and analyze the religious in hip hop culture—or, when scholars side step the category of religion in favor of other tropes and themes such as performance, protest and praise? What might such diversity of thought and approach signal about divergent theoretical and methodological approaches?

Some—such as Reverend Calvin Butts who a while back threatened to steamroll graphic rap CDs to protest the violence within the lyrics[1]—tried to resist the influence of hip hop, or at least tried to downplay the importance of hip hop for the survival of traditional religions. A more recent articulation of such moral policing might be found in Illuminati and New World Order suspicions of artists such as Jay Z,[2] concerns by religious communities over Kanye West's song "I am a God"[3] or West's "eponymously" titled 2013 album *Yeezus*,[4] or the pressure asserted by the pastor Jomo K. Johnson who publicly urged Philadelphia born rapper Meek Mill to apologize for his song "Amen."[5] Such moral critiques come at the expense of hip hop's ability to make use of religion or religious rhetoric, and dare we suggest, cut into hip hop's ability to instruct and shine a light on the moral improprieties of those within more "traditional" religious spaces; or, at least addressing such criticisms through a critical academic lens seems to suggest a prescient connection between so much of hip hop and religion: Where fan or religious adherent are concerned, today, many are left "feeling like they gotta sneak into heaven/when the reverend looking like a pimp and the pimp looking like the reverend."[6]

Critical attention to religion and hip hop suggests such critics (of hip hop) see no connection between thugs and the religious faithful, no connection between graffiti and the aesthetics of the "world" religions, and no connection between the way bodies are presented in religious ritual and the energy of bodies as they lock and pop, or krump. However, as some researchers have clearly demonstrated—thanks largely to early efforts in hip hop and religion scholarship—hip hop culture has also embraced these traditions, using the four elements of hip hop culture (i.e., dance, art, music, and lyrics) to make real for a post-civil rights audience the "truths" of various traditions. So arranged, hip hop culture can be a vehicle for maintaining and celebrating—while modifying—traditional religions. Run from Run-DMC becomes a preacher; Kurtis Blow becomes the pastor of the Hip Hop Church; DMX prays and preaches on albums; ScarFace talks about death and heaven; Erykah Badu promotes the teachings of the Nation of Gods and Earths, Kanye West and Eminem consider themselves rap "Gods" and the list continues.[7]

Still other artists critique these traditions, pointing out along the way the inconsistencies and hypocrisy they find embedded in the teachings and practices of these traditions. This stance is most graphic and explicit in relationship to the Christian tradition where the worst of scripture-sanctioned greed and mistreatment catches the ire of artists to call preachers out for their misdeeds. However, this doesn't always involve a rejection of these traditions, but rather a reconfiguration of them that gives them new truth. Take for example, Tupac Shakur as "Black Jesuz," or Kanye West's "Jesus Walks," or "I Am A God." More recently, Jay Z and Kanye West, in "No Church in the Wild," re-imagine religion by first dismantling all forms of authority that lead to the church and in place of this establish a new religion based on individual authority and "truth" expressed in community through an embodied appeal to mutually agreed upon consent.[8] All of them represent the maintaining of old religious, theological, philosophical, aesthetic language and symbols—i.e., Jesus, God, authority, Socrates, Plato, Picasso—but with a twist.

Hip hop figures are the contemporary representations of these figures, and the world with all its warts and troubles is the venue for the religious figures who don't hide from the world, don't condemn the world, but rather embrace the activities of the world. For some traditional religionists, some who have maintained allegiance to the Christian Church, for example, as presented to them through the years, what Tupac Shakur or Kanye West present isn't recognizable. For them, this turn in hip hop really presents a new religion—something too foreign and strange from their own ideological sensibilities to be worth anything of value. Scholars such as those presented in this volume don't shy away from this, but instead embrace the challenge and try to work through it—at times advocating for hip hop as a clarification of traditional and non-traditional religions, but in other instances, push for a very different understanding of the relationship between religion and hip hop culture. It is this relationship that we're most eager to understand, chart, play with and watch as religion and/in hip hop scholarship continues to grow and mature.

Hip Hop as Religion

Whether embracing these traditions or critiquing them, there are ways—as some of these essays argue—that hip hop is in relationship with religion. That is to say, religion is in hip hop, and hip hop in religion. Still other scholars and writers suggest that hip hop culture provides an alternative orientation, an alternative religious approach where the category of religion becomes refigured and rethought based on its movement and use in hip hop. Those holding to this position suggest that there are ways in which hip hop replaces (for those embracing it) traditional forms of religion in that it offers the thought, ritual structures, moral-ethical codes, and so on that guide life. At the extreme of this position is the argument that hip hop culture *is* a religion. The previous position—hip hop embraces while at times modifying religious traditions—doesn't require much theoretical work on the part of the study of religion and hip hop in that old ways of defining religion remain in place. Religion, for instance, can be understood in terms of institutions, doctrines and creeds. However, when one pushes this argument aside and suggests instead that hip hop is a religion, required is a different—a new—definition of religion.

Along these lines, thinking about hip hop as a religion has meant attention to a variety of other definitions of religion—such as religion as a life orientation, meaning-making, and a way of responding to the large questions and challenges of life. So conceived, religion isn't understood as something unto itself—a particular type of knowledge for instance—but rather it is understood as a way—a means by which people explore the meaning and function of human experience. This type of redefining privileges what religion *does*—in that religion is what it does for people in the world. An understanding of religion as the institutions, doctrines and creeds presented in the form of "world" religions is concerned with a clear sense of things that are sacred or set apart from ordinary life. However, this second definition of religion at work in the study of religion and hip hop culture is preoccupied with the mundane and ordinary dimensions of life and see in these religious images, concerns, ideas, and practices, a something more in the less at work.

The latter definition breaks free of the traditional distinction between the "sacred" and the "mundane" embraced by traditional definitions of religion and instead it finds in the many functions of hip hop a general wrestling with life that is full and complex. In this regard, hip hop culture—like the blues—privileges how bodies move through time and space, how these physical bodies (that are born, live, and die) encounter the world as the raw material for what is known as religion. That is to say, there is something "holy," so to speak in the activities, needs, and desires of human bodies moving through the world. In a word, traditional forms of religion embraced by some—e.g., Sunni Muslims, Christians, Hindus, Jews and so on—are rejected by others in favor of new religious options organic and intrinsic to their life circumstances. As KRS-ONE has marked so clearly through the creation of the Temple of Hip Hop, hip hop is a new consciousness, a new way of being—or one might say a new orientation for life complete with rituals, beliefs, and other markers of religion.[9]

The Study of Religion and Hip Hop Culture

Think about the articles you've read in this volume: in hindsight, moving across the articles by paying attention to the chronology of the articles—when they were written—also provides an interesting depiction of how issues related to religion and hip hop have changed over the years. As hip hop has grown, matured, and become global—its relationship to other cultural products such as religion has also changed. And, the reverse is true as well: as the study of religion has developed further (particularly as it relates to the communities involved in the development of hip hop—such as African Americans and Latinos/as) its ability to better imagine and capture the connections and synergies between religion and hip hop have also advanced. This is the nature of academic study, of scholarly inquiring, and careful attention to the patterns of conversation in this volume's articles sheds some light on this process.

Reflecting on the connections between hip hop culture and religion in this way clearly demands a different theory of religion such as that mentioned above—religion as a way of addressing the most fundamental questions of life as well as a way to explore the mundane and talk of the self and community, but it also means a different set of tools, or methods for study. And, as the various articles in this volume represent, this means attention to both the humanities and the social sciences—disciplines such as sociology and anthropology as well as theology, philosophy, history and ethics. All of these disciplines represent tools used to explore, unpack and explain what's taking place in hip hop culture and what this means for people interested in religion and hip hop. The more scholarly tools, the richer the conversation and the more we learn about the nature and meaning of hip hop *and, in, and as* religion.

Hip hop demands this sort of attention, and the results of this work are noteworthy, as the articles you've read here demonstrate.

We imagine the conversation regarding the intersections of religion and hip hop will only increase in detail and complexity. The range of participants will increase, as new generations of scholars and hip hop audiences also increase, and technology expands the ability to talk across the globe in real time. While the academy will likely remain the epicenter of this study of religion and hip hop culture, the process for securing access to that conversation will become more democratic. For instance, digital humanities and the emergence of "massive open online courses" (or MOOCs) will make topics like the study of religion and hip hop central across university and colleges campuses and will expand the audience beyond those who are officially enrolled as students at these institutions.[10] Academics who teach classes related to religion and hip hop (like the "Religion and Hip Hop Culture" co-taught by Anthony Pinn and Bernard "Bun B" Freeman at Rice University, with a student enrollment of 100 plus students) will have opportunity to share information and insights with a more diverse and literally global audience through these MOOCs. Pinn and Freeman's initial, traditional classroom based course also took students off campus to have conversation with the larger Houston community in alternate spaces, and this received significant media attention. Yet, providing a version of this course as a MOOC allows scholarship to follow the trails of globalization traveled by hip hop, and to do so in real time. Through such efforts, the "data" of religion and hip hop studies are opened exponentially, breaking down the distinction between art and artist, ethnography and ethnographer, even theologian and "god." While engineering, computer science, and some of the "natural" sciences have dominated earlier exploration of online—primarily free—courses, the humanities have now entered into this project. And the study of religion and hip hop culture stands to benefit in significant ways.

The above is particularly true, if one takes into consideration the manner in which hip hop culture and its fans have established a significant online presence, and have a keen interest in sharing information through digital formats—whether it be sharing music, viewing videos, or marking off community. As the production of hip hop has been democraticized through technology, with anyone with a laptop and the proper software being able to produce music and create an audience for their art or dance, the study of religion and hip hop will also need to move in this direction.

Online conversation through MOOCs and other means is even more compelling when one considers the ways in which the study of religion has also moved online. Scholars work to interrogate and explore megachurches and the prosperity gospel, for instance, both shaped by attention to technology used to promote materials and to forge virtual communities that allow people across the globe to mimic the dynamics of the prosperity gospel and to claim "membership" in megachurches such as Lakewood Church (pastored by Joel Osteen) in Houston they might never attend physically. Both hip hop culture and religion have gone virtual and viral, and along the way they have rethought how information is communicated and how community is formed. This volume gives a sense of this development as it relates to historical shifts, technological advances, and the very nature and meaning of globalization.

All this is to say, the future of the study of religion and hip hop culture will continue to include books, articles, conferences, meeting, and classes conducted in traditional university and college settings. But, it will also involve attention to and participation in digital and online knowledge production and sharing. Could it really be any other way, when hip hop culture emerges and grows through its manipulation of information and technology, and the missionary (i.e., expansion) impulse of religion often follows patterns of technological advancement?

In a word, hip hop and religion are ever changing to meet the demands of new generations living with new socio-economic, political, and cultural arrangements. Yet, they don't do this in isolation. They are organic and evolving cultural developments, or forms of expression that interact. They overlap, inform and influence each other. This new but growing area of study called religion and hip hop studies means to describe, analyze, and map the dynamics of this interaction. And this volume is but a small, though we hope useful, contribution to those efforts.

Notes

1. See for instance: http://www.nytimes.com/1993/06/06/nyregion/harlem-protest-of-rap-lyrics-draws-debate-and-steamroller.html. Accessed October 19, 2013.
2. http://flavorwire.com/newswire/jay-z-addresses-the-illuminati-rumors-again/ Accessed December 22, 2013.
3. http://www.christianpost.com/news/kanye-west-responds-to-i-am-a-god-critics-105260/ Accessed December 22, 2013.
4. http://blogs.wsj.com/speakeasy/2013/06/14/kanye-west-compares-himself-to-jesus/ Accessed December 22, 2013.
5. http://www.worldstarhiphop.com/videos/video.php?v=wshhXuoCv6mkQ67X6q2S Accessed December 22, 2013.
6. Talib Kweli feat. John Legend. "Around My Way." *The Beautiful Struggle*. Rawkus Entertainment, 2004.
7. DMX "Prayer," on 1998 "It's Dark and Hell is Hot": http://rapgenius.com/Dmx-prayer-lyrics; ScarFace, "Smile," on 1997 The Untouchables: http://rapgenius.com/Scarface-smile-lyrics; Erykah Badu, "On and On," on 1998 Baduizm: http://rapgenius.com/Erykah-badu-on-and-on-lyrics. Also, for Reverend Run: http://www.npr.org/2012/12/19/167623728/reverend-run-from-rapper-to-preacher. Kurtis Blow: http://www.villagevoice.com/2009-01-07/music/breaking-bread-with-kurtis-blow/ Accessed October 19, 2013. http://rapgenius.com/Kanye-west-i-am-a-god-lyrics; http://rapgenius.com/Eminem-rap-god-lyrics. Accessed December 22, 2013.
8. See: http://rapgenius.com/2pac-black-jesuz-lyrics; http://rapgenius.com/Kanye-west-jesus-walks-lyrics; http://rapgenius.com/Kanye-west-i-am-a-god-lyrics; http://rapgenius.com/Kanye-west-no-church-in-the-wild-lyrics. All accessed October 19, 2013.
9. See: http://www.krs-one.com/temple-of-hip-hop/ Accessed October 19, 2013. See also, KRS-One. *The Gospel of Hip Hop: The First Instrument*. New York: powerHouse Books, 2009.
10. Two of the major MOOC providers are edX (https://www.edx.org/) and Coursera (https://www.coursera.org/).

Contributors

H. Samy Alim

H. Samy Alim is Associate Professor in the Social Sciences, Humanities, and Interdisciplinary Policy Studies in Education (SHIPS), program faculty in Educational Linguistics and holds by courtesy appointments in Anthropology and Linguistics at Stanford University. Among other publications, he is the author of *Articulate While Black: Barack Obama, Language, and Race in the U.S.* (Oxford University Press, 2012) and *Roc the Mic: The Language of Hip Hop Culture* (Routledge, 2006).

Racquel Cepeda

Racquel Cepeda is an award-winning journalist, cultural activist, and documentary film-maker. She is the author of *Bird of Paradise: How I Became Latina* (Atria Books, 2013). Equal parts memoir about Cepeda's coming of age in New York City and Santo Domingo, and detective story chronicling her year-long journey to discover the truth about her ancestry, the book also looks at what it means to be Latina today. She is currently in production on *Deconstructing Latina*, a documentary focusing on a group of troubled teenage girls in a suicide prevention program who are transformed through an exploration of their roots via the use of ancestral DNA testing. Cepeda's writings have been widely anthologized and her byline has been featured in media outlets including *The New York Times, People,* the *Associated Press, The Village Voice, MTV News,* CNN.com, and many others. She has also contributed to WNYC, CNN and CNN's *Inside the Middle East* as a freelance reporter. Cepeda edited the critically acclaimed anthology *And It Don't Stop: The Best Hip-Hop Journalism of the Last 25 Years* (Faber & Faber, 2004), winner of the PEN/Beyond Margins and Latino Book Award. As the former editor in chief of Russell Simmons' *Oneworld*, Cepeda was responsible for the magazine's overhaul in September 2001, winning a Folio Award for best redesign and receiving accolades for her global take on urban culture.

Elonda Clay

Elonda Clay works as a Digital Librarian/Archivist at Philander Smith College in Little Rock, Arkansas while continuing her doctoral studies at the Lutheran School of Theology at Chicago. Her research interests include DNA ancestry testing, genetic-ethnic identifications, and the problem of origins, religion and hip hop, and religion and the Internet.

Judah M. Cohen
Judah M. Cohen is the Lou and Sybil Mervis Professor of Jewish Culture and Associate
Professor of Musicology at Indiana University. He has authored *The Making of a Reform
Jewish Cantor: Musical Authority, Cultural Investment*, and, with Gregory Barz, he co-
edited *The Culture of AIDS in Africa* (Oxford University Press, 2011). Recent publica-
tions include the "Jewish Music" article in the second edition of the *Grove Dictionary of
American Music*, and the "Music" entry for *Oxford Bibliographies in Jewish Studies*. He
has also published extensively on Caribbean Jewish history—including the book *Through
the Sands of Time: A History of the Jewish Community of St. Thomas, US Virgin Islands*
(Brandeis, 2012)— and is currently at work on a project involving musical theater and
World War II-era narrative.

Ian Condry
Ian Condry is a cultural anthropologist and Professor in Comparative Media Studies at
Massachusetts Institute of Technology. He is also chair of MIT's department of Global Studies
and Languages. He has written two books, *The Soul of Anime* (Duke University Press, 2013)
and *Hip-Hop Japan* (Duke University Press, 2006) both of which analyze "globalization from
below" from an ethnographic perspective. In 2006, he founded the MIT/Harvard Cool Japan
research project which explores the cultural connections, dangerous distortions, and critical
potential of popular culture (cooljapan.mit.edu). His new research explores the potential of
grassroots creative communities to offer new solutions to old problems in a time of economic
uncertainty and political dysfunction.

Greg Dimitriadis
Greg Dimitriadis is Professor in the Department of Educational Leadership and Policy in
the Graduate School of Education at the University at Buffalo, SUNY. He is the author of
several books including *Performing Identity/Performing Culture: Hip Hop as Text, Pedagogy,
and Lived Practice* (Peter Lang, 2001/2009) and *Critical Dispositions: Evidence and Expertise
in Education* (Routledge, 2012). He edits the book series *Critical Youth Studies* (Routledge).

Siphiwe Ignatius Dube
Siphiwe Ignatius Dube is a Post-doctoral Fellow in the Department of Practical Theology
at the University of Pretoria, South Africa, and a Research Fellow in the Centre for Africa
Studies, Gender Studies Programme at the University of the Free State (Bloemfontein, South
Africa). Dube's overall academic work examines how contemporary religious discourses
engage with gender (mostly critical masculinity studies), transitional justice (specifically the
role of religion in truth commissions), and popular culture (hip-hop and literature). Using
both critical discourse analysis and the social critical theory of the Frankfurt School as tools
for engaging the concept of "the ambivalence of religion," Dube's thinking explores how to
use this heterogeneous concept in productive ways for both the academic study of religions
and praxis application in social development projects. Dube is an author of numerous interdisciplinary articles and chapters on transitional justice and literature, hip-hop and religion,
masculinities and religion (Canada and South Africa), truth commissions (Canada and South
Africa) and feminist post-colonial literature and religion.

Michael Eric Dyson
Michael Eric Dyson, named by *Ebony* as one of the hundred most influential black Americans,
is the author of over sixteen books, including *Holler if You Hear Me* (Basic Civitas Books,

2006), *Is Bill Cosby Right?* (Basic Civitas Books, 2006) and *I May Not Get There With You: The True Martin Luther King, Jr.* (Free Press, 2001). He is currently University Professor at Georgetown University. He lives in Washington, D.C.

Juan M. Floyd-Thomas
Juan M. Floyd-Thomas is Associate Professor of African American Religious History in the Vanderbilt Divinity School and the Graduate Department of Religion of Vanderbilt University in Nashville, Tennessee. Dr. Floyd-Thomas is author of *The Origins of Black Humanism: Reverend Ethelred Brown and the Unitarian Church* (Palgrave Macmillan, 2008), *Making It Plain: Liberating African American Religious History* (Abingdon, 2014), and co-author of *Black Church Studies: An Introduction* (Abingdon, 2007) as well as several journal articles, book chapters, and other publications. He is currently working on several major research projects, including a history of African American religion and culture in twentieth-century Harlem. He is a member of several scholarly organizations and has lectured extensively both nationally and internationally.

Anthony Y. H. Fung
Anthony Y. H. Fung is Director and Professor in the School of Journalism and Communication at the Chinese University of Hong Kong and is also a Pearl River Chair Professor at Jinan University at Guangzhou, China. His research interests and teaching focus on popular culture and cultural studies, popular music, gender and youth identity, cultural industries and policy, and new media studies. He has published widely in international journals, and authored and edited more than ten Chinese and English books.

Margarita Simon Guillory
Margarita Simon Guillory is an Assistant Professor of Religion at the University of Rochester. Her research interests include American Spiritualism, Identity construction in African American Religion, and Social Scientific approaches to Religion. She has published articles in *Culture and Religion* and *Pastoral Psychology*. Her co-edited volume (with Drs. Stephen Finley and Hugh Page), *There is a Mystery: Esotericism, Gnosticism, and Mysticism in African American Religious Experience*, is currently under contract with Brill.

Marlon F. Hall
Marlon F. Hall is the Cultural Architecture for The Awakenings Movement, where he challenges ordinary people to live extraordinary lives through the power and love of Christ. Marlon has a joint degree from Fisk and Vanderbilt Universities in Anthropology and Political Science.

John B. Hatch
John B. Hatch is Associate Professor of Communication and the Wendt Ethics Professor at the University of Dubuque. Among other publications, Hatch is the author of *Race and Reconciliation: Redressing Wounds of Injustice* (Lexington Books, 2009).

Daniel White Hodge
Daniel White Hodge is the Director of the Center for Youth Ministry Studies and Assistant Professor of Youth Ministry at North Park University in Chicago. His research interests are the intersections of faith, Hip Hop culture, and young adult emerging generations. His two books are *Heaven Has A Ghetto: The Missiological Gospel and Theology of Tupac Amaru*

Shakur (VDM, 2009), and *The Soul Of Hip Hop: Rimbs, Timbs, and A Cultural Theology* (IVP, 2010). He is currently working on a book titled *The Hostile Gospel: Finding Religion In The Post Soul Theology of Hip Hop.*

Qurra Hussain
Qurra Hussain is a professional DJ, promoter and designer based in London. She has been DJing for over 13 years on the Hip Hop and World music stages and has produced and presented her own radio show and dabbles in music production and fashion design when she's not spinning. She currently holds three DJ residencies in London.

John L. Jackson, Jr.
John L. Jackson, Jr., is Dean of the School of Social Policy & Practice and Richard Perry University Professor at the University of Pennsylvania. Before coming to Penn, Jackson taught in the Department of Cultural Anthropology at Duke University and spent three years as a Junior Fellow at the Harvard University Society of Fellows. Jackson received his B.A. in Communications (Radio, TV, Film) from Howard University and his Ph.D. in Anthropology from Columbia University. As a filmmaker, Jackson has produced fictional films and documentaries that have screened all around the world, including Amsterdam, Jamaica, Trinidad and Tobago, Curacao, London, Puerto Rico, Toronto, and South Africa. He has published several books: *Harlemworld: Doing Race and Class in Contemporary Black America* (University of Chicago Press, 2001), *Real Black: Adventures in Racial Sincerity* (University of Chicago Press, 2005), *Racial Paranoia: The Unintended Consequences of Political Correctness* (Basic Civitas, 2008), *Thin Description: Ethnography and the African Hebrew Israelites of Jerusalem* (Harvard University Press, 2013), and (co-authored by Cora Daniels) *Impolite Conversations: On Race, Politics, Sex, Money, and Religion* (Atria/Simon and Schuster, 2014). His most recent film, co-directed with anthropologist Deborah Thomas, is *Bad Friday: Rastafari After Coral Gardens* (Third World Newsreel, 2012).

Rev. Cheryl Kirk-Duggan
Rev. Cheryl Kirk-Duggan is Professor of Religion and Director of Women's Studies at Shaw University Divinity School (Raleigh, NC). The 2009 and 2011 Shaw University Excellence in Research Awardee is author and editor of over twenty books and numerous articles; is an Ordained Elder in the Christian Methodist Episcopal Church, and holds membership in numerous scholarly organizations. The 2011 YWCA Academy of Women Honoree in Education, a 2011 Black Religious Scholars Group Honoree, and a 2012 Womanist Legend Awardee, her research and teaching is interdisciplinary, liberationist, theoretical, and practical. She garnered activists/scholars to respond to Katrina in *The Sky is Crying: Race, Class, and Natural Disaster* (Abingdon, 2006). She works in interfaith and ecumenical contexts. Her recent co-authored work with Marlon Hall, is *Wake Up!: Hip Hop, Christianity, and the Black Church*, from Abingdon Press, 2011. An avid athlete and musician who completed her first marathon in 2010, Kirk-Duggan practices hot yoga, loves to tinker with her flowers, volunteers around domestic violence and women's leadership empowerment, embraces laughter as her best medicine, and quests for a healthy, holistic, spiritual life. She has taught in the following contexts: two undergraduate programs, one in music, one in religious studies; and in a consortium working with doctoral students as core doctoral faculty. She currently teaches in a seminary within a university context.

Monica R. Miller

Monica R. Miller is an Assistant Professor of Religion and Africana Studies and Director of Women, Gender, and Sexuality Studies at Lehigh University. Among other publications, she is the author of *Religion and Hip Hop* (Routledge, 2012/2013) and currently serves as a Senior Research Fellow with the Institute for Humanist Studies (Washington, D.C.), Co-Chair/Founder of the "Critical Approaches to Hip Hop and Religion Group" (AAR), member of the Culture on the Edge international scholarly collaborative, and editorial board member of *Culture on the Edge: Studies in Identity Formation* book series (Equinox).

Felicia M. Miyakawa

Felicia M. Miyakawa is Associate Professor of Musicology and Assistant Director of the MTSU School of Music and teaches undergraduate and graduate courses in both "art" and "popular" music traditions. Before joining the MTSU faculty, Miyakawa taught music history review courses for graduate students at Indiana University and music history and music appreciation courses at West Valley College in Saratoga, California. The recipient of numerous MTSU research grants, Miyakawa's research areas include hip-hop music and culture, Black nationalism, American popular music, African-American music and literature, gender and pedagogy, and queer studies. She has presented papers at regional and national meetings of the American Musicological Society, the Society for Ethnomusicology, the International Association for the Study of Popular Music, the Society for the Scientific Study of Religion, and the Society for American Music, as well as at popular music conferences sponsored by the Rock and Roll Hall of Fame and Seattle's Experience Music Project. Her first book, *Five Percenter Rap: God Hop's Music, Message, and Black Muslim Mission*, was published in spring 2005 by Indiana University Press. Other publications appear in *American Music, Popular Music, Journal of Popular Music Studies, The Journal of American Ethnic History*, and the encyclopedia *Women and Religion in the World*. She is currently at work on her second book, a biography of the spiritual "Sometimes I Feel Like a Motherless Child."

Angela M. Nelson

Angela M. Nelson is Associate Professor and former Chair in the Department of Popular Culture at Bowling Green State University. She teaches classes on black popular culture, black popular music, black popular film, television situation comedies, and popular culture. Nelson has edited *"This Is How We Flow": Rhythm in Black Cultures* (University of South Carolina Press, 1999), co-edited *Popular Culture Theory and Methodology: A Basic Introduction* (Ray and Pat Browne Books, 2006), and published several articles and book chapters on different aspects of twentieth-century African-American popular culture. Her current research project examines black gospel stage plays as folk art and how they mediate race and religion.

James W. Perkinson

James W. Perkinson is a long-time activist and educator from inner city Detroit, currently teaching as Professor of Social Ethics at the Ecumenical Theological Seminary and lecturing in Intercultural Communication Studies at the University of Oakland (Michigan). Perkinson is the author of *White Theology: Outing Supremacy in Modernity* (Palgrave Macmillan, 2004), *Shamanism, Racism, and Hip-Hop Culture: Essays on White Supremacy and Black Subversion* (Palgrave Macmillan, 2005), and *Messianism Against Christology: Resistance Movements, Folk Arts, and Empire*, and has written extensively in both academic and popular journals on questions of race, class and colonialism in connection with religion and urban culture. He is in demand as a speaker on a wide variety of topics related to his interests and a recognized artist on the spoken-word poetry scene in the inner city.

Anthony B. Pinn

Anthony B. Pinn is currently the Agnes Cullen Arnold Professor of Humanities and Professor of Religious Studies at Rice University, founding director of Rice's Center for Engaged Research and Collaborative Learning and Director of Research for the Institute for Humanist Research (Washington, D.C.). He is the author/editor of thirty books, including *Noise and Spirit: The Religious and Spiritual Sensibilities of Rap Music* (NYU Press, 2003).

Steven J. Rosen

Steven J. Rosen (Satyaraja Dasa) is an initiated disciple of His Divine Grace A. C. Bhaktivedanta Swami Prabhupada. He is also founding editor of the *Journal of Vaishnava Studies* and associate editor for Back to Godhead. He has published more than thirty books in numerous languages, including the recent Krishna's Other Song: *A New Look at the Uddhava Gita* (Praeger, 2010); *The Jedi in the Lotus: Star Wars and the Hindu Tradition* (Arktos, 2010) and *Christ and Krishna: Where the Jordan Meets the Ganges* (FOLK Books, 2011).

Malka Shabtay

Malka Shabtay is an applied anthropologist who has worked for over 30 years with the Ethiopian Jewish community in Israel. She taught at the Ruppin Academic Center, the Institute for Immigration and Social Integration, and various other academic institutes. She combines research, consultancy and training for various organizations who are interested in applying cultural and cross-cultural perspectives in their work. She has published ten books and many articles. Current fields of interest: Ethiopian youth and young adults, domestic violence, new immigrant communities in Israel, and Jews as global people and Jews in Amazonia.

Dervla Sara Shannahan

Dervla Sara Shannahan is an independent researcher who has published on a range of subjects related to Islam and Muslim cultures; her recent research focuses on gender, inclusivity and UK mosques (*Journal of Contemporary Islam* and *Studying Islam in Practice*, ed. Gabriele Marranci). She is involved in the Inclusive Mosque Initiative, works as a trainee psychotherapist and is a Ph.D. candidate at Goldsmiths University, London.

Josef Sorett

Josef Sorett is an Assistant Professor of Religion and African-American Studies at Columbia University. As an interdisciplinary scholar of religion and race in the Americas, Sorett employs primarily historical and literary approaches to the study of religion in black communities and cultures in the United States. Sorett's current book project, *Spirit in the Dark: A Religious History of Racial Aesthetics* (Oxford University Press, forthcoming) illumines how religion has figured in debates about black art and culture. He is also editing an anthology that is tentatively titled *The Sexual Politics of Black Churches*.

Robin Sylvan

Robin Sylvan is the founder and director of the Sacred Center. His vision for the Sacred Center is the culmination of 25 years of spiritual practice and educational work. Sylvan received his B.A. at Fairhaven College, a small alternative college in Bellingham, Washington, where he did interdisciplinary, cross-cultural, and experiential studies in a variety of religious, spiritual, and artistic traditions. Sylvan then was Program Director for four years at The Ojai Foundation, a land-based educational foundation and workshop/retreat center in Ojai, California, where he worked closely with numerous lineage-holders in different religious and spiritual traditions, as well as prominent western scholars and artists. He is the author of *Traces of the Spirit: The Religious Dimensions of Popular Music* (NYU Press, 2002) and *Trance Formation: The Spiritual and Religious Dimensions of Global Rave Culture* (Routledge, 2005)

Martina Viljoen

Martina Viljoen is an Associate Professor in Musicology in the Odeion School of Music, University of the Free State. She graduated with an interdisciplinary doctorate combining the fields of musicology, philosophy, and studies on visual culture. She publishes locally and internationally on topics concerning hymnology, musicology, and the aesthetics of music, and was the guest editor of a special volume on critical theory and musicology in *The International Review of the Aesthetics and Sociology of Music*, June 2005. Viljoen serves on the advisory panel of *The International Review of the Aesthetics and Sociology of Music*, and regularly reviews articles, book chapters and books for academic publishers in South Africa and abroad. She has, over the past two decades, supervised a substantive number of doctoral, masters and honours studies, many of which have since earned accredited publication.

Joseph Winters

Joseph Winters is an Assistant Professor at UNC Charlotte in the Religious Studies department. His research interests lie at the intersection of African American Religious Thought, Religion and Critical Thought, and Literary Theory, and he is currently working on a manuscript (under review at Duke University Press), *Hope Draped in Black: Race, Melancholy, and the Agony of Progress*, in which he contests triumphant narratives of racial achievement using resources from African American literature and religious thought.

Permissions

Part I   Setting the Context, Framing the Discussion

Dyson, Michael Eric. "Performance, Protest and Prophecy in the Culture of Hip Hop." In *Black Sacred Music*, Vol. 5, pp. 12–24. Copyright, 1991. Duke University Press. All rights reserved. Reprinted by permission of the publisher. www.dukeupress.edu

Pinn, Anthony. "Making a World with a Beat." In *Noise and Spirit: The Religious and Spiritual Sensibilities of Rap Music*, ed. Anthony Pinn, pp. 1–26. New York: NYU Press. Reprinted by permission of the publisher.

Dimitriadis, Greg. "Hip Hop to Rap: Some Implications of an Historically Situated Approach to Performance." In *Text and Performance Quarterly*, Vol. 19, No. 4 (1999): 355–69. Reprinted with permission from Routledge/Taylor & Francis. The author would like to thank Norman Denzin, Judith Hamera, George Kamberelis, Cameron McCarthy, Peggy Miller, Paul Prior, and Jonathan Sterne for their helpful feedback on this project.

Alim, Samy H. "A New Research Agenda: Exploring the Transglobal Hip Hop Umma." In *Muslim Networks from Hajj to Hip Hop*, ed. Miriam Cooke and Bruce B. Lawrence, pp. 164–174. North Carolina Press, 2005. *From Muslim Networks from Hajj to Hip Hop*, edited by Miriam Cooke and Bruce Lawrence. Copyright © 2005 by the University of North Carolina Press. Used by permission of the publisher.

Part II   What's the "Religion" in Hip Hop?

Miller, Monica R. "Don't Judge a Book By Its Cover." In *Bulletin for the Study of Religion* (Equinox) Special Issue: "What's this 'Religious' in Hip Hop Culture?" Vol. 40, No. 3 (2011): 26–31. Reprinted by permission © Equinox Publishing Ltd 2011.

Winters, Joseph. "Unstrange Bedfellows: Hip Hop and Religion." In *Religion Compass*, Vol. 5, Issue 6 (2011): 260–270. Reprinted by permission. 2011 Joseph Winters. Religion Compass. 2011. Blackwell Publishing Ltd.

Jackson, John L. Jr. "Peter Piper Picked Peppers, but Humpty Dumpty Got Pushed: The Productively Paranoid Stylings of Hip-hop's Spirituality." In *Racial Paranoia: The Unintended Consequences of Political Correctness*. John L. Jackson. New York: Basic Books, 2008. Reprinted by permission BasicCivitas Books/Perseus Books Group.

Part III   The Religious Aesthetics of Hip Hop Culture

Simon, Margarita L. "Intersecting Points: The 'Erotic as Religious' in the lyrics of Missy Elliott." In *Culture and Religion*, Vol. 10, No. 1 (2009): 81–96. Reprinted by permission from Routledge/Taylor & Francis.

Clay, Elonda. "Two Turntables and a Microphone: Turntablism, Ritual and Implicit Religion." In *Culture and Religion*, Vol. 10, No. 1 (2009): 81–96. Reprinted with permission from Routledge/ Taylor & Francis.

Nelson, Angela M. "'God's Smiling on You and He's Frowning Too': Rap and the Problem of Evil." In *Call Me the Seeker: Listening to Religion in Popular Music*, ed. Michael J. Gilmour, pp. 175–88. Continuum, New York: 2005. Reprinted with permission © Michael J. Gilmour, 2005, *Call Me the Seeker*, Continuum US, an imprint of Bloomsbury Publishing Inc.

Viljoen, Martina. "'Wrapped Up': Ideological Setting and Figurative Meaning in African-American Gospel Rap." In *Popular Music*, Vol. 25, No. 2 (May, 2006): 265–282. Reprinted here with permission from Cambridge University Press. I am indebted to Anson and Eric Dawkins for permission to quote lyrics and musical transcripts from the WRAPPED UP music video. Written and Produced by Rodney Jerkins and the Dawkins brothers, Executive Produced by Raina Bundy.

Cepeda, Racquel. "AfroBlue: Incanting Yoruba Gods in Hip-Hop's Isms." In *Total Chaos: The Art and Aesthetics of Hip-Hop*, ed. Jeff Chang, pp. 271–277. Basic Civitas, 2006. Reprinted courtesy BasicCivitas Books/Perseus Books Group.

Part IV   Hip Hop and/in Religious Traditions

Floyd-Thomas, Juan M. "A Jihad of Words: The Evolution of African American Islam and Contemporary Hip Hop." In *Noise and Spirit: The Religious and Spiritual Sensibilities of Rap Music*, ed. Anthony B. Pinn, pp. 89– 128. New York: New York University Press, 2003. Reprinted courtesy New York University Press.

Alim, H. Samy. "Re-Inventing Islam with Unique Modern Tones: Muslim Hip-Hop Artists as Verbal Mujahidin." In *Souls*, Vol. 8, Issue 4 (2006): 45–58. Reprinted by permission of the University of Illinois–Chicago (http://www.uic.edu).

Miyakawa, Felicia M. "The Five Percenter 'Way of Life.'" In *Five Percenter Rap: God Hop's Music, Message, and Black Muslim Mission*, pp. 23–40. Bloomington: Indiana University Press, 2005. Copyright © 2005, Indiana University Press. Reprinted with permission of Indiana University Press.

Shannahan, Dervla Sara and Qurra Hussain. "Rap on 'L'avenue': Islam, Aesthetics, Authenticity and Masculinities in the Tunisian Rap Scene." In *Contemporary Islam*, Vol. 5, No. 1 (April 1, 2011): 37–58. Copyright © 2010, Springer Science + Business Media B.V. Reprinted with permission from Routledge/Taylor & Francis.

Sorett, Josef. "Believe Me, This Pimp Game is Very Religious: Toward a Religious History of Hip Hop." In *Culture and Religion*, Vol. 10, No. 1 (2009): 11–22. Reprinted with permission from Routledge/ Taylor & Francis.

Kirk-Duggan, Cheryl and Marlon Hall. "Put Down the Pimp Stick to Pick Up the Pulpit: The Impact of Hip Hop on the Black Church." In *Wake Up: Hip-Hop Christianity and the Black Church*, ed. Cheryl Kirk-Duggan and Marlon Hall, pp. 119–144. Nashville: Abingdon Press, 2011. Reprinted here with permission from Abingdon Press.

Hatch, John B. "Rhetorical Synthesis through a (Rap)Prochement of Identities: Hip Hop and the Gospel According to the Gospel Gangstaz." In *Journal of Communication and Religion*, Vol. 25 (2002): 228– 67. Reprinted here with permission from the *Journal of Communication and Religion*.

Hodge, Daniel White. "Where My Dawgs At? A Theology of Community." In *The Soul of Hip-Hop: Rims, Timbs and a Cultural Theology*, Daniel White Hodge, 104–124. Madison, WI: IVP Books, 2010. Taken from *The Soul of Hip Hop* by Daniel White Hodge. Copyright © 2010 by Daniel White Hodge. Used by permission of InterVarsity Press, PO Box 1400, Downers Grove, IL 60515. www.ivpress.com

Cohen, Judah. "Hip-hop Judaica: the Politics of Representin' Heebster Heritage." In *Popular Music*, Vol. 28, No. 1 (January 2009): 1–18. Reprinted here with permission from Cambridge University Press.

Shabtay, Malka. "'RaGap': Music and Identity Among Young Ethiopians in Israel." In *Critical Arts: A Journal of South–North Cultural and Media Studies*, Vol. 17, Nos. 1 and 2 (2003): 93–105. Reprinted with permission from Routledge/Taylor & Francis.

Part V   Hip Hop as Religion

Index

Note: 'N' after a page number indicates a note; 'f' indicates a figure.

AAR. *See* American Academy of Religion (AAR)
Ace of Base 372
Adams, Yolanda 237
Adorno, T. 81
advertising 156n26
aesthetics, of Tunisian hip hop culture 225–226
affirmation 275
African Americans: class division among, and rap music 15, 283n13, 283n15; communication style of 284nn24–5; generation gap among 300n19; and theodicy of black experience 130–131; use of term 281–282n1. *See also* black churches
African ceremonial music 156n21
African roots, of hip hop culture 411–414
Afrika Bambaataa 3, 57, 87, 415; on Nation of Islam 186–187; on "overstanding" 60–61n1; "Planet Rock" (song) 410; political consciousness of 186; as rap pioneer 409; and Yoruba tradition 160–161
Ahearn, Charlie 206, 347; *Wild Style* (1982) 2
Ahmed 217–218
Aidi, H. 228
AIDS. *See* HIV/AIDS
Aït-hamadouche, L. 219, 228
Akbar, Na'im, *Chains and Images of Psychological Slavery* 133
Akio, Gotō 350
Aladdin 225
Ali, Muhammad 412
Ali G. *See* Sacha Baron Cohen
Alim, H. S. 215, 230n2

Alim, S. 125
Allen, Ernest 34
Allen, Harry 17, 45, 54, 185, 215
American Academy of Religion (AAR) 4–5
Amnesty International 218
Anderson, B. 122
Anderson, Elijah 268, 283n16, 291
the Animals 343
Ansaaru Allah Community 206
apartheid 132
Appadurai, Arjun 339–340
appearances: vs. reality, in hip hop culture 89–90, 283n16. *See also* materialism
Arabo, Jacob "The Jeweler" 238
archeology 257–258
Aristotle 272
Armstrong, Louis 28
articulation theory 41
Asante, Molefi 134, 281
Ashanti 239
Atkins, E. Taylor 342
Atkins, Jeffrey. *See* Ja Rule
Atsushi, Innami 359, 361
Atwater, Lee 16
audience: as active agent 43; in early vs. later hip hop culture 45–47, 49. *See also* "you" pronoun
authenticity: vs. commodification 295; in hip hop culture 298; of J-rap 353; in Tunisian hip hop culture 217–220. *See also* realism
authority, in *The 50th Law* (50 Cent and Greene) 69
AZ 174–175

Bailey, E. I. 116, 125

Baker, Houston 29, 141, 395

Baker-Fletcher, K. 102, 103–104

Bakke, Ray 291

Bal, Mieke 145, 146, 147, 153, 156n10

Balti Hiroshima 230–231n7

Bambaataa, Afrika. *See* Afrika Bambaataa

Baraka, Amiri 25, 132–133, 160

Barcelona, Antonia 384

Barnes, Sandra 394

Barnes, S. T. 401

Baron Cohen, Sacha 314, 317n22

Base, Rob 120

battling: and cutting contests 117; definition of 117, 338; gender issues in 118; and implicit religion 121–127; and playing the dozens 117; as ritual process and practice 117–118; and "signifying" 117; social and political implications of 117; in turntablism 118–121, 409–410. *See also* turntablism

Bauman, Zygmunt 294–295, 301n22

Bayles, Martha 25

BDP. *See* Boogie Down Productions (BDP)

Beastie Boys 33, 307

Beatles 343, 358; *Sgt. Pepper* (album) 334

Becker, Howard 42–43, 47

Beckford, James A. 67

beliefs. *See* feelings and beliefs

Bell, C. 117

Ben David, Mordecai 306

Benson, George 358

Berger, A. A. 146

Berger, Maurice 305

Bernstein, Leonard 40

Berry, Chuck 27

Beta Israel community. *See* Ethiopian Jews

BET Gospel 155n3

Betha, Mason 238

Big Boi 33

Big Daddy Kane 206

Biggie Smalls 95

Bilbo, Theodore 134–135

Bililian Community. *See* World Community Al-Islam in the West (WCIW)

bin Olu Dara Jones, Nasir. *See* Nas

Bisman, Aaron 317n13

biting 127n3

Biz Markie 357

Bjork 371

black apocalypse 268

black churches: and community 277–278; and Don "Magic" Juan 247; generation gap in 248; and gospel music 26, 248; and hip hop culture 79, 247, 249–250, 256, 260–261, 267–268; materialism in 78, 82n3; as missionaries 249–252; parental role of 246, 248; prosperity gospel 238, 243n19; purpose of 248–249; recovery rhetoric of, vs. hip hop culture 268; shortcomings of 283n13; worship, and rap music 252–255; youth ministry 260–261. *See also* Christianity

black diaspora, and Ethiopian Jews 326

Black Hattitude 308–309

Black History Museum 185–186

black musical tradition: and existential concerns 22–25; and hip hop culture 76–77; mainstream culture's indebtedness to 25–26; as performative 43; sacred and secular in 26–28; spirituals as 22. *See also* blues music; gospel music; jazz; rap music; spirituals

black nationalism 34. *See also* Nation of Islam

black oral tradition: and hip hop culture 60; playing the dozens 117, 284n24, 412; and rap music 8, 12, 29–30, 412–413; and rhetoric 281; and signifying 412. *See also* linguistic technique and wordplay

black radio 14–15

Black Sacred Music: A Journal of Theomusicology (journal) 3, 34

black suffering: conceptions of, in rap music 136–137; and humanocentric theism 131–132; and slave mentality theodicy 132–134; in spirituals 136; and white supremacy theodicy 132, 134

Blakey, Art 342

Blood of Abraham 309, 312

Bloom, Alan 14

Blow, Kurtis, "The Breaks" (song) 12–13

blues music: and black racial identity 16; as devalued black musical tradition 15–16; disapproval of 23; Ellison on 24; and individualism 22; and rap music 413; and religion 26; and sexuality 23; and social issues 23–24; and spirituals 22–23; as subversive 24; theodicy of 130; white co-opting of 16

"body tricks" 118, 120, 121

Bone Thugs 235

Bono 27

Boogie Down Productions (BDP) 236; *By All Means Necessary* (album) 169–170, 236; *Criminal Minded* (album) 169, 236. *See also* KRS-One

boom boxes 48

bootleg tapes 45

Bourdieu, Pierre 69, 70–71

Boyarin, Daniel 304, 311

Boyd, Todd 171, 293

Brand Nubian 87; "Ain't No Mystery" (song) 200; and Five Percent Nation 173, 200, 204; "Love Me or Leave Me Alone" (song) 175; "Wake Up" (song) 78

bravado 285n35

Bray, Kevin 385

break dancing: African roots of 411–412; as appropriation of public space 348–349; as element of hip hop culture 60–61n1, 82–83n4, 408; generation gap in 349–350; and hip hop culture 44; in Japanese hip hop culture 346–349; as performative activity 348–349; transglobalism of 347; and West African possession dance 411–412; women in 349. *See also* dance

B-Real 164

Breen, Marcus 41

Breines, Paul 305

Brickle, Phil 252

Brod, Harry 305

Brooks, Dwight E. 279–280, 285n39

Brown, Bobby 351

Brown, James 77

Brown, K. M. 398, 400, 402–403

Buber, Martin 298

Buckshot Shorty, "Murder MC's" (song) 77

Buddhism 33

Burke, Kenneth 265, 273, 275

Burke, Miguel 274

Butler, Judith 66

Butts, Calvin 21, 74, 267, 283n14, 283n20, 422

Bynum, Edward 396–398, 403

Caesar, Shirley 104

Caldwell, Reginald 253

call and response: in early rap music 46; multilayered totalizing expression (MTE) process as 125; and turntable battles 123; and "Wrapped Up" (song/video) 149

Campbell, Anne 206–207

Campbell, Donald. *See* Don "Magic" Juan

Campbell, Joseph 268

Carlebach, Shlomo 306

Carter, Ron 76

chants. *See* collective delivery

Chapel, Gage 264–265, 280–281, 282n5

Cheney, Cherise 381, 383

Chernoff, John 43

Chic, "Good Times" (song) 12

Chille' Baby 269. *See also* Gospel Gangstaz

China: barriers to foreign artists in 371–372; Chou's popularity in 365; and corporate culture 372; Shanghai Media Group 372; state control of popular culture in 366–367, 371–372. *See also* Chou, Jay

China Mobile Company 370–371

Chou, Jay: "Baba, I Come Back" (song) 369; "Bullfight" (song) 367; as "Chinese" 368–371; and Chinese state control of popular culture 368; *Chopin of November* (album) 365; and corporate culture 370–371, 372; "Dong Feng Po" (song) 368; "It's My Site; It's My Command" (song) 370–371; "The Last Battle" (song) 369; marketing strategy of 367–368, 370–371; "In the Name of Father" (song) 367–368; popularity of 365; *Qilixiang*, or *Jasmine* (album) 365; as safe political icon 369–370; "Second Class of Year 3" (song) 367; "Shuang Jie Gun" (song) 369; "Snail" (song) 370; social vs. political issues in songs 369–370; state support of 370–371

Christian hip hop 90

Christianity: and community 290, 295–299; and Gospel Gangstaz 264, 268–281; hip hop culture as critique of 383–384; institutional failure of 383, 389; and Ja Rule 239; and KRS-One 79, 236–237; liturgical traditions 254–255; and missiology 249–252, 257–258; and Nas 79, 382; and non-religious spaces 296–297; and rap music 79, 83n17; as religion of oppressor 78; and Remy Ma 240; shift to, in hip hop culture 237–238, 240; and slavery 384; and West 238–239, 240, 243n17, 380; and white supremacy 383–384; worship, and rap music 252–255. *See also* black churches; gospel music

Chuck D 58, 135, 193, 325, 414. *See also* Public Enemy

Church of St. John Coltrane African Orthodox Church 28

Chutzpah 314–315

Clapton, Eric 359

Clarence 13X 78, 172, 199, 205. *See also* Five Percent Nation

class division: among blacks, over hip hop culture 15, 283n13, 283n15; in Japan 340

Clifford, J. 225

close readings. *See* textual criticism

CL Smooth 173

Cohen, Aviad. *See* 50Shekel

Cold Crush Brothers 47

collective delivery, in Run-DMC's songs 47

Coltrane, John 342; *A Love Supreme* (album) 28

Co-ma 121

Combs, Sean "Puffy" 386

Commentary 303

commodification: of hip hop culture 295; of rap music 46–50. *See also* materialism

Common: "The Bitch in You" (song) 178; as critic of gangsta rap 178–179; *Electric Circus* (album) 162; "G.O.D. (Gaining One's Definition)" (song) 178; and Ice Cube 178–179; Islamic faith of 178; "I Used to Love H.E.R." (song) 178; *Like Water for Chocolate* (album) 162; *Resurrection* (album) 33; "The Sixth Sense" (song) 178

community: and black churches 277–278; in Christian context 290, 295–299; and early rap music 45–46; and hip hop culture 290, 295–299; and identity 291; and spirituals 22. *See also* identity; individualism; space

complex subjectivity: definition of 126; and implicit religion 116, 126–127; Pinn on 75, 80–82, 126; and Shakur 80–81

Cone, James 136, 413

Connell, R. 215

conscious rap 87, 96n4, 177–178

conspiracy theories. *See* paranoia

consumerism and consumption: of Chinese popular music 367–368; in Japan 345; of rap music after Run-DMC 47–48. *See also* materialism

contexts of use: and audience as agent 43; Becker on art as joint activity 43; de Certeau on 41; as privatized 46–47

Cook, Nicholas 142, 143, 155n6, 156n12, 156n23, 156n26

Cooke, Sam, "A Change Is Gonna Come" (song) 26

Cooper, C. 324

Cooper, Carolyn 325

copyright, in U.S. vs. Japan 357–360

corporate culture 370–371, 372

Cosentino, Donald 394

Costello, Mark 29

Couch, Sean 382

Cox, Harvey 291

crack epidemic 267, 282–283n12

Craddock-Willis, Andre 413

Cray, Robert 16

Crazy-A 346–349, 357

Crazy Legs 347, 349–350

Cream 359

Cress-Welsing, Frances 87

Cross, Brian 34

Cross-Bronx Expressway 83n6

Crossley, S. 226–227

Crouch, Andre 26, 157n30

Crouch, Stanley 402

crucifixion 386

Cruise, Tom 339

Curry, Mary 161

Curtis, Edward 176

Cusic, D. 149

cutting contests 117

Cypress Hill 164

D'Ali 228

dance: and black musical tradition 43; West African possession dance 411–412; women in 50. *See also* break dancing

dancehall 127n2

Dancehall Queen (film) 325

D'Angelo, *Brown Sugar* (album) 163

Dassen Trio 352, 353

Davis, F. 156n21

Davis, Joel 335, 336

Davis, Ossie 171

Dawkins & Dawkins 141–154. *See also* "Wrapped Up" (song/video)

DC Talk 269

Dead Prez 87, 238

de Certeau, Michel 40, 41

Def Jam Recordings 47

de Mendoza Ibáñez, Francisco José Ruiz 384

Diallo, Amadou 58, 193

diaspora. *See* black diaspora

Dien, M. I. 223

diet 210n28

Disco Music Club (DMC) World DJ Championships 120–121

DJ Danger Mouse 358

DJing: as element of hip hop culture 60–61n1, 409; as spiritual experience 125–126; techniques of 409. *See also* battling; turntablism

DJ Jazzy Jeff and the Fresh Prince: *He's the DJ I'm the Rapper* (album) 15; "Parents Just Don't Understand" (song) 15

DJ Jin 360

DJ Kool Herc 409, 415

DJ Krush 348, 354

DJ Quick 291

DJ Yella 82n2

DJ Yutaka 351

DMX 91, 95

Dole, Bob 293
Dollar, Creflo 237–238, 242n14, 243n16
domestic abuse 246
Don "Magic" Juan 247
Dorsey, Thomas Andrew 26, 248
double consciousness 216, 224–225, 226, 228, 281
Douglass, Frederick 285n39
Dowdy, M. 220
DOZE Green 163
the dozens. *See* playing the dozens
Dragon Ash 360
Dr. Dre 82n2; "Been There, Done That" (song) 97n16
Dr. Dreck 314
dress code 206
Drewal, Henry John 161
Driscoll, Christopher 4
Dr. J$ 314
Drucker, Peter 261
drug abuse 267
DuBois, W. E. B. 224, 281
Dupri, Jermaine 238
Durkheim, E. 110
Dyson, Michael Eric: on gangsta rap 283n13, 283n15; *Between God and Gangsta Rap: Bearing Witness to Black Popular Culture* 3–4, 34; on Michael Jackson 27–28; on rap as deserving of serious attention 265; on rappers as griots 184; on Shakur 80, 399–400, 402, 403, 405
Dyson-Bey, Everett 402

E-40 56–57, 188–189
East End X Yuri 352, 358
Easy Irving 307–308
Eazy-E 82n2, 309
ECD 359
Eddy, Mary Baker 266, 282n7
education: and hip hop texts 56, 57, 187–188; and Jewish hip hop culture 307–308, 314–315
Ego 121
Ehrlich, Demitir 106
8 Mile (film) 291, 298
Elijah Muhammad 176, 204, 205, 206, 210n28
Ellington, Duke 28
Elliott, Missy "Misdemeanor": "Can You Hear Me?" (song) 107–108; *Cookbook* (album) 107; *Da Real World* (album) 109; the erotic in lyrics by 106–112; "Higher Ground" (song) 110–111; "Joy" (song) 107; "Lose Control" (song) 107; physical embodiment in lyrics 107; reciprocity in lyrics by 108–109; "Take Away" (song) 108–109; "Wake Up" (song) 111–112; "We Did It" (song) 109
Ellison, Ralph 24–26
embodiment: "body tricks" 118, 120, 121; in Elliott's lyrics 107; and rhetorical synthesis 282n8
Emerson, Ralph Waldo 236
Eminem 291, 298
Eric B. & Rakim 30
Ernst, Judith 54
the erotic: "admixture-notion" of 106, 112; boundaries of 105–106; in Elliott's lyrics 106–112; eros as power 103–104; eros vs. sexuality 104; and "Hush Harbor" 103–104; limits on complexity of 104–105; Lorde on 105–106, 110–111; and music 104–105; and orientation 103; polyvocal approach to 102; and religion 99–100, 103; in Shakur's lyrics 104, 105; Tillich on 105–106, 108, 109, 110. *See also* sexuality
Esposito, J. L. 221
Etan G 310, 314, 316n5
Ethiopian Jews: as Beta Israel community 322; and black diaspora 326; as blood donors 323; and hip hop culture 326; history of 322–323; marginalization of 326–328; methodology for research among 324; music subculture among youth 324; and racial identity 323–324, 326–327; and racism 323; and ragamuffin music 325; and rap music 325; and reggae 324, 325–326; violence in hip hop culture 326, 327; and women 327. *See also* Jewish hip hop culture
ethos 272–274
evangelism: of Five Percent Nation 207–209; of rap artists 30–33. *See also* Christianity
Eve 58–59, 193–194
evil: conceptions of 134–136; problem of 131. *See also* Satan; theodicy
existential concerns: and black musical tradition 22–25; as focus of religion 67–68, 80; and rap music 30
Exodus (film) 305
EZO 163

The Face 186
Faitlovitch, Jacques 322
Fantastic Five 47
Fard Muhammad 172–174
Farley, Christopher J. 283n19
Farrakhan, Louis 30, 170, 176–177, 179, 210n28
Farris Thompson, Robert 160, 161, 164, 346
fashion 349

fear, *The 50th Law* (50 Cent and Greene) on 70–71

feelings and beliefs, privileging of, in hip hop culture 89–90

Felton, Leo 92

female rap artists: in early rap music 410; and Five Percent Nation 181n29; as invisible in hip hop culture 240; and Islam 58–59, 193–194; and resistance to sexism 77–78; in Tunisian hip hop culture 227, 229. *See also* specific artists; women

Fiasco, Lupe 237; "American Terrorist" (song) 79

50 Cent 68–71, 91, 238; *Get Rich or Die Tryin'* (film) 95

50Shekel 303, 312, 313

The 50th Law (50 Cent and Greene): aims of 69; construction of authority in 69–70; on fear 70–71; and Green as co-author 68–69; New Age philosophy in 70–71; realism in 71

Fikentscher, K. 118

Fisher, Walter 265, 275, 279, 283n17

Five Percent Nation 30; "alphabet" of 173, 199–200, 202–203; among incarcerated 207; on black male leadership 175; and Brand Nubian 173, 204; Clarence 13X 78, 172, 199, 205; and conscious rap 87; evangelism of 207–209; family in 206; female adherents of 181n29; and gnosticism 172; goals of 208; individualism in 206; and law enforcement 180–181n19, 207; lessons 199–203; "mathematics" of 86, 173, 199–202; and Nas 382; and Nation of Islam 173, 199, 206; number 7 in 174; and numerology 203; and race 174; rap artist adherents of 180n12, 209; and rap music 87, 171–176, 208–209; Solar Facts 200–201; theology of 78, 86–87, 172–174, 198–203, 205, 208, 211–212n47; Universal Flag of 201–202; view of whites 174; view of women 175–176, 206–207; way of life 204–207; *The WORD* (newspaper) 207–208

Fleetwood, N. R. 225

Flores, Ysamur 394

Floyd-Thomas, J. 78–79, 187

Forbes, Bruce 379

Ford, Robert 2

Forman, Murray 2, 299n3, 399n11

Foucault, Michel 44, 69, 70

Fowles, J. 156n14

Francis, Sage 33

Franklin, Kirk 90, 269, 271, 280

Fredrickson, George M. 132

Freeman, Bernard "Bun B" 425

free-styling 76–77

Fried, Avraham 306

Friedman, Debbie 307

Frith, Simon 40

Fun-Da-Mental 219

Funky Four + One More, "That's the Joint" (song) 46

Fu-Schnickens, "Heavenly Father" (song) 74

gangsta rap: Boogie Down Productions (BDP) 169–170; Common's criticism of 178–179; criticisms of 74; Dyson on 283n13, 283n15; as normative black experience 267; origins of 82n2, 282–283n12, 410; rejection of social/political concerns 171; and signifying 171. *See also* rap music

Gang Starr 174, 237

Gangstas Wanted 217; "Arabi" 222, 228; "One-by-One" (song) 218, 221, 228

Gardell, Mattias 177, 203, 208–209

Gates, Henry Louis 77

Gaye, Marvin 104, 359; "What's Going On" (song) 26

Gee Money 119

genba 340, 341, 342, 348–350, 354, 363n9

gender issues: in battling 118; in Five Percent Nation thought 175–176; and Jewish hip hop culture 310–311; in Tunisian hip hop culture 215, 226–228, 229. *See also* masculinity; women

generation gap: in black churches 248; in break dancing 349–350; between Civil Rights vs. hip hop generations 300n19

Genuwine 108

George, Nelson 2, 34, 75, 267, 282–283n12

Giacomini, Nicholas. *See* MC Yogi

gift economy 123

Gilroy, Paul 50, 216, 235

Gladwell, Malcolm 90

gnosticism 172, 180n13

God: conceptions of 134–136; and problem of evil 131. *See also* theodicy

Goldscheider, Jeremy 312

the good 276

goodwill 273–274, 284n28

Goodwin, Andrew 145, 146

Gordy, Berry 47

Gore, Tipper 14

Gospel Gangstaz: bravado and self-confidence of 285n35; *Do or Die* (album) 269; emergence of 269; *Gang Affiliated* (album) 269; identity and credibility of 271–274, 281; as melding of

Christian message and hip hop 264, 268–281. *See also I Can See Clearly Now* (album)

gospel hip hop: and Butts 283n20; origins of 268–269

gospel music: and black churches 26, 248; Jesus as "lover" in 157n30; vs. rap music 267; and religion 25–26; and social issues 23; theodicy of 130; white co-opting of 36n16

graffiti: as element of hip hop culture 60–61n1, 82–83n4, 408; and hip hop culture 44; women in 50; and Yoruba tradition 162–163

Grand Master Flash 29

Grandmaster Flash and the Furious Five: conceptions of God in lyrics by 135; and DJing 409; on DJing as spiritual 125–126; "The Message" (song) 13, 76, 88, 135, 267, 410; "New York, New York" (song) 13; "Supperrappin" (song) 45

Grayson, Kent 125

Greater Mount Zion Baptist Church 253

Green, Al 26

Greene, Robert, *The 50th Law* 68–71

Grenz, Stanley 294

Gresson, Aaron 265, 268, 283n17

Grimes, R. L. 117

griots 184, 412, 415

Gross, J. 219

Grossberg, Lawrence 41

Grossman, Lori 312

Guru 174, 237

Gutstadt, Jonathan 314

Gypsy culture 250–252

Hager, Steven 45

Hakim 60

Haley, Alex 168

Hall, Marlin 4

Hall, S. 235

Hall, Stuart 41

Haman 316–317n7

Harmony 235

Haruo, Chikada 350

Hasni, Cheb 223

"Hate Me Now" (video): crucifixion in 386; as instance of metonymy 385–389; materialism in 387–388, 390; religious imagery in 389–390

Hawkins, Tramaine 26

Hebidge, Dick 325

The Hebrew Hammer (film) 303

HEEB magazine 304, 311, 315

Heineken Green Synergy DJ Competition 119–120

Heisei restoration 338

Hendrix, Jimi 27

Heron, Gill Scott 77

Heyward, Carter 298

Hick, John 131

Hidary, Vanessa 303

hijab 231n21

Hikaru, Utada 360

Hill, Lauryn 235; *The Miseducation of Lauryn Hill* (album) 408

Hime 361

Hinduism 333, 335. *See also* MC Yogi

hip hop culture: adversarial relationship of, with law enforcement 95; appearances vs. reality in 89–90, 283n16; and black churches 79, 247, 249–250, 256, 260–261, 267–268; and black musical tradition 76–77; and black oral tradition 60; break dancing as element of 60–61n1, 82–83n4, 408; and Christian worship 252–255; commodification of 295; and community 290, 295–299; as critique of black Christianity 383–384; elements of 60–61n1; evolution of, from performative to product 39; feelings/beliefs as privileged in 89–90; graffiti as element of 60–61n1, 82–83n4, 408; historicism of 18–19; homophobia in 81–82, 381; as interplay of art forms 44–45; in Japan 346–362; and jazz 76–77; Jewish 305–316, 325–327; Lindh as influenced by 91–93; and materialism 81–82, 90, 284n34; misogyny in 77–78, 81; as movement 1; origins of 44–46, 75–76, 267, 332; paranoia of 87–88; "post-soul" 293–295; rap music as element of 60–61n1, 82–83n4, 379, 408; recovery rhetoric of, vs. black churches 268; and religion 237–238, 240, 380; as religion 424; representation in 8; sampling in 77, 418; and social justice 57, 189, 381; and social/political issues 77; spatial awareness in 48, 291–292; spirituality of 414–417; as transglobal 55; and Yoruba tradition 160–164. *See also* DJing; graffiti; MCing; rap music

Hip-Hop Hoodíos 310, 311, 312, 317n15

hip hop imaginary 122–123

hip hop lyrics: metaphor in 57; as poetry 55–56; and *Qur'an* 187–189; "you" pronoun in 44–46, 48–49. *See also* linguistic technique and wordplay; specific artists and songs

hip hop studies: and American Academy of Religion (AAR) 4–5; diversity of 230n2; growth of 282n3; legitimation of 8–9, 60; in MOOCs 425–426; overview of 1–2; and religion 2–5, 421; sampling in 9; themes of 75–78

hip hop texts: and education 56, 57, 187–188; and *Qur'an* 55–57
Hiroshi, Egaitsu 347
Hiroshi, Fujihara 350
Hirsch, E. D. 14
historicism: of hip hop culture 18–19; and music criticism 41–42
Hi-Tek 190
HIV/AIDS 94
Hodge, Daniel White 4
Holiday, Billie 28
Holyfield, Evander 31
homophobia: in hip hop culture 81–82, 381; and Jewish culture 304–305
Horton, Willie 16
Hosokawa, Shuhei 342, 344
Hossam 219, 220
Houenou, Kojo Touvalou 61n2
Hughes, Langston 412
humanism 33
humanocentric theism 131–132. *See also* theodicy
humor, in Jewish hip hop culture 306–308, 314–315, 317n8
Hung, Chang-Tai 366–367
Hunter, Alberta 104
Hurricane G. 161
Hyams, Tor 314
hymns 143–144, 155n4
hypocrisy 90–91. *See also* appearances
Hythem 220, 223, 225–226, 229

IAM 59
Ibrahim 220, 223–225, 226
I Can See Clearly Now (album) 264; collapsed statement of 270–271; community in 277–278; credible identity projected in 271–274; encompassing conception of 270; ethos of 272–274; the good in 276–277; interpositionality in 279–280; realism in 275–276; recovery rhetoric in 280, 284n29; respect in 277; rhetorical synthesis in 265–266, 269–279; thematic development 274–279; unity of gospel and hip hop in 275; warfare in 278–279
Ice Cube 49, 82n2, 93–94; and Common 178–179; *Death Certificate* (album) 170; and Nation of Islam 170; "Westside Slaughterhouse" (song) 178
Ice Kid 120
Ice-T 40–41, 45
identity: in community 291; definition of 291; of Gospel Gangstaz 271–274, 281; and interpositionality 285nn39–40; and Jewish hip

hop culture 311, 312, 315–316, 317n15; and language 399n17; in post-soul hip hop culture 293–295; and space 291–293. *See also* racial identity; spatial identity formation model
ideology, concept of 142
implicit religion: commitment in 121–122; and complex subjectivity 116, 126–127; definition of 116; extensive effects of 125; integrating foci in 122–125; and turntable battles 121–127
independent labels 17–18
individualism: and the blues 22; in Five Percent Nation thought 206; in post-soul hip hop culture 294–295; and racial issues 268; and rap music 29. *See also* community
inner city. *See* urban life; urban space
interpositionality 279–280, 285nn39–40
intertextuality 156n15
Iron Sheik 194
Irvine, James R. 283n18
Irwin, A. C. 107
Isis 30
Islam: appeal of, in hip hop culture 237; and female rap artists 58–59, 193–194; hip hop as Lindh's introduction to 91–93; and hip hop culture 185–186, 237; Hi-Tek on 190; Mos Def on 54; and rap music 30, 78; in Tunisian hip hop culture 221–223; *umma* as borderless nation for 54. *See also* Five Percent Nation; Nation of Islam; Sunni Islam; *umma*
Islamic Studies 185
Ivy, Marilyn 344

Jackson, Curtis. *See* 50 Cent
Jackson, Jesse 293
Jackson, John 71
Jackson, Michael 27
Jackson, P. 79
Jackson, Ronald 265
Jacobs, Walter R. 279–280, 285n39
Jagoda, Flory 311
Jakes, TD 80
Jamel 227
Japan: class issues in 340; consumerism in 345; *enka* music in 344; history of popular music in 341–345; jazz in 341, 342–343; musical generation gap in 343–344; pop idol singers in 344–345; samurai in 339–341; syncretism in religion 339–340
Japanese hip hop culture: authenticity of 353; b-boys in 355–357; break dancing in 346–349; diversity of 360–361; families' competition in 354–355; fashion in 349; *genba* 340, 341, 342,

348–350, 354, 363n9; global standardization in 338; Heisei restoration 338; as Japanese 352–357, 363n5; as J-rap 352–353; local indigenization in 338–339; *moriagaru* 355; and music magazines 354; origins of 346; *oshare* 350; rap music's origins 350–351; and Run DMC 351; sampling and copyright in 357–360; *Samurai Champloo* (TV series) 361; and samurai imagery 338, 361–362; and women 353

Ja Rule 239

Jay Electronica 260

Jay-Z 89, 90, 358, 423

jazz: and cutting contests 117; and hip hop culture 76–77; in Japan 341, 342–343; and religion 28

Jensen, Richard 266

Jewish culture: Ethiopian Jews 322–328; hipster phenomenon 303–304; masculinity portrayed in 304–305, 315; Radical Jewish Culture movement 303, 304

Jewish hip hop culture: as addressing Jewish concerns 309–310; as educative 307–308, 314–315; and Ethiopian Jews 322–328; gender issues in 310–311; hipster phenomenon 309–312; humor in 306–308, 314–315; 317n8; and identity 311, 312, 315–316, 317n15; masculinity portrayed in 308, 309–311; origins of 305–309; and other musical genres 313–314, 317n15; parodies of rap songs 306–308, 314, 317n8; Purimspils raps 306; as transglobal 312–313; women in 311–312

jihad, dual meaning of 169

jihad of words: and black nationalist/Afrocentral rap 170; as discursive struggle against oppression 185; Five Percent Nation and rap music 171–176; Malcolm X 168; Nation of Islam 169–171; and social and political issues 169–171; Sunni Islam and rap music 176–179

Jim Crow ethics 134–135. *See also* racism

Johnson, Jomo K. 423

Johnson, Robert 23

Jones, Spike 343

Jones, William R. 130, 131, 133

J-rap. *See* Japanese hip hop culture

JT the Bigga Figga 56–57, 58, 188–189, 190–193

Judaism. *See* Ethiopian Jews; Jewish culture; Jewish hip hop culture

Jungle Brothers 87

Ju-Tang Clan 313

Kahf, U. 218

Kamel 218, 227–228, 230n6

Kan, Takagi 347, 350

Karim, Jamillah 60

katana 339. *See also* Japan

Keil, Charles 42, 43, 414

Kelley, Robin 48, 76

Kellner, Douglas 40–41

Kemp, Jack 266, 281, 282n5, 282n7

Kenji, Ozawa 352

Khalifa, Rashad 203

Kill Bill (film) 339

King, Barbara L. 236

King, F. W. 28

King, Martin Luther, Jr. 412

King, Rodney 410

King Giddra 338

Kingston Trio 343

King Sun 206; "Universal Flag" (song) 201

Kirk-Duggan, Cheryl 4, 102, 104–105

Kirkpatrick, Kwame 97–98n25

Kirkpatrick, Walter J. 283n18

Kitwana, Bakari 77, 91

Kligman, Mark 306

Kochman, Thomas 284n24

koinonia 277–278

Kool Moe Dee 87; conceptions of God in lyrics by 135–136; "Knowledge is King" (song) 135–136

Koran. *See* Qur'an

Kozinets, R. 124–125

Kramer, F. 394, 403, 404

Kramer, Lawrence 147–148

Krims, Adam 142, 152, 379

Krishna Das 336

KRS-One 29, 87, 283n16, 380, 410, 424; and Christianity 79; on knowledge 60–61n1; and Malcolm X 170; *Self Destruction* (album) 14; spiritual evolution of 236–237, 242n13; "Stop the Violence" (song) 14; "you" pronoun in 45. *See also* Boogie Down Productions (BDP)

Kundalini 396

kungfu movies 369

Kunjufu, Jawanza 87

Kweli, Talib 58, 190, 193

Kyllonen, Tommy 253, 257

Kyū, Sakamoto 343

Lambert, Eric 307

Lamp Eye 352–353

language: as arbitrary 88; as deliberately incomprehensible 89, 96n9; evolution of, from modern to postmodern 293–294; and identity 399n17; power of 70–71, 96nn6–7. *See also* linguistic technique and wordplay *langue* model 40

La Rock, Scott 169–170

Lash, Scott 293

The Last Poets 162, 413

The Last Samurai (film) 339

Lau, Andy 367

law enforcement: adversarial relationship of, with hip hop 95; and Five Percent Nation 180–181n19, 207

Lawrence, Martin 293

Lee, Bruce, *The Chinese Connection* (film) 369

Lee, R. D. 221

Lee, Spike, *The Autobiography of Malcolm X* (film) 170–171, 237

legitimation: of *The 50th Law* (50 Cent and Greene) 69; of hip hop studies 8–9, 60

Leviticus 252–253

Lil Kim 77

Lil' Raskull 83n17

Lincoln, Bruce 69

Lindh, John Walker 91–93

linguistic technique and wordplay: among African Americans 284nn24–5; "bad" as good 88; in hip hop lyrics 56–57, 188–189; of rap music 77; of Run DMC 88–89; "signifying" 77, 81; "tricknology" 96n5; use of "nigger/nigga" terminology 88–89. *See also* language; poetry

Li Peng 371

List, Ben 353

literacy: and rap music 18. *See also* language; linguistic technique and wordplay

Little Richard 26

liturgical traditions 254–255

L.L. Cool J.: *Bigger and Deffer* (album) 50; "I Can't Live Without my Radio" 48; "I'm Bad" (song) 47, 50

Lofton, K. 238

Lomax, Louis 205

Long, Charles 80, 102, 103, 116

Lorde, Audre 103, 104, 105–106, 110–111

Lubavitch, Chabad 310

Ludacris 238

ludic agency 124–125

Mac 230; "Just a Question of Time" (song) 221, 222–223, 229

Madhubuti, Haki 87

magazines 354

Mahan, Jeffrey 379

Main Source, "Live at the Barbecue" (song) 79

Maj, Barnaba 384

Makiko, Okada 359

Malcolm X 30, 412–413; *The Autobiography of Malcolm X* 168; *The Autobiography of Malcolm X* (film) 170–171, 237; commodification of 170–171; interpositionality of 285n39; jihad of words 168; and KRS-One 170; and Warith Deen Muhammad 181n32

marginalization, of Ethiopian Jews 326–328

Markham, Pigmeat 12

Marley, Bob 324

Martin, Ricky 371

Martin, Sallie 26

Masari 59

masculinity: and music production 49; portrayals of, in Jewish culture 304–305, 315; portrayals of, in Jewish hip hop culture 308, 309–311; racialization of 50; and rap music 48. *See also* gender issues

Mason, John 161, 402

massive open online courses (MOOCs) 425–426

materialism: criticisms of 227–228; in "Hate Me Now" (video/song) 387–388, 390; and hip hop culture 81–82, 90, 284n34; in *I Can See Clearly Now* (album) 276–277; of musical artists 82n3; in rap music 174–175; as spiritual value 238; and turntable battles 124–125; and West 238–239. *See also* appearances

Matisyahu 310–311, 312–313

Matsumura, Hiroshi 342

Mayfield, Curtis 26

Mays, Benjamin E. 134

MC Bell 348, 350

McCroskey, James C. 272, 273

McCutcheon, Russell T. 66, 67, 71

MC Hammer: "Pray" (song) 74; "Son of the King" (song) 235

MCing: as element of hip hop culture 60–61n1. *See also* rap music

McLeod, Kembrew 284n32

MC Lyte: "Cappucino" (song) 133; "Not Wit a Dealer" (song) 133

MC Paul Barman 314

MC Ren 82n2

MC Serch 307

MC Shan 15

McWhorter, John 93

MC Yogi 332–336; *Elephant Power* (album) 336; *Jivamukti* (album) 336

meaning. *See* existential concerns

Meek Mill 423

megillah 316n6

men: in Five Percent Nation thought 175; in Tunisian hip hop culture 215, 226–228

Men In Black (film) 151

metaphor: in hip hop lyrics 57; vs. metonymy 384

Meters Bonwe 372

metonymy: definition of 379; "Hate Me Now" (video) as instance of 385–389; vs. metaphor 384; rap music as 379, 385

Meyer, Leonard 42

M-Flo 360

Mic Jack Production 361

micronarratives 293–294

Middle Eastern music 181–182n35, 228. *See also* Tunisian hip hop culture

middle passage 22

Miller, Ivor 162

Miller, Matthew. *See* Matisyahu

Miller, Monica R. 4, 378, 379, 381–383, 388, 389

Million Family March 193

Million Man March 176–177, 190, 193

Minister Mase 238

misogyny: in hip hop culture 77–78, 81; in rap music 239; in Tunisian hip hop culture 227, 229. *See also* sexism

missiology 249–252, 257–258

Mitchell, T. 214

Mix Master Pauly 120

Moby 36n21

Moishe MC 308

Mojica, Vinia 162

Moltmann, Jürgen 295–296

Mongo Santamaria, "Afro-Blue" 161

MOOCs. *See* massive open online courses (MOOCs)

Mor, Ben 309

moriagaru 355

Morton, Jelly Roll 28

M.O.S.A.D. 361

Mos Def: *Black on Both Sides* 30; "Fear Not of Man" (song) 178; on hip hop and education 56, 57, 187–188; Islamic faith of 54, 78–79, 178; "Mr. Nigger" (song) 93–94; racism addressed in work by 93–94; and social justice 58, 193; on spirituality 30

MosEL 259–260

Moses, Robert 83n6

M.O.T. 307, 308, 314

Mr. Magic 86

Mr. Mystic 119, 123

Mr. Solo 269. *See also* Gospel Gangstaz

MTE. *See* multilayered totalizing expression (MTE) process

Muhammad, Elijah 30

multilayered totalizing expression (MTE) process 125

Murphy, Eddie 94

music. *See* black musical tradition; popular culture and music; specific types

music criticism: and articulation theory 41; contextual approaches to 41; and historicism 41–42; *langue* model as de-contextualized approach 40–42; micro- vs. macro-level analysis of 39–40; and performance theory 40–44. *See also* textual criticism

music industry, racism in 36n16

"musicking" 43

music production, women as excluded from 49

music videos: religious imagery in 36n21; Rose on 385; star narrative in 145–147. *See also* "Hate Me Now" (video); "Wrapped Up" (song/video)

Mutamassik 59, 194

Naoya 347

Nas: *Belly* (film) 95; and Christianity 79, 382; "The Cross" (song) 79; "Disciple" (song) 382; and Five Percent Nation 382; *God's Son* (album) 79; "Hate Me Now" (video) 378; "Heaven" (song) 382; "If I Ruled The World" (song) 77; "Life's a Bitch" (song) 174–175; and religious imagery 381–384. *See also* "Hate Me Now" (video)

Nation Conscious Rap: The Hip Hop Vision 185–186

Nation of Earths and Gods. *See* Five Percent Nation

Nation of Islam: and Afrika Bambaataa 186–187; among incarcerated 207; and Clarence 13x 172; and conscious rap 87; and "Don't Believe the Hype" (song) 19; and Five Percent Nation 173, 199, 206; and Ice Cube 170; and JT the Bigga Figga 58, 190–193; and Malcolm X 168; and Million Man March 176–177; move to orthodox Islam of 177; and numerology 203; and Public Enemy 169, 193; and racial paranoia 94; and Rakim 186; and rap music 87, 169–171; references to, in rap music 30; and World Community Al-Islam in the West (WCIW) 176. *See also* World Community Al-Islam in the West (WCIW)

Naughty by Nature, "Ghetto Bastard (Everything's Gonna Be Alright)" (song) 137

Neal, Mark Anthony 8

Nelson, Angela Spence 410, 413

Nelson, George 29

New Age philosophy, in *The 50th Law* (50 Cent and Greene) 70–71
Newcleus, "Jam On It" (song) 305
Newman, Paul 305
New Orleans Rhythm Kings 28
Nichols, Tony 119
Nkiru Bookstore 58, 193
Noble Drew Ali 209n2
nommo 134
Norek, Joshua. *See* Noriega, Josue
Norful, Smokie 237
Noriega, Josue 311
Notorious B.I.G. 235, 277
numerology 203
Nuruddin, Yusef 200, 203, 204, 210n13
Nuwine: *Ghetto Mission* (album) 31; on spirituality 31
NWA (Niggaz With Attitudes) 74, 291; "F— tha Police" (song) 16, 93; as gangsta rap 82n2; music of, as reflection of inner-city life 16–17; racism addressed in work by 93; *Straight Outta Compton* (album) 410

Ogilvy 370–371
Ogou: Achade 402–403; and Afrocentricity 396–398; and demonic diving 398–399; and political upheaval 396; and riots 394–396; and Shakur 399–405; as war god 398
oral tradition. *See* black oral tradition
Orbison, Roy 357–358
orientation: "decent" vs. "street" 283n16; and the erotic 103; religion as 116
Los Orishas 161
Orlando, V. 223
Osteen, Joel 426
Osumare, Halifu 55, 214
Otto, Rudolph 404
OutKast 33
Ouzgane, L. 215
"overstanding" 60–61n1

Palestine 218, 219, 229
PanBanegritude 61n2
paranoia: and conscious rap 96n4; conspiracy theories 88, 97n16; and feelings/beliefs as privileged over reason 90; and Felton 92; of hip hop culture 87–88; and Lindh 93; racial 88, 90, 91, 93–95; and "tricknology" 96n5; in West's lyrics 94–95, 97n21; white, regarding rap music 93
Paris 30
Parker, Lawrence. *See* KRS-One

parodies 306–308, 314, 317n8, 357–358
Patel, Joseph 274
Pattillo, M. E. 224
Paul 258, 260
Paul, Danny 307
P. Diddy 145, 148
Peace, Michael 269
Peirce, Charles Sanders 88
Pemberton, J., III 401
Pennycook, A. 217
performance theory 40–44
performativity: and black musical tradition 43; hip hop culture's shift from, to product 39; and rap music 45–46; textual criticism as ignoring 42; and Tunisian hip hop culture 220–221, 226. *See also* genba
Perkins, William 34, 55, 413
Perkinson, James 4, 393–394
Perry, Imani 77, 291, 380, 386
Perry, Matthew 341
Peter, Paul and Mary 343
Petrucci, Angelo 36n16
phenomenology 68
Phife Dawg 119
Pinn, Anthony B. 425; on complex subjectivity 75, 80–82, 116, 126; *Noise & Spirit: The Religious and Spiritual Sensibilities of Rap Music* 4, 21; on religion 81; on religion and hip hop 378, 379; *Why Lord: Suffering and Evil in Black Theology* 4
play, functions of 127
playing the dozens 117, 284n24, 412
poetry: hip hop lyrics as 55–56. *See also* linguistic technique and wordplay
The Police, "Wrapped Around Your Finger" (song) 148
political issues. *See* social and political issues
Pollock, Della 44
Poor Righteous Teachers 30, 78, 87, 174; "Can I Start This" (song) 175; "Strictly Ghetto" (song) 201
popular culture and music: functions of 366; history of, in Japan 341–345; and religion 379; state control of, in China 366–367, 371–372
possession dances 411–412
postmodernism, of rap music 142, 418–419
Potter, R. A. 146
Pough, G. 77
Pratt, Geraldine 291
Preachers in Disguise (PID) 269
President BPM 350, 351
Presley, Elvis 27

prophecy 380–381, 406n3

Public Enemy 29, 30, 351, 410, 414; "Bring the Noise" (song) 18; conceptions of God in lyrics by 135; "Don't Believe the Hype" (song) 19; on hip hop culture 93; *It Takes a Nation of Millions to Hold Us Back* (album) 18, 169; *Muse-Sick-N-Hour-Message* (album) 169; and Nation of Islam 169, 193; "Party for Your Right to Fight" (song) 18, 169; "Pollywanacraka" (song) 135; "Welcome to the Terrordome" (song) 136; "White Man's Heaven Is a Black Man's Hell" (song) 169; *Yo! Bum Rush the Show* (album) 18. *See also* Chuck D

public space: break dancing as appropriation of 348–349; politics of 48

Punx, Tinnie 350, 351

purification 275

Pushman, Parmita 335

Queen Latifah, "U.N.I.T.Y." (song) 77

Queen Mother Rage 30

Queen Pen 161

Qur'an, and hip hop texts 55–57, 187–189

R & B 26–27

racial identity: and belief 90; and blues music 16; of Ethiopian Jews 323–324, 326–327; and Five Percent Nation 174; and interpositionality 285nn39–40; social construction of 92. *See also* identity

racialization, of masculinity 50

racism: addressed in rap music 93–94; and Ethiopian Jews 323; and humanocentric theism 131–132; invisible 93–94; and Jim Crow ethics 134–135; in music industry 36n16; Public Enemy on 135; and recovery rhetoric 268. *See also* white supremacy

Radical Jewish Culture movement 303, 304

The Radical Rappin' Rebbes 307

Rae, Gina 295

ragamuffin music 325

raï 231n22

Rainey, Ma 23, 77

Rakim 186; "No Competition" (song) 174

Ramsey, Frank 119

rap artists: as educators 87–88; and evangelism 30–33; as griots 184, 412, 415; as priests 414; as prophets 380–381

rap concerts: as "taxed" 95; and violence 14

rap music: African roots of 411–414; airplay of, on black radio 14–15; and black nationalism 34; and black oral tradition 8, 12, 412–413; black suffering in 136–137; and blues music 413; call and response in 46; and Christianity 79, 83n17; and Christian worship 252–255; and class division among blacks 15, 283n13, 283n15; as commodity 46–50; as conservative 381; consumption of, after Run-DMC 47–48; criticisms of 21, 74, 267, 283n14; definition of 214; as devalued black musical tradition 15–16; East Coast vs. West Coast 49, 334; as element of hip hop culture 60–61n1, 82–83n4, 379, 408; elements of 333; and Ethiopian Jews 325; and existential concerns 30; and Five Percent Nation 87, 171–176, 208–209; God and Satan in 134–136; vs. gospel music 267; and Hinduism 335; as hybrid 29, 30; and independent labels 17–18; and individualism 29; and Islam 30, 78–79; in Japanese hip hop culture 350–351; language of, as deliberately incomprehensible 89; linguistic technique of 77, 88–89; and literacy 18; materialism in 174–175; as metonymy 379, 385; and Middle Eastern musical influences 181–182n35; misogyny in 239; and Nation of Islam 87, 169–171; negative public perception of 14; and oral tradition 8, 12, 29–30; origins of 12, 28–29, 44–46, 325, 408–410; parodies of, in Jewish hip hop 306–308, 314, 317n8; as performative 45–46; "pop" rap 15; popularity of 283n19, 408; as postmodern 142; and prophecy 380–381; racism addressed in 93–94; as reflection of inner-city life 12–13, 16–17; and religion 4; sacred and secular in 26–28, 34, 134; and sexism 17, 32, 239; slave mentality theodicy in 133; and social justice 186, 325; song length 45; as subversive 13–14; and Sunni Islam 176–179; technology of 418; transglobalism of 214; in Tunisia 214–230; and violence 14, 17, 93, 95; white paranoia about 93; white supremacy theodicy in 132; women as participants in 49–50. *See also* conscious rap; gangsta rap; hip hop culture; specific artists

Rasta Roots 119

reaffirmation 275

realism: in *The 50th Law* (50 Cent and Greene) 71; in *I Can See Clearly Now* (album) 275–276; of J-rap 353; and "keeping it real" 284n32. *See also* authenticity

reciprocity 108–109, 296

recovery rhetoric: of black churches vs. hip hop culture 268; in *I Can See Clearly Now* (album) 280, 284n29; and music 283n17

Red Alert 86

Redhead, Steve 43

Reed, Adolph 88

reggae 324–326

religion: and blues music 26; as complex subjectivity 75, 80–82; defining 422; and the erotic 99–100, 103; existential concerns as focus of 67–68, 80; and gospel music 25–26; hip hop as 424; and hip hop culture 237–238, 240, 380; and hip hop studies 2–5; and jazz 28; as orientation 116; and popular culture 379; and R & B 26–27; and rap music 4; and rock music 27–28; and sexism 32; as social construction 66–67; use of to lend authority, in *The 50th Law* (50 Cent and Greene) 69. *See also* implicit religion; specific religions; spirituality

religious imagery, in music videos 36n21

Remedy 313

Remy Ma, "Shesus Khryst" (song) 240

representation, in hip hop culture 8

respect 277, 283n16, 285n35, 291

rhetorical synthesis: Chapel on 282n5; definition of 264; elements of 266; and embodiment 282n8; in *I Can See Clearly Now* (album) 265–266, 269–279

rhetoric of music 282n4

rhetors 275

Rhymester 352, 355–357, 359, 360

Rigaud, M. 400

ritualising process: battling as 117–118; definition of 11

Rivers, Eugene 283n13

R. Kelly 91

Robertson, Roland 339

Rock, Pete 173

rock music 27–28

Rock Steady Crew (RSC) 346, 349, 356

The Roots 163, 177

Rose, Tricia 34, 102; on art and social world 81; *Black Noise* 1, 44, 186; on causes of marginalization 75; on hip hop and social justice 186, 325, 381; on hip hop's urban origins 76; on interplay of art forms 44–45; on masculinity of music production 49; on misogyny in rap music 77; on musical structures of rap 418; on music videos 385; on performativity 220; on rap as critique of oppression 388; on rap music 214

Rosenberg, Warren 305

Rosenthal, Andrew 307

Ross, Ricky 295

Roxette 372

Rubin, Rick 47, 50, 305

Run DMC: and Christianity 79; collective delivery in songs by 47; "It's Like That" (song) 47; in Japan 351; linguistic technique and wordplay of 88–89; "My Adidas" (song) 47; popularity of 305–306; "Proud to Be Black" (song) 13; *Raising Hell* (album) 13; and rap as commodity 46–50; and shift from performance to product 39; success of 13–14, 46; "Walk This Way" (song) 410

Rybacki, Donald 284n28

Rybacki, Karyn 284n28

Ryūichi, Sakamoto 345

Rza 59

sacred: and secular, in black musical tradition 26–28; and secular, in rap music 34, 134

Saevitz, David 309

Salewicz, Chris 325

Salt n Pepa 77, 410

sampling: definition of 282n11; in hip hop culture 77, 418; in hip hop studies 9; in U.S. vs. Japan 357–360

Sam's Club 97n21

samurai. *See* Japan; Japanese hip hop culture

Samurai Champloo (TV series) 361

Satan 134–136. *See also* evil

Saussure, Ferdinand de 88

Schachet-Briskin, Wally 307

Scha Dara Parr 352, 357

Schiller, Herbert 295

scholarship. *See* hip hop studies

Schorsch, Jonathan 303

Schwartz, Eric 314

Scott, Paul 21

Scott-Heron, Gil 12, 413

scratching 156n21

secular: and sacred, in black musical tradition 26–28; and sacred, in rap music 34, 134

secular humanism 131. *See also* humanocentric theism

Segal, George 314

Seicho-No-Ie movement 266, 282n7

Seikō, Itō 350, 351

Seiko, Matsuda 359

the self 293–295. *See also* identity 7A3 136

sexism: of Five Percent Nation 175–176, 206–207; and rap music 17, 32, 239; and religion 32. *See also* misogyny

sexuality: and black women 103–104; and the blues 23; vs. eros 104; and ragamuffin music 325. *See also* the erotic
Seymour, Jack 296
Shabak Samech 326
Shabazz, Lakim 206
Shaft, "Mucho mambo" (song) 148, 149, 153
Shakur, Tupac 66, 91, 235–236, 251, 257, 277, 291, 299, 423; "Black Jesus" (song) 80; and complex subjectivity 80–81; Dyson on 399–400, 402, 403, 405; the erotic in music of 104, 105; "Hail Mary" (song) 80; and Ogou 399–405; and racial paranoia 95
Shanghai Media Group 372
Shango, *Shango Funk Theology* (album) 160–161
Shiba, Shun'ichi 342
Shingō, Kazami 348
Shin'ichiro, Watanabe 361
Shlock Rock 306–307, 310, 314, 317n8
Shuren the Fire 361
Shusterman, Richard 141
Sieradski, Dan 317n13
Sigel, Beanie 184
"signifying" 77, 81; and battling 117; Potter on 146
signifying: and black oral tradition 412; and gangsta rap 171; and turntablism 118
silence 103
Simmons, Joey 31. *See also* Run DMC
Simmons, Russell 47, 50; *Life and Def: Sex, Drugs, and Money, + God* 33–34
Simon, Peter 324
Simone, Nina 28
Sincere Allah Merciful God 204
Sincero 230–231n7
Sister Souljah 30; *360 Degrees of Power* (album) 31
skelly 96n1
slave mentality: definition of 132–133; elements of 133; theodicy of 132–134
slavery: and Christianity 384; and spirituals 22; and Yoruba tradition 160
Small, Christopher 43
Smith, Bessie 12, 23, 77
Smith, Danyel 403
Smith, E. 79
Smith, Jada Pinkett 402
Smith, Jonathan Z. 67
Smith, Remy Martin 240
Smith, Theophus 383–384
Smith, Wilfred Cantwell 242n6
Smooth E 314

Snoop Dogg 32, 247, 343
SoCalled 310, 313
social and political issues: and battling 117; and blues music 23–24; and Chinese state control of popular culture 366–367; in Chou's songs 369–370; gangsta rap's rejection of 171; and gospel music 23; and hip hop culture 77; and hip hop's racial paranoia 88; and Jewish rap groups 308–309; in "jihad of words" 169–171; public space as 48; in Tunisian hip hop culture 217–220, 229
social hierarchy 123–124
social justice: and hip hop culture 57, 189, 381; and Mos Def 58, 193; and rap music 186, 325; and rock music 27
Soldierz At War 190
Solomon, Lenny 306, 307, 317n8
Solomon, Martha 282n8
Sorett, J. 79, 380
sound clashes 127n2
Soyinka, Wole 400–401
space: Christianity in non-religious 296–297; and identity 291–293; meaningful, for hip hop culture 291–292. *See also* public space; urban space
Spady, James 34, 55
spatial identity formation model 291f, 292
Specter, Phil 47
Spencer, John Michael 3
Spencer, Jon Michael 34, 283n19, 285n35; *Black Sacred Music* (journal) 34; on theodicy of the blues 130
Spicer, Jimmy: "Adventures of Super Rhymes" (song) 46; "Money (Dollar Bill Y'all)" 45
spinning. *See* DJing
spirituality: as based on faith over sight 90–91; of DJing 125–126; of hip hop culture 414–417; Mos Def on 30; Nuwine on 31; Simmons on 33–34; Sister Souljah on 31; Snoop Dogg on 32. *See also* religion
spirituals: black suffering in 136; and blues music 22–23; communality of 22; and slavery 22
Spoonie Gee, "Spoonin' Rap" (song) 45
Stanley-Niaah, Sonjah 127n2
Stannard, David 395
star narrative 145–147, 156n11
Stephen, Davis 324
Stetsasonic 87
Stone, Joe 307
Storahtelling 303
Stratton, Jon 307
street dancing. *See* break dancing

structuralist model 40
Subliminal 313
subversion 275
Suede 372
Sugarhill Gang, "Rapper's Delight" (song) 12, 28–29, 45, 46, 305, 410
Sugar Soul 360
Sun Africa 206–207
Sunni Islam: and Common 178; and conscious rap 177–178; and Lupe Fiasco 79; and Mos Def 78, 178; and rap music 176–179; and The Roots 177; and A Tribe Called Quest 177; and Tunisian hip hop culture 221. *See also* World Community Al-Islam in the West (WCIW)
Sunz of Man 59
Swados, Elizabeth 306
Swedenburg, Ted 57, 189, 219
Sylvan, Robin 381
Synatra, Ced 190
syncretism 247, 260, 280, 339–340, 345

tagging. *See* graffiti
Taiwan 371. *See also* Chou, Jay
Tate, Greg 171
Tate, S. 226
Taylor, Koko 23
T-Bone 147
technology: MOOCs 425–426; of rap music 418; sound based on 49; as "tricknology" 96n5
Terrill, Robert E. 285n39
Teven, Jason J. 272
textual criticism: as de-contextualized 40–42; as ignoring performative aspect 42
Tha Blue Herb 360
theodicy: of black experience 130–131; of blues vs. gospel 130; definition of 130; focus of 131; of slave mentality 132–134; of white supremacy 132
3rd Bass 307
Thompson, Ahmir "Questlove" 163
Thompson, John 142
Thornton, Sarah 43
Thurman, Uma 339
Tigay, Hillel 307
TikTokk 269. *See also* Gospel Gangstaz
Tillich, Paul 105–106, 108, 109, 110
Time Out New York magazine 303–304
T Men 216–217, 229
toasting 127n2
Tokyo B-Boys 349
Tone Loc, "Wild Thing" (song) 15
Toop, David 2, 34

Torres, Veronica 36n16
transglobalism: of break dancing 347; of hip hop culture 55; of hip hop's racial paranoia 91; of hip hop *umma* 57–60; in Japanese hip hop culture 338; of Jewish hip hop culture 312–313; of rap music 214; West on 363n7
Treach 137
Treacherous Three 47
A Tribe Called Quest 87, 119, 177, 235; "Verses from the Abstract" (song) 76
"tricknology" 96n5
Troubl' 121
Tru to Society 83n17
Tucker, C. Delores 21, 293
Tunisia: employment in 231n9; hijab in 231n21; liberalism of 221
Tunisian hip hop culture: aesthetics of 225–226; authenticity in 217–220; criticisms of materialism 227–228; double consciousness in 216, 224–225, 226, 228; female rap artists in 227, 229; interpretations of Islam in 221–223; as male-oriented 215, 226–228; methodology for research in 216, 230n6; misogyny in 227, 229; negative public perception of 223, 225; origins of 216–217; production in 231n24; rapper vs. Muslim identity in 223–225; situatedness of 217; social and political issues in 217–220, 229; staged selves in 220–221; vs. U.S. 215, 227; women in 226–227, 229
Turner, Richard Brent 168
Turner, Victor 127, 404
turntablism: battles and implicit religion 121–127; battling in 118–121, 409; and "body tricks" 118, 120, 121; commitment to 121–122; definition of 116; Disco Music Club (DMC) World DJ Championships 120–121; and gift economy 123; Heineken Green Synergy DJ Competition 119–120; and hip hop imaginary 122–123; and ludic agency 124–125; and "signifying" 118; and social hierarchy 123–124; subliminal dissing in 127n1. *See also* battling
Twilight Samurai (film) 340, 362–363n3
2 Live Crew 21, 74, 82n2, 357
2 Live Jews 307–308, 314
Tynetta Muhammad 203
Tyson, Christopher 399n19

U2 27
umma: agents of transglobal 57–60; as borderless Islamic nation 54, 185; as verbal mujahidin 184, 194

the unconscious 396–398
United Gospel Industry Council 36n16
urban life: in post-Civil Rights era 266–267;
    rap music as reflection of 12–13, 16–17;
    and violence as normative 267; and warfare
    278–279
urban space: anonymity in 294–295, 301n22;
    significance of 291–292; as site of hip hop's
    origins 76; typical conversation in 295
Usón, Ricardo Mairal 384
Utamaru 351, 356
Uttal, Jai 336
Uzi 339

the Ventures 343
verbal jihad. *See* jihad of words
Vibe magazine 27
Vibrastone 350
violence: and Ethiopian Jews' hip hop culture
    326, 327; as normative black experience 267;
    and public perception of rap 50, 93, 95; and
    rap music 14, 17; symbolic, in turntable battles
    118; and urban life as warfare 278–279
Virolle, M. 231n22
Virtue, Compton 90
Visagie, Johann 141, 154
Voll, J. O. 221

Wallace, David Foster 29
Walser, Robert 43
Wang, Jing 368
warfare 278–279
Warhol, Andy 29
Warith Deen Muhammad 176, 181n32
Washington, Jerome 258–259
Waters, Muddy 23
Watkins, Ralph 4, 255
Watts, Eric 284n34
WCIW. *See* World Community Al-Islam in the
    West (WCIW)
Webbie D 120, 124
Welch, Leona 257
Weld 15 228
West, Cornel: on globalization 363n7; on
    nihilism 174–175; on rappers' literacy 18
West, Kanye: and Christianity 79, 238–239, 240,
    243n17, 380; "Heard 'Em Say" (song) 94; "I
    am a God" (song) 423; "Jesus Walks" (song/
    video) 79, 238, 243n19, 380; and materialism
    238–239; paranoia in lyrics of 94–95, 97n21;
    Rolling Stone cover 238, 240
Wham 371

White, Kevin 253, 256
Whiteley, S. 229–230
whites: as co-opting black cultural
    productions 16, 36n16; as created by
    blacks 86, 96n2, 172
white supremacy: and Christianity 383; and
    reverse gaze 393; and Shakur as
    Ogou 403–405; theodicy of 132.
    See also racism
Wild Style (film) 293, 347
Williams, Hype 386; *Belly* (film) 95
Winbush, Angela 271
Wise, L. G. 83n17
Wise Intelligent 55–56, 57, 174, 187, 204, 205,
    209. *See also* Poor Righteous Teachers
women: in break dancing 349; in early vs. late
    rap music 49–50; and Ethiopian Jewish culture
    327; as excluded from music production 49;
    in Five Percent Nation thought 175–176,
    206–207; in hip hop culture 77–78; and "Hush
    Harbor" 103–104; and Japanese hip hop
    culture 353; in Jewish hip hop culture 311–312;
    as marginalized 118; and ragamuffin music
    325; in Tunisian hip hop culture 226–227,
    229. *See also* female rap artists; gender issues;
    misogyny; sexism
Woods, Joe 171
The WORD (newspaper) 207–208
wordplay. *See* linguistic technique and wordplay
World Community Al-Islam in the West
    (WCIW): as black Sunni Muslim collective
    176; and Nation of Islam 176; orthodoxy of
    176; and Warith Deen Muhammad 176. *See
    also* Sunni Islam
"Wrapped Up" (song/video): and call and
    response 149; danced religion in 153; as gospel
    rap 141; ideological tensions in 153–154;
    lyrics of 143–145; and *Men In Black* (film)
    151; and "Mucho mambo" (song) 148, 149,
    153; music of 147–152; rap section of 152,
    154; star narrative in 145–147, 156n11;
    structure of 142–143; tango elements in 153;
    title of 156n13; visuals in video 145–147; and
    "Wrapped Around Your Finger" (song) 148
Wu Tang Clan 309
Wuthnow, Robert 242n13

X-Clan 87

Yakuza 348
Yano, Christine 344
Yauch, Adam 33

yoga 33, 335
Yoga Toes Studio 332, 335
Yoji, Yamada 362–363n3
Yoruba tradition 160–164
Yosef, Ovadia 322
Young Missionary Temple Christian Methodist
  Church 252
"you" pronoun, in early vs. late rap music 44–45,
  48–49

Zeebra 351, 352, 360
Zekri, Bernard 185
Zhen Long Performance Company 372
Zhou Jielun. *See* Chou, Jay
Žižek, Slavoj 71
Zorn, John 303, 304
Zoubir, Y. H. 219, 228
Z-Pabon, Christie 124
Zulu Nation 57, 186, 409